Gunmen at Greyfriars

His Gunman Guardian
Gun Play at Greyfriars
Horace Coker's Dark Deed
The Gangsters Swoop
Ordered to Quit
Bunter Beats the Gangsters
The Vengeance of Bunter the Ventriloquist
The Bogus Beak

(Magnet issue numbers 1471 to 1478)

Gunmen at Greyfriars

By

FRANK RICHARDS

HOWARD BAKER
LONDON

GUNMEN AT GREYFRIARS

Frank Richards (The Magnet, 1936)

Originally published in single issues.

Hardcover edition, 1976

ISBN: 0 7030 0089 6

*Greyfriars Press Books are published by
Howard Baker Press Ltd., 27a Arterberry Road,
London, S.W.20, England.*

Printed by Litho Techniques (Kenley) Ltd.

Frank Richards

The writing phenomenon known to the world as Frank Richards (real name Charles Hamilton) died at his home in Kingsgate in Kent on Christmas Eve 1961 at the age of eighty-six.

By then it is estimated that he had written the equivalent of one thousand full-length novels.

His work appeared continuously for over thirty years in those famous Fleetway House magazines *The Magnet* and *The Gem*. Most famous of all was his immortal creation Billy Bunter, the Fat Owl of the Greyfriars Remove, whose exploits together with those of the other boyhood heroes Harry Wharton and Co., delighted generations of readers from 1908 to 1940.

The war unhappily saw the end of *The Magnet* but though the post-war years brought the return of Greyfriars stories in other formats nothing ever quite recaptured the evergreen magic of the original much-loved boys' paper. It was for this reason that, four years ago, W. Howard Baker presented the first of his now world-renowned faithful facsimilies.

The brilliant character studies of boys and masters created by Frank Richards ensured his own immortality. Apart from the boys of Greyfriars, not forgetting Horace Coker, the duffer of the Fifth, there was the unforgettable Mr. Quelch, the Remove form-master ('a beast, but a just beast'), the Rev. Dr. Locke, venerable Headmaster of the School, William Gosling, the crusty, elbow-bending school porter who firmly believed that 'all boys should be drownded at birth', Paul Pontifex-Prout, the pompous form-master of the Fifth, the excitable but kind-hearted 'Mossoo' (M'sieu Charpentier, French master), the odious Cecil Ponsonby, involved in murky goings-on at The Three Fishers, and peppery Sir Hilton Popper, irascible School Governor. All these characters and many, many more are to be found in the pages of these volumes.

Each of the Howard Baker editions contains a complete series of stories from *The Magnet's* great golden age. And each is a fitting memorial to the glowing imagination, the humour, the humanity and the well-nigh incredible industry of its brilliant author.

Frank Richards loved writing for the young, and affirmed that no writer could do any better work in life than this. Certainly none did it better than Frank Richards himself.

Sensational Schoolboy-Adventure Yarn featuring Harry Wharton & Co., of Greyfriars, "HIS GUNMAN GUARDIAN!"

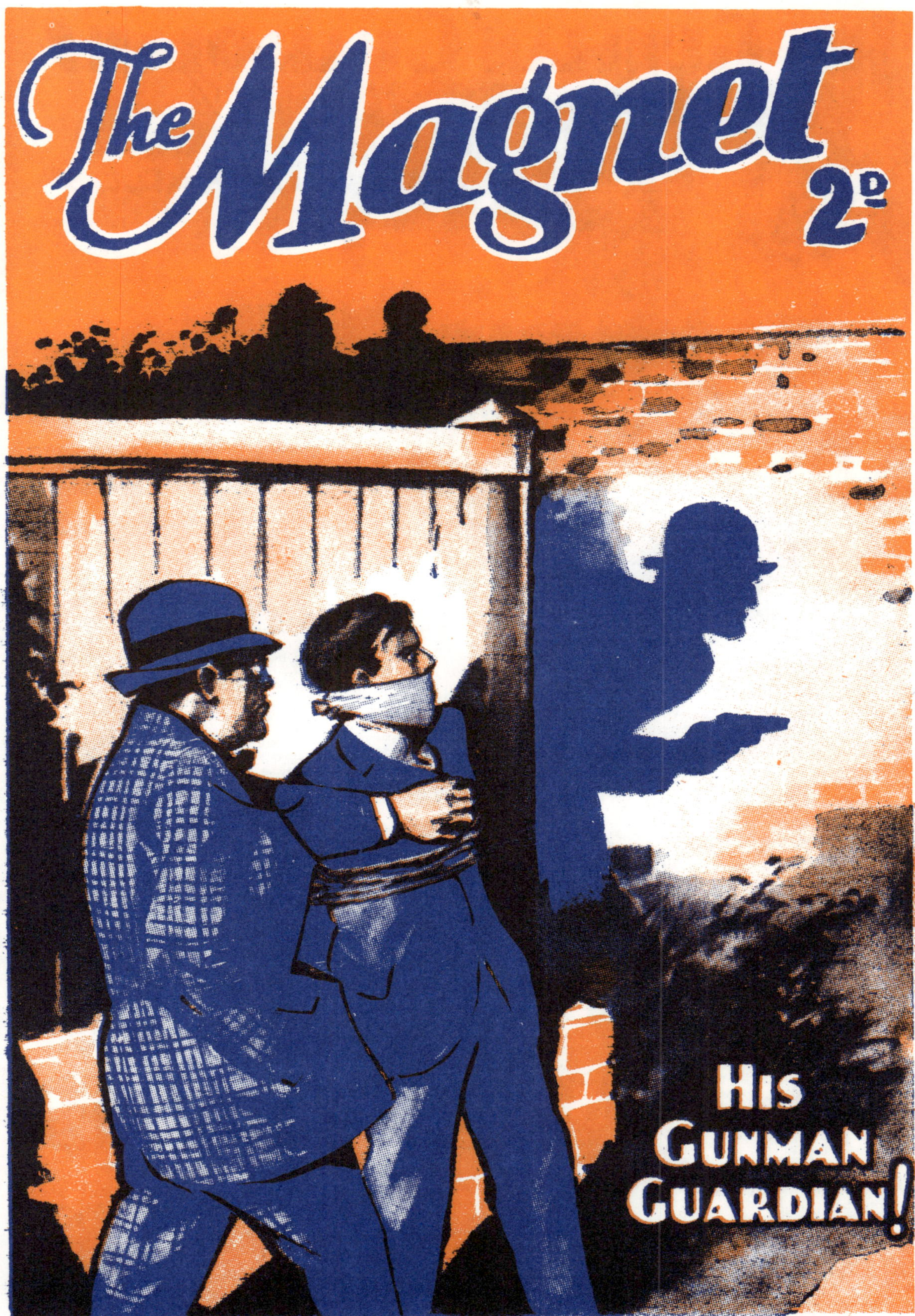

No 1,471. Vol. XLIX. EVERY SATURDAY. Week Ending April 25th, 1936.

FULL-O'-THRILLS YARN OF HARRY WHARTON & CO., INTRODUCING PUTNAM VAN DUCK and—

HIS GUNMAN GUARDIAN!

By FRANK RICHARDS

THE FIRST CHAPTER.
Bamboozling Bunter !

"FIVE shillings !"

"Right !"

Bob Cherry put his hand into his pocket.

Billy Bunter's eyes opened wide, behind his big spectacles.

It was not like Bob to expend cash quite so recklessly as this. Five shillings for a box of chocolates was rather a large sum for a junior in the Greyfriars Remove to "blow."

But Bob rattled two half-crowns on the counter of the school shop as if half-crowns were as cheap as blackberries.

"I say, old chap, is that for the train?" asked Bunter.

Greyfriars School was breaking up for Easter that day. The first bus had already started, loaded with fellows, for Courtfield Station. The second was about to start.

If Bob Cherry was laying in supplies to be consumed on the train it was a matter of deep interest to Billy Bunter. Bunter was going by the same train.

He had missed the first bus, because Harry Wharton & Co. had missed it. He was not going to miss the second—unless they did!

That morning Billy Bunter had been haunting the Famous Five of the Remove like a fat ghost. So long as they kept together his eyes and his spectacles hardly left them for a moment.

But when Harry Wharton and Frank Nugent went up to the studies, and Johnny Bull and Hurree Singh went to say good-bye to Mr. Quelch, and Bob Cherry headed for the tuckshop, Bunter was rather beaten. He could not keep them all under observation, unless he divided himself, like ancient Gaul, into three parts.

So he rolled after Bob, the tuckshop having an attraction for him at all times. He knew that they were all going together, so that was all right.

Mrs. Mimble pushed the box of chocolates across to Bob, who picked it up.

"Keeping it for the train, old fellow?" asked Bunter. Bunter would have been glad to sample the contents of that box on the spot.

"No fear !" answered Bob. "I fancy there won't be many of these chocs left by the time we're in the train, Bunty."

He walked to the door.

Bunter rolled after him.

"I say, old chap——" gasped Bunter.

"Run away and play, old fat man !"

"I say, I'll carry that box for you, if you like."

"Will you?" asked Bob.

"Pleasure !" gasped Bunter.

Not always an obliging fellow, Bunter would have carried a box of chocolates for anybody. His load, like Aesop's in the fable, would have grown lighter and lighter, the longer he carried it.

Bob was perfectly well aware of that little failing of Bunter's. But that morning he appeared to be in a very unsuspicious mood.

"Well, look here, Bunter, if you mean it——" he said.

"Yes, rather, old chap !"

"Well, take it up to Wharton's study, will you?" asked Bob. "Wait there till we come up."

"My dear chap," gasped Bunter, "I'd do more than that for a fellow I really like! Gimme that box."

Billy Bunter could hardly believe in his good luck when Bob handed him the box and he rolled off to the House with it under a fat arm.

Bob, with a cheery grin on his face, watched him roll into the House, and then walked down to the waiting bus.

There, within a few minutes, he was joined by his four chums: Wharton and Nugent, Johnny Bull and Hurree Jamset Ram Singh. They seemed to appear suddenly from nowhere in particular. And they were all grinning cheerily as they climbed on the bus.

Billy Bunter also was grinning cheerily as he climbed the Remove staircase.

The door of Wharton's study—No. 1 in the Remove—stood wide open. The study had a dismantled look. Fellows had been packing there.

Bunter rolled into the study.

Bob had told him to wait till the fellows came up. Bunter was quite prepared to wait idly.

Sitting in Harry Wharton's armchair he slid off the lid of the chocolate box.

As Bob had declared that there would not be many of those chocs left by the time they were in the train, the fat Owl of the Remove concluded that the Famous Five were going to dispose of them before starting.

He was more than willing to help. And his idea was to start early and avoid the crush.

A fat finger and thumb dipped into the box, and hooked out a luscious chocolate-cream. It was immediately transferred to Billy Bunter's capacious mouth.

Bunter gobbled !

Another and another and another followed.

Indeed, Billy Bunter was half-through the box before he quite realised what a gap he was making in the contents.

He paused, and listened for footsteps in the Remove passage. If the chums of the Remove were coming up to the study to whack that box of chocs before going for the train, it was high time they came. A little more delay, and that box was likely to be in the same state as Mother Hubbard's celebrated cupboard.

But they did not arrive.

Billy Bunter hesitated.

It is well said that he who hesitates is lost.

The fat finger and thumb hooked out another chocolate—and another ! It was really more than flesh and blood could resist—Billy Bunter's at least !

Choc after choc followed the downward path, and vanished.

"Oh crikey !" gasped Bunter, at length.

Only five chocolates remained in the box !

Even Bunter realised that he had rather plunged. The Famous Five were good-natured fellows, not likely to grouse at Bunter starting first on the chocs. But even very good-natured fellows might expect to have a whack in their own tuck.

Bunter had left them one each.

Manfully resisting further temptation, the fat Owl placed the box on the study table and wiped a sticky mouth with a grubby handkerchief.

He was feeling a little uneasy about what he was to say when the chums of the Remove come in to scoff those chocolates.

But they did not come in.

Footsteps were audible in the passage, and Billy Bunter stepped to the door and blinked out through his big spectacles.

But it was not one of the famous Co.

It was Herbert Vernon-Smith coming along from the stairs.

"I say, Smithy!" squeaked Bunter.

Smithy glanced at him.

"I say, are those fellows coming up?" asked Bunter.

"What fellows?"

"Wharton and his lot——"

"Eh? They're gone!"

Billy Bunter jumped almost clear of the floor.

"Gone!" he roared. "Did you say gig-gig-gig-gone?"

"I didn't say gig-gig-gig-gone—I said gone!" answered the Bounder. "They went on the second bus."

"The sus-sus-second bib-bib-bus!" stuttered Bunter.

"Yes; a quarter of an hour ago."

"Oh crikey! I was going with them!" gasped Bunter.

"Ha, ha, ha!"

"They've sneaked off while I was up here in the studies——"

"Ha, ha, ha!" yelled the Bounder.

"Oh, the awful beast! That's why he told me to bring those chocs up here, and wait till they came up!" gasped Bunter.

"You'll have to wait till next term!" chuckled Smithy, and he went up the passage laughing.

Billy Bunter did not laugh. His fat brow was corrugated in a deep frown, as he rolled hurriedly to the stairs. He had been "done"—diddled, dished, and done! Lured up to the studies by that box of chocs, he had sat there, scoffing chocs, while the Famous Five cleared off on the bus. Breathing wrath, the fat Owl of the Remove rolled out into the quad.

The second bus was long gone. A third and a fourth were filling. Among the crowd of Greyfriars fellows there was no sign of Harry Wharton & Co.

Evidently they were gone. By that time they were at Courtfield Station, catching the train.

"Beasts!" groaned Billy Bunter.

Billy Bunter had not quite decided whether he was going home with Harry Wharton, Bob Cherry, Johnny Bull, or Frank Nugent. It was going to be one of them, but he had not settled which. That doubtful point was now settled for him. It was not going to be any of them!

THE SECOND CHAPTER.

A Hot Chase!

HARRY WHARTON & CO. smiled as they sat down in their carriage in the train at Courtfield.

The platform swarmed with Greyfriars men, and there was a cheery buzz of voices, a trampling of feet, and a banging of luggage. Bob Cherry stood at the door, glancing along the platform. He would not have been surprised to spot at the last moment a fat figure and a pair of glimmering spectacles. Billy Bunter was a sticker, and it was not easy to make him come unstuck. But the fat and fatuous Owl of the Remove was not to be seen, and Bob chuckled and sat down as a porter came along to slam the door. The packed train rolled out of Courtfield.

"It was worth a bob each," remarked Harry Wharton, referring to the box of chocs that had kept Billy Bunter off the scene while the chums of the Remove got away on the bus.

"The worthfulness was terrific," chuckled Hurree Jamset Ram Singh.

"Bunter's finished the chocs by this time," remarked Johnny Bull. "The chocs are done—and Bunter's done!"

"Ha, ha, ha!"

"Just as easy to kick him, though," remarked Johnny.

Harry Wharton laughed.

"Not on breaking-up day," he said. "It was worth a bob each for a consolation prize for Bunty."

"Hear, hear!" chuckled Bob Cherry.

The train rolled on towards Lantham Junction, where the Famous Five were to separate for their various homes. Hurree Jamset Ram Singh, whose home was at Bhanipur, in far-off India, was going with Harry; the other members of the Co. joining him later at Wharton Lodge.

"Hallo, hallo, hallo! That sportsman's in a hurry," remarked Bob Cherry, who was looking from the window.

About half-way to Lantham the road ran parallel with the railway. On the road a little green Austin car was whizzing like a bullet.

It was going in the same direction as the train and easily keeping pace.

Only the driver was in the little car, and he was bent over the wheel and little could be seen of him, save his hat and shoulders.

But it could be seen that he was a boy, apparently no older than the juniors themselves, so that it was rather surprising to see him hurling along at top speed in a car.

The Famous Five gathered at the window to watch the little car; plenty of other faces along the crowded train were looking at it.

"If a bobby blows along, that chap will get pulled up short and sharp," remarked Frank Nugent. "I wonder how many he's doing?"

"Fifty at least," said Bob.

"Young ass!" remarked Johnny Bull.

"Oh, my hat!" gasped Wharton. "Look!"

In a spot where winter rains had sunk deep puddles the road had been made up with stones not yet pressed down by the steam-roller. The little car hit that bad patch suddenly and fairly rocketed.

It shot across to one side of the road, then to the other, zigzagging wildly. Several times it was on only two wheels—once or twice it seemed to the breathless juniors that it was on only one.

How the boy escaped disaster seemed a miracle. But he did not even slacken pace; he shot onward, rocketing.

"Some nerve!" said Bob.

The car steadied as the bad patch was left behind. It was now almost abreast of the carriage from which the Famous Five were staring. Suddenly the youthful driver seemed to become aware of the train on the embankment above the road and lifted his head and looked up.

"Great pip!" exclaimed Harry Wharton, as he saw the face—a rather good-looking face, though it had a razor-like keenness and alertness in its expression. "Know that chap?"

"That American chap!" exclaimed Bob. "What was his name?"

"Van Duck," said Nugent.

"That's it—Putnam van Duck!"

"The esteemed Van Duck that we met on the absurd steamer!" exclaimed Hurree Jamset Ram Singh.

Only for a second did the American boy glance up, then he was concentrated on his driving again; he needed to concentrate, considering the speed at which he was going.

Harry Wharton & Co. gazed at him with great interest.

They remembered Putnam van Duck, the son of the Chicago millionaire, Mr. Vanderdecken van Duck.

They had met him on the steamer, coming back from a holiday trip, and had wondered more than once whether they would ever see him again.

According to what he had told them, he was threatened with kidnapping by a gang of gangsters in the United States, and his millionaire "popper" had sent him travelling in charge of a hired gunman called Poker Pike.

Not liking the strict surveillance of Mr. Pike, Putnam van Duck had dodged his gunman guardian and hit the horizon, as he expressed it, only to be rounded up again by the faithful Pike.

Harry Wharton & Co. had not been aware that he was in England. Now that they saw him they wondered whether he was "hitting the horizon" again to get away from the too-careful care of Poker Pike.

It certainly looked as if he was in a hurry to get away from somebody, to judge by the speed at which he was hurtling the Austin along.

"Look!" roared Bob.

Far back down the road a big Daimler came booming into sight. It was going all out and lapping up the road.

Looking back at the Daimler, the juniors could see the face of the driver clear in the bright April sunlight.

It was a face that looked as if cut in hickory, with slits of eyes, a gash of a mouth, and a black bowler hat clamped down on the skull as if screwed there.

"Pike!" yelled Nugent.

"The jolly old gunman!" chuckled Bob.

Evidently it was a chase.

The millionaire's son was hitting the horizon, and his gunman guardian was in hot pursuit.

Fast as the Austin flew, the big Daimler was overhauling it hand over fist. Harry Wharton & Co. watched breathlessly.

Another mile on, road and railway parted company; but, to judge by the tremendous speed of the Daimler, the chase would be over by then. Poker Pike was driving as if on the race track, and the high-powered car fairly flashed along.

Putnam van Duck evidently knew that the Daimler was coming up behind. Fast as the green Austin had been going, it flew faster. It was very fortunate for both Van Duck and his pursuer that the road was a wide country road with little traffic.

"Oh!" gasped Bob suddenly.

It was sudden disaster to the Austin.

It had struck another bad patch and rocketed again, and this time it rocketed off the road on to the belt of grass that lay between the highway and the wood that bordered it on the farther side.

It seemed to the startled and horrified juniors for a few thrilling seconds that the little green Austin was whirling like a catherine wheel; it landed on its side in the grass.

But as it landed the American boy leaped clear.

They saw him standing, unhurt, shrugging his slim shoulders. Up the road came the big Daimler, booming.

Above the buzz of the train they heard the shout of the gunman.

"Say, you, Putnam van Duck——"

As the train rushed on the juniors

A GUNMAN TO CATCH A GUNMAN!

Putnam van Duck, son of a multi - millionaire, has been marked down as a victim by American gangsters, and his "popper" has sagely engaged a gunman for his defence!

---

leaned from the windows, staring back with breathless interest to see the last of the strange scene.

They saw the Daimler stop, and the lean, hickory-faced gunman leap down; they saw Putnam van Duck wave a slim hand at him as he did so, turn, and leap away into the shadowy greenery of the wood.

The Austin was left where it had rolled; the next moment the big Daimler was abandoned by the road-side, Poker Pike dashing into the wood in pursuit of the boy.

A few moments more and the whole scene was dropped behind as the train rushed on to Lantham.

"Well, my hat!" said Bob Cherry, as he sat down again. "Fancy seeing that kid again here! I wonder if jolly old Pike will get him?"

"We may see something of him these hols," remarked Harry Wharton. "He told us on the steamer that he would give us a look-in at Wharton Lodge if he came to this country."

"He won't find it easy to get shut of Mr Pike!" chuckled Bob. "By gum, I'd like to know how it's ended!"

But there was no guessing that. The juniors, as they ran on to Lantham, could only wonder whether Putnam van Duck was still hitting the horizon, or whether the hickory-faced gunman had rounded him up once more.

THE THIRD CHAPTER.
Left!

"TODDY, old man!" said Billy Bunter.

Peter Todd grinned.

Having witnessed the "escape" of the Famous Five, and Billy Bunter's subsequent search for the fellows who were no longer there, he was rather amused when the fat Owl rolled up to him. It did not need a great deal of penetration on Toddy's part to guess what was coming.

"Just going, old chap?" asked Bunter.

"Just!" agreed Toddy.

"I'm getting the next train," remarked Bunter. "Travel together, what?"

"Why not, as far as Lantham!" agreed Peter.

Bunter coughed.

"The fact is, I wouldn't mind coming on," he said.

"I should!" said Peter.

"After all, we're pals here," said Bunter, unheeding. "I was only joking when I told you that I wouldn't be found dead in Bloomsbury in the hols, Peter."

"Quite!" said Peter. "You'll be found dead in Bloomsbury, old fat man, if you're found there at all! That's a tip!"

"Oh, really, Toddy——"

"Good-bye!"

"Beast!"

Billy Bunter blinked morosely after Toddy's departing form.

Matters were getting serious.

Bunter had had one slight comfort. He had finished the last of the chocs in the box in Study No. 1.

That was so much to the good!

But it was time to go; and what was going to be done—or who was going to be done?

Lord Mauleverer had disappeared early, the Famous Five were gone; most of the other fellows were gone. The Bounder was not yet gone, but was going—in a big car his father had sent to take him home. Billy Bunter blinked at that car—but he had no more chance of getting in than the hapless Peri who looked in at the gate of Paradise.

Toddy was his last resource. His last resource had failed him. As Herbert Vernon-Smith stepped into his car the fat junior rolled over to him.

"I say, Smithy——" he squeaked.

The Bounder glanced at him.

"Fathead!" was his reply. Like Toddy, he guessed what was coming.

"I say, old chap, I've missed the bus——"

"What a treat for the fellows on it!"

"Like to give me a lift to the station?"

"I'm not going near the station!"

"Well, look here, if you drop me in London it will be all right!" said Bunter hopefully.

The Bounder chuckled.

"You want me to give you a lift, and drop you?" he asked.

"Yes, old chap!" said Bunter eagerly. Once ensconced in Smithy's car there was a chance, a very remote chance, of sticking on to Smithy. "You'll do it, old fellow?"

"Certainly!"

"Oh, good! You're a good chap, Smithy."

"None nicer!" agreed the Bounder. "I'll do it, like a shot! But I'll do it here."

"Eh?" ejaculated Bunter.

The Bounder, grinning, grasped the fat junior by the collar and swept him off his feet.

Having thus given him a lift, he dropped him.

Bump!

"Yaroooh!"

Smithy, chortling, rolled away in his car. Billy Bunter sat in the quad and blinked after him, spluttering for breath.

"Urrrgggh! Beast! Wurrrgggh!" gurgled Bunter.

Slowly and sorrowfully the Owl of the Remove picked himself up. He blinked round him through his big spectacles

Fellows were thinning out now. There was hardly anybody to be seen. Three Fifth Form men came out of the House --Coker and Potter and Greene.

Horace Coker, with his usual efficiency, had packed early and got it done; but having left out various things he had overlooked, he had had to do it all over again at the last moment: so Coker & Co. were late in leaving. A taxi-cab had been waiting about an hour for Coker, who was fortunately in a financial position to be indifferent to the mounting charges on the "clock."

"We've lost the train," Potter was remarking as they came out.

"You've lost it, you mean!" corrected Coker.

"Have I been waiting for you, or have you been waiting for me?" inquired Potter sarcastically.

"Don't jaw!" said Coker crossly. "If you'd reminded me about those things I left out, I should have put them in. But it's always the same—you fellows forget everything."

"But you forgot——" began Greene.

"Don't jaw, Greene! You're worse than Potter!"

"Look here, Coker——" said Potter and Greene together.

"For goodness' sake," said Coker, "don't jaw! Haven't you wasted enough time, or do you want to travel by a night train? Jaw, jaw, jaw!"

Coker led the way to the waiting taxi; Potter and Greene following him, and wondering, for the umpteenth time, whether it was rather a mistake to pal with Coker.

"I say, you fellows——" Bunter came up.

Coker gave him a glare. Already irritated by the forgetfulness of Potter and Greene he was in no mood to be patient with fags.

"Get out!" he rapped.

"I say, I'm going to the station——"

"Who's stopping you?" grunted Coker.

"I mean, what about whacking out the taxi?" asked Bunter. "Halves in the fare, what?"

Coker's glare became rather like that of the fabled Gorgon.

Not knowing Bunter so well as fellows in the Remove knew him, he was not aware that, if Bunter arrived at the station in that taxi, he would then discover that there was a shortage of cash, and that his half of the fare would have to be left over to the distant and uncertain future.

But the bare idea of a fag of the Lower Fourth having the unexampled cheek to propose travelling in his taxi aroused Coker's deepest ire.

Coker rather prided himself on having a short way with fags. His way with Bunter was exceedingly short.

Not taking the trouble to answer in words, he reached out at a fat ear and pinned the same with a sinewy finger and thumb.

"Wow!" howled Bunter. "Yow!"

Coker & Co. rolled off in the taxi, leaving William George Bunter clasping a burning ear and squeaking dolorously.

Nearly everybody was gone now. Mr. Quelch, looking out of his study window, glanced at Bunter with a surprised and expressive glance. The Remove master seemed to be wondering why he was not gone. Quelch himself would be going soon.

"Oh lor'!" mumbled Bunter.

He rolled up to the Remove passage, in the faint hope of finding some belated Removite there. Nobody was there—the studies were silent and deserted. Only a maid with a mop gave him a surprised look.

"Oh crikey!" said Bunter, as he negotiated the staircase again.

"Bunter!"

"Oh! Yes, sir!" gasped Bunter, blinking round at his Form-master.

"Why are you not gone, Bunter?" asked Mr. Quelch.

"I—I missed the bus, sir——"

"Fortunately, it is a very fine day, and it will be quite an agreeable walk to the station," said Mr. Quelch. "Good-bye, Bunter!"

Bunter rolled out into the quad.

Evidently it was time to go! Everybody else was gone, except the two or three fellows who passed the holidays at the school. The Owl of the Remove rolled dismally down to the gates.

Gosling, the porter, gave him a look. Gosling did not expect tips from Bunter; still, on the last day of the term, you never could tell; and there was a faint glimmering of hope in Gosling's ancient eye. It was very faint, and it died out as Bunter rolled on regardless. Gosling grunted.

The fat junior stood in the gateway. He looked back into the quad. Nobody was to be seen there except Mr. Mimble, the gardener.

"Oh lor'!" said Bunter. That magnificent residence, Bunter Court, was the only refuge now. Sammy Bunter, his minor in the Second Form, was long gone, joining Sister Bessie, of Cliff House, to travel home; Bunter was too late to travel with Sammy and Bessie. However, he did not miss them; he was going to see enough of Sammy and Bessie in the holidays.

He gave a last blink at the quad, and the House windows; and was about to turn away and depart when a hand tapped on his fat shoulder.

"Say, bo!" remarked a voice—a rather pleasant voice, in spite of its nasal accent.

"Eh!"

Bunter blinked round at the fellow in the road.

That fellow uttered a surprised exclamation.

"Fat Jack, by the great horned toad! Then this shebang is Greyfriars School —what?"

THE FOURTH CHAPTER.

Van Duck Blows In!

PUTNAM VAN DUCK gave Billy Bunter a nod and a grin. Billy Bunter gave Putnam van Duck an astonished blink through his big spectacles.

"And I don't want any cheek—see?" added Bunter.

"Say, I guess I got you right!" said Putnam. "Ain't you Fat Jack of the Boneyard?"

"No!" roared Bunter.

"Guess again!" said Van Duck. "I'll say you're the identical human balloon I met on the other side of the pond, with five guys that I sure want to see again. Are they hanging up?"

"If you mean Wharton's lot——"

"You said it!"

"They're gone!"

"Gone!" repeated Putnam. "This here show is Greyfriars, ain't it? I jumped to it that it was, seeing you loafing around."

"Yes, you ass! But we're breaking-up to-day for the Easter hols, and most of the fellows have gone."

"Sing me to sleep!" said Putnam.

"If you've come to see Wharton, you're too jolly late!" grinned Bunter.

to be kicked. And Billy Bunter would have been quite pleased to give him what he deserved.

On the other hand, he remembered that Putnam van Duck was the son of Mr. Vanderdecken van Duck, the Chicago multi-millionaire. He remembered that Putnam carried a "roll" of dazzling wealth.

Billy Bunter had in his pockets, at the moment, exactly the amount of his journey-money—that much and no more. Only that morning he had been disappointed about a postal order he was expecting. He did not even possess a single solitary copper to work an automatic machine for toffee or chocolate to comfort him on his journey home.

So Billy Bunter did not think of treating Putnam van Duck as he manifestly deserved. He rolled after him, and overtook him on his way to the House.

"I say, Van Goose!" he called out.

Before the horrified eyes of the Greyfriars juniors watching from the carriage window the Austin whirled like a catherine-wheel and then landed on its side in the grass. There were sighs of relief as Putnam van Duck jumped clear!

He remembered the keen, clear-cut face of the American boy whom he had met while on the holiday trip abroad with the Famous Five. But he was quite surprised to see the youth from Chicago turn up so suddenly, on the road by the school gates at Greyfriars. He had, in fact, forgotten Van Duck's existence till thus reminded of the same.

"Oh!" he ejaculated. "You!"

"Me!" agreed Van Duck. "I'll say I've been rubbering around to find Greyfriars, and I was jest going to ask you to put me wise, and pack me up in a Saratoga if you ain't Fat Jack, and——"

Bunter snorted.

On the steamer the young American had irritated him considerably by calling him by that peculiar name.

"Look here!" grunted Bunter. "My name's not Jack——"

"Nunk?" asked Putnam.

"And I'm not fat!" hooted Bunter.

"Search me!" ejaculated Putnam.

"They're all gone. You're not too late to see me, though."

Putnam van Duck looked at him. He did not look as if that was any great consolation.

"How did you get here?" asked Bunter.

Blinking up and down the road, he saw no sign of a vehicle.

"Hoofed it," said Putnam. "I guess I started in a car, but a guy got too fresh, and I'll say I've left that car strewn around." He glanced in at the gateway, and shrugged his slim shoulders. "Waal, if they ain't here, they ain't, and that's a cinch!"

"I'm here!" said Bunter.

"I guess that cuts no ice!"

Putnam van Duck walked in.

Billy Bunter blinked after him with a morose blink. This fellow, obviously, was a silly, cheeky ass, for he wanted to see Harry Wharton & Co., and did not want to see that much more fascinating fellow William George Bunter.

On that account the fellow deserved

Bunter remembered the American himself, but did not precisely remember his name. He knew that it was something like Van Goose.

"Eh!" Putnam spun round. "What the great horned toad are you giving me, Fat Jack?"

"Isn't your name Van Goose?" asked Bunter.

"Not so's you'd notice it!"

"I—I mean Van Drake. I knew it was something to do with a fowl of some sort," explained Bunter. "I say, Van Drake——"

"Guess again," said Putnam.

"I—I mean, Van Chicken."

"If you've got brains enough in your cabeza to mean anything you don't look it," said Van Duck.

"Oh, really, Van Turkey——"

"Search me!" said the millionaire's son. "Keep on guessing, big boy, and you'll get it right in a month of Sundays."

"The fact is, I don't quite remember your name."

"I'd guessed that one. Make it Van Duck"

"Oh, yes! I knew it was some silly name like that," agreed Bunter.

"Some what?"

"I mean, I knew it was a nice name—a really aristocratic name," said Bunter. "Some Americans have such weird names, you know. There's an American chap here named Fish. He, he he! Van Duck's better than Fish, anyhow.'

"We're Fish and Fowl, and you're Flesh—and plenty of it!" remarked Van Duck "Lots of it! Heaps of it! Oodles and oodles of it—what?"

"Well, look here!" said Bunter, changing the subject. "If you want to see Wharton. Van Goose—I mean Van Fowl—that is, Van Duck——"

"I sort of want to, and I've come here to chew the rag—a piece, with that very guy," answered Van Duck.

"I've told you he's gone. But——"

"But I guess there's plenty of guys around that can tell me where to cinch him. He told me on the steamer that he hangs up his hat at a place called Wharton Lodge. And I guess that's where I get off next."

"I can take you there," said Bunter.

"Oh!" said Van Duck.

"You see," explained Bunter, "I was going with Wharton for the hols to——"

"Playing golf?" asked Putnam.

"Golf!" repeated Bunter, staring. "No! Wharrer you mean?"

"What holes are you talking about, then?"

"Oh!" gasped Bunter. "Not holes—hols! The holidays, you know!"

"I get you! Carry on!"

"I was going with Wharton for the hols, but Toddy and Smith kept me talking. They hate to part with me, you know!"

"I don't know," contradicted Van Duck. "And I'll say that that sounds as if you're trying to string me along. How could any guy hate to part with you?"

Billy Bunter breathed hard. He was tempted to tell Putnam van Duck, on the spot, what he thought of him, of his nationality, his manners, and his customs quite a devastating opinion, if he had uttered it. But he did not give it utterance.

"Look here! I was going with Wharton for the hols, and I lost the train," he snorted. "I'm still going, and, if you like. I'll take you with me."

Putnam van Duck eyed him.

Having arrived at Greyfriars School too late to see the chums of the Remove, it had been his intention to inquire where Harry Wharton's home was to be found, and head for the same. So Billy Bunter's offer came in useful. If Bunter was going to Wharton Lodge, the stranger in the land could not want a better guide.

"Now you're talking," said Van Duck, more amicably "I'll tell a man, you're useful, if not ornamental. Can I rope in a telephone anywhere around to cinch a car?"

"Gosling will let you use the phone in his lodge."

"Who's Gosling? And where does he adorn the landscape?"

"This way!" said Bunter.

He led Van Duck to Gosling's lodge. The ancient Greyfriars porter stared at him; but when Bunter explained, willingly gave him permission to use the telephone.

"Ring up Courtfield Garage," said Bunter. "You can get a good car there. If you'd rather go by car than train, it will save time, and we'll whack out the exes—what?"

"I guess I can scare up enough cents to pay for a car," answered Van Duck. "I'll give you a lift in it, if you like."

"Well, I'd rather pay my whack," said Bunter.

"Oh, all O.K.! Pay half if you like."

"I—I mean, if you'd rather pay for the car, I don't mind in the least," said Bunter hastily. "Leave it at that!"

"I guessed that one, too," said Van Duck.

He rang up the garage and talked for a few minutes. Having finished with the telephone, he tipped Gosling for his service, and walked out of the lodge with Bunter—leaving Gosling blinking at a pound-note in his hand!

"My eye!" said Gosling.

Gosling had collected a good many tips that day. But a whole "quid" for so small a service made him open his ancient eyes. It even made him examine the note carefully, to make sure that it was a good one!

Billy Bunter's little round eyes glimmered behind his big, round spectacles. A fellow who could afford to chuck pound-notes about was a fellow that Billy Bunter wanted to know!

"I say, old chap," he gasped, "trot along to the tuckshop while we wait for the car It's still open——"

"I guess I ain't waiting."

"The car won't be here for a quarter of an hour!" urged Bunter "I say, ain't you hungry? My treat, you know——"

"I'm hoofing it to meet that car."

"What's the hurry?" demanded Bunter.

"Heaps! Say, that hombre on the telephone said he was coming from Courtfield—we can meet him on the road! Which way?"

"I'd rather not walk——"

"O.K.! I'll ask that porter guy."

"I mean, I'll walk with pleasure——"

"You're some lad at changing your mind, ain't you?" said Van Duck. "Waal, if it's going to be a pleasure to you, come on, and step out a few!"

Billy Bunter had to step out more than a "few," to keep pace with the brisk American. Putnam van Duck was slim and light, and a rapid walker. Billy Bunter was fat and heavy, and the laziest walker ever. But he was not going to let Van Duck get out of his sight. He exerted himself manfully, and puffed and blew along by the side of the American.

Van Duck glanced sharply out of the gates before starting. He glanced sharply up and down the road as he went. When they reached the road over Courtfield Common, he glanced, with equal sharpness, over the green expanse to right and left. Evidently he was on the alert—why, Bunter did not know. Neither did he care—being fully occupied in trying to breathe, while he exerted his fat limbs as they had seldom been exerted before.

"There's the car!" he ejaculated at last, in great relief, as a Rolls came whizzing from the direction of Courtfield. "I say, stop! Stop and wait for it to come up!"

Bunter stopped, and began to mop his perspiring brow. Putnam van Duck grinned, and came to a halt also—glancing sharply and suspiciously around, while the car came up. But there was no sign of Mr. Poker Fike on the horizon; and Putnam guessed that he had given the slip to his gunman guardian at last.

THE FIFTH CHAPTER.

Gun-Play!

BILLY BUNTER parked himself in the car, greatly relieved to be able to sit down and rest his fat and weary limbs. Putnam van Duck stood talking to the Courtfield chauffeur before getting in.

Bunter mopped his fat brow. The April sunshine was warm, and Bunter had been carrying his extensive weight at an unusual pace; and so he was in what a poet would have called a "melting mood."

But the fat Owl of the Remove, tired and damp as he was, was feeling satisfied. He was—he hoped, at least—booked for Wharton Lodge for the Easter vacation.

On his own, even Billy Bunter would have felt a little coy hesitation at barging in. Arriving there with Van Duck made it easier.

On the steamer, Harry Wharton had asked Van Duck to visit him at Wharton Lodge, in the Easter holidays, if he was in England then. Probably he would be glad to see him—there was, Bunter reflected, no accounting for tastes.

Billy Bunter's idea was to insinuate himself into Wharton Lodge, under the wing of the American.

It was worth trying on, at all events! If a fellow went out of his way to take the trouble to guide Wharton's guest to Wharton's home, the least Wharton could do would be to ask him to stay the night—and once installed in the house Bunter was prepared to trust to his fat wits for the rest. This was no new game to Billy Bunter.

But though the fat Owl was, as usual, thinking about himself and his own important affairs, he sat up and took notice as he heard what Putnam van Duck was saying to the chauffeur.

"Keep an optic open for a guy in a blue Daimler," Van Duck was saying. "I'm telling you that that guy is after this baby, and I don't want to meet him a whole lot. You get me?"

"Yes, sir!" said the chauffeur.

"I guess you'll know him, if you spot him," went on Van Duck. "That guy's got a face like a wooden image, eyes like chips of ice, and a mouth lik a rat-trap, and then some!"

"Yes, sir."

"If you raise that guy anywhere around, just let her rip!" said Van Duck.

"Yes, sir," said the chauffeur stolidly.

"How much will she do, when she means it?" asked Van Duck.

"Seventy, sir!"

"I guess that will make Poker Pike look foolish! Mind you keep tabs on a blue Daimler, and a guy with a face like a lump of hickory that's been hacked with an axe."

"Yes, sir."

Van Duck stepped in, and the car buzzed on. Whizzing round the end of the common, it took the Lantham road.

Billy Bunter blinked curiously at the American. He remembered that, on the steamer, Van Duck had been dodging the guardian his "popper" had placed with him to protect him from kidnappers. The American boy seemed to prefer taking a chance with the kidnappers to the too-faithful guardianship of Poker Pike!

"I say, is that man Pike after you?" asked Bunter.

"Sure!"

Putnam glanced rather anxiously along the Lantham road. It was on that very road that Poker Pike had chased him in the Daimler a few hours ago. He had dodged the bowler-hatted man in the wood, and picked up a lift on a motor-bus towards Greyfriars and walked the rest. He wondered whether Poker had got back to his car, and recommenced scouring the roads for him.

"If that guy is still rubbering around, in the timber, I guess it's O.K.," remarked Van Duck. "But that man Pike sure is some sticker!"

"All right, old chap!" said Bunter. "If he turns up, leave him to me!"

"Eh?"

"I'll handle him!" said Bunter reassuringly.

"Says you!" chuckled Putnam.

"Oh, really, Van Duck! I fancy I could handle that hooligan!" said the fat Owl. "If you'd seen me handling a big barge a week or two ago——"

"I guess I couldn't have!" grinned Van Duck.

"No; you weren't here then——"

"That cuts no ice! I guess I shouldn't have seen it if I'd been here!" chuckled Putnam. "Park it, old fat gink! Park it and sit on it!"

Billy Bunter grunted. This was rather an ungrateful reception of his generous offer of protection if the gunman turned up! Certainly, had Poker Pike turned up, Billy Bunter would have thought twice, or thrice, about handling one half of him!

The Courtfield car buzzed swiftly along in the direction of Lantham.

"Gee!" ejaculated Putnam suddenly.

The car was running past the end of a side lane, when from that lane a blue Daimler nosed out, with a hickory faced man, in a bowler hat, at the wheel.

Instantly Putnam ducked his head, dipping it low in the car, out of sight of the man in the Daimler.

So swift was his action, that he was in cover before even the keen eyes of Poker Pike sighted him.

But those eyes glittered at the fat face and glimmering spectacles of Billy Bunter!

Poker remembered Bunter as a member of Harry Wharton & Co.'s party on the holiday trip, when Putnam had dodged away from him on to the steamer in which the Greyfriars party were travelling.

Mr. Pike's icy slits of eyes glittered, and as the Rolls rushed past he turned the Daimler into instant pursuit.

He had not seen Putnam in the Rolls. But having lost Putnam, an acquaintance of Putnam's was the next best thing He wanted a word with Bunter.

He was not likely to get that word, however, if Putnam could help it.

Putnam barked at the Courtfield chauffeur.

"Say you! Hump it! That's the guy I was telling you about, and he sure is chasing me a few! Make her hum!"

"Yes, sir," said the stolid Courtfield man.

He did not understand in the least why his passenger was chased, or what it all meant, anyhow; but he was there to do what his passenger wanted and he did it. The Rolls was let out to a terrific burst of speed.

Fast behind came the Daimler, roaring.

Poker Pike, his brow corrugated over his slits of eyes, his gash of a mouth clamped on his unlighted cigar, bent over the wheel and made the Daimler whiz.

His first guess, at the sight of Bunter, had been that the fat junior might have seen something of Putnam, and might be able to put him wise. But as the Rolls roared away like a mad thing in swift flight, Poker Pike knew that it could not be Bunter who was fleeing at such a rate—and that Putnam was in the car, though he had not seen him there.

Assured of that, Poker Pike let out the Daimler in a race. Ever since losing Putnam in the wood, he had been scouring the roads—and now, by luck, he was on the trail again—and if he lost it once more, it was not going to be Poker's fault.

"I—I—I say, we—we—we're going jolly fast, you know," stammered Billy Bunter, through chattering teeth. "I—I say, is—is—is it safe?"

"Not a lot!" answered Putnam.

"Oh crikey! I say, slow down a bit, if——"

"And let that guy get a cinch on me?" grinned Putnam derisively. "Not in your lifetime, old-timer! Nope!"

"Ow!" gasped Bunter, as a jolt nearly tipped him off his seat. "Ow! I—I say—— Yow-ow-ow!"

Putnam looked back. The Rolls was whizzing—but the Daimler behind was whizzing, too. So far, it was keeping pace.

"Say, you!" hooted Putnam to the chauffeur. "Can this auto move? I'm inquiring of you! Can she move, or can she not? If she can't, get out and push! you hear me? Get out and push her!"

As the Rolls was doing over fifty, the Courtfield chauffeur fancied that she was "moving" already! However, he put it on, and now the Daimler dropped a little in the chase.

"I guess we're making Poker look foolish!" grinned Putnam, as he looked back. "Yep! I'll say that Poker is feeling like a piece that the cat brought in and left lying around. Oh! Jumping James!"

Bang!

"Ow!" gasped Bunter. "Is that a tyre!"

Putnam chuckled.

"If it was a tyre, big boy, while we're stepping out like this here, I guess you wouldn't be sitting there asking fool questions," he answered.

"What was it, then?" stuttered Bunter.

"Gun!"

"A gun!" yelled Bunter.

"Yep! I guess Poker's fanning us a few."

"Yaroooh!"

Bang!

Billy Bunter rolled off the cushions and plumped in the bottom of the car. There he gasped and gurgled and palpitated, while the gangster's gun spoke!

THE SIXTH CHAPTER.

Neck or Nothing!

PUTNAM VAN DUCK, looking back from the rear window, chuckled, his eyes gleaming with excitement.

The Courtfield chauffeur drove steadily on at a dizzy speed. The Daimler was dropping off—which was the reason why Poker Pike was handling his "gun."

Sprawling with his left hand on the wheel, a wicked-looking automatic in his right, Poker fired again and again at the fleeing Rolls.

He was not, of course, shooting at the occupants. His duty to Mr. Vanderdecken van Duck required him to recapture the wandering heir of millions of dollars; but certainly not to "shoot him up." He was "fanning" the fleeing car to puncture a tyre, if he could.

A punctured tyre, at such a burst of speed, was likely to be dangerous—certain to cause disaster. If that occurred to Mr. Pike, he did not reckon that it was going to stop him. He was going all out to rope in the millionaire's son who had been confided to his care; and that was that.

Putnam chuckled.

He was enjoying the excitement. He was fed-up to the back teeth with the watchful guardianship of the gangster; but being chased like this by the persistent Poker was quite interesting and thrilling. And he wondered what his popper, in far-off Chicago, would have thought of Poker's methods!

Chick Chew, the dreaded kidnapper, had marked out the millionaire's son as his prey; and it had been quite a brain-wave on Mr. van Duck's part to engage a gangster to guard his son and beat Mr. Chew at the game.

Poker Pike had been a gangster in the kidnapping line himself; so he knew the game, and was the man to put paid to Chick Chew, if anybody could put paid to him.

But clearly, in carrying out his duties as a guardian, Poker was rather dropping back into his old manners and customs as a kidnapping gangster!

Had Mr. Chew seen him hurtling along at fifty m.p.h., with one hand on the wheel, and loosing off bullets from an automatic with the other, Mr. Chew would certainly have reckoned that he was a rival kidnapper at work, and would hardly have guessed that he was a faithful guardian looking after his charge!

Bang, bang!

Spurts of dust kicked up round the Rolls. Horrified squeaks came from Billy Bunter!

"Keep her going!" yelled Putnam, as the car slowed.

"Level-crossing, sir!" said the Courtfield chauffeur over his shoulder.

"Aw, carry me home to die!" gasped Van Duck.

He stared ahead.

In the distance the railway crossed the road, and there was a signal-box and a level-crossing. That a train was coming was clear from the fact that the gates were beginning to move.

Putnam shut his teeth hard.

He looked back.

Poker Pike had ceased to fire. Perhaps he had spotted the obstruction ahead, and counted on the race as won.

Certainly, he had won if the Rolls was stopped on the near side of the railway. Long before the wide wooden gates reopened Putnam would be in his hands. And the gates had started to close across the road.

Putnam reached out and touched the Courtfield chauffeur's shoulder.

"Put her through!" he said.

"Sir!"

"I guess you got time!"

"But——"

"You got time if you make her hop! Make her hop, you hobo! You make her hit the high spots, pronto, or I'm telling you that I'll sure stick this hyer pin in the back of your neck——"

"But——"

"Put her through!" roared Van Duck. "You going to be beat in a race? I'm telling you to put her through. Ain't you ever stamped on the gas?"

"But——"

"Twenty pounds if you put her through! You get me?" hooted Van Duck. "That's a hundred dollars! Or this here pin in the back of your neck—as fur as it will go in with a big push! Now, then, feller!"

The Courtfield chauffeur did not answer again; he stamped on the gas! Twenty years before he had driven over shell-torn roads in Flanders, and he was still game. Twenty pounds was a large and attractive sum—and the pin in Putnam's slim fingers was also large, but not attractive at all! The Courtfield man went all out! It was neck or nothing now!

The car seemed almost to leave the ground as it flew!

The gates were on the move! If they closed too narrowly to allow the passage of the whizzing car, the chauffeur knew what would happen, and so did Putnam. But the signalled train was still distant, and the great gates swung slowly.

The Rolls rocked over the metals.

Was there time?

There was—just!

The car roared through—with a scrape and at the cost of a cracked mudguard! Onward, whizzing—while the gates behind closed and crashed, and locked in the face of the oncoming Daimler.

"I guess we've made the grade, old-timer!" yelled Putnam van Duck. "Keep her humming!"

The Rolls roared on.

Behind, the Daimler barely stopped in time to save a crash on the level-crossing gates. Mr. Pike said things, with emphasis!

Putnam van Duck sat down, grinning. Billy Bunter sat up, not grinning.

"Ow!" gasped Bunter. "Grooogh! I—I say, I—I wish I hadn't come in this beastly car! Oh dear! We're going to be smashed up—ooogh! Look here, you beast——ow!"

"Aw, sit it out!" smiled Putnam. "I'll tell you, this is the finest trip I've had in an auto for dog's ages! I guess we got Poker beat—he's sure losing a lot of time at that one-horse railway crossing way back."

"Will you stop this beastly car?" howled Bunter.

"Nope!"

"I'm not going to be shot to pieces by a mad Yankee, to please you!" yelled Bunter. "I want to get out!"

"Jump!" suggested Putnam.

"Beast!"

The car had slacked a little, but was still going very fast. To Billy Bunter's dizzy eyes the trees by the roadside seemed to merge into one continuous line. Certainly, he was not likely to jump.

But he was not staying in that car! Easter holidays at Wharton Lodge were of no use to a fellow if he did not get there alive. Bunter was keen on Easter with Harry Wharton & Co., certainly. But he cared less about his destination than about reaching it alive! On the latter point, in fact, Bunter was very particular indeed!

He heaved his weight up from the floor of the car, grabbed Putnam van Duck by the shoulder, and glared at him through his big spectacles.

"Lemme get out!" he howled. "See? I'm fed-up with you, you beast, and I want to gerrout! Stop this putrid car and let me gerrout!"

"Aw! Can it!" remonstrated Van Duck. "Ain't you hitting young Wharton's shebang along with this baby?"

"Lemme gerrout!"

Van Duck looked back. Cars were passing on the road, but none overtaking the Rolls. Far in the distance behind was a whirling spot of dust, coming on. Putnam guessed it was the Daimler, through at last, and taking up the chase again.

"Will you let me gerrout?" raved Bunter. "I tell you I want to gerrout! Beast! Will you lemme gerrout?"

"I guess I can waste a minute on you," conceded Van Duck. "And I'll mention that it's worth it, to lose sight of you. Say, you, go slow a piece and let this guy absquatulate."

The Rolls slowed and stopped, and Billy Bunter rolled out, with deep thankfulness. He rather overlooked the fact that he was being landed innumerable miles from everywhere. At the moment, all his desires were limited to one thing—getting out of that car! He got out, and gasped with relief.

Before he had gasped twice, the Rolls shot away, and vanished. He was still gasping when a Daimler shot by, and two slits of eyes turned on him for a fleeting second. Then pursued and pursuer were gone, and Billy Bunter was left on his lonely own—still gasping.

THE SEVENTH CHAPTER.

The Gangsters !

THE big Singer saloon stood by the road, outside the wayside inn, and Billy Bunter blinked at it as he came toddling along, hot and perspiring, in the warm April sunshine.

Bunter would have been glad of a lift in that car—or any car—even in a dust-cart! Almost, in a wheelbarrow. His fat little legs were curling up under him.

It was quite a warm spring afternoon. The road was sunny—and it was dusty. Passing cars had churned up the dust, and the wind, with a touch of the east in it, wafted dust all over Bunter. Warm, dusty, perspiring, tired, the fat Owl of Greyfriars rolled on; but he did not, like Iser in the poem, roll rapidly! He rolled slowly and wearily.

He had only a vague idea where he was.

He knew that Lantham had been left miles and miles behind, and he was in country quite strange to him. He was somewhere in Kent—he knew that. But Kent was rather a large spot to wander in.

The "garden of England" was looking quite nice in the sunshine, but Billy Bunter had no eyes for scenery.

Wearily he rolled on.

He almost regretted that he had dropped out of Putnam van Duck's car. Still, with a gunman behind, "fanning" it with bullets, that car was not really an attractive proposition. He quite regretted that he had not taken the school bus and the train at Courtfield. By this time he would have been home, at Bunter Villa, in Surrey. True, Bessie and Sammy were there! But any refuge would have been welcome to the tired Owl.

Stopping at the wayside inn, he blinked at it. He was in need—sore need—of refreshment, liquid and solid. Both were to be obtained there; no doubt the owner of the big Singer had stopped there for that reason. But in a hard and sordid world refreshments had to be paid for! And Bunter was in possession of his train fare, and nothing more!

He was hoping to sight a railway station. As fortune would have it, he sighted the wayside inn instead.

He blinked at the inn, and blinked at the car. If he spent his journey-money on refreshing the interior Bunter how was he to get home?

On the other hand, was there a chance

"I guess we've made the grade, old-timer!" yelled Putnam van Duck, as the Rolls reached the other side of the level-crossing in safety. "Keep her humming!" Behind, the pursuing Daimler barely stopped in time to save crashing into the level-crossing gates. "Ooooh!" gasped Bunter. "Groogh!"

of getting a lift—a less exciting life than the one Putnam van Duck had given him?

Bunter hesitated. But the aching void within settled the matter. He rolled past the Singer, rolled to a seat at a table under a tree in front of the inn, and sat down.

A ruddy-cheeked waiter came up.

Bunter ordered sandwiches, cake, and ginger-beer.

The die was cast!

The aching void was going to be filled. The journey afterwards had to be managed somehow.

Bunter tucked in. The waiter, who did not seem busy, was willing to talk. Bunter asked him to whom the car belonged.

"Two American gentlemen," said the ruddy-cheeked man. "They're in the bar now."

Bunter grunted. It seemed to be raining Americans in Kent that day! He had seen all the Americans he wanted to see, and one over!

"They've been inquiring about a car," went on the waiter. "Looking for a friend they've lost. They ain't found him."

"You don't know which way they're going when they leave?" asked Bunter.

"Don't I?" said the waiter. "They been asking about the quickest road to Surrey, at any rate."

Bunter's eyes gleamed behind his spectacles.

His home was in Surrey—at some distance from Wharton Lodge, in that county. If the two American gentlemen were heading for Surrey when they left that wayside Kentish inn they were going his way, and there was surely a chance of a lift. It was a roomy car, with room for two or three, as well as the two American gentlemen.

Hope springs eternal in the human breast! It seemed to Bunter a hopeful prospect!

Under the influence of that hope he gave further orders, and more cakes, and eggs on toast, and a pie, and more ginger-beer, followed the first consignment.

Bunter felt better and better, more and more hopeful, as he parked the invigorating foodstuffs.

By the time he had paid his bill he was left with exactly threepence in his possession. The waiter, as he received the cash, jerked his head towards the inn.

"There's one of them!" he remarked.

Bunter blinked round.

One of the American gentlemen was looking out of the inn. Bunter hoped to see a nice, genial, good-natured sort of tourist—the kind of genial man who could be touched for a long lift.

But his fat heart sank as he saw that American gentleman.

The man did not look nice, or genial, or good-natured. He was fat in figure, and fat people, as a rule, are good-natured. But this fat man looked a striking exception to the rule.

The face, fat as it was, was hard as iron. Not in features, but in general aspect, it bore a fleeting resemblance to Poker Pike's.

Indeed, Bunter, though he had little acquaintance with American gangsters, had no doubt that this fat man was of the same kidney as Mr. Pike.

One blink was sufficient to tell him that it was no use asking this man for a lift in his car. He did not look as if he had ever given away anything in his life, or ever contemplated the remotest possibility of doing so.

"Oh lor'!" murmured Bunter.

The waiter gave Bunter his threepence change. He lingered for a moment, but the threepence went into Bunter's pocket.

The waiter went back into the inn.

The fat man stood at the door, scanning the road for some minutes. His sharp eyes glided over Bunter for a second, taking no further notice of him.

Then he went back into the building.

"Oh lor'!" repeated Bunter.

He rose from the table under the tree. It was useless to linger; there was obviously nothing doing.

On the other hand, he had now parted with his journey-money, and he was a good ninety miles from home.

He rolled into the road, placing the Singer between him and the inn.

He had to get a lift! That car was going to Surrey. It was futile to think of asking the fat man for a lift. But there was ample room inside, and, as if to favour Bunter's design, there was an enormous rug sprawling over the interior of the car.

Bunter stopped at the door, his fat heart beating fast.

After all, if they spotted him they could only kick him out! Bunter had been kicked out of lots of places; it would be no new experience for him.

There was no eye on him. It was perfectly easy to get into the car and draw that enormous rug over him, screening him from sight.

If they got in, and drove off, without noticing him——

It was a chance, at least—and it was a case of any port in a storm. The Owl of Greyfriars made up his fat mind.

He opened the car door, slipped in, and shut the door after him. He squatted low, and bunched the big rug over him.

It was warm! It was stuffy! It was uncomfortable! But Billy Bunter was prepared to endure all these things, if only he got that lift to Surrey.

How long were the beasts going to be?

It seemed to the hidden Owl hours, but it was only ten or fifteen minutes before there was a sound of voices close at hand. Both of them had pronounced nasal accents, so he had no doubt that the two Americans had come back to their car.

Peering cautiously from under an edge of the rug, he had a glimpse of the fat man's massive back, standing by the wheel; and a glimpse of another man, in horn-rimmed spectacles, talking to him. And the horn-rimmed man's voice came clearly to his ears—and he barely repressed a squeak of surprise, that would have betrayed him had it been uttered.

"The jig's up, Chick! I'm telling you, Chick Chew, the jig is up! Them two guys are somewheres around, but we ain't hitting their trail any! Nix!"

Billy Bunter palpitated under the rug.

The fat man was Chick Chew!

He remembered that name!

It was the name of the Chicago gangster who was bent on kidnapping the millionaire's son. Bunter had almost forgotten what Putnam van Duck had told the chums of Greyfriars on the steamer about Chick Chew! He recalled it now.

He had no doubt as to the identity of the two "guys," to whom the horn-rimmed man referred. Obviously Putnam van Duck and Poker Pike! Chick Chew was on the track of the millionaire's son, though clearly he had lost that track for the moment.

"Oh crikey!" breathed Bunter.

But he did not breathe it aloud! He palpitated under the rug. Within six feet of him stood one of the most deadly and desperate gangsters of Chicago—the kind of man who thought absolutely nothing of taking a guy "for a ride," and putting him "on the spot."

Bunter wanted to be taken for a ride—but not in the gangster sense of those words. He did not want to be "put on the spot." Very much indeed he didn't!

Under the enveloping rug he imitated that sage animal, Brer Fox—and lay low and said nuffin'.

THE EIGHTH CHAPTER.

The Unseen Passenger!

"FORGET it, you Bud!"

Mr. Chew was speaking.

He snapped out the words as if he was biting off the syllables one by one. He had, as Bunter noticed, a most disagreeable voice. It had a tone in it like the filing of a saw.

"Forget it!" repeated Chick. "I'm telling you, Bud Parker, that I ain't letting up on this trail till I get a cinch on that gilt-edged bird! Jevver know Chick Chew get left? I'm inquiring of you."

"Nunk!" agreed Mr. Parker.

"You said it!" assented Mr. Chew. "First time I get left I'm throwing down the kidnapping game, and buying me a candy store. Yep! I ain't never got left yet! Not so you'd notice it, you, Bud Parker!"

"This here country ain't the States, Chick!" said Mr. Parker sadly and disapprovingly. "I'll say that a guy can't pull a gun in the street on this island without the whole block rubbering round like they was watching a circus. Now, if we was in the States we——"

"Park it!" said Mr. Chew. "Ain't that why Old Man van Duck has pushed his boy across the pond? Am I going to be beat so easy as that? I'm telling you, I'm getting a cinch on that infant, if he was packed up in Scotland Yard, with all the policemen sitting round him like fowls! Yes, sir!"

"But——" said Mr. Parker.

"You sure do spill a whole bibful, Bud!" said Chick. "I reckoned we had that young geck this morning, when he lit out in that little Austin, and Poker after him in a car! We lost them—but did we hit the Austin, packed up by the road, or did we not?"

"We sure did!" said Mr. Parker. "But——"

"It looks to me," said Mr. Chew, "as if young Van Duck has had too big a helping of Poker on his plate, and fancies shaking a loose leg. If that's the how of it, Bud, it's jest pie! Poker is sure a tough guy, and I guess he would shoot us up, as soon's he'd shoot up a policeman in Chicago. But if the young geck has throwed him down, we got that young geck dead to rights, once we've put salt on his tail! You get me?"

"He sure has got into a hole, and pulled it in after him, Chick."

"I'll get him! There ain't a lot of room in this island to dodge!" said Mr Chew. "I'll tell you, Bud, I'm nigh feared of letting out the car in this little island, fear of running over the edge! Sure!"

"Where are you looking for him?" asked Bud.

"Surrey!" answered Mr. Chew. "I'm leaving you here, Bud, to rubber around after him, while I look for him where I reckon he knows folks. Did you, or did you not, cinch a letter he wrote to Old Man van Duck?"

"I did!" said Bud.

"Did he, or did he not, mention in that letter that he had met up with some English guys, who'd asked him to meander in at a shebang called Wharton Lodge, in Surrey?"

"He did!" agreed Bud. "But I'll tell you, Chick, that that's a long step from here, and I don't see——"

"If you're going to tell me all the things you don't see, Bud Parker, I guess I shall be growing white hairs by the time you're through!" said Chick. "Pack it up! If I don't get noos of him in Surrey, I'll go over this small island with a small comb till I comb him out."

"You're the hombre to do it, Chick!" admitted Mr. Parker. "But——"

"I'll say you got billygoats in your family, with all them buts!" snorted Mr. Chew. "Park it, old-timer—park it!"

Billy Bunter heard the fat gangster squat in the driving-seat. Bud Parker stepped back.

It was a relief to the fat Owl that Mr. Parker was not coming in the car. There was little danger of discovery now.

"So-long, you Bud!" said Mr. Chew, with another snort "Mebbe, when you see me again there'll be a passenger in this here auto, travelling under that rug!"

He started the engine.

Evidently that big rug was in the car to screen a kidnapped prisoner, if Mr. Chew succeeded in getting a "cinch" on Putnam van Duck.

Equally evidently, Mr. Chew had not the remotest suspicion that there was already a passenger in the auto, travelling under that rug!

The car rolled away, leaving Mr. Parker looking after it through his horn-rimmed spectacles.

It ate up the miles.

Mr. Chew, as he drove, did not glance once into the interior of the Singer saloon. Not the faintest idea crossed his mind that a fat schoolboy, hard up for a lift, was stealing a ride there.

He drove fast.

Billy Bunter made no sound, and no movement! With every turn of the rapid wheels he was getting nearer and nearer to home That was a comfort. But the near proximity of the Chicago gangster was terrifying. He hardly dared to wonder what would happen if Mr. Chew discovered him.

Several times the car stopped, and he heard the rasping voice of the gangster inquiring the way

Every time it stopped, Bunter was tempted to dodge out.

But he dared not risk meeting the eyes of the gangster; especially as Mr. Chew, if he found him in the car, would guess at once that he had overheard his talk with Bud Parker, and that he was "wise" to him and his game. Terrifying visions of an automatic floated before Bunter's eyes, as he thought of that.

Moreover, he was heading for Wharton Lodge. As a destination, he preferred it vastly to Bunter Villa!

He had hoped to arrive there with Putnam van Duck, and insinuate an entrance under his wing. That had fallen through. But it was even a more promising prospect to arrive there with Chick Chew—if only Chick did not spot him in transit!

Exactly what Chick aimed to do at Wharton Lodge, Bunter could not begin to guess; but obviously he was not going to announce himself there as a gangster and kidnapper! But Bunter knew who and what he was, only too well. He would be able to tip Harry Wharton & Co. that the Chicago kidnapper was after their American friend.

After such a signal service as that, the least the beasts could do would be to ask him to stay on for Easter. Or, at all events, to refrain from booting him, if he stayed on without bothering to be asked.

It looked good to Bunter.

His first idea, in getting into the car, had been to get a lift to Surrey, within walking distance, if possible, of Bunter Villa. But, having discovered that Wharton Lodge was Mr. Chew's destination, Bunter did not take long to decide that that was going to be his destination also.

Hidden under the big rug, he rocked and jolted, while the Singer ate up the miles.

It seemed to him hours and hours and hours, if not days and days and days, before the car, after several brief stops, made a long halt.

He heard Mr. Chew alight.

Was it Wharton Lodge at last?

The gangster might have stopped somewhere to fill up with "juice." He might have stopped for lots of reasons! He might be at Wharton Lodge and gone into the house—or he might be standing by the car, his keen eyes ready to spot Bunter if he emerged!

It was a tormenting state of doubt.

Long minutes passed, and still the car remained motionless, and Billy Bunter remained as motionless as the car, hidden under the rug, afraid to stir.

But he stirred at last, as the sound of a familiar voice came to his fat ears from outside the car.

"That's a decent car, Inky!"

"Quitefully so."

Both voices were familiar—and reassuring. And Billy Bunter at long last pitched the suffocating rug aside and blinked out through his big spectacles—at the windows of Wharton Lodge, reddened by the sunset.

THE NINTH CHAPTER.

Chick Wants to Know!

COLONEL WHARTON, sitting by the window in the library at Wharton Lodge, glanced up from his paper as Wells, the butler, entered with a card on a salver.

He glanced at the card.

It bore a name he had never seen before:

MR. HANNIBAL CHEW.

"Hannibal Chew!" murmured the old military gentleman.

"An American gentleman, sir," murmured Wells. "He has just arrived in a car, sir, and desires to see you."

"Show him in, Wells."

"Very good, sir."

Wells retired; and a minute later ushered in a very fat gentleman, from whose fat face two keen eyes gleamed like a hawk's.

Colonel Wharton, laying down his newspaper, rose politely to bow to his unexpected visitor.

He had never heard of Mr. Chew before and never seen him, and now that he saw him did not much like his looks. But he bowed courteously.

"Mr.—er—Chew?" he asked.

"Yep!" Chick Chew bit off his answer. "Glad to meet you, sir."

"Your business with me?" hinted Colonel Wharton, without stating that he was glad to meet Mr. Chew. He wasn't!

The hawk-eyes gleamed round the lofty room for a second, taking in the whole apartment in that second. Then they fixed on the colonel.

"I guess you got my old friend Vanderdecken van Duck's boy staying here, sir!" said Mr. Chew.

"Who?" ejaculated Colonel Wharton.

"Young Putnam van Duck"

The colonel looked puzzled.

It did not occur to him that Mr. Chey had shot off this statement with the intention of surprising him into admitting that Putnam van Duck was there, if indeed there he was!

As Putnam was not there, however, the cunning Mr. Chew gained nothing by his abrupt opening.

"I think I have heard the name," said Colonel Wharton. "Yes, I have heard my nephew mention the name. But the boy is not here, Mr.—er—Chew"

"Nope?" asked Chick, disappointed

"My nephew is expecting some friends from school to stay with him for the Easter holidays, but I do not think that Van Duck is one of them."

"You mean he ain't coming along?"

"I am certainly not aware of it," said Colonel Wharton.

Mr. Chew's keen eyes gave him what he would have called the once-over. That piercing glance seemed almost to penetrate the colonel's old bronzed face.

Colonel Wharton was by no means so keen as Mr. Chew, who was as sharp as a razor. But he was quite keen enough to see that the unexpected visitor was scanning him, to ascertain whether he was telling the truth or not.

The bare idea of his word being regarded with the remotest doubt caused a flush to rise in the old bronzed face.

He had never met a man like Mr. Chew before. Probably Mr. Chew had never met a man like Colonel Wharton. To Mr. Chew it came quite natural to doubt any statement made to him. To Colonel Wharton it came as a painful shock to be driven to doubt any statement. It had not occurred to him to doubt Mr. Chew's statement that he was a friend of Van Duck's father.

What did occur to him was that this fat man was a particularly offensive kind of bounder.

However, one penetrating, gimlet-like glance satisfied Mr. Chew that the old military gentleman was not deceiving him.

"Then he ain't been here?" asked Chick.

"He has not!" said the colonel distantly.

"Mebbe you know the lad?"

"I do not know him," said Colonel Wharton. "If you are a friend of his father's, and have called expecting to find him here, I am sorry you are disappointed. But I see no reason——"

"Being over on this side, I reckoned I'd give old Van's boy the once-over," explained Mr. Chew. "But I don't aim to waste your time, sir. Mebbe you'll be able to put me wise where to spot that infant."

(*Continued on next page.*)

"I know absolutely nothing of him, sir," said the colonel. "To be exact, all I know is that my nephew and his friends, while on a holiday abroad, met an American boy named Van Duck, with whom they made friends. My nephew asked him to pay a visit here during the school holiday at Easter, if he happened to be in this country at the time. My nephew naturally told me this, but I have heard nothing of the boy since."

"You ain't wise to it that he's this side of the pond?"

"I have said that I know nothing of him" The colonel's manner grew stiffer and stiffer

"I guess I can put you wise to that, then," said Mr. Chew. "Young Van Duck is in England."

"Indeed!"

"Sure thing!" said Mr. Chew, with a nod. "And, missing him in London, I figured that he had moseyed off somewhere on a visit, and kind of reckoned that this was the shebang where he had hung up his hat."

"Evidently an error on your part, Mr. Chew."

Colonel Wharton's manner indicated that the interview was ended. But that cut no ice with Mr. Chew.

Frigid looks had no effect on that gentleman. He was not accustomed to retreating before anything less effective than a levelled gun!

"I'm telling you, sir," said Mr. Chew, "that I got the wind up some about my old friend Van's boy. Mebbe you've heard that a gang of kidnappers are after him."

Colonel Wharton smiled faintly.

"I believe my nephew mentioned that the boy had told him something of the sort," he answered. "If it is the case, there is no occasion for anxiety on this side of the Atlantic, Mr Chew."

"Nunk?" asked Mr. Chew, eyeing him.

"Scarcely," said the colonel. "In this country, sir, the police are well organised, and inaccessible to bribery, and I can assure you that they would make very short work of kidnapping gangsters."

"Says you!" remarked Mr. Chew.

"I doubt," said the colonel, "whether a Chicago gangster would venture to set foot in this country at all."

"Search me!" said Mr. Chew.

"At all events, no such character would ever think of carrying on a lawless enterprise here," said Colonel Wharton. "If Mr. van Duck's son is in England, his father may be absolutely assured of his safety."

"I'll tell all Chicago!" ejaculated Mr. Chew. He gazed at the colonel. "You don't figure that if a kidnapping guy was after that young gink, he would hop over the herring-pond and give your police his name and address and then ask them to catch him if they could?"

"Scarcely!" said the colonel.

"You're telling me!" murmured Mr. Chew. "You don't sort of opine that if you had that kid here, the guy who was after him would walk into this here shebang and walk him off under your nose, sir, at the muzzle of an automatic?"

Colonel Wharton laughed.

"Pray disabuse your mind of any such idea, Mr. Chew," he said. "Nothing of that kind is possible in a law-abiding country like this."

"Pack me up in a Saratoga!" said Mr. Chew, staring at the colonel. "And sit on the lid!" he added reflectively.

Colonel Wharton politely waited for him to go. But Mr. Chew was not going.

"I'll mention," he resumed, "that you don't seem to get the how of it, not a whole lot. I guess I feel anxious, more than a few, about that boy. But if he ain't here, and you ain't expecting him——"

"That is the case."

"Mebbe that nephew you mentionsd might know a little more," suggested Mr. Chew. "Mebbe you'd call him in and ask him."

"Really, sir——"

"You get me?" urged Mr. Chew. "If my old friend Van's son has hit up against trouble, I sure want to know. Mebbe that nephew will know where he's to be found. What's the matter with asking him?"

"I quite understand your anxiety, sir, though I assure you that it is unfounded, if the boy is in this country," said Colonel Wharton. "However, I have no objection to questioning my nephew as to whether he knows anything of Van Duck's present whereabouts."

"You said it, sir!" said Mr. Chew.

"I will send for him," said the colonel.

He touched a bell.

The door opened, and Wells' plump face appeared.

"Please ask Master Harry to step here, Wells!" said Colonel Wharton.

"Very good, sir!"

"Perhaps you will be seated, sir," added Colonel Wharton, as the butler retired.

"Sure!" assented Mr. Chew.

He sat down on the arm of an armchair, and crossed one plump leg over the other, his eyes on the door.

His hand slid for a moment to the back of his trousers, where—little as the colonel dreamed of it—an automatic reposed in a hidden pocket. Colonel Wharton, who did not believe that a Chicago gangster would venture to set foot in England, much less carry on his lawless enterprises, would have been astonished to learn what methods Mr. Chew was prepared to employ, if needed, to extract information from his nephew!

THE TENTH CHAPTER.

Startling

"I SAY, you fellows!"

Harry Wharton jumped.

So did Hurree Jamset Ram Singh.

They jumped almost clear of the ground in their surprise.

Taking a stroll on the terrace at Wharton Lodge after tea, they had noticed the Singer saloon standing on the drive, where Mr. Chew had left it. It was a handsome car, and they paused to look at it, aware that there was nobody in it—or, to be more exact, unaware that there was somebody in it.

A voice, coming from an apparently empty car, made them jump—especially the familiar voice of the fat Owl of Greyfriars, which they had not expected to hear again till next term.

"What——" gasped Harry Wharton.

"Who——" stuttered the Nabob of Bhanipur.

"Bunter!" howled Wharton.

He stared blankly at the stirring rug, which shifted, to reveal a fat face and a large pair of spectacles.

"The esteemed and idiotic Bunter!" exclaimed Hurree Jamset Ram Singh.

"Oh crikey!" gasped Bunter.

He heaved up from under the enveloping rug, set his spectacles straight on his fat little nose, and blinked at the two astonished juniors, gasping.

They gazed at him like fellows who could hardly believe their eyes—as, indeed, they hardly could.

Bunter had intended to blow in at Wharton Lodge for the "hols" if he could. Though he had been safely left behind at Greyfriars, owing to Bob Cherry's "astute dodge" with the box of chocolates, Wharton would not have been exactly surprised to see him blow in. But it was a surprise to see him arrive in a stranger's car, hidden under a rug on the floor. That was very surprising indeed.

The two juniors had had a glimpse of Mr. Chew as he went in, without taking any special note of him. But they knew that he was an American, and a man they had never seen before. It was really amazing to find Billy Bunter parked out of sight in his car.

"You fat villain!" exclaimed Wharton, when he had recovered his voice. "What the thump do you think you are up to?"

"Oh lor'!" gasped Bunter. He blinked to the right, and then to the left. "I—I say, where is he?"

"He? Who?"

"That villain!" gasped Bunter.

"What villain, you potty porpoise?"

"That Yankee kidnapper!" gasped Bunter.

Hurree Jamset Ram Singh tapped his dusky forehead significantly.

"The pottiness is terrific!" he remarked.

"Oh, really, Inky——"

"What are you doing in that car, you fat chump?" demanded Harry Wharton. "Does the owner know you're there?"

"No fear!" gasped Bunter. "I shouldn't be alive if he did! I say, where is he? Is it safe?"

"Safe?" said Harry blankly.

"Yes! I say, he's Chew," gasped Bunter—"Mr. Chew——"

"Missed a chew?" repeated Wharton, misunderstanding. "Who's missed a chew? Not you, if you had anything to chew!"

"You silly ass!" howled Bunter. "Chew—Mr. Chew—Chick Chew——"

"Chick Chew!" The name seemed familiar to Wharton "I've heard that weird name somewhere——"

Hurree Jamset Ram Singh chuckled.

"It is the absurd name of the idiotic kidnapper that the ludicrous Van Duck told us about on the steamer," he remarked.

"Oh, I remember! What about Chick Chew, you fat ass?"

"It's him!" said Bunter, breathlessly and ungrammatically

"Who's him, you blitherer?"

"That fat beast who was driving the car!" gasped Bunter. "I say, he's after Van Duck! I say, he knows he's here!"

"After Van Duck!" said Harry. "Van Duck isn't here, you owl!"

"Oh, don't be an ass!" said Bunter. "I jolly well know he's here. He told me he was coming here when I saw him at Greyfriars to-day, and it's hours and hours and hours since he left me on the road near Lantham, so he must have got here, and that ruffian Pike after him, and——"

"Well, if he was coming here, he hasn't got here," answered Wharton. "Did he drop in at Greyfriars after we left?"

"Yes; and I told him where you were, and he came here——"

"He hasn't come, ass!"

"Oh!" said Bunter. "I suppose that man Pike got him, after all, then! But, I say, that man Chew thinks he's here. I heard him say so while I was in the car. He's come here after him."

"What on earth makes you think the owner of the car is the kidnapper?" demanded Wharton.

With a herculean effort, Chick Chew broke loose from Harry Wharton and Hurree Singh, and made a bound for the French window. Next moment he crashed bodily through in a shower of broken glass!

"You silly ass, I heard him tell the other man so!" howled Bunter. "I tell you, he's after young Van Duck! I—I came specially to warn you. I didn't get into this car simply to bag a lift; I was thinking of Van Duck all the time, and running fearful risks to get here in time to warn you——"

"Chuck it!" said Harry.

"Oh, really, you ungrateful beast, I——"

"Is there anything in it, or is that fat chump trying to pull our leg, Inky?" asked the captain of the Remove.

Hurree Jamset Ram Singh shook his dusky head.

"The knowfulness is not terrific!" he answered.

"Look here, you fat ass, if you're not gammoning, tell us how you know," said the captain of the Remove.

Bunter had crawled out of the car. He stood blinking round him uneasily through his big spectacles. It was evident that he was in a state of great uneasiness, not to say blue funk.

"Where is he?" he demanded.

"He's gone in to see my uncle. Wells showed him in a few minutes ago. If you know anything about him——"

Billy Bunter gasped out an account of his startling adventures since he had been left behind with the box of chocolates at Greyfriars.

Harry Wharton and Hurree Jamset Ram Singh listened blankly. The fat Owl had finished when Wells appeared from the doorway.

"Master Harry——"

Wells broke off, with a surprised glance at Bunter.

"Yes!"

Harry looked round.

"The colonel desires you to step into the library, sir!" said Wells.

"Oh, all right! Is the man who came in this car still there, Wells?"

"Yes, sir!"

"What name did he give you?"

"The name on his card was Hannibal Chew, sir."

"Chew!" repeated Wharton. "My hat!" That piece of information bore out Billy Bunter's rambling statements. "Come on, Inky! You come in with me!"

"I say, you fellows," gasped Bunter—"I say, look out for his revolver!"

"Fathead!"

"Beast!"

The two juniors hurried into the house. Billy Bunter did not. Billy Bunter did not want to see Mr. Chew at close quarters.

"Here, Wells!" he said.

"Sir!" said Wells, eyeing him.

"Show me to my room!" said Bunter.

"Your room, sir?" repeated Wells.

"Yes. Buck up!"

"Are you staying, sir?" asked Wells.

"Yes! Of course I am!" snapped Bunter. "Haven't I told you to show me to my room, you ass?"

Wells coughed.

"I have had no instructions, sir, to prepare a room," he said. "Perhaps you will wait, sir, till Master Harry informs me——"

Billy Bunter gave him a devastating blink through his spectacles.

"That's cheek, Wells," he said.

"Indeed, sir!" said Wells.

"And I don't want any of it, see?" snapped Bunter.

"Yes, sir!" said Wells. "Thank you, sir!" And he glided away, and his portly figure disappeared by the service door.

"Wells!" hooted Bunter. "Look here, Wells——"

Wells was gone.

"Cheeky beast!" grunted Bunter. "They don't know how to keep servants in order here! I'd teach 'em!"

And as Wells did not show him to his room, Billy Bunter went upstairs to look for it himself, unaided!

THE ELEVENTH CHAPTER.
"Stick 'Em Up!"

"HERE is my nephew, Mr. Chew!" said Colonel Wharton.

Harry and Hurree Singh entered the library together. Hannibal Chew—or Chick, as he was known to his friends—rose from the arm of the armchair.

He gave the two schoolboys a penetrating look, which they returned with interest. Certainly, but for what they had just heard from Billy Bunter, they would have had no suspicion of the fat man.

Now they had very strong suspicions indeed.

According to Bunter, Putnam van Duck had been heading for Wharton Lodge, though he had not arrived there. Had he arrived, he would have been under the same roof as the man who had planned to kidnap him, and hold him to ransom. Escaping from his too-watchful guardian, Poker Pike, he would have walked right into the presence of the gangster.

"Harry," went on the old colonel, "this is Mr. Chew, a friend of Mr. van Duck——"

"A friend, uncle?" repeated Harry. "A friend of Van Duck's father?"

(*Continued on page* 16.)

THE HIKING HEADMASTER!

By DICKY NUGENT

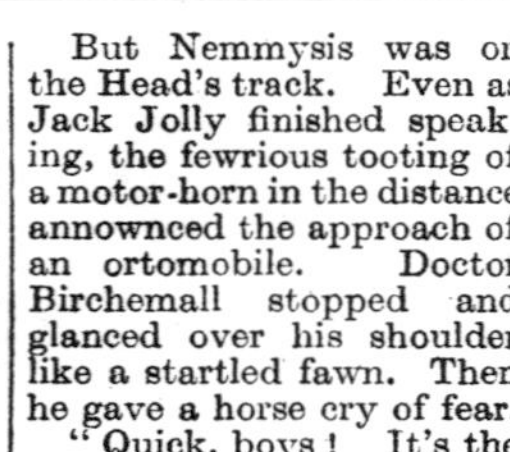

No. 185. EDITED BY

"I'm jolly glad we've left the Head behind!" grinned Jack Jolly, as he and his pals tramped down to the gates of General Jolly's manshun one bright Spring morning. And Merry and Bright and Fearless chimed in with a harty:

"Hear, hear!"

"We get enuff of the old fogey at skool, without having to put up with him on hollerday, too!" added the kaptin of the Fourth. "Like his cheek to invite himself to my pater's place!"

"Let's hoap he's gone by the time we get back!" chuckled Frank Fearless. "In any case, I'm looking forward to a cupple of days hiking—not to menshun the search we're going to make for that missing bar of gold that fell out of an airoplane somewhere over this part of the country last week! Won't it be a bit of luck for us if we find it and get the hundred pounds reward?"

"Yes, rather!"

"Hundred quid or not, it's a releef to be away from the Head!" grinned Merry. "We can—oh!"

He broke off with a gasp of serprize. Right in front of the St. Sam's juniors was the very man he was talking about—Doctor Birchemall, of St. Sam's! That alone was serprizing enuff; but what was still more serprizing was the Head's eggstraordinary attitude. Dressed in hiker's clobber, he was crawling about on all fours, nibbling the grass near the gates; and, as if that wasn't puzzling enuff, he was wearing round his neck a chain, the other end of which was tied to a stake in the ground!

"My hat!" gasped Jack Jolly. "He's set the billy-goat free and chained himself up in its place! What's the idea?"

At that moment, Doctor Birchemall spotted the juniors and beckoned them over. Jack Jolly & Co. obeyed the summons with alackrity. They were awfully anxious to find out the meaning of the Head's amazing behaviour.

"Good-morning, sir!" they corussed.

A look of fear came into the Head's greenish eyes.

"Not so loud, you yung idjuts, or they'll hear!" he wispered. "Lissen, boys: I'm in a fix. I am not, as you mite suspect, acting the goat——"

"My hat! What ARE you doing, then, sir?"

"I am adopting the guise of a goat—a distinction with a difference!" replied the Head. "To reveel the truth, boys, there are two detectives outside the gates, waiting to serve me with a writ for non-payment of income-tacks!"

"Few!"

"I threw them off the scent last nite, but when I got up early this morning, hoaping to hike my way to freedom, it was only to find them waiting outside for me! Luckily, I had this branewave," said the Head, with a feint smile. "I decided to take the place of the billy-goat so as to be near the gates! Now I am waiting for them to go up to the house. As soon as they do so, of corse, you won't see me for dust! Not so dusty, eh?"

"Grate pip! Wouldn't it be simpler to pay your income-tacks?" asked Frank Fearless.

"Unforchunitly, Fearless, I haven't the needful, or I would! I asked General Jolly for a loan; but he's as mean as they make 'em, and——"

The Head broke off, as the rattling of keys sounded from the direction of the gates.

"Locke, the lodge-keeper, is letting them in, sir," grinned Jack Jolly. "You'd better start nibbling the grass again, if you don't want them to be suspishus!"

"Thanks, Jolly; I will!" And the Head started making a pretence of chewing up tufts of grass with an air of relish.

It was really serprizing how closely the Head resembled a goat from a distance. Probably it was his lean, angular figger and beard that did it. Whatever the eggsplanation, he hoodwinked the two 'tecs all right, and they walked up the drive to the house without giving him a second glance.

The moment they were out of site, the Head flung off his chain and jumped to his feet.

"Worked like a charm!" he grinned. "Now for my getaway! Are you going hiking, too, boys?"

"Ye-es, sir, but——"

"Eggsellent! We can all go together! This way!"

Jack Jolly & Co. inwardly groaned. It was a bit thick, they reflected, to have the Head piled on to them like this just when they were fondly imagining they had escaped his klutches! But they couldn't very well argew the toss with such an important personage as Doctor Birchemall, so they relucktantly fell in with him—hoaping that it wouldn't be long before they all fell out!

It was soon pretty obvious that it was going to be no plezzure jaunt so far as the Head was conserned. The thought of the 'tecs who were after him seemed to inspire his feet and the juniors found that they were going to get no opportunity of searching for the missing bar of gold on which they had set their harts. At St. Sam's, Doctor Birchemall was used to weelding the birch, so perhaps it was not serprizing now to find him setting a spanking pace!

Mile after mile flashed by under his tireless nines, till Jack Jolly & Co. wondered when he was going to stop.

"If we go on like this," muttered Merry, "our legs will be worn to stumps and we shall all have bats in the belfry!"

"I'm sorry those 'tecs didn't bowl him out, and I only hoap he'll soon be caught!" mermered Jolly. "It's not kricket!"

But Nemmysis was on the Head's track. Even as Jack Jolly finished speaking, the fewrious tooting of a motor-horn in the distance annownced the approach of an ortomobile. Doctor Birchemall stopped and glanced over his shoulder like a startled fawn. Then he gave a horse cry of fear.

"Quick, boys! It's the cops!"

Jack Jolly & Co. looked back; and when they reckernised the same two 'tecs they had last seen walking up the drive to General Jolly's manshun, they felt as though a new hoap had dawned in their lives!

"They're only just in time!" grinned Frank Fearless, as he mopped his perspiring brow. "Another five minnits and we should all have been turned into grease-spots!"

"Don't be selfish, Fearless!" wimpered the Head, who was dancing about like a cat on hot brix. "Can't you think of some way to hide me?"

"Stand at the cross-roads with your arms up, sir," sujjested Jack Jolly. "Perhaps they'll mistake you for a signpost!"

"Ha, ha, ha!"

"What about climbing up into that tree, sir?" asked Bright, pointing to a tree at the side of the road.

The Head looked at it, then nodded eagerly.

"Good wheeze, Bright! I will! Bunk me up, some of you!"

Jolly and Bright gave the Head a helping hand to lift him into the tree before the 'tecs arrived, an
cupple of jiffies
Birchemall was clin
amongst the branc
the agility of a
And then, just
detectives' car race
the seen, an eggstra
thing happened.
shaking the tree, t
dislodged a brick t
lying on one of th
branches. The b
and hit him on the
and the Head overb
An instant later, he
downwards, to alig
a fearful wallop
heads of the two 't

Bang! Crash!

"Yarooooooo!"

"Ow-wow-ow!"

Somehow or ot
driver mannidged
the car to a stop
'tecs turned round
back, where the H
come to rest.

To their utter d
ment, they foun
hugging the brick t
caused his downf
grinning all over hi

"Good-morning,
men!" cried Docto
emall, cheerfully.
trubble to serve t
on me now. I
kindly drive me
nearest perlice-sta
settle my income-t
dispose of the
matter!"

"What the dicke

The Head held
brick and Jack Jol
jumped, as they sa
was of a pekuliar y
culler.

"See this
grinned the Head.
happens to be the
gold that dropped
that airoplane las
The finder is to r
reward of a hundre
—and the finder ha
be myself! Comp

WOULD YOU BELIEVE IT?

Peter Todd could hardly believe his ears when he heard Bunter say he did not like toffee—till Bunter added unless it had plenty of sugar in it. Dutton, who was making toffee over the study fire, did not hear Bunter. If he had, he might not have let the Owl share it. A "sticky" prospect!

The crew of the herring drifter which ran ashore at Pegg Bay were in a sorry plight, until Tom Redwing of the Remove pluckily swam out with a life-line. Redwing was brought up by the sea, and many of his leisure hours are spent by it. The rescue was quite in his "line"!

**Ten wickets for five r
Hurree Singh's ren
analysis when bowling
the Upper Fourth in th
Form match of the
Temple explained that
needed practice—but Bob
remarked that he has ne
them yet when they
"Collapse" of Temple**

S HERALD

STOP PRESS NEWS

'HARTON. April 25th, 1936.

"M-m-my hat!"
"Well, of all the luck!" jackulated Frank Fearless. We were after that our-elves, sir!"
"Sorry, and all that!" rfed Doctor Birchemall. Are you ready, officers? hen drive on! Ta-ta, oys! See you next rm!"
And a few seconds later e Head was being driven way to receeve his reward!
"Well, it's a pity we idn't bag that gold," re-arked Jack Jolly, as he nd his pals tramped off own the lane. "But ere's one good feetcher bout it. Now the Head's funds, we shan't see any-ing more of him this ollerday."
And when they thought over, the Co. decided that ter all it was worth every enny of a hundred pounds be released for the rest of e vack. from the dewbious elights of Doctor Birch-nall's company!

E'LL RAISE THE OOF OVER THIS!

Ogilvy, who hasn't spent penny of the pound his ncle gave him last month, iled in a recent singing st because he didn't eathe deeply.
Yet he seems to be able hang on to his note all ght!

PRIZES FOR PEA-SHOOTING

H. Vernon-Smith offers ve Free Feeds to the five ortsmen scoring the best ts from Remove study indows next week. Points warded for seniority of ctim and position of shot. op score if you hit a Beak the boko!

FOOD FOR THOUGHT AT THE ZOO!

Grins

PETER TODD

'Lonzy has recently become interested in the theory that man is descended from animal and, with a view to studying the theory, he has been spending half his holiday at the Zoo. I went along with him myself the other day and I must say I found plenty of food for thought.

I hadn't been inside the place more than a couple of minutes before I exclaimed: "What on earth is Skinner of the Remove doing in that cage over there?" It gave me a severe jolt when 'Lonzy told me that it was not Skinner but a wolf!

One exhibit I could have sworn was Coker. Only the sign outside its cage convinced me otherwise. It was a grizzly-bear.

Then there was a camel in the grounds that looked the living image of Fisher T. Fish, and a sea-lion that brought Mr. Prout to mind in a jiffy.

"'Lonzy, old sport," I said, as I rejoined my cousin; "there's not much doubt about the truth of your idea that men are related to animals——"

Then I broke off with a gasp, as I woke up to the fact that I was talking not to 'Lonzy but to an ostrich that looked exactly like him! And—would you believe it?—some of the keepers had got similarly mixed up and were trying to shoo 'Lonzy into a cage under the impression that he was an ostrich!

'M yes, there's food for thought at the Zoo right enough. Trot along and see for yourself, dear reader; but take identification papers with you!

(*We can't help suspecting that Peter is trying to pull our legs; but seeing what an old pal he is, we're printing his yarn just the same!*—ED.)

IT'S MORE THAN HOSKINS DOES!

A correspondent tells us that when Hobson of the Shell made a speech at the last meeting of the Senior Debating Society, he struck exactly the right note.

Hoskins, the Shell pianist, is green with envy!

HOLIDAY ROUTINE AT BUNTER COURT!

By BOB CHERRY

Cheery old Bunter has just been telling me what happens at Bunter Court at holiday time. So gather round, ye Bunter fans, and listen to the dope, just as I get it straight from the horse's mouth!

Breakfast is served by Hodgkinson, the butler, and the eighteen footmen in the luncheon-room or in any of the guests' fifty bed-rooms if the guests wish it. The best plate is always used—solid platinum, set with diamonds. The servants have to be content with the worst—mere silver plate.

After brekker, guests are wheeled in bathchairs to the terrace by Podgkinson the butler and the forty footmen. There they take their choice of the various amusements prepared for their pleasure. There is a string of hunters for those who yearn for a gallop through Bunter Park, and tennis, golf and cricket champions to play with those who feel like adjourning to the private courts, course and pitch respectively.

Lunch is served in the evening banqueting-hall by Dodgkinson and the sixty-five footmen. The best plate is again used—solid silver, studded with emeralds. The servants use the worst—mere platinum.

The afternoon is set aside for rest, in any of the seventy-five guests' bed-rooms. Dinner is served in the luncheon-room by Dodgkinson and the hundred-and-twenty footmen. Again the best plate is used—solid gold, set with sapphires. The servants use the worst—mere silver, studded with rubies.

Supper, Bunter mentioned, in a moment of absent-mindedness, is taken sitting on a pair of steps in the kitchenette.

It may strike you that there are one or two contradictions in this account of the routine at Bunter Court, but you must excuse Bunter for being a little vague; he hasn't visited this ancestral home of his just lately.

In fact, there are strong grounds for thinking that he never has visited it—except in his fat though brilliant imagination!

PREPARING for SUMMER at GREYFRIARS

By BOB CHERRY

If you imagine that Greyfriars is completely asleep this vac., lads, you're making a big mistake! I had a look in the other day to collect some kit I'd forgotten to bring away and I can assure you there's plenty going on!

What is making things move at Greyfriars is the near approach of Summer.

Some of you chaps would get an eye-opener to see what a hive of activity our playing-fields present just now. Mimble and a small army of assistants are working like Trojans to get the turf in trim; and if we don't start the season with pitches that are a joy to play on, it won't be for want of elbow-grease on their part!

Woodwork in every part of the School House is being adorned with a new coat of paint, two hard courts are being laid down beyond Little Side and the cinder-track is being renewed for Sports Day.

There's another kind of activity going on, too. Several masters have already returned from their holidays to prepare special syllabuses ready for the exams next July. Not so good, eh?

Ah, well! We can't expect to get the pleasures of the Summer Term without doing our quota of work. A certain amount of swot is a necessary evil; and I, for one, don't mind it when I think of the glorious prospect of fun and sport in the sunshine that goes with it.

GREYFRIARS FACTS WHILE YOU WAIT!

en Vernon-Smith said there a chestnut-tree on Courtfield nmon so widespread it would lter all the Remove except ater, "W. G. B." was an-ed! Bunter is certainly an size—but the giant chestnut beats him by several feet in h. The only "living" thing that does, says Smithy!

Mark Linley was telling Removites how, on his last visit to his home in Lancashire, he went down a coal mine, and was able to help when a miner was hurt by a fall of coal. Linley dragged off a heavy beam which had fallen from the roof on to the man, and was warmly congratulated. Marky "glowed"!

Removites represented the countries of their birth in a junior boxing tournament. Close finishes were the rule, Bob Cherry just defeating Tom Brown in the final to win the championship for England. Runners-up were Tom Brown (New Zealand), Delarey (South Africa), and Hurree Singh (India).

INCREDIBLE!

Snoop claims to be able to supply "inside" information on nearly everything. We can hardly believe it—knowing what a complete "outsider" he is!

(*Continued from page* 13.)

"Yes, and he has called under the impression that the boy was here. You remember telling me that he might visit you during these holidays——"

"I remember."

"I do not know whether you have heard anything of him since," went on the colonel. "But if you know anything of him, please tell Mr. Chew."

"Spill it!" added Chick encouragingly.

"I do know something more of him, uncle," said Harry quietly. "But I'm not sure that I had better tell Mr. Chew."

Colonel Wharton stared at his nephew.

"What do you mean, Harry? Mr. Chew is anxious about the boy, who appears to be threatened by kidnappers, as you told me. He desires to know where to find him, and if you can assist——"

"I know that Van Duck is threatened by kidnappers, uncle! And I know that the leader of the gang is named Chew!" answered Harry.

"Good gad!" ejaculated Colonel Wharton.

"The Chewfulness is terrific!" added Hurree Jamset Ram Singh.

Chick Chew straightened up, his face hardening, his hawk-like eyes alert. He looked, for the moment, like a jungle animal scenting danger.

"Mr. Chew seems to know that we met Van Duck, and asked him here," went on Harry. "But he does not seem to know that Van Duck told us about the Chicago kidnappers who were after him."

"Nope!" said Mr. Chew. "I'll say I was not wise to that, big boy! Did he say one of the crowd was named Chew?"

"He did!" answered Harry.

"I'll mention that there's a whole heap of Chews in the Yew-nited States!" said Chick. "You ain't figuring that I'm the Chew that young Van Duck told you was on his trail?"

"I am!" answered Harry.

"Forget it, bo!" advised Mr. Chew.

"Come, come, Harry," said Colonel Wharton. "What possible reason can you have for supposing——"

"Plenty of reason, uncle," said Harry. "If this Mr. Chew isn't the same Chick Chew that Van Duck spoke of——"

"Not so's you'd notice it!" interjected Hannibal.

"Then why," said Harry, "have you been hunting for Van Duck all over Kent in a car to-day?"

Chick fairly gasped. He was not easily taken aback, but this quite took the wind out of his sails. He had never seen this schoolboy before, and the boy had been here, in Surrey, while Chick was hunting in Kent. How the schoolboy knew anything of his proceedings that day was a mystery to Chick.

"Say, big boy, you dreaming?" he gasped.

"I think not," said Harry. "Why did you tell your confederate, Bud Parker, to go on hunting for him, while you came here to see whether Van Duck had turned up at Wharton Lodge?"

Mr. Chew almost fell down.

This looked like black magic to him. He had talked to Bud Parker standing by his car at the wayside inn in Kent, without, so far as he knew, any other car within hearing.

Yet this boy, nearly a hundred miles from the spot, knew what he had said to the other gangster!

His hawk eyes almost goggled at Harry Wharton. The colonel, equally amazed, stared blankly at his nephew.

"Say!" gasped Mr. Chew. "Can you beat it? I'm asking you, can you beat it?"

"And why," went on Harry, "did you tell Bud Parker that the next time he saw you, you might have a passenger hidden under that big rug in your car?"

"Fan me!" murmured the dazed Mr. Chew. "Fan me a few!"

"And why," continued the captain of the Greyfriars Remove, "did you tell Bud Parker that if you failed to find him here, you would go over the whole island with a small comb till you combed him out?"

Mr. Chew tottered.

"Afore this," he said, apparently addressing space, "I ain't never believed in them telepathic stunts! Now I'm sure getting it down! Yep!"

"If you're not after kidnapping Van Duck, why did you say all that to that bony man in the horn-rimmed spectacles?" asked Harry.

Mr. Chew moaned.

"Horn-rimmed specs and all!" he murmured. "Don't he know the whole bag of beans? He sure do! Carry me home to die!"

In his hectic career as a gangster in the great city of Chicago, Mr. Chew had doubtless encountered many surprises. But never had he been so utterly surprised as now.

If it was not telepathy or black magic, there was no accounting for what the old colonel's nephew knew of him and his proceedings that day!

He leaned a fat hand on the high back of the chair to steady himself. He gazed at Harry Wharton open-mouthed, revealing some expensive American gold-fitted dentistry.

"Say, big boy," he gurgled, "did a little bird tell you all that?"

"Harry!" gasped the colonel. "What can you possibly mean? How can you possibly know——"

Harry pointed to Mr. Chew.

"He looks as if I know!" he answered. "Uncle, that man is Chick Chew, a dangerous Chicago gangster, the man whom Mr. Vanderdecken van Duck is afraid will kidnap his son."

"Good gad!" said Colonel Wharton. "I cannot doubt it now, but——"

"Search me!" said Mr. Chew. "Search me, Charlie!"

Colonel Wharton made a stride towards him. Amazed as he was by the extraordinary fund of information in his nephew's possession, he could not doubt it. Mr. Chew's face was a confession.

The old military gentleman faced him, with knitted brows.

"So you are a kidnapper!" he exclaimed. "You are the gangster who has threatened to kidnap a boy and hold him to ransom!"

"Sort of!" gasped Mr. Chew.

"And you have dared to come here, here to my house, in search of information to help you in this dastardly rascality!" exclaimed the colonel, his voice trembling with indignation.

Mr. Chew pulled himself together. He had been taken quite off his balance. But he was very quickly himself again.

"You said it!" he remarked, in a casual tone. "And I'll mention that that young gink has said that he knows something of Putnam. I'll trouble him to spill it."

"What!" thundered the colonel. "Do you imagine, for one moment, that my nephew will give you any help in your lawless enterprise—that I would allow him to do so?"

"Kind of!" agreed Chick.

"Scoundrel!" boomed the colonel. "So far from that, you will be detained, as you have dared to venture here, and handed over to the police. And you will find that, in this country, the police cannot be corruptly influenced into releasing a dangerous desperado."

"You sure do spill a large mouthful!" said Mr. Chew. "I'll say you're some orator, when you get going! But time's money, old-timer, and I'm advising you to park it, and let me get through. I'm telling you I'm here for information, and I sure do want to know."

Colonel Wharton breathed wrath.

"Harry," he gasped, "go at once and tell Wells to telephone for a constable from Wimford! Mr. Chew, if that is your name, I shall detain you here till the constable arrives to take you into custody, and I warn you, sir, that I shall not hesitate to use force!"

"Ha, ha, ha!" roared Mr. Chew, greatly to the angry old soldier's surprise. "I'll pass it up to you, sir, for tickling a guy to death!"

But as Harry Wharton made a step towards the library door, Chick Chew's merriment vanished suddenly, and was replaced by a cold, hard, ferocious grimness. His hand shot to his hip, and reappeared with an ugly looking, black-muzzled automatic in the podgy fingers.

"Freeze on to that spot where you're standing, bo!" he said, snapping the words sharply through his American dentistry. "And you, sir, stick 'em up! You hear me toot? I'm whispering to you to stick 'em up!"

And the angry old colonel, making a stride towards the gangster, stopped suddenly, gasping, as the black muzzle of the automatic looked full in his bronzed old face, with the hawk eyes of Chick Chew gleaming over the barrel.

"Stick 'em up!" repeated Chick.

THE TWELFTH CHAPTER.

A Little Liveliness!

"STICK 'em up!"

Those words, familiar enough to Chick's own ears, sounded strange and startling in the quiet old library at Wharton Lodge.

Colonel Wharton stood as if transfixed.

Harry turned back from the door. Hurree Jamset Ram Singh stood stock still.

All three were under cover of the automatic. It needed only a pressure of Chick's podgy finger to spray them with bullets.

That he could even think of doing so seemed wildly unimaginable in that quiet country house, in the quiet English countryside.

But, unimaginable as it was, evidently it was in the gangster's mind. A chunk of Chicago, as it were, had been suddenly transferred across the ocean—and there it was!

Harry's teeth set hard and his eyes glinted. The nabob's dusky face set.

As for the old colonel, he stood rooted, staring in such amazement that his mouth was open, like that of a fish out of water.

It was not fear that rooted him. A man who had been through the War, from beginning to end, was not likely to be afraid of deadly weapons. But it was perfectly plain that Chick meant to shoot if a hand was lifted against him, and it was sudden death that looked the colonel in the face without a chance; bare hands were not much use against a levelled automatic.

"I said stick 'em up, bo!" bawled Mr. Chew.

Colonel Wharton gasped.

He did not "stick 'em up." Nothing would have induced him to obey the order of the gangster.

"Rascal!" he spluttered. "Impudent scoundrel!"

"Pack it up, old-timer!" said Mr. Chew. "You sit this one out! And I guess I ain't waiting long to see you reach for the roof."

Instead of raising his hands above his head, as ordered, Colonel Wharton clenched them hard. Even the grim automatic barely stopped him from hurling himself at the gangster.

"I will do nothing of the kind!" he thundered. "Do you flatter yourself for one moment that you can give orders to an Englishman in his own house—and a soldier, too, begad!"

"Just a few!" said Chick. "Put 'em up, old-timer, while you got time! Heap guys in Chicago could tell you that I'm a bad man to argue with!"

"Bah!" snorted the colonel.

"You putting up them fins?" growled Chick threateningly.

"No!" roared the colonel. "Shoot if you dare, you scoundrel!"

"I'll say you got sand!" said Mr. Chew. "There ain't a lot of guys that would stand on their hind legs chewing the rag with this baby when I got a gat in my grip! Nope! I guess I ain't honing to spill your vinegar all over this hyer expensive polished floor of yourn. Stand where you are, and park your chin-wag—you've said your piece!"

He glanced past the colonel, at Harry.

"Now, big boy, spill it!" he said. "Where'd you last see that young galoot Putnam? Shoot!"

"I shall tell you nothing!" answered the captain of the Greyfriars Remove steadily, though his heart was beating hard.

"Guess again!" suggested Mr. Chew. "Look at that old hoss—he'll sure be going off that deep end soon, and I'll have to strew him around with holes in him. You want to spill it—and spill it quick!"

"Scoundrel!" gasped the colonel.

"Aw, ain't I told you to park it?" remonstrated Mr. Chew. "Ain't I tipped you that you've said your piece? Sit it out, I'm telling you!"

"Rascal!" spluttered Colonel Wharton.

He made a movement. The cold, hard, hawk-eye glinted over the automatic, and the old soldier stopped again.

"I'll say you're the guy to ask for it!" said Chick, in a tone of cold, savage menace. "You'll sure cinch it soon, if you don't behave! Now you young gink, you going to spill it?"

"You will not utter one word to that scoundrel, Harry!" thundered the colonel.

"Not a word, uncle!" said Harry quietly.

The hawk eyes glinted at them.

Chick Chew, it was certain, was ready to shoot, if it came to shooting. But he had expected to gain his point by the mere terror of the levelled gun.

Chick was a reckless and unscrupulous rascal; but he was no fool, and he knew which side of the Atlantic he was on. What would have been a mere episode in his happy native city of Chicago, would have been sufficient to set the whole country in a buzz in the old-fashioned island in which he now found himself. In Chicago, gun-play was Chick's first resource; but on the old-fashioned side of the herring-pond it was his last!

There was a pause!

The colonel stood with clenched hands. Harry Wharton, near the door, stood quite still. Hurree Jamset Ram Singh, a few feet from his chum, rested his hand on a little table, where a book lay—Harry Wharton's "Holiday Annual."

The nabob's dusky fingers had closed on that volume, behind him.

His dusky face expressed nothing, but he was calculating his chances. The champion bowler of the Remove Eleven had an unerring hand. But it was a long chance to take, for nothing could have been more certain than that the gangster was ready to pull trigger on the instant if his safety was threatened.

The pause was brief.

The automatic swayed a little aside from the colonel, and Harry Wharton could almost have looked into the muzzle.

"I'm telling you, bo!" said Chick Chew, in a deadly tone. "I guess I ain't no baby-killer, but I got to get the goods! You're going to put me wise about that young gink Putman! I give you till that there clock has ticked off jest one minute!"

Harry Wharton did not answer; but he breathed hard. That he knew what would be useful to the gangster, Chick could guess, though he did not know what.

Wharton knew, from Bunter, that Putnam van Duck was on his way to Wharton Lodge; and might, indeed, arrive at any moment. Nothing would have induced him to tell what he knew. But the perspiration started out on his forehead as he looked at the black muzzle.

Colonel Wharton made a movement. The hawk-eyes gleamed round at him.

"You asking for it?" came in a deep growl from the gangster. "By the great horned toad I guess——oooooah!"

His eyes were off Hurree Singh. In fact, he had given the dusky schoolboy hardly any attention at all.

In that moment the nabob acted swiftly! His arm jerked—the volume flew through the air as swiftly as a bullet from Chick's own automatic.

It smashed on that automatic, hurling

(*Continued on next page.*)

GREYFRIARS INTERVIEWS

Our clever Greyfriars Rhymester is still going strong with his series of interviews. In the following snappy verses he introduces

DICK RAKE,

a real good lad of the Remove.

(1)

Dick Rake, though his temper is certainly short,
Is a pretty good sort on the whole.
He isn't outstanding at classes or sport,
At cricket he knows how to bowl.
If there is one thing at which Rake is a dab
It is physics, or otherwise, "stinks,"
He spends many hours in the chemistry lab.
Where he mixes most horrible drinks.

(2)

He'd just made a brilliant discovery when
I called round to see him to-day,
I found him at home in his study or den
With his study-mates out of the way.
He held a test-tube, and I saw with surprise,
That the tube was well-corked and sealed down,
'Twas brim-full of powder, which seemed to my eyes
To be coloured a kind of mud brown.

(3)

"My new high explosive!" he told me with pride,
As he deftly adjusted the cork.
"There's more than enough of this powder inside
To blow the whole school to New York!
In fact, it would blow up the county of Kent,
If you dropped it right here on the floor!"
I thereupon felt it was time that I went
And I made a swift move to the door.

(4)

"All right! I shan't drop it!" he said, with a grin.
I wasn't so certain of that!
However, I cautiously shuffled back in.
Too cautious! I tripped on the mat.
I made a wild plunge to recover my feet
And I bumped into Rake with a roar,
And then (with a word which I cannot repeat)
He let the bomb fall to the floor!

(5)

It burst! And the powder shot out in a stream!
I knew that my hair had turned grey!
And yet the school buildings to me didn't seem
To have shifted much farther away!
The county of Kent didn't show many scars
Of its horrible journey through space.
It might have been blown to the outermost stars,
But to me it looked just the same place!

(6)

"Some bomb!" I remarked, with a sniff of disdain.
"It burst like a packet of salt!"
Then Rake answered back. He was painfully plain
(His face has a similar fault).
He answered me warmly, but let it be said
That his manner was lacking in tact.
To throw a large book at a visitor's head
Is a most unaccountable act!

(7)

He followed the book with a bottle of ink,
Which I didn't object to so much.
But to start flinging eggs by the dozen, I think
Was really the finishing touch!
I wouldn't have minded as much as I did,
If the eggs had been fresh, but they weren't!
I wouldn't go through it again for a quid,
The beastly things ought to be burnt.

(8)

I might have overlooked the sickening smell,
I might have forgiven the yolk.
But when he was flinging the bomb-stuff as well
I thought it was far past a joke.
I then felt obliged to take action to stop
This highly uncivilised stuff,
And so with the aid of a shovel and mop,
I showed him that I'd had enough!

it from the gangster's hand, and the weapon clattered on the floor.

Chick, with a yell of rage, plunged after it.

As he stooped, the nabob leaped at him with the spring of a tiger of his native land. Both his fists crashed together on the top of Chick's head, and the gangster stumbled over and fell.

"Oh, good man, Inky!" panted Wharton.

He rushed forward to back up his dusky chum.

But the colonel was first. One active leap carried him to the sprawling gangster, and he grasped him as Chick scrambled furiously to his feet. The nabob's foot struck the automatic, sending it spinning across the room, far out of the gangster's reach.

Neither had Chick any time to reach for it. He was struggling in the grasp of the old colonel.

"Now, you scoundrel——" panted Colonel Wharton.

"Bag him!" panted Harry.

Both the juniors grasped hold of Chick. With three pairs of hands on him, the man from Chicago stumbled and staggered and struggled.

But, fat as he was, unwieldy as he looked, Chick was an active man, full of strength and full of beans.

It looked, for a moment or two, as if he must be overcome, and secured. But he suddenly hooked the colonel's leg, and the old soldier went over, bumping on the floor, gasping for breath.

Chick, with the two juniors clinging to him like cats, scrambled away to the window. The sound of the struggle had already drawn attention; and Wells, opening the door, stared into the room with amazed eyes.

The alarm was given, and the gangster was disarmed. Chick Chew was thinking now of only one thing—escape; or making his getaway, as he would have called it.

The french windows were shut. Chick reached them, and with a herculean effort hurled the two clinging juniors off.

But quick as he was, the colonel was on his feet by that time, and was coming on again, followed by the astonished Wells, and Harry and the nabob rallied at once. Chick had a split second.

But it was enough for the gangster, accustomed to desperate affrays and to swift action. His bulky shoulder crashed through the window, and the next moment he crashed bodily through it, in a shower of broken glass. From the smashed window startled eyes stared after him, as, running with the swiftness of a deer, he vanished into the shrubberies.

THE THIRTEENTH CHAPTER.

Bad Luck for Bunter!

"FAT Jack!"

"Beast!"

That exchange of compliments took place the following morning.

Billy Bunter, with his big spectacles glimmering in the April sunshine, was standing in the gateway of Wharton Lodge, blinking out at the wide world.

He was still there—though the future was a little uncertain.

As he had sagely calculated, Harry Wharton had asked him whether he would like to stop the night, and Bunter had.

For some reason or other Wharton had not followed it up with a request to remain for the rest of the vacation.

That was Bunter's fixed intention, if it could be managed. But it was not settled yet.

Having come down at eleven o'clock that morning, he had found that Harry and the nabob had gone out; which was annoying, for naturally, in such an uncertain state of affairs, Bunter wanted to get the matter settled.

Now, as he blinked out of the gateway to see whether the beasts were coming back, he sighted a slim, keen-eyed youth, who sauntered up the road, and who stopped at the sight of him.

It was Putnam van Duck.

"You again!" said Putnam. "I guess this is Wharton Lodge, then! What?"

"Yes!" grunted Bunter. "Seen those beasts?"

"Eh?" asked Putnam. "Who?"

"Wharton and Inky——"

"I ain't spotted them, but I guess I want to!" said Putnam. "Ain't they at home?"

"They've gone out!" grunted Bunter. "That's how they treat a guest here—clearing off before a fellow's up in the morning! I've a jolly good mind to clear off myself, before they come back. It would serve them right."

"It sure would!" agreed Putnam. "Nice for them, what?"

Snort, from Bunter.

"Look here, have you come here to stay?" he asked.

"Sort of."

"Well, you'd better not!" said Bunter. "You won't be safe here. See? That man Chew was here yesterday——"

"You're telling me!" said Putnam.

"There was a fearful row," said Bunter impressively. "He scared them all by pulling out a gun—as it happened, I wasn't in the room, or I'd have had it off him fast enough——"

"I sort of see you doing it," agreed Putnam. "I'll say you'd be a tin terror on ten wheels if you got going."

"Well, he was after you," said Bunter. "He smashed through a window and got away—as I wasn't there to stop him. He left his car behind, and the police from Wimford have been here, and taken it away. But I shouldn't wonder if he's hanging about. You can see you ain't safe here, Van Duck."

"That worries you a whole lot?" asked Putnam.

"Yes, of—of course. I jolly well don't want a gangster hanging about here while I'm here, I can jolly well tell you. The best thing you can do is to clear off at once!" suggested Bunter. "The further away you get the safer you'll be. You see that?"

Putnam chuckled.

He was a keen youth, but he did not need to be very keen to see that the safety Billy Bunter was worried about, was the safety of his own fat person.

Bunter did not like the idea of Mr. Chew in the offing. And he had no doubt that if Putnam van Duck stayed Mr. Chew would very soon be in the offing again.

He was, indeed, as anxious to lose sight of Putnam van Duck as Chick Chew was to get sight of him!

"Of course, I'm not thinking of myself at all!" Bunter explained.

"You wouldn't!" grinned Putnam.

"I never do!" said Bunter. "That's always been my fault—forgetting myself and thinking of others. I never get any gratitude, and I don't expect it. As for danger, that doesn't worry me—in fact, I like it. But as you wouldn't be safe here, Van Duck, you'd better not come in at all. I'll show you the way to the railway station, if you like."

"I guess I could find a station that I've just walked away from," said Van Duck. "But I sure ain't hitting it jest now."

"Now look here," said Bunter firmly. "Don't you come barging in where you're not wanted, see?"

Van Duck looked at him.

"Ain't this baby wanted around?" he inquired.

"No! I don't want to hurt your feelings, but the fact is, that after what happened yesterday, the old fossil——"

"Who's that?"

"I mean Colonel Wharton—grumpy old stick," said Bunter. "Savage temper, you know—stiff as a ramrod—looks at a fellow as if he wasn't there. Well, after that row yesterday, the old fathead told Harry that he'd better let you know, to keep away from here——"

"He sure did?" asked Putnam.

Harry Wharton and Hurree Jamset Ram Singh collared Mr. Pike and sent him hurtling into the ditch. There was a terrific splash as the gunman landed on his back in two feet of water and mud. "Gooooooogh!" gurgled Mr. Pike.

"Those very words!" said Bunter. "And Harry said—I hardly like to tell you what he said——"

"Oh, spill it!" urged Putnam. "I sure do want to know."

"Well, he said that of course he didn't want a pushing Yankee poking into the place——"

"Wharton said that?"

"Those very words! I hate telling you, old chap, but I can't help thinking it's better for you to know the truth," explained Bunter.

"The truth?" repeated Putnam. "Sure thing! Get on with it!"

"And Inky said—if you want to know what Inky said——"

"Shoot!" urged Putnam. "You've got me interested."

"Well, Inky said that he couldn't stand Yankees—you see, we've got one at Greyfriars, and he's a fearful tick—and he said he'd go, if you came. And Wharton said—— What are you grinning at?"

A wide grin overspread Putnam van Duck's face.

It was caused by the sight of Colonel Wharton, who was coming down the drive to the gates.

As Bunter had his face to the road, he naturally had his back to the drive within, and having no eyes in the back of his fat head, he did not, of course, see the old military gentleman coming.

Putnam, facing Bunter, and looking past him, saw the old colonel, and saw, also, that he was hearing Bunter's cheery remarks.

And the expression that was gathering on the old soldier's bronzed face, revealed the effect that those remarks had on him.

"Was I grinning?" asked Putnam. "Forget it, and carry on. I'll tell a man, I like to hear you talk!"

"Well, Wharton said, that if you showed up here he'd jolly well let you know at once where you got off!" said Bunter. "And the old ass——"

"Who?"

"I mean Colonel Wharton," said Bunter, in happy ignorance of the fact that Colonel Wharton, with a brow like thunder, was just behind him, "Colonel Wharton said—— Yaroooh! Yooop! Oh crikey!"

A grip like iron on the back of his collar caused Billy Bunter to break off with that wild splutter.

Spinning round in the angry old gentleman's grip, the fat Owl gazed at him in horror, his eyes almost bulging through his spectacles.

"Ooooogh!" he gurgled. "Leggo! Ooooogh!"

"You young rascal!" thundered the colonel.

"Urrrrrrggh!"

Still gripping the wriggling Owl by the collar, Colonel Wharton glanced at the smiling face of Putnam van Duck.

"I gather, from what this untruthful young rascal was saying, that you are my nephew's American friend," he said.

"You said it, sir!" assented Putnam.

"I am Colonel Wharton—I am very glad to see you here. There is not a word of truth in what this young rascal has been telling you——"

"I guessed that one, sir."

"My nephew has gone out, at the moment, but he will be delighted to see you when he returns," said Colonel Wharton. "As for you, Bunter——"

"Urrrrggh!"

"You untruthful, prevaricating, unscrupulous——"

"Wurrggh! Leggo! Oooogh!" gurgled Bunter. "I—I say, I—I wasn't—I mean, I never—groooogh! I didn't mean you were an old ass, sir! I—I was speaking of another old ass——"

"What?" roared the colonel.

"Not you at all, sir!" gasped Bunter. "Quite another silly old ass, sir—not you. And I say—gurrrrgggh! Stop shook-shick-shaking me! Urrggh!"

Shake, shake, shake!

"Urrggh! Wurrggh! Gurrggh!"

"Now," said Colonel Wharton, releasing the fat Owl's collar, "I think you have a train to catch, Bunter. I advise you to catch it at once. Please come with me, Van Duck."

"Sure!"

Putnam van Duck walked up the drive with Colonel Wharton. Billy Bunter, gurgling for breath, remained at the gateway, blinking after them in dismay through his big spectacles.

It was not uncommon for the fat and fatuous Owl of the Remove to put his foot in it; but never, or hardly ever, had he put his foot in it so disastrously as now. So far as Harry Wharton was concerned, it was still unsettled whether Billy Bunter was to stay or go. But so far as Harry's uncle was concerned it was evidently settled. Even Billy Bunter did not need a stronger hint than this to take his departure.

"Oh lor'!" gasped Bunter.

THE FOURTEENTH CHAPTER.

Punishing Poker Pike!

"PULL in, you!"

Harry Wharton and Hurree Jamset Ram Singh stopped suddenly. They were walking on the Wimford road, a mile from Wharton Lodge, when the bowler-hatted man stepped, as it seemed, from nowhere and faced them.

"Pike!" ejaculated Harry Wharton.

"The esteemed and ridiculous Pike!" murmured Hurree Jamset Ram Singh.

They smiled at the hard, serious, hickory face of the gunman, grim under the clamped-down black bowler. Mr. Pike did not smile He was a serious man, and had serious business on hand.

"I guess you're wise to me!" he remarked

"Quite!" said Harry, smiling. "We saw you yesterday, Mr. Pike, from the train, after young Van Duck on the Lantham road. Did you get him?"

Pike's slits of eyes scanned him sharply.

"I guess I never cinched that infant," he said. "But I'll mention that I'm sure cinching him soon That kid's popper pu. me in charge of him, and I guess he ain't shaking no loose leg without orders from Old Man Van Duck. Not so's you'd notice it, bo! Where is he now?"

"I haven t the foggiest!" said Harry, laughing

"I guess I'm asking you to talk turkey!" said Mr Pike. "I gotta see that kid safe! I'm telling you, Chick Chew is on this side, and he's after that boy like a politician after a bribe. Surest thing you know. You ain't standing between that boy and me seeing him safe."

"Not at all," said Harry. "If Van Duck's in as much danger as his father supposes, I think he's rather a young ass to keep away from you, Mr. Pike. But it's his own business, not mine."

"I'm asking you to put me wise," said Mr. Pike. "I guess you'll know. You're the crowd he made friends with on the steamer when he levanted last time. I saw him yesterday in company with one of the crowd—that fat guy with four eyes. Yep! Now he's in this quarter, and I see you here. I guess I can put two and two on paper and add them up! Surest thing, you know! That kid was aiming to join up with your bunch"

Harry Wharton made no reply to that.

As a matter of fact, Mr. Pike was quite right. But though Wharton was aware of Putnam's intentions, he was not aware of his present whereabouts. He had seen nothing of him since that glimpse from the train on the Lantham road.

"I been chasing that young guy a few!" went on Mr. Pike. "I'll say he's led me some dance! Up and down this here island till I figured we'd be falling off! I spotted him and lost him ag'in, and spotted him ag'in and lost him, more'n a few. Last night, I'll tell you, I lost him hereabouts. I guess he throwed down the car and took to the railroad. You get me?"

"We haven't seen him——"

"I sorted it out," went on Mr. Pike, unheeding, "that he put up for the night at a shebang down the line, and took a train in the morning. I got that froze! I been rubbering along that railroad till I got it from some guys that he was seen getting out at a little burg called Wimford. I'll mention I can see what's as plain as the dirt on a dago. You get me? That lad's moseyed along this-a-way to join up with the bunch he knowed on the steamer You know where he is. Spill it!"

Harry Wharton laughed.

"I've told you it's Van Duck's bisney, not mine, Mr. Pike," he answered. "If I knew where he was I should not tell you; but I don't know."

"Guess again!" suggested Mr. Pike.

"If you don't believe me, you ass——"

"I've been told a lot of things since I was a small child," said Mr. Pike.

"Mebbe I've believed some of 'em, not a whole lot."

Clearly Mr. Pike's training as a gunman had diminished his faith in the human species. He resembled Mr. Chew in that respect—as in many others. He happened at the moment to be on the right side of the law, and Mr. Chew on the other side; but in other points there really was not a lot to choose between them.

"Well, let it go at that," said Harry good-humouredly. "I know something about Van Duck's intentions, but I'm not going to tell you any more than I told Chick Chew yesterday. But I haven't seen him, and don't know where he is."

"You seen Chick?" Mr. Pike was instantly alert.

"He called at my uncle's house with a gun to ask about Van Duck," said Harry, laughing.

"Search me!" ejaculated Mr. Pike. "You telling me Chick got him?"

"No; he wasn't there. And Chick couldn't have got him, anyway. Chick was glad enough to get himself away, as it turned out."

"You're telling me!"

"The truth, Mr. Pike," said Harry, laughing again. "People do sometimes tell the truth, though it may seem rather hard to you to get that down."

"I ain't met a heap of them guys," said Mr. Pike simply. "And I'll say you ain't stringing me along so easy as you figure. Where's young Putnam?"

"Not knowing, can't say."

Mr Pike's hand slid into a pocket, which was sagging under a rather heavy weight but he withdrew it. His natural impulse to "pull a gun" had to be restrained in a land that was so hopelessly unlike his native land.

"I guess," said Mr. Pike, "that if we was in Chicago this minute I'd fan you a few for spilling them fables But we ain't."

"Just as well to keep that in mind," said Harry dryly.

"But," went on Mr. Pike, "you got to put me wise to young Putnam. You got to spill it or else I'm going to take you by the neck and twist you a whole lot. Surest thing, you know."

And Mr. Pike, proceeding from words to actions, made a sudden movement and grasped both the juniors at once in his wiry hands

His next proceeding would have been to "twist them a few," as he expressed it; but that intended proceeding was stalled off by the prompt proceedings of the two Greyfriars fellows.

Harry Wharton's fist came out like a bullet, landing on the jutting point of Mr. Pike's prominent jaw, and the gunman gave a startled yelp and staggered

Before he could recover from the jolt the two juniors collared him and rushed him over.

There was a ditch beside the road, fairly well filled by the spring rains. Mr. Pike went backwards into that ditch.

There was a terrific splash as he landed on his back in two feet of water over a foo. of mud

He disappeared entirely from sight, save for his feet, which stuck up out of the ditch, wriggling wildly.

In a split second, however, he emerged, struggling upright. His bowler hat, still firmly clamped on his bullet head, streamed with mud. His hickory face was masked with mud. His eyes and nose and ears were full of it. He gasped for breath and spluttered mud.

"Gooooooogh!" gurgled the gunman. He started scrambling frantically out of the ditch Leaving him to it, Harry Wharton and the nabob walked on towards Wharton Lodge. Behind them there was a continuous sound of gurgling, gasping and grunting. Mr. Pike was busy with the clinging mud for quite a long time

Looking back, a little later, the two juniors saw a muddy figure, in a muddy bowler hat, trailing along the road at a distance behind them.

They half expected Mr. Pike to follow on, for vengeance; but he did not seem to be thinking of that. And perhaps he had given up the idea of getting information by "twisting." Evidently he was shadowing them to their destination, with the idea in his mind that they would be leading him to Putnam van Duck

The two juniors exchanged a grinning glance.

"Cut!" whispered Harry. And the nabob nodded.

They ran to a roadside stile, and vaulted over. Immediately there was a sound of running feet on the road.

Cutting across a corner of the field, they hunted cover in a bunch of drooping willows.

Peering out of the willows, they had a view of a muddy face and a muddy hat over a stile. They suppressed their chuckles as they watched.

Poker Pike seemed at a loss as he scanned the field for unseen schoolboys. Finally, he seemed to make up his mind that they had run along the footpath to the next field; for he clambered over the stile, and hurried along that footpath.

When he disappeared into the next field, the two juniors emerged from their cover, and slipped back into the road. There, with smiling faces, they resumed their walk back to Wharton Lodge—leaving the persistent Mr. Pike to search field after field for them—in vain!

THE FIFTEENTH CHAPTER.
The Watcher in the Wood!

"VAN DUCK!"

"The esteemed Transatlantic Van Duck!"

It was a surprise for Harry Wharton and his dusky chum when they came in to lunch. Billy Bunter was not there! Putnam van Duck was!

The American grinned at them cheerfully as they shook hands.

"Guess I blew in!" he remarked. "You sort of remember asking me to give your show the once-over when we were on that steamer?"

"Quite!" said Harry. "And we're jolly glad to see you!"

"The gladfulness is terrific!" declared the Nabob of Bhanipur.

"My!" said Van Duck. "I guess I must be a sight for sore eyes, at that rate. I allow I had a long trip getting here. There was a guy wanted to tread on my tail, but I guess I dropped him along the railroad."

"We've seen Pike!" said Harry. "He doesn't know you're here—but he's not far away; looking for you."

"He sure is some sticker!" agreed Van Duck "I guess I ain't taking any little walks out, while he's rubbering around. I'm telling you, I'm fed-up to the back teeth with that hombre, and then some He's a good man, and I like him; but a little of him goes a long way."

"Well, I don't see how he can nose you out here," said Harry. "He's guessed that you came this way to see some of us; but he doesn't know my name, as far as I know; or my address, either. He can't barge into every country house in Surrey looking for you."

"I wouldn't put it past him!" said Van Duck. "He sure is a sticker, and he's got pop's orders; and I'm telling you when pop says jump, a guy jumps, and jumps hard and quick."

"You're all right here," said Harry, laughing. "But I'm not so sure about Chick Chew. Have you heard?"

"Yep: Fat Jack spilled it to me. And if you'd rather unload the trouble right now. shoot, and it's me for the railroad, pronto."

"Rot!" said Harry. "You're staying. The local police are looking for Mr. Chew, if he turns up in this quarter again He's gone."

Putnam chuckled.

"I guess your local police wouldn't worry Chick a whole lot," he said. "But Chick don't worry me so much as Poker.

(*Continued on next page.*)

COME INTO the OFFICE, BOYS—AND GIRLS!

Your Editor is always pleased to hear from his readers. Write to him: Editor of the "Magnet," The Amalgamated Press, Ltd., Fleetway House, Farringdon Street, London, E.C.4. A stamped, addressed envelope will ensure a reply.

DO I know of anything that travels quicker than light?—is a question that has been put before me on more than one occasion. At the moment of writing this chat I feel almost tempted to say: "Yes—news."

Only last week I made mention of the fact that, owing to numerous requests from readers, I was considering telling again the story of the early adventures of Harry Wharton & Co. Since then, I have been "snowed under" with letters on this subject. And to crown it all I actually received a "wire" yesterday, worded as follows: "Anxiously waiting to read about Wharton's early schooldays." Can I possibly, in the face of all this, do anything else but grant such a request? As your Editor and friend for the past twenty-eight years my sole aim has been to please you fellows, and in retelling this epic story, I feel sure that I will be doing many thousands of my supporters a really good turn.

Here, then, is the Great News! I have arranged for this wonderful story to appear in our popular companion paper—"The Gem Library," commencing with next week's issue. So look out for:

"THE MAKING OF HARRY WHARTON!"
By Frank Richards,

in next week's "Gem." Not one of my MAGNET readers should miss this rare treat, and I am telling you about it in plenty of time to enable you to give a definite order to your newsagent to reserve a copy of next week's "Gem" for you. There will be a mighty rush for this issue—out on Wednesday, April 22nd—and you simply must not miss it! So pass the good news round, chums. "The Making of Harry Wharton!" starts in next week's "Gem"!

Of course, the MAGNET will "carry on as usual" with bang-up-to-the-minute long complete school stories of Harry Wharton & Co. such as the ones Frank Richards is now giving us.

IF Billy Bunter ever gets into trouble with the police, chums, he can get a bit of comfort by reflecting on a case which has just happened in America. In this particular instance, a man was

TOO FAT TO GO TO GAOL!

He was sentenced for passing bogus cheques in Chicago. When he was taken to the gaol they couldn't get him in! Weighing 26 stone, the man was so fat that he couldn't pass through the doors. In consequence of this they had to get a special room near the prison for him. To crown it all the prison officials found that he was too large to fit any of the prison beds, and an extra-large size bed had to be made for him. I should think he'd prove a rather awkward prisoner for the authorities—just as Billy Bunter would, if he was unfortunate enough to find himself in the same position!

As I have pointed out on several occasions, some very curious things happen in this queer old world of ours. Here is a mystery which has just come to light in London. Can you imagine a man who has been

ON GUARD FOR 800 YEARS?

Takes a bit of believing—especially as he is a dead man! At a City church in Garlick-hill, the embalmed body of a man has stood to attention in a glass case just inside the door for approximately that period. Nor has he become a skeleton. There is still flesh on the body and hair on the head and eyelashes. A ghost of a smile is on the face. Who the man was no one knows, but it is claimed that he was a very important man of the twelfth century. Nowadays he is called "Jimmy Garlick." He was originally buried beneath the high altar of the church, which was subsequently destroyed by fire. One theory is that when the church was burned, chemically impregnated water was used to put out the fire, and this chemical water poured into the vault where "Jimmy" was buried, and thus embalmed him. But the actual truth will probably never be discovered, and in the meantime "Jimmy Garlick" still keeps his long vigil!

HERE is a selection of

THINGS YOU'D HARDLY BELIEVE

all of which have happened in the past few weeks:

Crimson Snow and Blood-red Rain fell a little while ago near Darbhange, in the Bihar and Orissa province of India. Several acres of land were covered, to the consternation of the natives, who fear it foretells some great calamity.

Yellow and Red Snow also fell in Switzerland, at Davos, Klosters, and in the Canton of Ticino. A microscopic analysis showed the presence of sand in the snow, and it is presumed that this sand was blown in huge quantities from the Sahara—one thousand miles away!

A Man Killed by a Trout. While fishing in the river Mur, in Austria, a retired Government official hooked a 7 lb. trout—a record for the river. It was too much of a shock for the official, and he fell dead. When he was discovered, the trout was still struggling on his line!

The Man who Walked 276,000 Miles! Philip Lewis. an Australian, has just completed this record walk. He has been wandering around Australia, preaching. In doing so, he has worn out 200 pairs of boots!

The Crazy Clock of Prague. Workmen in a Prague firm have sued their employers because they allege that the hands of the firm's clock always slip back a half-an-hour at six o'clock They are demanding overtime for all the extra half-hours which they have been forced to work because of the crazy clock!

Now for a reply to a query from Tom Harvey, of Whitstable, who asks me about

CHRISTOPHER COLUMBUS' DESCENDANT.

There is only one male direct descendant of Christopher Columbus, who discovered America. He is fifty-seven years of age now, and bears the same name as his illustrious ancestor. He lives in a spacious old palace in Madrid, Spain. But the curious thing is that he is not at all interested in travel He prefers to breed cattle and horses. Also he has only once visited America. That was in 1893, when he was a boy of fifteen. He was taken then to the Chicago World Fair, and spent three months touring the United States. But he says he has no desire to return there.

NOW we come to the all-important business of next week's programme. Another bumper twopennyworth? I'll say it is! And you'll fully agree with me when you read:

"GUN PLAY AT GREYFRIARS!"
By Frank Richards,

the second story in our grand new series featuring Putnam van Duck and his gunman guardian, Poker Pike. Wise as he is to the ways of gangsters, Poker Pike is far from wise to the playful ways of schoolboys like Harry Wharton & Co., of Greyfriars, who take a real delight in leading him up the garden! Fun as well as thrills you'll find in plenty in this first-rate yarn.

You'll enjoy, too, Geo. E. Rochester's closing chapters of "The Lost Squadron!" Particulars of the next great serial to follow I propose leaving over until next week. Rest assured. chums, it will be another winner!

Of course, our programme would not be complete without another "Greyfriars Herald" supplement, neither must we leave out our Greyfriars Rhymester who "sums up" in snappy verse Tom Redwing, of the Remove and a son of the sea. Ask your newsagent to reserve you a copy of next Saturday's MAGNET without fail

YOUR EDITOR.

I surely did get peeved with that guy and his gun."

"I'm not surprised at that," agreed Harry. "But surely, Van Duck, you'd be safer with Mr. Pike at hand, if Chew——"

"Forget it!" answered Van Duck. "Don't I keep on telling you I'm fed-up with that hombre? Chick ain't got me yet—and when he blows along it will be time to sit up and howl. Besides, I got to get shut of Pike, when I go to school——"

"School?" repeated Harry.

"Sure—Greyfriars!"

"You're going to Greyfriars?" exclaimed the captain of the Remove.

"Pop's sure fixing it up with your big chief there—and when you go back, this baby goes in the same packet. And I guess I don't want Poker and his gun fooling around at Greyfriars! You figure that they'd fit into the picture?"

"Oh, my hat! Hardly!" gasped Wharton.

The idea of Poker Pike and his inseparable automatic at Greyfriars School, rather took his breath away. Quite certainly Mr. Pike did not seem to fit into the Greyfriars picture!

"Pike's got to learn where he gets off!" said Van Duck. "If I can't keep clear of Chick on my own, I'll tell Pike—but not till then! That guy has got on my whole nervous system."

It was a very cheery party at lunch—not the less so, perhaps, because William George Bunter was conspicuous by his absence.

Van Duck was in great spirits; clearly in a state of exuberant satisfaction at having, at long last, dropped the watchful Mr. Pike. To Chick Chew, he seemed to give hardly a thought. No doubt he placed full reliance upon his ability to take care of himself.

Colonel Wharton seemed to have taken a liking to the brisk, cheery American; and Aunt Amy seemed quite pleased with him. Wharton and Hurree Singh were glad to see him again; and nobody doubted that he would be quite safe at Wharton Lodge. The colonel, in fact, was expecting to hear on the telephone any minute that the gangster had been taken into custody. That expected telephone call did not, however, materialise.

After lunch, the two juniors took their visitor for a walk; but Putnam declined to go outside the precincts of the estate. He was not thinking of Chick Chew—but of the persistent Poker!

They had a long ramble in the park; Putnam asking innumerable questions about the school he was going to join for the next term. When they were coming back towards the house in the golden sunset, the American boy stopped suddenly with knitted brows.

"I guess we're being piped!" he grunted.

"Piped!" repeated Wharton.

"I mean, there's a guy keeping tabs on us."

"I don't see——" Harry glanced round in surprise. He could see nobody.

"The seefulness is not terrific!" remarked Hurree Jamset Ram Singh.

Putnam pointed to a big elm-tree farther along the path they were following through the park.

It stood black against the sunset, its shadow falling far. Beside the shadow of the trunk was another shadow—projected by an unseen figure of someone standing under the tree, concealed from the juniors by the trunk.

"Oh!" ejaculated Wharton. "Who the dickens——"

"Poker!" snorted Van Duck. "Who else?"

"Or Chick!" suggested Harry. "It's somebody, anyhow, keeping out of sight—and the silly ass hasn't noticed that his shadow's falling across the path."

They stood looking at the shadow on the path ahead. It stirred as they looked at it. They could guess that the unseen watcher had heard their voices, and knew that they had stopped.

"It's sure Pike—waiting for me to pass to grab me!" muttered Van Duck. "There ain't no stalling off that guy Pike, I'll tell a man."

The shadow stirred again.

From its motions it looked as if the unseen watcher was coming closer to the elm trunk, to peer round it at them.

Whoever he was, it was clear that he had spotted them in the park and ensconced himself in cover there to waylay them as they came along.

A hat appeared from beyond the trunk.

It was not the black bowler hat worn by Mr. Pike! It was not the soft slouched hat of Chick Chew. It was a straw hat! And the band on it was familiar to the eyes of the juniors; it was the Greyfriars colours.

The mystery was elucidated the next moment. Following the hat came a fat head and a fat face; and a pair of large spectacles glimmered into view.

"Oh!" gasped Wharton. "Bunter!"

"The ludicrous Bunter!" ejaculated Hurree Jamset Ram Singh.

"Fat Jack!" exclaimed Van Duck. "And me figuring it was Poker!" He chuckled.

Billy Bunter blinked at them inquiringly. Then he came rolling round the tree.

"I say, you fellows——" he squeaked.

"You howling ass!" roared Wharton. "What are you playing at hide-and-seek for, you blithering bandersnatch?"

"How was I to know the old beast wasn't with you?" demanded Bunter.

"The who?"

"I mean the old hunks! I've been looking for you a long time, and when I heard you coming I thought he might be with you——"

"Ha, ha, ha!" roared Van Duck. Evidently it was dread that Colonel Wharton might have been with the party that had caused the fat Owl of Greyfriars to adopt such cautious and strategic tactics.

"Blessed if I see anything to cackle at!" grunted Bunter. "Nice way to treat a fellow, hanging about all day to see you, Wharton! If that's the way you treat a guest——"

"You fat ass!" exclaimed Harry. "I thought you'd taken your train long ago. Buzz off and take it!"

"Oh, really, Wharton——"

"The buzzfulness is the proper caper, my esteemed idiotic Bunter!" chuckled the Nabob of Bhanipur.

"Oh, really, Inky——"

"What are you up to, anyhow?" demanded Harry.

"Well, look here, old chap!" gasped Bunter. "I want you to explain to the old fossil! You see, he heard me calling him an old ass, and got into a temper, though I explained that I was speaking about another old ass, and not him at all! I suppose you can set it right with the old josser, old chap?"

"If you mean my uncle——"

"Yes, old chap; the old fathead was fearfully shirty, but if you put it to him, you know——"

"You'd better do that yourself," said Harry. "I won't kick you, as I'm not seeing you again till next term——"

"Beast!"

"Is that the colonel coming?" asked Van Duck, glancing along the path.

"Oh crikey!"

That was enough for Billy Bunter. He bolted! There was a crash in the underwoods as the fat Owl departed. He did not wait to see that it was not the colonel coming!

Chuckling, the three walked on, seeing no more of Billy Bunter! Whether he had, at long last, gone for his train, or whether he was haunting Wharton Lodge like a fat ghost, nobody knew.

THE SIXTEENTH CHAPTER.

Kidnapped!

HARRY WHARTON stirred in his sleep, moved uneasily, and half-opened his eyes. It was a late hour, and he had been sleeping soundly. But it seemed to him, vaguely, that a light had glimmered on his face as he slept.

But when he opened his eyes and glanced round drowsily, all was dark, save for the glimmer of starlight at the window.

With a grip on Van Duck's arm that was like a steel vice Chick Chew led his prisoner on. With hardly a sound they negotiated the passages and stairs, Chick every now and then turning on a glimmer of his flash-lamp!

He dismissed the fancy from his mind, turned his head on the pillow, and went to sleep again. In less than a minute he was as deep in slumber as before.

But it was not, if he had only known it, a fancy! In the dark shadow by the bed's head a shadowy figure stood—not stirring, till the schoolboy's regular breathing told that he was sound asleep.

Then Mr. Chick Chew, with an amazingly light step, considering his bulk, moved noiselessly to the door and passed with equal noiselessness into the passage outside, closing the door after him without a sound.

"I guess," Mr. Chew murmured to himself, "that I ain't buying that one."

Silently he moved to the next door and entered another bed-room.

Again the tiny beam of a small electric flash-lamp glimmered on the face of a sleeper. This time it was the face of Putnam van Duck.

Mr. Chew's beady eyes glimmered from rolls of fat. He had found what he wanted. He was buying this one, as he would have expressed it.

Putnam van Duck was fast asleep. But he came out of slumber, with a start and a jump, to find a cloth over his mouth, pressed there by a firm, heavy, podgy hand. A low voice whispered:

"Pack it up, big boy! You want a tap on the cabeza that will put you to sleep till sun-up, you only got to wriggle a few."

Putnam packed it up!

He was quick on the uptake, and he did not need telling in whose hands he was. He could see nothing but a bulky shadow looming over him, but he knew that it was Chick Chew.

He did not wriggle. The cloth over his mouth prevented a cry, but he would not have uttered one. He knew, better than the Greyfriars fellows, the ways of Chicago gangsters. He was well aware that Mr. Chew had a length of lead pipe ready, and that a single "tap" would stun him if he gave trouble—and that at the first hint of trouble that tap would be ruthlessly administered. A cracked head would not help him.

The gangster waited a few moments. Van Duck made no sound, and no movement, only watching the looming shadow with fascinated eyes. The gangster's voice came again, in the faintest of whispers.

"I guess you're wise to me, Putnam! Don't you imbibe any notion you're going to be hurt, if you behave like a good little man! I'll say you're too precious to be damaged. Old Man Vanderdecken, to home, is going to squeeze out a cool half-million dollars for you. But keep it parked, Putnam—keep it parked! I'd hate to crack your nut but if you give so much as a grasshopper's whisper, crack it goes, pronto!"

Putnam lay still.

The cloth was removed from his mouth. It had been placed there to stifle any involuntary cry when he woke. He was wide awake now, and he knew that the lead piping was ready.

"You get me?" came the gangster's murmur. "Don't squeal, big boy! For the sake of that good-lookin' cabeza of yourn, don't!"

"I ain't squealing a lot, Chick," answered Putnam, in as low a whisper as the gangster's. "I guess I'd be glad to be squinting at you over a gun, though, old-timer."

Chick chuckled softly.

"You're a spry lad!" he said. "I'll say you know where you get off—which is more'n your popper does, or he wouldn't have figured that he could beat Chick Chew. First time I'm beat at this game, bo, I throw it down and buy me a candy store! I ain't been beat yet."

"How'd you get here?"

"They make winders to houses, kid!" said Mr. Chew, "and I'll tell you I've given a bunch of guys the once-over before I arrove at you. Lucky for them they never woke. If they had they'd have gone to sleep again in some hurry. You get out and clamp on your rags!"

Putnam van Duck breathed hard and deep.

"I guess," he said, "that when you get me, Chick, you're roping in the world's prize boob. You sure are cinching the goob from Goobsville! Figure that if I hadn't throwed down Poker he would be on hand this identical minute, filling you up with lead, and you running to tallow all over the floor."

"I sure can do some shooting myself," grinned Chick Chew. "But I'll allow I'm pleased that guy ain't on hand with his gun. You getting ready to take a leetle pasear with me, Putnam?"

Putnam shrugged his shoulders.

"You said it!" he answered laconically.

He was perfectly cool. And he was as watchful as a cat for a chance, as he turned out of bed. But Chick Chew gave him no chance.

The bulky shadow hovered over the millionaire's son as he dressed. The short length of lead piping was ready, and any attempt at resistance, or to give the alarm, would only have meant that Mr. Chew would have had the trouble of carrying off a stunned prisoner, instead of walking him off on his feet. Putnam knew when there was a chance and when there was not, and he was like a lamb—though watchful as a cat!

He was angrier with himself than with the kidnapper. True, he had been fed up to the back teeth with Poker and his gun. But it was borne in very clearly on his mind now that Poker and his gun were exactly what he needed, if not what he wanted! He would have given a handsome slice of the Van Duck millions for a glimpse of the hickory face under the clamped-down bowler, at that moment.

But he had got rid of Poker Pike—too well! There was no help, and he was in the kidnapper's hands.

When he was dressed, Chick's fat hands groped over him and bound his arms down to his sides. Then the gangster inserted a gag into his mouth and tied it there.

"Only jest till you get clear, big boy!" the gangster whispered, almost apologetically. "I'd sure hate to tap you."

With a grip on the boy's arm that was like a steel vice Chick Chew led him to the door. Putnam did not need to be warned to walk softly; he knew that the alternative was to be knocked senseless and carried.

With hardly a sound they negotiated the passages and the stairs, Chick every now and then turning on a glimmer of his flash-lamp, his grip on Putnam's arm never relaxing for a second.

A cool breath of the spring night air came in at the open window on the ground floor. That was the way the gangster had entered, and it was the way both of them were to leave.

Chick lifted the boy from the window and followed him out. All was silent in the shrubberies glimmering under the April stars. Not a sound came from the house. The gangster had come and gone without alarm.

"This way, bo!" murmured Mr. Chew.

He led the millionaire's son away in the shadows. Five minutes later they stopped at a paling bordering the road.

Chick gave a low, cautious whistle. It was answered from outside the fence. Putnam realised that the gangster had a confederate waiting there.

Chick swung him over the paling, and he was received in other hands on the other side. The fat gangster followed, grunting for breath as he landed in the road. Putnam's eyes caught a glimmer of horn-rimmed spectacles.

"You sure cinched him, Chick!" whispered Bud Parker.

"I should smile!" answered Mr. Chew.

He stood for a long minute looking up and down the lonely, shadowy road, and listening. All was silent and still.

"I'm telling you, Bud," said Mr. Chew, "that this here game is pie, on this side. I'll say I'd never have pulled it off so easy on the other side."

"You said it!" agreed Bud.

"Jest pie!" said Mr. Chew with satisfaction. "And clam pie, at that, Bud! I guess we might have had the car here, with the engine running, and nobody'd took no notice!"

Bud grinned.

"You stick along here a few, Bud, and I'll soon have the car along," went on Mr. Chew. "You'll be ready to hop in soon's I get the auto."

"Sure!" said Bud.

The fat gangster disappeared down the road. Evidently the kidnappers had a car concealed at a little distance in some retired spot.

While Chick was gone to fetch it Bud Parker remained with Putnam in the shadow of the park fence, his grip on the kidnapped boy's arm.

And Putnam van Duck, unable to speak aloud, told himself silently that he was the world's prize boob and the goob from Goobsville for having shaken off the faithful, too-faithful Poker Pike. But, as it happened, the faithful Poker was not far away.

THE SEVENTEENTH CHAPTER.

Poker Pike Pulls Trigger!

"OH lor'!" groaned Billy Bunter. He groaned not once, but many times.

Bunter's luck was out. His spirits were down to zero.

The hour was late.

It was a lovely April night, stars glimmering in the blue vault of the sky, a silver edge of moon peering from fleecy clouds; but the beauty of the night was completely lost on the fat and forlorn Owl of Greyfriars.

Bunter like the Irish Emigrant in the song, was sitting on a stile. It was, in point of fact, the same stile over which Wharton and Hurree Singh had vaulted that day in giving the slip to Poker Pike. Bunter did not know that, and would not have been interested had he known; Bunter's fat thoughts were concentrated on his own woes.

And his woes were very woeful.

To a very late hour he had haunted Wharton Lodge, like a fat ghost revisiting the glimpses of the moon. Not till the last light in the last window had gone out had Bunter given up his vigil; then, at long last, had the fat Owl trailed sorrowfully away.

That unspeakable beast Harry Wharton might have placated that other still more unspeakable beast Colonel Wharton had Bunter got a word with him—but Bunter hadn't.

It took Bunter a good hour to cover a mile along the lonely, starlit road, then he spotted the stile and sat on it.

He had now been sitting on that stile a long time.

He was tired; he was lugubrious; and he knew that the last train would be gone at Wimford. All that was left for Bunter was to trail wearily into Wimford and knock up the inn.

Meanwhile, he rested his fat limbs and groaned.

Bunter had often taken chances—long chances—in making his arrangements for the school vacations. On this occasion chance would have favoured him but for the unfortunate circumstance of Colonel Wharton coming along while he was talking to Van Duck. Chance had let him down—with a bump! It had let him down more than once, but never so severely as now. He sat on the stile more sadly and sorrowfully than the Irish Emigrant and groaned.

"Oh lor'!" said Bunter, for the umpteenth time.

"Say, buddy, you sure do squeal a lot!" said a voice over his fat shoulder; and the Owl of Greyfriars nearly tumbled off the stile in his surprise.

"Oooh!" he squeaked.

He blinked round at a hickory face under a rather grubby bowler hat. Mr. Pike looked at him with his usual grim seriousness.

"I reckoned it was you, buddy," he said. "I'll say you're too wide to be forgotten. I'll tell a man I'm glad to meet up with you!"

Billy Bunter eyed him morosely. He was not glad to meet up with Mr. Pike. He did not care two straws about Mr. Pike.

"You silly ass!" he said. "You made me jump, barking in a fellow's ear like that!"

"I guess I'll make you jump a few more if you don't put me wise!" said Mr. Pike gravely. "Don't you figure on beating it; I'm mentioning that I want you. You get me?"

He put a leg over the stile and sat beside Bunter.

The fat junior blinked at him uneasily. There was a cold and quiet hostility in Mr. Pike's manner that made him apprehensive. Still, he was not thinking of "beating" it. He would not have been of much use in a foot race with the wiry gunman if he had been disposed to run—which he wasn't!

"Yesterday," went on Mr. Pike, "you was in that auto with young Van Duck. You was one of the bunch he was heading for. I got you card-indexed, the whole bunch of you. You was one of the crowd on the steamer, I guess. Yep. You was with him in the auto, though I reckon he dropped you way back. I'm asking you to whisper where that young gink is. You get me?"

"Oh!" gasped Bunter.

"I hit two of the bunch, and they tipped me into a ditch," remarked Mr. Pike. "I figured on piping them home, and they put up a getaway that left me beat. I sure did lose them, like I was a rural rube losing a roll on Broadway! Surest thing you know. I been rubbering around ever since, and I'll say there ain't much of this location I ain't rubbered over, looking round for some of that bunch of guys. I found you. Surest thing you know! You're one of the bunch. You're telling me! You don't want me to get busy and twist that fat head off'n your shoulders? Nope?"

"Oh!" gasped Bunter. "No!"

"Surest thing you know!" agreed Mr. Pike. "But that's jest what I'm going to do next if you don't spill the beans. Get me?" His icy slits of eyes glinted at the fat Owl. "Where's young Van Duck? Don't tell me you don't know, like them other guys; that ain't the stuff I want. Shoot!"

"Oh!" gasped Bunter. "I don't mind telling you. Serve the cheeky beast right! He's at Wharton Lodge."

"Where'll that be?"

"It's Wharton's place—about a mile from here, down the road." Bunter pointed with a fat finger. "They're all gone to bed hours ago."

"I guess that cuts no ice." The gunman slipped from the stile. "Get a move on, big boy."

Bunter stared at him.

"I'm not going there," he said. "The old fossil's too jolly shirty, unless Wharton——"

"Pack it up!" said Mr. Pike. "Mebbe you've told me the truth, and mebbe you ain't. I ain't one of them trusting guys you read about in books. You're going to lead me to that shebang, like I was a small boy and you was my loving nurse, by the hand. Surest thing you know! And I ain't parting with you none till I got Putnam under these here eyes what are looking at you, bo! Hump it!"

"But, I say—— Whooop!" roared Bunter, as Mr. Pike, grabbing him by a fat arm, hooked him off the stile.

Bunter landed in a heap.

"Ow! Wow!" he roared.

"Want some more?" asked Mr. Pike.

"Ow! No! Wow!"

Bunter scrambled to his feet.

He did not want to walk a mile back to Wharton Lodge; he had no hope whatever of being regarded in a favourable light at that establishment if he presented himself with a gunman who knocked up the house in the middle of the night.

But it was not a matter of choice. It was not what Bunter wanted, but what Poker Pike wanted that mattered.

Grunting, the fat Owl of the Remove rolled along by the side of the wiry gunman.

Possibly Mr. Pike was puzzled at finding the fat schoolboy out of doors at that late hour of the night on his lonely own, but that did not interest him; what interested him was that he had at last found a guide to Putnam van Duck—and he did not mean to lose that guide till he had cinched the millionaire's elusive son.

Bunter grunted and groaned as he rolled wearily along. That mile back to Wharton Lodge seemed to him unending.

"That's the place!" he gasped at last, as they came along by a tall park fence. "Keep on and you'll get to the gates——"

"I guess you're keeping on, too!" said Mr. Pike; and Bunter groaned and kept on.

He was too tired to run, even if he could have dodged—and he had no chance of dodging the gunman's keen, watchful eyes.

(*Continued on page 28.*)

MORE SENSATIONAL CHAPTERS OF OUR BIG THRILLER!

THE LOST SQUADRON!

In the Middle Watch!

SQUADRON-LEADER AKERS and Flight-Lieutenant Ferris are cast away on a desert stretch of land which has risen out of the depths as the result of a huge tidal wave.

After a series of thrilling adventures they meet more survivors, among whom are Coles, Huck, and a negro named Jim Crow, who have made a rich haul looting stranded derelicts.

At long last, ships come to the rescue of the castaways. Anxious to get clear with their booty, Coles & Co., together with the aid of Larsen, Crawley, and Baines, seize the tugboat Rosa, overpower the three seamen aboard, and make for the open sea. Running short of coal, they anchor to replenish their stock from one of the wrecks. During the first watch Crawley and Baines plan to double-cross the rest of the party and skip with the booty.

When Jim roused Coles and Huck in the middle watch to take over guard, he had something to tell them.

"Dem two guys, Baines and Crawley," he said, "have bin in de fo'c'sle more'n an hour to-night wid de three seamen I cain't see dat it means anyt'ing, but it might, so jest keep yore eyes skinned!"

Coles and Huck promised they would, and leaving Jim to turn in, they ascended to the bridge where they lounged against the for'ard rail, smoking and talking in low, rumbling tones.

From an idle and fruitless discussion as to what Baines and Crawley could have wanted in the fo'c'sle, they passed on to a review of their own chances of getting away with the booty which they and Jim had collected.

"I reck'n us'll do it," said Coles confidently. "Jim ain't no fool, an' if us kin only git this coaling over without bein' spotted, then we'll make America."

"We got a mighty tough break, picking like we did on a ship with empty bunkers," complained Huck.

"We suttinly did," agreed Coles. "But there was no other ship to pick on. We might have knowed, though, that the bunkers of a craft like this was bound to be low——"

He broke off suddenly, peering through the darkness in the direction of the fo'c'sle.

"What'n heck's that noise?" he demanded, as to their ears came a low, long-drawn moan.

"Guy snoring," volunteered Huck.

"That ain't a snore," returned Coles. "Listen!"

Tense and rigid, they listened with straining ears, and again from the fo'c'sle came a low groan.

"There's somethin' happened in there," said Coles decisively. "That guy sounds as though he's hurt bad. Come on, we'd better investigate!"

Drawing his automatic from his pocket, and with finger crooked in readiness round the trigger, Coles descended the bridge ladder, and followed by Huck, moved forward in the direction of the unlighted fo'c'sle.

As they neared it, they heard the groan again, and even the stolid and unimaginative Huck could no longer mistake it for snoring. It was the groan of a man in mortal pain.

"What's happened in hyar?" demanded Coles roughly, coming to a halt in the inky blackness of the fo'c'sle doorway.

No one answered, nothing stirred. Taking a step forward, Coles began to fumble for his matches in the pocket of his reefer jacket. Then suddenly he tensed, conscious of a presence near him in the darkness. He heard a soft step beside him, a sharp intake of breath, then before he could either cry out a warning to Huck or leap aside, something descended with crushing force on his skull and he sagged forward at the knees to pitch a limp and unconscious heap to the floor.

Simultaneously there came a muttered word, a rush of feet, and Huck was borne back against the bunks, rough hands and pressing bodies muffling his cry of surprise and alarm.

Beneath sheer weight of numbers he went to the floor. A match flared, giving him a momentary vision of distorted faces, then a boot crashed savagely against the side of his head and he passed into black oblivion.

"Got 'em!" said the shaking voice of Baines. "Light that cursed lamp, somebody!"

Again a match flared into life, and the fo'c'sle lamp was lighted, its sickly illumination disclosing Baines, Crawley, the three tugboat hands, and the huddled and prostrate forms of Coles and Huck.

"Get 'em tied up before they come round," ordered Crawley, straightening up from beside Coles, whose gun he had retrieved and slipped into his own pocket. "Sweet, wasn't it, the way the pair of 'em walked into the trap?"

"You've said it!" grunted one of the three seamen, as he helped his two companions to securely truss Coles and Huck.

"And now for the nigger," said Baines nervously, when Coles and Huck, bound hand and foot, had been unceremoniously flung on to separate bunks. "I only hope the brute's asleep."

"If he isn't there's one or two of us going to get hurt," said Crawley grimly. "Come on, and move as quietly as you can!"

Picking up a belaying-pin, he led the way softly from the fo'c'sle.

Reaching the companion ladder, the five stealthily descended in single file, Baines bringing up the rear.

The door of Jim's cabin was ajar, and from inside there issued the sound of full-bodied and hearty snoring.

"Sleeping innercent as a child," whispered Crawley, with a grin. "Now, listen! This cabin's fitted with electric light like the others, and the moment I switch on we'll rush him. Don't give him a chance. Let him have it as hard as you can paste it into him. Are you ready?"

His companions assured him in hoarse whispers that they were, and, stealthily pushing open the cabin door, the bare-footed Crawley stepped across the threshold.

Holding his breath, and with the utmost caution, he groped for the electric light switch. As his fingers touched it and closed on it he took a fresh grip on his belaying-pin.

Next instant the cabin was flooded with brilliant illumination. With a shout, Crawley leapt towards the bunk on which Jim was sleeping.

The shout awoke Jim, but before he could move, before he could stir, the belaying-pin had descended with crushing force on his skull.

With a moan, the negro relaxed and went limp.

Jubilantly Crawley swung on his companions.

"Got him!" he cried. "That's the three of 'em. Get him tied up!"

Swiftly the three seamen set to work, lashing Jim's arms behind his back and binding his legs and ankles.

"And now," said Crawley, when the job had been completed to their satisfaction, "the three of you had better get along to the stokehole and see about getting steam up. There's enough coal in the bunkers to get us back to Camelot."

"Wait a minute," growled one of the men. "What about the loot? It's in this cabin, isn't it?"

"Yes, there it is," said Crawley, indicating the two bulging sacks at the foot of Jim's bunk.

"Well, just to be on the safe side," said the other, "we're taking possession of that as well as the ship."

Crawley's eyes narrowed, and his hand moved towards the pocket in which reposed the gun he had taken from Coles.

"The stuff's all right here!" he snapped.

"That may be," returned the man, "but me and my two mates are going to put it where we can keep an eye on it. You've helped us to retake the ship, mister, because you say you reckon the game's up and that you're bound to be captured sooner or later. You're figgering on turning King's evidence. I don't say that ain't sensible of you. As a matter of fact, I think it is. But what I do say is we ain't trusting you any——"

"No?" rasped Crawley. "Then stick 'em up!"

As though by magic his gun had appeared in his hand and was covering the three seamen.

"You ain't trusting me, ain't you?" he jeered. "Well, I wasn't expecting you to. That's why I've got this gun. Make a move, just one of you, and I'll blow your brains out!"

He spoke out of the corner of his mouth to Baines.

"Get loaded up with as much of that swag as you can stow away about you," he ordered. "Then fill my pockets. I'll look after these mugs!"

With an almost frantic haste Baines got to work, stuffing his belt and pockets with jewel-cases and rolls of notes from the sacks. It was only when he could carry no more that he turned his attention to Crawley, who was still keeping the three seamen covered.

Taking care not to get between the men and the gun, Baines proceeded to cram Crawley's pockets full of the best of the swag, until at length Crawley brusquely called a halt.

"That'll do!" he snapped. "Put the key of the door in the lock outside!"

Hastily crossing the floor, Baines withdrew the key from the inside of the door and thrust it into the lock on the outside.

"We're going now," said Crawley, addressing the three seamen, "and we're taking the precaution of locking you in. But if you do manage to kick the door down before we get clear don't come after us, or'll you'll get a bullet, and I don't mean mebbe!"

Still keeping the men covered, he began to back towards the door.

Under the menacing threat of that blue-black barrel the trio could do nothing save stand motionless.

It was when he had almost reached the threshold that Crawley heard a slow and heavy step in the corridor outside, heard Baines gasp, then heard the deep and growling voice of Larsen say behind him:

"What is happening in here?"

Pursuit!

CRAWLEY halted, and for a moment he stood rigid. He dare not turn his head, dare not take his eyes from the three seamen, and in his heart he was cursing Larsen for this unlooked for and inopportune appearance.

"What are you doing, Crawley?"

Again the deep voice of Larsen growled from the doorway, and this time there was a suspicion in it, which made Crawley hesitate no longer.

"Tell him, Baines," he said, speaking over his shoulder, but still keeping the three men covered.

"D'you mean—d'you mean tell him everything?" gulped Baines.

"Yes, you fool!" snapped Crawley. "You know we were just going to his cabin to tell him!"

Baines knew nothing of the sort. What they had just been going to do was quit the ship, leaving Larsen to look out for himself. But, that plan having now been frustrated by the appearance of Larsen, Baines took his cue from Crawley and clumsily proceeded to explain what had happened.

"We kidded them three fellers into helping us to take the ship, Larsen," he said. "They thought we was going back to—to Camelot with them to turn King's evidence, but all we was after was the loot——"

"Yes, and now we've got it we were just coming to rouse you, Larsen," cut in Crawley. "We're clearing out with as much of the stuff as we can carry, and the only reason we didn't tell you before was that we knew you'd be no use in the scrap what we've had with the nigger and his two mates."

"Don't lie, Crawley!" said Larsen harshly. "You and Baines were going to quit like the dirty rats you are!"

"You're wrong, Larsen——"

"I'm not wrong!" grated Larsen. "You were going without me. I know the sort of snake you are, Crawley! Yes, and you, Baines! I'll talk to you later about this, when—when I'm stronger. I'll learn you to try to double-cross a man like me, Crawley!"

"I wasn't trying to double-cross you, Larsen," reiterated Crawley. "Honest, I wasn't. Baines knows——"

"Baines is as big a liar as yourself!" rasped Larsen. "There's a pair of you, and you haven't got an ounce of pluck between you. But I'm coming with you, Crawley. You don't get rid of me so easily!"

"We want you to come with us, Larsen," said Crawley with an effort. "Get hold of some swag, and we'll go."

Not yet had he seen Larsen, for not once had he taken his watchful gaze from the three seamen whom he was keeping covered; but now, as Larsen limped slowly forward into the cabin, Crawley shot a swift glance at him from out the corner of his eyes.

Far from being a prepossessing sight was Larsen, and fearful indeed must have been the punishment he had taken from Jim. His bearded face was still swathed in bloodstained bandages, his sunken cheeks were bruised and discoloured, and his bloodshot eyes were puffed and swollen.

He walked with dragging, shuffling step, and as he bent over the two sacks to help himself to as much loot as he could carry Crawley saw that his hands, raw and skinned, were shaking as though with the ague.

"You look in a pretty bad way, Larsen," observed Crawley.

"I'm not in so bad a way that I can't smash you, Crawley!" snarled Larsen.

Crawley made no further comment, but, waiting until Larsen had stuffed his pockets and belt as full as he could, he jerked his head in the direction of the door.

"Get up on deck and into the boat with Baines," he said. "I'll hold these fellers!"

"Yeah, git goin', Larsen," drawled the weak voice of Jim Crow from the bunk. "Git goin', case I gits dese ropes loosened an' whips you agin!"

So occupied had Crawley, Larsen Baines, and the three seamen been with their own affairs that they had failed entirely to notice Jim's return to consciousness, and his voice startled them considerably.

Larsen was the first to recover from his momentary surprise, and, limping to the side of the bunk, he stood glaring down at the negro.

"So you're awake, nigger," he grated, "and I've got you just where I want you!"

With the words, he drove his clenched fist with savage force down into Jim's upturned face, bringing blood spouting from squat nostrils and thick lips.

It was as foul and cowardly a blow as could well be imagined, and even Crawley felt sickened at the vicious brutality of it.

"That's enough, Larsen!" he said sharply, as Larsen raised his fist to strike again. "We've got no time to waste on the nigger. Leave him alone, and let's go!"

But Larsen paid no heed. The thrashing he had received from Jim had seared his mind as deeply as his body, and, with bruised and bearded lips asnarl, and bloodshot eyes ablaze with hate, he drove his fist again into the upturned face of the bound man.

"Stop him, Crawley!" croaked Baines from the doorway, and his face was ghastly. "Stop him, man!"

"Larsen" — Crawley's voice was metallic—"if you do that again I'll drop you!"

Larsen slowly turned his head, his blood-smeared fist upraised to strike again.

"You'll drop me?" he snarled. "You rat, you haven't got the pluck to shoot!"

With that he turned again to Jim.

"This time, nigger," he said slowly—and Baines shuddered at his voice—"I'm going to kill you! I'm going to smash your face right in!"

Then it was that the nearest seaman acted. Braving the menace of Crawley's gun, he leapt forward, and, seizing Larsen's upraised arm, whirled the man round, and drove his fist full into the convulsed and bearded face.

Simultaneously Crawley's gun spat lurid flame, but it was only to stop one of the other seamen who had rushed at him. Next instant he had leapt to the door and was outside with Baines, slamming shut the door behind him and turning the key in the lock.

"Come on, you fool!" he panted to Baines; and together they dashed up the ladder to the deck.

The boat was lying moored alongside

Printed in Great Britain and published every Saturday by the Proprietors, The Amalgamated Press, Ltd., The Fleetway House, Farringdon Street, London, E.C.4. Advertisement offices: The Fleetway House, Farringdon Street, London, E.C.4. Registered for transmission by Canadian Magazine Post. Subscription rates: Inland and Abroad, 11s. per annum; 5s. 6d. for six months. Sole Agents for Australia and New Zealand: Messrs. Gordon & Gotch, Ltd., and for South Africa: Central News Agency, Ltd.—Saturday, April 25th, 1936.

and, tumbling into it, they hurriedly cast off. Then, seizing the oars, they commenced to row frantically in the direction of the shore and were swallowed up in the night.

Meanwhile, down in the cabin, the three seamen had overpowered Larsen, and whilst two of them sat on him, the third was smashing the lock of the door by the simple expedient of kicking lustily at it with his heavy boot.

The overpowering of Larsen had not been difficult, for the man had been in no shape for a fight.

The lock of the cabin door yielding, rope was soon procured, and, trussed and bound, Larsen was carried to his cabin and flung on to his bunk.

A council of war between the three seamen then followed, and, abandoning any idea of going after Baines and Crawley, they decided to commence getting steam up right away with a view to setting off as soon as possible for Camelot.

"After all," said one of them philosophically, "we've got four of the fellers and most of the loot. It's not a bad haul, all things considered!"

After taking another look at their captives, they descended to the stokehole and started to rake out the fires and get them going again.

Jim, lying on his bunk, his face bruised and swollen, was thinking desperately. He had recovered somewhat from the nausea caused by Larsen's savage blows, and he realised to the full the plumb awful jam which he, Coles, and Huck were in.

Apart from having raided derelicts, the three of them would now find themselves faced with the much more serious charge of having seized a ship sailing the high seas on its lawful occasions. That was piracy—a hanging matter.

Something had got to be done, decided Jim, and done mighty quick. But what could be done? Bound and helpless as he was—and as he guessed Coles and Huck were—their chance of escaping the gallows was nil.

"Lordy, lordy," he groaned, "this chile am sure gonna swing!"

He lay quiet for a while, gathering his strength. Then slowly, and with a grim determination, he began to expand his mighty muscles, straining at his bonds until the rope cut into his flesh.

His lungs were filled to capacity; his heart was pounding madly. But, oblivious to everything save escape, he strained and strained with a terrible intentness, until at length sheer exhaustion caused him to relax and go limp.

A while he lay, drawing great breaths into his labouring lungs; then tentatively he began to move his arms and legs, testing the tightness of the rope which bound him.

As far as he could discover, it had yielded not the fraction of an inch. But nothing daunted, he went to work again, straining at the bonds until the perspiration started out in beads on his forehead and his great knotted muscles formed his black and glistening skin into the semblance of moulded, quivering iron.

But he had been tied by expert hands, and the taut rope, cutting deeper and deeper into his arms and legs, would not yield. Time and again Jim tried to loosen it, but at length, weak and exhausted, he relaxed and confessed himself beaten.

Well, it was to be a hanging, then. He, Coles, and Huck would swing together. Perhaps Larsen would be with them, for if Larsen had not been guilty of raiding derelicts, he had, at least, been in on the seizing of the Rosa.

And what about Crawley and Baines? Would they be caught? Almost certain to be, sooner or later, reflected Jim. The only chance of getting clear had been to get the Rosa coaled and put to sea.

He had been a fool ever to have brought Larsen into the game. And Larsen had been a fool ever to have trusted Crawley and Baines.

"Yeah, I guess us is all rogues together," mused Jim—"all rogues together!"

A while he lay, staring up at the low ceiling of the cabin. Then, as strength slowly returned to him, he heaved himself up on the pillow, and raising his head, looked about him.

The cabin contained only a chair and a small dressing-chest. On a hook behind the door hung oilskins and a sou'-wester, and on one wall was nailed the dingy picture of a ship, cut from some periodical.

But it was the dressing-chest which held Jim's attention. On it was a comb, a hairbrush, and a small cheap shaving mirror. Long and earnestly Jim gazed at that mirror. Then, suddenly swinging his bound feet to the floor, he cautiously rose and straightened up.

It was all he could do at first to maintain his balance, but eventually he began to find what, with grim humour, he termed his "sea-laigs." That done, he groped behind him with his fingers, and, after pulling the blankets to the floor, he took a hop forward in the direction of the dressing-chest and swayed perilously.

He managed to keep his balance, however, and another hop took him a few inches nearer the chest. Another hop, and then another, and he began to feel more confident. But it was slow work, and he knew that at any moment he might be disturbed by one of the seamen coming to take a look at the prisoners.

The negro reached the chest without mishap, however, and, leaning against it, he picked up the shaving mirror with his teeth. Still holding it, he turned away and commenced the return journey to the heap of blankets lying on the floor by the side of the bunk.

Reaching them, he dropped to his knees; then, lowering his head, he carefully dropped the mirror so that it lay face upwards. That done, he shuffled forward until one knee was pressing on the glass. Then, slowly and deliberately, he exerted pressure with his knee until there came a sharp crack and the glass splintered into pieces.

Shuffling backwards, Jim surveyed the broken fragments; then, selecting the piece he wanted, he bent his head and picked it up with his teeth. Laboriously he turned about, still on his knees, and with the piece of broken glass held tightly between his teeth, he lowered his head and inserted one splintered corner of the fragment into the crack between the floorboards.

Now came one of the most difficult and delicate parts of Jim's task. He could move his knees slightly, and, shuffling into position, he raised his right knee an inch or so from the ground and pressed it down on the glass, wedging it more firmly between the floorboards.

His knee was bleeding profusely by the time he had completed the job to his satisfaction. But he paid no heed to that as jubilantly he stretched himself out full length on the floor and began to work the rope which bound his arms up and down on the rough edge of the piece of glass.

Time and again he paused to strain at his bonds, and time and again he returned to his sawing. Then suddenly he felt something give, and this time, after he'd stretched his mighty muscles to their utmost and then relaxed, the rope fell loosely away from about his arms and he knew that they, at least, were free.

It took the negro some minutes to disentangle his arms from the coils, but he managed it at last. Then he set feverishly to work to untie the knot of the rope which bound his legs.

When that was done he rose stiffly to his feet and stood a moment gingerly massaging his bruised limbs and ankles. Then, with grim and purposeful stride, he quitted the cabin, and, bounding up the ladder, gained the deck.

He knew where he was going, knew what he intended to do. Crossing the deck to the port rail, he stood for a moment staring shorewards through the greying light of early morning.

Next moment his arms flashed up and he dived, his lithe, black body cleaving the water with scarcely a ripple. Then with powerful strokes he struck out for the beach.

The cold salt water refreshed him probably more than anything else could have done, and by the time he had reached the beach he was beginning to feel more like his old self.

The negro gained the shore near where Baines and Crawley had beached the boat after their flight from the Rosa, and, making his way to the boat, he scanned the firm sand for footprints.

He found them easily enough, two pairs of tracks leading southwards along the beach, and grimly he set off in pursuit, walking swiftly with long, raking stride.

He knew that it would take a few hours yet for the Rosa to get up steam, and in the meantime he was determined to catch up with Baines and Crawley, and, after relieving those two gents of the booty they had stolen, give them something to remember him by.

Not only had they ruined all his plans, but they had cleared off with a good part of the loot which he, Coles, and Huck had spent long and laborious hours in wresting from the safes of stranded ships, and for which they had eventually risked not only their liberty but their lives.

O.K., then! Baines and Crawley would find that treachery such as theirs was a game which did not pay.

They were keeping to the beach, obviously because the going was easier there than inland.

Like a black Nemesis, Jim stalked along their trail, increasing his pace until he was almost running.

Only once did he stop, and that was to pick up a long piece of seaweed which he stripped until all that was left was the tough and supple black stem—a deadly weapon in such hands as his.

Then on he went again, following the tell-tale footprints in the sand. That Baines and Crawley would be hurrying, he knew, but they had not had more than an hour's start at the most, and they would be moving at nothing like the rate he was.

The light was growing stronger now, but there was no sign of his quarry ahead, and eventually Jim broke into a run.

(On no account, chum, miss the concluding chapters of this thrill-packed yarn. You'll find 'em in next week's great value-for-money issue of the MAGNET.*)*

HIS GUNMAN GUARDIAN!

(Continued from page 24.)

But suddenly those keen eyes left Bunter, as if Poker Pike had totally forgotten his fat existence.

To Billy Bunter's astonishment, the gunman made a sudden dart towards the high fence at the side of the road, pulling a gun from his pocket as he did so.

Bunter blinked after him blankly.

He had seen nothing in the shadows, his eyes not being so keen as Poker Pike's.

Bunter did not know that there were two shadowy figures crammed close to the park palings in the shadows; that one had his arms bound, and that the other—a man in horn-rimmed spectacles —was holding him by the arm.

But Poker Pike knew. He had spotted Bud Parker and his prisoner.

It seemed like a nightmare to Bunter.

He saw the gunman dash across the road, gun in hand; he heard a startled voice; and then perceived a moving shadow by the fence—and then came flashes, stabbing the darkness, and the roar of a firearm. With a squeak of terror, the fat Owl flung himself down in the grass by the road.

Nobody heeded him. Poker Pike was rushing down on Bud Parker, firing as he rushed, splashing lead along the road and the fence.

Bunter heard a yell, and the sound of running feet. Louder sounded the roar of Poker Pike's automatic.

Bang, bang, bang!

The fat Owl blinked round in terror. In the starlight a man in horn-rimmed spectacles was running frantically up the road, with Poker Pike loosing off lead after him—bullets spattering up the dust round him as he ran.

"Oh crikey!" gasped Bunter.

A figure, gagged, with arms bound, lurched out of the shadow of the park fence.

"Oh crikey!" repeated Bunter, as he recognised Putnam van Duck.

Bang! roared Mr. Pike's final shot.

Bud was gone.

He had not waited for Chick Chew to get back with the car. The arrival of Mr. Pike, with his ready gun, had quite altered his plans. Never had Mr. Parker made so prompt a get-away.

He was gone; and Poker turned to Putnam.

"Say! I'll mention that you're my antelope, with the hide on!" he remarked. "I'll tell a man, I ain't losing you agin, you Putnam van Duck!"

"Oh crikey!" said Bunter, for the third time.

He crawled to his feet.

THE EIGHTEENTH CHAPTER.

All Right for Bunter!

Knock, knock!

Wells, half-dressed, opened the door.

Colonel Wharton, in flowing dressing-gown, looked down from the stairs over the banisters.

Harry Wharton and Hurree Singh, in pyjamas, stared on either side of him.

"Good gad!" said the colonel.

"Great pip!" said the colonel's nephew.

And the Nabob of Bhanipur murmured that the great-pipfulness was terrific.

Wells almost fell down as Putnam van Duck walked in, and, following him, came a wiry man with a hickory face, with a grubby bowler hat screwed down on his bullet head. And last, but not least, came a fat youth with a hopeful but uneasy blink behind his big spectacles.

"What!" gasped Colonel Wharton.

"I'll say I'm sure sorry to wake the whole caboodle!" said Putnam van Duck. "I ain't jest been out for a leetle pasear this time of the night. Chick got me out of a window."

"Good gad!"

"And Pike blew along and got busy with his gat, and here I am again," said Putnam. "I guess Chick's side-kicker has gone to tell Chick to call again. He sure has fallen down on it this time. Now, sir, if you've had enough trouble to my tally, I'll sure beat it pronto."

"Nonsense!" gasped Colonel Wharton. "You will go back to bed, and every precaution shall be taken——"

"I guess Poker's precaution enough, sir," grinned Van Duck. "I got to tell you, sir, that this guy is the galoot my popper put to keep tabs on me, and he won't quit."

"Not so's you'd notice it," remarked Poker Pike stolidly.

Slowly it seemed to occur to Mr. Pike that he was indoors in an establishment different from the "joints" to which he was accustomed, and he removed his hat.

"Your—your guardian can be accommodated here, my boy," said the colonel. "Certainly he shall stay."

"Surest thing you know," remarked Mr. Pike calmly.

"Wells, you will see——"

"Certainly, sir!" gasped Wells.

"I say, you fellows——"

"Who is that?" rapped the colonel, staring at Bunter grimly.

"That fat guy brought Pike along, jest in time to catch Bud Parker before Chick came back with the auto," said Putnam. "But I sure don't know why he blew in here on my tail! You want anything—you, Bunter?"

"Oh, really, Van Duck——"

"I'll mention that the butler guy's waiting to shut the door, and you're on the wrong side of it," remarked Van Duck.

"Beast! I say, you fellows!" Bunter blinked up at the two juniors, grinning down from the stairs. "I say, I've lost my train, and—and—I mean, I came back to—to—to save that beast from the other beast."

"Wells, Master Bunter will stay the night," grunted the colonel.

"Yes, sir."

Wells closed the door.

Bunter was on the safe side of it. Fortune, after all, had smiled on the fat Owl of the Remove. Colonel Wharton, perhaps, fancied that he was going on the morrow. Bunter fancied that he wasn't. And Bunter was right —he didn't.

* * * * * * *

What Chick Chew thought and said when, coming back with the car for the kidnapped millionaire's son, he met his confederate in frantic flight, was not known at Wharton Lodge.

Probably what Mr. Chew said was something very emphatic.

Anyhow he had, as Putnam put it, fallen down on his enterprise. No doubt he was going to try again—it being a matter of personal and professional pride with Mr. Chew not to register defeat. Aware of that, Putnam van Duck quite threw down the idea of parting with his gunman guardian, and made up his mind to tolerate Mr. Pike and his gun.

"I guess I got to chew on Poker," he told Harry Wharton. "I guess Pop was right. Poker's the guy to put paid to Chick. I got to chew on that guy for keeps."

"But at Greyfriars——" said Harry. "When you come to the school——"

"I'll say Poker'll come, too"

"Oh, my hat!" said Harry.

He chuckled at the idea of the gunman at Greyfriars, keeping "tabs" on a new fellow in the Remove. There was no doubt that Poker Pike and his gun would cause rather a sensation at Greyfriars. It made the new term unusually interesting to look forward to.

THE END.

(Enjoyed the yarn, chum? Thought you would! I guess you're looking forward to the next story in this grand new series. Note the title: "GUN PLAY AT GREYFRIARS!" and make a point of ordering next Saturday's issue of the MAGNET *well in advance!)*

WHEN THE GANGSTERS CAME TO GREYFRIARS!

No. 1,472. Vol. XLIX. EVERY SATURDAY. Week Ending May 2nd, 1936.

SPARE A MOMENT FOR A CHEERY POW-WOW? THEN—

COME INTO the OFFICE, BOYS—AND GIRLS!

Your Editor is always pleased to hear from his readers. Write to him: Editor of the "Magnet," The Amalgamated Press, Ltd., Fleetway House, Farringdon Street, London, E.C.4. A stamped, addressed envelope will ensure a reply.

AS a kick-off to this chat of mine, chums, I feel that I must once again draw your attention to the grand yarn telling of Harry Wharton's early schooldays which appears in this week's issue of our companion paper, the "Gem." This splendid treat will appeal specially to new readers of the MAGNET who would like to know how Harry Wharton first came to Greyfriars, how he quarrelled with Frank Nugent, and the exciting adventures at Greyfriars that changed his whole character.

"THE MAKING OF HARRY WHARTON!"

is undoubtedly one of the very finest stories ever written. This splendid story also tells how Billy Bunter, the world's funniest and fattest laughter-merchant, first found a footing in the Remove Form. If you have not already purchased a copy of this week's "Gem" I should advise you to do so right away as this particular issue will sell like hot cakes!

Do you know what is

THE SMALLEST BOOK IN THE WORLD?

"Constant Reader," of Coventry, asks me if I can answer this question. Yes, the smallest volume in the world was sold by auction in London recently. It is a translation of the Rubaiyat of Omar Khayyam. It is only a quarter of an inch in length, and its weight is just over one grain! It is printed with minute copper plates. The pages have been stitched by hand and bound with leather. Needless to say, it is impossible to read the book without the aid of a powerful magnifying glass. The book was printed in Massachusetts in 1932. So tiny is the type, that when the book was being printed, work had to stop whenever a motor-car passed by the printing establishment. It was found that the vibration of a passing motor-car was sufficient to blur the type!

Now let's talk about something big. What is

THE BIGGEST ARTIFICIAL LAKE

in the world? G. K. D., of Bridport, asks me that. It is the new lake which has just been completed at Boulder Dam, on the Colorado River, Arizona, U.S.A. The lake hasn't filled up yet, and it will take between four and five years to do so. But when it is filled, it will be 115 miles long. In certain parts the depth will be as great as 1,000 feet, and it will spread into distant valleys and canyons. The newly-constructed Boulder Dam is one of the big engineering feats of the world. It is the highest embankment in the world, and stands in seven million tons of massed concrete. No less than 1,800,000 horse-power will be created by it, and this will be distributed over the States of Arizona, Nevada, and Southern California. Passenger boats will ply on the lake, new industries will be created, and the district—once a mass of barren rocks and mountains—will become a tourists' paradise!

Harry Farmer, an Australian reader of Sydney, has sent me along a paragraph which he thinks will interest fellow-readers of the MAGNET. It might well be headed

SNAKES ALIVE!

A resident of Bungowannah, South Australia, decided to have a day's duck shooting. His wife and his two sons went with him. As well as ducks, they found the place infested with poisonous snakes. Before they could settle with the ducks, they had to deal with the snakes. Many people might have beat a hasty retreat, but not this family. Snakes or no snakes, they weren't going to be done out of their day's hunting. So they "sailed in" on the snakes.

Before the day was out the four of them had killed seventy-two poisonous snakes—and had managed to get a large "bag" of ducks!

Good hunting, eh, chums?

Here is another paragraph that might interest my readers. It concerns

AN INTERESTING AMATEUR EDITOR,

who lives at Union, New Jersey, U.S.A. Clark Johnston is only a schoolboy of nine years of age, but he already edits, prints and publishes a newspaper of his own, called the "Boulevard Bugle." It is printed by means of a typewriter and a duplicator, but it hasn't much of a circulation. As a matter of fact, Clark turns out only sixteen copies a week, but these are eagerly snapped up by his schoolfellows.

In a recent issue this juvenile editor printed an article wishing good luck to King Edward VIII, and posted a copy to the King.

HERE'S a yarn which comes from Tanganyika, and will appeal to animal lovers. It's about

THE MAN WHO PALLED UP WITH A LION

He's an African native, and he says he has been friends with this particular wild lion for years. Furthermore, the lion appreciated his friendship so much that whenever it made a "kill" it always left a portion of its prey for this elderly native.

Of late, lions have been making themselves a nuisance in the Tabora district by raiding stock. The native authorities therefore constructed a number of traps to catch the lions. This particular lion was caught in one of the pit traps. The native found him and, by means of a ladder, went into the trap and helped the lion to escape. Unfortunately, the authorities did not agree with the native, and the result was that he was fined fifty shillings in a native court for saving the lion!

Here is an item that will interest those of you who are film fans. The very latest in cinemas is

PARACHUTING CINEMAS.

How would you like your cinema fare literally dropped on you from the skies? This is what is happening in certain rural districts of Russia. Operators, projectors and films are carried by aeroplane to districts which are far off the beaten track. As the aeroplane passes over the selected spot, the operators and the apparatus are dropped by parachute, and film shows are then given. The films are generally "silent" ones, and music is supplied by an accordion. Some of the collective farms where these shows are given are forty miles away from the nearest railway, and the people working upon them would probably never see a cinema show unless it was delivered to them in this unusual manner.

JUST to finish up this chat, here are a few more

THINGS YOU'D HARDLY BELIEVE!

The Ticking Cow! A farmer in New Jersey lost his watch. Months later, one of his cows was slaughtered—and the watch was found inside it, still ticking away merrily! Every time the cow breathed she had wound up the watch one notch!

Another Snake Yarn. A resident of Tarago, New South Wales, was quietly reading when, looking down, he spotted a big tiger snake. He was able to reach for his gun and shoot it. He had just disposed of the snake when thirty more snakes wriggled into the room. They were the young offspring of the snake he had shot. Luckily the Australian managed to dispose of these, too—a bag of thirty-one snakes in a few minutes!

A Million Pounds of Hidden Treasure! A Russian refugee claims to know the whereabouts of a million pounds' worth of hidden treasure in gold roubles. He says it was buried in the mountains after the fall of Port Arthur in the Russo-Japanese war. He also says that unless he can get the treasure, he will carry his secret to the grave.

A Dream of Wealth. A doctor in Austria dreamed that he received a shoal of letters headed with the number 13.49.1. He bet on these numbers at a gambling resort—and won £800.

I have left a little space to tell you something about next week's programme:

"HORACE COKER'S DARK DEED!"
By Frank Richards,

is the title of the next complete yarn in our grand new series. The great Horace is on vengeance bent and things happen! I do not wish to delve more into the plot for fear of spoiling your enjoyment. Anyway, the tale itself is a real good one, and will be voted on all sides as one of Frank Richards' best. The "Greyfriars Herald," too, is bang up to standard. Next we come to more snappy verses by the Greyfriars Rhymester, and last, but not least, the opening chapters of our grand new tale of modern piracy—further particulars of which appear on page 26 of this issue. Why not give a regular order for the MAGNET, chums? It will save you being disappointed!

YOUR EDITOR.

GRAND SCHOOL YARN OF FUN AND THRILLS—BY THE PRINCE OF STORY-TELLERS!

GUN PLAY at GREYFRIARS!

By FRANK RICHARDS

Poker Pike, bodyguard to Putnam van Duck, is rather like a fish out of water at Greyfriars. But when the gangsters come to Greyfriars, Poker Pike is on the job!

THE FIRST CHAPTER.

Going Back to Greyfriars!

"FULL!" said Bob Cherry.

"What!" roared Coker.

"Full!" repeated Bob.

Why Coker of the Fifth looked so fearfully annoyed, indeed, enraged, was rather a puzzle to the chums of the Greyfriars Remove.

The carriage was full! Bob's statement to that effect was hardly needed—Coker could see that the carriage was full.

That carriage seated six, and there were six fellows in it. Harry Wharton, Frank Nugent, Hurree Singh, Johnny Bull, and Bob, going back to Greyfriars for the new term, and Putnam van Duck, of Chicago, a new fellow.

Lantham Junction swarmed with Greyfriars men, who mostly wanted to go by that train, rather than wait for the next. Still, everybody couldn't go by that train, and Coker of the Fifth was one of those that couldn't. At all events, he couldn't go in a carriage that was already full!

When Coker looked in and saw six fellows in six seats, it was up to Coker to pass on. Coker was not a whale on arithmetic, but he could, of course, count up to six correctly. But instead of passing on, he glared in at the window at the Remove fellows in towering wrath.

"What did you say?" he roared.

"Full!" repeated Bob.

"By gum!" gasped Coker. And he gripped the door-handle, to wrench the door open. "I'll teach you to call me a fool, you cheeky young tick!"

"Wha-a-t!" stuttered Bob.

"Ha, ha, ha!" came a yell from the rest of the carriage.

Evidently Coker had misunderstood!

Bob had simply been making a plain statement that the carriage was full. Coker's impression was that the junior was telling him what he thought of his intellect. Hence his wrath!

"I say——" gasped Bob.

But there was no time to explain.

Horace Coker wrenched the door open. He barged in. Bob, hurled headlong by that hefty barge, was strewn along the floor of the carriage amid innumerable feet. He yelled as he was strewn.

"Now, then——" roared Coker.

But Coker got no farther than that, the whole carriage rose on Coker. Harry Wharton and Frank Nugent grasped his arms. Johnny Bull and Hurree Singh seized his ears, which were large and gave a good hold. Putnam van Duck took possession of his neck. Bob, sprawling among dust and feet, grabbed his legs.

Coker collapsed.

Coker of the Fifth, when he was wrathy, did not count odds. But the odds, counted or uncounted, were there, and too many for Coker. For a whole minute the interior of that first-class carriage was the scene of a first-class shindy. Coker hardly knew what was happening. What he next knew, clearly, was that he was dropping on the platform of Lantham Junction and dropping rather hard.

Bump!

"Ooooogh!" gasped Coker.

He sat up dizzily.

His hat was gone, his necktie hung at the back of his neck, and his collar was curled round one ear. He had a dismantled look.

"Oooogh!" he repeated breathlessly. "I—I—I'll—ooogh!"

"Ha, ha, ha!" came from the fellows along the platform. Witnesses of Coker's sudden descent from the carriage seemed amused thereby.

"Coming in to have some more?" asked Harry Wharton.

"Oh, do!" said Johnny Bull.

"Lots more on tap, Coker!" chuckled Frank Nugent.

"Oodles and oodles, if you're honing for it!" grinned Putnam van Duck.

"Urrrggh!" gurgled Coker. He staggered to his feet.

Potter and Greene of the Fifth rushed up.

"Oh, here you are, Coker!" exclaimed Potter. "Come on, we've got a carriage along——"

"Those cheeky young rotters——" gasped Coker.

"Come on!" urged Greene. "No time to rag with fags, Coker."

"Those cheeky young ticks——"

"Look here, our places will be bagged——"

"Think I'm going to let a cheeky fag call me a fool!" roared Coker. "I'm going to smash him! See? Smash him to small bits! You fellows lend me a hand."

"You silly ass!" howled Bob Cherry "I never called you a fool——"

"Why, you lying young sweep——"

"I said 'full'——" shrieked Bob.

"Yes, I heard you say fool, and I'm going to jolly well smash you for it," hooted Coker, recklessly splitting his infinitive. "Come on, Potter! Come on, Greene! You handle the other little brutes, while I whop that cheeky tick!"

And Coker rushed to the assault.

Potter and Greene did not come on. They scudded off, to make sure that their places on the train were not bagged. They seemed to consider that more important than scrapping with a mob of fags.

Coker, unheeding, charged.

The doorway of the carriage was crammed with juniors on the defensive. Harry Wharton & Co. packed their goal, so to speak

Coker of the Fifth was heavy and hefty, and full of beans. But really, he had no chance. He broke on the Remove defence like a wave on a rock.

Instead of smashing through, knocking cheeky juniors right and left, which was his intention, he went backwards on the platform again, which was far from being his intention.

Crash!

For the second time, Coker hit the Lantham platform with his burly back, and tapped it with his bullet head.

"Man down!" chortled Johnny Bull.

"Ha, ha, ha!"

"Come on, Coker!"

"Have some more!"

Coker sat up as a porter came along and slammed the carriage door. The train was full up and about to start. Coker, breathless, sat up and blinked at it. Bob waved a parting hand from the open window.

"Good-bye, Coker!"

"Ooooogh!" gasped Coker. He picked himself up, and tottered to the carriage. Even yet, Coker did not seem to have had enough.

"Stand clear, there!" shouted a porter.

"Chuck it, fathead!" said Bob, holding the handle of the door inside. "We're starting, you frabjous ass!"

The engine was screaming. Doors were shut along the train. Even Coker realised that there was no time to deal with the heroes of the Remove as they deserved. He glared in at the window.

"You cheeky young scoundrels!" he spluttered. "You wait till we get to Courtfield! Just wait, and I'll jolly well—gurrrrrggggh!"

Coker did not mean to say that. He said it involuntarily as Putnam van Duck reached through the open window and nipped his prominent nose between a finger and thumb that felt like a steel vice.

"Wurrrgh!" gurgled Coker. "Oogh! Led do my dose—gurrrggh!"

"Ha, ha, ha!"

"Urrrrgh!"

"I'll say you've asked for it, big boy!" said Putnam van Duck cheerily. "I'm pulling that probiscus a few."

"Yurrrgh! Led do—grooogh!"

The train was moving. Coker had to move as the train moved, with that vice-like grip on his nose. For a moment or two Coker was led along by his nose. Then Putnam, releasing him, pushed, and Coker sat down for the third time.

He was still sitting clasping his nose with both hands and gurgling horribly as the train ran out of Lantham and the Removites lost sight of him.

He had told the juniors to wait till they got to Courtfield—but clearly, if they did, they would wait in vain, for Coker was not going to Courtfield on that train. He was left behind at Lantham, nursing a crimson beak—which was still flaming red when Coker got on the second train.

THE SECOND CHAPTER.

A Surprise for Loder!

"I SAY, you fellows!"

"Blow away, Bunter!"

"I say, sorry I missed you at Lantham——"

"Nobody else is!"

"But here we are again!" said Bunter, unheeding. "I'll go on to Friardale with you. I say, got any chocs?"

"No!"

"Got any toffee?"

"No!"

"I say, there's lots of time to dodge into the buffet here before we get on the local."

"Good—dodge in."

"You fellows coming?"

"No!"

"Beasts!" said Billy Bunter.

The fat Owl of the Remove blinked morosely at the Famous Five through his big spectacles. He had descended from another carriage when the train stopped at Courtfield, where the Greyfriars fellows had to change for the local train for Friardale and the school.

Bunter had intended to join up with his old pals at Lantham. They had seen him. Bunter, fortunately being short-sighted, hadn't seen them. But he saw them now, and here he was!

"This way, Van Duck! said Harry Wharton to the American boy. "We get over the line for the local."

"I say, you fellows——"

"Roll off, Bunter!"

"I say, I was packed in a carriage with a lot of Sixth Form cads," said Bunter. "Looking for you fellows, you know, I had to jump in at the last minute, and the carriage was full of seniors. That beast Loder pulled my ear. He made out I trod on his foot! He's come back this term a worse bully than ever."

"Shut up, you ass!" said Bob Cherry hurriedly.

Loder of the Sixth was standing with Carne and Walker, of that Form, only a few yards away. He glanced round at Bunter.

Bunter, happily unaware of the proximity of the bully of the Sixth, rattled on unheeding.

"Rotten bully, you know! I'd have knocked him down if he hadn't been a prefect! It's a bit thick, isn't it, the Head making a rotter like Loder a prefect! I say, what's the matter with you fellows? What are you making faces at a chap for? What——Yarooooh!"

A finger and thumb closing on Billy Bunter's fat ear made him jump and utter a yell simultaneous with the jump.

"Ow! Leggo, Coker, you beast!" howled Bunter. "Oh, is it you, Loder? I—I say, leggo my ear! I—I say——Yaroooh!"

"What were you saying about me?" asked Loder of the Sixth, grimly compressing his grip on the fat ear.

"Ow! Nothing! I was only saying——yaroooh! I mean, I never said a word, only——whooop! Leggo my ear! Wow!"

Billy Bunter hopped.

Harry Wharton & Co. looked at Loder. But for the fact that he was a prefect of the Sixth Form, they certainly would have up-ended him on the platform on the spot. But Sixth Form prefects were not to be lightly handled by juniors of the Lower Fourth.

Loder was looking cross. Perhaps he had come back for the new term in a bad temper. Anyhow, he was in a bad temper now. Still, even a good-tempered fellow might have been annoyed by hearing Bunter's description of him.

He nipped Bunter's fat ear like a pair of pincers with finger and thumb.

Bunter almost danced.

"Yow-ow-ow!" he howled. "I say, you fellows, make him leggo! Wow! Oh lor'! Yow-ow-ow!"

"Say, who's that guy?" asked Van Duck, staring at the scene.

"That's Loder!" answered Harry. "He—— Oh, my hat! Here, hold on!"

Van Duck stepped towards Loder of the Sixth and caught him by the arm.

"Forget it, bo!" he said. "I guess that fat guy's had enough, and a few over. Take a rest, see?"

He jerked at Loder's arm, and Bunter's fat ear was released.

Loder, in sheer astonishment, glared at the American boy. As he had never seen him before, he could guess that he was a new boy for Greyfriars. Indeed, only that circumstance accounted for his cool cheek in interfering with the lordly and lofty proceedings of a Sixth Form prefect.

"Why, you—you—you——" gasped Loder. He wrenched his arm away from Van Duck, and grabbed the youth from Chicago by the collar.

"Hold on, Loder!" exclaimed Harry Wharton. "Van Duck's a new kid!"

Loder of the Sixth did not heed.

Holding Putnam van Duck by the collar with one hand, he smacked his head with the other.

Even a prefect of the Sixth was not entitled to smack a fellow's head; but Gerald Loder did not always stop to consider whether he was entitled to do a thing before he did it, and he did it—hard!

"Aw, wake snakes!" roared Van Duck, as Loder smacked. "Say, you pesky geek—— Yooo-hooop!"

Smack, smack, smack!

Harry Wharton & Co. exchanged glances. They did not want to begin the term with a row with a Sixth Form prefect. And although Loder was exceeding the limit, it was a very dubious and perilous matter to handle a prefect. Before they could make up their minds what to do, a man in a black bowler hat which seemed screwed down on his bullet head, pushed through and grabbed Loder by the neck.

"Oh!" gasped Bob Cherry. "Jolly old Pike!"

It was Poker Pike, the gunman hired by Van Duck's "popper" to guard him from kidnappers.

Mr. Pike had been travelling in the carriage next to that occupied by the chums of the Remove. He had alighted when they did. So he was right on the spot when he was needed.

Van Duck knew little of Public schools, of the prefectorial system, and of what an important person a Sixth Form prefect was. Mr. Pike knew less. And he cared less still.

All Mr. Pike knew was that Putnam van Duck, entrusted to his charge by Mr. Vanderdecken van Duck, the multi-millionaire of Chicago, was having his million-dollar head smacked. It seemed to Mr. Pike time for him to horn in, as he would have called it. He horned in.

Loder of the Sixth, with a grip on his collar that there was no resisting, was plucked off his feet.

He gave a gasping howl as he went.

In his native city of Chicago it was Mr. Pike's way to depend chiefly on his "gun." But he had already learned that he was in a strange land where guns were looked on with disfavour. He had learned, with surprise and disapproval, that in England a guy could not flourish a six-gun without attracting an extraordinary amount of attention—let alone "shoot up" another guy and walk away as if nothing had happened!

Still, Mr. Pike could use his hands as well as his gun. And he was as strong as a horse, or nearly so.

Having fastened an iron grip on the back of Loder's collar, he swept him off his feet with a single jerk of his sinewy, wiry arm.

Loder, in a state of spluttering amazement, found himself in the air, swinging round.

The astonished spectators hurriedly jumped back out of reach. Billy Bunter, however, did not jump quite in time.

"Whoop!" roared Bunter, as Loder's feet established contact with his fat ribs. Bunter went over like a fat ninepin.

Loder swung on.

Revolving on his axis, as it were, the gunman swung Loder round and round by his collar, with a grim and serious face, evidently seeing nothing of a comic nature in the lesson he was giving him.

But from the swarm of Greyfriars fellows on the platform there came a yell of laughter.

"Ha, ha, ha!"

"And the rowfulness will also be preposterous!"

"Say, Poker, you guy, let up on that geek!" shouted Putnam.

"Ha, ha, ha!"

A buzzing, excited crowd surrounded the scene. But they kept out of reach of Gerald Loder's whirling feet.

"Oooooooogh!" came in a suffocated gurgle from the bully of the Sixth.

"Ha, ha, ha!"

"Let up, Poker, I'm telling you!" yelled Van Duck.

"You said it!" agreed Poker.

He let go Loder's collar, and the hapless Sixth Former dropped on the platform. He rolled there, spluttering.

Mr. Pike looked down at him with his grave and serious eye.

"I guess that lets you out, feller," he said. "You don't want to lay a paw on that Putnam van Duck—not while this guy is around!"

"Ha, ha, ha!"

Harry Wharton & Co. were almost weeping with merriment as they went along the platform. They could foresee high old times at Greyfriars if Poker Pike was going to take care of his charge in this way.

Leaving Loder sprawling and spluttering, Mr. Pike followed them.

Vanderdecken van Duck was very urgent in the matter, and it really appears that the boy is in danger of kidnapping."

"In this country, sir——"

"It is a fact, Mr. Quelch. You have, of course, heard of the kidnapping of wealthy men's sons which appears to be carried on in the United States as a sort of industry—a very extraordinary industry Well-known people have left that country, Mr. Quelch, and come to live in England for no reason but to protect their sons from professional kidnappers."

"I am aware of it, sir. But at a school like Greyfriars—really, sir, I cannot imagine any danger." Mr. Quelch gave a sniff. "It is unthinkable,

"Wurrrggh!" gurgled Coker, as Putnam van Duck reached through the open carriage window and nipped his prominent nose between a finger and thumb that felt like a steel vice. "Ooooogh! Led do by dose—gurrrggh!" "I'll say you asked for it, big boy!" said Van Duck, as the train began to move.

"Oh, my hat!" gasped Bob Cherry.

"Grooogh!" gurgled Loder, half suffocated, and wholly amazed and flabbergasted. "Oooogh! Owwoch!"

Walker and Carne ran forward. They had never seen Mr. Pike before, and certainly had no idea that he had been sent to school with a new boy as his guardian against kidnappers.

"Here, chuck that!" exclaimed Walker.

"Stop that, you hooligan!" shouted Carne.

They clutched at Mr. Pike together. Hardly glancing at them, Poker Pike swept round his left arm and knocked them both over like skittles.

He did not even pause in swinging Loder! Gerald Loder, like the music in the song, went round and round.

"Here we go round the mulberry-bush!" chuckled Bob Cherry.

"Ha, ha, ha!"

"The roundfulness is terrific!" chortled Hurree Jamset Ram Singh.

THE THIRD CHAPTER.

Some Shindy!

"EXTRAORDINARY!" said Mr. Quelch.

"Very!" agreed the Head.

The Remove master pursed his lips. The headmaster looked thoughtful and a little worried.

"Extremely unusual!" said Mr. Quelch.

"I agree," said Dr. Locke. "But Mr. sir, that the most lawless American kidnapper would venture——"

"It would appear so, Mr. Quelch; yet such is actually the case," said the Head. "I learn that this boy, Van Duck, has been passing the Easter holidays at the home of a boy in your Form—Wharton—and while he was there an attempt was made to kidnap him, which was only prevented by his guard."

"Indeed, sir?"

"Yes, indeed, Mr. Quelch! Mr. van Duck had the very singular idea of engaging a man of similar character to the gangsters to guard his son—on the principle, I suppose of setting a thief to catch a thief." The Head smiled faintly. "It appears to have been a success Certainly this man Spike—I think his name is Spike—saved the boy from kidnapping at Wharton Lodge."

"But here, sir——"

"Mr van Duck was so very earnest in the matter, sir, and so very anxious for his son's safety, that I have consented to allow the guardian to take up his residence at the school during the term."

"If you have consented, sir, there is nothing more to be said," observed the Remove master, carefully suppressing another sniff.

"The situation is, indeed, very unusual," said Dr. Locke. "But no doubt the man Spike—or Pike—I am not sure whether his name is Spike or Pike—will be tactful, and will keep himself in the background, and be very careful not to attract undue attention."

"I should certainly hope so, sir."

"I have not yet seen the man, Mr. Quelch," said the Head. "I understand that, although he has been a gangster himself, he is very faithful to his charge —quite devoted. I have arranged for him to have a room in Gosling's lodge, where he will be out of contact with the boys. Indeed, if he exercises a certain amount of tact and reticence, probably most of the boys will remain unaware that he is in the school at all."

"I hope so, indeed!" said Mr. Quelch.

"No doubt he will be careful not to bring himself into prominence in any way," said the Head "I shall, indeed, when I see him, impress the necessity of this upon him very carefully. I shall—— Bless my soul! What is that disturbance in the quadrangle?"

Dr. Locke glanced towards his study window in surprise and annoyance.

On the first day of the term some latitude was allowed. Fellows fresh back from the holidays were liable to be a little exuberant before they settled down for the new term.

Still, there was a limit, and the sudden uproar in the quadrangle, almost under the headmaster's window, sounded rather beyond the limit.

"What ever can that mean?" exclaimed the Head.

"Something unusual appears to be going on," remarked Mr. Quelch. "I will ascertain, sir."

He rose and stepped to the window of the Head's study Dr. Locke rose and followed him there.

From the quad came roars of laughter. A swarm of fellows of all Forms was to be seen. Mr. Quelch spotted the Famous Five of his own Form howling with laughter; but those cheery youths for once did not seem to be mixed up in the disturbance, whatever it was.

Near the old stone fountain, in the middle of the green old quad, the crowd was thickest. There, above a sea of heads, arms and legs, could be seen waving in the air—a pair of arms and a pair of legs!

Somebody, it seemed, was being carried along, and objecting strenuously to the process. Whoever it was, he was being borne directly towards the fountain, amid a roaring mob of Greyfriars fellows.

"Extraordinary!" ejaculated the Head. "What—who——"

"I cannot imagine."

"Ha, ha, ha!" came a roar. "Poor old Coker! Ha, ha, ha!"

"It is a Fifth Form boy, I think," said the Remove master. "The boy Coker—a rather troublesome boy in Mr. Prout's Form But what——"

He threw open the window.

"Wharton!" he called out.

The head boy of his Form was within hearing.

"Oh! Yes, sir!"

Harry Wharton turned his head.

"What is going on here, Wharton?" exclaimed Mr Quelch. "What is the cause of this disturbance?"

"I—I think Coker's getting a ducking, sir."

"Wha-at?" stuttered the Head. "Is—is—is that Coker of the Fifth Form who is—is being carried along in that—that extraordinary manner? Upon my word! Who—who—who can be doing this?"

"Who is that man, Wharton?" exclaimed Mr. Quelch, glimpsing the bowler-hatted man who was carrying Coker of the Fifth like a bundle, heedless of the hefty Horace's wild struggles

"Mr. Pike, sir!"

"Pike!" repeated Mr. Quelch.

"Pike!" said the Head faintly.

They gazed, petrified.

Amazing as the scene was to the headmaster and the Remove master, the explanation was really quite simple. Coker of the Fifth, after arriving at the school, had spotted the new boy who had pulled his nose at Lantham.

Nothing could have been more natural than for Horace Coker to collar that youth and proceed to give him on the spot what any fellow richly deserved for pulling a nose so important as Coker's.

But barely had Coker's grasp closed on Putnam van Duck than Mr. Pike's grasp had closed on Coker, with the result that so astounded the Head as he stared blankly from his study window.

Mr. Quelch smiled a faint, sarcastic smile.

"So that is Mr. Pike, sir?" he said. "That is the man who is to remain here as guard over the new junior in my Form——"

"Bless my soul!" said the Head.

"The man who will, no doubt, be careful not to bring himself into prominence in any way——" remarked Mr. Quelch.

"Bless my soul!"

"Whose tact and reticence will cause most of the boys to remain unaware of his presence in the school!" murmured the Remove master.

"Really, Mr. Quelch——"

"I fear, sir, that there can be few persons within these walls who are not already aware of the presence of Mr. Pike!" said the Remove master.

"I—I—I fear so!" stammered the Head. "I—I—— Goodness gracious, Mr. Quelch, what is he doing with that Fifth Form boy?"

The question hardly needed asking, and did not need answering at all. Mr. Pike's action answered it.

Having reached the fountain, he dropped Coker of the Fifth bodily into the foot of water in the wide granite basin.

Splash!

There was quite a waterspout as Coker of the Fifth landed there. From the whole excited mob in the quadrangle came a roar:

"Ha, ha, ha!"

"Bless my soul!" said the Head faintly.

Leaning from the window, he gazed with a petrified gaze.

Coker struggled up in the fountain basin. He struggled to his knees, drenched and dripping, dazed and dizzy. Mr. Pike gave him a grave and serious look from the slits of eyes under his clamped-down bowler.

"I guess," said Mr. Pike gravely, "that you don't want to man-handle that Putnam van Duck! Not while this guy is around. No, sir! I should say surely not. I'm telling you to chew on that!"

"Goooooogh!" gasped Coker.

"Grooogh!"

"Ha, ha, ha!"

"Chew on it!" advised Mr. Pike; and turning, he walked away, leaving Coker of the Fifth to scramble out of the fountain, amid shrieks of laughter

---

THE FOURTH CHAPTER.

An Interrupted Whopping!

"BEAT it, you!" exclaimed Putnam van Duck, in exasperated tones.

Harry Wharton and Frank Nugent grinned.

They were in Study No. 1 in the Remove, unpacking books and other things, with the new junior. They had learned from Mr. Quelch that the new boy was to be quartered in Study No. 1 with them, to which they had no objection, being already on the friendliest terms with the youth from Chicago. Fisher T. Fish, the Yankee junior in the Remove, was far from popular; but Van Duck seemed quite a different sort of American, and all the Famous Five had taken to him.

They had not been ten minutes in the study when a hickory face under a black bowler hat looked in at the door.

Mr. Pike, having been accustomed to wearing his hat in the Chicago "joints" where he had, till recently, "hung out," saw no reason, apparently, for changing his manners and customs at Greyfriars School. At any rate, the black bowler remained clamped on his bullet head, as if it grew there.

Van Duck gave him a glare.

His experience at Wharton Lodge, when Chick Chew, the kidnapper, had so nearly got away with him, had made him realise the value of Poker Pike as a guardian. He admitted that his popper had guessed correctly in appointing Mr. Pike to take care of him.

Nevertheless, he was in a rather fed-up state with Poker, and objected strongly to having the gunman incessantly treading on his tail, as he described it.

It was clear that Mr. Pike, with all his gifts as a guardian, lacked tact. His solid brain seemed capable of assimilating only one idea at a time.

The idea being fixed in his bullet head that he had to watch over Putnam van Duck, he disregarded all other considerations. Greyfriars School, to Mr. Pike, was simply a joint where Putnam happened, for the time, to be hanging up his hat; merely that, and nothing more.

"You pesky bonehead, you!" went on Putnam. "You figure you're a schoolboy yourself, or what? You ain't no business horning in here! Beat it, and beat it pronto! You want to disappear! Get me?"

Mr. Pike stood immovable in the doorway.

He seemed to be ruminating.

"I guess I got to keep tabs on you, you, Putnam van Duck!" he said, after a thoughtful pause.

"Nobody's allowed in the studies, Mr. Pike," said Harry Wharton, laughing. "You really will have to clear."

Mr. Pike took absolutely no notice of that intimation. But having given Study No. 1 the once-over, he gave Putnam a curt nod, and walked down the passage to the stairs. There he sat down on a settee on the landing.

Remove fellows stared at him curiously. Shell fellows and Fourth Formers came to give him a look. Fifth Form men glanced out of the games study, and grinned at him.

Mr. Pike remained quite unmoved under the general scrutiny. He sat like a rock, chewing an unlighted cigar.

In Study No. 1 Wharton and Nugent grinned, and Putnam van Duck frowned. A fat face and a big pair of spectacles glimmered in at the door.

"I say, you fellows——"

"How did Bunter know we were unpacking a cake?" asked Frank Nugent.

"Oh, really, Nugent!" Billy Bunter rolled in. "I say, that looks a decent cake! Not so good as the one I was bringing back from Bunter Court, though! You should have seen that cake——"

"Well, let's see it!" suggested Nugent.

"I forgot to pack it, after all!" said Bunter. "But they'll send it on, and then I'll whack it out with you fellows, same as you're whacking out this one with me."

"Are we?" asked Frank.

"Looks as if we are!" remarked Wharton, as Bunter helped himself to a slice, about a third of the cake, at one fell swoop.

Bunter gobbled.

"Not a bad cake!" he said. "Hardly like the cakes I get at home; but not bad! But I say, you fellows"—Bunter's voice came rather muffled, through cake—"I say, I never came here to see if you had a cake. I say, Loder's coming."

"Oh, bother Loder!" said Harry.

"I say, I heard him asking about that new kid," grinned Bunter. "He's found out that Van Duck's in the Remove, and I fancy he's coming up after him."

"Bless Loder!" said Nugent.

"Say, is that guy Loder a big noise hereabouts?" asked Van Duck.

"He's a Sixth Form prefect," said Harry Wharton, "and a prefect is a big noise in any school, old bean! They have whopping privs."

"What the great horned toad are whopping privs?" demanded Van Duck.

"Privilege to whop!" explained Wharton. "That means that they cane juniors."

"Like masters?" exclaimed Van Duck, with a whistle.

"Exactly."

"Pretty mouldy stunt, I guess!" said Putnam. "Mean to say that that guy can cane me if he likes?"

"Certainly he can—and very likely will! Of course, a prefect has to have a good reason for whopping. But Loder's an artful dodger, and he's always got a good reason. Anyhow, you gave him one, grabbing hold of him to stop him pulling Bunter's ear at Courtfield."

"Gee!" said Van Duck.

"You can't cheek prefects here, Van Duck," said Bunter, with his mouth full. "You've got altogether too much cheek, old chap! You'll get it taken out of you at Greyfriars! Do you good, you know."

"That's Bunter's way of expressing thanks for butting in to help him!" explained Nugent."

"Ha, ha, ha!"

"I say, you fellows, I don't want to be here when Loder comes up," said Bunter. "He's in a rotten temper! I shouldn't wonder if he's been losing money on gee-gees in the vac. You know him! I'll take a bit of that cake with me, if you don't mind. It tastes rather good."

Bunter had already had a third of the cake. That, however, was only a taste, to Bunter.

"Take the lot!" said Nugent, with deep sarcasm.

"Oh, all right!" said Bunter, deaf to sarcasm. He picked up what was left of the cake, and started for the door.

"You fat villain!" yelled Nugent.

"Oh lor'! Here's Loder!" gasped Bunter, as a heavy tread was heard in the passage, and he bolted, cake and all, as Gerald Loder appeared in the doorway.

Loder looked in, with a grim brow.

"Oh, here you are!" he said, fixing his eyes on Putnam van Duck, with quite a deadly look in them.

"Sure!" assented Van Duck, eyeing him warily.

Loder had his official ashplant under his arm. It was evident that he had come up to Study No. 1 to use the same.

Having already smacked Van Duck's head for his cheek, as he regarded it, Loder would no doubt have been satisfied to let the matter drop, but for the consequences that had accrued.

Who Mr. Pike was, and why he had intervened, Loder did not know. But he knew that he had been handled, and made to look ridiculous before a swarm of Greyfriars fellows, and he put it down to Van Duck's account. Having arrived late, he had seen nothing of Mr. Pike at the school, and did not know that he was there. Loder's offended dignity had to be avenged, also his bad temper had to be wreaked, and Van Duck was the only available victim.

He slipped the ashplant down into his hand, and stepped into the study. Van Duck, watching him, backed away.

"I don't know who you are," said Loder grimly, "and I don't care—but you're going to learn here that you can't cheek prefects! Bend over that chair!"

"What for?" asked Van Duck.

"I'm going to whop you!"

Van Duck looked at the other two juniors.

"That O.K. in this joint?" he asked. Greyfriars School was a strange proposition to the boy from Chicago, and prefects with "whopping privs" quite new to him; but he was ready to play the game according to the rules, so to speak, and he was quick on the uptake.

"I'm afraid so, old bean," said Harry. "You see, Loder is a prefect of the Sixth, and you grabbed hold of him and stopped him, and that's cheek in a junior. You have to bend over."

"I guess I ain't got no kick coming, if it's O.K.," said Putnam. "A guy only wants to know."

And he obediently bent over the chair.

Loder flourished the cane, and brought it down with a swipe.

Putnam van Duck was tough. But this was, as he would have described it, a new one on him! He gave a yell that ran the length of the Remove passage.

Loder grinned.

Swipe!

The cane came down again.

"Aw, wake snakes!" gasped Van Duck. "Yoo-hooop!"

There was a swift tread in the passage. A bowler hat appeared in the doorway. Loder's cane was going up for a third swipe, when Poker Pike stepped swiftly in and grasped him by the shoulders.

"Wh-a-at—who-o-o-o——" stuttered Loder, as he was swung away as easily as an infant.

He stared round blankly at the gunman.

"You!" he stuttered, recognising the man who had handled him on the platform at Courtfield. "You! Let go! What are you doing here? Let me go at once, you scoundrel!"

"I guess," said Poker, "that I warned you! Didn't I put you wise on the railroad depot not to get fresh with that Putnam van Duck?"

"Let me go!" shrieked Loder, struggling.

Putnam van Duck jumped up.

"Poker, you pesky gink, you beat it!" he shouted. "You hear me howl? You beat it, and keep on beating it—see?"

Unheeding, the gunman hooked Loder of the Sixth to the door. In amazement and rage, the bully of the Sixth struggled and struck at him. His fist landed on the hickory face, without producing the slightest effect on Poker. It was quite a hard knock; but it did not make Mr. Pike even wink.

Mr. Pike jerked Loder off his feet, tucked him under his arm, and carried him away down the passage to the stairs.

The Sixth Former yelled, and roared, and struggled as he went. Fellows in the passage and in the doorways of the studies, stared and yelled with laughter.

"Hallo, hallo, hallo!" roared Bob Cherry, from No. 13. "Jolly old Pike on the warpath again!"

"Ha, ha, ha!"

A swarm of excited juniors followed as Mr. Pike carried Loder across the landing, and went downstairs with him —kicking and struggling like a fractious infant under the gunman's sinewy arm. Loder was no weakling; but he had no chance at all in the gunman's iron grip. He kicked, he struggled, he yelled, and he roared; but he went, and a yelling crowd followed down the stairs.

THE FIFTH CHAPTER.

Called to Order!

"THE Head!"

"Oh crumbs!"

"Ow! Help!" Loder was yelling. "You fellows—— Ow! Help! Lend me a hand! Draggimoff! Ooooh!"

Dr. Locke swept on the scene, with rustling gown and thunder in his brow. His eyes almost bulged from his head at the sight of a Sixth Form prefect, tucked under Poker Pike's powerful arm, kicking and wriggling.

"What—what—what does this mean?" gasped the Head. "Man—Spike—I mean Pike—release Loder at once! Do you hear me? Release him instantly! How dare you lay hands on one of my prefects?"

Poker Pike looked at the headmaster. He kept Loder pinned under his right arm; but he raised his left, and touched the brim of his hat. Even the hard-boiled gunman was impressed a little by the majestic Head.

"I ain't met up with you afore, bo!" he said genially. "You the king-pin in this joint?"

"The—the what?"

"It's the headmaster, Pike!" breathed Harry Wharton, over the banisters.

"Sure!" said Poker, with a nod. "I get you, big boy!" He gave the Head a nod. "O.K., chief! This young gink got rather fresh, and I reckoned it was time to horn in. Get me?"

"Release Loder at once!" commanded the Head.

There was a pause! Poker Pike thought it over, and his mental processes, unlike his actions, were slow.

However, it was clear that those processes led him, finally, to decide that the "king-pin" of the "joint" was a man to be obeyed; for he released Gerald Loder. He released him rather suddenly, and Loder went to the floor with a heavy bump and a howl.

"Now, sir, explain yourself!" exclaimed the Head. "I sent for you some time ago, but you were not to be found——"

"I guess I been keeping tabs on young Putnam!" said Poker, with a nod. "I ain't letting that young geek get fur out of my sight! Nope! But if you're honing to chew the rag, I ain't stopping you."

Dr. Locke opened his lips again, but he paused. He had to explain to Mr. Pike where he got off, as Poker himself would have put it. But he preferred not to have the interview in the midst of a buzzing, staring crowd of excited Greyfriars fellows.

"Follow me, please!" he rapped.

"Treading on your tail, sir!" answered Mr. Pike cheerfully; a reply that made the Greyfriars fellows chortle. And he followed the Head.

Loder staggered to his feet.

He tottered away to his study. His face was crimson with rage and mortification; and he was only too keenly conscious of the chuckles that followed him. It was likely to be a long time before Greyfriars forgot the sight of Gerald Loder carried downstairs, tucked under Poker Pike's arm.

Mr. Pike followed the headmaster into his study. Arrived there, Dr. Locke looked very expressively at the bowler hat that was still screwed down on the bullet head.

It did not seem to occur to Mr. Pike to take it off. He sat down on a corner of the Head's writing-table, and crossed one tightly trousered leg over the other —a proceeding that made the Head gasp a little. Sitting there, in that elegant attitude, Poker chewed his stump of a cigar, and waited stolidly for Dr. Locke to speak.

"Really!" gasped the Head, at a loss.

"Spill it!" said Mr. Pike encouragingly.

"Wha-a-t?"

"Shoot!" said Mr. Pike.

"Bless my soul! Mr. Pike, you are sent here by Van Duck's father to guard him against kidnapping. I have consented to allow you to remain in the school, and you will stay here——"

"Surest thing you know!" assented Mr. Pike.

"But you must learn, sir, to keep the peace, and to behave yourself with tact and discretion!" snapped the Head. "You have laid hands on one of my prefects——"

"That guy got too fresh, sir!" explained Mr. Pike. "I piped him lambasting young Putnam, and horned in. O.K.!"

"Prefects in this school, Mr. Pike, are entitled to administer canings to junior boys," said the Head. "You had no right to intervene, and you must never let anything of the kind occur again!"

"Sez you!" remarked Mr. Pike.

"What—what do you mean?"

"You're telling me!" said Mr. Pike.

"Certainly, I am telling you how you must conduct yourself here," said Dr. Locke. "Your rooms have been prepared in the porter's lodge. I will send the page with you, to show you there. And I impress upon you, Mr. Pike, that there must be no more disturbances of any kind. In such a case, it will be necessary for you to leave."

"Says you!" repeated Mr. Pike, unmoved.

"Certainly I say so, and you must remember it!" said Dr. Locke. "I quite understand that you are new to our ways here, and can make allowances; but there must be no more disturbances —nothing at all of that kind. I trust that I make myself clear."

"Clear as mud!" said Mr. Pike.

"Van Duck is here, like any other boy —the fact that he is a millionaire's son, and perhaps a person of some consequence in his native country, makes no difference—none whatever!" explained the Head. "You must not dream of interfering on his account."

"You're sure spilling a bibful!" said Mr. Pike.

"Eh! What? Your duties here are strickly limited to protecting the boy from enemies outside the school!" said the Head. "Bear that in mind! Now I will send the page with you." He touched a bell. "You will not return to this building unless specially sent for."

"I got to keep tabs on Putnam!" said Mr. Pike.

"I do not quite follow your meaning. Tabs are not worn by Greyfriars boys," said the Head. "Van Duck will dress exactly like the other boys. Neither is any boy at Greyfriars allowed the attentions of a personal servant."

Mr. Pike looked at the Head, and the Head looked at Mr. Pike.

"I guess Old Man Vanderdecken sent me here to keep tabs on Putnam!" insisted Mr. Pike.

"That is absurd!" said the Head. "Mr. Van Duck can have had no such intention. I repeat that tabs, or any kind of personal decoration, cannot be worn by Greyfriars boys!"

"I don't seem to get you," said Mr. Pike, puzzled.

"I think I speak plainly enough," said the Head. He glanced round as Trotter appeared in the doorway. "Trotter!"

"Yessir!"

"Please conduct Mr. Pike to Gosling's lodge."

"Yessir!" gasped Trotter.

Trotter's eyes opened so wide at the sight of a man with his hat on, sitting on the Head's writing-table, that they looked like falling out of his face.

Mr. Pike detached himself from the table.

"I don't quite get you, feller," he said slowly. "I got to keep tabs on Putnam, and that's a cinch. No hoodlum ain't going to cinch that young geek while I'm drawing old man Vanderdecken's pay. No, sir! I guess I'm going to see that baby safe."

"Quite so—quite so! I fully approve," said the Head. "Now please follow Trotter."

"You said it, sir," said Mr. Pike.

He followed Trotter.

There was a roar when he appeared in the quad.

"Hallo, hallo, hallo! Here he is!"

"Here's the jolly old gunman!"

Quite an army of Greyfriars fellows followed Mr. Pike to Gosling's lodge. They were quite disappointed when the door shut on Mr. Pike and his bowler hat.

Poker Pike had the spotlight at Greyfriars that day. The Head had hoped that, by the exercise of tact and reticence, he would keep himself out of the public eye—to such an extent that Greyfriars fellows would hardly know that he was there at all. That hope, it was clear, was going to be disappointed. Mr. Pike had many gifts, but it was plain that tact and reticence were not included in the list.

In fact, though it was the first day of term, and on the first day of term fellows naturally had plenty of things to talk about, Van Duck's gunman guardian reigned as the chief, if not the sole topic. Poker Pike had the spotlight, and it was probable that, unless he changed his manners and customs very considerably, he would keep it.

THE SIXTH CHAPTER.

Unexpected!

"HENRY'S beginning badly," remarked Bob Cherry.

There was a chuckle in the Remove Form Room.

"Henry," otherwise Henry Samuel Quelch, master of the Remove, had not

Fastening an iron grip on the back of Loder's collar, Mr. Pike swept the Sixth Former off his feet and swung him round and round. The astonished spectators jumped back out of reach, with the exception of Billy Bunter. "Whooop!" roared the fat junior, as Loder's feet established contact with his fat ribs. "Ooooogh!"

arrived to take his Form. When the Lower Fourth came in after morning break, Mr. Quelch was not there, so they marched into the Form-room, prepared to wait for Henry quite as long as Henry might keep them waiting. Nobody was fearfully anxious to settle down hard to the term's work.

"I say, you fellows, there was a phone call for old Quelch," said Billy Bunter. "I heard the bell go in his study."

"Let's hope the other man will keep him talking," remarked Herbert Vernon-Smith. "I can do without quite a lot of Quelch."

"Hear, hear!" grinned Skinner.

"Yaas, begad!" remarked Lord Mauleverer. "Jolly decent chap, whoever he is, to ring Quelch up when a lesson's just startin'."

"What about a spot of leap-frog?" asked Bob Cherry.

Bob found it difficult to keep still, even when a master was present—impossible when the master was absent.

"Fathead!" answered Harry Wharton. "Quelch may blow in any minute. And he's not in the best of tempers this morning."

"Beaks never are first day of term," sighed Bob. "And I fancy Van Duck's jolly old gunman got on Henry's nerves yesterday."

"Where is that jolly old gunman?" asked Peter Todd. "I haven't seen him this morning."

"I have," chuckled Bunter. "He asked me where Van Duck could be found. I believe he was looking for him in first lesson."

"Ha, ha, ha!"

"Did you put him wise?" grinned Fisher T. Fish.

"Oh, I told him how to find our Form-room," said Bunter. "You see, if he comes barging in, it will interrupt class. Even if it's only for a few minutes, it's so much to the good."

"Hallo, hallo, hallo! Here comes Henry!" said Bob, as footsteps were heard coming up the corridor.

Few of the juniors were in their places. But there was a rush to get into them as the footsteps came along to the door. Whether it was the worry of beginning term, or the effect of the gunman, or both, it was certain that Mr. Quelch was not in his bonniest mood. And nobody wanted to attract the Remove master's gimlet eye specially to himself.

But it was not the angular form of Henry Samuel Quelch that appeared in the doorway of the Remove-room. It was the thickset, stocky, wiry figure of Poker Pike, gunman guardian of the millionaire's son. And there was a general chortle from the Lower Fourth.

"Jolly old Pike!" chuckled Bob.

"The esteemed and ridiculous Poker!" grinned Hurree Jamset Ram Singh.

"Aw, carry me home to die!" murmured Putnam van Duck.

The Remove welcomed the sight of the gunman. Some fellows, like Bunter, would have welcomed any interruption to work. All the fellows wondered what would be the effect on Mr. Quelch, if he arrived and found the man from Chicago there. There might be trouble; there might even be a "row," which was quite a delightful prospect to most of the young rascals of the Greyfriars Remove.

Mr. Pike looked in, his hickory face serious as usual. He gave Putnam van Duck a nod.

"Aw, there you are!" he grunted. "I guess I been rubbering around looking for you, you Putnam van Duck."

"You pesky goob!" roared Van Duck. "You ain't allowed in here."

"Forget it," said Mr. Pike, and he marched in. Looking round for something to sit on, he spotted Mr. Quelch's high chair at the Form-master's desk, and sat on that.

Sitting on it he tilted it back at a rather dangerous angle, in order to rest his legs across the top of the high desk.

Mr. Pike was accustomed to such attitudes in the joints he frequented at home in Chicago. But it looked rather out of place in a Form-room at Greyfriars School, and it made the Removites yell.

"Look here, you gink Pike!" yelled Putnam van Duck. "You got to beat it! I'm telling you, you can't horn in here!"

"I got to keep tabs on you, Putnam," answered Mr. Pike.

"Will you beat it?" yelled Van Duck.

"Not so's you'd notice it," answered Mr. Pike.

"Look here, Mr. Pike!" exclaimed Harry Wharton. As head boy he felt impelled to weigh in. "You really can't stay here."

Mr. Pike glanced at him.

"What's biting you, bo?" he inquired. "Pack it up!"

"But I tell you——"

"Don't spill any more," said Mr. Pike. "You make me tired."

"I say, you fellows, Quelch will go off at the deep end when he finds that ruffian here," chuckled Billy Bunter.

"I'm telling you to absquatulate, you Pike!" roared Van Duck.

Poker Pike did not take the trouble to answer again. Tilted back on the high chair, with his legs sprawling across Mr. Quelch's desk, he chewed his stump of a cigar, unregarding.

There was a deep breath among the juniors as hurrying feet were heard in the corridor a few minutes later. Mr. Quelch, having got through his talk on the telephone, was hurrying to take his class.

"Now look out for the fireworks!" murmured Bob Cherry.

Mr. Quelch hurried in a little breathless, and evidently in a state of annoyance. He was the soul of punctuality, as a rule, and hated being late for class.

Had he found leap-frog going on, there was no doubt whatever that Henry Samuel Quelch would have come down hard and heavy on the leap-froggers. Fortunately all the Remove were in their places.

Not noticing the stranger within the gates for the moment, Mr. Quelch glanced at his class.

"I am sorry that I have been detained for a few minutes," he said. "We will now proceed without further delay."

He stared at his class. He could not mistake the breathless expectation in every face there. Something, he realised, was "on," though he did not know for the moment what it was.

His grim face set severely. If his Form fancied that there was going to be any relaxation of discipline on the first day in the Form-room, Mr. Quelch was the man to undeceive them on that point.

There was quite a row going on in the Third. Wiggins had not yet got his Form into order. Books were dropping, and desk lids slamming. But nothing of that kind was practicable with Mr. Quelch.

He gave his Form a long, long look. But every fellow was quiet in his place, only looking breathlessly expectant.

Puzzled and irritated, Quelch turned towards his desk. Then he understood, as he became aware of the presence of Poker Pike.

"What—what—who—what——" stuttered Mr. Quelch, as he gazed at the gunman.

Poker Pike did not move from his elegant and rather precarious position. But the bowler hat nodded genially at Mr. Quelch.

"What—what—what are you doing here?" exclaimed Mr. Quelch.

"Setting around," answered Poker affably.

"Upon my word!"

"Keepin' tabs on Putnam," added Mr. Pike "You horn in with them young rubes, feller; I ain't going to interrupt you none. I guess I know how to beyave, and I ain't chewing the rag in this here joint."

"Ha, ha, ha!" came a yell from the Remove.

Mr. Quelch whirled round at his class.

"Silence!" he hooted.

Then he fixed his eyes on Poker again.

"Leave this Form-room! Do you hear me? Leave this Form-room at once!"

"You mean beat it?" asked Mr. Pike.

"Eh? What? I mean go—go at once!" gasped the Remove master.

"Forget it, feller!" said the gunman. "I sure ain't worrying you any, setting around! Pack it up, bo!"

"Will you go at once?" almost shrieked Mr. Quelch.

"Not so's you'd notice it."

Mr. Quelch stepped up to his desk, picked up his cane, and swished it threateningly. The Remove watched him breathlessly. His face was almost crimson.

"Leave this Form-room!" he rapped, and he tapped the gunman on the shoulder to emphasise that order.

"Whurrrooooh!" roared Poker.

In his precarious, balanced position, with the high chair tilted back, and his feet on the desk, that tap on the shoulder did it.

Poker Pike went over backwards.

Having lost his centre of gravity, the well-known law of gravitation did the rest. Under the influence of that well-known law, so ably expounded by Sir Isaac Newton, Mr. Pike shot towards the centre of the earth as unerringly as Sir Isaac's apple.

He did not, of course, reach the centre of the earth, the floor of the Remove Form Room stopped him in transit.

It stopped him suddenly and hard.

Crash! Crack!

His shoulders hit the floor first; the back of his head hit it a split second later. It sounded like a postman's knock.

"Yurrrrooop!" roared Mr. Pike, sprawling dizzily on his back.

"Oh!" gasped Mr. Quelch, staring.

And from the Remove came a roar: "Ha, ha, ha!"

THE SEVENTH CHAPTER.

The Remove to the Rescue!

MR. QUELCH stared down at Mr. Pike.

Mr. Pike stared up at Mr. Quelch

The Remove rocked with merriment.

"Upon my word!" stuttered Mr. Quelch. "I—I am sorry you—you have fallen down but—but you must leave this Form-room at once——"

"Carry me home to die!" gasped Mr. Pike.

He scrambled to his feet.

He stood rubbing the back of his head. It was a hard and solid head, shaped like a bullet, and nearly as hard. But that crack on the floor seemed to have hurt it; it had even dislodged the bowler hat—without which Mr. Pike had not, so far, been seen in the school.

"Search me!" said Mr. Pike.

He picked up the black bowler and clamped it on his head again—he clamped it down hard—then he turned to Mr. Quelch with a glint in his icy slits of eyes.

"Feller," he said, "you're the guy to ask for it, and that ain't no dream! But I ain't going to shoot you up."

"Wha-a-at?" stuttered Mr. Quelch.

"Nunk!" said Mr. Pike. "Old Man Vanderdecken put it to me—no gunplay, 'cept when kidnappers is around. I'll say I feel powerful inclined to fan you a few, but I ain't going to do it."

"Upon my word! I——"

"But I'll tell all this little island," went on Mr. Pike, "that I ain't the guy to be throwed about like I was a sack of potaters! No, sir! Surest thing you know! I ain't going to pull no hardware on you, but I sure am going to beat you up a piece."

To Mr Quelch's amazement and horror, the gunman advanced on him with his knuckly fists clenched.

Quelch backed away, wondering whether this was some fearful dream.

Quelch was no coward. But he was long past the age for a rough-and-tumble, even had such a thing been imaginable in a Form-room at Greyfriars.

"Man!" gasped Quelch.

"I guess you got it coming to you, feller!" said Mr Pike, following him up. "You sure have asked for it, hombre!"

"Goodness gracious——"

"You locoed gink, Poker!" shrieked Putnam van Duck. "Hold in your hosses, you pesky bonehead!"

Unheeding, the incensed gunman followed Mr. Quelch as he backed in almost dizzy horror across the Form-room.

"This is where we barge in, I think," remarked Harry Wharton.

"What-ho!" grinned Bob Cherry.

"Come on!" shouted Johnny Bull.

"Back up, Remove!" yelled the Bounder, always ready for a shindy.

Five or six fellows rushed out of their places and rushed at Poker Pike; after them rushed a dozen more.

They were none too soon.

The horrified Form-master had backed up to a wall, where he stood waving Mr. Pike off with his hands as if he were a bluebottle.

But Mr. Pike was no bluebottle to be waved off. He was closing in on Henry Samuel Quelch when the rush of the Removites stopped him.

That sudden charge sent Mr. Pike staggering and just saved Mr. Quelch from a punch that would undoubtedly have done serious damage.

Leaning on the wall, Quelch spluttered for breath. While he spluttered most of his Form were busy.

Billy Bunter, Skinner, Snoop, and one or two other fellows kept their places, but nearly all the Remove joined in.

Many hands were needed to deal with Mr. Pike. The man who had carried Loder of the Sixth, wriggling under his arm, was not easily handled by juniors; but many hands made light work.

The Famous Five collared him all at once. Vernon-Smith, Redwing, Peter Todd, and Squiff got hold. Struggling, Poker Pike went over and crashed on the Form-room floor a second time.

"Cinch him!" yelled Van Duck.

"Bag him!" gasped Bob Cherry.

"Sit on him!"

"Jump on him!"

"Roll him out!"

"Whoo-hoo! Hoooh!" gasped Johnny Bull, as Mr. Pike's knuckles caught him on the jaw. Johnny went over like a skittle.

But the gunman was down, and the swarming juniors kept him down. He was active, strong, and witty, but the Remove were many too many for him.

With two or three fellows grasping each arm and each leg, even the hefty gunman struggled in vain.

They surged to the door, half-carrying and half-dragging Poker Pike. Putnam van Duck was foremost in the fray, but all the fellows were eager for front seats. It was a tough struggle, but it was ever so much more entertaining than Latin grammar.

"Chuck him out!" gasped Harry Wharton.

"Boot him!"

"Ha, ha, ha!"

"Say, you, Putnam van Duck, you leago my years!" yelled Poker Pike, in wild wrath and indignation. "Ain't I here to keep tabs on you?"

"You locoed geck!" snapped Van Duck. "You got to learn where you get off, Poker—and this is jest the spot!"

"I guess—— Ow! I reckon—— Whoop! I'll say—— Yurrrrooooop!" howled Poker.

"Ha, ha, ha!"

"Out he goes!"

"Goodness gracious!" gasped Mr. Quelch feebly "Upon my word! Oh dear! G-g-g-g-goodness gracious!"

A struggling mass reached the doorway of the Form-room; a bowler hat was left behind, rolling.

In the doorway Mr. Pike rallied. But it booted not; he was hurled forth, and landed in the passage in a sprawling heap.

The Removites packed the doorway as he sprawled and gasped for breath.

Putnam van Duck shook a warning finger at him.

"Now you beat it, you big stiff!" he roared. "You get me? Beat it—and beat it pronto! And keep on beating it!"

"Urrrrrrggh!" gurgled Mr. Pike.

He sat up, blinking.

"My boys!" gasped Mr. Quelch. "My bib-bib-bib-boys——"

"Carry me home to die!" gasped Mr. Pike.

He picked himself up.

Standing in the passage, he gasped for breath, and eyed the breathless mob of schoolboys in the doorway.

He was clearly debating, in the depths of his slow and stolid brain, whether to charge back into the Remove-room. Harry Wharton & Co. stood ready to stop the charge, if it came. Some of them had had some rather hard knocks in the tussle, and it was certain that there would be some more, if Poker Pike charged. But they packed the doorway and stood ready.

"Will you beat it, you geck!" howled Van Duck. "You figure you can kick up a rookus here, like you was in a joint back in Chicago! Beat it!"

Mr. Pike nodded slowly. Apparently he had made up his mind to beat it He turned and went down the passage, stopping at the end, and sitting down in the window-seat there. And he sat there without his hat!

"Boys," gasped Mr. Quelch, "go to your places!"

The juniors moved back from the doorway. Mr. Quelch looked out into the passage. He frowned at the sight of the gunman in the window-seat. Mr. Pike, it seemed was going to "keep tabs" from that spot.

Quelch breathed hard, and shut the door of the Form-room.

"Silence!" he barked.

The Remove was in a buzz of excitement. No doubt Mr. Quelch was grateful to his boys for coming so promptly to his rescue. But such an extraordinary scene in his Form-room was intensely irritating and exasperating to the Remove master. He barked at the Remove—indeed, he looked really as if he might bite! The buzz died away, and the juniors took their places.

After which, during third school, Quelch carried on as if nothing had happened. But when the Remove were dismissed, Quelch was seen to direct his steps towards the Head's study, no doubt to acquaint his chief with Mr. Pike's startling proceedings that morning—from which the Removites deduced that Poker's days at Greyfriars were probably numbered.

THE EIGHTH CHAPTER.

Inky!

"YOUR hat, sir!" said Peter Todd politely.

Mr. Pike was seated on the bench outside Gosling's lodge, where he had his quarters.

He sat hatless.

His black bowler had been left behind, in that tussle in the Remove Form Room; it had rolled, unregarded, under the desks. As Poker Pike seemed to live, move, breathe, and have his being in that hat, some of the fellows had rather expected him to come back for it.

But he had not come; and after the Remove were dismissed, he went back to the lodge, still without it. His greasy, well-brushed hair glimmered in the sunshine as he sat—still "keeping tabs." Nobody, kidnapper or otherwise, could have come in at the gates without Poker Pike giving him the once-over.

His hickory face expressed satisfaction as Toddy came up with the hat in his hand and presented it.

Five or six fellows who had followed Peter, were grinning—Billy Bunter, especially, exploding in a series of chuckles like a fat Chinese cracker.

They seemed to see something comic in Peter taking the gunman's hat back to him. Peter's face, however, was as serious as Mr. Pike's own, and nobody could possibly have guessed, from Peter's face, that he had spent ten minutes carefully packing ink under the inside lining of that hat.

Certainly, Mr. Pike did not dream of suspecting it.

He was "wise" to the ways of gangsters and gunmen; nobody could have taught him anything about bootlegging, or racketeering, holding up a guy for his roll, or putting a 'rival gangster "on the spot." But he was not so wise to the playful ways of schoolboys.

Quite unaware that the hat had been tampered with, Poker Pike jammed it on his oily head, jamming it down with firmness. He seemed comforted when it was fixed there again. He thanked Peter with a nod, and resumed chewing his unlighted cigar and watching the gate.

"He, he, he!" chuckled Billy Bunter. "I say, you fellows, wait till it begins to run——"

"Shut up, fathead!" said Peter.

"Oh, really, Toddy——"

"I give him about ten minutes," remarked Peter, when the juniors were out of Mr. Pike's hearing, "then he will begin to look like a zebra."

"Ha, ha, ha!"

It was quite a warm day, and where Mr. Pike sat was a sunny spot. Two or three drops of perspiration glistened on his forehead, under the brim of the clamped-down bowler.

If Mr. Pike noticed any dampness about his brow, he naturally attributed it to the same cause. He had no suspicion that ink was oozing through the lining of his hat, mixing with the oil on his hair, and beginning to streak his forehead.

Harry Wharton & Co., taking a trot round the quad before dinner, came on the group of juniors, who were watching the gunman from a distance, with smiling faces.

"Hallo, hallo, hallo! What's the jolly old joke?" inquired Bob Cherry.

"He, he, he!" cackled Bunter. "Look at Pike!"

The Famous Five looked.

"What the dickens——" exclaimed Harry Wharton, in astonishment.

Poker Pike was sitting, unmoved, on the bench by the porter's lodge. If he noticed the juniors at all, he gave them no heed.

The expression on his hickory face was thoughtful. Perhaps he was still thinking, in the slow depths of his solid brain, about the "rookus" in the Remove Form Room, and whether to get on with beating-up the schoolmaster guy!

In a place so strange to him as Greyfriars School, Mr. Pike realised that he had to walk delicately, like Agag of old. He was by no means satisfied with the outcome of that "rookus," and now he was putting in a big "think."

But there was something on Mr. Pike's face besides a thoughtful expression. There was a red streak of ink running over his left ear to his left eye. Several streaks of red and black were dawning on his forehead.

Peter had used ink, both red and black, and plenty of both. As the lining of the hat pressed on Mr. Pike's hard skull, the ink oozed slowly through, and now it was beginning to give Mr. Pike's countenance a highly decorative appearance.

He was obviously quite unaware of it Harry Wharton & Co. looked at him blankly.

"He's got his hat again!" remarked Bob.

"And something in it!" chuckled Hazeldene.

"Somebody been japing him?" asked Harry, laughing.

"I fancy so!" said Peter Todd gravely. "I believe some fellow parked ink in that hat, before handing it back to him."

"Ha, ha, ha!"

That outburst of merriment drew Mr. Pike's attention at last. He looked at the group of juniors rather grimly.

"Hallo, there's that ruffian!" Coker of the Fifth came along, with Potter and Greene. "Great pip! Look at him! Ha, ha, ha!"

Coker of the Fifth disliked Mr. Pike. His ducking in the fountain had annoyed Coker extremely. Coker was annoyed to learn that the man was allowed to remain within the walls of Greyfriars. But at the sight of the streaky face, looking more and more like a zebra's every moment, Coker forgot his wrath, and burst into a roar

"Ha, ha, ha!" roared Coker, and Potter and Greene grinned.

Mr. Pike's expression grew grimmer. But at that moment Trotter came down from the House, and headed for the porter's lodge. He had a message for Mr. Pike.

At the sight of the streaky face, Trotter jumped and stared.

"Oh, my eye!" ejaculated Trotter.

"What's biting you, bo'?" asked Poker.

He rose from the bench. The look on his streaky face made the House page jump back about a yard at one jump.

"Oh, nothing!" gasped Trotter. "The 'Ead wants to see you in his study. He's sent me to tell you."

And Trotter cut off, grinning.

"Oh, my hat!" murmured Peter Todd, in dismay.

It had seemed, to the playful Peter, quite a lark to decorate Mr. Pike in that extraordinary way. But he had not foreseen that Poker would be called in to see the Head.

"Oh crumbs!" said Bob, with a gasp. "If he goes in to the Head like that——"

"Ha, ha, ha!"

Mr. Pike was starting for the House. He passed the group of juniors, who strove to subdue their merriment as he came by. Coker of the Fifth, however, saw no reason for subduing his merriment. He roared.

"Ha, ha, ha!"

Poker Pike turned towards Coker.

"Say, big boy, you sure do snicker a whole lot!" he remarked. "You asking for a lambasting?"

"Ha ha, ha!" roared Coker.

He almost doubled up with mirth, at a close view of Mr. Pike's streaky countenance.

"I guess," remarked Mr. Pike, "that you've sniggered more'n a few, and I'll say you make me tired! You got it coming!"

He made a stride at Coker of the Fifth. Before Coker quite knew what was happening two hands that seemed made of iron were grasping him. Coker was hefty, and he was beefy; but he crumpled up in that iron grasp.

"O o o o g h!" spluttered C o k e r. "Leggo, you ruffian! Potter—Greene—whooooop!"

"Oh crumbs!" gasped Nugent.

"Here, you chuck that!" exclaimed Potter.

Unheeding, Mr. Pike dropped on one knee and "made a knee" for Coker with the other. Across that knee Horace Coker sprawled, face down.

He kicked and struggled and roared.

Mr. Pike swept up his right hand. It came down on Coker's trousers like a flail! It landed with a whack that rang across the quad like the report of Mr. Pike's own six-gun!

Smack!

"Yoo-hooop!" roared Coker. A moment ago Coker had been roaring with merriment. He was still roaring. But now it was not with merriment.

Whack! came from Mr. Pike's heavy hand again.

"Yaroooh!"

"Ha, ha, ha!" shrieked the juniors.

Whack!

"Whoooop!"

Coker's legs kicked wildly in the air. Potter and Greene made a quick forward movement—and then a quicker backward one, as Mr. Pike's flail-like arm swept round, and they barely missed it.

Smack!

"Yoo-hoo-hoooop!"

"Ha, ha, ha!"

"I guess," said Mr. Pike, with his usual gravity, "that that lets you out, big boy!"

He pitched Coker off his knee. Horace rolled and roared. Mr. Pike walked off towards the House, leaving Coker roaring with wrath and anguish, and the other fellows with laughter.

THE NINTH CHAPTER.

Poker Pike is Puzzled!

"HA, ha, ha!"

"Look!"

"What's that game?"

"It's the wild man from Borneo!"

"Ha, ha, ha!"

The quadrangle was crowded with fellows; and the eyes of every fellow in the quad turned on Mr. Pike as he progressed towards the House.

Mr. Pike had not been long at Greyfriars, but he had already caused considerable entertainment there. But this was the climax! Now he had, so to speak, brought down the house!

He was puzzled, and he was getting angry. There was a glitter in his slits of eyes as he stared round at innumerable laughing faces.

It was not the best of manners, perhaps, to burst into a yell of laughter at the sight of Mr. Pike. But the fellows really could not help it. By this time more and more of the ink had oozed out of the hat. A black streak was oozing down Mr. Pike's pug nose. It gave him a most remarkable aspect.

Quite unconscious of it, Mr. Pike was only surprised and annoyed. His grim face grew grimmer and grimmer. On the steps of the House, Loder and Walker of the Sixth were standing, and, like the rest, they burst into a yell as Mr. Pike and his remarkable face dawned on them.

"Ha, ha, ha!"

Mr. Pike gave them a glare as he came up the steps. That glare might have had a terrifying effect, but for the streaks of ink that made the gunman look like a zebra. But Poker Pike, at the moment, did not look terrifying—he looked comic, and the two prefects only laughed the louder.

"What on earth is the man doing that for?" asked Walker, chuckling. "Is he potty, or what?"

"Must be, I think!" said Loder. "Potty or tipsy! Ha, ha, ha!"

"You guys surely do hone to snicker!" said Poker Pike. "I guess I'll hand you something to snicker for."

He made a grasp at Loder and Walker. The fact that they were Sixth Form men and prefects mattered not a boiled bean to Poker Pike. He got Loder by the collar with one hand, Walker by the other.

Crack!

Two heads came together with a loud concussion. Two fearful yells were blended into one!

"Yoooooooop!"

"Ha, ha, ha!" came a howl from the swarm of fellows in the quad. It was the first time that the Greyfriars fellows had seen two Sixth Form prefects having their heads knocked together!

Loder and Walker, yelling frantically, wrenched themselves away from Poker Pike. They got away—leaving their collars in Poker's hands.

Collarless, they scrambled out of his reach. Mr. Pike was left standing on the steps, staring at the two crumpled collars in his hands.

"Search me!" ejaculated Mr. Pike.

He threw the collars into the quad, and marched on into the House. Mr. Prout, the master of the Fifth, met him as he entered.

Prout, hearing the uproar in the quad, was coming out to see what was going on. He met Poker Pike face to face, and jumped at the sight of him. In his surprise Prout would have jumped clear of the floor had he had a little less weight to lift.

"Who — who — what — what ——" stuttered Prout. He stared at the streaky face with starting eyes.

Mr. Pike gave him a resentful glare.

"What's got you, you old gink?" he demanded.

"Wha-a-t?" stuttered Prout. "What—what does this mean? Are you mad? What do you mean by appearing here with a face like that?"

Mr. Pike breathed hard.

His best friend had never called Mr. Pike handsome. If his face had been his fortune, he would have been extremely hard-up. Still, such as it was, it was his face—a poor thing, but his own, so to speak.

Unaware of the unusual decoration on his face, Mr. Pike considered Prout's remark very personal and very unpleasant. Even in a Chicago joint, where manners were far from polished, nobody had ever asked Poker Pike what he meant by going about with a face like that! It would, indeed, have been a perilous question to put to a guy so handy with a gun as Mr. Pike.

"Why, you fat old geck!" said Poker. "You ornery, dog-goned old stiff, I guess your own face looks like a piece that the cat brought in. I'd sure hand you a sockdolager, if I didn't figure that it would burst you all over this here shebang! Pack it up! You get me? Pack it up, while you're still in one piece, you pesky old bonehead!"

He gave Mr. Prout a push on his portly chest.

Mr. Pike was really a considerate man. Had he handed Prout a "sockdolager," as he was tempted to do, Greyfriars might have been in need of a new master for the Fifth Form.

He gave him a push instead—but there was a lot of beef in a push from the hefty gunman.

Prout staggered back as if a battering-ram had tapped him. He staggered, stumbled, and sat down; with a bump that almost shook the floor.

"Oooooogh!" gasped Prout.

He sat and gasped, in a dizzy state. Poker gave him a glare, and walked on to the Head's study.

Reaching the fountain, Mr. Pike dropped Coker bodily into the wide granite basin in which was about a foot of water. Splash! There was quite a waterspout as Coker landed there. From the excited mob in the quadrangle came a roar. "Ha, ha, ha!"

Arrived there, he opened the door and walked in. Poker had not learned to tap at doors before entering in his native haunts in Chicago.

Dr. Locke was seated at his writing-table, by which stood Mr. Quelch. The Remove master was looking very grim; the headmaster very worried.

Both of them jumped at the sight of Poker Pike.

Mr. Pike did not remove his hat. Had he done so, he would have found it dripping with ink, and would have discovered the cause of the hurricane of merriment that had accompanied him on his way to the House.

But it did not occur to him to remove his hat. He lived in that hat; indeed, it was uncertain whether he took it off when he went to bed!

With the black bowler screwed down on his skull, and streaks of red and black ink oozing from under it, Mr. Pike faced the two masters—who fairly goggled at him.

"Bless my soul!" said the Head faintly.

"Upon my word!" gurgled Mr. Quelch.

Poker eyed them none too agreeably. He was getting angrier and angrier.

"I guess you allowed you wanted me to horn in!" he said gruffly. "I'll say I've come! Shoot!"

"You—you—you are Mr. Pike!" stuttered the Head. Really, Mr. Pike was hardly recognisable in his decorated state. "What—what does this mean, Mr. Pike? Why have you done this?"

"Ain't you sent for me?" demanded Poker.

"Yes, yes!" gasped the Head. "But—but—but—your face——"

"My face?" repeated Poker, in a voice rather like the growl of a tiger.

He had not expected this from a courteous old gentleman like the Head! Anyhow, he had had enough about his face from the stout old guy he had sat down in the passage. He did not want any more.

"Mebbe you'll put a guy wise what's the matter with his face, you old gook?"

"Are you mad?" hooted Mr. Quelch.

"I guess," said Poker, "that if any guy here is locoed, it ain't this baby. I'll tell a man!"

"Your face——"

"Forget my face!" roared Mr. Pike. "I guess if you went digging in a scrap-heap, you'd dig up a better-looking face than the one you've got on, dog-gone you! And then some!"

"But——" stuttered the Head. "Your—your face——"

"I'm telling you," hooted Mr. Pike, "that I've heard enough about it, and a few over, and then some more! You get me? I'm whispering to you, you pesky old mugwumps, that if any guy at home talked to me that-a-way, his friends would have to go around picking up what was left of him! And for jest one Continental red cent, I'd wade in and beat you up a few! Surest thing you know!"

Mr. Pike glared at the headmaster and the Remove master.

They gazed at him.

"But——" gasped the Head.

"But——" gasped Mr. Quelch.

"Pack it up!" roared Mr. Pike. "Pack it up, and put the lid on! I've had jest all I want!"

"B-b-b-but——" stuttered the Head.

"Aw, can it!" snarled Mr. Pike.

He swung round to the door. In great wrath, he tramped out, slamming the door after him with a terrific slam.

"Bless my soul!" said the Head faintly.

"Goodness gracious!" murmured Mr. Quelch

Mr. Pike tramped out of the House, with a black brow under his bowler hat. In the sunshine of the quad his streaky face showed up to great advantage, and a yell greeted him.

"Ha, ha, ha!"

"Here's the jolly old zebra!"

"I say, you fellows—— He, he, he!"

Mr. Pike gave an almost deadly glare round. He looked like running amuck in the laughing crowd.

Putnam van Duck rushed up to him.

"Poker, you locoed gink," he shrieked, "what's the game? What you playing this fool game for, you bonehead?"

"What game, dog-gone you, you Putnam van Duck?" howled the exasperated Poker. "What the great horned toad——"

"Your face——" gasped Putnam.

"My face!" yelled Poker. "Great jumping toads, you whisper jest one word about my face, and I'll sure hand you a few!"

"What have you inked it for?" yelled Putnam.

"Eh?"

"Like you was a Red Indian with his war-paint on!"

"What?"

"What you done it for, you locoed bonehead?"

In great surprise, Mr. Pike passed his hand over his face. His hand came away streaked with red and black, and he gazed at it in still greater surprise. That rub on his face changed the inky streaks into a general smudge, and there was another howl:

"Ha, ha, ha!"

"Say, this here has got me beat!" said the amazed Poker. He passed his hand over his astonished face again, smudging ink right and left, amid shrieks of laughter. "Say, how come?"

He took off his hat and stared at it. It dripped mixed inks. The amazement

(*Continued on page 16.*)

DO YOU LIKE GOING BACK TO SCHOOL?

Asks TOM BROWN

If you don't, you jolly well should! That's Mr. Prout's idea about it, anyway! I ran into the jolly old Fifth Form master down at Brighton, and in a few pompous sentences he told me just what he thought about it.

"The notorious reluctance of juveniles to return to their studies after a vacation is entirely inexcusable, Brown," he snorted. "Every boy should embark on the term's labours with the same zest as he embarks on the recreative avocations of a holiday. *Joie de vivre* can be experienced in the competitive struggle in the Form-room just as much as in the sporting arena! Hah!"

Dunno about you, lads, but it was a new one on me! Up to that moment, I'd never considered the possibility of getting joy out of French irregular verbs, for instance, or the theorems of dear old Euclid. But Prouty seems to think we ought to get a real kick out of them, anyway, and, for all I know, some of you may.

As nobody seems to be staying near me this vac., I haven't been able to collect fellows' opinions on this burning topic. So I've taken the liberty of putting answers into the mouths of a few of our leading lights. Voila!

BILLY BUNTER: Like going back to school? Beast!

HORACE COKER: I'd like it if the school treated me with the respect rightly due to its most illustrious member. But it doesn't—so I don't!

GERALD LODER: So long as they don't "saddle" me with responsibility and "spur" me on to swotting, I don't mind a "bit."

BOB CHERRY: What-ho! I like everything! Whoopee!

CECIL TEMPLE: What—what? School? Oh, gad! What?

WUN LUNG: No savvy!

LORD MAULEVERER: Snore!

No. 186. EDITED BY HA

THE SPARTANS of ST. SAM'S!

First Instalment of a Rib-Tickling New Serial

By DICKY NUGENT

"Bravvo, Jolly!"

It was a horse voice that echoed across Little Side, and it made Jack Jolly turn as red as a pony!

Looking over his shoulder in the direction from which it had come, he saw that the speaker was Burleigh, the burly kaptin of St. Sam's. Burleigh, who had rolled across from the Skool House while Jack Jolly & Co. were practising the igh jump, gave an encurridging wave.

"You're shaping jolly well, Jolly!" he growled, as he sawntered over. "If you jump like that on Sports Day, kid, the Junior High-Jump will be won by St. Sam's as easy as winking!"

"Thanks, awfully, Burleigh!" said Jack Jolly, closing one eye at his pals.

"Now let's see what you can do, Fearless!" ordered Burleigh.

Frank Fearless nodded and walked back a few paces in readiness. Like the rest of the company, he looked a fine fizzical specimen. His square shoulders and straight limbs and angular figger were those of an all-round athlete.

"Stand clear, you fellows!" he cride. Then he took a short run, soared into the air like a rocket, and cleared the bar by inches. This was no small feet, and there was a roar of applawse from Burleigh and the rest of the company.

The next moment there was a very different kind of roar. Just as Fearless jumped, Mr. Lickham, the Fourth Form master, came cycling fewriously across the turf, and, as luck would have it, he arrived on the seen at the very moment when Fearless descended!

Crash! Thud! Wallop!

"Yarooooo!" howled Mr. Lickham, as Fearless came down on him like a sack of potatoes.

"Oh, crumbs! It's Lickham!" cride Jolly. "Reskew, St. Sam's!"

"Ha, ha, ha!"

Jolly and Merry and Bright soon piled in and sorted out Mr. Lickham and Fearless from the bike. Luckily, the master of the Fourth appeared to have suffered little in the way of injuries, apart from a few cuts and nocks.

"I was just bringing a message to you, Burleigh!" said Mr. Lickham. "The Head wants you at once—you and any other athletes I can find. He's waiting for you outside the pavilion

on B collect there- dresse runni on Sp "S better marke kids c perha "B leigh Ane left I rushe "B Docto they pavili "A "S I've want Birch ing s to the have the whom Kapti repres agains Sports you'v I mus "D they'r of ath asked prize. Do shook "N not. matte baked throu of Spo will and a that Burlei farely when steak "Y

COW TURNED REMOVITE INTO ARTIST!

Says HARRY WHARTON

Frank Nugent always imagined he was something of an artist till this vac. Then he started painting a landscape near my uncle's place, and soon learned that he wasn't. A famous artist of the modern kind happens to live near by, you see, and he chanced upon Nugent while Frank was doing his stuff. And he told Frank just where he was wrong!

"Art!" That's not art!" he groaned. "Why, it's no better than photography! Why don't you take a snap and have done with it?"

"What's wrong with it?" Frank asked.

"Everything; that's all!" answered the cheery artist. "You're putting it on the canvas just as it is—like some dashed surveyor, measuring it up as a building site. Art, my boy, should express the soul of the artist! To paint a real picture, you should put into it what you *feel*—not merely what any beast of the field with a pair of eyes can *see*!"

And that was that! It gave Frank quite a severe jolt for the time being, I can tell you!

Now we come to the really juicy part of the tale. On the following day, Frank ran short of green paint and left his easel with the canvas on it for a few minutes while he sprinted down to the village for a fresh tube. Imagine his dismay when he returned, to find that a cow had wandered up and started licking his artistic effort, wiping out most of the scene and turning it into a fearsome mix-up of colours.

He chased the offending animal away and ruefully stood in front of his ruined work, wondering what to do.

Just at that moment up rolled the afore-mentioned modern artist once more. The artist stopped and looked; and then he jumped!

'My boy!

What's come over you?" he gurgled.

"Well, you see, sir——"

"Don't try to explain! If you try to explain Art, you kill it! My boy, you're painting a masterpiece! It's going to be a work of genius! I heartily congratulate you!"

And with that, the artist walked away, fairly chortling.

And Frank didn't have the nerve to call him back and tell him that the "genius" was in reality one of the beasts of the field to which he had referred so disparagingly the day before!

NO WONDER HE "SIZE"!

Temple, of the Upper Fourth, says that ready-made clothes are so unreliable in measurement that the mere thought of them makes him shudder!

They give him fifty "fits"!

WOULD YOU BELIEVE IT?

When Billy Bunter came in, bursting with the story of how he had saved a man from drowning in the Sark, he seemed surprised nobody believed him. It came out that Tom Redwing had got the man out—Bunter had only lent a hand in dragging him through shallow water! Bunter's boast was "shallow"—as usual!

"Nap" Dupont tells how last vac. he took part in a wild boar hunt in his native France. The boar, one of the few left to-day, invaded a village—and "Nap" ran considerable risk getting near it. Though the most excitable fellow in the Remove, "Nap" is by no means lacking in courage. He goes "wild"!

When Bolsover major picked quarrel with Sir Jimmy Vivis the one-time waif promptly p up his fists. Despite his advan age in weight and reach, Bolsov had his work cut out! "Bully Bolsover is tough—but Sir Jimn Vivian's "tough" early li made him a "tough" opponen They shook hands after fo rounds!

HERALD

STOP PRESS NEWS

RTON. May 2nd, 1936.

fe has
skool
re all
els or
ist like

if I'd
e," re-
"You
e, too,

Bur-

& Co.
n and
rleigh.
cride
, when
t the

n fakt,
han I
Doctor
crush-
To get
eigh, I
tching
thletes
Sports
sen to
Sam's
rs on
e mess
e job,

think
e lot
sir?"
n ser-

hemall

I do
mince
half-
re put
ng test
Sam's
oup—
of fish
ll you,
es me
rage,
t is at

seem

to be in a stew about it, sir," admitted Burleigh. "But let me assure you, sir, that there's nothing for you to worry your fat over. The fellows I've selected are the best athletes at St. Sam's, and I'm certain they'll beat the pick of St. Bill's or St. Pete's."

"Yes, at hopscotch or marbles, p e r h a p s!" snorted the Head. "Unforchunitly, Burleigh,

however, those two games don't figger on the programme. What I want to see is athletes who will carry all before them in running, jumping, throwing the kricket ball, et settera!"

"Then I'll show you such men here and now, sir!" cride Burleigh. "Tallboy! Strapper! Jolly! Fearless! Stand fourth!"

The fellows named stood fourth and Burleigh himself stood fifth. Together, they made as fine-looking a crowd of sportsmen as you could have met in a day's march. They had iron jaws and muscles of steel and harts of gold; and you could tell at a glance that they would always be on their metal.

"Now you'll see for yourself, sir," growled Burleigh. "You go first, Tallboy. Do the quarter-mile."

Tallboy set his teeth. An instant later, he was off like a boolit from a gun. Long before the Head had time to air his views any more, Tallboy was back again, having done the quarter-mile like a flash of litening!

A bust of applawse greeted his amazing performance. But not from Doctor Birchemall. The Head meerly smiled sinnically.

"What made you take so long over it, Tallboy?" he asked. "Why, a snail could have done it in that time!"

"My hat!" gasped Tallboy.

"Strapper!" grunted Burleigh. "Show us what you can do in the long jump!"

Strapper nodded and took a breef, preliminary run, then jumped. The crowd farely gasped as they saw that he had covered almost the entire length of the cricket-pitch! Surely, they thought, after that, the Head would smother any further criticisms he had intended to make. Much to their disgust, however, the only thing the Head smothered was a yawn!

"What a feeble jump!" he eggsclaimed. "Why, it's no more than any common or garden kangaroo could do!"

Burleigh frowned.

"You're jolly hard to satisfy, sir. But you haven't seen everything. Just watch these two yungsters and see if they don't strike you as the best you've ever seen for their age. Do the hundred-yards hurdle run, Jolly, will you? And you, Fearless, show the Head the high jump. After that, sir, I myself will throw the cricket ball for your bennyfit."

Jolly and Fearless hastened to carry out Burleigh's commands; and after they had given brilliant performances, Burleigh concluded by throwing a kricket-ball completely out of site.

All that Doctor Birchemall did, however, was to larf mirthlessly.

"If it wasn't so tragick, Burleigh, it would be funny!" he cride. "These boys are simply N.G. As to your own paneful effort, I don't suppose for a moment that you threw the ball more than about half a mile!"

"Grate pip, sir!" eggsclaimed Burleigh. "What more do you want?"

The Head's eyes gleemed.

"Plenty more, Burleigh!" he replied. "I want my skool to be represented by super-men! I want a team of athletes that will make everyone say the spirit of ancient Sparta has descended on St. Sam's!"

"My hat! And how do you eggspect to get them, sir?"

Doctor Birchemall grinned.

"By deposing you from the post of Sports Kaptin, Burleigh, and putting in your place someone I know who combines superyewman fizzical strength with incredible o r g a n i s i n g a b i l i t y and the supreme will to win!"

Burleigh stared.

"Mite I ask the name of this jeenius, sir?"

"Certainly. His name is Alfred Birchemall!"

"You?" gasped Burleigh.

The Head grinned and nodded.

"Little me! Why not?"

For a moment Burleigh and the crowd gazed at the Head speechlessly. Then they yelled.

"Ha, ha, ha!"

"The Head—Sports Kaptin, you know!"

"You're pulling our legs!"

"I'm not!" declared the Head indignantly. "You wait till the St. Sam's Spartans really get going! Yah!"

With that, he tramped off to the tuckshop for a much-needed glass of pop, leaving the crowd still larfing fit to bust.

Try as they would, they couldn't believe that the Head really meant it. But soon, had they known it, they were to get konvincing proof that Doctor Birchemall was in deadly earnest over the Spartans of St. Sam's!

(Don't miss Dicky Nugent's mirth-provoking account of Birchy's Spartans in next week's instalment.)

H. VERNON-SMITH explains

WHY BLENKINSOP WILL NEVER SEE GREYFRIARS

I met Bertram Blenkinsop during the vac. Nice lad, with thick glasses and a kiss-curl hanging over his forehead; had a slight lisp and wore mittens because it was chilly, and he suffered from a bad circulation. His mater told me he was coming to Greyfriars next September. She asked me quite a lot of questions about the dear old school.

"Do they air the blankets well?" was her first question.

Fairly well, I told her, considering that they were stored in a damp crypt and only hung out to air when it was raining. Mrs. Blenkinsop looked a little alarmed.

"Are the beds nice and springy?" she asked.

"Not really," I beamed. "But then you can't expect wooden planks to be awfully springy, can you?"

"And do the masters always see that the boys wear their flannel chest-protectors!"

I had to admit regretfully that they didn't. They pinched them to make into overcoats for their pet Pomeranians, I explained.

Mrs. B. began to show signs of distress. She asked about the boys. Of course, there were no bullies amongst them?

On this point I was able to reassure her completely. The old-fashioned bully who roasted new boys in front of the Common-room fire and hung them up by their ears, had died out, I said. Nowadays, new boys were merely kicked downstairs occasionally, or beaten unconscious with cricket-stumps. In fact, things had greatly improved so far as bullying was concerned.

I told her lots more like that just to put her at her ease. Quite a pleasant little chat we had, in fact. I began to look forward to young Bertram settling down at Greyfriars.

But now I hear he won't be coming after all. I was puzzled to know why, at first, but I think I've fathomed it out now. Mrs. B. must have got scared over an indiscreet remark I let drop at the end.

I told her that mittens had been abolished at Greyfriars—in favour of muffs!

GREYFRIARS FACTS WHILE YOU WAIT!

Vernon-Smith attended
struction classes in
ast vac., it being his
to fly his own private
oon as he is old enough.
," Mr. Samuel Vernon-
w "Smithy" to school
ginning of the term—
. Vernon-Smith, being
aire, employs a pilot!

Alonzo Todd has a passion for long words. Asked to write an essay on the biggest creatures on earth, most Removites merely mentioned the elephant and the whale. "Lonzy," however, went back to prehistoric times and referred to the titanotheres, the brontosaurus, and the zeuglodon. What were they? "Lonzy" will tell you!

At the Courtfield Fair, Bob Cherry broke all records at the coconut-shies — knocking down six juicy coconuts with only seven balls! Bob is a dead shot, and he had only one "miss." When Bob and his chums walked off with the coconuts, however, the proprietor sadly "missed" them! He'll "shy" at Bob next time!

(*Continued from page 13.*)

in his inky face made the Greyfriars fellows yell.

"Ink!" said Poker dazedly.

"Ha, ha, ha!"

"It's sure ink——"

"Ha, ha, ha!"

"Can you beat it?" said Poker, in wonder.

"Ha, ha, ha!"

Slowly the truth dawned on Poker's solid brain as he gazed at his inky hat.

"I guess that pesky young guy doctored this here hat afore he handed it up to me!" he said. "Yep! I'll say that's the how of it! Surest thing you know. And I'll mention that I'm going to cinch that young guy, and beat him up a few! I'm sure going to lambaste that galoot!"

And Poker stamped away, to search for Peter Todd. And it was fortunate for the playful Peter that Poker did not find him.

THE TENTH CHAPTER.

Snaffled!

"I GUESS I got to lose him!" groaned Putnam van Duck.

"I guess, calculate, reckon, and opine that you dog-goned well have!" said Bob Cherry, with great gravity.

And there was a chuckle in the Rag.

It was some days later, and a half-holiday, and the Famous Five and their new American chum were talking it over. A run up the river, that bright and sunny spring afternoon, seemed a good idea to the chums of the Remove, and it was an attractive idea to Putnam. He had not yet seen much of the surroundings of Greyfriars—which, naturally, he wanted to do.

But there was, so to speak, a lion in the path—in the shape of the gunman guardian, Poker Pike.

Mr. Pike was, as Bob described it, understudying Mary's little lamb, whose fleece was white as snow; for everywhere that Putnam went, that gunman was sure to go!

True, he had not "horned" into the Form-room again. Mr. Quelch, under the Head's gentle persuasion, had agreed to overlook what had happened there, on the strict condition that it never happened again. And it seemed to dawn on Poker that his charge would be safe in lesson-time under his Form-master's eye, not requiring "tabs" to be kept on him in the Form-room.

But in the quad he kept a wary eye on Van Duck; and if the American junior went out of gates, after him went Poker, treading on his tail, as Putnam put it.

Every now and then he would look into Study No. 1, at tea-time or in prep, or into the Rag, giving Putnam the once-over to make sure that he had not been spirited away somehow.

Certainly, under that watchful care it seemed unlikely that Chick Chew, the kidnapper, would have any chance of getting away with the millionaire's son.

But Putnam could not help feeling that Poker overdid the watchful stunt. His friends felt the same.

It was a standing joke in the school, though fellows soon got used to seeing the serious, hickory face, under the immovable bowler, pop up in all sorts of places, at all sorts of times.

Now that the juniors were planning a run up the Sark on the half-holiday, they all knew that Poker would be on the trail as soon as they started. And they all agreed that Poker was superfluous.

Putnam guessed that he had got to lose him for the afternoon, and his friends agreed that it was so.

"Soon's we beat it, we're going to see that guy Poker treading on our tail," said Putnam. "I'm confiding to you guys that I don't want any more Poker on my plate. I've had enough, and then some!"

Whereupon six heads were put together, and a plot was plotted, amid many chuckles. And when the plot had been duly plotted and cut and dried, the juniors left the Rag, and Bob Cherry went to look for Poker Pike.

He found him walking in the quadrangle, getting a good many glances from Greyfriars fellows, most of them amused, though Coker of the Fifth frowned at him severely

"Hallo, hallo, hallo! Mr. Pike," Bob greeted him cheerily, "got your gun about you?"

"I guess it ain't fur away, bo!" answered Mr. Pike. "I'll say my hardware'd show up, pronto, if a galoot about Chick Chew's size came cavorting around!"

"You haven't seen him about yet?" asked Bob.

"Nope!"

"Shall I tell you where to spot him?" asked Bob.

Mr. Pike became attentive at once. With sudden alertness, he whipped hand to hip to make sure that his six-gun was there and ready.

"You seen him?" he rapped. "I'll say I been surprised that Chick ain't horned in yet. He ain't the guy to let up on a racket once he's got his molars into it! You see that hombre?"

"Well," said Bob, with a grave and serious face, "it's a bit suspicious to spot a man hiding in the woodshed, isn't it?"

"I'll say so!" said Mr. Pike, still more alert.

"I've never seen Chick Chew," went on Bob. "But is he a big, fat man, with a nose like a pimple and a mouth like a coal-mine, and gold-stopped teeth, and plenty of them?"

"You said it!" exclaimed Mr. Pike eagerly. "Where's that guy?"

Mr. Pike was aware that Bob Cherry had never seen Chick Chew. It did not occur to him for the moment that Bob Cherry had received a complete description of him from Harry Wharton, who had. So it naturally appeared to Mr. Pike that Bob had now seen the kidnapper about Greyfriars.

Bob certainly did not say so. He had no intention of saying so. If Mr. Pike drew incorrect conclusions from his remarks, that was Mr. Pike's own affair.

"I'll show you to the woodshed, if you like," said Bob. "But, look here, I shan't go in with you if Chick Chew's there and he's got a gun! Do you think he would have a gun?"

"I should smile!" answered Poker.

"Well, then, I'll take you there, but I shall jolly well stay outside!" said Bob. "That all right?"

"You young bonehead!" said Mr. Pike. "You figure that I'd let a schoolboy horn into a rookus with that hombre? I guess I want you to point out the spot and keep clear! Get to it!"

"This way!" said Bob.

And he led the gunman away to Gosling's woodshed.

The door of that building was closed, and the key was in the outside of the lock. Gosling sometimes kept that shed locked, but as often as not he left the key there. It was there now.

"That's the shed!" said Bob.

"You stick here!" said Mr. Pike briefly.

Bob remained at a distance. He watched the proceedings of Van Duck's gunman guardian with keen interest.

Poker Pike pulled out his six-gun and gave it a glance, and gripped it firmly in his right hand. Then, with cautious tread, he approached the door of the woodshed. His slits of eyes were on the little window of the shed. He was watchful as a cat.

If Chick Chew, carrying on his kidnapping stunt, had insinuated himself within the precincts of the school, and taken cover in the woodshed to wait for an opportunity, Poker was the man to root him out, round him up, and fill him full of lead if he did not put up his hands when ordered to do so.

But knowing the gangster as he did, Poker rather expected him to spot the enemy bearing down, and to open the ball by potting at him from the window. So it was with extreme wariness that Poker Pike approached the woodshed.

There was no alarm, however, and he reached the door and threw it open. Then, with uplifted gun, he marched in.

Had a fat man with gold-stopped teeth been in that shed, there was no doubt that Poker would have put paid to him. As it happened, however, nobody was there—and Poker Pike glared round in vain for a kidnapper.

Slam!

Click!

The gunman spun round towards the door.

"Search me!" he ejaculated.

The door had slammed and the key had turned!

Poker Pike was not only alone in the shed, but he was a prisoner there! As that fact dawned on him, Poker replaced the gun in his hip-pocket. He realised that he had not to deal with a kidnapping gangster, but with playful schoolboys who were pulling his leg!

"Carry me home to die!" murmured Poker.

He banged fiercely at the door. There was a chuckle audible outside.

"Snaffled!"

It was Bob Cherry's voice.

"Ha, ha ha, !"

"Say, you young ginks," roared Poker Pike, "you let me out of this here shebang! How you figure I'm going to keep tabs on that Putnam van Duck?"

Nobody answered that question. There was another chuckle, and a sound of retreating footsteps.

Leaving the watchful gunman locked in the woodshed, Harry Wharton & Co. walked cheerfully down to the school raft, to get their boat out into the river.

"Search me!" gasped Mr. Pike. "I'll tell a man, this is the bee's knee! Say, you pesky young gecks, you want to let a guy out of this here shebang! You hear me whisper?"

But answer there came none.

Mr. Pike, breathing hard, examined the window. There was no escape that way for a guy of Mr. Pike's dimensions. He wrenched at the door. It was immovable—as immovable as Mr. Pike's own bowler hat!

He breathed wrath. Mr. Pike was a little slow on the uptake; but he had a pretty clear idea that this was a trick to keep him busy, while Putnam, for once, took a trip out of gates without his gunman guardian treading on his tail!

Mr. Pike thought it out. Then he pulled the six-gun from his pocket again. Taking aim at the lock of the door, he loosed off lead.

Bang, bang, bang!

The unusual sound roared all over Greyfriars. The Head, in his study, started. Fellows in the quad—fellows at cricket practice—fellows up and down and round about—stared round them. Some thought it was a car backfiring somewhere.

Bang, bang, bang!

It was not a backfire! It was Mr. Pike shooting the lock of the woodshed to pieces. Having done this, he hurled the door open, and rushed forth in search of Putnam van Duck!

THE ELEVENTH CHAPTER.

On the River!

"HERE, clear out!" snapped Coker of the Fifth.

A good many fellows were going on the river that bright spring afternoon. Among them was Horace Coker, of the Fifth Form. Coker was taking out his handsome, expensive boat, with the help of Potter and Greene—what time the Famous Five were getting their roomy old tub down to the water. And Coker, of course, was annoyed by such microbes as Remove juniors getting between the wind and his nobility!

"Gerrout of the way!" snapped Coker.

"Fathead!" answered Bob Cherry politely.

"Barge 'em over!" growled Coker.

"Oh, don't row!" urged Potter.

"Shut up, Potter!"

"Look here——" began Greene.

"Shut up, Greene!"

Coker had a short way with fags. Now his friends in the Fifth were getting the benefit of it.

"I said 'Barge 'em over!'" continued Coker. "Come on!"

Potter and Greene did not come on. They had set out for a pull on the river, not for a shindy with the Remove. They left the barging to Coker.

He barged! But, as it turned out, Coker of the Fifth proved to be, not the barger, but the bargee, so to speak! For six juniors barged all at once, and Coker of the Fifth was strewn end-wise along the school raft—roaring.

The chums of the Remove slid their boat into the water, and crowded in.

A fat figure came rolling in pursuit.

"I say, you fellows!" yelled Billy Bunter.

Bob took an oar to push off. Coker, sitting up, was gasping for breath. Billy Bunter came to the edge of the raft.

"I say, wait for me!" he gasped. "I'm coming! I—I want to help you look after Van Duck, you know, in case those kidnappers get after him."

"I'll say you'd be a lot of use!" chuckled Putnam.

"Oh, really, Van Duck! I say, keep that boat in, Cherry, you beast—I mean, wait for me, old chap——"

"Ha, ha, ha!"

"Blessed if I see anything to cackle at!" howled Bunter. "Look here, I'm coming! I—I'm really anxious about Van Duck——"

"Oh, hop in, fathead!" said Harry. "Buck up! We want to get off without having to stop and slaughter Coker."

"I say, got the grub on?" asked Bunter.

"What grub?"

"Isn't it a picnic?"

"A picnic! No!"

"Mean to say you haven't got any tuck?" hooted Bunter.

"Ha, ha! Not a ghost of a doughnut!" chuckled Bob. "Jump in, if you're coming, old fat man!"

Billy Bunter did not jump in. He gave the grinning juniors a devastating glare through his big spectacles.

"You silly asses! I thought it was a picnic! I'm not coming! If you think I'm going to slog about, rowing that rotten old tub up the river, you're jolly well mistaken, I can jolly well tell you!"

"What about looking after Van Duck?" grinned Johnny Bull. "Ain't you anxious about Van Duck?"

"Ha, ha, ha!"

"Blow Van Duck!" snorted Bunter. "Van Duck can go and eat coke!"

The fat Owl's concern for Van Duck seemed to have evaporated suddenly at the discovery that it was not a picnic.

"Here, gerrout of the way!" Coker had arrived. He slung Billy Bunter aside, and the fat junior, with a yell, sat down on the planks. "Now, you cheeky young sweeps——"

Coker would have boarded the Remove boat the next moment. But at that moment Bob shoved off with his oar.

Instead of shoving off from the raft, however, he planted the end of the oar on Coker's broad chest, and shoved off from that.

Under the force of that hefty shove, the boat shot out into the Sark, and Horace Coker shot over backwards and distributed himself along the raft.

(Continued on next page.)

GREYFRIARS INTERVIEWS

A life on the ocean wave may suit some people—but it doesn't appeal to our long-haired poet who, in the following brilliant verses, introduces

TOM REDWING,

the sailorman's son, of the Remove.

(1)

A life on the ocean wave, my lads,
Is Redwing's constant plan,
He loves the sea, although his dad's
A fine old sailorman.
It's odd that he should love the sea,
It proves he does not shirk,
If Tom was anything like me
He wouldn't love his work.

(2)

John Redwing owns his gallant craft,
And Tom will own one, too.
A boat of deep or shallow draught,
A cruiser or canoe!
Don't talk of steam when Tom's about,
Such things he does not heed.
"Just let me shake my canvas out,"
Says he. "I'll show you speed!"

(3)

And whether through the tempest dark,
Or sunlit summer seas,
Be sure that Tom will steer his barque
With certainty and ease.
He'll know his vessel through and through
And love her stem and stern,
And then whate'er the wind may do
He'll know which way to turn.

(4)

He took me for a sail to-day,
A dinghy was our boat,
And as we gaily sailed away
He told me, while I wrote,
Exactly how to sail a ship
And manage her white wings,
And showed me, too, throughout the trip,
With ropes and spars and things.

(5)

Of course, I didn't understand
A single thing he said.
I wrote them down with shaking hand,
But now they can't be read.
"You hoist the foc's'le!" he cried,
"And weave the mizzen mast,
Then batten down the poop inside
And make the bo'sun fast!

(6)

"You then wind up the starboard watch,
Belay it, if you like,
And splice and reef the after-hatch,
And furl the marlinspike!
The stuns'ls and the tons'ls spread
Abaft the lazarette,
Then drop two points the for'ard lead,
And there you are—all set!"

(7)

I promised I'd remember this
When next I went to sea.
"We need six knots or we shall miss
The blessed tide," said he.
"And when we've tied the knots!" I cried,
"They'll have to be undone!
With six big knots to be untied,
What chance have we of fun?"

(8)

He let me steer the little craft
When it was getting late.
Said he: "The sail is fore-and-aft,
So mind you keep her straight!"
What happened after that, I've found,
Can hardly be described,
But Redwing says I "brought her round
Until the darn thing gybed!"

(9)

The boom caught Redwing on the ear,
I'm sorry to record,
And poor old Redwing—well, I fear
He went clean overboard!
I think my steering might be blamed,
Tom Redwing thinks so, too.
"And that's the last time!" he exclaimed,
"I'll sail a boat with you!"

"Ha, ha, ha!" yelled the juniors, as Coker was distributed.

"Ooooough!" gasped Coker. "I—I—I'll—— Yooough!"

"When you've finished, Coker," said Potter, with deep sarcasm, "we might get this boat out! I thought we were going for a row!"

"Ooogh!" spluttered Coker, as he staggered up. "Don't jaw! Ooogh! I'll smash 'em! Ooogh! I'll—— Ooooogh!"

"Hallo, hallo, hallo!" yelled Bob Cherry suddenly. "Look!"

A running figure came in sight. In great surprise, the juniors in the Remove boat stared at Poker Pike.

As they had left him locked in the woodshed, and had taken away the key, they had not expected to see Mr. Pike again so soon! But there he was! Evidently it was not easy to lose him!

"Row, brothers, row!" chuckled Frank Nugent.

"Ha, ha, ha!"

The juniors pulled, increasing the distance between the boat and the raft, as Poker Pike came panting up. The gunman waved excited hands at them.

"Say, you guys, you pull in!" shouted Poker. "You hear me? I guess I want that Putnam van Duck! You hear me toot?"

"Aw, take a rest, Poker!" called back Van Duck.

"Pull!" said Harry W h a r t o n, laughing.

Poker Pike stood staring after them. With a dozen yards of water between, they were safely out of the reach of the gunman, and it looked as if Mr. Pike was beaten to it. Grinning back at him, the juniors pulled up the river.

But Mr. Pike was not beaten yet.

Coker & Co. got their boat into the water. They were pushing off, when Mr. Pike, with a sudden leap, landed in among them, making the boat rock as he landed. His weight sent it spinning out into the river.

"What the thump!" ejaculated Potter.

"What the dickens!" gasped Greene.

Coker fairly roared with wrath.

"Here, you! Get out of this boat! You hear me? You cheeky ruffian, gerrout of this boat! What the thump do you mean? Pitch him out, you men!"

"I guess," said Poker Pike, with his usual serious calmness, "that I got to get after that Putnam van Duck! You guys foller that boat."

"We're going down the river!" gasped Potter.

Mr. Pike shook his head.

"You a i n ' t!" he contradicted. "You're going arter that Putnam van Duck, and I'm mentioning it!"

"Look here!" bellowed Coker.

"Pack it up!" said Mr. Pike tersely. "You get after them guys! Get me? I ain't honing to damage you any, but if you don't get after them guys pronto, I'm going to beat you up a few! Get to it!"

Coker, almost foaming, hurled himself at Mr. Pike. The next moment he was in the bottom of the boat, hardly knowing how he got there. Mr. Pike gave the startled Potter and Greene a grim look, brandishing a fist that looked like a lump of wrought iron.

"You getting after them guys?" he inquired.

Potter and Greene decided on the spot that they were!

They did not want what had happened to Coker to happen to them! They exchanged a furious look, and settled down to the oars.

Coker lay gasping. Mr. Pike sat in the stern, and Potter and Greene pulled as if they were rowing in a boat race, in pursuit of the Remove boat. And a crowd of fellows on the raft and the towpath stared, as the chase swept out of sight up the Sark.

THE TWELFTH CHAPTER.

Chick's Chance!

"THE jig's up, Chick!"

"Not by long chalks, Bud Parker!"

"I'm telling you——"

"Park it!" snapped the fat gangster.

Chick Chew was leaning on a tree on the towpath by the Sark, a mile or more from Greyfriars School.

Smoking a long cigar, Chick was gazing meditatively at the sunny river, rippling between green banks, clothed in woods.

Bud Parker sat in the grass, his horn-rimmed spectacles gleaming in the sunshine. His look was pessimistic.

Ever since the gangsters had crossed the "pond," on the track of the millionaire's son, Bud had been pessimistic. He was in a strange land, where guns were at a discount. Even the police did not pack guns, and yet somehow managed to keep law and order in a way never dreamed of in Chicago.

Mr. Parker had the deepest contempt for a country where a "cop" was armed only with a truncheon, which he hardly ever had to handle. Yet he realised that these unarmed "cops" somehow did their job in a way that made the gangster game much more difficult than it was on the other side of the pond.

Bud would have been glad to throw down the whole thing and get back to Chicago, where a gangster had a chance. But Mr. Chew was as determined as ever. He was not going to be beaten. His professional pride, as America's greatest kidnapper, was at stake!

"We ain't bitten it off yet," said Mr. Chew. "But we're going to bite it off, you Bud! We nearly had that gilt-edged gink at that place in Surrey. Now they've parked him in a school——"

"And Pike watching him!" said Bud.

"I guess," said Mr. Chew, "that Poker Pike can't be keeping tabs on him all the time. I guess that young guy will be wandering around a few. And when he goes wandering around, I'll mention that he is going to meet up with this bunch."

"Says you!" grunted the horn-rimmed man.

"Yeah!" said Mr. Chew.

He glanced along the towpath.

"We was piping him the day he left that shebang with the other young ginks," he went on. "I got it firm that he was at Greyfriars—ringing up a schoolmaster guy there, the first day, and getting it straight. We know where he is. All we got to do is to rope him in."

"And that's a heap!" said Bud.

"Any fine day," said Mr. Chew, "he may be wandering around. This very afternoon, as like as not, he'll be giving this here river the once-over."

"Says you!" repeated Mr. Parker pessimistically.

"This very minute," went on Mr. Chew, "there's a boat coming up, and I wouldn't be a heap surprised to see young Putnam in it."

"You got another guess coming, Chick!"

"Aw, can it, you Bud!"

Bud grunted, and Chick Chew watched the river. His look grew more and more intent as he watched the boat pulling up the Sark.

"Jumping toads!" ejaculated Mr. Chew, at length.

"Pipe him?" asked Bud sarcastically.

"You said it!" breathed Mr. Chew.

"Wha-a-t!"

Bud bounded to his feet. He stared at the boat on the sunny Sark, still at a distance.

Six schoolboys were in it. The gangsters had seen them all before. They knew the Famous Five by sight. Better still, they knew Putnam van Duck.

"Search me!" gasped Bud.

His eyes nearly popped through the horn rims of his spectacles, in his surprise.

Mr. Chew grinned, with a gleam of American dentistry.

"Did I mention we might pipe him wandering around, or did I not?" he inquired.

Bud gave his great chief a look almost of veneration.

"Chick," he said, "I pass it up to you!"

"I'll buy it!" said Mr. Chew.

He backed round the tree on which he had been leaning. Bud Parker followed him quickly.

The boat was still at a distance. The schoolboys had seen nothing of the gangsters on the bank; but wariness was second nature to the kidnappers. Very quickly they were in cover, cautiously watching the boat.

Four of the juniors were pulling. Frank Nugent and Putnam van Duck sat in the stern, the former steering. The gilt-edged schoolboy's face showed up clearly in the bright spring sunshine. Chick and Bud watched that face as the boat drew nearer.

The oarsmen were pulling hard. It was a rather big and roomy old boat, but it moved swiftly under the pull of four oars.

Coker's craft had been dropped behind and was out of sight beyond the winding banks of the Sark. But Harry Wharton & Co. had no doubt that the persistent Poker was still in chase, and they were losing no time.

Putnam was very keen to get away from the ubiquitous Poker on that half-holiday, and lose him for a time. His friends cheerfully backed him up. Certainly none of them had the remotest suspicion that the gangsters were anywhere in the neighbourhood of Greyfriars School.

It was difficult to imagine danger lurking in that quiet, sunny English countryside. The whole thing seemed rather a "lark" to the juniors, and they were getting away with the lark. Coker's boat had been pressed into service for pursuit, but they were dropping the pursuit.

Voices floated to the hidden gangsters as the boat pulled nearer, drawing in a little towards the bank.

Mr. Chew had spotted Van Duck's intended game. But his game was afloat, and Chick was ashore, and he had yet to solve the problem of getting hold of Putnam van Duck. He was debating in his mind whether to "hold up" the boat's crew at the muzzle of an automatic, and order them to pull in to the bank. But he was not quite sure that it would work. He was not pessimistic, like Mr. Parker; but his faith in gun-play as a method had been a little shaken.

Holding up a guy at the end of a gun worked all right in Chicago. Such a guy would put up his hands automatically, as it were, playing the peculiar game according to the rules.

In this strange land it was different. And if these schoolboys disregarded the

"Oh, my eye!" ejaculated Trotter, as he reached the school porter's lodge with a message for Poker Pike. "What's biting you, bo?" asked Poker. The look on his streaky face made the school page jump back with a grin. "Oh, nothing!" he gasped. "The 'Ead wants to see you in his study!"

levelled gun, what was Chick going to do?

Really, he was not prepared to sweep the boat fore and aft with death-dealing lead! Such a proceeding would have made altogether too tremendous a sensation in the sleepy little island which was so unlike Chicago.

The gangster's gun was, in point of fact, chiefly bluff; and if a guy "called" the bluff, the gangster was rather at a loss.

Debating this difficult matter in his mind, Mr. Chew watched the approaching boat, and listened to the cheery, boyish voices that floated to his ears on the breeze.

"We've beaten them, you men!" came Bob Cherry's voice.

"Yes, rather!"

"Beaten them to a frazzle, I guess."

"They been racing with some other school kids, I reckon!" murmured Bud Parker; and Mr. Chew nodded.

"I fancy they're still after us!" came Harry Wharton's voice. "Look here! We don't want Coker's boat barging after us all the afternoon. Pull in, and let them pass."

"They'll spot us!"

"Not if we shove the boat under these willows and keep doggo till they've gone on!" said the captain of the Remove.

"Ha, ha, ha!"

There was a yell of laughter, and the boat pulled into the bank—at a spot where thick bunches of willows drooped, within a stone's throw of the spot where Chick and Bud stood behind the tree.

The idea of keeping "doggo," and letting the persistent Poker pass on up the river, hunting for a boat that was not there, appealed to the juniors' sense of humour.

Mr. Chew, watching, could scarcely believe in his good luck. His problem was solved for him.

The Remove boat slid into the bank, and the six schoolboys scrambled ashore. The boat was pushed under the willows, where the drooping branches quite hid it from sight from the river. Coker's boat was not yet round the lower bend. There was plenty of time.

"Give them ten minutes," said Harry Wharton. "We'll watch them pass from the trees—keep in cover!"

"What-ho!"

Chuckling, the chums of the Remove backed into the trees along the towpath. From that cover they were going to watch the river, and watch Coker's boat pass, with the watchful Mr. Pike in it. After it was out of sight, they could resume their own trip, untroubled further by Mr. Pike.

They grinned as they watched.

So did Chick Chew.

"I guess," he whispered to Mr. Parker, "that we got these here babes in the wood jest where we want them."

"I should smile!" murmured Bud.

"Pull your gun, old-timer—but don't you be too sudden with it—we ain't in Chicago now!"

"Don't I know it?" grunted Bud.

"I guess a few sockdolagers from the butt will keep them young rubes quiet, if they horn in," whispered Chick. "We got to get a cinch on young Putnam, and walk him through this here timber to the car. Easy as pie, and as good as clam pie! Did I mention we was going to cinch that guy, you Bud, or did I not?"

"You surely did!" assented Mr. Parker.

Harry Wharton & Co., as they watched the river from the edge of the wood, heard a sudden rustle behind them. They glanced round.

"Hallo, hallo, hallo!" yelled Bob Cherry. "Look out!"

"Great pip!"

There was a rush.

Chick Chew's grasp was on Putnam van Duck, when the American junior, with a swift spring, eluded it, and bounded out into the towpath.

In an instant he was running down the towpath. After him thundered the fat gangster. After Chick tore Bud Parker.

"T h e—t h e kidnappers!" stuttered Harry Wharton.

"That blighter Chick!" gasped Bob.

"They're after him!"

"Come on!"

The Famous Five rushed down the towpath, after the pursuing gangsters, who were at the heels of the fleeing millionaire's son.

Big and fat as he was, Chick ran fast and hard, and it was clear that Putnam van Duck had little chance of escape. The Famous Five tore in pursuit. How this was going to end they did not know; but they knew that they were going to stand by Putnam van Duck to the finish.

THE THIRTEENTH CHAPTER.

Gun Play!

"YOU cheeky rotter!" gasped Coker.

Poker Pike did not answer. He was a man of few words, and he saw no occasion for chewing the rag. If Coker of the Fifth started trouble, Poker was prepared to stretch him in the bottom of the boat again. So long as he merely blew off steam, Poker did not mind. He was a considerate gunman.

"You dashed ruffian!" hissed Coker.

Potter and Greene did not speak. Their feelings, indeed, were too deep for words.

Besides, they needed their breath to pull. Mr. Pike was keeping them at it, hard!

If they slacked down, the gunman's icy eyes were turned on them, with such a significant look, that Potter and Greene pulled again, with all their beef.

"You rotten rascal!" hooted Coker.

Mr. Pike, watching the river for the

boat ahead, allowed Coker's remarks to pass him by, like the idle wind which he regarded not.

He was deeply anxious to spot the Remove boat, hidden from his sight by the windings of the river. Potter and Greene were doing their best; but four oars beat two, and the junior boat was far ahead. It was a worry to Mr. Pike, and he had neither time nor inclination to bother about Horace Coker and his indignant wrath.

Coker was the man to proceed from words to deeds—in fact, it was usually his way to act first and think afterwards, if he thought at all. But he did not handle Mr. Pike as he longed to do.

Once was enough, even for Horace Coker! One smite had landed the hefty Horace on his back, and it had been five minutes before he felt able to resume the perpendicular. He did not want another of those mighty smites. Poker Pike was too large a proposition for him, and even Coker understood it.

So—little as it was his custom—Coker contented himself with words. They were bitter words, angry w o r d s, emphatic words; but they had no more effect on Mr. Pike than water on a duck's back.

Potter and Greene pulled, while Coker raged like the heathen of old. Potter and Greene would have preferred to swipe Mr. Pike with the oars. But they were disinclined to have their features pushed through the back of their heads. And Mr. Pike meant business—cold business from the word go, as he would have said.

His press-gang methods infuriated the Fifth Formers. Coker could barely restrain himself from punching. Fortunately he managed to do it. Potter and Greene rowed hard, suppressing their fury. Poker Pike w a t c h e d anxiously for a sight of the Remove boat.

He did not sight that boat. Indeed, but for the interposition of the gangsters, there was no doubt that Coker's boat would have pulled past the spot where the Removites had landed, and that Mr. Pike would have gone onward to explore the upper reaches of the Sark for the fellows who had stayed astern of him.

But suddenly, as he watched the river, a running figure on the towpath dawned on Mr. Pike.

His slits of eyes gleamed with alertness.

It was Putnam van Duck running his hardest! Fast on his track, the next moment, appeared another figure—that of a fat man, running still harder, and gaining on the American junior.

Then, behind Mr. Chew, appeared Bud Parker, going all out—and trailing in the distance, five schoolboys, running breathlessly.

"Search me!" said Mr. Pike.

He rose to his feet, his hand flying to his hip. Coker's tirade was cut short by astonishment. Potter and Greene stared at the gunman, and rested on their oars.

"You guys, you pull in to the bank!" barked Mr. Pike. "Pronto!"

Then the Fifth Formers saw the chase on the towpath.

"Oh crumbs!" said Potter.

"Oh crikey!" said Greene.

"Oh scissors!" ejaculated Coker.

"You hear me toot?" snapped Mr. Pike. "Pull in, you gecks! I got to get that Putnam van Duck!"

Potter and Greene pulled for the bank. Standing up in the boat, Mr. Pike calmly and coolly took aim with his six-gun.

Bang!

The report of the revolver rang across the river, and echoed through the woods. Chick Chew gave a sudden bound.

His eyes, as he chased, were on Putnam van Duck. He had not wasted a glance on the river. He did not even know there was a boat there till Poker Pike's gun roared.

He gave an astonished yelp, and a wild jump, as a bullet kicked up earth at his feet. Losing his footing, he stumbled, and rolled in the grass of the towpath.

Bang!

Bud Parker let out a yell that would have done credit to a Red Indian. The bullet that cut through the crown of his hat, grazed the top of his head. It was enough—and more than enough—for Mr. Parker.

Without stopping a second, Bud Parker swerved, and shot off the towpath into the wood, and vanished.

Bang, bang!

"Search me!" spluttered Chick Chew.

He scrambled wildly up, with hot lead from Poker Pike's six-gun spattering earth round him.

Putnam van Duck, running like a deer, got ahead. Chick glared after him as he ran, and glared at the gunman standing in the boat. As he glared, another shot whizzed by an inch from his ear.

He spluttered with breathless rage. He had caught Putnam without his gunman guard; but that faithful guard, it was clear, had not been far away. Here he was, taking pot-shots at Mr. Chew from Coker's boat!

Resuming the chase of the fleeing millionaire's son, with Poker raining bullets at him from the river, did not seem a practical proposition to Mr. Chew.

He gave Poker Pike an astonished and infuriated glare, and for a second groped for his automatic. But he remembered in time that he was no longer in Chicago, and left the automatic where it was! He swerved off the towpath and darted into the wood.

Bang!

Poker's gun roared after him as he went. The bullet clipped the rim of the disappearing slouched hat.

Coker's boat bumped into the rushes under the bank. Mr. Pike leaped ashore, the smoking six-gun in his hand. But the gangsters were gone—running, and not likely to stop running till they reached their car and started the engine!

THE FOURTEENTH CHAPTER.

Out of Bounds!

"LOOK out!" gasped Bob Cherry.

"Oh crumbs!"

Harry Wharton & Co., racing down the towpath, stopped, panting for breath. They had forgotten Poker Pike; but they were reminded of him as they heard the six-gun roar.

They stopped—as they did not want to stop any of the bullets that were whizzing across the towpath.

But as Mr. Pike stepped on the bank they came on. The gun-play was over, and Mr. Pike, with sedate carefulness, was reloading his six-gun. In the distance Putnam van Duck had stopped, and was looking back. Seeing how matters stood, the American junior walked back to rejoin his friends with a cheery grin on his face.

Coker & Co. pushed off in their boat. They were glad, at least, to have done with Mr. Pike. Whether Mr. Pike wanted that boat any longer they did not know; they pushed off in haste, in case he did!

Mr. Pike had no further use for Coker and his craft. He had found Putnam van Duck—though in a rather unexpected manner. Having found him, he was freezing on to the gilt-edged youth.

"Well," remarked Van Duck, with a chuckle, "I'll say that was some rookus! And then a few!"

"Lucky Mr. Pike turned up!" remarked Harry Wharton.

"The luckfulness was terrific!" grinned Hurree Jamset Ram Singh. "The esteemed and absurd kidnappers were nearer at hand than we supposefully considered!"

"You said it!" agreed Putnam. "I'm telling you, Poker, I'm glad to see your face jest about now, though it ain't a sight for sore eyes, and that's a cinch. You sure got that bunch hopping like they was sent for."

Poker Pike nodded. Having reloaded his gun, he packed it away at his hip. The gangsters were gone, and very unlikely to be seen again. They were looking for a chance to kidnap Van Duck; but not for a pitched battle with his gunman guardian.

"The fact is, we were rather fatheads!" said Bob Cherry. "You oughtn't to have come out without your jolly old shadow, Van Duck, and we oughtn't to have helped you."

"Boneheads!" agreed Putnam. "But I never reckoned that Chick was rubbering around in this vicinity. I guess we're sticking to Poker now."

"Surest thing you know!" said Poker. That detail was already settled in Mr. Pike's mind. "Now I got a cinch on you agin, I'll say I ain't letting up, you Putnam van Duck."

"Like a trip on the river, Mr. Pike?" asked Harry, with a laugh. "Come on, let's get back to the boat."

The Greyfriars fellows walked back to the willows, where the boat had been hidden. Mr. Pike's solemn face expressed nothing as the boat was pulled out of its hiding-place; though no doubt he guessed the trick the playful juniors had intended to play on the pursuer.

But Mr. Pike had nothing more of that kind to expect. The chums of the Remove had succeeded in "losing" him that afternoon; but they had been very glad to find him again, as matters had turned out.

When the Remove boat pushed off, Mr. Pike sat in the stern—an honoured guest. He was not exactly merry or bright company, with his serious hickory face under his immovable bowler hat; but he was indispensable.

Whether the juniors agreed or not, Poker was going to keep "tabs" on the millionaire's son till he was safe within the school gates again. Fortunately, they agreed.

It had been an exciting interlude, but it was over; and the juniors pulled cheerily on their way up the river, what time two disappointed and disgruntled kidnappers were packing into a car on the Courtfield road and hitting the open spaces!

Coker & Co. had gone down the river, and were out of sight. Far from the school, the juniors had the Sark to themselves, so far as Greyfriars fellows were concerned. They pulled on till Popper's Island came in sight.

That island was "out of bounds"—a little circumstance that juniors sometimes forgot on a half-holiday. Putnam van Duck had never seen that little wooded island in the broadest reach of the river, opposite Popper Court woods; and they were going to show him over it.

Bob Cherry scanned the banks as they approached it.

"All serene!" he remarked. "No jolly

old keepers about—and jolly old Popper is away! Safe as houses!"

The boat nosed in under the trees at the landing-place on the island, and was tied up. The juniors scrambled ashore, followed by Poker Pike.

There was a path through the thickets to the glade in the centre of the island, under the branches of a big oak-tree. The Removites followed it, while Poker Pike, watchful as ever, stood scanning the river and the opposite bank, to make sure that there was no sign of the kidnappers.

"Hallo, hallo, hallo!" ejaculated Bob Cherry. "Somebody else knows that old Popper is away from Popper Court."

He glimpsed a straw hat through the thickets. Evidently Popper's Island was already tenanted.

That, however, did not matter to the juniors. Any other Greyfriars fellow there was as much out of bounds as the juniors, while common-or-garden members of the public had no concern with them. They walked on cheerily into the glade.

A startled exclamation greeted them.

Two fellows were seated on a log under the big oak-tree. They were Loder and Walker of the Sixth.

"Oh, my hat!" ejaculated Harry Wharton, in dismay.

It had not occurred to the juniors that prefects might be on the island. Prefects of the Sixth Form were not subject to "bounds" like juniors; though certainly Sir Hilton Popper, had he discovered them on his island, would have made as much fuss about senior trespassers as any other.

What two Sixth Form men were doing on the island was rather a mystery—or would have been but for a lingering scent of cigarette-smoke in the air, and the fact that Gerald Loder hastily shoved something out of sight, into his pockets, as the juniors appeared. But neither cigarettes nor cards were to be seen.

Loder and Walker jumped up from the log, and stared at the newcomers. Walker coloured—and Loder glared.

"Sorry to interrupt, Loder!" said Bob Cherry politely.

And the juniors grinned. All of them knew that the two black sheep of the Sixth had been smoking and playing nap in that secluded spot, far from the eyes of authority. Loder and Walker would not have remained prefects long had their headmaster witnessed their proceedings.

"You young rascals!" exclaimed Loder. "Out of bounds—as usual! Get off this island at once! I shall report this to your Form-master!"

"I guess you'll get reported about the same time!" remarked Putnam van Duck. "You're here, too, ain't you? You kind of look as if you are."

Loder's eyes fixed on the American junior with a deadly glare.

He had not forgotten the episode in Study No. 1 on the first day of term.

As a prefect, invested with "whopping privs," Loder might have completed the interrupted whopping at a later date; but he had never done so, for the simple reason that he did not care to risk being tucked under Mr. Pike's arm again. The Head had solemnly warned Poker Pike not to interfere with the prefects in the execution of their duties; but Loder did not feel at all sure that that would cut much ice with the gunman.

Now, however, Putnam was there without his gunman guard. Mr. Pike, who was standing by the boat watching the river, was out of sight, and Loder did not know that he was on the island at all.

"You cheeky little scoundrel!" said Loder, in measured tones. "We came here to look for juniors out of bounds, as we are quite prepared to explain to the Head. But you are breaking bounds, and you will be reported; but, first of all, you're going to have a lesson about cheeking a prefect!"

A light walking-cane lay on the log. Loder picked it up and stepped towards the juniors.

"Look here, Loder——" began Harry Wharton.

"Hold your tongue!" snapped Loder. "I'll give you six all round, if I have any lip from you! Van Duck, bend over and touch your toes!"

"Guess again!" said Putnam.

"Are you going to bend over?" roared Loder.

"Not so's you'd notice it."

Loder made a stride at him: and as Putnam dodged, swiped with the stick. There was a terrific yell from Putnam as he caught the swipe on his shoulders. It rang over the island, and both banks of the Sark.

It was followed by a rapid footstep in the thickets. The next moment a hickory face and a bowler hat dawned on Loder, and he was grasped, and swept off his feet, in the wiry hands of Poker Pike.

THE FIFTEENTH CHAPTER.
Not Reported!

"CAN it, you!" said Mr. Pike.

"Ow! Leggo!" panted Loder. "You ruffian! You—you—— Ooogh!"

"Hold on!" gasped Harry Wharton.

"I guess I'm holding on," remarked Mr. Pike.

He was, and the bully of the Sixth crumpled helplessly in his sinewy hold.

"I mean, let go!" said Harry. "Loder's a prefect——"

"I guess I ain't wise to what that

(Continued on next page.)

The Story You Have Been Waiting For!

It tells of the Early Adventures of Harry Wharton at Greyfriars and starts in This Week's GEM!

"THE MAKING OF HARRY WHARTON!"

You'll Revel in Reading About Harry Wharton, the Obstinate, Hot-headed New Boy of Greyfriars!

Spread the Good News Around Among Your Friends. This Grand Story appears in the GEM now on sale. Price 2d.

I have pleasure in announcing this new feature which I know will have a very special interest for all "Magnetites"—"THE MAKING OF HARRY WHARTON!" This grand story, written, of course, by the inimitable Frank Richards, will relate the very earliest adventures of Harry Wharton, from the time when he first entered the great Public school, Greyfriars, as a new boy—and what an unusual type of new boy he was!

I felt that I could not give my loyal chums of the MAGNET a greater treat than this magnificent yarn, which will answer the questions which pour in upon me every week from hundreds of companion-paper readers. What were Harry Wharton, Billy Bunter, Frank Nugent, and Bob Cherry like in those early days? How was the famous Co., now known as Harry Wharton & Co., first formed?

These, and many other similar questions, will be answered by Frank Richards himself in "THE MAKING OF HARRY WHARTON!"—which begins in this week's GEM. It will, I promise you, be a real treat for all who read it, and will knit closer the ties which unite the readers and the Editor of the famous Companion Papers in a common bond of loyalty and good fellowship. THE EDITOR.

might happen to be," said Poker. "But I'll say he ain't lambasting that Putnam van Duck, s'long as this here baby is looking after him. Nope!"

"Will you leggo?" shrieked Loder.

Had he been aware that Poker Pike was on hand, the bully of the Sixth certainly never would have administered that swipe. Evidently the Head's solemn warning on the subject had "cut no ice" with Mr. Pike.

Walker of the Sixth made a move forward to Loder's aid. But one glint from the gunman's icy eyes made him step back in a hurry.

"Look here——" began Walker.

"Pack it up, you!" snapped Poker.

"Let me go!" yelled Loder, struggling frantically. "You ruffian, I'll have you turned out of the school for this. I'll have you kicked out of Greyfriars. Do you think you can handle Sixth Form men, you hooligan?"

"Surest thing you know," answered Poker.

"Ha, ha, ha!"

The juniors chuckled. But they were feeling rather uneasy. Loder, after all, was a prefect, and he had a good case to put before the Head. He had caught the juniors out of bounds. Putnam had cheeked him, and he was acting within his rights and powers. And Poker, in stopping him, was disregarding the headmaster's solemn warning.

For the moment Loder was helpless; but when they got back to Greyfriars the case was going to be very much altered.

Certainly the juniors knew that Loder and Walker were black sheep, and had no doubt why they were on the island that afternoon. Had the Head known as much as the juniors knew, it would have been the "sack" for both the sportsmen of the Sixth.

But there was no proof of that, and Loder was on safe ground. Whoppings all round, and the "boot" for Mr. Pike, seemed to be the probable result of this unfortunate encounter.

Loder wrenched furiously to free himself from the gunman's grasp. But that grasp was like iron.

"Let me go!" raved Loder. "You ruffian—— Yaroooh!"

Mr. Pike did not seem to like the names Loder was applying to him. Holding Loder with one hand, he smacked his head with the other.

"Oh crikey!" gasped Bob Cherry.

"Yooop!" howled Loder. "Oh, my hat! You—you—you—— I'll have you turned out of the school this very day! Wait till I see the Head! Ow!"

"Forget it!" said Mr. Pike stolidly. "I guess I'm a fixture at that pesky school, so long as that Putnam van Duck hangs up his hat in the shebang. Surest thing you know."

"Oh crumbs!" murmured Harry Wharton.

There could be little doubt that when Loder reported this to the Head, Mr. Pike would be politely but firmly told to quit. How he fancied that he could remain, if the Head ordered him to go, was rather a mystery. But it was quite clear that he did.

"You—you fool!" panted Loder. "I tell you, you fool, that—— Yarooh!"

Smack!

"You don't want to talk to me that-a-way," said Mr. Pike seriously. "I guess I ain't taking all that back-chat, feller. Nunk!"

Loder, foaming with rage, twisted round in Poker Pike's grip, and struck at the hickory face with all his strength.

His fist crashed hard.

Mr. Pike blinked. Even the tough gunman was not impervious to a hefty blow like that at close quarters. He blinked, and blinked again.

"I'll say you're the guy to ask for it, feller," said Mr. Pike. "You surely are one hog, and don't know when you've had enough. Mebbe a dip in the water will cool you down a few."

With a grip on the back of Loder's collar, Poker Pike jerked him along the path through the thickets to the water.

Loder struggled frantically as he went.

He clutched at bushes and trees; he struggled and twisted and kicked, but the grip on his collar was irresistible, and he went along in a scrambling heap.

"Oh, my hat!" yelled Bob Cherry. "Look!"

"Ha, ha, ha!"

From Loder's pockets, as he twisted and scrambled and rolled, all sorts of things were shed. The pack of playing cards which he had thrust hastily out of sight when the juniors arrived, came unexpectedly to light.

Cards were shed in a shower, dropping all along the path as if Loder was leaving a "scent" in a paper-chase.

A cigarette-case opened as it dropped, shedding cigarettes. They scattered among the cards.

"Oh gum!" gasped Walker, staring in horror at that unexpected revelation. He rushed after Loder—not to the rescue, but to gather up those evidences of guilt, and get them out of sight.

Bob Cherry promptly put a foot in his way. Walker tripped over it, and went headlong.

"No, you don't, Walker!" grinned Bob. "We'll take care of Loder's property for him. It will be awfully interesting to the Head when he reports us at Greyfriars."

"Yes, rather!" chuckled Johnny Bull.

"The ratherfulness is terrific!"

With many chuckles, the juniors followed Loder and Mr. Pike, gathering up cards and cigarettes. Walker staggered to his feet

"Look here, you young rascals!" he stammered. "Look here! Hand those things over to me, and—and I'll get Loder to let the matter drop—see?"

"That's all right; we'll take care of them," grinned Bob. "And if you butt in, Walker, we'll send you where Pike's taking Loder. You can't come the jolly old prefect in the giddy circumstances."

James Walker was only too well aware of that.

So far from reporting the juniors to their Form-master, or to the Head, Walker was only anxious that nothing should be heard of the affair at Greyfriars now. Visions of a stern-faced headmaster, pronouncing the dread words: "You are expelled," rose before Walker's mind.

No doubt they would have risen before Loder's, too, but Gerald Loder was too busily occupied to think of anything but what was happening to him at the moment.

Jerked along by the collar, strewing the ground with cards and cigarettes as he went, Loder reached the landing-place. Close in under the trees the water was shallow; but if there was not much water, there was plenty of mud Into the muddy shallows Mr. Pike landed Loder, with a swing of his powerful arm.

Splash.

"Ooooooch!"

Loder sat in water up to the shoulders. His legs disappeared in soft, clinging mud as the Sark rippled round him.

He sat and spluttered wildly.

"I guess," said Mr. Pike solemnly, "that lets you out, you Loder! Yep! You don't want to hand out sockdolagers to this guy. You get me?"

"Oooooch!" spluttered Loder.

He scrambled wildly to his feet, stirring up a sea of mud. As he would have scrambled back to the island, Mr. Pike raised a warning hand.

"Stick there!" he said. "I guess you got a boat somewhere, and your side-kicker can mosey round with it and pick you up. Don't you come any nearer, feller. You'll get damaged, a few."

Loder stood with water up to his knees, drenched and dripping. His straw hat floated away down the Sark.

"You—you—you——" he panted.

"Park it!" said Poker Pike. "I guess you can howl to the other guy, and he can fish you out. You ain't coming back here."

"Walker!" yelled Loder. "Where are you, you fool? Bring the skiff round, you dummy! Do you hear, you idiot?"

The Sixth Form skiff was on the other side of the island. Walker, thus politely adjured, went for it, and sculled round the little island. Loder clambered savagely into it when it arrived.

He sat and streamed water and mud. There was a chuckle from the island, and Loder glared back at a bunch of grinning juniors. He shook a wet and muddy fist.

"Wait till you get back to the school!" he yelled. "Just wait! The minute you get back, you go to the Head!"

"Right-ho!" yelled Bob. "We've got something for him, Loder!"

He held up a handful of playing-cards. The other fellows, grinning, followed suit. Loder's eyes almost popped from his face at the sight of his pack of cards, thus displayed to his startled gaze.

"Oh!" he gasped. "You—you—— Give me those cards! Throw them into the skiff! Do you hear?"

"That's all right, Loder!" said Harry Wharton reassuringly. "We're going to hand them to you when we see the Head——"

"In the Head's study!" grinned Bob.

"And the cigarettes along with them!" said Nugent.

"Ha, ha, ha!"

"For goodness' sake, shut up, Loder!" hissed Walker. "Those young scoundrels have got us in a cleft stick. If you want the sack, I don't! Shut up!"

Walked rowed away. Loder sat staring back, with a furious muddy face. Bob Cherry hurled his handful of cards after the skiff, and they scattered over Loder as he went, and fluttered round on the water. There were plenty more left for evidence—if required!

But it was pretty certain that they would not be required! Loder was not likely to make a report to any master at Greyfriars—in the circumstances. He was likely to be only too eager to keep the whole matter dark.

"Good-bye, Loder!" yelled the Removites.

"Ha, ha, ha!"

Harry Wharton & Co. were left in possession of Popper's Island.

And when, later, they returned to Greyfriars in time for calling-over, they did not expect to be called before either

Coker was about to board the Remove boat, when Bob Cherry planted the end of an oar on the Fifth Former's broad chest, and shoved off from that. Under the force of that hefty shove, the boat shot out into the Sark—and Horace Coker shot over backwards. "Ha, ha, ha!" yelled the juniors.

Form-master or headmaster for having been out of bounds! And they were right! In Hall, Loder of the Sixth gave them a black look—and that was all! Loder had said nothing—and, in fact, his chief anxiety was that the juniors should not say anything, either! Which was quite satisfactory to the cheery chums of the Remove.

THE SIXTEENTH CHAPTER.

Poker Pike Plays Cricket!

"STICK him in the field!" suggested Bob Cherry.

Harry Wharton laughed.

"Know anything about cricket, Mr. Pike?" he asked.

Poker looked thoughtful.

Putnam van Duck did not know much about the great game, and his friends in the Remove were only too glad to instruct him. But Putnam, of course, could not walk down to Little Side after class in flannels without Poker Pike walking after him. Fellows on the cricket ground stared at the gunman in his black bowler—rather conspicuous among the junior cricketers.

Many of them grinned. But Mr. Pike's face was quite serious and solemn. If he looked incongruous there, he did not feel incongruous. Nothing mattered to Poker except keeping tabs on the son and heir of the Chicago multi-millionaire.

"Keep off the grass, you!" Van Duck hooted at him; to which Poker turned a deaf ear. Then Bob suggested sticking him in the field. Which, as Mr. Pike was determined to stick there, was really not a bad idea.

"Cricket!" repeated Mr. Pike. He nodded slowly. "Yep! I guess I read a book about it once."

"Great pip! That's good!" exclaimed the captain of the Remove, in surprise. He had not supposed that a gunman from Chicago would know anything about cricket, if he had ever heard of the game at all! It was quite surprising to hear that Poker Pike had read up the subject.

"Yep!" said Poker, with another nod. "I ain't no big reader, but I guess I read that book when I was a small nipper. Surest thing you know! Wrote by a guy named Dickens, and I'll mention that he was no slouch of a writer guy."

"Dickens!" repeated Harry. "I never heard that Dickens wrote anything about games——"

"Ha, ha, ha!" shrieked Bob Cherry. "I don't think Dickens wrote about this sort of cricket!"

"Sure!" said Poker. "I'll tell you, it was some book—I guess it was called 'Cricket on the Hearth,' if I don't disremember."

"Ha, ha, ha!" yelled the juniors.

Evidently Poker was, after all, unacquainted with the game. The cricket he was thinking of was the cricket that chirped on the hearth—quite a different kind of cricket!

"Oh dear!" gasped Wharton. "Cricket on the hearth is a bit different from cricket on Little Side, Mr. Pike. This is a game. Played with a bat and a ball——"

"On a pitch!" said Bob Cherry.

Mr. Pike glanced round him, puzzled.

"I guess I don't see no pitch!" he remarked.

"You don't see it?" exclaimed Bob. As Mr. Pike was standing on it, and was blessed with good eyesight, that was a surprising statement.

"Nope! There ain't no pitch hereabout that I can see! Where'd that pitch be?" asked Poker.

"Under your feet!" gasped Bob.

Mr. Pike jumped a little as he glanced down. He was quite unaware that he was treading on pitch. The suggestion startled him.

"Aw, pack it up!" he grunted. "I ain't walking in no pitch, I ain't! I guess I'd feel it sticking to my boots if I was. You young guys may be powerful smart, but I'll tell a man you can't string me along."

"Oh, scissors!" gasped Bob, realising that there was another misunderstanding. "Not pitch—pitch! A cricket pitch——"

"If there was any pitch here, I guess I'd pipe it as soon's the next guy!" grunted Poker. "Pitch is black, I reckon, and I can't see nothing but green."

"Ha, ha, ha!"

"You ornery bonehead!" snapped Van Duck. "They call the location where they play cricket a pitch."

"You're telling me!" said Poker.

"Stick him in the field!" said Bob, grinning. "Make him useful as well as ornamental."

"Will you go into the field, Mr. Pike?" asked Harry, smiling.

"I'll call that a fool question," answered Mr. Pike. "Ain't I in this here field already, along of you guys?"

"Ha, ha, ha!"

Evidently Mr. Pike had much to learn on this abstruse subject.

"If you mean the next field, you can forget it!" said Poker. "I'm sticking in this hyer field, to keep tabs on that Putnam van Duck."

"I don't mean the next field!" chuckled the captain of the Remove.

"Fielding's a part of the game. You see, one fellow slings down the ball, and another fellow whops it with the bat, and a fellow keeps wicket, and other fellows stand round to stop the ball going into the next county. That's called fielding."

"Sho!" said Mr. Pike.

"Put him in the deep field," said Bob. "The dear man will be out of the way there, anyhow."

"Where's that deep field?" asked Mr. Pike suspiciously. "Looks to me all on a level."

"Ha, ha, ha!"

Apparently Mr. Pike guessed that the "deep" field was on a lower level than the rest! Really, it was a natural mistake for a guy who knew as much about cricket, and the language thereof, as he knew about the language spoken in the planet of Mars.

"This way!" said Harry, laughing, and he guided the gunman to the spot selected for him. Poker went slowly, glancing back every now and then. He did not mean to be led out of sight of Putnam van Duck.

Really, it was improbable that Chick Chew would make any attempt on the millionaire's son, in bright daylight, in the midst of a crowd of schoolboy cricketers. But the cautious Poker was taking no chances.

However, he found that he was not led out of sight of the junior. He was satisfied to stand where Harry Wharton placed him.

It was not, of course, a match, or certainly the Remove fellows would have shifted Mr. Pike right off the ground, gun and all. Six fellows a side were putting up some practice, for the benefit of Van Duck—who, though he knew little of the game, was quick on the uptake and keen to learn. It did not matter which side Mr. Pike supported, as he was not likely to be of much use to anybody; the chief consideration was to keep him out of the way.

"Now," said Harry, "if the ball comes this way, you stop it. Catch it if you can—but stop it, anyhow."

"I get you!" agreed Mr. Pike. He seemed willing to learn, and willing to oblige. Perhaps he was rather keen to learn some of the strange manners and customs of this strange country, to relate to his gun-slinging friends when he got back to Chicago. "What'll I do with it when I stop it? Do I keep it?"

"Keep it?" gasped Wharton. "Nunno—not exactly! You send it back to the bowler."

"Who's that?"

"The chap who bowls—Inky, at the present moment."

"I get you!" assented Mr. Pike. "I seen some bowling—I've played ten-pins back in Chicago."

"Oh! This is a bit different from ten-pins! But you'll soon catch on. Anyhow, don't let the ball pass you if you can help it. You see, the batsmen will be running all the time the ball's away."

"They run after the ball?" asked Poker.

"Oh! No! They run between the wickets. Those stumps sticking in the ground are called wickets. Now, you stick here, and—and keep tabs on the ball, see?"

"Surest thing, you know."

Mr. Pike stood—alert and watchful. Hurree Jamset Ram Singh took the ball, to bowl to Bob Cherry. All the cricketers were grinning. And though cricket practice among the juniors seldom drew attention, on this occasion quite a number of fellows strolled over to Little Side to look on. Mr. Pike, in his bowler hat, was a conspicuous and remarkable object on a cricket field. Grinning fellows looked on, to watch his performance.

But Poker Pike did not grin. He saw nothing to grin at. He took cricket as seriously as he took everything else. He gave his bowler hat a shove to jam it a little more tightly on his bullet head, though it already seemed to be screwed there. Then he stood alert. He was not going to let the ball pass him if it came his way—if he could help it.

It did not come his way at first. But when Hurree Jamset Ram Singh sent down the last ball of the over Bob Cherry delivered a terrific swipe at it, and sent it right down to Poker Pike like a bullet from his own six-gun.

Mr. Pike stopped it!

He did not even see it coming, alert as he was! But he stopped it, because he was directly in the line of its flight! He stopped it with his waistcoat.

Bang!

"Yurrrroooooooh!" roared Poker Pike.

He leaped clear of the ground and sat down with a heavy bump. He pressed both hands to his waistcoat as he sat.

"Urrrrggh!" he gurgled.

"Ha, ha, ha!"

"Some fielding!" yelled the Bounder.

"Ha, ha, ha!"

"Urrrggh!" gasped Poker Pike, staggering up. "Carry me home to die! I guess I'll hand that guy a sockdolager or two! Urrgh!"

"Send that ball in!" shouted Harry Wharton.

Mr. Pike blinked at him. His first impression seemed to be that it was a case of assault and battery, and that it was up to him to hand the batsman a few "sockdolagers." His second impression was that this was the way cricket was played.

"Aw!" he gasped. "Is that how you play this here game? I'll say I don't like it a whole heap—it sure does shake up my eats!"

"Ha, ha, ha!"

"Send that ball in!"

"I get you!" said Mr. Pike, and he picked up the ball. He had been told to send it back to the bowler—and he did so, delivering it with a quick throw straight at Hurree Jamset Ram Singh's dusky head.

The Nabob of Bhanipur had barely time to dodge it. It whizzed past his head and caught Herbert Vernon-Smith on the ear.

The Bounder's yell could have been heard all over Greyfriars.

"That O.K.?" called out Mr. Pike. He only wanted to know.

"Oh crikey!"

"Ha, ha, ha!"

"You mad idiot!" yelled the Bounder. "Do you want to brain a chap? Ow!"

"Ha, ha, ha!"

"Ain't that right?" hooted Mr. Pike. "I got one of 'em!"

"Ha, ha, ha!" shrieked the cricketers.

Poker Pike apparently had the idea that cricket was run on gun-play lines, and that the ball was a weapon of offence, with which fellows were to be knocked over, if possible. His own brief experience seemed to bear out that theory.

Smithy rubbed a damaged ear and glared. The other fellows doubled up with merriment.

Harry Wharton wiped away his tears, and explained matters a little further to Mr. Pike. He was willing to learn; but Rome was not built in a day. However, he got it into his solid brain that fellows were not to be knocked over with the cricket ball. That was so much to the good.

"I get you!" he said. "I get you O.K. I got to stop that ball! I ain't got to do nothing but stop that ball! I guess I'll put it through."

After which Mr. Pike was more alert and watchful than ever. He watched for the ball like a cat watching for mice. He did not want another bang on his waistcoat, shaking up his eats, as he described it.

His watchfulness was rewarded. The next time the ball came Mr. Pike's way it would have missed him by yards and travelled onwards fast and far—but Poker Pike had his eye on it!

He did not jump at the ball! He did not stir from where he stood! His hand flew to his hip.

Poker Pike was no cricketer, but he was a handy man with a gun! In his own haunts in Chicago he was well known to be sudden on the draw!

Bang!

It was not an easy shot! But Mr. Pike could handle a gun!

There was a shattering crack as the cricket ball got the bullet and flew to fragments!

The cricketers stood petrified.

Poker Pike, with the smoking six-gun in his hand. stood grinning with satisfaction.

"I guess I stopped it!" he remarked. "That O.K.?"

"Oh crumbs!"

"Oh crikey!"

"Oh scissors!"

"Ha, ha, ha!"

"You dangerous maniac——"

"Put that gun away!"

"Aw, pack it up!" exclaimed Poker indignantly. "Ain't I stopped that ball, like I was told?"

"Ha, ha, ha!"

"I think," gasped Bob Cherry, "that we shall want a new ball if we're going on with this! And I think we'd better persuade Mr. Pike to sit it out."

There was a howl of laughter round the field. The Greyfriars fellows had rather expected entertainment, when they saw Poker Pike at cricket. But they had not expected fireworks. Mr. Pike's new method of fielding quite took them by storm, and they howled and yelled.

"Ha, ha, ha!"

Gently but firmly Mr. Pike was led off the field. He declined to go far—he had to keep tabs on Putnam. But he was shifted off the ground, and, giving up the idea of mastering the mysteries of the game of cricket, he sat it out.

THE SEVENTEENTH CHAPTER.

Alarming!

"I SAY, you fellows!"

"Buzz off, Bunter!"

"But I say——"

"Hook it!"

On the table in Study No. 1 lay a cake—a large cake—a huge and luscious cake! Five juniors were regarding it with admiration and appreciation. It had arrived for Putnam van Duck, and Putnam was going to whack it out with his friends.

But Putnam van Duck, having been called into Mr. Quelch's study, was not there, and until he arrived his friends could not very well start on the cake.

So they waited for him.

Several times, while they waited, Billy Bunter had blinked into the study with longing blinks through his big spectacles. He had, however, rolled away at last and disappeared.

Now he had returned! He barged into Study No. 1 with excitement in his fat face.

(Continued on page 28.)

OUR BIG THRILLER !

THE LOST SQUADRON!

The Golden Day !

SQUADRON-LEADER AKERS and Flight-Lieutenant Ferris are cast away on a desert stretch of land which has risen out of the depths as a result of a huge tidal wave.

After a series of thrilling adventures they meet more survivors, among whom are Coles, Huck, and a negro named Jim Crow, who have made a rich haul looting stranded derelicts.

At long last ships come to the rescue of the castaways. Anxious to get clear with their booty, Coles & Co., together with the aid of Larsen, Crawley, and Baines, seize the tugboat Rosa, overpower the three seamen aboard, and make for the open sea. While replenishing their stock of coal from one of the wrecks, Baines and Crawley double-cross the rest of the party and skip off with the booty. Armed with the tough stem from a lengthy piece of seaweed, the negro is soon racing along the sand, hard on the heels of the precious pair.

Suddenly he came upon his quarry. Rounding a big outcropping of rock, he saw, less than fifty yards away, Baines and Crawley seated on the sand, cooking their breakfast over a fire of driftwood. Near by, lying at drunken angle, was the rusty hull of a derelict, and it was evident that it was from there that they had obtained the food.

Jim saw them before they saw him, and he stepped quickly back behind the rocks. It did not take him more than a few moments to make up his mind what to do. Moving up the beach behind the rocks, he made a detour which brought him out behind the derelict, on the other side of which, in blissful unconsciousness of the big negro's presence, Baines and Crawley were frying tinned bacon and boiling coffee.

Taking a fresh grip on his sjambok of seaweed, Jim rounded the hull and stepped into view.

Crawley had his back to him, and it was Baines, squatting by the fire, coffee mug in hand, who saw him first. If Baines had suddenly seen an apparition, he could not have registered more terrified amaze.

His eyes opened wide, so did his mouth, and the mug of steaming coffee fell from his nerveless hands, its contents deluging the fire in a miniature and sizzling upheaval of smoke and sparks.

"What'n heck's wrong with you?" demanded Crawley angrily.

"L-l-look !" gulped Baines.

But Crawley had no time to look, for in that same moment a great hand closed on the back of the collar of his reefer jacket, jerking him to his feet.

Wheeling round, Crawley found himself face to face with Jim Crow.

"You?" he gasped.

"Yes, sah, it's me !" said Jim grimly.

Dropping his seaweed, the negro pulled the gun from out of Crawley's belt and thrust it into his own.

"I'll jest take care of this li'l automatic," he went on, retrieving his seaweed without loosening his grip on Crawley. "An' now jest shed yore jackets, both of youse, an' empty yore trouser pockets. D'you hear me, Baines?"

"Y-yes; all right, Jim," stammered Baines, proceeding to peel off his jacket.

"Go on, Crawley, git busy," ordered Jim, releasing his hold on Crawley.

For a moment Crawley hesitated, eyeing Jim and the wicked-looking length of seaweed in the latter's hand. Then slowly he took off his jacket, and throwing it to the sand, proceeded to empty his trouser pockets.

"Where'n thunder have you come from?" he snarled.

"From de Rosa," purred Jim. "Surely you ain't forgotten how you left me dere, Crawley?"

No, Crawley had not forgotten, for when next he spoke his voice was unsteady.

"What—what are you figurin' on doin'?" he demanded.

"I'm figurin' on giving you an' Baines the biggest hiding either of you has ever had," answered Jim. "An' if you've discarded all de stuff what you stole from Coles, Huck an' me, I'm starting in right now."

He stepped quickly forward, and Crawley let out a scream of pain as the sjambok of seaweed whistled through the air and thudded cruelly into his back.

Baines was already fleeing and Crawley followed suit. But Jim was far swifter of foot than either of them, and mercilessly he flogged them along the beach bringing from them howls of pain and curses of impotent rage.

Only when the seaweed was broken and useless did Jim desist, and coming to a halt, he stood with hands on hips grimly surveying the fast receding forms of Baines and Crawley.

Then, with a grin on his lips, he turned about, and after collecting the booty discarded by the precious pair, set off back the way he had come, heading in the direction of the Rosa.

What Jim intended to do when he reached the Rosa he did not know. All he did know was that now the Rosa had been re-taken by the seamen his plans were completely and hopelessly wrecked.

He was a fool, he told himself, to return to the Rosa at all. But he was not going to desert Coles and Huck. If they were going to be punished then he was going to stand by them and take his punishment along with them.

He trudged along the beach, plunged in gloomy thought, but making resolutely towards the bay in which the tug lay at anchor.

Reaching it at length, he seated himself on a boulder and, with chin cupped in hands, sat gazing at the small black-hulled vessel which he had so fondly hoped to sail to America.

A wisp of black smoke was drifting lazily from the long slender smoke stack and he could see a man moving about by the galley. Otherwise, there were no signs of life on board at all, and by that he guessed that Coles, Huck and Larsen were still lying bound and helpless in their bonds.

What was to be done? It wouldn't be long now before the Rosa weighed anchor and stood southwards down the coast to Camelot. Should he chuck the whole game up and go quietly aboard and surrender? Or should he go aboard and in one last glorious fight endeavour to win freedom for Coles and Huck?

"Guess I dunno what to do," Jim mused dejectedly. "I'se so plumb tired an' weary an' sick ob eberything."

He was silent awhile, then:

"Lordy, lordy but dis ain't like you, Jim. Be a man. Be white. Go an' git Coles an' Huck outa dat fo'c'sle!"

Yet somehow the idea of another scrap did not appeal to the negro.

"Dere's bin enuff of dat rough stuff," he muttered. "We're beat—licked holler—so we may's well admit it an' quit. But, somehow, it ain't fair to Coles an' Huck. They'll be relying on ol' Jim——"

Abruptly he broke off and rose to his feet. Coles and Huck would be relying on him. That was good enough. They were his mates and he wasn't going to let them down. He would do his best to get them out of the fo'c'sle, and if he failed—well, he'd go down fighting.

"It's the on'y thing a feller can do," he told himself, moving down the beach to where the tug's boat lay. "Ain't dey my pards?"

Pushing the boat into deeper water, he clambered aboard and, picking up an oar, turned the bows towards the tug. Then seating himself, he proceeded to scull leisurely in the direction of the Rosa.

Once he looked over his shoulder. The three seamen were gathered by the port rail of the Rosa watching him. But coolly he continued with his rowing, his powerful arms sending the boat cutting through the water.

It was when he was half-way between the beach and the tug that he suddenly rested on his oars, his head inclined in a listening attitude.

Yes, he had not been mistaken. For faint and from far away to the south was coming the drone of powerful aero engines. That the machine or machines were heading towards the Rosa was evident, for steadily the noise was growing in volume.

Shipping his oars, Jim turned in his seat and gazed into the southern sky. The three seamen on the tug had also heard the engines, for they were staring in the same direction.

Then flying low and coming up at a terrific speed, Jim saw a great black-winged and triple-engined monoplane.

At less than five hundred feet it roared over the Rosa, then, as it banked and came about, the thunder of its engines died away, and its nose went down for a landing.

With engines ticking over, it landed on the water to seaward of the tug, and came cruising in towards the vessel. Then its engines were switched off, and a voice hailed Jim from the cockpit.

"Boat ahoy! Put us aboard!"

For a moment Jim hesitated, then, unshipping his oars, he sculled steadily in the direction of the monoplane, bringing the boat alongside one of the giant floats.

Two leather-clad men had swung themselves down from the cockpit and were waiting for him.

Jim grinned at sight of one of them.

"Why, if it ain't Mr. Akers!" he exclaimed. "How am you, boss?"

"I'm very well, Jim," replied Akers, following the other leather-clad man into the boat. "How are you?"

"None too great, Mr. Akers, an' dat's a fact," replied Jim, pushing off from the float. "You wanna go aboard de Rosa, I'se 'pect?"

"Yes, Jim," replied Akers, settling himself in the stern-sheets. "Have you any idea how she happens to be here?"

"We bringed her, sah!" replied Jim simply.

"That's just what I thought," nodded Akers. "What on earth made you do such a stupid thing?"

"Well, you see, Mr. Akers," exclaimed Jim, sculling slowly towards the tug, "we wasn't aware dat she didn't have no coal in her bunkers. We was figgerin' on taking her to America."

"With the stuff which you took from the derelicts?"

"Yes, sah!"

"You're a fool, Jim."

"I knows dat, sah!"

"Who else is aboard with you?"

"Dere's Larsen an' Coles an' Huck an' de three hands what we captured along wid de ship," replied Jim. "Baines an' Crawley was aboard, but dey left kind of sudden in de early hours of dis mawnin', sah!"

"Why?"

"Well, it's a queer sort of story, Mr. Akers," said Jim, resting on his oars. "At de moment Larsen, Coles, an' Huck is lying aboard dere bound an' helpless, an' dem three fellers what you see standing by de rail is waiting to knock me over de haid as well. Afore I puts you an' dis other gen'elman aboard, p'raps I'd better tell you all about it an' put you wise as to how de land lays."

"Yes, perhaps you had better, Jim," assented Akers gravely. "This, by the way," he indicated his companion, "is Captain Lester, who has flown over from Canada in that machine you see there."

"Pleased to meet you, cap'n," acknowledged Jim, then turning to Akers, he proceeded to unfold in detail all the events which had happened since he, Coles, and Huck, had seized the Rosa with the aid of Larsen, Baines, and Crawley.

Akers listened in silence and without comment until Jim reached the point where he had fought with Larsen on the bridge.

"You slammed him properly, Jim?" he inquired.

"I sure did, sah!" responded Jim.

"I wish I'd seen it," said Akers regretfully. "Yes, go on!"

Jim proceeded, coming at length to the events of that particular morning, and telling how he had chased Baines and Crawley, then returned to the Rosa in two minds whether he should attempt to rescue Coles and Huck, or bow to the inevitable and quietly submit to sharing with them whatever punishment the future might have in store.

"But you could have cleared off on your own?" exclaimed Captain Lester, staring.

Jim looked at him.

"Sah," he said with dignity, "dem two fellers is shipmates ob mine!"

Rebuffed and confused, Captain Lester could only look helplessly at Akers, as, dipping his oars into the water, Jim resumed his sculling towards the Rosa.

Coming neatly alongside, Jim waited until Akers and Captain Lester had swung themselves up on to the low deck, then he followed, the mooring-rope in his hand.

"I don't know who you are or what the nigger's been telling you," began one of the seamen addressing Akers, "but he's the feller who grabbed this tug at Camelot——"

"I know all about it," cut in Akers, a trifle curtly. "Jim, go below. I'll send for you in a few minutes."

"Yes, sah," said Jim, and obediently he disappeared below.

Turning to the three seamen, Akers

Printed in Great Britain and published every Saturday by the Proprietors, The Amalgamated Press, Ltd. The Fleetway House, Farringdon Street, London, E.C.4. Advertisement offices: The Fleetway House, Farringdon Street, London, E.C.4. Registered for transmission by Canadian Magazine Post. Subscription rates: Inland and Abroad, 11s. per annum; 5s. 6d. for six months. Sole Agents for Australia and New Zealand: Messrs. Gordon & Gotch, Ltd., and for South Africa: Central News Agency, Ltd.—Saturday, May 2nd, 1936.

then explained who he and Captain Lester were.

"The object of our present flight was to locate you," he said. "We knew from your skipper that your bunkers were almost empty, and we were pretty certain we'd find you somewhere along the coast."

He thereupon questioned them as to what had happened since the night the Rosa had been seized by Jim and Larsen, and their four companions. It was not that Akers doubted what Jim had told him, or that he wanted corroboration of the negro's story. It was merely that he wanted to hear the seaman's version of the affair.

And they gave it without sparing Jim in the slightest. In fact, they could say nothing good about Jim at all, which, under the circumstances, is perhaps not to be wondered at. Anyway, Akers listened to them in silence, then sent for Jim.

"Now, look here," he said severely when Jim was standing in front of him, "you and your precious friends have been guilty of a most serious crime in seizing this ship. You realise that?"

"Yes, sah," said Jim humbly.

"You were the ringleader, of course?"

"Yes, sah."

"You will probably be sent to prison."

"Yes, sah!"

"Where are the money and valuables you took from the derelicts?"

"Most of dem are aboard heah, sah, an' de rest is in de boat alongside."

"You realise where this looting has landed you, don't you?"

"Yes, sah!"

"Have you any regrets?"

Raising his head, Jim looked Akers full in the eyes.

"I wish now," he said fervently, "dat I never stood in on it. I wish now dat I had never left de Boston. I wish dat I had gone wid you an' Mister Ferris, like what Sam did. I wish all dat now, but I ain't whining, Mister Akers. I'll take what's comin' to me!"

Akers' eyes softened as he looked at the big negro.

"Well, I'll tell you what's coming to you, Jim," he said. "You, Coles, Huck and Larsen are going to work your passage back to St. John's, down in the stokehole of this vessel. Captain McAllister, the master, is on his way here now, and, judging by the towering rage he's been in ever since you stole his ship, I don't envy you your trip across the Atlantic."

"Is Captain McAllister coming?" exclaimed one of the seamen in surprise.

"Yes," replied Akers. "There are about fifty ships anchored off Camelot at the moment, and on sighting you we wirelessed them your position. Captain McAllister replied that he was leaving for here at once, with the remainder of his crew."

"Oh, golly!" groaned Jim. "An' den it's de police when us gits across?"

"If you behave yourself, Jim," said Akers, "there won't be any police when you get across."

"But, Mister Akers," stammered Jim, "you—you doan't mean——"

"I mean, if you behave yourself, as I say," said Akers, "you'll hear nothing further of this business. You're more of a fool than a rogue, Jim. You've gone to a lot of trouble collecting loot, and you've lost it all. You've gone to a lot more trouble collecting this ship, and you've lost that, as well. The only persons whom you've really inconvenienced are Captain McAllister and his crew, and I think we can safely leave them to deal with that little matter on the way across."

Mercilessly the negro flogged Baines and Crawley along the beach, bringing from them howls of pain!

"Mister Akers," stammered Jim hoarsely, "you—you'se a white man! I—I dunno how to thank you——"

"You can thank me by not being such an ass in future, Jim."

"Mister Akers," said Jim fervently, "I won't never be an ass no more. No, sah, not never! An' if eber I sees a feller what's tempted to do wrong I'll give him such a bashin' dat he won't never feel tempted no more!"

. . . . . .

Three days later, having flown across the Atlantic with Captain Lester, who had refuelled from one of the stranded tankers, Akers spent long hours closeted with the Canadian Prime Minister, at Ottawa.

Akers made a full report to him of all that had happened, and left with him the rough chart of the new land which had risen from out the depths of the sea. Then he returned to his hotel, where, during the ensuing week, he was joined by Ferris, who had crossed aboard the Texan.

Another summons came to Akers to attend at Parliament House, and there he received news which staggered him, and rendered him almost speechless with emotion.

"I have been in communication with all Prime Ministers and Governor Generals throughout the British Empire," the austere and white-haired Premier informed him, "and we have decided that on this land which has arisen from out the sea we will build a new England. We will cultivate wherever possible, and build new harbours and great cities."

His voice trembled as he went on:

"England is gone, the world is saying, England is dead! Do they not know that England can never die, that England is immortal? Humbly asking God's blessing on our work, we, the sons of England, will transform that barren land into a new and glorious country which will be the envy of all peoples, and a fitting tribute to the greatest nation the world has ever known."

That night, with Ferris by his side, Akers stood on the balcony of his hotel. He was very quiet as he stood there gazing eastwards towards where, far across the sea, lay that dead and silent land of rock and sand.

To Akers it was no longer a vista of dreariness and desolation. Instead, he saw a land of towering skyscrapers and mighty cities, of vast harbours and great aerodromes, a land where all was new, and fine, and splendid—a golden land of infinite promise—the mighty hub around which the world revolved.

England!

THE END.

(In next Saturday's MAGNET *you'll find the opening chapters of a smashing story of modern piracy that's going to grip you right from the commencement to the fall of the curtain. Don't miss this great treat, chums!)*

GUN PLAY AT GREYFRIARS!

(*Continued from page 24.*)

"Bunk!" hooted Bob Cherry. "This is Van Duck's cake, you fat cormorant——"

"Eh! Who's talking about a cake?" snorted Billy Bunter. "I say, that man Pike——"

"What about Pike?"

"I say, you fellows, you'd better go and stop him! He's flourishing that gun of his at Loder——"

"What?" roared the Famous Five.

"I say, you'd better go and stop him!" gasped Bunter. "Go and stop him before he shoots Coker's head off——"

"Coker's?" yelled Johnny Bull.

"I—I mean Loder's——"

"Ha, ha, ha!"

"Blessed if I see anything to cackle at!" howled Bunter. "I can jolly well tell you Wingate's life is in danger——"

"Ha, ha, ha!"

That Billy Bunter was inventing this yarn out of the sly depths of his own fat brain nobody in the study doubted. It was a rather palpable dodge to get them out of the study while Bunter had a go at the cake.

But the laughter died away as a loud report rang suddenly from the quad, echoing in at the open window.

Bang!

"Great pip!" ejaculated Bob Cherry.

For an instant the Famous Five stood as if spellbound. Then they rushed out of the study, shoving Bunter aside.

If Poker Pike was loosing off his six-gun in the quad evidently he had to be stopped—if possible. Greatly alarmed, the juniors rushed down the passage and tore down the stairs and pelted out into the quad.

"Ooooough!" gasped Bunter.

The rush of the juniors from the study had left him sitting down. He heaved up his weight, gasping for breath.

Then he rolled to the table, his little round eyes gleaming behind his big, round spectacles. He grabbed up the cake, and stopping only to break off one chunk and cram it into his capacious mouth, he rolled to the door with it. Harry Wharton & Co. were already out of the House, and the coast was clear!

But was it? As Billy Bunter rolled out of the study, with that large and luscious cake in his fat hands, there was a footstep from the direction of the stairs. Bunter blinked round in alarm.

"Oh lor'!" he gasped.

His eyes almost popped through his spectacles at the sight of Putnam van Duck.

The American junior had arrived at a rather unfortunate moment for the grub-raider of the Remove.

"By the great horned toad!" ejaculated Putnam; and he accelerated. "Say, big boy, what you figure you're doing with that cake?"

"I—I—I wasn't going to scoff it!" gasped Bunter. "I—I wasn't going to get it away to the box-room, Van Duck! I—I—I was—was—was—— I was going to—— Whoop! Yooop! Stop pulling my nose, you beast! Wooogh!"

"I guess that cake sort of belongs to this study!" remarked Van Duck; and he led Bunter back into Study No. 1 by his little fat nose.

"Urrrrggh!" gurgled the Owl of the Remove.

The cake was landed on the table again.

"Where are the guys gone?" asked Putnam. "I guessed they was here waiting for me."

"I—I say, you'd better get after them, Van Duck!" gasped Bunter. "They've gone to stop that man, Pike, shooting old Quelch——"

"Wha-a-at?"

"Honest Injun!" gasped Bunter. "He was flourishing his gun at Quelch in the quad, and——"

"And I've just left Quelch in his study, too!" grinned Van Duck. "Try again!"

"I—I mean Loder—that is, Coker——"

"That's what you mean, is it?" asked the junior from Chicago. "Now I guess I'll put you wise as to what I mean. I mean to rub your head in the coal-locker for cinching my cake——"

"Ow! Leggo!"

There was a tramp of feet in the passage. Harry Wharton & Co. came in, rather breathlessly.

"Ow! I say, you fellows, make him leggo!" howled Bunter. "I say, I wasn't going to snaffle that cake! I say, if you don't go and stop that man, Pike, he will be shooting old Prout. He was flourishing his gun right in Prout's face and—and you heard it go off——"

"It wasn't Pike's gun, you fat ass!" said Bob Cherry. "It was that fat-headed minor of yours, Sammy Bunter, letting off a cracker under the study windows."

"And we jolly well know why!" roared Johnny Bull. "You put him up to it, you fat spoofer, to get us out of the study while you snaffled the cake."

"Oh!" gasped Bunter. "I—I say, you fellows. I—I haven't spoken to Sammy to-day. I never went to look for him, after I saw this cake here, and I never knew that Toddy had a cracker in his desk, and I certainly never took it out—I—I wouldn't, you know."

"Oh crikey!"

"I hope you can take a fellow's word!" said Bunter warmly. "I never asked Sammy to let that cracker off under the study windows, and never promised him half the cake if I got it! Nothing of the kind! I—I haven't seen my minor to-day, at all. He wasn't in the Rag when I spoke to him there and——"

"Ha, ha, ha!"

"Blessed if I see anything to cackle at! I say, you fellows, hadn't you better go at once—with that man, Pike, flourishing his gun at the Head——"

"Ha, ha, ha!"

"You needn't worry about that cake," said Bunter. "I'll look after the cake while you're gone. I will, really!"

The juniors gazed at Billy Bunter. His deep-laid scheme for snaffling that cake had alarmed them—till they discovered that the alarming bang only came from a cracker, and not from Poker Pike's six-gun! They gazed at him—and then they collared him.

There was a heavy bump in the Remove passage as Billy Bunter departed from Study No. 1. It was followed by a loud roar.

Then the juniors gathered round the cake, which was cut. As large slices were handed round, a fat face and a large pair of spectacles blinked in at the door.

"I say, you fellows——"

"Do you want some more?" roared Bob.

"I—I say, it—it was only a lark, you know," gasped Bunter. "I—I thought it would—would amuse you, you know. He, he, he! I—I say, old chaps, I'd like a chunk of that cake! I would, really!"

Hope springs eternal in the human breast Apparently, Bunter was still hoping for a whack in the cake!

As it happened, that hope was fulfilled! Bob Cherry picked up a chunk of cake and stepped to the door. Bunter rolled in, with outstretched fat paw. But it was not in that fat paw that he received the chunk. Bob Cherry grabbed him with his left hand, and with the right, crammed the chunk of cake down the back of the fat Owl's neck.

"Ow!" howled Bunter, wriggling frantically. "Ow! Stoppit! Beast! Ooogh!"

"Have some more?" asked Bob.

"Ow! No! Beast! No!"

"Ha, ha, ha!"

Billy Bunter wriggled out of the study. He did not want any more cake. Taken internally, it was nice. Taken externally, it was horrid. Very much indeed, Bunter did not want any more! The cake was finished without further assistance from Billy Bunter!

THE END.

(*Now look out for: "HORACE COKER'S DARK DEED!" the next yarn in this grand new series featuring Putnam van Duck and his gangster enemies. It's full of fun and exciting situations. Be wise and order your copy in good time, chums!*)

Meet CAPTAIN VENGEANCE, Modern Pirate, Inside!

No 1,473. Vol. XLIX. EVERY SATURDAY. Week Ending May 9th, 1936.

HORACE COKER'S DARK DEED!

By FRANK RICHARDS

He came quickly towards the juniors with a grim look on his face; they backed away from the stairs, trying to look as if they had never thought or dreamed of sliding down the banisters in all their young lives. Unfortunately, Loder of the Sixth was not of a trusting disposition, and he had a dislike for those cheery members of the Lower Fourth. He had not seen them come down, but he had heard them—and he knew.

"You young sweeps!" said Loder. "Sliding down the banisters—what?"

"No harm done, Loder," ventured Bob.

"You might have broken your necks!" said Loder. "Not that that would have mattered much! But what about House rules?"

Bob did not answer that question; really there was no answer to be made. He had rather forgotten House rules—good and necessary rules, as Bob was ready to admit. Still, a fellow did rather forget rules at times—especially when he had an exuberant nature, and was always full of beans, like the cheery Bob.

Loder, standing by the newel post, regarded the dismayed five with malicious satisfaction. This meant a report to Mr. Quelch, and lines or a gating, if not a whopping—which was a satisfaction to the bully of the Sixth.

"I'll take you to Quelch now——" he recommenced.

He was interrupted.

"Look out!" yelled Bob.

Loder did not catch on in time. He had caught the Famous Five, and he was not aware that a sixth fellow was following their example and following their descent of the banisters.

Van Duck had started before he noticed that Loder was there. Once started, there was no stopping.

It was a long banister, with a wide curve in it. It was not easy to negotiate. A fellow could have fallen off at any point, but he could not have jumped off safely till he reached the end.

Had Loder of the Sixth looked round in time and seen Van Duck coming he might have jumped clear, but he did not look round in time.

Putnam van Duck came like a bullet. He flew down the banisters and flew off the end and failed to jump clear, like the Famous Five, because Loder was in the way. He landed on Loder!

Crash!

Bump!

It seemed to Loder of the Sixth that a battering-ram had hit him. Van Duck was not a heavy-weight, but he came with a terrific impetus. Loder was knocked spinning.

He spun two or three yards before he crashed—and when he crashed it was a terrific crash.

"Ooooh!" stuttered Van Duck breathlessly.

He crashed a split second after Loder—and it was on Loder that he crashed, sprawling right over him.

THE FIRST CHAPTER.

Follow Your Leader!

"COAST'S clear!" said Bob Cherry.

"But——"

"Nobody's about——"

"But——"

"Oh, come on!"

Bob did not wait for a third "but." He swung himself on the broad, smooth oaken banister and went sailing down.

"Fathead!" said Harry Wharton.

But he followed. Where one member of the Famous Five of the Greyfriars Remove went the rest were sure to follow.

Venturesome fellows liked to descend the big staircase sitting on that long, smooth oaken banister and sailing down at headlong speed. A fellow whizzed down at a dizzy rate, lifted his leg over the massive newel post at the lower end, and jumped off to the floor—and it was quite exciting and exhilarating, but rather dangerous.

A fellow who lost his nerve after starting would have been booked for a fall that would have done a great deal of damage.

For which reason sailing down the banisters was strictly forbidden at Greyfriars and liable to punishment.

Bob Cherry rather forgot that. A glance down having revealed that there was, for once, nobody about—neither beaks nor prefects—it seemed to Bob too good a chance to be missed.

So down he went—whizzing!

Harry Wharton, having remonstrated in vain, followed, and whizzed after him. After Wharton went Johnny Bull, then Frank Nugent, and then Hurree Jamset Ram Singh. Five fellows were sitting on the banister all at once, one after another, all whizzing. Putnam van Duck, the American junior, who was coming downstairs with his friends, paused.

"Gee!" he ejaculated, staring at that sudden, startling acrobatic performance.

Van Duck had plenty of nerve; he was not afraid to follow where others led—but this was a new one on him, and for a moment or two he stood and stared.

It was a rapid performance. Almost in a second Bob was down to the newel post, lifting a leg over it, and shooting off, to land lightly on his feet. After him shot the rest of the Co., landing, one after another, actively, lightly, and successfully.

Then Van Duck prepared to start.

Unlike his fellow-countryman, Fisher T. Fish of the Remove, he had heaps of pluck. It was a dangerous game—and he knew it—but he was not going to get left. He swung on the banister to go.

At the same moment there was a startled and dismayed exclamation below.

"'Ware prefects!"

The lower hall was not so deserted as Bob Cherry had supposed at that cursory glance from the landing. From the big window alcove Loder of the Sixth stepped out.

He had been looking out into the quad, scowling at the sight of a bowler-hatted man who was walking there, but at the sound of five fellows jumping, one after another, Gerald Loder looked round and stepped forth.

From one point of view, this was fortunate. The old oaken floor was hard to fall on; Loder was much softer. Van Duck's fall was broken by Loder.

Judging by Loder's agonised howl, he was broken, too.

Harry Wharton stared on in dismay. Breaking the rules was serious; breaking a Sixth Form prefect was still more serious.

"Oh, my hat!" gasped Bob.

Harry Wharton ran forward to give Putnam a hand up. The American junior staggered breathlessly to his feet.

"Carry me home to die!" he gasped. "What the great horned toad did that pesky geck get in the way for? I've sure collared a million bumps and a few over—and then some!"

"Urrrggh!" came a moan from Loder.

"Hurt, Loder?" asked Bob.

It was quite a superfluous question. Only too plainly Loder of the Sixth was hurt. Still more plainly, he was wildly enraged.

He staggered up, gasping and spluttering; he turned to Putnam van Duck with a deadly glare.

As a prefect, Loder was entitled to report these delinquents to their Form-master; he was entitled to order Van Duck to "bend over" and take "six" for having floored him. But he was too enraged to think of what he was entitled to do. Had he had his ashplant with him, no doubt he would have used it—hard. But he hadn't. He leaped at Van Duck, almost like a tiger, smacking his head right and left—which no Greyfriars prefect was entitled to do. The smacking of heads was absolutely "taboo" at Greyfriars School.

He did not merely smack—he banged!

"Yurrroop!" roared Putnam.

A bang on the right side of his head gave him a list to port, and a bang on the left righted him again; another bang was coming which would have floored him—for Loder was too savagely exasperated to think or care what he was doing—but Putnam dodged that third bang, cut across to the open doorway, and scudded out into the sunny quad.

"Stop!" roared Loder.

Stopping for more bangs was the last thing that Putnam van Duck was thinking of. He flew.

After him flew Loder in fierce pursuit.

"Oh crumbs!" gasped Bob Cherry.

And the Famous Five, in a state of great dismay, followed on into the quad to see what was going to happen.

THE SECOND CHAPTER.

Poker Pike Horns In!

POKER PIKE glanced round.

The bowler-hatted man was walking sedately in the quad, on the path by the elms, when Putnam van Duck flew out of the House.

Some of the Greyfriars fellows smiled when they passed him.

The idea of a Chicago gunman being posted at the school to guard the son of a Chicago millionaire from kidnappers, rather amused them.

But as Poker Pike had been at Greyfriars since the first day of the term they were getting used to the sight of him, with his serious hickory face under the brim of the tight-fitting bowler hat, that seemed never to part company with his bullet head, even indoors. Even the fact that he was known to "pack a gun" had ceased to thrill them.

Mr. Pike was prepared to "pull" that gun if danger threatened the son of Vanderdecken van Duck, entrusted to his watchful care. The millionaire had hired him for that purpose, and Poker was a dutiful "guy."

Protecting Putnam from Chick Chew, the "star" kidnapper of the great United States, was Poker's present duty, and he did it with thoroughness.

There had been some trouble, because Poker seemed to consider it his duty to protect Putnam, not only from threatening kidnappers, but from everybody else who got too "fresh."

He had even interrupted a Sixth Form prefect who was whopping Putnam, and carried that prefect—Loder, of the Sixth—struggling and kicking under his arm, which had led to a long and serious "jaw" from the Head, who had had to impress on Mr. Pike just where he got off, so to speak.

Now, looking round, Mr. Pike saw Putnam van Duck in full flight, and, raging on his track, Loder of the Sixth.

His slits of eyes glinted, and his gash of a mouth set hard. His brows knitted under the clamped-down bowler.

He made a stride towards the scene.

Then he stopped.

Poker was not a man easily impressed, but the headmaster of Greyfriars had impressed him. Also, Mr. van Duck had directed him to respect and obey the headmaster in every particular.

His impulse, at the sight of his charge chased by Loder, was to "cinch" Loder and beat him up a few. But the Head's stern injunctions weighed on his mind, and he paused.

SENSATION at GREYFRIARS!

Some person unknown has had the effrontery to drench the Head with ink, and the question is being asked up and down the school—WHO DID IT?

As he stood undecided, Van Duck flew past. After him came Loder, as if he were on the cinder-path.

Poker Pike stepped abruptly into his way.

He was not going to cinch Loder, or beat him up; but he was going to stop him. Poker reckoned that no reasonable guy could find fault with that.

He stepped suddenly in front of Loder, and stood like a rock, and Loder crashed like a wave on a particularly hard rock, and almost broke like a wave.

It was a terrific concussion.

Loder was going at great speed, stared at on all sides, forgetful of everything but his desire to get hold of the junior who had floored him. It was a most injudicious exhibition of excitement and bad temper on the part of a Sixth Form prefect, but Loder was too enraged to think of appearances.

Going at top speed, his impact would have hurled almost any other man off his feet. But Poker stood like a rock, and the concussion did not seem even to shake him. It more than shook Loder!

Loder staggered back, crumpled, and rolled over from the shock. He rolled at Mr. Pike's feet, gasping.

"Man down!" gasped Bob Cherry, as the Famous Five came trooping out of the House.

"That jolly old gunman!" gasped Frank Nugent.

There was a shouting of voices all over the quad. Fellows rushed up from all quarters.

"I say, you fellows!" yelled Billy Bunter. "That gangster's at it again! He, he, he!"

"Ha, ha, ha!"

Gerald Loder sat up dizzily. Mr. Pike was looking down at him with a calm and serious face. Putnam van Duck came to a panting halt at a little distance, looking back, ready to dodge again if Loder resumed the pursuit.

"Oh!" gasped Loder. "Ow! Oooogh! You rotten ruffian! Ooogh!"

"Pack that up, big boy!" advised Mr. Pike. "I got orders from the king-pin of this here caboodle not to beat you up, but you don't want to ask for it none."

Loder staggered up.

He gave the man from Chicago a deadly glare. Loder would have liked nothing better than to have planted his fist full in the hard-boiled hickory face, and sent Mr. Pike spinning. He would have tried it on, but for the knowledge that the punch would have hurt his fist more than it would have hurt Poker's face!

Instead of hitting Mr. Pike, he moved to go round him and get after Putnam van Duck.

But Mr Pike moved at the same moment, and the bully of the Sixth found him still in the way.

Loder moved again, and Mr. Pike moved again. The stocky figure still barred Loder's way.

"Will you get out of my way, you ruffian?" howled Loder.

Mr. Pike shook his head.

"Nope!" he answered. "Not if you're 'gunning' after that Putnam van Duck. I guess I'm here to look after that young guy."

"You cheeky fool!" roared Loder.

"Can it!" said Mr. Pike warningly. "I keep on telling you not to ask for it, you, Loder!"

"Get out of my way!" yelled Loder.

"I should smile!" answered Mr. Pike.

Putnam van Duck, a dozen yards behind the gunman, grinned. About fifty fellows, gathering round the scene, grinned also. Loder made another move to walk round the gunman. Mr. Pike promptly headed him off.

He had his hands in his pockets, resisting the temptation to beat Loder up a few. At home, in Chicago, Mr. Pike would have beaten up any guy who fooled around like this—if he had not, indeed, pulled a gun on him. But Poker, greatly to his credit, was trying to accommodate himself to the strange manners and customs of the strange land in which he now sojourned. He wasn't going to beat Loder up if he could help it, but he was not going to let him go "gunning" after Putnam van Duck.

Loder was almost dancing with rage.

"Will you let me pass?" he howled.

"Not so's you'd notice it!" answered Mr. Pike.

"I'll knock you down if you don't stand aside!" bawled Loder.

"Aw, forget it!" advised Mr. Pike. "You couldn't chew it if you bit it off!"

"Ha, ha, ha!" yelled the Greyfriars fellows. Mr. Pike's flow of language never ceased to entertain them. According to what they learned in their school books, America was one of the English-speaking countries; but the variety of English that Poker Pike had brought from Chicago bore little resemblance to the language spoken at Greyfriars.

"You cheeky ruffian!" yelled Loder.

"Park it!" said Mr Pike.

Again Loder attempted to circle round the obstruction. Again Mr. Pike barred his way.

Prudence failed Loder. In his fury, fanned to white heat by the laughter of the crowd of fellows behind him, he forgot that Mr. Pike was too large an order for him.

He made a spring at the gunman, hitting out fiercely with both fists.

Crash!

"Oh crikey!" gasped Bob Cherry.

Mr. Pike had shoved his hands into his pockets, perhaps to help him resist his natural inclination to knock Loder into the middle of next week, or further along the calendar. So the sudden attack took him off his guard.

Both Loder's fists, with all Loder's weight behind them, landed in his hickory face before he could whip out his hands.

Mr. Pike went over backwards. He went over an uprooted tree. His bowler hat crashed on the quad, and his feet flew into the air.

"Yurrrooogh!" gasped Mr. Pike, as he crashed.

He was knocked down! Loder of the Sixth had knocked him down! And as he sprawled on his back, Loder rushed past.

"Oh, my hat!" exclaimed Harry Wharton. "What next?"

"Look out!" shrieked Bob.

Poker Pike was on his feet with a bound. His hickory face was grim with wrath. His hand flew to his hip. In amazement and horror, the Greyfriars fellows saw that he was pulling a gun.

"Pike!" yelled Wharton.

"Stop!"

"You mad fathead!"

"Stop him!"

"Oh crikey!"

Mr. Pike did not heed. His six-gun had leaped into his hand, and the muzzle bore on Loder of the Sixth.

Bang!

Loder leaped clear of the ground with a yell of terror, as a bullet smashed up earth at his feet. He spun round, his eyes starting from his head, almost jabbering with terror. Mr. Pike strode at him, with levelled gun, and grim face over it.

THE THIRD CHAPTER.

Jump!

THERE was a roar of excitement in the old quadrangle of Greyfriars.

The report of Poker Pike's six-gun had awakened every echo, and startled every ear in the school.

Windows were crammed with faces, looking out.

Dr. Locke was seen at his study window, his eyes almost popping through his glasses. Mr. Quelch, the Remove master, was at his window; Prout, master of the Fifth, was leaning out, amazed. Startled faces stared, and startled voices sounded on all sides.

Poker Pike did not heed. Neither did Loder! The smoking gun in the gunman's hand transfixed the bully of the Sixth with terror.

His impression was that Poker had fired at him, and was going to fire again. Of course, Poker hadn't! Poker was a handy man with a gun, and he could plant a bullet just where he liked. He had chosen to plant that one at Loder's feet—certainly very close, but a miss was as good as a mile!

"Now, you pesky gink!" roared the exasperated Poker. "I guess I'm going to fan you a few! You get me? Dance, you geck, dance!"

Bang!

The six-gun roared again.

"Yarooooh!" roared Loder.

He leaped a foot in the air.

The bullet took a chip of leather from his boot. Loder actually felt it as it chipped his boot. He was not hurt. But he was frightened almost out of his wits.

"Jump, you gink, jump!" roared Mr. Pike. "I guess I'm fanning you a few, and if you don't jump, and keep on jumping, I guess you'll want crutches! Surest thing you know! Jump, you gink! Dance, you geck! You got it coming!"

Bang!

"Urrgh! Help! Yoop!"

Loder yelled—and jumped!

With bullets crashing at his feet, he had to jump!

There was an alarmed yell from Putnam van Duck.

"Poker, you geck! Pack it up! You hear me? You can't fan a guy here, you gink! You figure that you're fanning a hobo in a Chicago joint, you pesky bonehead! Can it!"

But Poker Pike did not heed. He banged again with the six-gun, and Loder gave another convulsive bound.

"Oh, my hat!" gasped Bob.

"It's all right!" stuttered Wharton. "He's not going to hurt Loder. It's his idea of a game!"

"Some game!" grinned Bob.

"The gamefulness is terrific!" chuckled Hurree Jamset Ram Singh.

Bang!

Loder bounded.

Breathlessly, the Greyfriars crowd looked on. Had Mr. Pike been shooting at Loder, plenty of fellows would have rushed on him to stop him, taking the risk of the gun.

But everybody except Loder could see that he was not being "shot up." And even Loder could see that he was all right so long as he jumped. He jumped for his life!

Some of the fellows had heard of the peculiar game of "fanning." They had heard of it as a wild and woolly custom of the wild and woolly West. They had never expected to see it in the quadrangle of Greyfriars School. Now they saw it!

Bang!

Loder leaped nearly a yard into the air.

"Ha, ha, ha!"

Coming down after that terrified leap, Loder stumbled, and sat. He sat suddenly and hard, and yelped.

Mr. Pike, his gun emptied, glared at him over the smoking revolver.

"You pesky galoot!" he said. "I guess that lets you out! You beat it! You head for that shebang, and hunt cover, and I guess I give you till I get this gun loaded! Absquatulate, you geek! Hoof it, you gink! Get going, you doggoned big stiff!"

Loder leaped to his feet.

He forgot vengeance on Putnam van Duck. He forgot everything but that terrifying gun. He ran for the House.

Loder was not a first-class man on the cinder-path, but he ran now as no fellow had ever run for the School 100 yards. His feet scarcely touched the ground. He flew.

A roar of laughter followed him.

"Ha, ha, ha!" yelled the juniors.

"Put it on, Loder!" roared Coker of the Fifth.

"Hook it, Loder!" howled Vernon-Smith.

"Ha, ha, ha!"

It did not take Mr. Pike long to reload a six-gun. But he had no further use for that gun. Loder beat him to it. Before Mr. Pike was ready to resume "fanning," Loder reached the House steps.

He went up those steps with the bound of a kangaroo. He bolted into the House, like a scared rabbit into a burrow.

He had no time to look where he was going. He neither knew nor cared what might be in front of him. What was behind him was enough for Loder to think about.

Had he reflected, he might have guessed that the Head would be hurrying out to intervene in that amazing and alarming scene in the quadrangle. But he had no time to reflect.

He bounded headlong into the House, just as Dr. Locke, in hot haste, reached the doorway. There they met!

It was a sudden and unexpected meeting on both sides.

Loder, when he had crashed into Mr. Pike in the quad, had broken like a wave on a rock. He had better luck crashing into the Head! The headmaster did not stand rock-like, in Poker's style. The Head went backwards, spinning.

Loder, halted by the shock, stood spluttering. Dr. Locke lay extended, gazing up at him, wondering if it was an earthquake, or whether Greyfriars School had fallen in on him.

"Oh!" gasped Loder.

"Ooooooogh!" said the Head faintly. "Woooogh!"

Other masters were speeding doorward. Mr. Quelch and Mr. Prout rushed to the overturned headmaster. Mr. Capper and Mr. Wiggins, Mr. Hacker and M. Charpentier, followed them fast. There were plenty of helping hands for the Head! He needed them. He was quite winded.

"You clumsy young rascal!" Prout hooted over a plump shoulder at Loder.

"Loder! How dare you!" gasped Mr. Quelch.

"I—I—I——" stammered Loder helplessly.

Sympathetic hands lifted the headmaster. They stood him on his feet. He stood unsteadily, supported by Quelch and Prout—Capper, Wiggins, and Mossoo hovering round with anxious sympathetic murmurs.

"Urrrggh!" was the Head's first remark.

"My dear sir——" exclaimed Mr. Quelch.

"Grooogh!"

"My dear Dr. Locke——" gasped Prout.

"Urrgh! Loder! You—you—you—you clumsy, stupid, reckless—urrrgh!"

"I—I——" stuttered Loder.

There was a yell at the doorway. It was the voice of Herbert Vernon-Smith, the Bounder of Greyfriars.

"Look out, Loder! He's coming!"

"Ha, ha, ha!"

It was a false alarm. Poker Pike was not coming! But it was enough for Loder of the Sixth! He bounded away—shouldering M. Charpentier as he passed in his haste, and sending the little French master tottering.

"Ciel!" squeaked Mossoo. "Mon Dieu! Je crois—urrggh!" He clutched at Mr. Hacker to save himself, and caught the master of the Shell round the neck. They staggered together.

Loder did not heed. He bounded on, reached his study, slammed the door after bounding in, and turned the key in the lock.

Not satisfied with that, he dragged the study table to the door, and backed it up with the armchair. Then, feeling a little safer, he had time to gurgle for his second wind.

Dr. Locke did not proceed into the quadrangle. He was in no state to deal with Poker Pike! Had the Chicago gunman loosed off a whole battery of machine-guns, the Head would hardly have heeded in his present winded state.

He tottered back to his study between Quelch and Prout, sympathetically supported on either side. And for quite a long time afterwards the Head seemed to be imitating the young man of Hythe who was shaved with a scythe and did nothing but wriggle and writhe!

In the quad, Poker Pike packed his gun and resumed his sedate pacing. He seemed to regard that trifling incident as over and done with.

The Greyfriars fellows, rocking with laughter, did not take the same view. Fanning a guy with bullets was O.K. in Chicago, no doubt; but it was wildly out of place in a school quad—and everybody but Poker Pike guessed that something was coming to the Greyfriars gunman!

"Well, you know these schoolmasters!" said Coker disparagingly. "They think they know everything. I don't suppose for a moment that Dr. Locke would listen to advice from a Fifth Form man—even me! Fatheaded, if you like, but there it is."

"Oh!" gasped Potter and Greene.

"That man Pike," went on Coker, "has got to have a lesson. Having him here is all rot. I don't suppose that young ass, Van Duck of the Remove, is really in any danger from kidnappers—and I don't see that it matters, anyhow. He cheeked me, I know that; and I know that that man Pike ducked me in the fountain for whopping him I'd have mopped up the school with him, only the actual fact is, you fellows, I can't handle him."

Coker made this statement as if he expected it to surprise his friends very much.

Putnam van Duck came like a bullet. He flew down the banisters, and flew off the end—and failed to jump clear, because Gerald Loder was in the way! Crash! It seemed to the Sixth Former that a battering-ram had hit him. "Oooooh!" gasped Van Duck. "Urrrggh!" moaned Loder.

But they were well aware that even the beefy Horace could not have handled one half of Poker Pike—or even one-quarter! Still, it was rather surprising that Coker could see that obvious fact! Coker's usual idea was that he could handle anybody, and that it was only his good nature that kept him from being a regular terror.

"I've tried," said Coker, "and he pitched me about like a bundle of rags. You know what happened on the river the other day. He floored me easily. As for you fellows, you knew better than to try tackling him at all. He can handle me as easily as I could handle either of you chaps!"

Potter and Greene looked at Coker. They were not so sure that Horace Coker could handle them so frightfully easily!

"Thrashing the rotter," went on Coker, "is what I'd like: but what's the good of thinking of it when it can't be done? There are more ways of killing a cat than choking it with cream. That man's made himself dashed unpleasant—well, I'm going to try to be a bit unpleasant, too!"

Coker's friends thought that he would not have to try very hard to effect that result!

"Easy as falling off a form!" repeated Coker. "He ducked me in the fountain. I'm going to duck him—only more so—see? He ducked me in water—I'm going to duck him in ink!"

"Eh!" ejaculated Potter.

"What?" stuttered Greene.

"I've got it all cut and dried," said Coker. "Just listen! That blighter Pike has his quarters in Gosling's lodge. I fancy the Head's idea was to keep him as far away from the House as possible.

THE FOURTH CHAPTER.

Coker Knows How!

"EASY as falling off a form!" said Coker of the Fifth.

Potter and Greene looked doubtful.

"I mean, of course, if you do exactly as I tell you, and don't start thinking for yourselves!" added Coker.

This made Potter and Greene look still more doubtful. Horace Coker of the Greyfriars Fifth had unbounded confidence in himself. His friends had less! In fact, much less—if any!

"I suppose," said Coker, with a touch of sarcasm, "that Fifth Form men aren't going to take cheek and dashed impudence from a ruffian out of a Chicago slum, and smile! That cheeky ruffian has got to be put in his place! The Head ought not to allow him here. I've told you that before."

"Why not tell the Head?" suggested Potter, with a private wink at Greene.

There's a side-door at the porter's lodge, as I dare say you know, that opens into his room—that's the door he uses! There's a porch, with a roof, over that door; and what about you sitting on top of that porch, Potter——"

"Eh?"

"With a big can of ink——"

"What?"

"And mopping it over his head——"

"Oh crikey!"

"Or Greene could do it!" said Coker. "Either of you could do it all right. You haven't much gumption; but any fool can do a thing, if he's careful to carry out instructions. You see that?"

"Oh!" said Potter and Greene together.

"I've got all ready for it," continued Coker. "I've collected a lot of ink, and parked it in a tin pail, in those rhododendrons near Gosling's lodge. I got it all ready before lock-up. All that remains is to carry out the wheeze. Either of you—I don't mind which!"

Coker did not mind which; it was immaterial to him. But Potter and Greene looked as if they minded very much.

"I say, hadn't we better get along to the games study?" asked Greene uneasily.

Prep was over in the Fifth, and Potter and Greene would have gone already had not Coker kept them while he used his chin.

"Yes, come on," said Potter. "Blundell's got something to say about the cricket, and we don't want to miss it. See you later, Coker."

"Don't go!" said Coker calmly. "I've not finished yet."

"But——"

"And don't jaw! I've thought all this out," went on Coker, heedless of his friends' longing glances at the door. "After dark, that man Pike goes rooting all over the shop—keeping tabs, as he calls it, in his wierd lingo. He fancies the kidnappers are coming after that young Yankee in the Remove at all hours of the day and night. Beaks are always running into him when they take their trots in the quad of an evening. And——"

"It's after lock-up, Coker!" Potter pointed out. "Of course, I—I'd like no end to sit on top of that porch with a can of ink! Just the thing I'd really enjoy doing! Hem! But as we're not allowed out of the House after lock-up——"

"We can get out all right!" said Coker.

"I say, there'd be a row——"

"I'm not suggesting that you should call on Prout and tell him what we're up to!" said Coker sarcastically. "Keep it dark, of course. Now, have you got it clear? That ruffian Pike will be rooting about the House and the quad as usual to-night; but sooner or later, of course, he will go indoors. That's where you get him, Potter"

"Do I?" murmured Potter.

He seemed to doubt it.

"Only Pike uses that side door at the porter's lodge. No chance of making a mistake in the dark I know you'd make a mistake if you could; but it's safe as houses! Sitting on top of that porch, you mop the pail of ink over him as soon as you hear him coming—see?"

Potter and Greene was silent. It was clear that Coker had been thinking this out with deep cunning!

He had it all cut and dried! Really, it looked good. Still, they did not seem keen on it. Breaking House bounds did not appeal to Coker's friends as much as it did to Coker. Also, even if the pail of ink was successfully mopped over the objectionable Mr. Pike, there was some doubt as to what might happen afterwards. Coker did not seem to have thought of that. Potter and Greene thought of it.

"Got it clear?" asked Coker. "Mind, this is only a beginning; we're going to keep on ragging that ruffian Pike till he gets fed-up and gets out of the school. I'd rather thrash him, as I've said. But I'm hardly up to his weight. Ragging him is the idea! We're going to rag him right out of Greyfriars—and this is the start."

"Um!" said Potter and Greene.

They did not like Mr. Pike. They had had one sample of his heavy hand, and hadn't liked it at all! Ragging him out of Greyfriars struck them as quite a desirable sort of thing, and they were prepared to stand round and cheer while somebody else got on with it. But they were not prepared to rag him personally—especially after what had happened to Loder of the Sixth that afternoon!

Coker rose from the armchair. He seemed to have finished talking—which was a relief, as far as it went. But if action was to follow discussion, Potter and Greene really would have preferred Coker to go on talking.

"Come on!" said Coker.

He led his friends from the study.

Potter and Greene exchanged a glance. They did not want a row with Coker, and it was clear that there was going to be a row if they refused to back him up in this enterprise. Still more they did not want to enter into a hostile encounter with the Greyfriars gunman. It was a difficult position.

However, they followed Coker.

Blundell of the Fifth called to them as they passed the open door of the games study. Potter and Greene paused.

"Come on!" said Coker testily.

Potter and Greene suppressed their feelings and came on. They went downstairs, and Coker led them to the Fifth Form Room.

Form-rooms, of course, were deserted at that time, only an hour before dorm. They were supposed to be kept locked; but as Prout always forgot to lock his Form-room, that was all right.

Coker tramped in, followed by Potter and Greene. He closed the door, and led them across to the window.

The May night was fine, but dark. There was no moon, and hardly a star in the dark sky. Nothing could have been more favourable for Coker's enterprise.

It was important, of course, not to be seen! Breaking House bounds, by way of a window, meant lines, and probably detentions—as well as a lengthy jaw from Prout—worse than either detentions or lines. And ragging the man from Chicago was not an enterprise of which beaks would have been likely to approve!

But the quadrangle was dark and deserted. Unless Poker Pike was "rubbering" around, on the watch for kidnappers, there was nobody about.

Coker pushed up the window.

"Safe as houses!" he remarked. "I hope you've got it clear! You'll climb on the porch, Potter, and I'll hand the pail up to you. Greene and I are going to wait round the corner. We shall be ready to cover your retreat—you'll have to get away afterwards, you know. Quite likely that ruffian will be shirty, and will get after you."

Potter thought it probable!

"If he does we'll barge him over, see?" explained Coker. "You can leave that to me! Now, come on!"

Coker led the way. He clambered through the window, held on to the sill, and dropped. It was quite a short drop from the Form-room window to the ground. But Coker, of course, lost his footing, and tumbled over.

Bump!

"Ooooh!" gasped Coker.

There was a faint chuckle from within the open window. Then there was a faint whisper. Then, if Coker could have heard it, there was a faint sound of tiptoe tread!

Horace Coker picked himself up. He grunted and stared up at the window. Potter and Greene were not following him out.

"Come on!" hissed Coker.

No reply. Coker breathed hard!

"Are you coming?" he yelped.

Still no reply! If Potter and Greene heard, they did not heed. Probably they did not hear—very probably, for they were already out of the Form-room and on their way to the games study.

"Potter!" hissed Coker. "Deaf? Greene!"

Coker could not venture to shout to them. A shout would have been heard by other ears; and even Coker realised that it would be injudicious to draw general attention to the fact that he was outside the House after lock-up. He breathed wrath.

"Are you silly idiots deaf?" he hissed. "Are you coming? Can't you hear me? How long are you going to keep me waiting? You blithering idiots—you silly asses—you potty chumps—you frabjous, footling fatheads—are you coming, or are you not coming?"

Evidently the answer was "not." There was no answer, and they did not come. Coker, at last, grabbed the sill again, lifted himself, and glared into the dark interior of the Form-room. He was quite perplexed.

"Are you there?" he breathed.

Stony silence! Potter and Greene were not there!

Slowly it dawned on Coker's powerful brain that they had only waited for him to give them a chance to cut off, and leave him on his lonely own! If Coker was keen to carry on with his remarkable scheme for making Mr. Pike tired of Greyfriars School as a residence, Coker had to play a lone hand! Either Coker, alone, unaided like Coriolanus of old, had to mop that pail of ink over Mr. Pike—or Mr. Pike had to be left to go on the even tenor of his way unmopped!

THE FIFTH CHAPTER.

Poker Pike Gets It in the Neck!

"OH!" gasped Billy Bunter.

Bunter was startled.

After prep that evening, most of the Remove fellows were gathered in the Rag. The chief topic there was the "fanning" of Loder of the Sixth in the quad that afternoon; and what the probable result was likely to be for Poker Pike.

Putnam van Duck was worried. It was true that he was fed-up to the back teeth with Poker and his watchfulness. He could hardly walk ten yards outside the House without finding Poker on his trail. Even inside the House the watchful gunman cropped up in all sorts of places, at all sorts of times, to give him the once-over, and make sure that he was still there!

Still, his popper, back in Chicago, was very keen on Poker keeping "tabs" on him; and after what had happened, it looked as if Poker might be politely, but firmly, requested to depart from Greyfriars.

Personally, Putnam would not have mourned to see the last of his gunman guardian. But he knew that Chick Chew, the star kidnapper of the United States, was likely to get busy if Poker went—and he did not want his popper to be alarmed for his safety. So Putnam was worried.

Billy Bunter happened to blink out of the window. That blink was followed by his startled gasp.

Flattened on the window-pane was a human face!

Really, it was startling!

Billy Bunter blinked at that face at the window, his little round eyes almost popping through his big round spectacles.

"Oh!" he gasped. "Ooogh! I say, you fellows—— Oh crikey!"

A dozen fellows looked round.

"What the dickens!" exclaimed Vernon-Smith, in astonishment, as he spotted the face at the window. "Who the thump——"

"I say, you fellows, is it a burglar?" gasped Bunter.

"Fathead!"

The Bounder ran to the window and threw up the sash. A hickory face, under a bowler hat, looked in!

"Pike!" ejaculated Vernon-Smith.

"Sure!" assented Poker. The bowler hat gave a nod.

"You silly idiot!" yelled Bunter. "What the thump do you mean, making a fellow jump out of his skin?"

Mr. Pike did not answer that question. The window being open, he put his bullet head and his bowler hat inside, and his slits of eyes scanned the interior of the room.

There was a chuckle from the juniors. It was only Mr. Pike's watchfulness! He was dutifully keeping tabs on Putnam van Duck; and giving the Rag the once-over, no doubt with a lingering misgiving that the millionaire's son might have been spirited away since he had last seen him.

"Say, you guys, where's that Putnam van Duck?" inquired Mr. Pike.

Van Duck was seated in an armchair which had its back towards the window. He was, therefore, invisible to his gunman guardian's anxious eyes.

"You howling ass!" exclaimed the Bounder. "Do you think the kidnapper has come down the study chimney after him?"

"I wouldn't put it past him!" answered Poker.

"Ha, ha, ha!"

"Say, is that young guy around?" demanded Poker.

Putnam van Duck grinned and sat where he was. He was tired of Poker and his once-overs. Once-over was not so bad; but the twice-over, and the thrice-over, and the dozen times over, got on his nervous system. He sat tight and left Mr. Pike to go on inquiring.

The hickory brow puckered anxiously under the brim of the bowler hat.

"Say, put me wise!" snapped Poker Pike. "If that young guy ain't around, I guess I got to get on his trail! I'll mention that I ain't setting around while Chick Chew gets away with that Putnam van Duck! Surest thing you know."

"Van Duck's all right, Mr. Pike!" said Harry Wharton, laughing.

"The rightfulness is terrific, my esteemed and idiotic Poker!" chuckled Hurree Jamset Ram Singh.

"Says you!" retorted Mr. Pike. "I guess I want to see that baby! Yep! I sure do want to give him the once-over."

Leaning his elbows on the window-sill, Poker Pike pushed his head and his bowler hat farther in to survey the room.

Herbert Vernon-Smith grinned, stepped closer to the window, and suddenly jerked down the sash.

Mr. Pike gave a convulsive bound as it shut on the back of his neck.

There was a shriek of laughter from the juniors.

"Ha, ha, ha!"

"Yurrrooop!" gasped Mr. Pike. He felt, for a moment, as if he had been guillotined. He wriggled wildly.

Had Mr. Pike's hands been inside, the Bounder would have had reason to regret playing that little trick. But Mr. Pike's hands were outside. Only his head was inside, the rest of him barred off by the shut sash.

He heaved frantically; but he could not raise the sash with the back of his neck. Poker Pike was a prisoner!

"Let up, you young geek!" he roared. "Say, you pesky gink, you going to let up on a guy?"

"Not so's you'd notice it!" said the Bounder, answering Mr. Pike in his own language. "I guess I got you, Poker Pike; and I'll say you're cinched a few, and then some."

"Ha, ha, ha!"

"He, he, he!" cackled Billy Bunter. "I say, you fellows, have that hat off him! Nobody's ever seen it off!"

"Ha, ha, ha!"

Poker wriggled wildly. But the Bounder kept a hand on the sash, and the gunman, hefty as he was, had no chance.

Billy Bunter rolled up to him—undaunted by Mr. Pike's infuriated glare. So long as Mr. Pike's hands were outside the window, Bunter was bold as a lion.

He jerked the bowler hat off Poker's head. A well-oiled crop was revealed, glistening in the light.

Bunter waved the hat in the air.

"I say, you fellows, it comes off!" he squeaked.

"Ha, ha, ha!"

Really, it might have been doubted whether Poker Pike's hat did come off; he was never seen to remove it, and fellows had almost wondered whether it grew on his head! But it was off now! It was not, after all, a permanent fixture; evidently it was at least semi-detached!

"Pass!" yelled Peter Todd.

Billy Bunter tossed the bowler hat into the air. Skinner caught it with his foot as it came down, and "passed" to Peter, who passed in turn to Bob Cherry.

There was a scramble after the hat! It passed from foot to foot, all over the Rag, amid howls of laughter.

Poker Pike spluttered with wrath.

Outside the window his legs thrashed wildly. His wild wriggling gave him quite a pain in the back of his bull-neck. But he could not wriggle loose. He was held fast by the jammed sash, and he could only splutter and gurgle and gasp, as he watched the juniors playing football with his hat.

Up and down and round about the Rag went that hat, passed from foot to foot. It showed signs of damage after a time.

"Say, you ginks, will you let up on that hat?" shrieked Poker Pike. "I'm telling you to let up!"

"Pass!" roared Squiff.

"On the ball!" shouted Hazeldene.

"Ha, ha, ha!"

"Gee!" chuckled Putnam van Duck. "I'll say this is the bee's knee! I'll tell a man it's the grasshopper's side-whiskers, and then some."

"You Putnam van Duck!" roared Poker, as the American junior, rising from the armchair, came into his view. "You young scallawag, you get a cinch on this winder, and let a guy out!"

"Forget it, Poker!" answered Putnam cheerfully. "You poked your cabeza in where it wasn't wanted, and you can sure park it there."

"You doggoned young geek!" hooted Poker.

"Pass that hat!" roared Bob Cherry.

"Ha, ha, ha!"

Poker Pike could only wriggle in wrath. Generally he was a "guy" who could take care of himself, and a little over; but this time he had got it in the neck—right in the neck! Amid roars of laughter the game of football went on, with Poker's hat, which was getting more and more damaged, and every moment looked less and less like a hat.

THE SIXTH CHAPTER.

Splash!

HORACE COKER breathed wrath and indignation as he peered into the deserted Fifth Form Room from the dusky quad. Slowly he dropped back from the sill, a deep frown corrugating his rugged brow. Potter and Greene had let him down. And Coker was inclined to go after them, tell them what he thought of them, and follow it up with knocking their heads together.

But that, though satisfactory in its way, would not have helped on his campaign against the Greyfriars gunman. And Coker, angry and indignant as he was, kept to the matter in hand. Leaving the House behind him, Coker scuttled away across the quad.

He had been left to carry on alone; and Coker was not the man to turn back when he had set his hand to the plough. He was going to carry on.

Once away from the lighted windows, it was very dark in the quad. From the direction of the Rag, the room where the juniors most did congregate, Coker heard sounds of merriment as he went—some sort of shindy seemed to be going on among the fags. But he did not heed it. Fags were miles, if not leagues, beneath Coker's lofty notice.

He reached Gosling's lodge.

A light burned in the ancient porter's window, and he had a glimpse of William Gosling inside through the curtain.

Passing on round the little building, Coker cautiously annexed the pail of ink he had left concealed in the shrubbery.

It was a small size in pails, but it held quite a lot of ink. There was a good gallon in it. Coker had plenty of money, which he spent lavishly on anything that took his fancy. This time, it appeared, his fancy had run to ink.

Pail in hand, he approached the side door of the lodge, with redoubled caution. There was no light in Mr. Pike's room there. That looked as if he was out of doors.

He was, as a matter of fact, or, to be exact, his head was indoors, and the rest of him out of doors. All of him, at any rate, was at a good distance from his quarters.

This suited Coker. Had Mr. Pike been in, Coker would have had to wait for him to come out; and he mightn't have come out. As he was out, it was certain that he would go in sooner or later. The sooner the better, once Coker was in a position to receive him.

Coker had no doubt that he had, as was his custom, gone round scouting—on the watch for kidnapping gangsters. Nobody else at Greyfriars supposed for a moment that Chick Chew and his gang would ever make any attempt on Putnam van Duck in the school. But Poker Pike took no chances. At any moment of the day and night his bullet head and his bowler hat were liable to pop up anywhere. Coker had observed the manners and customs of the gunman, and laid his plans accordingly.

Having satisfied himself that Poker was not at present on the spot, Coker of the Fifth stopped at the porch outside the side door.

That porch had a solid wooden roof, with a slight slant on it. Its sides were trellised and easy to climb.

A fellow posted on top of that porch had anyone who came to the door below at his mercy. It was as Coker had told his friends, as easy as falling off a form.

It was not easy to make even an easy climb, burdened with a pail of ink. Coker missed his friends now. His plan had been for one fellow to climb up, and another to hand up the pail, which was simple. It was not so simple to climb up carrying the pail.

Essaying to do so, Coker slipped, and there was a gush of ink from the tin pail. Coker breathed hard as he felt it splash his trousers.

It made them feel uncomfortably damp. And it wasted the ink. About a quart had splashed over Coker's trousers.

He set the pail on the ground and groped in his pocket, where he remembered he had some string. Had Coker intended to provide himself with string he would no doubt have forgotten to do so. But it happened to be there, and it came in useful.

He tied one end of the string to the handle of the pail. The other end he looped over his wrist.

Then he clambered on the porch.

This time it was easy. The darkness was deep, and Coker knocked his head once or twice on projections, and murmured things. But he landed safely on the roof of the porch.

Then, with great care, he pulled up the pail by means of the string. It banged twice on the trellis, shedding a splash of ink each time. About another quart was missing by the time Coker landed his fish.

Still, there was more than half a gallon remaining. Half a gallon of ink was a good amount to land on any man's head. Even a quart would have made anyone sit up and take notice. Half a gallon was enough to do the job fairly thoroughly.

Squatting on the porch, pail in hand, Coker waited and watched, and listened for footsteps. Watching was not of much use in the deep dark. He could see little or nothing. But he was certain to hear a footstep when it came. And nobody, of course, ever came to that door, excepting Mr. Pike. When Mr. Pike came, Coker was bound to hear him, and he was ready for him.

So far, he had been glad that the gunman was off the scene, giving him a chance to get through with his preparations. Now that he was ready, he waited impatiently.

It was less than an hour to dorm, and he had, of course, to be in the House at bed-time. Coker was a reckless ass, but certainly he did not want Mr. Prout to miss him when the Fifth Form went to roost.

When was the brute coming?

Already he had been absent some time. He might come back any minute. Coker, as the minutes passed, wished he would buck up.

He was, of course, quite unaware that Mr. Pike, in those moments, was unavoidably detained with a window-sash shut down on the back of his neck. Mr. Pike was unable to return to his quarters till the juniors were done with him; and they were not done with him yet. But Coker was in a state of blissful ignorance of what was going on in the Rag.

He waited, with intensifying impatience.

He was eager to get on with the good work. A lot of the fellows had declared that Poker Pike would get "booted" for his gun-play performance in the quad that afternoon. The Head was sure to come down heavy for it. That was all very well, but it was certain that he had not been booted yet. The Head, so far, seemed to have taken no steps. Coker was taking steps, and he was going to take more, too, keeping on with it till the obnoxious and obstreperous Poker had had enough.

"Blow the brute!" muttered Coker impatiently.

It was not a comfortable position, squatting on top of the porch. Ink was sticking his trousers to his legs. Coker was not enjoying this. But he was a sticker, and he stuck!

At last—at long last—there was a sound of footsteps.

Coker's eyes gleamed.

Someone was coming.

All he could see in the dark was a faint shadow as it moved. He waited. If it was old Gosling coming out of his lodge for something or other, he would pass on, and all well. If it was Poker Pike, he would come up to the side door; then there would be no mistake.

Coker listened intently.

The footsteps came directly to the side door of the lodge. Below him, as he peered down, a dim figure loomed in the dark—about to pass under the porch of the door.

That was Coker's moment!

The tin pail was lifted—and upended! Out from the pail shot, at one fell swoop, more than half a gallon of black ink!

It landed fairly on the head beneath Coker!

Splash!

There was a sudden gasp below.

"Urrrrrgghhh!"

Drenched, dripping, smothered with ink, the dim figure reeled, staggered, and sat down, with a bump.

Coker did not linger.

He had not thought much about consequences. But Coker, though he was not bright, was too bright to remain within hitting distance of a Chicago gunman after smothering him from head to foot with ink.

He made a bound from the top of the porch, landed on his feet, tumbled over headlong, picked himself up, and ran.

Behind him, as he ran, horrid sounds woke up the echoes of the night—sounds made by a man who seemed to have an impediment in his speech. Some of the ink, it seemed had gone into the recipient's mouth.

"Urggh! Hurrrggh! Gurrrrgggh!"

Coker grinned as he ran.

Almost in a twinkling he was back at the House, scrambling into the Fifth Form Room.

To shut the window, get out of the Form-room, and bolt, was the work of only a few seconds. Coker was safe back while his hapless victim was still gurgling horribly in the darkness at Gosling's lodge.

THE SEVENTH CHAPTER.

Horrid for the Head!

TO say the headmaster of Greyfriars School was astonished would be to put it mildly.

Astonished was not the word. Amazed—astounded—would be nearer the mark. Flabbergasted would perhaps express it better

Life is full of surprises. Unexpected things are always happening. No doubt Dr. Locke had had his share of life's surprises. But this one beat all the rest hollow—knocked them into a cocked hat.

Dr. Locke, indeed, hardly knew what was happening, at first, so utterly was he taken aback.

Gerald Loder made a spring at Poker Pike. before the gunman could draw his hands from his pockets, hitting out fiercely with both fists. Mr. Pike went over backwards, like an uprooted tree, and his feet flew in the air. "Yurrrooogh!" gasped the gunman, as he crashed.

Having thought the matter over and decided what he had to say to Mr. Pike, the headmaster had walked down to Gosling's lodge, to see Mr. Pike, and say it. Gun-play, to which Mr. Pike was so happily accustomed in his native Chicago, could not possibly be permitted at Greyfriars School, under any circumstances whatever. Either Mr. Pike had to give his faithful promise never to handle a firearm again within the walls of the school, or he had to go—and go at once. The Head intended to speak politely, but firmly—very firmly indeed.

Such were the thoughts in his majestic mind as he arrived at the side door of Gosling's lodge. But those thoughts—and, indeed, all thoughts—were driven out of his mind by what happened next. He was about to step into the porch to knock at the door when it happened.

It seemed, for an awful moment, as if the dark skies had opened their floodgates on him. Fluid of some sort splashed and poured down on him from above.

Taken quite off his balance, the Head stumbled back, and sat down, gurgling horribly.

Fluid—he did not realise for the moment that it was ink—streamed all over him. It drenched him. It smothered him. He dripped with it.

Coker, having spilt so much, had rather wondered whether there was enough left in the tin pail to give Mr. Pike a good drenching. He need not have had any misgivings on that point. There was enough—quite enough! It happened to be Dr. Locke, not Mr. Pike, who got it. But there was no doubt about the thoroughness of the drenching.

Sitting there in the dark, streaming ink, the Head gurgled. He saw and heard nothing of Coker's flying leap and flight. Ink was all over him; he was conscious only of ink. He lived and had his being in a world of ink.

"Hurrgggh! Gurrggh! Wurrggh! Mooooough!" gurgled and mumbled the amazed headmaster.

He sat and gasped, and gurgled. Slowly he gathered his startled wits. He staggered to his feet.

"Bless my soul!" he gasped. "What—what—who—what—— Bless my soul! It—it—it is—I think—ink! Urrrggh!"

He gazed round him almost wildly. It was not the floodgates of the sky that had unexpectedly opened on him. He had been drenched with ink! It was an outrage—an unprecedented outrage! Astonishment, flabbergasted amazement, began to turn to wrath.

Who had done this? It was long past lock-up. The Greyfriars fellows were all in the House. It could not have been one of them, even if it was imaginable for any Greyfriars fellow to play such a trick on his headmaster. Who could have done it?

"Bless my—gurrrgh—soul!" mumbled the Head. "The—the rascal! The ruffian! The—grooogh! Oogh! Who can have—ugh!— Who—ooogh!"

There was a sound of an opening door. Gosling, in his lodge, had heard something.

The Head staggered away, leaving a pool of ink on the ground, but taking more with him. He came into the light as Gosling opened his door and the illumination streamed forth.

"Who——" began Gosling. "What is——"

He broke off as he saw the Head, and gave a startled howl.

"Gosling——" gasped the Head, as he totteringly approached.

Gosling backed into his doorway.

"'Ere, you keep orf!" he roared. "Wot I says is this 'ere, you keep orf! Out of it, you blooming nigger!"

Gosling backed in and slammed the door. The astonished Head heard the sound of a shooting bolt.

He did not quite realise that, with black ink smothering his face, he was unrecognisable, and rather a startling object, to see suddenly in the dark.

Gosling bolted himself, and then bolted the door!

"Bub-bib-bless my soul!" gasped the Head.

He tottered to Gosling's door and knocked. He was in need of immediate help, and he did not in the least understand Gosling's strange actions.

"Gosling!" he called out. "Gosling!"

"You 'ook it!" came a howl from the porter within. "You 'ear me! Wot I says is this 'ere, you 'ook it or I'll telephone for the perlice!"

"Gosling——"

"'Elp!" roared Gosling, as the Head knocked again. "'Elp!"

"Gosling!" shrieked Dr. Locke. "It is I, the headmaster——"

"'Elp!" yelled Gosling. "There's a wild nigger! 'Elp!"

"Are you mad, Gosling? Or have you been drinking? It is not a negro—it is Dr. Locke——"

"'Elp!"

"Upon my word!" gasped Dr. Locke. "Gosling, I shall discharge you for this! Open your door at once, you stupid man!"

"'Elp!"

"Gosling——"

"'Elp!"

Dr. Locke turned away. There was no help from Gosling. Gosling seemed to want help himself—or, at least, "'elp!" The inky headmaster tottered away to the House.

He shed dripping ink as he went. He passed the lighted windows of the Rag and heard a roar of laughter from that apartment. Something was going on there. But he gave that no attention.

He tottered on.

"What—what—who——"

It was Mr. Prout's voice. The master of the Fifth was taking his usual stroll in the quad when he suddenly spotted the Head, in the gleam of light from many windows.

Prout jumped almost clear of the ground.

"Who—what——" he stuttered.

"Mr. Prout!" gasped the Head.

He approached the Fifth Form master, who backed away as swiftly as Gosling had done. There was no doorway at hand for the alarmed Fifth Form master to dodge into, but he backed promptly, waving fat hands at the inky headmaster, as if to wave him off, like a wasp.

"Keep your distance!" spluttered Prout. "Keep your distance! I will strike you—I will knock you down if you dare——"

"Prout!" shrieked the Head.

"Who are you?" thundered Prout. "How dare you enter these premises? Keep your distance! I am not afraid of a black ruffian! I will knock you down——"

"Prout! I am Dr. Locke——"

"Wha-a-t?" stuttered Prout.

"I have been smothered with ink——"

"Wha-a-t——"

"Mr. Prout——"

"Upon my word!" Prout recognised the voice at last, if he could not recognise the face. The face, indeed, was quite unrecognisable. "Is—is—is it indeed Dr. Locke? My dear sir, forgive me! I did not know—I did not dream—I fancied it was some dreadful negro—I—I—— Goodness gracious! Who has done this?"

Prout gazed at his chief in horror.

"I—I do not know!" said the Head feebly. "I saw no one. But—pray assist me to the House, my dear Prout. I—I—I——"

"An unparalleled outrage!" gasped Prout. He gave his chief a helping arm. "An absolutely unprecedented outrage! Pray allow me."

Prout navigated the tottering headmaster to the House. Five minutes later the news spread like wildfire.

Somebody had been ragging the Head! Somebody had been lying in wait for him at Gosling's lodge, and had mopped tons and tons of ink over him! The Head had been nearly drowned in ink!

Everybody buzzed with excitement! Two Fifth Form fellows in the games study looked at one another with almost ghastly faces when they heard. Potter and Greene remembered Coker! They gazed at one another in mute horror. But everybody else buzzed. Such a happening was, as Prout had justly said, unparalleled and unprecedented. Greyfriars School fairly thrilled with the startling news.

THE EIGHTH CHAPTER.
Who?

"STOP that row!"

That was Coker all over.

Sixth Form prefects might have noticed that an unusual uproar was going on in the Rag, and barged in to quell the tumult. They might have brought ashplants along, and handed out swipes from the same.

But no Fifth Form man had any right whatever in the junior quarters. No fellow who was not a prefect had any right to interfere, though the juniors had been making as terrific and discordant a din as the jazziest of jazz bands on the radio. And it was not so bad as that!

Certainly there was plenty of noise. Twenty fellows could not play football with a hat indoors without making a noise. Chairs went over—a table rocked—fellows slipped and stumbled and bumped—they shouted, and they cheered. No doubt a prefect would have looked in sooner or later. But, as it happened, it was Coker who looked in.

When Coker of the Fifth threw open the door of the Rag, and looked in, and told the Remove to "stop that row," the Remove stopped it. Not that they were in the least disposed to obey orders from Coker of the Fifth. But his cheek in barging in, and giving them orders, called for prompt treatment.

Poker Pike's hat had been reduced to a state of ruin. The next item on the programme was to reduce Coker of the Fifth to the same state.

Twenty or more glares were turned on the Fifth Former. Heedless of glares, Coker stepped into the Rag, frowning.

"You noisy young sweeps!" he snapped. "Do you know you can be heard all over Greyfriars? Stop it, see?"

"You cheeky ass!" roared Johnny Bull. "What are you butting in here for? Collar him!"

"Bag him!" shouted Bob Cherry.

"Scrag him!" yelled Vernon-Smith.

There was a general move towards Coker. The remains of Poker's hat lay unheeded on the floor.

"Say, you young ginks, you letting up on a guy?" yelled Poker, with another frantic squirm, under the shut sash.

Coker jumped.

He stared across the Rag at the window, and nearly fell down at the sight of the gunman's red and furious face, and his bullet head, pinned down by the window-sash on the back of his neck.

Coker could not believe his eyes.

Hardly five minutes ago he had drenched and smothered that bullet head with ink at Gosling's lodge—or, at any rate, he believed that he had.

Yet here was the bullet head jammed in the window of the Rag, without a sign or a spot of ink on it.

The ghost of Poker Pike could not have startled Coker more than Poker did in the flesh, at that moment.

"Why, what—what——" gasped Coker. "Who—who—who is that? Is—is—is that—that—that—that man Pike?"

Harry Wharton & Co., about to hurl themselves at Coker, and give him what he was asking for, stopped, in sheer surprise.

"Is—is—is that Pike?" gasped Coker blanking.

"Don't you know him when you see him, fathead?" asked Harry Wharton. "Do you think it's his ghost, ass?"

"Has—has he been there long?" gasped Coker. Coker was not quick on the uptake; but it was dawning on him that it could not have been Poker Pike who had got the ink.

Getting rid of that ink would have taken time. Whoever had got that ink had a good hour's washing before him, at least. And there was not a spot on Poker.

"About half an hour!" answered Harry.

"Oh crikey!" gasped Coker.

That settled it! If Poker Pike had been jammed in the window of the Rag for half an hour, or half that period of time, evidently Poker Pike had been nowhere near Gosling's lodge when Coker mopped the ink!

Somebody had got it! Who? Somebody, it was certain. Coker had heard that somebody's horrid gurgles as he fled. Who?

"Say, you pesky young guys," roared Poker Pike, "I'm telling you to let up on a guy, or I sure will beat you up a few!"

Coker stood goggling at him.

He might have stood goggling at him for quite a long time, petrified with astonishment. But he was interrupted.

The Removites interrupted him.

They interrupted him by collaring him on all sides, and Coker was up-ended on the floor of the Rag.

He roared as he smote the floor, and the mystery of the ink was banished, for the moment, from his mind. He had nearer and more pressing matters to think of now.

"You cheeky little ticks!" howled Coker, struggling in many hands. "Leggo! I'll wallop the lot of you!"

"Roll him over!" yelled Skinner.

"Bump him!"

"I say, you fellows, lemme get at him! Give a fellow a chance!" squeaked Billy Bunter.

"Scrag him!"

"Ha, ha, ha!"

Nearly every fellow in the Rag lent a hand! If Coker of the Fifth fancied that he had the authority of a prefect, and could give orders to the Remove, they were the fellows to undeceive him on that point. They did so—promptly, drastically, and effectually.

Coker rolled and roared.

Putnam van Duck picked up the wreck of his gunman guardian's hat. He went to the window with it and jammed it on Poker's bullet head, grinning cheerily at the exasperated Poker.

"I guess you can beat it, Poker!" he remarked. "I'll say we're through with you, big boy. You keep your cabeza parked in your own shebang, see? Don't you put it in here any more."

"You pesky young geck!" gasped Poker. "You ornery, dog-goned, pie-faced, slab-sided young mugwump——"

"That'll be enough!" said Putnam. "You beat it, old-timer." He shoved up the sash, and Poker Pike was able to get his head out at last. Poker had a severe crick in the neck by that time.

"I guess——" began Poker sulphurously; but Putnam slammed the window shut, and cut short the flow of his remarks.

Then he joined the Removites, and lent a hand with Coker.

Coker of the Fifth was going through quite an exciting time. It was being impressed upon him that it was injudicious to butt into the Rag and issue commands to the juniors there.

"Roll him over!"

"Bump him!"

"Scrag him!"

"Sit on his head!"

"Gurrrggh!" gurgled Coker.

Wingate of the Sixth looked in at the open doorway of the Rag. His arrival was fortunate for Coker. Coker's state was rapidly approximating to that of Poker Pike's hat!

"Stop that!" called out the captain of Greyfriars sharply.

"'Ware prefects!" exclaimed Skinner.

"All right, Wingate!" gasped Harry Wharton. "Only giving Coker what he came in specially to ask for!"

"Stop that row at once, you young sweeps!"

"Well, perhaps Coker's had enough," remarked Bob.

"Urrrggh!"

Coker staggered up as the Removites released him. He looked as if he had had enough. He felt as if he had had too much.

"What the thump are you rowing here with the fags for, Coker?" asked the Greyfriars captain testily. "Clear off, you ass!"

"Urrrggh!"

Coker tottered to the door. Wingate frowned at him as he went.

The Removites eyed the head prefect of Greyfriars rather uneasily. They realised that there had, as a matter of fact, been rather an uncommon uproar in the Rag, first with Poker Pike's hat as a football, and then with Coker of the Fifth.

But it was not on that account, as they soon learned, that Wingate had looked in. As Coker tottered away, the Greyfriars captain fixed a stern and searching look on the mob of juniors.

"Any of you young rascals been out of the House?" he demanded.

"Not since lock-up, of course," answered Harry.

"Oh, of course!" said Wingate sarcastically. "I'm quite aware that no fellow of the Remove would dream of such a thing!"

"Honest Injun!" said the captain of the Remove. "Has anything happened out of the House, Wingate?"

"Yes!" grunted Wingate. "Something jolly serious has happened! Somebody has been ragging the Head."

There was a general jump.

"Ragging the Head!" gasped Wharton.

The idea of "ragging" the Head, or even of thinking of such a proceeding, rather took the juniors' breath away. It was an unthinkable thing.

"Some mad ass seems to have waited for him at Gosling's lodge, and mopped a can of ink over him!" said Wingate. "Goodness knows who—some young lunatic, anyhow! Nobody here been out of the House?"

"Nobody!" answered Harry.

"No fear!" said Bob.

"We've been rather busy here for some time, Wingate!" drawled the Bounder, and there was a chuckle.

"Well, whoever did it is booked for the sack!" growled Wingate.

And he turned and left the Rag, leaving the Removites in a buzz of surprise and excitement.

THE NINTH CHAPTER.

Keep It Dark!

"URRRRRGGGH!"

That sound of gasping was audible in Coker's study as Potter and Greene arrived.

Coker had gone up to his study after leaving the Rag. He felt that he needed a rest. He collapsed into his armchair, and gasped and gurgled for breath. In that winded and breathless state, Coker was fully occupied with his own little troubles, and he remained, so far, unaware of the thrilling news with which the whole House was buzzing.

Potter and Greene looked in.

"Oh, here he is!" said Potter.

They came into the study, gazing at Coker. Coker gazed back at them. He noticed the horror in their faces, but had no idea of its cause.

"Been in a row?" asked Greene.

Coker looked as if he had been in a row. He was dusty all over, his tie was gone, and his collar hung under one ear. His hair was like a mop.

"Yes!" gasped Coker. "Those cheeky young scoundrels—— Ooogh! Didn't you fellows hear that fearful row in the Rag? Ooogh!"

"There's always a row in the Rag," said Greene. "Have you been rowing with the fags?"

"Urrgh! I looked in to tell them to stop that din!" gasped Coker. "They set on me—urrggh—ragged me—ragged a Fifth Form man, you know! Pretty state of things Greyfriars is coming to! Oooogh! Quelch doesn't whop those scoundrels enough! I've a jolly good mind to tell him so! Ugggh!"

Potter and Greene exchanged a glance.

Having seen Coker started on his expedition to Gosling's lodge, they had been absolutely horrified when they heard what had happened to the Head. They could not doubt that Coker had got the wrong man in the dark. But the discovery that he had been scrapping with juniors in the Rag gave them a ray of hope.

"So you've been in the Rag?" exclaimed Potter.

"Urrgh! Yes! Wurrgh!"

"Thank goodness!" said Greene. "Then you never went to Gosling's lodge, after all! Thank goodness!"

"Eh—of course I did!"

"You did?" exclaimed Potter and Greene together.

"Of course I did!" grunted Coker. "I went into the Rag after I came back. What are you goggling at, you dummies? You know I was going. You let me down like rotters!"

Potter and Greene stared at him. That ray of hope vanished. Coker had, after all, carried on! So there was no doubt about what had happened!

"You let me down!" repeated Coker. "And a pretty muck you've made of the thing, too! I never got that brute Pike, after all!"

"Oh, you awful ass!" groaned Potter.

"I can't quite make it out," said Coker. "It puzzles me. You see, I had it all cut and dried. Nobody ever goes to that door except that man Pike. Well, when somebody came to the door, what was I to think?"

He glared at his dismayed chums.

"All your fault, of course! If you'd been with me, it wouldn't have happenned! Letting a fellow down! I thought I had him; but when I went to the Rag to stop that thundering row, there he was—those young sweeps had him there, with his head jammed in the window—Pike, you know! You could have knocked me down with a feather when I saw him! Up to that minute I thought he'd had the ink! Somebody had it!"

"S-s-somebody!" groaned Greene.

"Yes." Coker nodded. "Somebody had it—Gosling, perhaps——"

"Gig-gig-Gosling?"

"Well, I can't make it out, but I don't see who else it could have been," said Coker. "Gosling was in his lodge when I got there. I saw him through the curtain. He may have come round to Pike's door to speak to him. I don't see why he should, and, of course, I never expected anything of the kind. But somebody did——"

"Oh dear!" moaned Potter.

"Whoever it was, he got the ink right on his topknot!" said Coker. "Serve him jolly well right for barging in where he wasn't wanted, if you come to that! I suppose it was that old ass Gosling. If it wasn't, I just can't make out who it was. But it wasn't Pike! You see, it couldn't have been, as those fags had him stuck in that window all the time!"

"No!" gasped Greene. "It wasn't Pike! Oh lor'!"

"Oh, you mad ass!" moaned Potter.

"Don't be a dummy, Potter! It was all your fault! I couldn't see who it was, of course—I'm not a cat to see in the dark! If you fellows had been there, helping a chap——"

"You don't know who it was yet?" gasped Greene.

Coker shook his head.

"No—unless it was Gosling. Can't make it out! Nobody ever goes to that door except Pike. I suppose somebody had to see him this evening—goodness knows who! I hope it wasn't a master!"

Coker started a little as that idea came into his mind.

"You—you—you hope it wasn't a master!" stuttered Potter.

"Well, that would mean a fearful row!" said Coker. "But it can't have been, of course. Old Prout may have been prowling in the quad, but he wouldn't have any reason for going to see Pike——"

"The Head had a reason!" groaned Potter.

"The Head?"

"I dare say he was going to see him about that row this afternoon when he played the goat with Loder of the Sixth. Anyhow, he went."

"The Head?" repeated Coker mechanically.

"The Head!" said Potter and Greene.

Coker gazed at them. He forgot his bumps and bruises, his shortage of breath—he forgot everything in the overwhelming horror of that communication.

"The Head?" he breathed. "You—you mean to say—you—you mim-mim-mean to s-s-s-say that—— Oh crikey!"

"The whole House is buzzing with it!" said Potter. "Can't make out why you haven't heard—too busy playing the fool with the fags, I suppose! They're searching all over the place for a fellow who's been out of the House since lock-up."

"Oh crumbs!"

"The Head got it!" groaned Greene. "It's the sack, of course! They're looking for a man to sack!"

"Oh crikey!"

"Prout found the Big Beak tottering about in the quad, smothered with ink; took him for a nigger at first, I hear, and——"

"Oh scissors!"

Coker sat, petrified with horror.

The dreadful seriousness of the situation was borne in, even on Horace Coker's almost impenetrable intellect. He had drenched his headmaster with ink! It was Dr. Locke's majestic napper that had received the contents of the tin pail! Horror held Coker spellbound!

A rag on the headmaster was not only awfully bad form, it was awfully dangerous; it meant the "sack." And this was no common rag; it was the limit in rags—the very outside edge. A pail of ink on the headmaster!

Coker sat almost stunned.

Potter and Greene could only gaze at him. Their looks showed that they took it for granted that Coker was done for; he was as good as bunked already!

Coker found his voice at last.

"It was a mistake, of course! How could I know the Head was going there? I can't see in the dark. I say, sure it was the Head?"

"Sort of! It's all over the House."

"I—I wonder if—if the Head would understand that—that it was a—a—a mistake if—if a fellow explained——" said Coker haltingly. "It—it's the sort of mistake any fellow might make, you know, in the dark——"

Coker's voice trailed away. He realised that, mistake as it was, it was the kind of mistake a fellow was expected not to make.

And he could not even explain the mistake without admitting that he had been out of House bounds after lock-up, lying in wait for Mr. Pike with a pail of ink. That was not the sort of admission a fellow could make to a headmaster—especially a headmaster whom he had swamped with ink!

"This has got to be kept dark," said Coker at last. "Don't you fellows gabble."

"Kept dark!" repeated Potter. "I can see it being kept dark! The whole House——"

"Don't jaw!" Coker was recovering a little. "Nobody knows that I was out of the House. It was rather lucky Wingate finding me in the Rag when he did; it was very soon afterwards, and—and it's a sort of alibi really. He didn't know I'd only just got there."

"Well——" said Greene.

"Don't gabble!" said Coker. "It's all right! Nobody's likely to fancy that a Fifth Form man would do such a rotten thing as to rag his headmaster. Taking it for a rag on the Head, they'll never think of the Fifth. See?"

"I—I suppose there's a chance——" said Potter.

"Don't you fellows jaw, that's all!" said Coker. "Keep it dark!"

"If you're going to try to keep it dark," said Greene, with sarcasm, "you'd better go and change your bags. You look as if you'd been swimming in ink."

"All your fault!" said Coker. "If you'd been there to hand up the pail——"

"If they find a fellow with ink on him——" said Potter.

"I know that as well as you do, Potter—better!" Coker jumped out of the armchair. "I'll cut off to the dorm and change. Don't you fellows say a word. You know what you're like for gabbling——"

"Look here——"

"Don't jaw! And don't gabble!" Coker went to the door; at the door he turned back and added impressively: "Mind you don't gabble!"

Then he departed. When the Fifth Form went to their dormitory a little later Coker was in spotless trousers—and the inky pair were safely hidden from sight at the bottom of his box. Later they had to be got rid of; such deadly evidence could not be got rid of too soon. But for the moment it was all right; Coker had recovered his confidence, and Potter and Greene could only hope for the best.

THE TENTH CHAPTER.

Loder, the Detective!

THE next day there was one topic at Greyfriars School.

Who had ragged the Head? Who had inked the Big Beak? Who, in the name of wonder, had mopped gallons and gallons and gallons of ink over the august and majestic napper of the headmaster? And why?

"Why" was a more baffling question than "Who." For why had any fellow, granted that he was idiot enough, wanted to do it?

Apart from the peril of such an exploit, it was rotten bad form, rotten bad taste—the sort of thing that wasn't done. Nobody could brag of such an exploit; any Greyfriars man would have kicked the fellow who had done it readily and willingly. It was the rottenest thing that had ever been known to happen in the school. So why? Who could have wanted to ink the Head?

Nobody was likely to guess that a fellow had inked the Head without wanting to.

It was clear that someone had ambushed him in the dark. The inky pail was found; all sorts of inky tracks and traces were found. Someone, it was surmised, had watched the Head go, tracked him, and got him in the dark with that pail of ink.

The whole thing, as Loder of the Sixth remarked, had evidently been planned from the beginning. The pail of ink must have been got ready. No fellow was likely to have a pail of ink at hand ready for use at a moment's notice. It was not the sort of thing a fellow kept by him It had been specially got ready for the Head, of course.

Loder of the Sixth was putting in some deep thinking on this subject. It seemed to Loder that he saw light.

Three fellows in the Fifth knew the truth, but they buried their knowledge deep. Nobody thought of Coker in connection with the matter.

Loder was not thinking of Horace Coker; he was thinking of quite a different person—no other than Poker Pike, the gunman.

Probably the wish was father to the thought. But it seemed very probable to Loder. The man who had made him dance in the quad was capable of anything and everything—from inking a headmaster to holding up a bank.

The outrage had occurred at Mr. Pike's door. Who could have been there but Pike? The Head had spoken very severely to Poker on some occasions; and Loder had no doubt that he was revengeful. Loder's way of judging was to judge others by himself. Nobody, so far as could be learned, had been out of the House at the time. But Pike, of course, was out of the House; and as he was always prowling about after dark, very likely he had spotted the Head on the way to the lodge. It seemed so probable to Loder that he wondered that everybody else did not guess it at once.

Nobody did—but Loder.

Gerald Loder was not a very dutiful prefect; he was, in fact, rather a slacker and a black sheep. But he could be very keen on duty sometimes. He was very keen now to discover the perpetrator of this awful outrage—if it was Poker Pike.

Masters and prefects, that day, were inquiring and investigating right and left. Only Loder had a clue—or thought he had.

He followed it up with a success that quite surprised him.

After morning lessons he went down to Gosling's lodge and looked at the scene of the outrage. There were still plenty of traces of ink about. A dozen fellows were looking at them when Loder arrived. Ink, evidently, had been splashed about on a liberal scale.

Gosling was in his doorway; he was eyeing the little crowd that had gathered. The Bounder, among the juniors, was speaking as Loder came up.

"Must have been gallons of it," Smithy remarked. "If I were a prefect I should be looking for a chap with ink on his clobber."

"A chap who got ink on his clobber would have sense enough to change his clobber, I fancy," remarked Skinner.

"Then I should jolly well look for a fellow who changed his clobber this morning!" grinned the Bounder.

Loder made a mental note of that remark. It seemed to him a very sensible remark. He resolved to ascertain as soon as he could whether Poker Pike had changed any article of attire that morning. That would be easy to ascertain at a single glance, for Poker always sported the same garments. Loder felt quite obliged to Smithy for the hint.

He stopped to speak to Gosling. It was known that the tin pail which had been found in an inky state had been abstracted from Gosling's woodshed; the ragger had borrowed it for his purpose.

"I suppose you've no idea who took that pail from your shed yesterday, Gosling," Loder began.

"Which I ain't," replied Gosling. "If I knowed I'd know who was fooling about 'ere last night, Mr. Loder."

"Did you miss it from your shed?"

"Not till it was found lying about this morning."

"Does that man Pike ever go to your woodshed?"

Gosling blinked at him. That question rather revealed the drift of Loder's suspicions.

"He's been there at times," answered Gosling dryly. "Lent me a 'and sometimes with the roller. He's got his ways, but he ain't a bad sort."

"Did you see him there yesterday?"

"No," said Gosling.

"Did you notice anybody else hanging about anywhere near the woodshed yesterday?"

"No, I didn't!" said Gosling. "'Cept Master Coker, what I passed coming away."

Loder made a note of the name.

Coker was not an observant fellow; still, if he had been near the woodshed, he might have observed anybody who was about, such as Mr. Pike!

"Where is Pike this morning?" asked Loder. "I haven't seen him about as usual."

"Been down to Courtfield to buy a noo 'at!" answered Gosling.

Loder started.

"A new hat!" he repeated.

"Yes, he's back now, if you want him!" said Gosling.

Loder turned away, his eyes gleaming! Poker Pike had worn the same hat—in fact, lived in it night and day—ever since he had been at Greyfriars School. Why had he bought a new hat, the very next morning after the outrage with the ink?

There was only one answer to that question! He had splashed his hat with ink, swamping the Head, and dared not let such a clue be seen! Could anything be clearer? Loder had noted Smithy's suggestion that the ragger might change inky clobber! Pike had changed his hat! If that was not proof that that ruffian had inked the Head, Loder would have liked to know what proof was.

"I say, you fellows!" It was a squeak from Billy Bunter, as the side door of the lodge opened, and Mr. Pike walked out. "I say, he's got a new hat!"

"Ha, ha, ha!"

Mr. Pike walked by the juniors—in a new hat—and gave them a rather grim look as he passed. Mr. Pike had lived perpetually in the same hat since arriving at Greyfriars. But that game of football in the Rag had done it! Poker was not, perhaps, particular about his hats, but even in the cheapest joint in Chicago he could not have worn that

Held fast by the jammed sash, Poker Pike could only splutter and gurgle and gasp, as he watched the Removites playing football with his hat. "Say, you ginks, will you let up on that hat?" he shrieked. "I'm telling you to let up!" Amid roars, the game of football went on.

bowler which had been used as a football by the playful juniors.

The juniors, who knew—better than Loder!—why Mr. Pike was sporting that new tile, chuckled. Poker frowned as he walked on. Loder's eyes followed him, fairly gloating.

It was a new hat! There was no mistake about it! Its newness shone in the May sunshine. It was not merely a clue! It was proof!

Loder, quite sure of his ground now, hurried away in search of Coker of the Fifth—to learn whether Coker could tell him anything—little dreaming what Coker could have told him, had he liked!

THE ELEVENTH CHAPTER.
No Information from Coker!

"WHAT about those trousers?" asked Potter.

"Yes, those bags!" said Greene.

They were anxious.

So was Coker!

A pair of trousers, drenched with ink, were safely tucked away at the bottom of Coker's box in the Fifth Form dormitory. There, of course, they were safely out of sight. Still, there they were. If, by some horrified chance, they came to light, the game was up for Coker.

The discovery that a fellow had drenched his trousers with ink at the time that some person unknown had drenched the headmaster with ink, would not have left much mystery about the matter.

So long as those inky trousers remained in the House there was danger! Suppose a Head's Inspection took place! Such things happened without a notice beforehand. That would be the finish!

"It's all right!" said Coker. "I'm going to get rid of those trucks. I thought of burning them in the study, but—it might attract attention——"

"Oh crikey!" said Potter, aghast at the idea. He had no doubt that such a proceeding as that would attract attention—quite a lot of it!

"Or I could bury them somewhere!" said Coker thoughtfully. "It would have to be after dark, of course."

"Of course!" said Potter.

"The first thing," said Coker, "is to get them safely out of the House! I can stick them in some cranny somewhere, to be got rid of later. Only a fellow might be noticed going out with a bundle."

It was rather a worry!

"I think I've got the idea, though," Coker went on. "I'll get up to the dorm. You fellows go round and stand under the window. I'll drop the bundle down to you. See?"

"Um!" said Potter and Greene.

"One of you can keep watch, and the other catch the bundle," said Coker. "Whistle if anybody comes along, and I'll wait. See?"

It seemed a sound scheme. Potter and Greene went out of the House—passing Loder of the Sixth coming in as they went.

Coker headed for the stairs.

It was a rule at Greyfriars, as at most schools, that fellows did not go to the dormitories in the day-time without leave from a master. Coker, in view of the business he had in hand, certainly did not want to draw a beak's attention to the fact that he wanted to go up to the Fifth Form dorm. Neither did Coker care about rules, anyhow.

He went regardless. It was, as a matter of fact, a rule that was often forgotten. Still, any fellow who was seen on the upper stairs was liable to be called to order.

Coker, ascending the upper staircase, was about six steps up when his name was called.

"Coker!"

Horace glanced round. It was Loder's voice.

Standing on the stairs, Coker looked down at Loder! He breathed hard and deep!

Had Prout, his Form-master, spotted him and called him down, it would have been annoying. This was more than annoying. Coker did not think much of the Sixth, and often said so. It was very irksome to Coker, considering what an important fellow he was, to be under the authority of prefects! He could have knocked Loder into a cocked hat, with one hand! To Coker's masterly intellect, that seemed a good reason why Loder should refrain from exercising authority in his direction.

"Well?" snorted Coker.

"Come down!" said Loder.

Coker glared.

"Throwing your weight about, as usual?" he jeered.

That was not the way for a fellow to speak to a prefect! But, strange, to relate, Loder showed no signs of anger.

He was not, in point of fact, spotting Coker breaking the rules, and exercising authority. He was thinking of far more important matters.

"I want to speak to you, Coker," he said, quite civilly.

"You can speak where you are!" said Coker.

"I don't want to shout! Look here, Coker, it's rather urgent—come down!" said Loder. "I've been looking for you."

"Oh!" said Coker, mollified. He realised that this was not a case of "throwing weight about."

Coker came down. Potter and Greene, by that time, were waiting under the

(*Continued on page* 16.)

TREATING 'EM ROUGH!

In which our pet juvenile "orther," Dicky Nugent, continues his "grate" new serial:

"The SPARTANS of ST. SAM'S!"

The GREYFRIA

No. 187. EDITED BY H.

"Which it's time to get up, sir!"

Snore!

"Time to get up, sir!" repeeted Binding, the page, raising his voice slitely and poking his head further round the door of Doctor Birchemall's bed-room. "It's six o'clock—the time as you told me to call you, this 'ere mornin'!"

Snore!

Binding looked rather worried. The Head had given very deffinite orders that he was to be awakened at six on this particular morning; and anyone at St. Sam's who failed to see that the Head's orders were carried out stood in grave risk of being carried out himself—on a stretcher! After a moment's hezzitation, Binding trotted into the bed-room and shook the Head by the shoulder.

Snore!

Still Doctor Birchemall slept on, wearing a seraffick smile on his dial. As a matter of fakt, he was dreeming that somebody had sent him a tuck hamper and that he was bizzily engaged in skoffing the contents. It took a lot to wake the Head out of a dreem like that.

Binding got desprit. Bending over the bed, he grabbed the Head's beard, which was lying over the top of the idadown, and gave it a sudden and violent pull. The ruse suxxeeded; Doctor Birchemall awoke in a trice and sat up in bed with a howl of angwish.

"Yarooooo! Leggo my wiskers!"

"Six o'clock, sir!" said Binding. "Which I'm sorry if I got your goat!"

"You'll be sorrier still next time you get my goatee!" growled the Head. "Now hop it, Binding—or, as the vulgar would put it, you may go!"

"Yessir!" grinned Binding; and he went.

After he had departed, Doctor Birchemall got out of bed and dressed. He dressed in a somewhat serprizing fashion, for, instead of putting on his customary outer garments of sober black, he donned flannel trowsis and a swetter. There was a mischeevous gleem in his eyes as he did so.

"Ha, ha!" he muttered with a leering larf. "The rain of Birchemall, the new Sports Kaptin of St. Sam's, has begun! The day is yung and the boys who are destined to win fame and honner in the realm of sport are still in the Land of Dreems! Little do they dreem how soon they are going to be turned into Spartans under my stern system of training!"

Setting his mortar-board on his head at a jawnty angle and tucking a birch under his arm, Doctor Birchemall went fourth.

His first visit was to the Sixth Form Passidge, where the seniors had their sleeping quarters. Now you would have thought as he was looking for athletes that he would have called on such mitey men of valler as Burleigh and Strapper and Tallboy. But the Head had his own ideas about who was going to represent St. Sam's in the forthcoming sports contests. He ignored the giants of the Sixth completely and went straight to the study occupied by Weekling, the least athletic fellow in the Sixth!

Doctor Birchemall grinned as he perseeved that Weekling was fast asleep. Going to the handbasin in the corner, he filled a jug with water. Then he crossed over to the bed and, with a swift movement, upended the jug over Weekling's head.

Swooooosh!

"Yarooooo! Help! Perlice! Groooo!" shreeked Weekling, leaping up from his bed to find water streeming down him. Then he saw Doctor Birchemall, and at that uneggspected site, his eyes almost bolted out of their sockits.

"Good-morning, Weekling!" grinned the Head. "Rather a wet one, eh, what?"

"W-w-what's the idea, sir?" stuttered Weekling, dazedly.

"The idea, Weekling, is that I am paying you the honner of enrolling you in the St. Sam's Spartans! From now until Sports Day, morning, noon and nite, you will be undergoing a stern and gruelling training that will turn you into a veritable king among athletes. Put on a pair of running shorts and a jim vest, Weekling, and report to me in the quad!"

"M-m-my hat!"

"Shorts and jim vest only, mark you!" said the Head, sternly. "No socks or shoes or other luxuries as worn by the mollycoddles who have hitherto posed as athletes at St. Sam's! And fall in quickly—or you and I will fall out!"

So saying, Doctor Birchemall marched briskly out of Weekling's study, leaving Weekling almost parrilised with dismay and disgust.

The Head's call on Weekling was a prelood to many similar calls. Throwing water over Weekling seemed to have wetted the Head's appetite for recroots, and fully a score of unforchunit St. Sam's fellows were awakened that morning by a jug of cold water from the Head.

The funny thing about it was that Doctor Birchemall seemed to be selecting the weekest and puniest fellows in the skool to be his Spartans! He chose Swotter and Skellington and Waystead and Littlegrub, for instance—four of the most hoapless duffers at sport in the Sixth. From the Fifth he gathered in Starveling, Rattler and Cofhard, and from the Fourth, Weazer and Lackbrawn and Weede. The crowd that evenchally assembulled in the quad. certainly consisted of the worst fizzical specimens at St. Sam's—and standing there with bare feet in the thinnest of jim costumes made them look even worse than usual!

Despite the fakt that it was nowhere near rising-bell, half the skool turned out to watch the amazing parade, and there was a respectful cheer as Doctor Birchemall came galloping out of the House. The cheer jolly soon changed to a roar of larfter, though, when the Head tripped up on the bottom step and came a cropper on the end of his nose.

Bang!

"Wooooop!"

"Ha, ha, ha!"

Jack Jolly & Co., of the Fourth, assisted the Head to his feet, and when he had somewhat recovered, he addressed his recroots. The effect of his speech was rather spoiled becawse he had to hold a handkercheef to his dammidged nasal organ.

"Poys!" he cride. "I ab goig to stard trading you to become Spartans! I wad every poy to udderstad that froh dow till Spords Day he will sped all his time hardening his body and developing his muscles. Do you here?"

"W-w-we here, sir!" stuttered the amatcher Spartans, whose teeth were farely chattering with the cold.

"All serede, thed!" said the Head. "... dow begid with ... jerks. Addenshud ...

And then the S... of St. Sam's went ... the hoop with a v... The Head made th... and skip and jump ... themselves into kn... they didn't know ... they were on their h... their heals!

It was a commic... site to the onlooker... it wasn't so funny ... Spartans. Most o... were not at all ... fizzical jerks, and th... ing of their joint... out across the qua... the rattle of machi... going off. To make ... worse for them, ... Birchemall went ... gingering them u... his birch, and the ... reports from their ... joints were soon n... with sharp yells ... from their lipps.

"Arbs raise! ... bend!"

Crack! Bang! Bang! Crack!

Swish, swish!

"Yarooooo!"

"Help!"

"Have mersy, si...

But the pleas ... Head's viktims fell ... ears. The Head ... on regardless, and ... breakfast-time did ... a halt. By that t... would-be athletes ... as though they'd ... through a mang... sorrier-looking set ... tans could hardly ... been imagined!

As the grinning ... swarmed back to th... House, Jack Jolly, ... Fourth, notissed B... the late Sports ... strolling along with ... set eggspression ... rugged fizzog.

"You don't thi...

WOULD YOU BELIEVE IT?

Performing a "tap" dance in the Remove Form Room before the class, Fisher T. Fish drew a round of applause. Fishy is certainly slick with his feet—but when Mr. Quelch came in suddenly, Fishy looked more "sick" than "slick." He "danced" again—in a different way!

When Skinner broke bounds the other night to go to the Cross Keys, he did not notice that the moon had a ring round it. Returning, Skinner got a drenching—he had not heeded the sign. As he had lost at cards, too, Skinner was "damped" in more senses than one!

To reduce Bunter's girth ... increase his height, the ... medico suggested Bunter ... stand properly, pulling i... fat stomach. Bunter trie... soon decided he couldn't ... the treatment. He "pulle... at the tuck-shop for refres... instead!

ARTON.

May 9th, 1936.

ad is seriously thinking putting up those freeks represent St. Sam's in Sports, do you, Burh ?" asked Jack Jolly. 3urleigh shrugged.

I'm afraid he will, y," he replied. "Once ctor Birchemall sets his ad on a thing there's no pping him."

My hat!" eggsclaimed nk Fearless. "Someg ought to be done ut it."

Something *will* be done ut it!" said the deed Sports Kaptin, meany.

nd as Jack Jolly & Co. down to breakfast they ldn't help wondering it deep skeem was evolvin Burleigh's brane.

You will hear all about leigh's amazing wheeze rustrate Doctor Birchem- plans in next week's alment of this amusing al!)

ANSWERS TO ORRESPONDENTS.

OTTER & GREENE th).—"Coker wants to ome a racing motorist. you think we ought to him?"

Ve advise you not to nd in Coker's way!

. OGILVY (Remove).— 'ibley says he wants a sician in his concerty; yet he won't let me my concertina."

Ve can only tell you to "accordionly."

ONSTANT READER rd).—"What did Bunthink of Vernon-Smith's n feed last week?"

e described it afterds as simply "gorge".

BOB CHERRY says—

BATSMAN BUNTER MEANS BUSINESS, *BUT——*

I nearly threw a fit the other afternoon, when I ran into our one-and-only Prize Porker, tramping down towards the practice-nets in spotless flannels and with a cricket-bat tucked under his arm.

"Whither away, old fat bean?" I inquired, wonderingly.

"To the nets—to practise batting!" was Bunter's crisp answer.

"Well, you certainly need plenty of practice!" I chuckled. "But I never knew you to roll up to any kind of sport before, unless it was compulsory. What's the big idea?"

"Just that I've made up my mind to be the best batsman in the Remove—in fact, the best in the school!" said Bunter. "Owing to Wharton's rotten jealousy, I've never had a place in the Form team, and for that reason I've treated the game with contemptuous indifference—neglected it, in fact. But now I've decided to change all that."

"You have?"

"What-ho!" Bunter chuckled. "I'm going to practise batting until there's nobody in the school who can hold a candle to me. Then even Wharton won't be able to stop me from getting my just reward—a place in the Remove Eleven, if not in the First Eleven itself!"

"Oh, crumbs! Are you really serious?"

"My mind is made up," Bunter answered, loftily. "Nothing will stop me from sticking to practice, day in and day out. Nothing on earth will keep me from the nets this afternoon, I can tell you!"

"Come over to the tuckshop with me, old sport, and have a few jam tarts."

Bunter jumped slightly.

"Tuppenny ones?"

"Threepenny ones, if they've got 'em!"

"I say, Bob, old chap, this is awfully decent of you," grinned Bunter. "Thanks, I will!"

"But what about your net practice?" I hooted. "What about training?"

"Ahem! Perhaps, on consideration, it's hardly worth the fag. I'll give the other chaps a chance instead and chuck up the idea altogether!"

And that gives you an idea of what Bunter's like when he really means business!

WE LOVE OBLIGING LODER!

Declares HARRY WHARTON

Loder has started the new term well—by fagging the Remove!

Judging by the steely look in his eyes when he first tried it on, he thought we should be fearfully annoyed at this. We had every right to be, of course. It was settled donkey's years ago that the Remove were not to be fagged.

But Loder got a surprise. We weren't a bit annoyed. The reason is, you see, that we simply love obliging Loder!

Bob Cherry, for instance, said that it was a real pleasure to make his toast for him. It's true that the "toast" looked like lumps of charcoal and that Loder's carpet got burnt in the process, but that couldn't be helped.

Vernon-Smith, too, remarked that he was delighted to fetch up some tuck from the school shop for Loder. Admittedly, by some unforeseen chance, the tuck he gave Loder had been tampered with, so that there was ink in the cakes, mustard in the chocs., and soap in the candy. But accidents are always liable to happen, aren't they?

Then again, the job of polishing up Loder's furniture gave Tom Brown quite a lot of pleasure. A peculiar mischance led to his putting glue on the chairs instead of furniture polish, so that Loder and his guests all became stuck as soon as they sat down. But who would have thought of that happening?

It made Johnny Bull awfully happy to lay the fire for Loder. Somehow or other he managed to get a lot of fireworks mixed up with the wood, but that didn't spoil his happiness in any way!

On the whole we have to admit that Loder isn't altogether satisfied with his Remove fags. In fact, there's a rumour going the rounds that he may chuck it now at any moment.

We do hope he won't. We love obliging Loder. We're getting so much fun out of it that life will seem quite blank when Loder doesn't allow us to oblige him any more!

HAVE A HEART, MR. PROUT!

Begs SQUIFF

On Tuesday morning there was a low, distant rumbling heard in every part of the House soon after rising-bell. The alarm was immediate and widespread. Fellows, in all dorms. paused in their washing and dressing, and those who hadn't turned out sat up in bed wondering what the dickens it could be.

Pictures fell off walls, ornaments fell off mantelpieces, and bits of plaster came down from ceilings all over the place. We were quite scared for a few seconds, I can tell you.

After the first half-minute it got rapidly worse, and it wasn't long before every part of the building seemed to be shivering and shaking. Those who were dressed rushed out to investigate. And what do you think was the cause of all the trouble?

It was Mr. Prout, of the Fifth, doing slimming exercises in his bed-room!

Every morning since that day we've had to put up with the same thing, and, to my mind, it's time someone tackled him about it. The noise doesn't matter much now we know what it is, of course. What I'm thinking about is the danger. Think what a mess it would be if the entire House collapsed one morning and we were all buried in tons of debris!

Have a heart, Mr. Prout! Let me make a personal appeal to you, sir! For the sake of all of us and the sake of the good old school buildings, do your skipping out of doors in future.

All other considerations aside, look what a treat you'll be giving the boys!

THE KEY TO THE PROBLEM!

Loder is on the tiles a lot lately. They say that all the Head's warnings that he'll be locked out have merely resulted in his getting indifferent.

Presumably getting in different ways every night!

GREYFRIARS FACTS WHILE YOU WAIT!

giant yew-tree in the garden is known to be than 1,000 years old. Old e, the Head's gardener, it in splendid trim—he is good for 2,000 years! Mimble's gnarled features nearly] as old as the yew itself!

When it was time for compulsory cricket practice, Lord Mauleverer was "snoozing" in his study—whereupon Johnny Bull played a fanfare on his cornet in the doorway. Against all expectations, "Mauly" coolly slept on! Johnny Bull had to be "fanned"!

Dr. Locke, the kindly headmaster of Greyfriars, finds relaxation in a game of bowls, at which he is no mean performer. A silver cup in his study commemorates the winning of a local championship by a team captained by Dr. Locke. The Head's "cup" was full that day!

(Continued from page 13.)

dormitory windows. They had to wait! Probably they would not wait long.

It could not be helped! Coker could hardly proceed to disinter those inky trousers from his box with a prefect about—especially if he made that prefect irritable and suspicious, by marching up to the dormitory under his eyes and regardless of his authority.

"Well?" said Coker.

"I'm looking for that rotter who inked the Head last night——" began Loder.

"Wha-a-at?"

"And I think I've found him!" went on Loder.

"Eh?"

"I fancy I can put my hand right on him. For goodness' sake don't jump like a kangaroo!" exclaimed Loder irritably. "What the dickens is the matter with you, Coker?"

Coker had jumped nearly clear of the floor!

"You—you—you can put your hand on him?" he gasped.

"I fancy so!"

"Oh crikey!"

"Nobody else seems to have thought of him," went on Loder. "But I got on to it at once, and I think I've got something like proof."

"Proof?" said Coker faintly.

He gazed at Loder.

"Yes. I fancy the rotter will be kicked out of the school to-day," said Loder. "I've got it pretty clear against him."

"Oh!"

"I want you to help me," said Loder.

"Me?"

"Yes, you! I fancy you may be able to."

Coker could only gaze. Certainly, he could have helped Loder—quite a lot! But he really had no desire to do so!

"You see," said Loder, "the rotter who did it got ink on him——"

"Ink on him?"

"He was bound to, swamping ink about from a pail! He seems to have splashed it on his hat."

"His hat?"

"Yes, his hat! What are you goggling like that for? Nothing surprising in his getting ink on his hat is there, when he was splashing a pail of ink about?" snapped Loder.

"You—you don't mean his trousers?" stuttered Coker.

"No; he hasn't changed his trousers, so far as I know."

Coker gasped, casting a surreptitious glance down at his own spotless bags.

"Has—has—hasn't he?" he articulated.

"If he has, I haven't noticed it. But he has changed his hat—I'm absolutely certain on that point."

Coker breathed again.

For an awful moment, of course, he had fancied that Loder had spotted him, and was about to march him off to the Head as the discovered culprit!

Now he realised that Loder was on quite another track! Coker had changed his trousers after that awful episode! He had not changed his hat!

Loder was not after a fellow who had changed his trousers! He was after a fellow who had changed his hat! Horace Coker could only wonder dizzily who the fellow was!

"That's proof enough, in my opinion," went on Loder. "But I want to make absolutely sure. I dare say you know that the pail that was used belongs to Gosling, and was taken from his woodshed."

Coker knew it only too well.

"I've been speaking to Gosling——"

"Oh!" gasped Coker.

He remembered that he had passed Gosling the previous afternoon, when he had been hanging about the woodshed, looking for a chance to annex a receptacle for gallons of ink!

He had brought that ink in bottles; but could not, of course, distribute it over his victim from half a dozen bottles! Gosling's tin pail had served his turn!

"Gosling noticed you yesterday——" went on Loder.

"Oh!"

"Near the woodshed——"

"Ah!"

"That's why I've been looking for you," explained Loder. "Now, I want you to think and remember carefully, Coker! Did you see anybody near the woodshed while you were about?"

"Um!"

"Somebody got that pail from the shed," said Loder. "Gosling generally leaves the place unlocked during the day; but it's locked at night. That pail was got before dark—see? Well, if you saw anybody hanging about, I want to know who it was. Did you see that man Pike?"

"Pip-pip-Pike!"

"That scoundrelly gunman! He did it——"

"Did—did—did he?"

"I'm absolutely certain that he did!"

"Oh!"

"But if you happened to have seen him about while you were near the woodshed, that would clinch it!" explained Loder. "See?"

"I—I—I see!"

"Well, did you see him?"

"N-n-no!" stuttered Coker. "I—I don't remember seeing him! No! I never saw anything of him there! No!"

Loder knitted his brows. He had hoped for information from Coker! It seemed that Coker had none to give.

"Look here, Coker, think it over carefully," he said. "You don't like that gunman brute any more than I do. I remember he ducked you in the fountain the first day of term for whopping that cheeky young tick Van Duck. You're bound to do anything you can to help get the scoundrel who inked the Head——"

"The—the what?"

"The scoundrel—the utter rotter, who inked the Head!" said Loder. "I suppose you know it was a dirty trick, and only an absolute rotten outsider would have done it!"

"Oh!"

"Well, try to remember if you saw that gunman anywhere near Gosling's woodshed yesterday while you were about!" urged Loder.

Really, it might almost have been supposed that Loder was urging Horace to remember it, whether it had happened or not!

But Horace shook his head.

"I never saw him!" he answered.

"Then I'm wasting my time!" growled Loder. "I suppose you're too dunder-headed a fool to see anything if it was right under your nose! Or perhaps you don't want the rotten rascal to be found out?"

"No—I mean—I—I—mean, I never saw anything of Pike——"

Loder gave an angry snort.

"Oh, get out, you dummy!" he snapped. "I shall report you to Prout for going up to the dormitory without leave."

Loder stalked away.

"Oh crikey!" murmured Coker, as the prefect went. He wiped a bead of perspiration from his brow. He was feeling quite faint.

When Loder was gone, Coker re-started after the interval, as it were, and scuttled up to the Fifth Form dormitory, regardless of the impending report to Prout. He disinterred a bundle from his box, whipped to the window, and looked down.

Unfortunately, by that time Potter and Greene were tired of waiting, and had gone. Nothing was to be seen of either of them.

Coker, with feelings too deep for words, interred the bundle in his box again, and quitted the dormitory. The opportunity had passed, owing to that ass Loder butting in, and the fatal trousers still remained to be dealt with.

THE TWELFTH CHAPTER.

Not Poker!

"BLESS my soul!" said the Head. He adjusted his glasses and stared at Loder.

That dutiful prefect had made his report. No other prefect had any report to make; but the others, of course, were not gifted with such detective ability as Gerald Loder.

The Head was surprised; almost as surprised as he had been the previous evening, when the ink descended on him like a bolt from the blue.

The good old Head had hoped, if not quite believed, that it was no Greyfriars fellow who had perpetrated that outrage. Improbable as it seemed, he had thought that perhaps some extraneous intruder had been within the school walls. Certainly he had not thought of Poker Pike.

"Bless my soul!" he repeated. "Are you serious, Loder? Bless my soul! I cannot imagine anything of the kind—a man, even such a very unusual man as Mr. Pike—playing a foolish trick like a very thoughtless schoolboy! Impossible, Loder! In fact, absurd!"

Loder bit his lip.

He hoped to gain distinction by being the one and only prefect to solve that baffling mystery. He hoped to see the Greyfriars gunman ordered to quit. But this was not encouraging.

"I think, sir, that there is something like proof," he said. "It happened at Pike's door. Nobody but he could have known you were there. He is a rough character, capable of—of almost anything. Whoever did it, sir, must have got splashed with ink—that's practically certain. He has bought himself a new hat this morning. I think it looks pretty clear, sir."

It looked clear enough to Loder in the bitter state of his feelings towards Poker Pike. It was by no means so clear to the Head, who, of course, did not share those feelings in the least.

Indeed, the Head could see—what Loder did not quite realise—that personal dislike had something to do with Loder's theory.

"Impossible!" he repeated.

"I hope, sir, that you will question the man, at least!" said Loder. "Let him explain why he has, on this special morning, discarded the hat he was wearing yesterday. He must have a reason."

Dr. Locke pursed his lips.

"That is undoubtedly a coincidence," he said. "But—well, I will send for the man and speak to him, Loder. You may remain here."

Dr. Locke rang for Trotter, and the House page was dispatched, to request Mr. Pike to step in.

Mr. Pike was prowling in the quad at the moment, so Trotter was not long in finding him. He arrived at the Head's study in a few minutes.

The Head glanced at his hat as he came in, Mr. Pike, according to his invariable custom, keeping it on his head!

Obviously, it was a new hat!

"I guess a young guy allowed you wanted to chew the rag with me a piece!" remarked Mr. Pike, taking a seat, in an easy attitude, on the corner of the Head's writing-table.

"Oh! Yes!" gasped the Head. He did not always find it easy to follow Mr. Pike's meaning. "Quite so! I desired to speak to you. You have heard of what happened last night, Mr. Pike, at your door?"

"Surest thing you know!" assented Mr. Pike. "I'll say the whole bunch is chewing the rag about that very thing."

"May I ask whether you were indoors at the time?"

"Nope!"

"You saw nothing of the occurrence?"

"Nonk!" said Mr. Pike. "I guess if I had been around, I'd sure have given the guy a sockdolager or two! But I sure was not on the spot."

Loder's lip curled.

"Will you tell Dr. Locke where you were?" he asked, as the Head paused.

Poker glanced at him.

"Sure, if he wants to be put wise!" he answered. "I was looking in at a winder, giving young Putnam van Duck the once-over."

"It doesn't take long to look in at a window," sneered Loder.

"That's all you know, and it ain't a lot," retorted Mr. Pike. "I guess I was looking in at the winder a good half-hour, and then some—and I'll say that it seemed longer."

Loder shrugged his shoulders, and the Head raised his eyebrows. Mr. Pike's statement struck them both as somewhat extraordinary. They did not know the peculiar circumstances in which Mr. Pike had looked in at the window of the Rag.

"You bought a new hat this morning," said Loder.

As the Head did not speak, Loder took up the questioning.

"Yep!" assented Mr. Pike.

"Will you tell Dr. Locke why?"

Poker stared at him.

"I guess the king-pin of this here outfit ain't interested in my hats," he answered, in surprise. "He sure ain't sent for me to ask me about that."

"You had a reason," said Loder.

"You said it."

"What was the reason?"

Mr. Pike blinked at him, and blinked at the Head. Not dreaming for a single instant that he was suspected of being the mysterious mopper of ink, he was utterly astonished. However, he answered.

"I guess the old hat was a goner," he said. "I'll say I was sorry to lose that hat. It was a good hat, and it set me back six dollars when I bought it in Chicago. But it sure was a back number."

"You mean something happened to it last night to spoil it?" asked Loder, feeling quite like a questioning detective-inspector.

"Surest thing, you know," assented Mr. Pike.

"Bless my soul!" said the Head.

He did not, and could not, believe that Mr. Pike had mopped ink over him. But really it was beginning to look as if there was something in Loder's circumstantial evidence.

Loder's eyes gleamed. He was sure of his ground, and he felt that he was extracting the truth from the delinquent, little by little.

"About what time last night was the hat spoiled?" asked Loder.

And the Head gave quite keen attention now.

"I sort of disremember exactly," said Mr. Pike. "I guess it would be about nine."

"About the time that Dr. Locke was drenched with ink at your door?"

"That very time," agreed Poker.

"Bless my soul!" repeated the Head.

"I think it's pretty clear now, sir," said Loder. "But seeing the hat will be conclusive."

"I don't get you," said Mr. Pike, more and more puzzled. "What's all this chin-wag about a guy's hat?"

"Where is the old hat now?" asked Loder.

"I want to know," answered Poker, meaning thereby that he did not know in the least. "I chucked it into a dust bin. Mebbe it's there yet, if you're powerful interested in my old hat."

"If you will send Trotter, sir——" Loder turned to the Head.

"One moment!" said Dr. Locke. "Please tell me, Mr. Pike, in what manner your hat was spoiled? Was it splashed with ink?"

"Ink!" repeated Mr. Pike. "Nope! Wusser'n that, I'm telling you! But I ain't complaining about it, sir. I can take a joke with the next man. Boyees will be boyees, I guess!"

The Head started; and Loder stared.

"Boys!" repeated the Head. "Do you mean that your hat was spoiled by some of the boys, Mr. Pike?"

"You said it, sir—me with my neck jammed in a winder, and them young gecks kicking that hat about all over the shebang," said Mr. Pike. "I'll say it didn't look a lot like a hat when young Putnam lammed it on my cabèza agin. Nunk!"

"Bless my soul! Please tell me exactly what happened, Mr. Pike!"

(Continued on next page.)

GREYFRIARS INTERVIEWS.

This week our long-haired poet gives you a pen-picture in verse of a fellow who is handy "with his mits,"

RICHARD RUSSELL,

the fighting man of the Remove.

(1)

Dick Russell has a solid claim
To figure in our Hall of Fame,
For in the gym in fighting trim
He boxes with a will;
His strength and science are immense,
He's cool and full of common sense,
And in the art of self-defence
We all admire his skill.

(2)

Bob Cherry is the only chap
Who ever beats him in a scrap,
And even Bob admits the job
Is rather more than tough!
While as for me, I shouldn't stand
A single chance in all the land
To fight and get the upper hand
If Russell cut up rough.

(3)

That was, of course, the reason why
I thought I'd keep a wary eye
On Russell while in tactful style
I paid my weekly call.
If Russell started hitting out,
I'd no desire to stop a clout
Upon my somewhat tender snout—
No! No desire at all!

(4)

However, he was quite polite
And showed no tendency to fight
As I barged in and, with a grin,
Inquired how did he do.
He did not land an uppercut
Upon my solar plexus, but
He answered: "Not so bad, old nut!
Walk in and take a pew!"

(5)

I soon discovered why his tone
Was like a dulcet gramophone;
He wanted me, I found, to be
A catspaw, more or less!
Said he: "Old Coker's coming soon,
He told me so this afternoon,
And so I'm waiting for the coon!
And ready, too, I guess!

(6)

"If Coker wants to find a row,
He'll find it here, and find it now!"
He said as he invited me
To take a cricket stump.
"Stand there, against the door!" he said,
"And when you hear old Coker's tread,
Bring down the stump upon his head—
But please don't kill the chump!"

(7)

He took a poker from the shelf
And joined me at the door himself;
On either side we stood, and tried
To keep our ears alert.
He facing me, I facing him,
We stood in silence, keen and grim,
Till Coker's tread, far off and dim,
Was heard! Now he'd be hurt!

(8)

We raised our weapons in the air,
The door was opening—and there
Was Coker's scowl and Coker's growl!
He strode into the room!
Then he tripped upon the study mat
And, pitching forward, landed flat
Upon his toes and nose—and that
Was how we met our doom!

(9)

For as we brought our weapons down,
Instead of meeting Coker's crown,
My cricket stump fell with a bump
Upon Dick Russell's bean!
His poker banged upon my brow,
And down we fell together! Wow!
And so we're in the Sanny now,
While Coker laughs unseen!

"Mind, I ain't complaining!" said Poker. "I guess I don't want them young ginks called up on no carpet. Boyees will be boyees, like I said. If that's a cinch, I ain't no objection to putting you wise."

"Certainly—certainly!" said the Head. "It is not a question of that. I simply desire to know what occurred."

"I'll shoot, then," said Poker.

And he briefly related what had happened at the window of the Rag, in the very moments when Dr. Locke was getting the ink at Gosling's lodge.

Loder turned almost green as he listened.

Dr. Locke bit his lip with vexation. He had said that Loder's accusation was absurd. Now he knew it.

Loder, in fact, had succeeded in proving an "alibi" for the gunman. As Mr. Pike had been fixed at the Rag window, with his head jammed under the sash, at the very time that the ragger was at work with the ink, obviously Mr. Pike could not be the ragger. Unless, indeed, he had the remarkable and unusual gift of being in two places at once.

"I remember," said the Head, "that I noticed that some uproar was going on in the junior room when I returned from the lodge. I am sorry, Mr. Pike, that the boys should have——"

"O.K.!" said Mr. Pike cheerfully. "Boyees will be boyees! I ain't got no kick coming, sir."

He looked inquiringly at the Head.

"You wanted to chew the rag a piece?" he asked. "Spill it!"

It did not even occur to Mr. Pike that he had been under suspicion, and that the matter for which he had been sent for was now dealt with and done with.

"Ah! 'Hem! Another time, Mr. Pike," said the Head, a little confused—"I am sorry to have troubled you—another time——"

"Jest as you like, sir," said the wondering Poker; and he slid off the table and walked out of the study, still with his hat on.

When he was gone, Dr. Locke turned to Loder.

"Have you anything further to say, Loder?" he asked coldly. "Any further absurd and nonsensical accusations to make?"

Loder breathed hard. Apparently he had none. At all events, he had nothing to say. He was glad to get out of the Head's study.

He heard the Head give a pronounced sniff as he went. That was all the reward he received for displaying so much zeal in tracking down the unknown delinquent. Really it was not very encouraging to a zealous prefect.

THE THIRTEENTH CHAPTER.

Inky!

"INKY!" shouted Bob Cherry.

Coker of the Fifth started violently, and spun round with a flushed face, staring at Bob.

Bob did not notice him.

Bob was, in point of fact, calling to Hurree Jamset Ram Singh, who was commonly called "Inky" by his friends, on account of his beautiful complexion.

Coker possibly was aware of that circumstance, if he had thought about it, which he did not. He was not thinking of the Nabob of Bhanipur; he was thinking with a worried brow of his inky trousers, not yet disposed of.

"Inky!" roared Bob.

Bob had just come down from the studies.

All the Famous Five had been rather busy since class that day. They had "impots" to write. Putnam van Duck and his five friends had been awarded two hundred Latin lines each for their exploit of sliding down the banisters, which, of course, Loder had reported to Mr. Quelch.

Those lines had to be handed in after tea, and, as so often happened with impositions, they had been left rather late.

But the six juniors had wired in and done them at last. Bob, as the slowest worker of the Co., finished last, and now he had come down to look for his friends.

Spotting the dusky Nabob of Bhanipur in the distance across the quad, Bob naturally hailed him. Equally naturally he hailed him by the name by which Hurree Singh was known to his pals. He did not even see Coker, and Coker did not notice him till he shouted: "Inky!" Then Coker noticed him immediately and emphatically.

"Inky!" roared Bob.

Coker had a guilty conscience. That was why he took it for granted that Bob was shouting at him.

How this little beast knew anything about the matter that was wrapped in mystery, Coker could not guess. But evidently he knew, as he was shouting "Inky!" at him in the quad—or, at least, Coker supposed that he was.

Coker strode towards him, red and angry and apprehensive.

"Shut up!" he hissed.

"What?" Bob stared at him. "What's biting you, Coker? Can't I call Inky if I want to?"

"You'll get jolly well kicked if you call after a Fifth Form man in the quad, you cheeky young sweep!"

"Wha-a-a-t!" stuttered Bob.

"How did you know?" demanded Coker.

"What and which?" asked the astonished Bob.

"You know what I mean!" breathed Coker. "Keep your cheeky mouth shut, see? You call Inky again, and I'll jolly soon shut you up!"

Bob simply stared at him blankly.

Coker was the man to barge in, in all sorts of matters that did not concern him; seldom or never had he been known to mind his own business. But it seemed rather over the limit, even for Coker, to barge in when a Remove fellow was merely calling to a fellow in the quad!

"You silly, cheeky ass!" gasped Bob Cherry "I'll jolly well call Inky as much as I like, and as often as I like!"

And he immediately suited the action to the word, just to show Coker that he was nobody.

"Inky! Inky! Inky!" he roared.

"My esteemed Bob——" came Inky's answer, as he came trotting up.

"Here, hands off!" roared Bob, as Coker, alarmed and enraged, collared him. "You mad ass—— Yaroooh! Rescue, Remove!"

"I'll give you Inky!" panted Coker. "I'll jolly well give you Inky, you cheeky little beast!"

"Yaroogh! Rescue!" yelled Bob, struggling manfully.

Hurree Jamset Ram Singh rushed in at once. A dusky hand gripped the back of Coker's collar and jerked him backwards from Bob.

Harry Wharton and Frank Nugent came speeding from one direction—Johnny Bull from another.

They arrived in a bunch and hurled themselves on Coker.

They did not delay to ask questions. Questions, in fact, were not needed. Coker of the Fifth was asking for more trouble, and they had plenty more for him if he wanted it. They handed it out.

Coker was strewn on the hard, unsympathetic earth. He was strewn hard. He roared as he was strewn.

Feet, planted on Coker, pinned him down! It seemed to amuse the cheeky young rascals of the Remove to use Horace Coker as a doormat. They chuckled as they trod.

"Dear old Coker!" said Nugent. "Always asking for it. What's the matter with him this time, Bob?"

"Blessed if I know!" gasped Bob. "I was calling Inky, and he suddenly pitched into me. Blessed if I think Coker's quite sane."

"Lemme gerrup!" came gurgling from Coker.

"You silly ass, Coker!" said Harry Wharton, in wonder. "What the thump does it matter to you if Bob calls Inky?"

"I'll call Inky all day long, and all night, too, if I jolly well want to!" snorted Bob.

"Oh, shout it out!" said Coker bitterly. "Get a man sacked! Sneaking little beasts!"

"Wha-a-at?"

In sheer astonishment, the chums of the Remove gazed down at Coker. They withdrew the pinning boots, and Coker sat up, gasping. Then he tottered to his feet.

"Rotten little sneaks!" gasped Coker. "I've whopped you often enough, but you can't say you haven't deserved it! Now you've got a chance to get your own back! Make the most of it!"

"Is he potty?" asked Frank Nugent.

"The pottifulness seems terrific!" remarked the Nabob of Bhanipur.

"What the thump do you mean, Coker?" roared Harry Wharton. "Who's sneaking? What the dickens are you driving at?"

"You know jolly well!" snorted Coker. "I can't imagine how you've found out——"

"Found out what?" yelled Johnny Bull.

"Oh, don't gammon!" snapped Coker. "You know jolly well, when you howl out 'inky' at a chap! Have you been sneaking into my dorm?"

"Y-your dorm!" stuttered Wharton.

"If you've seen the trousers——"

"Trousers?"

"Anyhow, you've nosed it out somehow!" said Coker contemptuously. "Well, go and tell the Head, if you like, that I did it! I shan't deny it! Go and sneak—it would be more manly than giving a fellow away by yowling at him in the quad!"

The chums of the Remove gazed, dumbfounded, at Coker. They could not doubt to what Coker alluded. Coker was owning up that he was the man who had inked the Head! Why, the juniors could not imagine.

It was an amazing surprise to learn that the culprit was Coker of the Fifth! It was more amazing for him to tell them, unasked, what they had not thought of suspecting!

"Well, my only hat!" gasped Wharton. "You—you—you did it, Coker? It was you who—who—who——"

"You know it was!" snarled Coker. "I dare say you don't know it was a mistake in the dark, and I meant it for that Chicago blighter, Pike——"

"Oh crikey!"

"But the Head got it! How you

found it out beats me! Go and give a man away!" growled Coker. "I'm not asking you to keep it dark! Catch me asking favours of scrubby little scoundrels in the Lower Fourth! But don't howl it at me in the quad—I'll jolly well smash you if you do!"

"Who was howling it at you?" hooted Bob.

"Eh? You were!" snarled Coker.

"I? I——" stuttered Bob.

"Yes, you—howling 'inky' at the top of your voice—I dare say twenty fellows heard you, as I suppose you meant them to!" sneered Coker.

Bob Cherry gasped. His friends gasped. They saw Coker's misapprehension now. They gazed at Coker—they gazed at one another—and they burst into a yell:

"Ha, ha, ha!"

"Laugh!" said Coker, with sardonic bitterness. "It's funny to see a man sacked for making a mistake that any fellow might have made in the dark! Laugh!"

"Oh dear!" gasped Bob, wiping his eyes. "You'll be the death of me yet, Coker. Do you think I was calling 'inky' to you?"

"I know you were!"

"Nothing of the kind, you ass!"

"Ha, ha, ha!"

"Oh, don't gammon!" growled Coker. "You couldn't have been calling it at anybody else—nobody else is inky, I suppose?"

"Ha, ha, ha!"

"I was calling Inky!" shrieked Bob.

"Yes, I know you were calling 'inky'——"

"I mean Inky—not 'inky'!" howled Bob. "I mean Hurree Singh! See? This chap—this here blessed inky-complexioned Indian prince as ever was! Got it now?"

"Eh?"

"Ha, ha, ha!"

"Oh scissors!" gasped Harry. "We call Hurree Singh Inky, Coker. Bob was calling to Hurree Singh—calling him Inky! Ha, ha, ha!"

"It is an absurd and ludicrous name applied to my ridiculous self!" chuckled the Nabob of Bhanipur.

"Oh!" gasped Coker.

"Ha, ha, ha!"

Coker gazed at the almost hysterical juniors. They were nearly weeping. Slowly Coker realised it.

"Oh!" he repeated.

"Ha, ha, ha!"

"Then—then—then you never knew!" stuttered Coker.

"Not till you told us!" answered Harry.

"Ha, ha, ha!"

"Oh!" said Coker.

"All serene, you born idiot!" said the captain of the Remove. "We never knew till you told us—but we're not telling anybody else. Not a word about this, you fellows!"

"No fear!" said Bob.

"Oh crumbs!" said Coker. "Of—of course, when I heard that young tick shout 'inky,' I thought——"

"You thought?" asked Bob.

"Yes, I thought——"

"What did you do it with?"

"Ha, ha, ha!"

"I don't want any cheek!" roared Coker. "If you think you can be cheeky, because you know about it, I can jolly well say—— Yarooh! Yoohoop!"

Coker did not mean to say that. He said it involuntarily as the Famous Five sat him down on the quad again, cutting short his flow of eloquence.

"Don't tell anybody else, Coker, old man!" advised Harry Wharton. "We're keeping it dark; but I wouldn't tell everybody. Come on, you fellows!"

"Ha, ha, ha!"

And the Famous Five, almost weeping with merriment, scuttled off before Coker could get on his feet again.

THE FOURTEENTH CHAPTER.

Danger Ahead!

WHO did it?

Up and down, and round about, that question was still being asked—and, so far, nobody had been able to supply the solution to the riddle.

The masters discussed the strange mystery in Common-room, at almost endless length. Each was certain of one thing only—that the rascal who had mopped ink over the Chief Beak was not in his particular Form! Beyond that they knew nothing.

Prefects were keen on the hunt. Loder had lost all his enthusiasm, and now that it had been proved—by his own investigations—that Poker Pike had had nothing to do with it, Loder did not care two hoots who had inked the Head, and whether he was found out or not. But the rest of the

(Continued on next page.)

august body of the Sixth Form prefects kept going.

Juniors debated the matter with keen interest. In the Shell and the Fourth they had little doubt that a Remove man had done it. In the Remove they were divided in opinion, whether it had been done by a Shell fellow or a Fourth Former.

Five fellows knew. They had had it from Coker! But they kept it awfully dark—as dark as Potter and Greene were keeping it! They did not even tell their American chum, Van Duck.

Such an awful thing could not be kept too dark! Nobody wanted to see old Coker sacked—especially as it appeared that he had not meant to rag the Head at all, but had, with his usual fat-headedness, got him by mistake!

Mistake or not, the culprit's fate was fixed, if it was spotted! And if Coker of the Fifth hoped that the excitement would die away he was disappointed.

No doubt, if no discovery was made, it would be forgotten, in time. But a good deal of time was required. Headmasters were not half-drowned in ink every day! It was a tremendous sensation. Instead of the affair dying away it seemed to ripen.

The hunt was up! Kind-hearted old gentleman as the headmaster was, he could not possibly let a matter like this pass. He hoped that the investigation would prove that the culprit was no Greyfriars fellow But if it proved that a Greyfriars man was guilty, it was the "long jump" for that hapless Greyfriars man!

Smithy's surmise that the unknown ragger might have stained himself with ink, which had appealed to Loder, had occurred to others. It transpired that search was being made for fellows who had inky stains on their clobber.

That, as Bob Cherry remarked, incriminated the whole of the Second and Third Forms! Most of them, at least, were of the ink, inky!

Skinner solemnly warned Billy Bunter to wash! True, Bunter had no actual ink on him. But, according to Skinner, if the prefects saw Bunter's neck they might think it was black with ink!

Which made the Removites chuckle, and Bunter snort! Skinner, of course, exaggerated. Even Bunter's neck was not quite so bad as that.

The feelings of Horace Coker may be more easily imagined than described when he heard that inky clobber was being looked for. Those inky trousers were still wrapped up in a bundle, in Coker's box.

Loder, in his annoyance, had reported Coker to Prout, and Coker had been given two hundred lines for going up to the dormitory without leave. Lines did not worry Coker much; he was past caring about lines.

But Prout, reminded of forgotten duties by the incident, locked the door of the Fifth Form dormitory, so that it was impossible for any fellow to go there without asking leave!

This thoughtfulness on the part of Mr. Prout was not likely to last long. But for the moment it was fatal! For the inky trousers were now locked up, and Coker had no chance of getting at them till bed-time.

Those dreadful trousers remained, as irrefutable evidence against Coker, if some unfortunate chance brought them to light! Coker's worried thoughts were haunted by inky trousers.

And he had cause for alarm. After tea that day Billy Bunter burst into Study No. 1, in the Remove, with startling news.

"I say, you fellows!" gasped Bunter. "I say, they're going to cop him, if he is a Remove man."

"And how?" asked Putnam van Duck.

The Famous Five were not interested; they knew that it was not a Remove man.

Billy Bunter chuckled.

"I say, I've just seen the prefects going up! Quelch has gone with them. They're going to search the junior dormitories, beginning with the Remove."

"What on earth for?" asked Harry Wharton.

"Inky clobber!" grinned Bunter. "Everybody's clobber is going to be looked at, every box is going to be nosed into. See? They think the fellow, whoever he was, must have got ink on him—and changed afterwards, of course. A fearful lot of ink was slopped about, you know. If it was one of you chaps, you're booked."

"You silly ass!" grunted Johnny Bull. "We were all in the Rag at the time, kicking Pike's hat about!"

"It wasn't a Remove man!" said Harry. "They won't find anything in our dorm. I—I wonder if they'll search the senior dormitories."

"Sure to, if they draw the junior dorms blank," said Bunter. "I fancy they'll be going through the Fifth tomorrow; and then, very likely, the Sixth Form Rooms. I say, you fellows, I wonder if it was a Sixth Form man? I thought very likely it might have been Loder——"

"Loder!" gasped the juniors.

"Well, he was nosing about Gosling's lodge to-day, and asking Gosling a lot of questions," said Bunter. "He seemed very anxious to find out if Gosling had seen anybody near his woodshed—where the pail was taken from, you know. Looked to me as if he was worried about something."

"Oh, my hat!"

"Jolly good thing if Loder was sacked—what?" said Bunter cheerfully. "Do you fellows think it was Loder?"

"Ha, ha! No."

"Well, it looks like it to me," said Bunter.

Herbert Vernon-Smith looked in at the door.

"You fellows heard?" he asked. "They're up in our dorm—going through our boxes, I hear. I say, Skinner was in the Rag at the time, wasn't he?"

"I think so," answered Harry. "Why?"

"Well, he seems worried," grinned the Bounder.

The chums of the Remove left the study and joined a crowd that was gathering in the passage. The news was spreading that the Remove dorm was being searched by prefects, for a possible clue to the culprit. Harold Skinner undoubtedly looked very uneasy. So much so that a good many glances were cast at him, and fellows exchanged significant looks.

There was a general move down the passage to the landing, to the foot of the dormitory stairs. But the Removites were able to go no farther than that. Gwynne of the Sixth stood on the upper staircase, to bar off intruders.

"I suppose a fellow can go up, Gwynne?" said Skinner.

The prefect gave him a look.

"Not unless he's sent for," he answered, in a very significant tone.

"He, he, he!" from Bunter.

"You ass, Skinner!" muttered Snoop. "What the dickens did you do it for? You must have been potty!"

"Idiot!" was Skinner's answer.

Wingate of the Sixth looked down the stairs.

"Skinner's wanted!" he called out. "Send Skinner up!"

"Skinner!" called Gwynne.

Skinner slowly ascended the upper staircase. There was a buzz in the thickening crowd on the landing. Fellows of all Forms were gathering there, and the excitement was growing.

"So it was a Remove man, after all!" said Hobson of the Shell. "I rather fancied that it was."

"I guessed that, first thing!" remarked Temple of the Fourth.

"Oh, rather!" said Dabney.

"You silly asses!" hooted Bob Cherry. "Do you think a Remove man would rag the Head?"

"Looks as if the prefects think so," grinned Temple. "Why have they sent for Skinner?"

That was rather a puzzle. Excitement was intense, and only Gwynne on guard prevented an eager rush up the stairs to see what was going on in the dormitory. The general conclusion was that a clue had been found, and that Skinner was the man!

"Hark!" exclaimed Frank Nugent suddenly.

A sharp yelp was heard from above. It was repeated. It sounded like a fellow getting swipes from a cane. The crowd on the landing exchanged glances.

That's Skinner!" breathed Bob.

"Quelch is there, you fellows!" breathed Billy Bunter. "I noticed he had his cane under his arm. But, I say, he can't be letting Skinner off with six! Everybody thought the chap would be sacked——"

"Hallo, hallo, hallo! Here he comes!"

Skinner came back down the stairs to the landing. Every eye was fixed on him. He wriggled painfully as he came. Evidently, he had been caned by his Form-master. But it was not a caning; it was the "sack" for the man who had ragged the Head. It was quite perplexing.

"I say, ain't you going to the Head?" squeaked Billy Bunter.

"You fat idiot!" answered Skinner.

"Ain't you going to be sacked?" demanded Hobson.

"Fathead!"

"Why did they send for you, Skinner?" asked Harry Wharton.

Skinner snarled.

"The silly fools found a packet of cigarettes, rooting through my box!" he answered. "I knew it was there, and if I'd known they were going up to the dorm——"

"Ha, ha, ha!"

"Ow!" said Skinner. "Wow! The silly idiots—wow!"

"Ha, ha, ha!"

Evidently Harold Skinner was not "the man." He had not been afraid that the prefects would find inky clobber in his box. He had been afraid that they would find his packet of cigarettes. And they had!

There was a roar of laughter as Skinner wriggled painfully away.

Half an hour later, Mr. Quelch came down—grim, but satisfied. Nothing of an inky nature had been found in the dormitory occupied by his boys. The prefects remained in the regions above —going through other junior dormitories with other Form-masters.

It was close on prep when that lengthy and laborious search finished—drawing blank! Fellows went to the studies to prep, highly excited. No clue had been found in the junior quarters, and the search was dropped. Would there be a search of the senior quarters? And would anything be found there if there was?

It was a deeply interesting question to the juniors. It was still more deeply interesting to Coker of the Fifth! To him, indeed, it was more than interesting—it was horrifying and terrifying!

He knew that the idea had been mooted. He knew that Prout was already booming indignantly on the subject. The Fifth, in Prout's opinion, were above all imaginable suspicion in such a matter. Junior masters did not see this!

It was unlikely! But it might happen next day, if nothing was discovered. And if it happened, what about those trousers?

There was only one resource! Those trousers had to be got rid of that night—somehow, or anyhow! A bundle dropped from a window in the dark, after all the fellows were asleep, could be picked up in the quad by a fellow who got out early, before rising-bell! It was risky—but it was the only way! Coker went to bed that night with the rest of the Fifth—but not to sleep!

It was a late hour. Stars glistened in the sky; but it was dark in the quad, especially where the shadows of the trees and buildings fell. Chick Chew, star kidnapper of the United States, was on the spot.

Chick had found more trouble in the kidnapping business since he had hit England, than he had ever experienced in his own happy land. Bud Parker

COME INTO THE OFFICE, BOYS AND GIRLS!

Your Editor is always pleased to hear from his readers. Write to him: Editor of the MAGNET, The Fleetway House, Farringdon Street, London, E.C.4. A stamped, addressed envelope will ensure a reply.

WHICH is the stronger animal, a lion or a gorilla? David Franks, of West Ham, asks me that question. As a matter of fact, there isn't much to choose between them. A famous explorer has just related how he witnessed

A BATTLE TO THE DEATH

between a lion and a gorilla. The lion had been stalking a baby gorilla, but, before the lion could leap upon it, the father gorilla appeared. The gorilla beat its chest loudly like a drum and emitted its appalling roar. Incidentally, I wonder if you know that the amount of energy required to emit that roar is said to be as much as would break a man's neck? The lion, swinging round, charged the gorilla. The gorilla, leaping aside, gripped the lion by one of its hind legs, snapping it immediately. The next moment, the two of them were locked together in a death-grip. In a few seconds the fight was over. The gorilla was almost torn to pieces. But the lion did not survive. It was so terribly injured that it could only limp away a few yards, and then fall. Its neck was so mauled that the beast bled to death where it lay. So it seems that when these two kings of the jungle meet, honours are even.

Here's a true yarn from America. In Kansas City,

POLICEMEN MUSTN'T WEAR MOUSTACHES!

They've all been told to shave them off. The reason is that the moustaches have caused so many fights between police and civilians that the police director has banned moustaches for good. The whole trouble started when a "speed-cop" grew a fancy little moustache. It looked so comical that people used to roar with laughter when they saw it, and even pass rude remarks. This was more than the speed-cop could stand. He would jump off his motor-bike and go for whoever dared to laugh at him. Apparently, moustaches are not popular in Kansas City, for when other policemen began to grow them, they, also, came in for uncomplimentary remarks. So many free fights were caused between the police and the civilians, that the only way to stop the whole business was to prevent the police from wearing moustaches. So peace has at last been restored!

Talking of restoring peace reminds me of the fact that I have restored peace with the many thousands of my readers who have been constantly asking me to republish stories dealing with the early adventures of Harry Wharton. This grand new feature—under the title of "THE MAKING of HARRY WHARTON!"—commenced in last week's issue of our grand companion paper, the "Gem." If any of my chums have not yet taken advantage of this great treat I should advise them to do so now. The "Gem," by the way, is on sale every Wednesday, price 2d.

Just room for some

REPLIES IN BRIEF!

When Were Tithes Instituted in this Country? Tithes are the payments which farmers are compelled to make for the upkeep of the churches. They were instituted by the first Archbishop of Canterbury about the year 600.

Who Built the Taj Mahal? The "Pearl Mosque" was built nearly 300 years ago by Shah Jehan as a mausoleum for his wife. It is known as the eighth wonder of the world.

How Many Books are there in the British Museum? It is difficult to say, for new books are being added every day. There are considerably over four million volumes, making it the largest library in the world.

I suppose you are all wondering what I have in store for you next week. Well, you'll certainly enjoy:

"THE GANGSTERS' SWOOP!"
By Frank Richards,

the fourth yarn in our grand new series. Poker Pike is finding it a real hard job "keeping tabs" on Putnam van Duck. As to what actually happens in this all-thrilling yarn I leave you to learn in due course. Believe me, chums, you'll find it a real top-notcher!

As usual, there will be another full-of-chuckles edition of the "Greyfriars Herald," a contribution by our clever Rhymester, and more chapters of our great new story of modern piracy which you will find is going to surpass all previous MAGNET serials for thrills, drama, and exciting adventure.

YOUR EDITOR.

THE FIFTEENTH CHAPTER.
One for His Nob!

"OW, pack it up!" snapped Chick Chew.

"I guess——" muttered Bud Parker.

"Can it, you!"

The fat gangster peered through the thick shadows of the Greyfriars quad. Bud Parker, his "side-kicker" in the kidnapping game, blinked round uneasily through his horn-rimmed spectacles.

was frankly discouraged. Bud would willingly have thrown down the whole game and streaked for home. Not so Mr. Chew! Mr. Chew was going to cinch the son of the Chicago millionaire, if it cost him a leg! The word failure did not exist in Chick Chew's vocabulary.

Standing under the shadowy elms, the two kidnappers watched the great facade of the House. Innumerable windows glimmered in the starlight.

Not a light burned. All Greyfriars was sunk in silence and slumber.

"I guess it's O.K.," murmured Mr. Chew. "I'll say it would be as easy as pie, if Old Man Vanderdecken hadn't coughed up that idea of hiring Poker Pike to keep tabs on his boy. Yep! But I guess we're buying it, you Bud, all the same, Poker or no Poker!"

"Mebbe he's around!" muttered the uneasy, horn-rimmed man, "and I'm telling you, that guy Poker is pesky sudden on the shoot——"

"Park it!" growled Chick. "I guess even Poker goes to sleep, times. You keep here, you Bud, and if you spot any guy rubbering around, you pass him a tap on the cabeza with the butt of your gat, and keep him from singing. I guess I'll be back afore you san say no sigar in mine!—and I'll mention that I'll have that young geek Putnam rolled up in a blanket, this side up with care! I ain't never got left yet—and I ain't going to begin, in this here one-horse country. Nope!"

Leaving the uneasy Bud on the watch under the shadowy elms, Chick Chew made a cautious approach to the House.

Cool and confident as he was, Chick was glad when he got into the cover of the deep shadow of the building.

He could not help feeling how exceedingly unpleasant it would be to hear the sudden bark of Poker's six-gun breaking the silence of the spring night.

Watchful as he was, Poker certainly had to get an allowance of sleep. But it was quite probable that he might prowl a few at night!

That, indeed, was Poker's invariable custom, had Chick only known!

Chick hoped that he was at the moment, asleep; but he took every precaution, in case he was awake and wary.

Fat as he was, the gangster moved lightly and swiftly, and dodged into every available cover as he approached the House—and did not breathe freely till he was wrapped in dark shadow under the walls.

His plan was carefully mapped out—to get into the school, search there for Putnam van Duck; tap him on the head to keep him quiet for a necessary length of time; roll him in a blanket, and walk off with him!

Only from the watchful gunman did he fear peril, and if he eluded the watchfulness of the gunman, it was pie—and clam pie at that!

Getting into the House presented little difficulty to Chick. He had played many parts in his time, before he burst into fame as the star kidnapper of the United States. In earlier and humbler days he had cracked safes and picked locks.

Locked doors and fastened windows only made Mr. Chew smile. Even bolts and bars did not stop him, and only checked him for a time.

But bolted doors, of course, meant delay, even to a master-hand at the game like Chick. He moved round the building, looking for an easily accessible window.

His footsteps made no sound as he moved, and the darkness covered him like a cloak. Bud, watching across the quad, might feel uneasy—but Chick was full of cheery confidence.

Even if the gunman was awake, and wary, and watching, he wasn't going to see Chick in the dark. Once he had reached the building Chick felt safe. A sound, certainly, might have given the alarm in the silence of the night. But Chick was going to make no sound.

When he had selected his window, that window was going to open noiselessly under his skilled hand. It was going to be left open for the passage of the tapped and blanketed millionaire's son, when Chick got him! There was not going to be any noise—unless something unexpected happened—as, indeed, something unexpected so often does!

It was the unexpected that happened now!

It was so utterly unexpected, that even the wary gangster was taken totally by surprise. The wariest gangster that ever put a guy on the spot could not have foreseen or guarded against this amazingly unexpected occurrence.

Chick had calculated all chances! Poker Pike might be rubbering around—he had reckoned on that! Some master might be up late—he had reckoned on that! Even a "cop" might have been roped in to keep tabs on the school—Chick had reckoned on that possibility. He had, he fancied, reckoned up everything in the list!

But he had not reckoned on a bundle suddenly falling out of the dark sky and crashing on his head!

No guy could have foreseen that!

If Chick Chew had been asked to name the thing that might possibly cramp his style that night, the very last thing he would have thought of, would have been Horace Coker's trousers!

He had never heard of Horace Coker! Had he heard of him, he would never have envisaged the possibility of Coker throwing his trousers, tied up in a bundle, out of window in the middle of the night.

It was not the sort of thing that was often done! It had never come within the scope of Chick's experience before, wide as that experience had been. It was the very last thing he could have thought of!

Yet it was what happened.

Coker—as ignorant of Chick below, as Chick was of Coker above—dropped that bundle from the window of the Fifth Form dormitory, breathed a sigh of relief—and then gave a startled jump.

Coker had supposed, of course, that the bundle would fall on the earth, and remain there till morning—when, at the earliest possible moment, he would get out of the House, pick it up, and scud down to the river with it.

Instead of which, the bundle had fallen fairly upon the head of Chick Chew; knocking him spinning.

The bundle was neither very large nor very heavy. But, descending from so great a height, it landed with terrific force. It fairly crashed on the gangster's head. From the startled Chick there came a howl that woke nearly every echo of Greyfriars School.

"Yooooo-hoooooop!" howled Chick.

He crashed.

"Oh crikey!" gasped Coker.

He put out his startled head, and stared down. He could see nothing. But he could hear. Something, he could guess, was happening. He did not know what.

Chick Chew staggered up dizzily.

The bundle that had knocked him over had fallen beside him.

Chick did not heed it. He did not even worry about the amazing mystery of its descent from a dark sky. He knew that his startled howl must have reached any wakeful ear in the school, and probably startled a good many sleeping ones out of slumber. He had given himself away—with a vengeance! He had spilled the beans!

Panting, he listened. If Poker was around——

He was!

Bang!

It was the roar of a six-gun!

A running figure loomed up in the gleam of the stars. It was little more than a dim shadow, crowned by a bowler hat. It was Poker Pike, burning the wind towards the spot where the uproar had sounded.

Probably he glimpsed the gangster. Anyhow, he burned powder—flash on flash, crack on crack!

"Search me!" gasped Chick.

Carrying off Putnam van Duck was now, in the way of stunts, a back number—as dead as the dodo. Chick knew that he would be a lucky gangster if he carried himself off, with the alarm given, and Poker Pike loosing off lead with a generous liberality.

Chick ran, and Bud ran, and Poker ran, and rapped out lead at the same time.

Windows opened, voices shouted; the whole school was awakened.

Coker, from the window of the Fifth Form dormitory, stared. He had no idea that his trousers had started that terrific row.

He had not seen what occurred—only heard the result. Startled voices floated up to the window; some of the masters and prefects were turning out. Coker hoped fervently that none of them would happen to spot a bundle lying in the shadow of the wall.

THE SIXTEENTH CHAPTER.

At Last!

"I SAY, you fellows, what's up with Coker?"

"Coker?" repeated Harry Wharton.

"Look!" grinned Bunter.

The Famous Five looked round at Coker. As a matter of fact, a good many fellows had looked at Coker already that morning. Since breakfast Coker's proceedings had been rather attractive of attention.

Coker was going up and down and round about by the wall of the House, staring into corners, looking round buttresses, scanning window-sills, peering into shrubbery. Coker seemed to be in search of something.

"I say, I asked him what he had lost, and he called me names!" said Billy Bunter. "He's fearfully shirty! If he's been dropping money about, I'd help him look for it with pleasure; but when I told him so, he was simply ill-bred——"

"Perhaps he knows you think findings are keepings!" grinned Bob Cherry.

"Oh, really, Cherry——"

Harry Wharton & Co. went over to Coker. Poker Pike was in the quad, and they noticed that he had his eyes on Horace, watching him very curiously indeed. His serious, hickory face was quite intent under his bowler hat.

Coker did not notice the Greyfriars gunman. He did not heed anybody or anything in his search for that bundle. He had not found it yet.

Coker was out of the House that morning before the rising-bell had given three clangs. But the early bird was not destined to catch the worm. There was no bundle to be seen. The trousers had vanished.

It was dismaying.

Had the trousers vanished for good, of course, that would have been all right. But Coker could not hope that.

The trousers were somewhere. The bundle, Coker supposed, must have gone farther than he intended to throw it; it had fallen somewhere or other, but he could not spot where. He had searched till the breakfast-bell went—in vain. He searched again after breakfast—still in vain!

"I'll call Inky all day long, and all night, too, if I jolly well want to!" snorted Bob Cherry, pinning Coker down with his foot. "Oh, shout it out!" said Coker bitterly. "Get a man sacked! I'm not asking you to keep it dark that I inked the Head! But don't howl out 'inky' at me in the quad or I'll jolly well smash you!"

Where were those trousers?

It was a baffling mystery. Coker had dreaded that the bundle might be spotted and picked up. But that could not be the explanation, for the discovery of a bundle containing a pair of trousers drenched with ink would have spread like wildfire through the school.

Everyone would have known that it was a clue to the man who had inked the Head, and before this the garments would have been traced to their owner, and Coker would have been up before the Beak. But what had happened? Where and O where were the trousers?

Coker, having searched every possible and impossible spot, was searching the lot over again. He really seemed to hope to be able to conjure the trousers there by sheer force of looking.

"Lost anything, Coker?" asked Harry politely.

Coker glared round at him.

Billy Bunter had not over-stated the case in saying that Coker was shirty. He had under-stated it. Coker was in a state of suppressed rage and fury, mingled with apprehension and alarm. He was simmering—almost boiling.

"Shut up and clear off, bother you!" snorted Coker.

"Don't they learn nice manners in the Fifth!" remarked Bob Cherry.

"The nicefulness is terrific!" chuckled the Nabob of Bhanipur.

"If you want me to smash you——" began Coker, in a roar. Then he checked the roar, remembering that these juniors knew the secret, and were keeping it dark. "Here, I say, you can help me to look, if you like. I've lost my trousers!"

"What-a-at?" stuttered the five together.

"Trousers! They're gone!" breathed Coker.

"But you've got them on!" gasped Frank Nugent, wondering whether Horace was wandering in his mind.

"Eh—what? You young idiot! Not these trousers!" snapped Coker. "The other trousers——"

Harry Wharton & Co. blinked at Coker. Knowing nothing of the thrilling adventures of those trousers, they were naturally astonished

"You—you've lost a pair of trousers?" gasped Bob Cherry. It was the very last thing the juniors expected to hear that a fellow had lost in the quad. "Mean to say you came out in two pairs of trousers this morning, and lost one——"

"You young ass! No!" hooted Coker. "Haven't you any sense? I chucked them down from the dorm window last night in a bundle."

"You—you—you chick-chack-chucked a pair of trousers out of a window at night?" stuttered Bob.

"Yes. I was going to field them first thing in the morning, and bury them somewhere, or drop them in the river," said Coker. "But—they're gone!" Then, as he saw the blank amazement in the juniors' faces, he snorted. "You young asses! If they find those bags, my number's up! Don't you understand?"

"But why?" gasped Harry Wharton.

"Think they won't guess how the ink got on them, you young fathead?"

"Oh!" gasped Harry. "Was there ink on them?"

He began to understand.

"Do you think I should chuck trousers away for fun?" snorted Coker. "Don't be a sillier young idiot than you can help!"

The juniors grinned. Their idea was that, if there was a silly idiot on the spot—as certainly there was—it was not one of themselves.

It had not occurred to Coker to mention that the trousers were inky—which really was the important point.

"There was a row last night," went on Coker. "I hear that that gunman spotted the kidnappers after young Van Duck—or fancied he did—and started banging away at them. The row started after I'd chucked the trousers down. I wouldn't have done it if I'd known what was coming, but I never heard a sound till I'd dropped the trousers. Then somebody yelled, all of a sudden, like billy-ho! Hardly a second after I'd dropped the trucks, you know! I can tell you it startled me!"

"The bundle can't have been found!" said Harry. "Some of the masters came out when the row started, but if they'd found the bags—inky——"

"It's not that," said Coker. "I should have heard about it before this. But what's become of the bundle?"

"According to Pike, the kidnapper was around," said Bob. "But I suppose he never stopped to kidnap your trousers?"

"Ha, ha, ha!"

But Coker did not laugh. It was no laughing matter to Coker. Those unhappy trousers were irrefragable evidence of guilt. They were somewhere—but where?

"It's all that rotten gunman's fault!" groaned Coker. "If he hadn't cheeked me, I should never have gone after him

(*Continued on page* 28.)

CAPTAIN VENGEANCE!

By JOHN BREDON

THE FIRST CHAPTER.

Nemesis Island!

NEMESIS ISLAND lay green and golden in the intense sapphire blue of the Indian Ocean; like a giant tropical lizard basking in the sun.

Coconut-palms, tall, slender, graceful, thrashed their feathery tufts to the song of the monsoon. Green tamarisks waved. White sands lay cracked and baking in the sun. Silver surf creamed and boomed along the razor-edged coral reefs that guarded the channel into the little half-moon bay that was the sole and only landing-place of Nemesis Island.

Above the long wooden jetty, with its palm-thatched goods sheds, rose the high observation tower of the white prison buildings. In the interior, dense tropical jungles enfolded the quarries and plantations where the wretched convicts toiled out their hopeless lives under the whips and guns of the overseers.

Nemesis Island!

It is said that every crook and criminal, every spy, adventurer, and political refugee, gives a shudder at the very mention of that dreaded name.

Nemesis Island is a by-word as the most terrible penal settlement in the world. It belongs to the republic of Varland, a small European power in the Baltic. To its living death have been sent murderers and criminals of all nations, the worst men in the world, for Varland was the Mecca of every runaway crook with money in his pocket—until Morgan Drake, mystery man of the British Secret Service, induced its government to pass a law against them that was as sudden as it was unexpected.

Under a striped awning that shielded him from the blinding rays of the afternoon sun, lolled Governor Zarda, huge, bald, and yellow of countenance, with black, beady eyes that were almost hidden in rolls of fat; like a great humped hog heaped into a basket chair. Silently he levelled a pair of binoculars at a tiny speck that was cutting an arrow-head of foam through the shimmering, unruffled sea.

A smile of gloating satisfaction creased the governor's heavy, bloated features as he recognised one of the motor launches belonging to the settlement. With a podgy finger he pressed an electric bell-push at his elbow. Next moment, from the stately white house with the green sun-blinds that was Governor Zarda's quarters, came a broad and powerfully built man in the straw hat and canvas slacks of a convict, with the crimson dagger of Varland and the number 333 branded in red on his rugged, massive chest.

"You observe, No. 333?" gloated Governor Zarda, turning his gleaming monocle upon the silent convict. "That is our launch. They have captured the negro who tried to escape. No man ever gets away from Nemesis Island, No. 333—no man has ever done so, or ever will!"

Complacently the governor smirked as he swabbed the sweat-band of his solar topee.

Fortunately for his peace of mind as he made that arrogant boast, Governor Zarda did not possess the gift of seeing into the future. Still less had he the power to read the thoughts that were hatching in No. 333's teeming brain, as the convict stared out across the flashing ocean. Silently the governor and No. 333 watched as the prison launch foamed alongside the landing pier.

"Tell the prison lieutenant to bring in his cattle, No. 333," continued Governor Zarda, mopping his moistured brow. "I have entertainment for them. They shall see their negro comrade lashed into bleeding ribbons. That will teach the scum how hopeless it is to think of escape!"

"At once, Excellency!" The face of No. 333 was a mask of grim immobility as he passed into the office to seek out the prison lieutenant

It was a remarkable countenance, incidentally; strong, ruthless, cunning, with a jaw of iron, and pale blue eyes that were hard as flints.

A few years before No. 333 had been Von Eimar, the world's master-spy, the man on whose head a dozen governments had set a price. Now he was Convict No. 333—but, having still the brain of Von Eimar, he had been excused the brutalising work in the quarries or plantations, and, becoming the governor's secretary, now knew more about the secrets and organisation of Nemesis Island than did Governor Zarda himself.

The prison siren brayed out its insistent, brazen note. From quarries and plantations the guards were herding the cowed and shackled convicts—drooping listlessly in their rusty chains and in the blazing glare of the sun, into the dusty, arid square beneath the governor's house.

"No man escapes from Nemesis Island!" That was Governor Zarda's confident and oft-repeated boast; and, up till now, he had no occasion to unsay it.

At night the prisoners were huddled into a barbed-wire enclosure that was studded with concrete watch-towers equipped with machine-guns and powerful arc-lamps. The barriers were charged with electricity from the prison power-house, and to touch them meant death. By day the convicts toiled in chain-gangs, overlooked by inhuman task-masters, whip in hand and gun in belt. If one broke his fetters and slipped away into the green, poisonous mangrove swamps or tangled jungle, the shark-infested Indian Ocean still hemmed him in.

The negro runaway was half-dead. For two days, without food or drink, he had been afloat on a miserable raft that he had constructed out of bamboo poles and palm fibre. A hovering aeroplane, sent out by the governor, had spotted him, and the launch had brought him in. In any case, he had had no chance. Nemesis Island was hundreds of miles from the nearest shipping routes.

Now, drooping and faint, he was being lashed up to the terrible triangle beneath the governor's window. His fellow convicts, sullen, crushed, yet dully resentful, were lined up under the rifles of their guards to watch his punishment.

Lash, lash, lash!

With the feral cruelty of a diseased mind, Governor Zarda laughed softly to himself and rubbed fat fists as he watched the black's tortures from the window.

Some of the prisoners of Nemesis Island were not present at the "entertainment." One of these was No. 333 —Van Eimar, as has been said. Another was No. 186, who had once been the notorious doctor and poisoner of Brussels, Dr. Nieuwe.

Since the regular prison doctor had died of tropical fever—or, possibly, something else—No. 186 had been in charge of the prison hospital.

"Is all well?" asked No. 186, a tall, thin, stooping man, with a narrow, swarthy face and pointed "imperial," peering through his rimless pince-nez as Von Eimar met him in the dispensary.

"Yes. It's our best chance," breathed No. 333, his eyes glittering beneath narrow lids. "The guards are all in the square. We may not have another chance like this for weeks. Come on!"

A warder, with a revolver holstered to his belt, was nodding drowsily in a chair by the door that led to the hospital ward. He rose to his feet as the convicts approached.

Von Eimar wasted no time in words. As the unsuspecting warder opened his mouth to speak Von Eimar slipped past him and let fly with a powerful fist.

Taking a terrific pile-driver just behind his right ear, the man flopped out with not so much as a groan.

"Good!" grunted No. 333, stooping to possess himself of the man's revolver-belt. "Not so bad, eh? Now for a sudden recovery of your patients, doctor!"

Mutiny!

THERE were nearly thirty men sweltering in the confined and breathless heat of the prison hospital, besides a couple of convict orderlies.

At a word from Von Eimar all but half a dozen leaped from their beds and stood tensed and alert.

Sick men? Dying of tropical fever? Not they! Except for those six genuine cases, there were not two dozen more healthy fellows, nor greater villains, than the group of evil-browed felons that crowded round Von Eimar and the doctor.

Simple as the plot was, it was carefully planned and carried out. It was easy for Von Eimar, who had access to every record and card-index in the governor's office, to pick out a number of the most hardened and ruthless scoundrels in the convict settlement to join him in his desperate enterprise. And what was easier than for his confederate, Dr. Nieuwe, to report these men as being sick, after first handing them a potion to give them the hideous, yellow appearance of tropical fever?

And what a crowd they were, too! "Killer" Moran, for instance, Chicago gangster, bootlegger, racketeer, kidnapper, and hold-up man, with a dozen cold-blooded murders to his record! His brutal, gorilla face and beetling brows stamped him for what he was. And Luis Ramiro, the flashing, dark-eyed South American! Mikhail Lebedoff, the Russian ex-naval artificer and engineer! They were all of a kidney, except, perhaps, the tall, good-looking, straight-limbed Englishman, of about thirty, whose temples were already greying with the horrors of Nemesis Island, and the little bow-legged Cockney, who had found himself in the convict settlement because of his broad-minded views on the subject of property.

"No talking!" exclaimed Von Eimar briefly. "You know our plan. Every man knows what he has to do? Good! Then follow me, and keep quiet!"

Through a maze of empty, white-washed corridors, No. 333 led his men up a vertical iron ladder to the flat leads of the single-storied prison buildings. Stooping, with their heads ducked low under the parapet, they hurried in a snaking line towards the lofty control tower that dominated the settlement.

A sentry was lounging idly by the door at its base. As they swarmed round a corner he made a sudden grab for his rifle, but at the sight of Van Eimar's murderous eyes squinting down the sights of a levelled automatic, he thought better of it and raised his hands, dropping the weapon. Moran and Luis Ramiro lashed his arms behind his back with cord, gagging and binding the man with quick and scientific efficiency.

The turret-door was of reinforced steel, but the forcing of locks was child's play to Mikhail Lebedoff, expert safe-cracker since his expulsion from the Russian Navy. Up the narrow, twisting stairs bounded two of the mutineers to surprise and overpower the solitary operator in the wireless transmission station above.

"No man escapes from Nemesis Island!" Such is the proud boast of Governor Zarda—until Convict 333, the world's master-spy, turns the tables on his captors and becomes CAPTAIN VENGEANCE!

The lower floor of the control tower was the arsenal, and swiftly the rebel convicts armed themselves. Racks of glistening, well-oiled rifles were promptly emptied. Over naked shoulders were slung ammunition bandoliers and revolver-belts loaded with cartridges. Killer Moran swung on to one shoulder a light machine-gun, which he knew so well how to use.

Lolling on the stone balcony-rail of his window, Governor Zarda heard a rapid tramping of bare feet in the passage-way. Surprised, he flung a glance over his humpy shoulder into his office.

Then he stood appalled!

The office door was flung violently open, and the governor's eyes almost popped from under twitching, hairless lids as he saw the gap crammed with a mob of armed villains, headed by Von Eimar, who had levelled his gun.

"Wha—what——" stuttered Governor Zarda, not daring to trust his bulging eyes.

"Silence, you fat pig!"

The barrel of Von Eimar's gun was jammed into the governor's fat and palpitating ribs. There was none of the convict secretary's habitual deference about him now. It was not out of politeness that he picked up the governor's fallen cigar, where it was burning a hole in the expensive carpet, thrusting it between those flabby lips; nor when he jammed the dangling monocle back into Zarda's terror-brimming eye.

With a swing of his powerful arm, he forced the now abject governor back through the window.

All unsuspicious of the tense drama that was being enacted above them, convicts and prison guards were massed in the square before the whipping-post, all facing the window. The negro was drooping upon his leashed wrists, already unconscious, perhaps dead. Still the whip coiled around his black, criss-crossed shoulders.

"Now!" snarled Von Eimar, keeping well behind the governor's bulky figure as his iron grip squeezed that trembling elbow. "Tell your dogs of warders to line up under the window! Then give the order 'Ground arms!' Quick, you son of a pig!"

The hidden automatic drove into Governor Zarda's fleshy back.

As in a dream, Governor Zarda fumbled in the folds of his ample sash for a whistle. Every face was upturned to the balcony as he winded a call upon it. Von Eimar and his confederates hung well in the background, out of sight, the arch-mutineer screened by the mosquito-curtains of the window.

In a thin, piping voice, utterly unlike his usual rich and domineering tones, the governor spoke as Von Eimar instructed him.

Surprised, but obedient, the prison guards filed forward under the governor's window, lowering their rifles to the ground, but watchful, hands upon the butts under their holster-flaps.

Then, in a snapping voice, Von Eimar spoke:

"Let 'em see your ironmongery, Moran!"

With a wicked, ugly grin, Killer Moran swung the muzzle of his light machine-gun between the shoulders of Von Eimar and the governor; sights aligned, drum clicked into position, his thick fingers crooking round the trigger.

Surprised ejaculations escaped from the row of sun-helmeted guards at that unexpected development.

"Surrender, you scum!" suddenly bawled Von Eimar, heaving the governor aside and hanging his brawny body over the balcony. "We've got you cold! No tricks, you rats! One hand to a gun, and I'll drop each man where he stands!"

A wave of Von Eimar's podgy hand to that black, hovering death-muzzle was sufficient. The guards raised their hands above their heads.

Left to himself, Killer Moran would have mown down those horrified warders with as little compunction as if they had been a row of ninepins. But Von Eimar, cold, hard, and ruthless as he could be upon occasions, was not one that loved murder for its own sake.

Lovingly, Moran cuddled his itching finger round that trigger that, at a twitch, could release a stream of murderous lead. But he knew better than to defy Von Eimar's expressed order.

"Now, men!" roared Von Eimar, to the equally stupefied convicts massed behind the guards. "Where are your wits? Disarm the dogs! Quickly! Make them prisoners! Are you afraid, you fools?"

His staccato voice broke the spell.

With a prolonged, bestial howl, rattling their irons as they rushed, or, rather, hobbled, the delighted prisoners converged in a dense mob upon their paralysed guards and overseers.

Disarmed, stripped of their uniforms, cursed, kicked, buffeted, and spat upon, the luckless guards would have been trampled underfoot and clawed limb from limb had not Von Eimar intervened to save them.

"Take them to the cells!" he thundered, above the howling, raving clamour. And it says much for the man's dominant personality that his commands prevailed.

The dusty, naked, and bleeding warders, now prisoners in their turn, were dragged off by their jubilant, triumphing captors and locked in the row of iron-barred cells under the prison buildings—black, horrible dens that were used for solitary confinement.

Then bedlam was let loose on Nemesis Island. Three hundred mutinous convicts, babbling with joy, swarmed over the entire penal settlement, looting, destroying.

Wild shouts echoed as they broke into the engineering shop for tools to release them from their irons, to which many of them had been linked in files perpetually for years.

Furiously they stormed into the liquor stores and maddened themselves with raw spirits.

Never had such sights been seen before on Nemesis Island.

Grim, masterful, and forbidding, Von Eimar stood upon the broad staircase that led from the hall of the governor's house, with the shrunken prison governor cowering in his grip.

He had seized upon the governor's monocle, screwing it into his own pale blue eye, and he looked a strange sight, stiff and upright like a Teutonic officer, the felon brand scarring his naked breast, and the governor's topee tilted upon his square, shaven head.

A mob of half-naked convicts, their evil faces flushed and distorted, flourished knives, rifles, and billets of wood as they howled and lusted for Governor Zarda's blood.

"Give him to us, the mangy old wolf!"

"Kill the dog, kill him!"

"We'll tear him to bits!"

"Lash him to the triangle and do to him as he did to the nigger!"

These and worse threats in half a dozen different languages were hurled at the terror-stricken governor as he stood with quaking paunch and flexing knees.

With hairy, naked, perspiring breasts, branded with numbers and the crimson dagger of Varland, wrists scarred with shackle-marks, backs scored by the lash, the rebel convicts came tramping in a dense mass up the stairway.

Fierce yellings changed to brutal laughter as they saw their late tyrant, half-mad with panic, crouching away behind Von Eimar's straddling legs.

Von Eimar took a pace forward, his little eyes narrowed. Behind him, their faces dark and grim, grouped the little band of mutineers who had effected the conspiracy.

"Back, you pig-dogs!" Von Eimar growled like a savage mastiff, baring his teeth. "Governor Zarda lives. I say so. I need him alive for a special purpose!"

In surprise the would-be murderers halted, daunted for a moment by that fierce, dominant glare; and then a snarl of wild-beast anger mingled with coarse and derisive mirth rumbled from their hoarse throats.

With a curse, a gigantic half-caste Malay spat out something inarticulate, thrusting forward with bare, splay-toed feet as he flourished a heavy iron bar.

Von Eimar grinned, showing white, gold-filled teeth like a spitting cat. The drink-misted eyes of the mutineers hardly saw his clenched fist move, so suddenly did he swing it up. But it crashed under the half-caste's chin with a jolt that almost snapped his spinal cord, and the brute slumped down among the legs of his startled and wavering companions.

Then, as the excited rabble hung back in a doubting mass, sullen, resentful, yet subdued by Von Eimar's cold and measuring glance, a telephone-bell on a near-by stand buzzed suddenly into whirring life.

Von Eimar, scowling, lifted the receiver from its hook.

"Well?" he barked into the transmitter, revolver levelled, one eye upon the seething mob that filled the hall.

His face darkened as a clear English voice came over the wires from the observation post at the top of the control tower. It was the English ex-naval lieutenant who was speaking.

Von Eimar listened to what the man had to say; then, replacing the receiver, he addressed the seething mob.

"Men!" he said in a snapping voice, which cut like steel through the noise and babble. "Listen to me, you pack o' fools! You'll have something more to think about presently than making a jigsaw puzzle of Governor Zarda!" Sneering, he laughed in their faces. "There's a ship heading for the island, my friends! A warship! She's making for the harbour. and when she reaches it——"

The Captured Cruiser!

THE incipient storm collapsed like a pricked bubble. In terror the convicts crowded up to Von Eimar, begging of him to know what he intended to do now that this awful gulf yawned at their feet.

With a wave of his podgy hand the arch-mutineer quelled them.

"Leave this to me, men," he said coolly. "I am leader here! Is that agreed? Very well! Obey my orders implicitly if you wish to get out of this trap."

With that he made his way to the control tower, followed by his lieutenants and the whole throng of the now subdued and dismayed insurgents.

With a pair of binoculars in his hands, a cigar sticking out from the corner of his mouth, Von Eimar leaned against the iron railing of the observation tower, apparently in no way disturbed by the danger that threatened to wreck all his carefully prepared schemes.

Beneath him on the flat prison leads massed the convicts. a sea of anxious faces all staring at that grim, grey warship, with its plume of drifting smoke and creaming bow wave, that was steaming slowly towards the island harbour.

"It's the cruiser Zermac," announced Von Eimar gravely "The flagship of the Varland Navy—on a world tour, so I understand I hadn't calculated on this. The supply ship, on which I intended we should make our escape, isn't due for two days!"

"Awkward!" commented Ronald Westdale, the tall Englishman who had first observed the unexpected cruiser. "I don't know how many men she carries, but you can't expect our lot of underworld rats to put up a fight against disciplined Navy men."

"A crack in our gearbox, an' no error!" supplemented Hilarity Hinton, the cheery, irrepressible Cockney, whose spirits could not be damped either by the horrors of Nemesis Island or by the imminence of death. "This is where we split, as the pea-pod said to the basin!"

"Perhaps!" Von Eimar ruminated, as though speaking to himself. "Perhaps not! I think I have a plan—yes, it might work. Donner! I'll make it work!"

As Admiral Mericski, of the Varland Navy, came alongside the pier in his swift motor-pinnace it was too dark for him to see anything unusual about the guard of honour which was drawn up with rifles and fixed bayonets to receive him. They wore the cool, white uniforms of prison guards, their scarred, ugly faces shaded by sun helmets, and in the dim, uncertain light there was nothing to show that they were convicts disguised.

At the head of the jetty stairs stood Governor Zarda, looking very sick and pale in his splendid, epauletted uniform. Beside him, arm-in-arm, was a sturdy, square-set man in neat white ducks—none other than Von Eimar—wearing a monocle that shone against the quay lights.

"This is an unexpected pleasure, Admiral Mericski," purred Von Eimar, smiling cordially. "Pray excuse Governor Zarda. He is greatly sick—of a tropical fever—and speech is too much for him; it might bring on a fatal stroke."

Governor Zarda licked his trembling lips as the barrel of Von Eimar's automatic prodded him in the small of his back.

Admiral Mericski stared in haughty surprise.

"And who, in the name of Satan, may you be, sir?" he demanded.

"If you will accompany us to Government House I can explain, my dear admiral," returned Von Eimar blandly.

The admiral stared haughtily, and at last condescended to pace along beside Von Eimar and the governor, clanking his sword importantly as he went.

As soon as they were in Governor Zarda's private office, Von Eimar laughed gutturally. Slipping the automatic into his pocket, he slapped his hands. The folding doors were flung open, to reveal Killer Moran, scowling as he chewed, and a dozen ragged and half-naked convicts, armed with rifles and bayonets.

Admiral Mericski was staggered.

"What means this?" he gasped, uncomprehendingly. "Is this some form of a joke?" Angrily he swung upon Governor Zarda, who had collapsed weakly into a swivel chair. "If so, I must say that it is in the worst possible taste. I am offended! Perhaps you, sir, can enlighten me," he added, turning to Von Eimar. "Order those ruffians away, whoever they are!"

Von Eimar beamed through his monocle.

"Certainly I can enlighten you, admiral," he said smilingly. "It is a joke, to be sure, though one that I fear you will not appreciate. Let me introduce myself. This morning I was No. 333, a guest of the Republic of Varland, on Nemesis Island. A few years ago I was Von Eimar, international spy. You will have heard of me, I imagine. To-night I am Captain

Printed in Great Britain and published every Saturday by the Proprietors, The Amalgamated Press, Ltd. The Fleetway House, Farringdon Street, London, E.C.4. Advertisement offices: The Fleetway House, Farringdon Street, London, E.C.4. Registered for transmission by Canadian Magazine Post. Subscription rates: Inland and Abroad, 11s. per annum; 5s. 6d. for six months. Sole Agents for Australia and New Zealand: Messrs. Gordon & Gotch, Ltd., and for South Africa: Central News Agency, Ltd.—Saturday, May 9th, 1936.

Vengeance, the pirate, and your cruiser, my dear admiral, is to be my private man-o'-war." He pressed a fat thumb upon the soda-water siphon at his elbow. "A drink, my dear admiral? I fancy you will need it?"

Admiral Mericski seemed to be on the verge of an attack of apoplexy. Thunderous rumbles and gurgles sounded in his plump throat. He strove to speak, but he could form no words.

"Ruffians," exclaimed Von Eimar, turning to Killer Moran and his men, "the admiral has requested me to order you away. Go, then, and take these two other ruffians with you!"

With an ugly smile upon his gorilla face, Killer Moran took the Admiral by the elbow.

"Aw c'mon, baby!" drawled the giant American gangster, chewing as he spoke. "This way, ol' palooka! Don'tcha be frightened, admiral boy! Guess we ain't gonna take yuh for a ride—not unless yuh git ferocious! Nope, sirree! We'll take yuh for a nice li'l sea-trip, instead!"

Like a man in a dream, Admiral Mericski suffered himself to be led away.

At a poke from a bayonet, none too gently administered, Governor Zarda heaved his great bulk from the chair and waddled hopelessly behind him.

• • • • • •

A minute later a man in the uniform of a prison official approached the coxswain in charge of the admiral's pinnace.

"The admiral's orders," he said, saluting, as he handed the petty officer a folded note. "All the crew except the duty men are to be landed at once, without arms. They are to be lodged in the governor's fort. Here are Admiral Mericski's official instructions to the commander."

If the coxswain was surprised at the unusual order, it was not for him to question it. At a word from him the outboard engine was started up, and the pinnace foamed back smartly to the hawsered cruiser.

The commander who acted under Admiral Mericski was puzzled. But his instructions were explicit and peremptory. The admiral himself had penned them, at Von Eimar's dictation, with a revolver held to his head as an encouragement. Promptly, therefore, the commander issued orders for the lowering away of the boats, and he himself accompanied the first boat-party to the shore.

The trap worked like a charm. As the sailors passed unarmed through the narrow sally-port of the battery they found themselves suddenly dazzled by blinding searchlights. Stern voices ordered them to throw up their hands if they didn't want to be riddled by machine-gun bullets.

Group after group was hustled through the frowning prison gates, clamped into the irons discarded by the convicts, and locked into different casements of the fort.

It was after midnight, when the officer of the watch, pacing the bridge of the cruiser, was surprised to see a number of motor-launches speeding towards the Zermac.

The boatswain's whistle piped smartly. Duty men lined the cruiser's well-deck as Governor Zarda and Admiral Mericski came climbing the accommodation-ladder, arm-in-arm with Von Eimar, who chatted amiably with them as his monocle shone in the deck-lights.

The lieutenant of the watch advanced to meet them, and then gaped foolishly at the ragged and branded mob of convicts that scrambled up the steel sides of the cruiser.

"Wha-what——" he exclaimed, in bewilderment.

"T-tell your men t-to surrender, officer!" gasped Admiral Mericski, forked beard quivering ludicrously as he spoke. "That is an order. D-don't do anything rash, for Heaven's sake!"

Cheering, and brandishing knives and guns, a sea of armed convicts poured over the bulwark rails from the boats crowding below.

The officer and the watch made no resistance. Indeed, they had very little chance, being unarmed. In stupefaction they allowed themselves to be bound with their own lanyards, and hustled off to the cruiser's brig under the foredeck.

Swarms of excited convicts overran the captured cruiser. Into the gun-turrets they climbed, along the superstructure past the squat black funnels and deck-houses, swinging up the ladders from the well deck on to the quarter deck, dropping down vertical iron ladders to overpower the engine-room hands, and the firemen and trimmers who were banking the fires in the stokehold below.

Never was a proud warship subdued more easily. The crew of the Zermac had a courage fully equal to that of their admiral and the island prison governor. Inside ten minutes the convicts were masters of the entire vessel.

Von Eimar tramped up the steel ladder rungs to the bridge, a satisfied smile lighting his broad Teutonic features. He threw open the door of the chart-house and entered.

"Ruffians!" exclaimed Von Eimar "Take these two other ruffians with you!" "Aw, c'mon, baby!" drawled Killer Moran, taking the admiral by the elbow. "Don'tcha be frightened, admiral boy, we ain't gonna take yuh for a ride, not unless yuh git ferocious!"

Next moment, however, he halted in blank amazement.

"Teufel!" he rapped out, in surprise.

A smooth-faced, athletic youngster of about fifteen, with fair hair and frank, grey eyes was studying a chart by the glow of the electric bulb. He wore, not the uniform of the Varland Navy, but a white yachting suit, and his appearance was distinctly English.

"Donnerwetter!" exploded Von Eimar, grunting in his throat.

The boy looked up. He was as amazed as the escaped convict leader himself.

"Von Eimar, the spy!" cried the lad, rising from the chart-table.

For once in his life Von Eimar lost his iron self-control. A white blaze of anger consumed him.

"Yes, I am Von Eimar, the international spy!" he thundered stamping into the room with a strong fist closing over the butt of his revolver. "And you are Roderick Drake, the son of Morgan Drake, the British Secret Service agent, who sent me to the living death of Nemesis Island!"

Fierce passion distorted his livid face, and Roderick Drake, looking straight into those glaring eyes, saw murder in their depths as Von Eimar unholstered his gun, and squinted along the sights on the barrel.

(Face to face with the son of the man who had sent him to the penal settlement on Nemesis Island, Von Eimar has revenge in his reach! Look out for startling developments in next week's thrilled-packed chapters of this powerful pirate yarn!)

HORACE COKER'S DARK DEED!

(*Continued from page 23.*)

with that ink, and shouldn't have got the Head by mistake! By gum, if I get through this, I'll make that brute sit up! I'll rag him right and left till I rag him out of the school! I'll give him something botter than ink next time—a bucket of tar——"

"Mind the Head doesn't get it, Coker!"

"Ha ha, ha!"

"Oh, shut up!" snapped Coker. "Look here, if you've got any idea what can have become of those dashed trousers——"

Harry Wharton glanced round. At a little distance Poker Pike was standing, with his keen slits of eyes fixed intently on Horace Coker. For some reason he was keenly interested in Coker that morning, and Harry Wharton fancied he could guess why.

"What about Pike?" he asked.

"Pike!" repeated Coker.

"I mean, he was prowling about, and if anybody spotted the bundle, he was the man to spot it. Then he might hang about to spot a fellow looking for something here—and that's what he's jolly well doing now!"

"Oh!" said Coker.

He stared across at the Greyfriars gunman. Poker certainly was the man likeliest to have spotted the bundle if it had been spotted. But why he should have kept such a discovery dark was rather a mystery.

"Oh!" repeated Coker.

"Hallo, hallo, hallo! There's the bell!" exclaimed Bob Cherry, as the bell rang for first school; and the Famous Five cut off to the House.

Coker did not follow. Prout would be ratty if he was late in the Form-room, but that did not matter; what mattered was trousers.

Looking at the gunman, he discerned a faint grin on the hickory face. Coker made up his mind at last and approached the gunman.

"Look here——" he began.

"Looking," said Poker laconically.

"Did you——" Coker paused.

"Shoot!" said Poker.

"Did you——" Coker paused again.

"Spill it, big boy!" said Poker. "You the guy that chucked a bundle out of a winder last night?"

"Did you find it?" gasped Coker.

"Jest a few!" agreed Poker. "I'll say it was that bundle dropping that made Chick Chew let out a howl like he was Sitting Bull on the war-path and put me wise that he was around. Surest thing you know!"

"Oh!" gasped Coker.

"I guess I rubbered around a few after they hit the horizon," said Poker. "I sure did spot that bundle and cinched it, and I'll mention that I stared some when I piped what was in it. Yourn?"

Coker hesitated.

He disliked that gunman—disliked him intensely. It was his fixed intention to rag him out of the school—if he was not himself, unfortunately, sacked before he could carry out that fell intention. In these circumstances, he felt a natural coyness about placing himself at Poker's mercy. Yet he realised that he already was at Poker's mercy if Poker had the fatal trousers.

"Yourn, I reckon!" said Poker, as Horace did not speak. "I guessed I'd spot a guy looking for that bundle in the morning, and I sure was around early, and I'll say I've been watching you a few. Them trousers was parked full of ink, and I guess I don't need telling why a guy wanted to lose them. I'll say you're the guy that got the king-pin of this here outfit the other night at the door of my little caboose with a pail of ink. Surest thing you know!"

Coker breathed hard.

"Boyees will be boyees," went on Poker; "and I ain't the galoot to give a boyee away. Nope! But I'll tell all this here island it was a dirty trick to pass up on a mild old guy like that schoolmaster."

"It—it was a mistake!" gasped Coker. "I never meant it for the Head: I'd have mopped it over myself sooner! I—I meant it for somebody else."

"That lets me out," said Poker, with a nod. "If you never meant it for that schoolmaster guy, I ain't shouting it out any. But who'd you reckon you'd get with that can of ink at the door of my caboose?"

Coker did not answer that question. Really it hardly needed an answer.

"Carry me home to die!" ejaculated Poker Pike. "Why, you ornery young geek—you pie-faced, slab-sided, goldarned, pesky gink—you figured on getting this baby with that doggoned ink! Surest thing you know!"

Coker stood dumb.

There was a long pause.

"Search me!" said Poker at last. "I'll say you was asking for more'n you could chew if you'd bit it off—and then some! But if you never aimed to get the schoolmaster guy, that lets me out. I guess you can have them trousers."

"Oh!" gasped Coker.

He followed Mr. Pike to the lodge. At the sight of the bundle Coker felt like a shipwrecked mariner who saw land. The trousers—those terrible trousers—were in his hands at last! Coker made quick time down to the river.

* * * * *

Harry Wharton & Co., when they saw Coker of the Fifth again, beheld a cheery smile on his rugged features.

From which they deduced that it was all right.

And it was!

Coker had a hundred lines, not to mention a "jaw," from Prout for being late for class that morning. But lines and jaw left Coker unmoved, in his happy relief. Those trousers—those wretched trousers—were gone; sunk, full of stones, at the bottom of the Sark, and no clue remained to connect Coker with the mysterious mopper of ink.

The hunt was still going on. That day, in spite of Prout's indignant boom, there was a search in the Fifth Form dormitory. Coker did not mind. Coker only smiled. Nothing would ever be known now. That was all right!

"That gunman chap isn't a bad sort," he told Potter and Greene.

"Eh?" said Potter and Greene.

"The fact is I rather like him," said Coker.

Potter and Greene could only stare at their great leader.

"He's got some funny ways," said Coker. "But I tell you he's a good sort in his own way. You can take that from me! Don't let me hear any more rot about ragging him, or anything of that kind! I shan't stand it!"

"We never——" gasped Potter.

"It was you!" hissed Greene.

"Don't jaw!" said Coker. "What fellows you are for jawing! Jaw, jaw, jaw!"

THE END.

(*The next yarn in this full-of-thrills series is entitled: "**THE GANGSTERS' SWOOP!**" It's the brightest and most sparkling yarn you could wish to read, so make sure and order next Saturday's* MAGNET *in good time!*)

Harry Wharton & Co. in another Thrilling Schoolboy Adventure . . "THE GANGSTERS SWOOP!" By Frank Richards

No. 1,474. Vol. XLIX. EVERY SATURDAY. Week Ending May 16th, 1936

The GANGSTERS SWOOP!

By FRANK RICHARDS

FEATURING THE WORLD-FAMOUS HARRY WHARTON & CO., OF GREYFRIARS.

THE FIRST CHAPTER.

Bunter is Too Obliging !

"SHUT that door!" roared Bob Cherry.

"I say——"

"Shut it!"

"I say, you fellows——"

"Shut that door!" yelled six or seven voices in chorus.

"But——" howled Billy Bunter.

"You fat ass, shut that door!"

Instead of shutting the door of Study No. 1, Billy Bunter blinked in, through his big spectacles, at the crowd of juniors there.

He blinked through a cloud of flying fragments of paper.

Harry Wharton & Co. were busy. They were tearing up paper for "scent" in a paper-chase that was due on the morrow.

On the study table was a stack of paper—old exercises, disused books, newspapers—anything and everything that could be collected for the purpose.

The Famous Five were all there, and Putnam van Duck, and Smithy, and several other fellows—and many hands made light work. A large basket was filling with torn paper—till Bunter opened the study door. Then it began to unload a little.

It was a fine May day, but there was a keen wind blowing in the quadrangle. There was a strong draught coming along the Remove passage. The study window was wide open.

So when the door was open also, something like a gale blew through the study, scattering torn paper in clouds. Which was rather exasperating to the fellows who had torn it up. They did not want to crawl over the floor gathering up innumerable fragments. So they all yelled to the fat Owl of the Remove to shut the door.

Instead of which, Billy Bunter stood in the middle of the open doorway, blinking at them.

"Will you shut that door?" shrieked Harry Wharton.

"Look here——"

"Bang it on his silly nose, Smithy—you're nearest!"

The Bounder reached out, grasped the door, and hurled it shut. Billy Bunter made a swift backward leap, just in time. Never had his fat little nose had a narrower escape.

"The silly ass!" growled Bob Cherry, as fragments of paper fell like snowflakes. "What the dickens does he want? It's past tea-time!"

"Maybe he's honing to lend a hand with this job," suggested Putnam van Duck.

There was a chuckle in Study No. 1.

Van Duck was a new fellow. That accounted for his suggestion. No fellow who had been long at Greyfriars School, and become well acquainted with Billy Bunter, would have fancied that he was keen to lend a hand in a job of work.

Whatever Billy Bunter wanted, it was not a job. Bunter was unemployed as often and as long as he could manage it; and he had never been known to be genuinely seeking work.

But it seemed that he wanted something; for about a minute later, the door opened a few inches, and he blinked cautiously in.

"I say, you fellows——" came his squeak. Along with it came the draught from the passage, and a fresh scattering of fragments.

"Get out!" roared Johnny Bull.

"But I say——"

"Slaughter him!" howled Frank Nugent.

Two or three fellows jumped up. With that gale from the passage scattering the fragments, they looked like having a paper-chase in the study, without waiting for the morrow. Which was not at all what they wanted.

"I say, I've got a letter!" yelled Bunter. "I say, there was a letter for Van Duck, and I've brought it up——"

"Chuck it in, then, fathead, and shut that door!"

"But I say——"

Bang!

Billy Bunter jerked back his head like a tortoise popping back into the shell, as a whizzing cushion crashed. The door shut again.

"Beasts!" came a howl through the keyhole.

Putnam van Duck, who was seated on the box under the window, busily ripping old newspapers, sat up and took notice.

"Say, if there's a letter for me, I guess I want it," he remarked. "Maybe it's from my popper, back in Chicago."

"'Tain't!" came the voice through the keyhole. Evidently Bunter heard the American junior's remark through that aperture.

"How'd you know, you fat clam?" called out Van Duck.

"The postmark's London!" squeaked Bunter, through the keyhole. "And the fist ain't your father's, either!"

"How'd you know my popper's fist?"

At which there was another chuckle

in Study No. 1. The boy from Chicago was learning a lot of things at Greyfriars, but he had yet a lot to learn about William George Bunter.

"Bunter sees the outsides of all the letters, and the insides of a good many," explained Bob Cherry.

"Beast!" came through the keyhole.

"Well, he's an obliging guy to bring the letter up for me!" remarked Van Duck. "Chuck it in, Bunter! Might be from old Coot——"

There was yet another chuckle.

"Bunter's always obliging to millionaires and things!" said Bob. "He scents a remittance in that letter!"

"Beast!"—through the keyhole.

"Shove it under the door, Bunter!" called out Harry Wharton.

"Shan't! There may be money in it!" retorted Bunter, through the keyhole. "A chap oughtn't to be careless with a letter with a remittance in it. I'm going to give it to Van Duck!"

The door reopened.

Bunter rolled in—extracting a letter from his pocket as he did so. He blinked round the study with the letter in his fat hand.

It did not seem to occur to him to shut the door while he handed over the letter. Bunter was not bothering about torn paper blowing in the wind. He was thinking of what might be inside Van Duck's letter—and the chance of securing a small loan from a fellow who had just received a remittance. It was not Billy Bunter's way, as a rule, to be fearfully obliging; but a millionaire's son was the sort of fellow Bunter liked to oblige.

Owing to a disappointment about a postal order he was expecting, Bunter was short of cash. He wanted to be present when that letter was opened. If it contained, as seemed very probable to Bunter, a remittance, Bunter wanted a whack in the crumbs that fell from the rich man's table. Bunter, as usual, was on the make!

"I say, here it is," said Bunter. "I say, Van Duck—I say—whoop! I—I—yarooop! Leggo, Inky, you beast! Woo-hoop!"

Hurree Jamset Ram Singh jumped up and grabbed the Owl of the Remove. Nobody in the study cared twopence whether there was a remittance in Van Duck's letter or not; unlike Bunter, they were bothered about the "scent" blowing all over the place. The Nabob of Bhanipur grabbed Bunter by the back of a fat neck.

"Chuck that letter over, Bunter!" said Van Duck.

"Yarooh!"

"And buck up with the chuckfulness, my esteemed fat idiot!" said Hurree Jamset Ram Singh, administering a hefty shake.

"Urrrggh!" gurgled Bunter. "Beast! Urrgh! Leggo! I'm chucking it, ain't I?"

He chucked the letter over to the American junior at the window. Then he left the study—swiftly. A swing of Hurree Jamset Ram Singh's arm spun him into the passage, and the door slammed on him.

A howl sounded from the Remove passage. At the same moment there was a howl from Putnam van Duck.

"Gee—my letter——"

He grabbed at the letter as it flew. But that letter, borne on the draught through the study, flew past him, and out at the open window. It was gone before Bunter, swift as Bunter's departure was.

Putnam van Duck jumped up, and stared from the study window. He had a glimpse of an envelope flying on the wind, and then it vanished.

"Search me!" gasped Van Duck. "That pesky bonehead—— I guess I got to get after my letter!"

"You'll find it in the quad!" said Harry Wharton; and Van Duck cut across the study to the door.

It opened and shut quickly. A fat hand caught at Putnam's sleeve as he ran towards the stairs.

"I say, old chap——" gasped Bunter.

"Leggo, you fat clam!"

"But, I say——"

Bump!

With his letter flying about in the wind in the quad, Putnam had no time to waste on Bunter. He grabbed the fat junior, and sat him down in the Remove passage—hard.

"Sit down, you pesky bonehead!" grunted Van Duck; and as Bunter sat, he cut down the passage to the staircase.

"Ow! Beast!" roared Bunter. "Catch me bringing up letters for you again, you rotter! Urrrggh! Beast!"

In Study No. 1, Harry Wharton & Co. continued tearing up "scent," expecting Putnam to come back every minute. But he did not come back. The sportive winds of May were whirling that letter into unknown spaces, and the American junior was hunting for it, and hunting in vain.

ON THE SCENT!

To Harry Wharton & Co., of Greyfriars, it seems absolutely impossible to think that kidnappers could be looking out for a chance to grab a schoolboy on a paper-chase. But kidnapping Putnam van Duck means a ransom of half a million dollars from his "popper," the multi-millionaire of Chicago, and that makes all the difference!

THE SECOND CHAPTER.

Rounding Up the Slackers!

"OUT you come!" roared Bob Cherry.

He was looking into the doorway of Study No. 12 in the Remove.

On an expensive sofa in that luxuriously appointed study was stretched the elegant figure of Lord Mauleverer.

It was the following afternoon—a bright, sunny May afternoon, and a half-holiday at Greyfriars. The Remove run was about to start, and a crowd of fellows, in running shorts, were gathering in the quadrangle

On a fine, keen day hare and hounds appealed to most of the fellows in the Greyfriars Remove—a strenuous Form. But there were exceptions.

It was a rule that every fellow in the Form had to join up, though fellows who disliked the strenuous life generally managed to tail off very early in the run.

Some preferred not to start if they could possibly get out of it. Lord Mauleverer, the laziest man ever, was one; Billy Bunter, emphatically, was another. Skinner & Co. preferred cigarettes in their study—a preference they were not allowed to gratify.

Harry Wharton, as captain of the Remove, was going round hunting out slackers and shirkers, and Bob Cherry was lending him a hand—an energetic hand! Everything that Bob did had a spot of energy in it—a considerable spot. Whether he liked a fellow, as he did Mauly, or whether he loathed him, as he did Skinner, it was all the same to Bob; they were all going to line up for the start, at least, whatever they might contrive to do later.

Perhaps Mauly had forgotten that the paper-chase was on, or perhaps he hoped that the paper-chasers would forget him. Anyhow, his lazy lordship had retired to his study after dinner, and was now reposing on his sofa, with a silken cushion under his noble head, gazing out of the study window at the blue sky in dreamy contentment, till Bob Cherry happened, rather like an earthquake and a thunderstorm rolled into one.

"You're not changed, you ass!" roared Bob. "Buck up! Get a move on! Jump to it! Do you want to stick on that sofa while we're doing miles and miles and miles and miles and miles?"

"Yaas!" assented Lord Mauleverer.

"Tired?" asked Bob.

"Yaas!"

"What's made you tired?"

"You!" said his lordship plaintively.

Bob chuckled.

"I'll give you something to cure all that, old bean!" he answered. "If you feel that you can't get off that sofa—is that how you feel?"

"Yaas!"

"I'm the man to help you!" said Bob.

He came across the study, and his lordship eyed him apprehensively. His lordship's apprehensions were well-founded.

Bob grasped the end of the sofa, heaved at it, and tilted it over. There was a howl as his lordship rolled off his expensive sofa, and landed with a bump.

"Oooooh!" howled Mauleverer.

"Feel that you can get going now?" asked Bob.

"Ow! Wow!"

"Still tired?"

"Ow! Yaas! Wow!"

"Race you down the Remove passage!" said Bob. "I'll give you a start—with my foot—like that——"

"Yarooh!"

"And like that!"

"Keep off, you dangerous maniac!" yelled Mauleverer.

And he bounded out of the study, followed by the chuckling Bob.

Harry Wharton was coming out of Study No. 14, helping Fisher T. Fish, the American junior. Unlike his fellow-countryman, Putnam van Duck, who was very keen on the strenuous life, Fishy wanted to give the paper-chase a miss. Fishy had some accounts to do that afternoon—he loved to spend a holiday at accounts. It was really rather "fierce," as he would have expressed it; for Fishy was not sure what had become of a halfpenny he had missed, and he was very anxious to trace that missing halfpenny

But it booted not! Fishy's pencil went in one direction and his account-book in the other as the captain of the Remove helped him out of the study. He helped him by a rather long ear, to the accompaniment of fiendish howls from Fisher T. Fish.

"You pesky boob, will you leggo my year?" Fishy was yelling.

"Hallo, hallo, hallo!" roared Bob.

"Another tired man? Leave him to me, old top! Stand steady, Fishy—and see if I can land you at the stairs with one kick!"

Fisher T. Fish did not stand still. Wharton let go his ear, and he flew! Fishy had no desire whatever to see whether Bob could buzz him the length of the passage with one kick!

"Any more?" grinned Bob.

"Skinner hasn't turned up!" said Harry, laughing.

"Come on!"

Skinner's study was No. 11. The door of Study No. 11 burst open as if a battering-ram had hit it when Bob arrived there.

Skinner, Snoop, and Stott were in the study.

They were gathered round the table, with impot paper before them and pens in their hands. They looked busy.

"Hallo, hallo, hallo!" roared Bob Cherry. "You fellows know that we're just starting? Get down and change!"

Skinner glanced round.

"Sorry!" he answered. "I've got lines for Loder!"

"Same here!" said Snoop. "You know that beastly bully, Loder of the Sixth! No good telling him that we want to go on a paper-chase when he's given us lines!"

"Oh!" said Bob, rather nonplussed.

He did know, only too well, what a very unpleasant fellow Loder of the Sixth was.

Stott, who was not quite such a slacker as his friends, looked sheepish. He laid down his pen, and rose from the table.

"Look here, I'm going!" he said.

Snoop sneered, and Skinner shrugged his shoulders. Stott passed Bob, and went out of the study. Harry Wharton looked in.

"Come on, Skinner and Snoop!" he said.

"Lines for Loder!" said Skinner.

That was good enough for Bob Cherry, who was as unsuspicious as he was strenuous. The captain of the Remove was not quite so trustful as Bob. A Form captain had duties to do, and had to keep an eye open.

"That's all right, Skinner!" he said. "Lines can't stop a chap joining up for a run! I'll explain to Loder of the Sixth."

"That won't stop him giving me six if I don't take in the lines!" said Skinner. "I'd rather get them done, if you don't mind."

"But I do!" pointed out the captain of the Remove. "You're joining up for the run, old bean! But I'll tell you what—I'll cut down and see Loder, and ask him to give you leave first, if you like."

That offer did not seem to please Skinner. It made Snoop look quite alarmed. Snoop laid down his pen.

"May as well go!" he said.

"Why, you spoofing slackers!" roared Bob Cherry. What the captain of the Remove had guessed at once now dawned on Bob. "You haven't got lines for Loder at all! It's just spoof to get out of the run! Bag them!"

"I say, I'm going!" gasped Snoop.

And he cut out of the study in a hurry, and joined the other slackers on the way to the changing-room.

Skinner gave the captain of the Form a bitter look. As he had no lines to do for Loder of the Sixth, he certainly did not want that prefect asked to give him leave. Loder would have been annoyed by the use of his name for purposes of spoof, and would no doubt have made the lines a reality, as well as adding, in all probability, a swipe from his ashplant!

"Look here," said Skinner savagely, "I'm not coming—see? There's a beastly east wind, and I don't like it! I've got a pain in my foot, too!"

"Which foot?" asked Bob.

"The right!" grunted Skinner.

"I'll give you one in the other foot to match!"

Bob Cherry lifted his own foot—a large size in feet—and brought it down, and Skinner jerked his left foot away just in time.

Whether he had a pain in his right foot or not, he certainly would have had a pain in his left had that hefty stamp landed on it.

"You silly ass!" yelled Skinner. "Keep your hoofs to yourself! Look here, I'm jolly well not going——"

"Take his other ear, Harry."

"Yaroooh!" roared Skinner, as his ears were captured.

Wharton and Bob walked out of the study with Skinner's ears. Needless to state, the rest of Skinner accompanied the ears.

"Seen Bunter?" called out Johnny Bull from the landing.

"Hasn't he turned up?"

"No; can't find him anywhere."

"The fat porker! Help Skinner down to the changing-room while we look for him."

But it was useless to look for Billy Bunter.

Generally that fat and fatuous youth was seen oftener than any Greyfriars fellow could possibly desire to see him. Now he was conspicuous by his absence.

Studies and passages were drawn blank. He was not in the Rag or hiding in the Form-room. He could not be seen in the quad, and every fellow who was asked had seen nothing of him. Billy Bunter had vanished.

That he was dodging the Remove run was certain, but in what secluded spot he had parked his fat person for that purpose was a mystery. Up and down and round about went half a dozen fellows, looking for Bunter; but they found him not! He had vanished as completely as Van Duck's letter, blown away the previous day, though it was certain that Billy Bunter had not blown away—the most powerful of hurricanes would hardly have been equal to his weight!

Bunter had to be given up. Wingate of the Sixth was to start the run, at the appointed time, and the captain of the school could not be kept waiting. Of all the slackers in the Remove, Billy Bunter was the only one who succeeded in escaping—but Bunter had made a success of it! Harry Wharton gave him up at last and joined the fellows in the quad.

"Can't find Bunter?" asked Smithy.

"No—he's keeping doggo somewhere, the fat slacker," growled the captain of the Remove.

"I can tell you how to catch him!" grinned the Bounder.

"How?"

"Make a noise like a postal order."

"Ha, ha, ha!"

"Fathead!" said Harry. "I'll kick him when we come back! Now, then, you men, ready! Wingate will be here in a tick! Got your 'scent,' Van Duck?"

"Sure!" answered Putnam.

Harry Wharton and Putnam van Duck were to be the hares, the rest of the Remove the pack. All was ready now for Wingate to come down to the gates to give the signal for starting. But before Wingate of the Sixth arrived someone else arrived on the scene—Poker Pike, the Greyfriars gunman.

THE THIRD CHAPTER.

Poker Says "Nope!"

"WHAT'S this here stunt?" Poker Pike asked that question.

Mr. Pike had been sitting on the bench by Gosling's lodge, with his eye on the gates, while the Removites were gathering there.

Poker Pike, when he was not prowling round the quad or the Cloisters, the playing fields or the tennis courts, generally had his eye on the gates.

It was rumoured in the Remove that he was paid an enormous salary by the Chicago millionaire for keeping guard over his son at Greyfriars School.

Large or small, there was no doubt that Poker earned that salary, and earned it conscientiously.

He watched over the safety of Putnam van Duck night and day, often causing Putnam extreme irritation thereby.

Chick Chew, star kidnapper of the United States, had made no fewer than three attempts to kidnap the son of the multi-millionaire; and Poker had put paid to every one of them.

The headmaster, when he gave leave for the gunman guard to take up his quarters at Greyfriars, had hoped that Mr. Pike would exercise tact and reserve and rather keep out of the public eye.

Instead of which Poker had become a very prominent character at Greyfriars, and very often had the spotlight.

Still, even Poker Pike was forgotten sometimes, and Harry Wharton & Co., in fixing up the paper-chase that Wednesday afternoon, had not bestowed a single thought on the Greyfriars gunman.

Van Duck, naturally, was going to take part in the Form run; nothing would have induced him to stand out. In fact, he couldn't have stood out—without being rounded up like Skinner & Co., unless he had found some deep hiding-place like Billy Bunter. Which certainly would not have suited that very keen and energetic youth from Chicago.

Like the other fellows, he had forgotten his guardian. And, like them, he was reminded of him when the hefty gunman, with his black bowler hat jammed down on his bullet head, lounged on the scene. Poker Pike was not a man to be forgotten long.

Having inquired what the stunt was, Poker Pike stood with his hands on his hips, eyeing the juniors with his keen slits of eyes. His hard-boiled hickory face wore its usual serious expression. Evidently he was on the alert at the sight of Putnam preparing to go on a cross-country run. To Mr. Pike's suspicious and wary mind the whole countryside was haunted by American kidnappers on the watch for the millionaire's son.

"That blessed gunman!" exclaimed Bob Cherry. "Van Duck, old bean, you'd better tell him that this is where he gets off."

"Poker, you big stiff," yapped Putnam van Duck, "you beat it! See? You beat it pronto! You're too numerous! Vamoose!"

Poker did not "vamoose." He stood like a rock. Wingate of the Sixth could be seen coming down from the House. The run was booked to start. But that did not matter to Poker Pike. He stood immovable in the way.

"I guess I want to know, you Putnam van Duck!" said the gunman. "I figure from your outfit that you're aiming to burn the wind with this bunch of young guys. That it?"

"You said it!" agreed Putnam. "It's a paper-chase, you geck, if you know what that is! Absquatulate!"

"I guess not!" said Poker, with a grave shake of the head. "You can't do this, big boy. I'm telling you! I got to keep tabs on you, and I'll say you got to sit it out."

Van Duck snorted! The other fellows grinned.

"Forget it!" growled Van Duck. "I'm going!"

"You ain't!" contradicted Poker. "How'd I keep tabs on you and you beating it all over the horizon? Mebbe that galoot Chick Chew is around this afternoon—I'll say he ain't the hombre to lose chances. I ain't aiming to cable Old Man Vanderdecken, in Chicawgo, that Chick has cinched his boy! Surest thing you know."

"It's all right, Mr. Pike," said Harry Wharton, laughing. "Chick Chew won't bother Van Duck in a crowd like this."

"Mebbe," said Mr. Pike—"and mebbe not! I ain't taking chances! Boyees will be boyees—and I guess you'll scatter, and never think of Chick till he gets a cinch on that young geck. You wash it out, you Putnam."

"Go and chop chips!" was Putnam's answer.

"Here's Wingate!" said Frank Nugent. "All ready, Wingate!"

"Line up," said the Greyfriars captain. "Ten minutes start for the hares. Now, then—— Here, what do you want?" He stared at Poker Pike.

"I'll mention I want that Putnam van Duck!" said Poker. "I guess he ain't hitting the horizon with that bunch."

Wingate laughed.

"That's for Van Duck himself to settle, Mr. Pike," he said. "I don't suppose the kid will be in any danger in a mob like this. There is no order for him to keep in gates, and he will do as he pleases."

Poker shook his head.

"You got another guess coming!" he replied. "Old Man Vanderdecken van Duck sure has put it up to me to keep tabs on him. I guess if he wants a walk I'll walk with him—but I ain't running none. I'll murmur that he's going to sit it out."

"It's for you to settle, Van Duck!" said Wingate.

"I'm going!" roared Putnam.

"That's that, then! Get going!"

The two hares made a move. So did Poker Pike! Poker's move was swift, and he grabbed the shoulder of the millionaire's son.

"Forget it!" he remarked.

"Leggo!" yelled Putnam.

"I guess not."

"Will you leggo?" shrieked Putnam.

"Not so's you'd notice it!" said Poker calmly. "Chew on it, big boy! I got to keep tabs on you."

"Let him go at once, you ass!" exclaimed Wingate.

"Park it, you!" said Poker.

There was a buzz from the Remove crowd. Some of them were laughing, but some were getting wrathy. Time was being wasted, and Poker, who very often "horned in" where he was not wanted, had never been so much in the way as now.

But it was clear that he meant business. His grasp on Van Duck's shoulder fastened like a vice.

"Chuck it, Pike, you fathead!" roared Bob Cherry.

"Up-end the cheeky ass!" exclaimed the Bounder impatiently.

"Roll him over!" said Peter Todd

"Barge him out of the way!" exclaimed six or seven fellows at once.

"Hold on!" rapped Wingate. "Better call Quelch!"

Wingate, as head prefect and captain of the school, was a person of authority. But, to Mr. Pike, he was only a schoolboy like the rest. Wingate, fortunately, was a good-tempered fellow, and could be patient with a stranger within the gates, who did not understand Greyfriars manners and customs

An order from Mr. Quelch, the Remove master, would have been enough, no doubt It was the easiest way out. But Quelch, as it happened, was not available.

"Quelchy's gone out, Wingate!" said Harry. "He went out after dinner with Prout."

Bob Cherry grasped the end of the sofa, heaved at it, and tilted it over. There was a howl, as Lord Mauleverer rolled off his expensive sofa, and landed with a bump. "Oooooooh!" howled his lordship. "Feel that you can get going now?" asked Bob cheerily. "Ow! Yaas! Wow!"

"Oh!" said Wingate. "Well, we can't bother the Head! Pike, you ass, let go that kid at once!"

"Forget it!" answered Poker.

Wingate's good temper failed him a little. He came up to the gunman, with a rather grim expression on his face.

"Chuck it, now!" he snapped. "Take your paw off Van Duck's shoulder!"

The Removites looked on breathlessly. The captain of Greyfriars was not the man to take no for an answer. But it was only too clear that Poker Pike's answer was going to be in the negative.

"Poker, you gink——" urged Putnam.

"Pack it up, you Putman van Duck," answered Poker. "You ain't beating it none! You hear me talk!"

"Will you let that kid go?" snapped Wingate, losing patience.

"Nope!" answered Mr. Pike.

"I shall have to make you, then!"

"Forget it, bo'!"

"Last time of asking!" snapped Wingate.

And as Mr. Pike's grasp remained immovable on Van Duck's shoulder, the Greyfriars captain grasped Mr. Pike, to drag him off.

Big and strong as the captain of Greyfriars was, his wrench at the gunman did not even make him stir. Poker stood rock-still! But, as Wingate wrenched again, the gunman swung round his left arm, and the big Sixth Former went spinning.

"Oh!" gasped Wingate, as he spun.

He tottered a couple of yards, under the impetus of that hefty shove, stumbled, and fell.

What would have happened when he got on his feet was never known, for, before he could rise, the whole Remove rushed at Poker Pike.

Poker was hefty and wiry, strong almost as a horse. But even Poker had no chance against the swarm of juniors.

They grasped him on all sides and dragged him bodily over; and Poker yelled as he hit the county of Kent.

"Bag him!" yelled Bob Cherry.

"Down him!" yelled Johnny Bull.

"Sit on him!"

For a couple of minutes there was a wild mix-up. Then Poker Pike, still resisting, was on his back, with about a dozen feet planted on him, pinning him there, and three or four fellows sitting on him.

Under the Removites, the Greyfriars gunman heaved like the mighty ocean. But he heaved in vain!

THE FOURTH CHAPTER.
Poker in the Pack!

"KEEP him there!" gasped Harry Wharton.

"What-ho!" chuckled Bob.

"We've got him!" grinned the Bounder.

Smithy's foot was planted on Mr. Pike's bull neck, and Poker gurgled under the pressure.

"Safe as houses!" chortled Peter Todd. "Get going!"

"Ha, ha, ha!"

"Say, you ginks, you let up!" came a suffocated howl from Poker Pike, wriggling under many feet. "I'm telling you to let up! Don't I keep on telling you I got to keep tabs on that Putnam van Duck?"

"Forget it, old-timer!" chuckled Putnam. "This is where you get off, Poker."

"Come on!" said Harry, laughing.

The two hares trotted down the road. Poker made another mighty heave—in vain! Most of the pack were pinning him down, and they were not going to let him go till the hares had had their start. After which it would be too late for Poker to horn in again.

Wingate, rather breathless and not in the best of tempers, gave the wriggling gunman a very grim look. However, Poker was safely held, and the Greyfriars captain left it at that.

Harry Wharton and Putnam van Duck trotted down Friardale Lane, and disappeared from sight towards the wood. Wingate looked at his watch. The pack waited for the signal to start.

The pack was not quite so numerous now. Two or three fellows had taken advantage of the excitement to slip away unnoticed. Fisher T. Fish had scuttled off to get back to his accounts, and Skinner had disappeared somewhere in the quad.

Bob Cherry, certainly, would have had an eye on them, and would have rounded them up had he been less busy. But Bob was very busy with Mr. Pike—his foot was on Poker's waistcoat, jammed hard. So Fishy got back to his study—and Skinner dodged behind the elms—and both escaped!

Time was up at last, and Wingate gave the signal to start. Bob Cherry blew a blast on a bugle.

Innumerable feet were withdrawn from Poker Pike—they were wanted for other purposes now. The pack went streaming down the road on the trail of the hares—leaving Mr. Pike sitting up breathlessly in the dust.

"Search me!" gasped Mr. Pike.

He grabbed at his bowler hat, which had fallen off in the tussle. He jammed it down on his bullet head before he rose to his feet Then he scrambled up.

Wingate gave him a glance and went in at the gates. Poker did not heed Wingate. He stood staring after the streaming pack.

"Carry me home to die!" he ejaculated.

What Poker would do when he was released, the Removites neither knew nor cared. But Mr. Pike knew what he was going to do!

It was his business to "keep tabs" on the millionaire's son. The millionaire's son was already far away, cutting across country with the captain of the Remove, leaving a trail of torn paper. There was only one thing for Poker to do—he started running after the pack.

Poker was not clad for running. But he had a turn of speed, and he was soon on the tail of the pack.

Bob Cherry glanced back at the sound of pounding footsteps behind him. He gave a yell.

"Hallo, hallo, hallo! He's after us!"

"Oh, my hat!" exclaimed Vernon-Smith, glancing over his shoulder. "He's joining up for the paper-chase!"

"Ha, ha, ha!"

Poker came pounding on. He joined the running pack as they reached the stile that gave admittance from the lane into Friardale Wood. Bob Cherry gave him a welcoming yell.

"Come on, old bean! The more the merrier!"

"I guess I ain't letting that Putnam van Duck get fur out of my sight!" panted Poker. "I'll say I'm going to rope in that young gink!"

"Right-ho!" chuckled Bob. "We're all after him, to rope him in if we can—nobody's going to stop you now, old scout!"

"Ha, ha, ha!"

The pack chuckled as they went on. As one of the pack, Poker was welcome to catch the hares if he could! But the juniors did not think it likely that the gunman would be in at the death. In coat and trousers, boots and bowler hat, Mr. Pike did not seem, to them, likely to keep in the running long. Much lighter attire was needed for a run across country extending over many winding miles.

But Poker was a sticker. He was a serious guy, and took his duties seriously. Certainly, he was not so keen on paper-chases. But he was going to catch Putnam van Duck, if he could. So he ran with the pack, amid a chorus of chuckles.

The paper trail left the footpath and wound among the trees of Friardale Wood. In the thickets, fellows who were not keen on the run disappeared. Snoop was the first, and then Lord Mauleverer sat down on a log to rest for a moment or two—and that moment or two lasted a good half-hour before his lazy lordship got going again—and then his footsteps carried him homeward.

Stott tailed off, breathless from the effect of too many cigarettes in the study. Hazeldene conked out next, perhaps for the same reason. But the pack was still numerous when it came to the plank bridge over the stream in the wood.

The paper trail crossed the stream.

and the pack headed for the bridge. Only one fellow could cross at a time, and Bob Cherry reached it first and trotted over. The Bounder was second, when Poker Pike, reaching it at the same moment, shouldered him aside to pass ahead.

Keen as all the fellows were on hunting the hares, the keenest Remove man was not so keen as Poker. With streams of perspiration running down under his bowler hat, Poker barged on hard and fast. He was not going to waste any time with schoolboys getting in the way.

His hefty shoulder sent the Bounder spinning, and Poker leaped on the plank. There was a howl of rage from Vernon-Smith as he sat in the shallow stream. Poker, unheeding, barged across the plank.

Smithy was up in a second, his running shorts soaked and dripping. The Bounder did not care for that, but he did care for being shouldered out of the way. He leaped on the plank with a spring like a tiger, flew after the gunman, and barged him in the middle of the back.

Poker had reached the middle of the stream at the moment that Smithy reached the middle of his back!

He went headlong.

There was a terrific splash as the gunman took a header into the water! The water splashed right and left on the pack as they followed the Bounder across the plank.

"Yurrrggh!" gurgled Poker.

He went right under for a second, then he was on his feet, standing with the stream flowing past under his armpits. Streaming by in single file across the plank bridge, the juniors howled with laughter as they passed him.

"Wet?" howled Peter Todd.

"Damp!" chuckled Frank Nugent.

"The dampfulness is terrific!" chortled Hurree Jamset Ram Singh.

"Ha, ha, ha!"

"Urrrrgh!" gasped Poker. "I guess I'll beat that pesky young guy up a few! Gurrrggh! And then some! Wurrggh!"

"Ha, ha, ha!"

The whole pack had streamed past by the time Poker scrambled out of the water.

Looking back a few minutes later, the Removites howled with laughter at the sight of the gunman.

Drenched and dripping, squelching water from his boots at every step, Poker Pike was still coming on! He could not have felt happy, but he was not going to be beaten! More than a ducking was required to deter Poker Pike.

He was breathless, he was wet, his drenched clothes were sticking to him, his hickory face was crimson under the dripping bowler, but—like Charley's celebrated aunt—he was still running!

THE FIFTH CHAPTER.

Awkward for Bunter!

BILLY BUNTER leaned back in Mr. Quelch's armchair, rested his feet on Mr. Quelch's hassock, and grinned.

Bunter was taking it easy.

It was no wonder that the Remove fellows had failed to find him when they were rounding-up the slackers. Nobody had thought of looking in a master's study. Fellows were not supposed to enter Masters' Studies without leave—and few fellows were ever anxious to do so!

Certainly Billy Bunter would not have risked stepping into his Form-master's study, even to dodge a paper-chase, had Mr. Quelch been anywhere about the House or the school. But he was aware that Quelch had gone out after dinner, with Prout, the Fifth Form master, for a long walk.

Quelch being safely off the scene, and Quelch's study certain never to be searched by juniors, it really was the safest spot that the fat slacker could have selected.

What Quelch would have said—and done—had he suddenly come in and found the fat junior taking it easy in his armchair in his study, hardly bore thinking of. But there was no danger of that. Henry Samuel Quelch was miles away, walking Mr. Prout off his portly legs!

So Bunter, grinning, took it easy! He could hear the voices of Remove fellows in the quad, but he was careful not to show himself at the window. The voices died away at last, and he knew that the paper-chasers were gone.

But he was in no hurry to move. He could not be too careful in such an important matter. He was not going to run the slightest risk of being rounded-up, after all, and forced to exert his fat self. For half an hour after the Removites had started, the fat Owl remained sprawling in Quelch's armchair.

Then at last Bunter rose and took a cautious survey from the window. There were plenty of fellows to be seen on a half-holiday, but none of them were Removites.

Coker of the Fifth was walking and talking with Potter and Greene of that Form. Temple, Dabney & Co. could be seen, heading for the tuckshop. Sammy Bunter of the Second Form was sucking toffee under one of the elms. Hobson of the Shell, with a cricket ball, was demonstrating a rather tricky action in the bowling line to his friends Hoskins and Stewart. In the distance, Sixth Form men could be seen at games practice. Hacker, master of the Shell, was strolling with his hands tucked under his coat tails, and his usual worried expression on his face.

All these things Billy Bunter saw, from Mr. Quelch's study window, without interest. What interested him was the fact that no Removites were to be seen. Evidently the danger was over.

Suddenly, however, he spotted a Removite. But it was not alarming, for it was Skinner that he spotted.

He grinned at the sight of Skinner.

Evidently Harold Skinner had succeeded in dodging, as well as Bunter. Skinner owed that to Mr. Pike and his obstreperous intervention. Having changed, Skinner was sauntering at ease in the quad—happy to have escaped the exertion of a cross-country run.

The sight of Loder of the Sixth coming along with Walker and Carne caused Bunter to pop back from the window.

Loder was not likely to care whether he joined up for a paper-chase or not; but it was not safe to let a prefect spot him in a master's study.

All was clear now, and Bunter decided to vacate that study.

He rolled over to the door, and opened it a few inches, to peer out, to make sure that the coast was clear.

Unfortunately for Bunter, it wasn't.

A murmur of voices was audible farther along the passage. He recognised the tones of Capper and Wiggins, masters of the Fourth and Third.

Capper was talking to Wiggins, in the latter's study doorway.

Billy Bunter shut the door again, quickly and noiselessly. He dared not let other beaks see him emerging from his Form-master's study at a time when, obviously, he had no business there.

"Beasts!" murmured Bunter.

He waited impatiently. Five minutes later he reopened the door a few inches—only to hear a third voice added to the two. Monsieur Charpentier had joined the two masters, and was taking part in the conversation at Wiggins' door.

Bunter shut Mr. Quelch's door again. He snorted angrily.

Having escaped the paper-chase by taking refuge in Quelch's study, he now had to escape from Quelch's study, and there was a lion in the path—or, rather, three lions in the path, in the shape of two Form-masters and a French master.

It was very irritating for talkative beaks to choose that time and place for talking—very awkward for Bunter. He could not possibly emerge while they were there. He would be reported to Quelch, and there was a strict rule on the subject of entering Masters' Studies without leave.

"Beasts!" repeated Bunter.

He went back to Quelch's armchair and sat down again. As he had to wait, he preferred to sit it out.

Coker of the Fifth had been heard to say that when the beaks got together they cackled like a lot of old hens! Really it seemed like it! Bunter wondered how long that cackle was going on at Wiggins' door.

Buzzzz!

The telephone bell interrupted his reflections on that subject.

"Oh lor'!" gasped Bunter, in alarm.

Bunter did not often move quickly. But a jumping kangaroo had nothing on Bunter as he bounded to the telephone and hooked off the receiver.

Quelch could not possibly come in to take that call. He was miles off the scene. But if the bell was heard, someone would come in and take it—and discover Bunter there! And certainly it would be heard if it went on ringing! Bunter dreaded that even that single buzz might have been heard by the three masters down the passage.

He stood gasping, the receiver in his hand. That beastly bell stopped, but Bunter did not bother about the person who had rung up. He stood listening, with thumping heart, for a sound from the passage.

Luckily there was no sound. Wiggins' doorway was well away down the passage, and that single buzz had not reached the group of masters—all busy "cackling." One or two repetitions would certainly have dawned on them. But there was going to be no repetitions. Bunter was going to take care of that.

He breathed more freely, as there was no sound of alarm. All was well so far. Relieved on that point, Bunter had leisure to remember that there was somebody on the phone, expecting to be answered.

He had to answer that somebody! It was no use replacing the receiver and leaving the unknown to ring up again! He had to shut the beast off somehow! It was easy to tell him, whoever he was, that Quelch was out, and not expected in till tea-time. So Bunter put the receiver to a fat ear, and found that somebody was talking on the phone, and had, no doubt, been talking all the time Bunter was listening for an alarm from the passage.

". . . and put him wise that his popper's old friend will be there to give him the glad hand——"

That was what Bunter heard, and it was rather puzzling. He could guess, from the phraseology, that it was an American speaking. But he could not make head or tail of the rest.

"Hallo!" gasped Bunter into the transmitter. "I—I say, I didn't catch that. Who's speaking?"

"Say, didn't you hear me tooting all this time?" demanded a rather annoyed and indignant voice over the wires.

"No! Yes! I—I mean there's rather a row going on!" gasped Bunter. "I—I mean who is it?"

"Ezra Coot!"

"Ezra Coot!" repeated Bunter. The name sounded familiar to him. It came into his fat mind that he had heard Putnam van Duck mention it. It was the name of an American business man in London, a friend of Van Duck's father.

"Sure! That's Mr. Quelch, I reckon," went on the voice. "I guess I'll sing it over agin if you haven't got it, Mr. Quelch. I sure want to see Putnam. And I guess he's put you wise about my letter to him yesterday—what?"

"Oh!" gasped Bunter.

The fat junior had forgotten about Van Duck's letter, which had blown out of the window of Study No. 1 in the Remove the previous day and had never been found. He remembered it now.

That letter, apparently, had been written by this Ezra Coot, who was following it up on the telephone.

Had Putnam read that letter and known that he was to be called on the phone by his father's old friend that afternoon, no doubt he would have stood out of the paper-chase; as it was, he was gone.

"Say, I got the right number, ain't I?" demanded the nasal voice over the wires. "Mr. Quelch, at Greyfriars School?"

"Oh, yes!" gasped Bunter.

He was about to add that Quelch was out and was not expected back till tea-time, but he paused in time.

If this Ezra Coot wanted to see Putnam van Duck, the fact that Quelch had gone out would not stop him; he would keep on ringing till he got in touch with somebody at Greyfriars, that was certain.

That did not suit Bunter.

Mr. Quelch and Ezra Coot and Putnam van Duck mattered nothing; what mattered was that the telephone-bell should not draw anyone to the Remove master's study to discover Bunter there.

While the dismayed fat Owl was wondering how he could bar off this obnoxious Coot the nasal voice went on:

"I guess you remember my name, Mr. Quelch. I rang you up first day of your school term to ask if my old friend's son had arrived safe and sound."

Bunter remembered that there had been a phone call for Quelch the first day in the Form-room that term. It had made Quelch late for class.

"Oh!" he stuttered. "Yes—quite!"

"I wrote Putnam yesterday and told him I'd be in Courtfield to-day on business and would be sure glad to make his acquaintance," went on the voice.

"Mum-make his acquaintance!" stammered Bunter.

"Sure! I ain't met up with Vanderdecken's son yet, and I'll be pesky glad to see him and make his acquaintance," said Mr. Coot. "I figured on coming along to the school, but time don't allow. I got my train to catch after I get through my business at Chunkley's here."

"Oh!"

"But Vanderdecken's written me from Chicawgo and asked me to give his boy the once-over, and I guess this is an opportunity. I get through my business here at four, and I can give young Putnam till half-past. Tell him to mosey along to the Courtfield Hotel at four and have tea with his father's old side-kicker. You get me?"

"Oh, yes! I—I—— Yes!"

"I told Putnam to show you that letter, sir, and put you wise. I reckon he ain't forgot—what?"

Certainly Putnam had never shown Mr. Quelch that letter, as he had never seen the inside of it himself; but the man on the phone, of course, knew nothing of the happenings in Study No. 1 the day before.

"I guess Putnam will be glad to see a friend he's heard his popper talk about a whole lot back in Chicawgo. Anyhow, you tell him, sir, to come along to the Courtfield Hotel at four if he wants to see me. If he ain't turned up by half-past, I got my train to catch, and I shall have to give him a miss. But I'd sure like to see him."

"Oh, yes!"

"That's the whole packet, sir. I won't waste your time. Good-bye!"

The man at the other end rang off. Billy Bunter was left blinking at the telephone.

THE SIXTH CHAPTER.

Bunter's Brain-wave!

"BEAST!" murmured Billy Bunter.

He put up the receiver and grunted.

He had been alarmed. Every moment while Mr. Coot was talking on the phone he had dreaded to see the study door open. It was all very irritating to Bunter.

However, all was safe. No one had come to the study, and he had got rid of Ezra Coot by the simple expedient of allowing him to believe that he was speaking to Mr. Quelch.

That was all right so far as it went. Mr. Coot had gone away satisfied, and was not likely to ring up again.

According to what he had stated, he was going to wait for Putnam at the Courtfield Hotel from four till half-past, and if he did not come would then catch his train. That did not matter very much. He couldn't have seen Putnam that day anyhow, as the American junior was miles away on a paper-chase

A tea at the Courtfield Hotel was going begging Bunter was rather sorry that that letter had been lost.

Had Van Duck been there he might have been persuaded to take a pal along to tea with his father's old friend. Bunter would have been willing—more than willing—to go to tea with a rich American.

Still, there was not much in that. Had Van Duck taken a pal to tea with him, it was pretty certain that he would have picked one of the fellows in his study. Fascinating fellow as Bunter was, the kind of fellow to make any tea party a success, there was little chance that Putnam would have selected him.

Bunter went to the door again and listened. "Cackle" was still going on down the passage.

He returned to Mr. Quelch's armchair and sat down, fervently hoping that no other beast would ring up on the phone while he was there.

Bunter was getting more and more impatient. Quelch's study had been a useful refuge, but he was tired of it.

He was, in fact, getting hungry. And while all the fellows were out of gates on a paper-chase there was a chance for a hungry Owl to do a little scouting in the Remove studies. Bunter was accustomed to make the most of such opportunities as a snapper-up of unconsidered trifles. Even a solitary doughnut, or a few bullseyes, would have been welcome.

Apart from that chance, the afternoon presented rather a dreary prospect to Bunter. No Remove man, so far as he knew, was within gates, excepting Skinner—and Skinner was not the fellow to ask a fellow to tea, or to lend him a half-crown, or even a humble bob, on a postal order he was expecting.

If the hares and hounds came in late for tea, as was more probable than not, there was only tea in Hall for Bunter—and even that was hours off.

It was a serious matter to the fat Owl, whose life was one long series of food problems, one after another.

And all the while there was a ripping spread going begging. It made Bunter feel quite bitter to think of that.

He remembered what he had heard Putnam say on the subject of Mr. Coot. Ezra Coot was rich; as a pal of a millionaire was pretty certain to be. Bunter could not doubt that it would be a really handsome spread at the Courtfield Hotel—the best that money could buy. Putnam was going to miss it; but he did not care a lot about such things, anyhow. Billy Bunter cared more than a lot. He could not help thinking of that wasted spread.

"Oh crikey!" ejaculated Bunter suddenly.

He sat upright in Mr. Quelch's armchair, his little round eyes glistening behind his big round spectacles.

A sudden idea had shot into Bunter's fat brain—a brilliant idea—so brilliant that it positively dazzled him. It was an absolute brain-wave.

Bunter grinned.

That gorgeous spread need not be wasted. Bunter was the man who would enjoy it most. And why should he not?

Ezra Coot had said that he had never met Putnam van Duck, and wanted to make his acquaintance. He had lived many years in London; and until recently, of course, Putnam had lived on the other side of the Atlantic. If he had never met Putnam he could not possibly know him by sight.

Suppose a fellow turned up at the hotel in Courtfield at four o'clock. Was not Mr. Coot certain to believe that he was the fellow to whom he had written, and to whose Form-master he had telephoned? He had never seen either Van Duck or Bunter. Why should he not suppose that Bunter was Van Duck if he turned up in Van Duck's place?

It was, indeed, scarcely possible that he could suppose anything else, in the circumstances.

"By gum!" breathed Bunter.

It was a positively dazzling idea.

Billy Bunter jumped out of Quelch's armchair. With this great scheme in his fat brain he simply had to get out of that study.

Once more he opened the door and listened for sounds. The "cackle" at the door of Mr. Wiggins' study had died away at last. But there was a quick tread in the passage, which Bunter knew was Mr. Hacker's.

Back popped Bunter! Hacker had had to choose that awkward moment for coming in, after his walk in the quad!

Bunter had Quelch's door shut, just in time, before Hacker passed. He shook a fat fist at the passing master of the shell—behind the door!

Really, it looked as if Bunter would never get out of that study! And he had to get to Courtfield by four, if he was going to capture the spread intended for Putnam van Duck! It was

Coming along at full pelt, the " hounds " bumped into Coker and sent him sprawling. But they were not to escape with impunity. Coker seized Bob Cherry by the ankle and brought him down. " Oh crikey ! " gasped Bob, as he sprawled. " Leggo, you mad ass ! Leggo ! "

a long walk to Courtfield—miles across the common! And owing to that sad disappointment about a postal order, Bunter lacked not only a taxi-fare, but even the few coppers necessary for a lift on the motor-bus. Time and tide wait for no man, and here was Bunter a prisoner in his Form-master's study, unable to escape.

That passage, sometimes, was quite deserted for quite a long time. It had been deserted when Bunter dodged into the study. Now it seemed to be thickly populated with beaks.

Hacker's jerky tread having died away, and a door closed up the passage, Bunter tried again. Opening the door a few inches, he listened anxiously. He had the pleasure—or otherwise—of hearing the voice of Mr. Lascelles, the games master. Bunter loathed Harry Lascelles, who was maths master, as well as games master, maths being the most awful thing in existence, from Bunter's point of view. But never had he loathed them so much as now.

He was speaking to Wingate of the Sixth—Bunter recognised Wingate's voice replying.

There was nothing unusual in the captain of the school coming along to speak to the games master. They often consulted about the games. But it was frightfully annoying to Bunter. Gladly he would have knocked together the heads of Wingate and Mr. Lascelles, had that been practicable.

Closing the door once more, Bunter gave that up as a mode of egress. It was clear that the passage was going to be haunted by the beaks for an indefinite length of time. He crossed to the window.

If nobody was at hand he might drop from the window unperceived. It would not matter if juniors saw him; it was all right so long as beaks and prefects were not about. Beaks were not likely to be at hand in that direction, with so many of them haunting the passage.

Bunter blinked from the window cautiously.

Temple, Dabney & Co., of the Fourth, were still in sight. Dicky Nugent and some other fags of the second Form were scampering at a distance. They did not matter. No Sixth Form man was to be seen anywhere near.

Bunter resolved to chance it—after a long and searching stare out of the window. It did not occur to him to look downward. No master or Sixth Form man could have stood under the window without his head showing above the broad stone sill. It did not occur to Billy Bunter that a junior might be standing there, with his head just below the level of the high sill.

He had forgotten Skinner, and if he had remembered him he could not have guessed that Harold Skinner, tired of loafing about, was leaning on the wall under that window. Bored, with nothing to do, Skinner leaned there idly, thinking that he might as well have gone on the paper-chase.

Happily ignorant of that, Billy Bunter prepared for swift action. If he did not want to be seen leaving Quelch's study by the door, still less did he want to be seen leaving it by the window. Speed was essential.

He acted quickly, when his fat mind was made up.

He grabbed the window-sash and shot it up, bundled out, and dropped over the stone sill, with very unaccustomed rapidity.

He expected, of course, to land on the earth. His expectations were not realised.

He landed on Skinner.

Skinner, hearing the window open above his head, was just looking round, when Bunter happened!

He did not know that it was Bunter. He was taken quite by surprise. All he knew was that something large, and heavy, thudded right on his head, squashing him down to the ground.

That large and heavy something sprawled over him, knocking every ounce of breath out of him, and squeaking with surprised alarm.

"Oooogh!" squeaked Bunter.

"Gurrrggh!" gurgled Skinner faintly.

"Oh crikey!"

Bunter sat up. He did not realise, for a moment, that he was sitting on a face.

Skinner did!

Skinner realised it with great clearness.

"Ooooogh!" gasped Bunter. "What—ooogh——"

"Urrrrgh!" came a suffocated gurgle from beneath Bunter as the hapless Skinner wriggled like a worm beneath the heel!

"Oooogh! Ow! What—oh crikey! Oooogh! Yaroooop!" yelled Bunter. "I'm bitten! Ow! What's biting me? Yaroooh!"

Bunter fairly bounded. He was off Skinner's face in a twinkling.

THE SEVENTH CHAPTER.

Hard Pressed !

TA-RA-RA-RA-RA!

Bob Cherry blew a blast on the bugle.

Up the towpath by the Sark, between the green woods and the

shining, rippling water, streamed the pack. Fluttering on the towpath were the fragments of torn paper. But the paper trail was not needed then, for the hares had been, for a moment, sighted—running swiftly up the river, past Popper's Island.

They vanished again, by a bend in the winding bank, but they had been spotted. The pack had high hopes of catching them, far from home.

"Come on!" panted the Bounder.

"Put it on!" gasped Peter Todd.

There were miles yet to run—up the river, and across Courtfield Common—before the hares headed for home. The pack were eager to bag them half-way on the run, and this looked like a chance. They tore on, by the shining river.

The pack had thinned out by this time. Even keen fellows had been unable to keep up the pace. Some had tailed off and taken short cuts back, others were keeping on, far in the rear. Nine or ten were still running with Bob, and behind them, sweating and breathless, ran Poker Pike!

People who saw the paper-chasers pass glanced at them—and stared at Poker Pike! It was an interesting, but not an unusual sight to see a crowd of cheery schoolboys on the run. But it was very unusual indeed to see a hickory-faced man in a bowler hat running with the pack!

Poker did not care for stares or smiles. He was quite indifferent to the impression he made on the public. But he was not feeling good. He was hefty and muscular, and had good wind, but the run was telling on him. His clothes were drying in the sunshine, but they were still damp and clinging, and they were far from being a suitable garb for a cross-country run.

For which reason Poker had discarded his coat, and was running in his shirt-sleeves!

He had gained a much-needed breathing-space while he stopped for a minute to remove articles from his coat pockets and transfer them to his trousers pockets. He simply could not keep on in that coat; he had to leave it behind and risk its loss. But he left it with empty pockets, hanging on a branch in Friardale Wood.

Then he re-started, running more easily, it was true, but collecting still more startled stares from people on the river or the towpath. At the tail of the pack, he pounded resolutely on.

Looking back every now and then, the juniors grinned at the sight of the crimson, perspiring face under the black bowler. Poker, quite unintentionally, was adding a little comic entertainment to the paper-chase.

Once or twice the pack distanced him, but the paper trail was a sure guide, and Poker kept grimly on.

To the juniors it was an absurd possibility that kidnappers could be looking out for a chance to grab a schoolboy on a paper-chase. But it seemed very far from impossible to Poker.

He knew the reputation of Chick Chew, the star kidnapper, the gangster who never admitted defeat. In the great United States, Chick had never been known to fail, and he was reputed to have made a huge fortune in his peculiar profession.

Kidnapping Putnam van Duck meant a ransom of half a million dollars from his popper, the multi-millionaire of Chicago. That was a sum for which it was worth while to put up a real tussle—even if Chick had not had his professional pride to consider in this matter.

Poker would not have been surprised to find Chick Chew, or some of his side-kickers, turning up at any point on the trail. He would not have been surprised had one of the hares, instead of being run down by the pack, vanished into a motor-car driven by Chick Chew or Bud Parker or Tug Keary, or some other of the kidnapping gang.

Breathless, but with unshaken determination, Poker pounded on, much to the entertainment of the Removites ahead of him.

"There they are!" yelled the Bounder as he had another glimpse of the hares on the bank between Popper's Island and the Popper Court Woods.

"Put it on!" gasped Tom Redwing.

"We've got 'em!" breathed Bob.

The hares vanished again. Green branches on the winding bank hid them. But the pack were more than confident now.

Still more confident would they have been, had they seen what was happening beyond the curve of the bank ahead.

Harry Wharton and Putnam van Duck went round that curve full tilt, still dropping handfuls of paper from the bags of "scent." Both of them knew that it was touch and go now. Hard pressed, they spurted.

As that towpath was used by members of the general public, and anybody might have come along at any moment, it behoved the hares to look where they were going—to look before they leaped, as it were.

But with the pack whooping close behind, the hares rather forgot the need of care and caution. It was quite a sharp bend by the river, and they came round full pelt; and never knew that anyone else was on the path till the crash came.

Coker of the Fifth was not to blame—that was certain. Often and often, in his little troubles with the juniors, Horace Coker was the man who hunted trouble. This time Horace was absolutely blameless; but he found the trouble, all the same, just as if he had hunted for it in his usual style.

Coker was sauntering down the towpath, thinking—certainly not of Remove fellows and their fag paper-chase—but of the great game of cricket. He was thinking what an absolute idiot Blundell was. The captain of the Fifth had a practice game on that afternoon, in which Potter and Greene, Coker's pals, were wanted, and Coker wasn't.

While Potter and Greene played cricket, Coker, if he liked, could have looked on and seen them doing it—which he didn't want to do in the least. Walking by the Sark, Coker of the Fifth was wondering, sardonically, how that absolute idiot Blundell expected to win matches, when he left out the best man in the Form—and not only the best man in the Form, but the best man in the school. Then the hares arrived, like a couple of bullets, and Blundell and cricket and all things else were driven out of Coker's mind, as he was hurled headlong, and strewn at full length on the towpath.

Harry Wharton and Putnam van Duck staggered back from the shock.

Wharton reeled against a tree by the path, panting. Van Duck sat down, with a bump, in the grass.

Coker lay on his back, staring dizzily at a blue sky, with a first hasty impression that the crack of doom had sounded, and that the Universe was falling into pieces around him.

Fortunately it wasn't.

The solid earth was still in its usual place when Coker dizzily sat up on it. He blinked at two breathless juniors.

"You idiot!" gasped Wharton.

"You pesky gink!" gurgled Van Duck.

Which was adding insult to injury, for Coker was not to blame for that collision; really, the juniors were to blame.

But they were naturally exasperated, for the hounds were coming on fast, and there was not a second to waste. The question of who was to blame mattered less than the fact that precious moments were lost.

"Ooooch!" gasped Coker. "Ow! My hat! Ow! Knocking a fellow over—— Oooooh! Why, I'll smash you!"

Coker got on his feet, somehow. He was winded by the shock, and he gurgled for breath. But smashing the cheeky fags who had knocked him over was, of course, too important a matter to be postponed. He tottered at them.

"Get on!" gasped Wharton. "Never mind that ass!"

"You said it!" panted Putnam.

They were rather winded by the shock as well as Coker, but not so badly as Coker. Swerving to right and left they dodged Coker, who was luckily too winded to deal with them as they deserved.

Leaving Coker gasping, they ran on, resuming the distribution of "scent," and covering the ground at great speed.

Coker, gurgling, gazed after them.

They vanished from sight almost in a moment. Coker, struggling for breath, was in no state to pursue.

Neither was he given long to think about it. Round the bend by the river came the pack, whooping.

The hares had met Coker face to face. The hounds came at his back as he stood staring after the vanished hares.

Like the hares the hounds had rather forgotten that the general public might be walking on that towpath. Like the hares they came round the bend full pelt.

For the second time Coker of the Fifth was strewn on the grass, though this time the charge came from the rear.

He went over on his face, and Bob Cherry and Smithy and Redwing, leaders of the pack, sprawled blindly over him.

Before they knew what had happened, or was happening, Peter Todd and Squiff, Tom Brown and Russell and Ogilvy, were sprawling over them in turn.

The rest of the pack came to a hurried halt.

"Hallo, hallo, hallo!" spluttered Bob Cherry. "What—who——"

"That fool Coker——" hissed the Bounder.

"That idiot Coker——"

"That blithering chump Coker——"

"Yooop!" roared Bob as, leaping up and running on, he was caught by the ankle, and brought down again, with a terrific crash

It was Coker who had grasped.

The hares had floored Coker, and escaped with impunity. The hounds had floored him again; but they were not to escape with impunity, if Horace Coker could help it. He had grabbed one of them, at any rate.

"Oh crikey!" gasped Bob, as he sprawled. "Leggo, you mad ass! Leggo!"

"I'll smash you!" gasped Coker. "I'll smash the lot of you! I'll jolly well mop up the whole crew of you!"

He scrambled up. Letting go Bob, he grasped at Smithy and Redwing, who were nearest, and got them by the necks. There was a loud crack as two heads came knocking together. There was a louder yell.

"Barge that idiot over!" howled Peter Todd.

Some of the hounds were running on. But most of the pack turned their attention to Coker. He was giving them all his attention, and they had to give him some.

They gave it promptly and efficaciously. Smithy and Redwing were struggling in his grasp, when Bob and Nugent, Johnny Bull and Hurree Jamset Ram Singh collared Horace, and hooked him over.

The odds were overwhelming; but Coker of the Fifth was not the man to count odds. He was the man to put up a fight against the most terrific odds. And he did.

For two or three minutes Coker raged in the midst of the Removites, keeping them very busy. But the odds were too overwhelming, even for the hefty and infuriated Horace.

He was left on the towpath at last, sprawling, breathless, quite at the end of his resources. The pack, panting, ran on, leaving him for dead, as it were.

The hapless Coker lay gurgling for breath in a fearfully untidy state, as a man in shirtsleeves and a bowler hat came trotting by. Poker Pike gave him a surprised stare, but did not stop. Almost as breathless as Coker, but determined as ever, the Greyfriars gunman charged on after the pack. Coker was left with the towpath to himself; and it was a long, long time before he resumed the perpendicular.

Forgetting Coker, the pack whooped on, off the towpath to the wide, open spaces of Courtfield Common. The paper trail lay ahead; but the hares had gained valuable minutes, when every second was precious—owing to Coker. They were far out of sight as the pack panted along the paper trail across the common.

THE EIGHTH CHAPTER.
Rival Spoofers!

HAROLD SKINNER looked at Billy Bunter, under the window of Mr Quelch's study, with a deadly look.

Billy Bunter was wriggling painfully, and he seemed to be hurt; but he was not hurt so much as he was going to be. Skinner's temper was never very good, and sitting on his face had not improved it in the least. Kicking Bunter across the quad, and back again, seemed quite a good idea to Skinner.

"You fat, foozling freak!" said Skinner. "What the dooce do you mean by jumping out of a window on a fellow's head?"

"Ow!" moaned Bunter. "Wow! Wharrer you mean by biting a fellow like a mad dog, you beast? Ow!"

"I'll jolly well——"

"Oh crikey!" exclaimed Bunter.

It was not Skinner's threatening words that caused him to exclaim. It was the sound of three o'clock chiming out from the clock-tower.

Three o'clock, and Mr. Coot's visitor was expected at the Courtfield Hotel at four! And there was a long, long walk between.

"I—I say, Skinner, old chap!" gasped Bunter, backing hastily away as Harold advanced on him. "I say, lend me four bob for a taxi fare, will you?"

Skinner stared at him in sheer astonishment. Under no circumstances whatever, would he have lent Billy Bunter four bob. In the present circumstances he was less likely to do so than ever. Dropping on a fellow's head, and sitting on his face, was really not the way to get that fellow into an unusually generous mood.

"Mad?" asked Skinner.

"Well, look here, lend me a tanner for the bus!" gasped Bunter—moderating his transports, as it were.

"I'll lend you four bob, as soon as a tanner!" said Skinner. "Just as soon! But at present I'm going to lend you a boot!"

Bunter backed away again.

He did not want the loan of Skinner's boot! That was quite useless to him. And he had no time to waste on a row with Skinner.

"Keep off, you silly beast!" he hooted. "I'm in a hurry! I shall be late for tea if I don't get off! You might lend a chap a tanner—I'll settle out of my postal order when—when it comes! I say—— Keep off, you beast!"

Bunter made another backward jump as Skinner followed him up. Bunter had no time to waste on Skinner; but Skinner had some to waste on Bunter. He seemed quite bent on that idea of lending Bunter his boot!

"Don't play the goat, you fathead!" howled Bunter. "I tell you, I've got to get to Courtfield by four, or I shall miss the spread——"

"Sticking somebody at the bunshop?" jeered Skinner. "Who? All the fellows are out on the paper-chase."

"I'm not going to a fag spread!" answered Bunter disdainfully. "And it isn't at a mouldy old bunshop, either. I say, Skinner, look here." Another bright idea struck Bunter—it seemed to be his day for brain-waves. "I say, I could take a pal if I liked. You stand the taxi, and I'll take you! What?"

Skinner paused.

He did not give up that idea of lending Bunter his boot! But he postponed the performance till he ascertained whether there was anything in this.

Skinner, like Bunter, was hard-up that afternoon! The black sheep of the Remove had lately placed all his available cash on a horse that was absolutely certain to win.

Unfortunately, that horse had come in eleventh. He had not run off with the race—only with Skinner's cash!

Tea in Hall—the last resource of the stony—was Skinner's prospect, as well as Bunter's that afternoon.

Certainly he was not prepared to stand a taxi, as Bunter suggested. But he was prepared to hear whether Bunter could stand a spread. That, too, was improbable, but it was worth while to make sure. There was lots of time for kicking Bunter, if there was nothing in it.

"I mean it!" said Bunter impressively. "A first-class feed at the best hotel in Courtfield! Everything of the best, and as much as you like."

"Gammon!" said Skinner.

"Only I've got to get there by four!" said Bunter. "It's a jolly long walk across the common! You stand the taxi—and come with me, see?"

"I'll come with you like a shot, if you're telling the truth!" grinned Skinner. "Of course, you might be—accidents will happen! Tell me about it first."

Billy Bunter blinked round cautiously through his big spectacles. He did not want other ears to hear.

There were very few fellows at Greyfriars to whom Bunter could have propounded so extraordinary a scheme for getting a free tea, without danger of being kicked. But Skinner was one of the few.

He was quite as unscrupulous as Bunter, without having the excuse of being such a duffer.

"Keep it dark, you know!" murmured Bunter. "It's rather a secret! Ever heard of a man named Coot?"

"Coot!" repeated Skinner blankly. "Coot! I believe I've heard that American chap mention the name—some man who may be coming down to see him some time, I believe. What on earth about Coot?"

"He's standing the spread!" breathed Bunter. "He's in Courtfield to-day, on business; and he's standing it, at the hotel——"

"He's asked you?" exclaimed Skinner

"Not exactly asked me," admitted Bunter. "But I'm jolly well going—and I can take a pal, if I like! Van Duck would very likely have taken a pal—might have taken Wharton or Nugent! Luckily, they're all out. I say, keep it dark, old man! You'll have to back me up, of course! You'll call me Van Duck, see?"

"Call you Van Duck!" repeated Skinner, wondering whether William George Bunter was wandering in his fat mind.

Bunter winked.

"You see, he's going to think I'm Van Duck!" he whispered.

"You look like him, don't you?" said Skinner. "A lot! Is he going to believe that Van Duck has grown double width since he's been at Greyfriars?"

"Oh, really, Skinner! He's never seen Van Duck—wants to make his acquaintance, see? Van Duck can't go—he's out with the fellows! Well, why shouldn't I go—and you with me? See?"

Skinner gazed at the fat Owl of the Remove. This sounded to him as if the fat junior's wits were going astray.

But as Bunter proceeded to explain about the lost letter, and the call he had taken on the telephone, Skinner's expression altered.

He could see that there was, after all, something in it.

"By gum!" said Skinner. His eyes glistened. "Why, if the man's never seen Van Duck, he might take any chap for him—any chap who went along in his name."

"Safe as houses!" said Bunter complacently. "You see, the mere fact of the fellow turning up will show that he is Van Duck—so far as old Coot can tell. He doesn't know that the Yankee never had his letter, and he can't possibly guess that I was in Quelch's study and took his call. See?"

Skinner nodded.

He was not thinking of kicking Bunter now! He was thinking of quite other things. But he did not tell Bunter of what he was thinking!

"Why, if any man in the Remove walked up at four and said he was Van Duck, how would the old bean know he wasn't?" said Bunter, grinning. "Of course, he'd never dream it wasn't the right chap."

"Never!" agreed Skinner.

"And he's going straight back to London—he said he was catching a train, and had only half an hour for Van Duck! Safe as houses! Even if he mentions it afterwards to Van Duck in a letter, nobody will know who went."

"Right as rain!"

"And I can tell you, it will be a spread!" said Bunter. "American millionaires do you all right! Better than doorsteps and dishwater in Hall, what?"

Skinner chuckled.

"As Inky would say, the betterfulness is terrific!" he answered.

"Only there's no time to lose!" said Bunter anxiously. "It's a jolly long walk to Courtfield. You stand the taxi—it will only be four bob, and we can call it on Quelch's phone, see? You're going to have a whack of a spread worth pounds."

"Come up to the study!" said Skinner.

"Haven't you got the tin about you?"

"No!"

"Well, look here, I'll wait for you here." Bunter did not like stairs.

"I mean, I've got some toffee in my study——"

"Oh, all right, old chap! Come on!"

Even with the prospect ahead of a gorgeous spread stood by an American millionaire, Bunter fell to the lure of toffee!

He followed Skinner into the House and up to the Remove passage. That passage was quite deserted.

Except for Fisher T. Fish, happy and busy with his accounts in Study No. 14, at the end, there was not a single Remove fellow on the spot.

Skinner paused at the doorway of Bunter's study, No. 7. He opened the door of that study and glanced in. It was, as he expected, vacant.

Bunter blinked at him impatiently.

"I say what are you wasting time for, Skinner?" he yapped.

Skinner's answer was not in words.

Taking hold of the fat Owl's fat shoulders, he gave him a sudden spin, sending him headlong into the study.

Bunter, with a startled yell, rolled.

Skinner swiftly whipped the key out of the lock inside, and jammed it into the lock outside. As Bunter sat up he slammed the door, turned the key, and slipped the latter into his pocket.

There was a roar from Bunter in the study.

"Skinner, you beast——"

No answer from Skinner—unless a sound of retreating footsteps, dying away towards the stairs, could be taken as an answer.

Bunter, equally astonished and enraged at this extraordinary trick, dragged frantically at the doorhandle and yelled.

"Skinner, you beast! Skinner, you rotter! Let me out, you tick! Let me out of this study, you cad! Do you hear?"

Skinner did not hear—being downstairs by that time. Anyhow, he would not have heeded.

"Beast!" roared Bunter. "I shall be late at Courtfield! I say, it's no good if a fellow doesn't turn up by four."

He banged on the door and yelled frantically through the keyhole. But he realised that Skinner was gone.

"Oh crikey!" gasped Bunter.

The game was up—for Bunter! He could see now that Skinner had been pulling his fat leg, in pretending to fall in with his scheme. This, it seemed, was Skinner's retaliation for having his face sat on!

Bunter had been a prisoner in Quelch's study, and had escaped by the window. Now he was a prisoner in his own study—but there was no escape by a window thirty feet from the ground! This time he was a study prisoner for keeps!

He gasped with wrath. Minutes—precious minutes—were passing, and that gorgeous spread at Courtfield was fading away like the unsubstantial vision of a dream.

"Oh, the beast!" groaned Bunter. "Rotter! Toad! Tick! B e a s t! Blighter! Worm! Oh lor'!"

He could hardly find words for Skinner's iniquity.

And he did not guess, as yet, the full depth and extent of that iniquity! While the hapless Owl raged in Study No. 7, Skinner was swinging out of the school gates, to start for Courtfield.

It was a good idea—a real brain-wave of Bunter's—Skinner admitted that. But Bunter was not the fellow to carry it out.

The fat and fatuous Owl would have given away the deception before he had opened his mouth twice—in Skinner's opinion, at least. A much more artful fellow than Bunter was required to carry out such a spoof successfully—a fellow, for instance, like Harold Skinner!

Skinner could get brain-waves, as well as Bunter! And—cheerfully leaving the fat Owl of the Remove to rage in a locked study—Skinner started to walk to Courtfield, to carry out Bunter's scheme on his own, and stick Mr. Ezra Coot for the spread intended for Putnam van Duck!

THE NINTH CHAPTER.

The Man who Watched the Road!

"ALL right now?" said Harry Wharton breathlessly.

"O.K.!" agreed Putnam.

The hares had fallen into a gentle trot.

Behind them, the paper trail wound among the bushes and furze of Courtfield Common. During the long run there had been only one spot of danger—when Coker of the Fifth had butted in—fortunately for the hares, though rather unfortunately for Coker. He had delayed the pack long enough to give the hares the chance they needed—and they had made the most of it.

From that time they had kept well ahead, and when they looked back, from a knoll on the common, they saw nothing of the pursuers. So they ventured to fall into an easy trot, as they headed for the road over the common, by which the way lay back to Greyfriars School.

"I guess we've got them beat!" added Putnam van Duck.

"Well, I fancy we may see something of Bob, or Smithy, or Squiff!" said Harry. "But we can take it easy for a bit."

Taking it easy, they trotted on to the long, white road, that lay like a ribbon across the green common, from Friardale and the school to the town of Courtfield.

They struck the road about midway between Courtfield and the school, and at that spot a small, black, closed car stood by the roadside.

The chauffeur was standing by it, staring steadily in the direction of the distant school, as if in expectation of seeing someone coming from that direction.

Harry Wharton did not take any particular notice of either the car or the driver, but Putnam gave the latter a rather keen "once-over."

"I guess that hombre hails from my side!" he remarked.

"Eh?"

"I mean he's Amurrican."

"Oh!" said Harry, and he glanced at the man—a stocky, clean-shaven man, with keen eyes in an alert face.

The man turned as he heard the schoolboys approaching, and watched them come off the common into the road. Then, as they would have passed on, he stepped towards them, touching his cap.

"I guess you'll excuse me!" he began, and Wharton smiled. The guess confirmed Putnam's remark that the man was an American.

They came to a stop.

"Yes," said Harry. "Anything we can do for you?" It was rather puzzling what the man wanted, but he concluded that a foreigner might be doubtful about the way to somewhere.

"Mebbe!" said the clean-shaven man. He was eyeing the two juniors very keenly, and Wharton noted that Van Duck's face was equally keen.

It came into his mind, suddenly, that Van Duck had reason to be alert, if he fell in with strange Americans. Certainly this man was neither Chick Chew nor Bud Parker, both of whom Van Duck knew by sight. But Chick had a good many "side-kickers" in the kidnapping game, and an American standing by a car on a rather lonely road, only a mile from Greyfriars, would certainly have made Poker Pike suspicious.

"I guess I'm waiting here for a boy from the school," explained the driver. "Mebbe you belong to Greyfriars?"

"Yes," said Harry.

"One of you might be the feller, then, though I didn't look for him in that kit!" said the clean-shaven man.

"We're on a paper-chase," said Harry, with a smile.

"What's the name of the fellow you want?" asked Van Duck. "This chap is Wharton, and I'm Smith!"

Harry Wharton repressed, with difficulty, a start of surprise. Van Duck generally spoke with a slight nasal intonation, which betrayed the fact that he came from the other side of the "pond." Now, however, he spoke very carefully, without that nasal sound in his voice. And he gave his name as Smith!

Wharton was quick on the uptake. He did not need telling that Van Duck scented danger in that black, closed car and the waiting driver. Poker Pike after all, had been right!

Both the juniors saw the shade of disappointment that came over the sharp American face as Van Duck gave the names.

"I guess neither of you ain't my bird!" he said, and he stepped back to the car.

"But what chap do you want?" asked Harry. "We'll give him the tip you're waiting for him, if we see him. What's his name?"

"Oh, Jones!" said the driver. "If you see Jones, tell him to get a move on."

"Right-ho!"

The hares trotted on towards the school. They trotted more swiftly than before. Putnam made the pace, and Wharton kept up with him.

A glance over a shoulder showed the clean-shaven young man standing again as the juniors had first seen him, staring along the road after them.

"By the great horn spoon!" murmured Van Duck.

"You think——" muttered Harry.

"I guess it's a cinch! There ain't a lot of Amurricans hanging about this quiet spot—and he's waiting for a fellow from the school. I guess that guy Poker was on the right mark!"

Putnam chuckled.

"Did you pipe his face when I said our names? I guess he was honing to hear that one of us was named Van Duck."

"But——" said Harry.

"I guess I gave him the straight goods—I'm a Smith on one side of the family!" grinned Putnam. "And mopper's name is mine as much as popper's, I guess."

"But I can't make it out," said Harry. "If he's one of that gang, what possible reason can he have for supposing that Van Duck—you—may be coming along this road this afternoon?"

Putnam shook his head.

"That let's me out!" he answered. "I can't guess that one, sure! Mebbe Chick's been working some game—or mebbe the feller's just cruising on the

Before Poker Pike could fire at the running gangsters, Bob Cherry gave him a hefty charge, and sent him crashing to the ground. There was a roar of rage from Pike, as the gangsters disappeared among the trees!

chance of a guy walking out on a half-holiday! Anyhow, I'll lay Rockefeller's millions to a continental red cent, that if he'd been wise to it that I was little me, he'd have roped me into that car."

"But if Chick Chew set him to watch for you, surely he'd set a man who knew you by sight——"

"If he did, wouldn't I likely know him by sight, too, and give him a wide berth?" grinned Putnam.

"Oh! Yes, I suppose so. But—— Blessed if I can make it out!" said Harry. "If it's as you think, that man's got some special reason for believing that Van Duck will come along here this afternoon—and how the dickens——"

"Ask me another! But if he wasn't one of Chick's gang, I'll eat Poker's gun, and then some!"

Much puzzled, Wharton trotted on by the American junior's side. The car and the man beside it dropped out of sight.

"Gee!" ejaculated Putnam suddenly. "I guess that's one of the bunch, ahead of us—I mean, the pack!"

"Skinner!" exclaimed Harry.

A Remove fellow was coming along the road from the direction of the school. It was Harold Skinner—and Wharton frowned as he recognised him.

"It's all right," he said, "Skinner can't catch us—he never followed the trail. I don't suppose he started at all."

Certainly Skinner showed no sign of having done any hard running that afternoon. He was quite fresh, and walking with unusual quickness.

He started a little at the sight of the two hares coming down the road. It was rather an awkward meeting for Skinner, as one of the hares was his Form captain, whose duty it was to see that slackers did not slack.

Skinner would have passed on without stopping, but the hares stopped.

"All serene," said Skinner uneasily. "I can't catch you, you know! I haven't followed on. I conked out rather early."

"Very early, I fancy!" said Harry contemptuously. "Did you start at all?"

"Every fellow was bound to start, wasn't he?" said Skinner blandly. "But I told you about the pain in my foot. It came on rather bad after a mile, and I had to chuck it."

"If you started, and did a mile, all right!" said the captain of the Remove. "That's not bad for a slacker."

"Well, I did!" grunted Skinner. "But the pain in my foot——"

"That hasn't stopped you from taking a walk."

"It's passed off, luckily," said Skinner, still bland.

"If you did a mile——"

"I've told you I did!"

"That would be as far as Giles' mill. Did you get as far as the mill?"

"Just!" agreed Skinner. "I sat down there a bit to rest my foot before I started back to the school."

Harry Wharton laughed.

"Try again!" he suggested.

"What do you mean?" demanded Skinner.

"I mean, that we never went within a mile of Giles' mill, and that any fellow who followed the trail can't have seen the mill this afternoon."

"Oh!" ejaculated Skinner.

Van Duck chuckled. Skinner was fairly caught.

"So you were pulling my leg?" he snarled.

"Exactly!" assented Wharton coolly. "I jolly well knew you never started. I suppose you cut while Pike was kicking up that row at the gates, or Bob would have bagged you. You know as well as I do, Skinner, that a man can't cut a Form run. You get a batting."

"Oh, go and eat coke!" snapped Skinner, and he tramped on, leaving the hares to resume their trot to the school.

THE TENTH CHAPTER.

"Got!"

THE man who stood by the small black car fixed his eyes, with a glint in them, on a schoolboy coming up the road across the common at a quick walk.

Skinner, as he came on, glanced at him carelessly. But the clean-shaven man's glance at Skinner was not careless—it was keen, searching, scrutinising. And as Skinner reached the spot where the car stood by the roadside, the man stepped towards him, touching his hat.

"'Skuse me, sir!" His manner was very respectful. "If you're the young gentleman from the school, sir—the one I'm waiting for——"

Skinner stopped. He was half-way to Courtfield, and he would have been glad of a lift in a car for the rest. Skinner was a better walker than Billy Bunter, but he was no whale at any kind of exertion. The man spoke with an American accent, which Skinner noted at once, and it occurred to him, naturally, that he might have some connection with the American at the Courtfield Hotel.

"You're waiting for a Greyfriars fellow?" he asked.

"You said it, sir! If you are Mr. Van Duck——"

(*Continued on page 16.*)

BURLEIGH'S BRANE-WAVE!

Another rollicking instalment of "The Spartans of St. Sam's!" By the Second Form literary genius,

DICKY NUGENT

GREYFRIA
No. 188. EDITED BY H

One fine day, a cupple of weeks after the St. Sam's Spartans had commenced their commical career, Doctor Birchemall came galloping fewriously down to the Sports Ground on horseback. He held the rains in one hand, a pistle in the other, and a long, croollooking whip in the other; and there was a grim, determined eggspression on his skollarly fizzog. Those who were near enuff heard him muttering into his beard as he galloped across the quad.

"If I don't turn my Spartans into champion sprinters this afternoon," he was muttering darkly, "then I'll eat my Sunday worst mortar-board!"

A grinning crowd followed the Head of St. Sam's to the Sports Ground to see the fun. There they found the St. Sam's Spartans lined up on the running-track. The fellows couldn't help larfing when they looked at Doctor Birchemall's so-called athletes. So anxious was the Head to win the inter-skools sports without the help of Burleigh's followers that he had left out all the fellows Burleigh had previously chosen and roped in the weakest and puniest fizzical spessimens at St. Sam's in their place! The result was that they looked more like a collection of old crocks than a squad of Spartans!

Litening flashed from the Head's eyes as he rained in his steed and hailed them in a voice like thunder.

"Ho, there, you sons of dogs!" he roared. "Prepare for an afternoon of strenuous sprinting! I'm going to make sure that the efforts of those who march under my banner shall never flag! Woe betide the lazy lubbers who lag behind!"

"Mersy, sir!" wimpered some of the sprinters.

"Mersy be blowed!" cride the Head, with a leer. "Are you ready?"

The unforchunit Spartans nodded, and Doctor Birchemall raised his pistle.

Bang!

"Yaroooo!"

The Head's hand had wobbled as he fired, with the result that he had fired point-blank at himself! Forchunitly, however, the bullet passed through his brane and did no dammidge.

Any hoaps the sprinters mite have built up of that little axxident making things easier for them were soon dashed to the ground. The Head came galloping after them in a cupple of jiffies, lashing out with his whip for all he was worth.

"Skamper along, Skellington!" he yelled encurridgingly. "Wade in, Waystead! Lead on, Littlegrub! Step on it, Starveling! Bless my sole! What are you all dawdling about for?"

This was insult added to injury with a vengenz, for the Spartans were running as fast as their flabby legs would carry them, whereas Doctor Birchemall was perched comfortably on the back of his horse. But it would have been asking for trubble to point out that to the Head, so the Spartan sprinters wisely refraned—and ran for dear life to avoid the Head's whip instead!

Burleigh of the Sixth joined the spectators as the sprinters finished the course for the second time. His eyes farely flashed fire as he noted the feeble, flagging footsteps of the Head's chosen athletes. Cleaving his way to the front of the crowd, he ran on to the track and coolly brought the Head's horse to a halt.

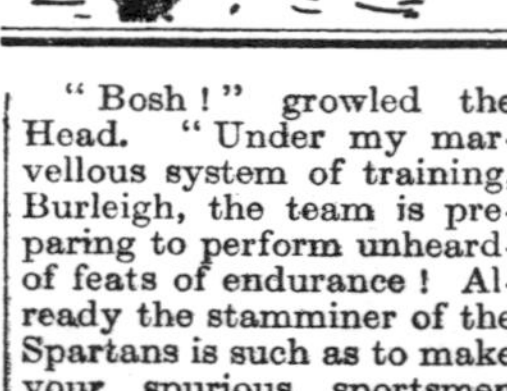

"Stop!" he cride dramatickally. "I'm not going to see those fellows tortchered like this without a protest, sir! Why, every one of them has got the stitch! Look at the way they reel!"

Doctor Birchemall knitted his brows.

"I don't quite cotton on, Burleigh!" he said.

"Then you must be wool-gathering, that's all, sir!" said Burleigh bluntly. "Sir, the time has come to end this sollum farce! If the skool is to win the sports you and I must patch up our differences!"

The Head grinned sardonically.

"Know any more funny stories, Burleigh?" he asked.

Burleigh culfered fewriously.

"Nothing funnier than the story that will be told after Sports Day if your so-called Spartans are allowed to represent St. Sam's!"

"Bosh!" growled the Head. "Under my marvellous system of training, Burleigh, the team is preparing to perform unheard-of feats of endurance! Already the stamminer of the Spartans is such as to make your spurious sportsmen look meer spineless spoofers in comparison! Just look at them!"

He pointed proudly down the track, fondly imagining that the Spartans were still on the run. But, grately to his chagrin, he found that every single Spartan had collapsed! They were all lying about in various parts of the track, puffing and blowing like grampuses! Burleigh couldn't help grinning as he looked at them.

"My hat! By the look of them, sir, the only kind of race your Spartans will win is an ambulance race—with the Spartans on the stretchers!"

"Ha, ha, ha!"

"Silence!" yelled the Head as the crowd roared with larfter at Burleigh's sally. "I'll have the lazy yung raskals on their feet again in a cupple of shakes, beleeve me!"

"I daresay you will," said Burleigh, with a skornful glance at the Head's instrument of tortcher. "But let me tell you, sir, that all the whips you can lay your hands on won't make athletes out of those rabbits!"

"Rats!"

"No, rabbits!" said Burleigh, jerking his thumb in the direction of the Spartans. "Sir, let me make a last request to you to abandon this vencher and allow the old brigade, led by myself, to take over the sports once more!"

"Nothing doing, Burleigh!"

"But I want to appeal——"

"Ring off!" said the Head rudely. "It's no good of you arguing the toss, Burleigh, so you may as well save your breth. Gee-up!"

He gave his steed a flick with the whip and trotted off again.

It was the Head's last word on the subject—there was no doubt about that; and as Burleigh tramped off the track his face was very grim and stern. He had made up his mind what to do. He wasn't going to stand for it; he wasn't going to take it lying down, but he was going to sit up and take notiss at last!

"Tallboy! Tuffnut! Jolly! Follow me!" he said gruffly as he walked towards the Skool House. Tallboy and Tuffnut, of the Sixth, and Jolly, of the Fourth, fell in and followed their leader, and on the way to the House, Burleigh collected all the rest of the old team of athletes he had been training for the sports before the Head had interfered.

When he reach Skool House, Burle the crowd straight Sixth Form Room. locked the door and speaking, and in jiffies the fellows lissening intently to account of Burleigh's wave.

"Fellow - sports cride Burleigh. " seen for yourselve Doctor Birchemall my plea to abolli Spartans and allow compete for St. Sa the sports. He tre with utter kontemp

"Shame!"

"There is only on left for us to do, that said Burleigh. " this—to pretend w team from another and to compete f honners *against t Sam's Spartans as everybody else!"*

"M-m-my hat!"

"But the Hea reckernise us!" Jack Jolly.

Burleigh smiled.

"No he won't. thought of that a You see, we shall disguised—disguised even our own mother reckernise us."

"Grate pip!"

"Well, what d think of the idea n asked Burleigh.

For several secon fellows were too se to say a word. The denly they all jum their feet, cheering l very dickens!

"Good old Burlei

"Hooray!"

"Hip, hip, hooray

"Wonderful whee Jove!"

"Brilliant branew George!"

WOULD YOU BELIEVE IT?

A stand-up fight between Bob Cherry and Bolsover major, whom Bob had caught twisting a fag's ear, lasted five rounds. By then Bolsover had one eye closed, and his other nearly so. Bob is not styled Remove champion for nothing—and Bolsover's bullying had made him see red! But when Bolsover admitted his fault, Bob was quick to offer his hand. A "handy" pal!

Lord Mauleverer kept Removites awake searching for his new pyjamas the other night—and it was not till Peter Todd jerked the bedclothes off Bunter that they came to light! Bunter had coolly "borrowed" them, splitting the jacket up the back to make it fit! Mauly nearly had a "fit"—while the Removites went into "fits" of laughter!

A registered letter for Billy B provoked the Owl to great ex ment. He felt sure it contain a fat remittance! opening it, however, nothing a loose penny stamp fell o whereupon, Bob Cherry no that the letter was postma "Aberdeen." Later, Ski admitted getting a pal to pos It was too bad of Skinner

ARTON. May 16th, 1936.

Burleigh smiled.
"Glad you like it, chaps! Now I'll see about getting entry officially reckoned. We'll call ourselves team from St. Alf's. , remember—mum's the word! None of you must breathe a syllable about it!"

"No fear!"

"Rely on us, old chap!"

"Well, that's that," said Burleigh, with a sigh of relief, as the meeting broke up. "We know how we stand now, and we've at least got something to train for. Keep yourselves as fit as fiddles—and then on Sports Day you'll be ready to face the music!"

And, having given the chaps that wise advice, Burleigh went off to settle details of his brilliant brainwave!

(Now is Burleigh's "brainwave" going to work in practice? For the answer read next week's instalment of this mirth-making serial!)

ANSWERS TO CORRESPONDENTS.

"INQUIRER" (Remove): "What sort of ink was it that fell on to Loder of that booby-trap Saturday?"

We don't know for certain, "Inquirer," but if it's any help to you we understand that Loder saw red!

DUPONT (Remove): "Bolsover says he is going to knock my head off. What shall I do?"

The best advice we can give you, old chap, is not to lose your head!

HOW BUNTER BEAT TREE-CLIMBING CHAMPS!

By
PETER TODD

I hope that you chaps who have always said Bunter was too weighty for tree-climbing will now admit you were wrong. Those of you who were at the final of the Tree-climbing Championship certainly won't have any doubts about it! In fact, it's not going too far to say that you'll remember Bunter as a tree-climber for the rest of your lives!

In actual fact, the Championship had already been decided when Bunter put in an appearance. The test tree was a very tall oak in the meadow opposite Major Thresher's orchard, and Bob Cherry and Dick Russell, the finalists, had both done their stuff and come down again, Bob having succeeded in sticking his flag a few inches above Russell's, and thus winning the day.

Blundell of the Fifth, the judge, was just holding up Bob's hand in the sign of victory, when along came Bunter.

That's putting it mildly; what I should say is along flew Bunter! He covered the ground at a speed that was simply staggering, and he made straight for the old oak-tree.

Up he went like a fat frog that was animated by clockwork! Bob blinked and Russell rubbed his eyes. Bunter was climbing up by the same route as they had taken themselves—and doing it a jolly sight quicker, too! They simply gasped when they saw him go without a single stop right to the top of the tree a good three feet beyond Bob's winning flag!

Well, there it was, anyway! Whether you like it or not, it goes down to posterity now that Bunter beat the tree-climbing champs at their own game!

Oh, I almost forgot to tell you why he did it.

The explanation was that whilst scrumping in Major Thresher's orchard Bunter had spotted a bull coming towards him, and the oak-tree happened to be the first haven of refuge he reached!

Chaps have since been pulling his leg, because the bull turned out to be a tame one belonging to old Thresher that often wanders around the grounds.

Be that as it may, Bunter has succeeded in beating the tree-climbing champs!

CRICKETERS, BE GENTLEMEN!

Urges BOLSOVER MAJOR

The old-fashioned courtesy that used to be part of the charm of cricket is fast dying out. If the Greyfriars game is anything to go by, there's about as much politeness in cricket nowadays as there is in all-in wrestling.

It saddened me, I can tell you, when I took a stroll round the playing-fields last Wednesday. As I passed Big Side I saw Loder stop a ball with his nose. Did he bow to Fitzgerald, the bowler, and murmur, "My fault, sir"? Not a bit of it! He just danced up and down the turf yelping like some blessed dog and calling Fitz all the names he could think of—including a lot that I myself had never thought of before!

Then on Little Side I saw Smithy swing back his bat to make a late cut and catch Wicket-keeper Hazeldene an awful whack on the napper! Did he profusely apologise? Nothing of the kind! What he did was to laugh till the tears ran down his cheeks!

These incidents—typical of the sort of thing you can see any day of the week—make me feel it's high time something was done to bring back good manners to cricket. I've made up my mind to do all I can to help, anyway.

If I find anyone showing bad manners in any game where I'm playing, I'm going to walk right up to him and say: "If you don't learn better manners, you pie-faced pest, I shall give you a oner on the boko!" If that warning doesn't teach him to act like a gentleman, I shall roll the pitch with him, then jump on him!

(Looks like cricket will become a regular riot if Bolsy carries out his threat. May we suggest, Bolsy, that you alter your tactics and start by cultivating a few manners yourself?—Ed.)

FISH FAVOURS SCIENTIFIC FEEDING

Says FRANK NUGENT

Fisher T. Fish gave a lecture on "Malnutrition" in the Rag last week. Malnutrition, to save you the fag of looking it up in a dic., means under-feeding. And Fishy, in his lecture, maintained that practically every boy in the British Isles is suffering from under-feeding. Not because we don't eat enough—oh dear no! The trouble is, according to Fish, that we don't eat the right things.

"What I believe in and what I'm hyer to advocate," declared Fishy, "is scientific feeding—eatin' the right things in the right proportions!"

When he had finished and asked for questions, the first question was from Tom Brown.

"How could we learn to feed scientifically?" Browny asked.

Then Fishy smiled. Looked as if he had been waiting for that question.

"You've said it, Browny!" he chortled. "Jest to save you all the trouble of studyin' the science of correct feedin' for yourselves, you see, I've made up hampers of food sufficient to last any guy two days. These hampers are guaranteed to contain jest the right quantity of fat, protein and carbohydrate required to keep a guy as fit as a fiddle—an' I'm retailin' 'em at the amazingly low price of one shilling each. Cash with order, of course! Who wants one?"

It's surprising how Fishy still gets away with it sometimes. He had quite a rush of orders.

In due course his customers received their hampers. And what do you think they found inside them? You'll never guess, so here's the list:

1 packet of lard.

1 bag of flour.

1 bag of split peas.

That was all the hampers contained.

Fishy stoutly maintained, when the complaints flowed in, that it was no swindle. The fat, protein and carbohydrate content was O.K., and the quantity sufficient to last two days. But, in spite of his indignant protestations, his customers weren't satisfied till he had been rolled all round the Rag and bumped in every corner!

GREYFRIARS FACTS WHILE YOU WAIT!

and shy of "heroics," Wingate, Captain of the Scouts, was glad when the presentation of the Scouts' silver medal for saving a man from drowning was finally over. Sir Popper, Governor of the school, "gassed" on for some time—little wonder that Wingate would have liked to "drown" him!

Wun Lung has his own ways of "paying out" fellows who bully his young brother, Hop Hi, in the Second. After Bolsover had cuffed Hop Hi, he found the leaves of his Latin grammar gummed together. Wun Lung offered him a "crib" in class next day—but it was an exercise purposely filled with errors! Bolsover's exercise was like a Chinese puzzle—and no "error"!

Mr. Prout is ever ready to recount how during a recent summer vac., he went tarpon fishing off Florida, U.S.A. Bunter, happening to point to the photograph of the biggest "catch" made by the expedition, had to listen to the whole story. Bunter said he would almost rather have had the caning Mr. Prout had originally promised to give him!

(*Continued from page* 13.)

As he was going to present himself to Mr. Ezra Coot as Van Duck, Skinner was prepared, of course, to lay claim to that name.

He nodded coolly

"Did Mr. Coot send you to meet me?" he asked.

He mentioned the name of the American gentleman intentionally, so that this man should have no doubt that he really was Van Duck. Any other fellow coming along the road, of course, would have known nothing about Mr. Coot—so far as this man could know.

Skinner was a keen and observant fellow, and he did not fail to note the flash of satisfaction in the man's sharp eyes. Quite plainly, the man was very glad to have met Van Duck on the road!

"That's the how of it, sir!" he said. "Mr. Ezra Coot, at the Courtfield Hotel——"

"He's expecting me at four!" said Skinner calmly.

Skinner had no doubt about being able to carry off that "spoof" successfully, much as he doubted Billy Bunter's ability to do so. Still, he was glad to put it to the test before meeting Mr. Coot himself!

If he satisfied this man, who had come from Mr. Coot, it was pretty certain that all would go well when he met Ezra.

Indeed, Ezra Coot could hardly entertain the slightest imaginable doubt on the subject, if his visitor arrived in the car he had sent to meet Van Duck on the way!

"You said it, Mr. van Duck, sir!" The clean-shaven man was obviously very satisfied. "You see, sir, I met up with Mr. Coot in Courtfield, and when he said he was expecting his old friend's son, coming from the school, I allowed I'd run down and meet him up the road, and give him a lift. It's an honour, sir, to meet the son of Mr. Vanderdecken van Duck."

Skinner suppressed a grin.

He had no doubt that a pushing American would be glad of a chance of establishing contact with the son of the multi-millionaire of Chicago.

That was the impression he received from this American's remarks. Perhaps it was the impression the American intended him to receive!

"That's all right," he said. "I'll be glad of a lift."

"My car's quite at your service, sir!"

"Thanks!" said Skinner, airily.

The man opened the door of the car for Skinner to step in As he did so, he looked past Skinner, as if in expectation, or perhaps apprehension, of seeing someone else coming up the road.

But the road was quite deserted.

Across the green common a scattered crowd of schoolboys in running kit came into sight. The pack was arriving on the paper trail. The high wind had scattered that trail a little on the wide common, and there had been some delay; but the hounds had picked up the "scent" again, and were coming on fast.

The man with the car, however, did not look at them He had stopped the hares, on the chance that one of them might be Van Duck; but now that he had Van Duck—as he believed—in his presence, he was not interested in any other schoolboys.

Skinner followed his glance down the road. He had the impression that the man with the car expected to see him followed by somebody. It did not occur to him, at the moment, that the man was uneasy lest Poker Pike might be in the offing, keeping "tabs" on the millionaire's son.

But no one was to be seen on the road.

Skinner stepped into the car.

He sat down, in a very cheerful mood. All was going well!

He was getting a lift into Courtfield; he was going to arrive early at the hotel; and he was going to bag the magnificent spread intended for Van Duck! And it was an added satisfaction, to Skinner's peculiar nature, that Billy Bunter, who had schemed and expected to bag that spread, was locked in his study at the school, disappointed and furious.

But Skinner's satisfaction was brief.

Having sat down in the car, he expected the man to shut the door, step into the driving seat, and drive on to Courtfield.

His expectations were not realised.

What happened was nothing like that! It was, indeed, something that made Harold Skinner wonder whether he was dreaming—a particularly horrid and terrifying nightmare.

The clean-shaven man did not shut the door He stepped into the car after Skinner. In utter horror and amazement and dismay, Skinner saw him jerk a revolver from his hip. He grasped it by the barrel in his right hand, and with his left grasped Skinner's collar.

"Don't yaup." His voice came with a snap. "You ain't going to be hurt none, if you keep quiet! Jest a yaup, and you won't give another! You get me?"

Skinner could only gaze at him in stony horror.

Almost stunned with amazement and terror, he could hardly believe that this was really happening.

But he kept quiet!

Astounding, unbelievable as it was, he knew—knew only too well—that a cry, an attempt at resistance, would be followed instantly by a crash on his head from the heavy metal butt of the pistol—which would put it out of his power to give further trouble.

White as chalk, he goggled at the man.

"Keep it parked!" came the snap again.

Unresisting, Skinner was twirled off the seat to the floor of the car. The man jerked the door shut.

The blind were drawn on the windows, and the interior of the closed car was invisible to any passer-by.

Skinner, frightened out of his wits, was as unresisting in the man's hands as clay in the hands of the potter.

Dazed with astonishment, he felt a cord passed round his wrists, and then his ankles, and knotted. Then a gag was fastened in his mouth.

Utterly helpless, he huddled on the floor of the car, and the man drew an ample rug over him, completely screening him from sight.

Skinner saw nothing more. But he could hear. He heard three sharp, loud blasts on the motor-horn in swift succession. Then he heard the buzzing of the engine. The little black car jumped into motion.

It roared away.

What direction it was taking, Skinner did not know; but he was certain that it was not in the direction of Courtfield.

Obviously, the man was not taking him to tea with Mr. Ezra Coot in this extraordinary way!

What did it mean?

What could it mean?

He was kidnapped!

And as that word came into his mind, along with it came the explanation. Nobody, it was certain, would possibly want to kidnap Harold Skinner of the Remove. He was kidnapped as Van Duck!

He had given the name of Van Duck—he had artfully and cunningly made this man believe that he was Van Duck—and the man, so far from coming from Ezra Coot, was one of the kidnapping gang, on the look-out for a chance to "cinch" the millionaire's son.

Skinner groaned through the gag.

He had been given no chance to explain. Indeed, had he done so, the man would hardly have believed him. If he had denied that he was Van Duck, after laying claim to that name, the rascal would have taken it for a palpable falsehood.

Tea with a rich American was very much off the programme now. He was not going to the Courtfield Hotel; he was going to some hidden and remote den of the kidnapping gang.

The car roared on.

Tea with Mr. Coot! Skinner—now that it was too late—was keen enough to realise that there was no tea with Mr. Coot—no Mr. Coot at all!

The whole thing was a trick to get Putnam van Duck out of the safety of the school.

It was a trap, and Skinner, the sharpest and most cunning fellow in the Remove, had walked into it.

Possibly Van Duck would have walked into it, but for the lost letter. That lost letter had never been written by the genuine Mr. Ezra Coot. The telephone call that Bunter had taken in Quelch's study had not come from the genuine Ezra, but from a scheming rascal using his name It grew more and more clear to Skinner that the whole thing, from beginning to end, was a "plant."

And he had walked into it!

What was going to happen to him now?

Billy Bunter would have walked into it, but he had fooled the fat Owl and taken his place—for this! Wriggling under the enveloping rug, Skinner groaned, a muffled groan under the gag. Many times Skinner's artfulness had over-reached itself. But never so disastrously as now.

Billy Bunter, boiling with fury in Study No. 7 in the Remove, pictured the artful Skinner sitting down to a magnificent spread with a spoofed American at the Courtfield Hotel. It had dawned on Bunter's fat brain at last what Skinner's game was.

But if Billy Bunter could have known the facts, he would have been exceedingly glad that he was locked in Study No. 7. It was not nice, but it was nicer than being tied up under a rug on the floor of a rushing motor-car in the hands of Chicago kidnappers.

THE ELEVENTH CHAPTER.

O.K.!

"SKEERED?" sneered Chick Chew.

"I guess," said Bud Parker, "that I'd ruther be back in Chicawgo, Chick. I ain't making no pretence of liking this country."

Chick snorted contemptuously.

The fat gangster was standing, leaning on an old beech, in a clump of trees on Courtfield Common. Bud Parker stood near him, his eyes watchful as a scared rabbit's through his horn-rimmed spectacles.

Bud was uneasy. He had been uneasy ever since the gangsters had transferred their activities from their native haunts to the dangerous side of the Atlantic—dangerous for gangsters!

In a one-horse island where cops did not even pack guns, Bud might have been expected to consider gangstering an easy job—mere pie. But he did not. He had a wholesome respect for the British Police Force, in spite of their lack of guns. Shooting up cops was all very well in Chicago, but in this dog-goned island a cop could not be shot up without setting the whole country on its hind legs, rubbering after the guy with the gun. And Bud, though he packed his accustomed automatic, had not the slightest intention of using it until he was safe back on the other side of the pond.

It was difficult for Bud to believe that there really existed a country where a guy couldn't buy his way out of the "stone jug." But he was driven to believe it. And he had a deep dread of finding himself inside a "stone jug" in a land where the way out was not for sale.

"I'll say you're some Dismal Jimmy, Bud!" said Mr. Chew. "I ain't shouting out that we've had a whole heap of luck so far. Nope! This ain't the country that I'd pick out of a heap for our game. Surely not! If I was picking and choosing, I'd sure leave this here island on the counter. But Old Man Vanderdecken has parked his boy in this pesky island—yep or nope?"

"Yep!" agreed the uneasy Bud.

"Are we going to cinch half a million dollars for that infant, or are we not?" demanded Chick.

"Sure—if we get him!"

"Did you say 'if'?" growled Chick. "You pie-faced bonehead, I'm telling you to forget it! Did you ever know me let up on a racket when I'd once got my molars into it?"

"Nope!" admitted Bud.

"Did I ever get left?" continued Mr. Chew, whose method of argument seemed to be the Socratic one of asking questions. "I'm inquiring of you, Bud Parker?"

"We ain't never throwed it on this side yet," said Mr. Parker. "I'm telling you, Chick, this ain't Chicawgo, nor it ain't Noo Yark, nor even 'Frisco. I'll tell a man, I surely dislike seeing a cop around. They don't pack no guns, sure. But they're on the level. And I'm shouting out to you, Chick, that a cop on the level is more trouble than a cop with a gun!"

"Aw, can it!" grunted Chick. "We ain't getting cinched by no cops! And if we was——"

Bud shivered. It was clear that he really hated the idea of getting "cinched" by a man in blue.

"Mebbe," said Chick, "we can't buy cops and we can't buy judges in this pesky one-horse island, what I guess some mangy cat left lying around. But we can buy lawyers here, same as in the Yew-nited States."

"Mebbe," said the pessimistic Bud. "But I ain't figuring that that will cut a lot of ice if they get us."

Chick gave another grunt.

"Mebbe," he said, "we win up this very day. Ain't we got it all cut and dried?"

"Ain't we had it all cut and dried afore?" asked Bud, taking up the Socratic method himself. "Ain't we slipped up on it every time? I'm inquiring of you, Hannibal Chew?"

"One swaller," said Mr. Chew, "don't make a summer! I allow it ain't so easy here as in the States. There ain't the room here for a guy to move around without falling over some other guy. But we're getting through. Ain't I wrote to that guy Putnam, using the name of old Coot in London in a fist that old Coot would sure figure was his own if he piped it?"

"Sure!" assented Mr. Parker.

"Ain't I told Putnam, in that there billy-doo, that Coot'd be calling him to-day on the phone, and so making it sure that he wouldn't write no answer and put the old guy in London wise in the racket?"

"Yep!" agreed Mr. Parker.

"And ain't I phoned to his pesky schoolmaster this afternoon and fixed it up O.K. for the young guy to mosey along to Courtfield and take tea with old Coot what's a hundred miles away?"

"You said it."

"Waal, then, you bonehead, what's the matter with Hanner?" demanded Mr. Chew warmly. "Ain't it working? Ain't Tug waiting on the road with a car, ready to meet up with young Putnam when he comes along?"

"Sure thing!"

"Ain't he a man what young Putnam's never seen? And ain't the young guy sure to hop into that car when asked so to do?"

"Mebbe."

This time Mr. Parker gave a qualified assent.

"And if he don't hop in, ain't Tug the guy to pass him one on the cabeza and throw him in?"

"I'll say so."

This time the assent was unqualified.

"And ain't Tug going to give three hoots on the klaxon, to put us wise when he's got that young guy?" pursued Mr. Chew. "And ain't we

(Continued on next page.)

GREYFRIARS INTERVIEWS

Our clever Rhymester is still going great guns. The latest victim to come under his eagle eye . . . and pen is
HURREE JAMSET RAM SINGH,
Nabob of Bhanipur, the Hindoo junior of the Remove.

(1)

Of highest caste in all his land,
A Prince of wide dominions,
He comes from India's coral strand
And has his own opinions
About the English climate, which
Is certainly much cooler
Than that which smiled upon the rich
And powerful young ruler.

(2)

Good-[illegible] full of sense,
He's [illegible] !
His popularity's [illegible]
Save with [illegible]y.
Week in, week [illegible] not heard
From this good-tempered chappie
One snappish or ill-natured word,
He's always calm and happy.

(3)

The language Inky speaks is queer,
It regularly dazes
Strange visitors when first they hear
His weird and wondrous phrases.
"Terrific!" is the word he loves,
And all things are "terrific,"
From battleships to boxing-gloves,
From Poles to the Pacific!

(4)

A moonshee wise and full of lore
Taught Inky English grammar,
He should have taught himself before
He started in to hammer
His verbs and proverbs, both so odd,
Into his hopeful pupils,
He should have been clapped into quod
Without the slightest scruples.

(5)

So Inky's tongue is queer and quaint,
While ours is full of knowledge,
And Inky's words are like what ain't
Not spoke at this here College.
But on the field of play his fame
Is quite another story,
At any kind of outdoor game
He shines in brightest glory.

(6)

I found him bowling at the nets
Upon a pitch of matting,
And I had very few regrets
That I was not there batting,
For when he bowls in Larwood style,
His lightning-like expresses
Can shift your stumps about a mile,
As everyone confesses.

(7)

"Take up the batfulness," he said,
"And hit the bowling smiteful!"
And when I shook a cautious head
His grin became delightful.
"I wagerfully bet," said he,
"A bag of doughnuts niceful,
If you will bat, I'll bowl you three,
And hit the wicket twiceful!"

(8)

I took him on and grasped the bat,
He bowled a daisy-cutter,
I shut my eyes and lifted that
To the pavilion gutter.
"Well donefulness!" he grinned, and then
He swiftly bowled a second,
The off-stump vanished from my ken,
About one mile, I reckoned.

(9)

"Gosh! What a snorter!" was the cry
I made to Inky's chuckles,
He bowled his third express, and I
Late-cut it (with my knuckles).
I jumped about upon the pitch
In pain and indignation,
But still, I got the doughnuts, which
Were ample compensation!

waiting here ready to horn in if that Poker Pike is treading on his tail?"

"I should smile!" assented Mr. Parker.

"Waal, then, chew on it and get happy!" said Chick. "I'm telling you any minute we'll hear Tug hooting to put us wise that he's got that young guy. Three hoots mean that he's got him. I'm telling you, we're going to hear three pesky hoots."

Mr. Parker did not answer. He seemed to doubt it.

"And then," said Mr. Chew cheerfully, "we walk our chalks around a few to pipe whether that guy Poker is around offering trouble. I ain't denying that he's a bully boy with a glass eye when it comes to handling a gat, and he'd think no more of throwing lead at Tug than he'd think of shooting up a cop on the side walk in Chicawgo. But I guess I can throw lead a few, if it comes to that!"

"I ain't liking it!" grunted Mr. Parker. "I ain't liking it at all! This ain't no country where a guy can throw lead."

"Ain't I wise to that?" growled Chick. "I guess I ain't pulling no gun jest for greens! Nunk! But if Poker is around, horning in, I got to handle a gat! So've you! I'm telling you, three toots on the tooter means that Tug has got young Putnam—and four toots means that Poker is horning in. And if there's four toots on that there horn, Bud Parker, you pull your gun and follow me, and burn powder like you wos in a rookus in Chicawgo. You hear me whisper?"

"You said it!" mumbled Bud. Clearly he did not like the idea.

Chick snorted, and chewed his cigar.

Bud listened in undisguised trepidation.

The clump of trees, where the two gangsters stood in cover, screened from the public view, was some little distance back from the road.

Known so well by sight to Poker Pike, and to a good many Greyfriars fellows, Chick had to be very careful not to be seen in the vicinity of Greyfriars. But he was on the spot—if he was wanted.

His plans had been laid so carefully that he had little doubt that Putnam van Duck would walk straight into the trap. Like many cunning schemers, he did not allow for the chapter of accidents.

The only danger, Chick reckoned, was that Poker Pike might be keeping tabs, to the extent of shadowing the millionaire's son on his way to Courtfield.

If that proved to be the case, Chick was ready to wade in—gun in hand! He shared, certainly, Mr. Parker's misgivings about gun-play in a country where guns were so much at a discount. He would have avoided gun-play, if possible. But if gun-play was imperatively called for, Chick was the man to answer the call!

The gangsters listened.

It was getting towards four o'clock, and if Putnam had fallen into the trap, it was time he did the falling. Bud evidently had doubts—but if Chick had any, he did not allow his dubiety to appear in his fat face.

Suddenly from the direction of the road came the sharp, loud, clear hoot of a motor-horn.

Honk!

Bud started. Chick listened.

Honk!

"That's two!" breathed Bud.

Before he had the words out, the third hoot came, loud and clear.

Honk!

Bud listened, almost in anguish, for a fourth honk. Three hoots meant that the schoolboy millionaire was kidnapped in the black car, safe and sound. Four meant danger. Was a fourth coming?

If it came, Chick was ready to dart out of the clump, and speed on the scene, gun in hand—loosing off lead as soon as he spotted the gunman. And Bud had to back his play, repugnant as the game was to him. The sweat started out on Bud's forehead, over his horn-rimmed glasses, as he listened.

But there was silence—save for the sound of a distant car, growing more distant. Silence is said to be golden—but never had it seemed of such pure gold to Bud Parker.

Chick Chew grinned.

"What'll I be telling you, you Bud?" he asked.

"He's sure got him!" breathed Bud.

"Yep!" grinned Chick. "He's got him—Tug's got him! And that guy Poker ain't around none. Three toots on the horn if he got him safe—four if Poker was around. Did you hear three or four, you Bud?"

"Three!" said Bud.

"You said it!" agreed Mr. Chew. "Are we pulling off this here stunt, or are we not, Bud Parker?"

"I'll say we are!" said Mr. Parker, deeply relieved.

"Yep!" said Mr. Chew. "Old Man Vanderdecken can sure start counting out half a million dollars, Bud—he'll be handing them over soon. I'll say we're earning them harder than we used in Chicawgo—but we're cinching them, Bud! If you want to see a guy that never gets left, you want to give this baby the once-over! I'll tell a man this is jest clam pie! I'm asking you, Bud Parker, whether it is O.K., or whether it is not O.K."

"O.K.!" said Mr. Parker.

"You said it!" smiled Chick. "I guess Tug's a mile off by this time, and we want to beat it easy and quiet across this here bit of prairie. We got the Daimler parked a mile off, and I guess we can hit it without any galoot getting wise to us. I allow that this ain't a stunt that calls for publicity."

Chick Chew heaved his heavy bulk away from the beech, and left the clump on the side farthest from the road.

Bud followed him.

A mile away, in a secluded lane, the gangsters had a car waiting, which they could reach by cutting across the common without coming out into a road. It was, as Chick declared, a stunt that did not call for publicity—and the less they met the public view, the better. Leaving the trees, they started at a quick walk across the open green common—and as they did so, there was a yell of surprise.

"Hallo, hallo, hallo! That's Chick Chew—they're the kidnappers! Collar them, you fellows!"

A dozen schoolboys in running kit, following a paper trail, were swooping down towards the clump of trees as the gangsters emerged. Chick and Bud met the Greyfriars pack fairly face to face.

THE TWELFTH CHAPTER.

Bob Cherry Butts In!

BOB CHERRY was in the lead. Close behind him came Nugent and Johnny Bull, Hurree Jamset Ram Singh, and the Bounder. Strung out after them were Squiff and Tom Brown, Peter Todd and Redwing, and two or three other fellows.

Bringing up the rear, panting and perspiring, was a hickory-faced man in shirtsleeves and a bowler hat.

The paper trail ran at a short distance from the tree-clump. The hares had passed that clump, without seeing anything of the gangsters, deep in cover in the midst of the trees.

Neither had the gangsters seen anything of the hares.

If they had heard the light running footsteps at a distance on the grass, that sound had only caused them to hug cover the closer!

Certainly it had never crossed Mr. Chew's mind, keen as he was, that the millionaire's son he wanted, running as a hare in a paper-chase, had passed within twenty yards of him!

Chick was good at guessing, but that was one of the things that he could not be expected to guess!

Of the hares, Mr. Chew knew nothing. Of the pack, he learned more than he wanted to know. They would have passed the thick clump of trees, a dozen yards off, had not the gangsters emerged when they did.

But as they emerged, Bob Cherry saw them at once, and, swerving towards the trees, he yelled to his comrades.

Chick and Bud stopped dead, staring.

"The kidnappers!" yelled Bob.

"The esteemed Chew!" panted Hurree Jamset Ram Singh.

"That gang!" gasped Johnny Bull.

"You're leaving the trail!" shouted Smithy.

"Come on!" roared back Bob. "The kidnappers—bag 'em!"

From Mr. Pike, in the rear, came a gasp. His slits of eyes were on the gangsters at once.

Ever since Putnam van Duck had started, as a hare, the resolute Poker had kept up the chase—with the firm belief in his mind that Chick was surely somewhere around watching for a chance to cinch the millionaire's son. And here was Chick!

"Search me!" gasped Poker.

He was tired. He was perspiring. He was sticky. He was almost at the end of his tether. His bowler hat felt like a band of iron on his burning brow. But at the sight of the gangsters he woke to new life. He raced.

"Carry me home to die!" gasped Mr. Chew.

He was surprised.

In fact, his sharp eyes almost popped from his fat face at the sight of the Greyfriars gunman at the tail of the Greyfriars pack.

He had been prepared for an encounter with Poker on the road where the car waited, keeping tabs on Putnam and giving Tug trouble. But he was utterly amazed at seeing him coming at a panting run across the common, in his shirtsleeves at the tail of a running crowd of paper-chasers.

It was clear that Poker knew nothing of the kidnapping scheme—carried out with such complete success! He was on the spot by accident! Running in a schoolboy paper-chase—the very last thing that the astonished Chick would have expected to see the grim-faced gunman doing!

Chick was so astonished that his fat jaw dropped, revealing gleams of gold from his expensive American dentistry.

"Beat it!" panted Bud.

Bud beat it promptly. Mr. Chew was not long after him—about the tenth of a split second!

"After them!" yelled Bob.

"Tally-ho!" roared the Bounder.

Paper-chase and hares were forgotten for the moment.

With Bob in the lead, the whole pack swooped down on Chick and Bud. Only swift retreat saved them from clutching hands.

They darted away, with the pack whooping after them.

Fast after the pack came Poker Pike.

Poker had been feeling as if he had hardly a run left in his legs, wiry as they were. He would have given half the princely salary paid by Mr. Vanderdecken van Duck just to sit down for a couple of minutes and rest his weary limbs, and fan his crimson face with his bowler hat. But he forgot all that at the sight of the gangsters. He found new energy from somewhere. He accelerated; he raced; he flew.

He passed Bob Cherry and took up the lead, instead of panting at the tail. After him flew the juniors.

"They got him!" Poker gritted between his teeth. "They sure was around—and they got him!"

Bob gave a breathless chuckle as he caught the words.

"Where have they got him?" he gasped. "In their waistcoat pockets?"

Poker did not answer. He had little breath left, and he needed it all for running.

If the gangsters had "got" Putnam, as Poker guessed, it was clear that they had disposed of him somehow; he was not with them.

But Poker had no doubt of it!

He had feared it, all through the paper-chase; it had haunted him along all those weary, sticky miles. Obviously, the hares must have passed near the gangsters, as the paper trail had led the pack right on to them. That was enough for Poker. They had got him!

And Poker was going to get them!

His lungs were almost bursting. His legs were nearly falling off. Sweat ran in streams down his hickory face. His bowler hat felt now more like a ring of fire than a band of iron. But he flew on.

It was fortunate for Mr. Chew and his horn-rimmed side-kicker that they were fresh, and good at sprinting. Good as they were at the game, the pack would have had them had the meeting taken place earlier. But long, hard miles lay behind the hounds—and every mile had told! Hard as they ran, they did not gain on the fleeing gangsters.

Poker Pike, wonderful to relate, did gain. He shot ahead of the panting pack, much to their astonishment.

But even Poker, though he gained, could not keep it up. Ahead of the running gangsters appeared a fringe of trees, along a sunken lane, at the edge of the common. That was where the Daimler was parked out of sight. That was their objective. They flew for the car. Poker, gaining on them by a tremendous spurt, came almost within clutching distance.

But they flew on—and Poker sagged. He ceased to gain; he lost ground, though still ahead of the pack.

Grim and hard the hickory face set, in its sea of perspiration. Poker halted. He dragged the gun from his hip.

"Hallo, hallo, hallo!" gasped Bob Cherry, a dozen yards behind. "Oh crikey! Chuck that, you mad ass!"

If Poker heard, he did not heed. Up went his six-gun to a level, glinting in the May sunshine.

The pack, in sheer horror, came to a breathless halt, staring. They had forgotten Poker Pike's gun. Poker hadn't!

The gun was aimed, Poker's finger on the trigger. Perhaps remembering that he was no longer in Chicago, even at that breathless moment, Poker aimed at Chick Chew's flying fat legs. In his happy native city, no doubt, his aim woulld have been to hit the gangster where he lived, as he would have expressed it. Now he was content to roll him over, with a bullet in the leg.

"He—he—he's shooting!" gasped Nugent.

"Oh crikey!"

"Oh crumbs!"

Before Poker Pike could pull trigger, however, Bob Cherry gave him a hefty charge, and sent him crashing to the ground.

There was a roar of rage from Poker Pike as he scrambled to his feet. Roaring with rage, he rushed on again. But there was no chance now. The running gangsters disappeared through a fringe of trees.

Three minutes later Poker stumbled down into the shady lane. It was only to hear the buzz of a car and to see the Daimler disappearing in the distance.

Poker Pike stood staring after the car as the pack gathered in the lane. He brandished his useless gun.

"Gone!" gasped Bob Cherry.

"The gonefulness is terrific!" panted the Nabob of Bhanipur.

"They—they had a car!" breathed the Bounder. "Might have guessed that one. They're gone!"

Poker gave a groan.

"They got him! They sure cinched that Putnam van Duck! And Old Man Vanderdecken paying me to keep tabs on him! He sure will figure that I've sold him out!"

(*Continued on next page.*)

"But——" gasped Bob.

"I guess you young guys put this across me!" roared Poker. "Didn't I put you wise at the start? Didn't you set on a guy and keep him cinched while that Putnam van Duck walked his chalks? Yep! I'll say so! And ain't I going to beat you up a few? Surest thing you know!"

"Here, look out——" yelled Bob.

"Oh crumbs!"

"Barge him over!"

"Great pip!"

Convinced that Putnam had fallen into the hands of the kidnappers, and that he had failed in his trust, Poker's next idea was to "beat up" the fellows who had put it across him! He parked his gun and charged at the pack.

They scattered.

They could feel for Poker, in the distressing circumstances. They would willingly have consoled him; but they were not prepared to give him the consolation of "beating them up."

"Hook it!" gasped Bob.

The pack scattered and ran. They headed back across the common, to the deserted paper trail. After them charged Poker.

It was rather fortunate for all concerned that Poker was at an end of his running resources. He dropped behind in the race.

He was far in the rear when the juniors hit the paper trail again. They followed it fast, and Poker's bowler hat dropped out of sight when they reached the Courtfield road.

After that loss of time there was no hope of catching the hares. But the pack ran hard, anxious to learn whether anything really had happened to Putnam van Duck, as Poker firmly believed.

On that score their fears were relieved as they came panting up to the school gates. For there, cheerful and smiling, the hares stood, waiting to welcome them home.

THE THIRTEENTH CHAPTER.

Skinner in a Scrape!

"LIGHT down!"

Skinner did not know how long he had lain, tied like a turkey, under the enveloping rug, in the black car. It seemed to him like centuries; but certainly it was nothing like so long as that!

But the car had stopped at last.

The rug was jerked off, a knife slit through the cord on his wrists and ankles, the gag was jerked away, and Skinner was free.

In a dusky twilight, he blinked dizzily at the clean-shaven man, who told him curtly to light down.

Skinner tottered from the car.

His first impression was that it was night, or, at least twilight. But he discerned that the duskiness was due to the fact that he was inside a closed building. Looking round, he saw that it was a garage.

Tug had closed the garage doors after running the car in. Skinner had a dim view of the garage—that, and nothing more. Where it was, to what building it was attached, he had not the faintest idea. All he could feel sure of was that it was at a great distance from Greyfriars School.

He tottered, leaning on the car and gasping. The terror in his face drew a contemptuous sniff from Tug. He did not seem to have expected such a total loss of nerve on the part of Putnam van Duck!

"Take a cinch on your nervous system, big boy!" said Tug. "You ain't going to be chewed up in this here shebang! This here is a home-from-home, where you'll sure be looked after like you was in your popper's mansion."

"I—I say——" gasped Skinner.

"I guess I had to treat you rough!" said Tug. "I hadn't no time to lose, with mebbe that guy Poker rubbering around. But you're O.K. now! You jest got to sit down and wait for Chick to trickle in."

"I—I say, let me go!" gasped Skinner. "If you think I'm Van Duck you——"

"Hay?"

"I'm not Van Duck!"

Tug stared at him. As Skinner had told him, on the Courtfield road, that he was Van Duck, he was not likely to believe that statement.

"I'm not!" groaned Skinner. "Oh crikey! I say, I give you my word that I'm not Van Duck! You've made a mistake——"

"I guess you're the guy that's doing that!" grinned Tug. "I'll say it's a big mistake to figure on stringing me along that-a-way, young Putnam."

"I'm not Putnam!" groaned Skinner. "It was a lark—just a lark. I was pretending to be Van Duck——"

"Keep it up!" said Tug. "I'll say you'll go on pretending."

"But I'm really not——"

"Can it!" said Tug tersely. "Can it, and put the lid on the can! You come this way, young Putnam!"

He gripped Skinner by the arm and led him to the back of the garage, where he opened a small door; it led into an adjoining room. Tug pushed Skinner into it.

That room, he saw at a glance, had been prepared for an unwilling occupant. It had a window, across which iron bars had been newly screwed; outside the window was a closed and locked shutter. Bedstead, table, chairs, and other articles of furniture stood about, evidently placed there recently for the kidnapped junior.

This, it was clear, was designed as Putnam van Duck's abode while Chick carried on negotiations with his popper for the ransom. Now it was going to be Skinner's abode. It might have been Billy Bunter's, had not Skinner so artfully ousted the Owl of the Remove. From the bottom of his heart Harold Skinner wished that he had not been quite so artful Bunter was welcome to this—more than welcome!

"I say, do listen to a fellow!" moaned Skinner. "I'm no use to you if you want that Yankee chap! I'm not Van Duck!"

"Carry on!" grinned Tug.

"I'm not at all like him!" gasped Skinner. "If you knew Van Duck by sight you'd jolly well know——"

"You're telling me—because you're wise to it that I ain't never seen you afore!" grinned Tug. "Carry on, bo! Say, you'd like me to believe that you ain't the bird we want?"

"Yes!" gasped Skinner.

"And, not being the bird we want, you'd like me to let you beat it here and now?" asked Tug.

"Yes! You see——"

"Mebbe you'd like me to run you back to where I picked you up, and drop you there, to hoof it back to your school?" suggested Tug.

"Oh, yes!" gasped Skinner.

"That's what you want?" asked Tug.

"Yes, yes!"

"Well," said Tug, "I guess there ain't no harm in your wanting, and you can sure keep on wanting, young Putnam van Duck. Keep on wanting all you want!"

And Tug chuckled.

Evidently he did not place the slightest faith in Skinner's denial of identity. It seemed too palpable to Tug. It sounded to him the thinnest story he had ever heard.

He would not have been surprised had Putnam van Duck sought to bribe him to let him go before Chick returned to make sure of him, but he really was surprised that Putnam should try such a flimsy tale as this; it was altogether too thin.

Skinner stood overwhelmed with dismay. Little as the clean-shaven man believed him, he certainly was not Putnam van Duck. What was going to happen to him when the leader of the kidnapping gang discovered that a mistake had been made?

Skinner had read a good deal about American gangsters; he had obtained quite a lot of lurid information from the films on that subject. He was feeling almost sick with apprehension.

Certainly he had rather made fun of Van Duck's supposed danger from kidnappers at Greyfriars, but that was when he was safe at school. He was not feeling like making fun now—now that he was in the power of the gangsters in Van Duck's place

Tug went to the door. Skinner jumped after him.

"Look here," he panted, "I tell you I'm not Van Duck! I'm Skinner—that's my name! I've got letters in my pocket to prove it——"

"Cute!" assented Tug. "All fixed up ready to back up this yarn if you was cinched by a guy what wasn't wise to your frontispiece. Cute!"

"Oh, you fool!" gasped Skinner. "You idiot! I'm not Van Duck! I tell you I'm no use to you!"

"You'll do!" grinned Tug. "We'll sort of make you do."

"But I'm not Van Duck!" shrieked Skinner, as the gangster prepared to close the door on him.

"And you a cute American!" said Tug, with playful reproach. "Ain't you cute enough to know that that sort of dope ain't no use? I'm sure s'prised at you, young Putnam van Duck! I'll tell a man! If there's a guy that could string me along with a tale like that I'd like to see the colour of his hair—I sure would!"

And, with a cheery chuckle, Tug drew the door shut, and Skinner heard a key turn in the lock on the other side.

"Oh crikey!" gasped Skinner.

He sat down on the edge of the bed.

He was a prisoner! For how long? Until Chick Chew turned up and discovered that he was the wrong bird. What was going to happen then?

THE FOURTEENTH CHAPTER.

Bunter Asks for a Batting!

"I SAY, you fellows——"

"Bunter!"

"Bat him!"

"I say, don't you play the goat!" roared Bunter.

Hares and hounds were home after a hard run. They had splashed and changed in the changing-room and come up to the studies to tea. The Remove passage, so silent that afternoon, rang to footsteps and cheery voices.

Six fellows were in Study No. 1—the famous Co. and the American junior. They were doing full justice to ham and eggs and other good things when the Owl of the Remove blinked in through his big spectacles.

Bunter's fat existence had been rather forgotten during the paper-chase. But as the chums of the Remove were reminded of it they were reminded also of the fact that Bunter had dodged the run, and was, therefore, entitled to a batting on the bags. Which was not what Bunter had come to the study for, by any means!

"There's a fives bat on the bookcase, Bunter," said Harry Wharton. "Hand it over, and then bend across the fender."

"Oh, really, Wharton——"

"Don't make a chap get up for it after a hard run," said Harry. "You might hand over the bat; it's for you, you know."

"Beast!"

The chums of the Remove chuckled. Bunter, not a very obliging fellow at the best of times, was really not likely to oblige by handing over a fives bat intended for his own tight trousers.

"You cut the run, you fat slacker!" growled Johnny Bull.

"Oh, really, Bull! The fact is, I—I forgot," said Bunter. "I was—was awfully keen on it, but I fell asleep; I was fast asleep in Quelch's armchair in his study, you know, when I heard you fellows starting——"

"Ha, ha, ha!"

"So you were hiding in a beak's study!" exclaimed Bob.

"Oh, no! I—I went there to—to borrow a—a book; I'd lost my Latin grammar, and I wanted one particularly——"

"On a paper-chase?"

"Yes—I mean no! I mean I went there to see the time by Quelch's clock, to make sure of not being late starting. As for dodging the run, of course I never thought of such a thing. I hope I'm not a slacker, like that cad Skinner!"

"Oh crumbs!" gasped Bob. "He hopes he's not a slacker!"

"The hopefulness is terrific."

"Being fast asleep, I forgot all about it," went on Bunter. "If you think I heard you starting, you're quite mistaken. I never heard Bob say 'Where's that fat slug?'"

"Oh, my hat!"

"Nothing of the kind, you know! Sorry I missed the run. Still, you were pretty lucky, Wharton; you'd hardly have got home without being caught it I'd been in the pack. Same with you, Van Duck."

"Search me!" gasped Van Duck. And the Famous Five chuckled. So far from catching a hare in a paper-chase, it was rather doubtful whether Billy Bunter could have caught a tortoise. It would have had to be a very aged tortoise.

"But never mind that," said Bunter. "It was rather rotten of you fellows to start without me really. But never mind that. I say, I'll have some of that ham; it looks good. I say, I suppose you're going to bat Skinner for cutting the run, Wharton?"

"Yes, rather—same time as you get it!"

"Oh, don't be an ass!" grunted Bunter. "I was fearfully keen on it. That cad Skinner cut it from sheer slacking. I say, give it to him hard, won't you? Look here, I'll lay it on if you like, if you fellows hold Skinner. I'll make him jolly well squirm!"

The tea party in Study No. 1 stared at Bunter. A batting was due to Skinner for slacking, but nobody expected Billy Bunter to be keen on seeing a slacker batted. He might have been expected to have a fellow feeling for a fellow slacker. A fellow feeling is said to make us wondrous kind. But it was clear that Bunter had no kindness to waste on Skinner.

"What has Skinner done, fatty?" asked Frank Nugent, laughing.

Bunter gobbled ham and eggs.

"The awful cad!" he said. "He did me out of a spread! Locked me in my study, you know, to keep me out of it! I was sticking there till Mauly came in. Hours and hours—three-quarters of an hour, at least. Fancy that!"

Bunter talked with his mouth full. If he had been done out of one spread, he was taking care not to be done out of another.

"Rotten luck, you know!" he went on, his fat voice a little muffled by

(*Continued on next page.*)

COME INTO THE OFFICE, BOYS AND GIRLS!

Your Editor is always pleased to hear from his readers. Write to him: Editor of the MAGNET, The Fleetway House, Farringdon Street, London, E.C.4. A stamped, addressed envelope will ensure a reply.

FUNNY things happen over in Fisher T. Fish's country! But I think one of the most curious clubs to be found over there is the club for

DRAWING THE LONG BOW!

In other words—The Liars' Club, of Burlington, Wisconsin. Believe it on not, chums, in this club they actually give a gold medal each year to the member who succeeds in telling the "tallest story"! And what yarns some of them spin! One member, who lives in New Mexico, claimed to be so "quick on the draw," that he could stand in front of a mirror, and whip out his six-gun quicker than his own reflection could do!

Another club member claimed to have succeeded in growing buck-wheat mixed with Mexican jumping beans. When he made the buckwheat into pancakes, the jumping beans caused the pancakes to turn themselves!

All the members are not Americans, however. For instance, a London member weighed in with a story about an Irish fisherman. He tried hard to catch fish, but couldn't. So, as a last resort, he threw snuff into the water. This caused the fish to sneeze so hard that they hammered themselves to death on the rocks!

Finally, there was another story about a sea captain whose ship was called, appropriately enough, the Prevaricator. He claimed to have sailed over the Sahara Desert on the heat waves! What's more, he made the voyage pay for itself by catching smoked herrings on the way!

I think that's enough "tall stories" to be going on with!

Ever thought of keeping your own menagerie, chums? There are, of course, a large number of private menageries in this country. But menagerie keeping is a most expensive hobby. However, a resident of Llanelly has solved this problem. He possesses

A CEMENT MENAGERIE,

which is certainly a new one on me. This man is seventy-three years of age, and for the last four years he has been adding to his "menagerie." He has constructed a great number of coloured and life-like effigies of animals and birds—making them all of cement. They are placed around the lawn and forecourt of his house, and so natural do they look that many visitors receive a shock when they first spot them.

Who is

THE OLDEST MAN IN THE WORLD

still living? That is the question which "Curious," of Brighton, propounds to me this week. The oldest living man is caimed to be Ali Shefleyaga, a Turk, who is aged 137. He is a forester in the village of Karabey, in Kurdistan. Ali has three wives and eleven children. But, despite the fact that he is so old, he has not given up learning. On the contrary, he has just taught himself to read and write a new language. In his younger days Ali used to read and write the old Turkish script, but that has been changed. So the old man has learned the new Turkish alphabet with Latin characters. Good luck to him!

DON BRADLEY, of Chelsea, asks me an interesting question this week, concerning

SKYSCRAPERS MADE OF GLASS?

He wants to know if any have yet been constructed. Up to the present, no. But many architects are experimenting with glass as a building substance, and, as a matter of fact, several houses have already been constructed of glass bricks. These glass bricks are opaque, so, while they allow daylight to pass through the walls, people outside can't see through them. It is claimed that they insulate the building against cold in winter. Another big advantage is that they are fireproof. Besides being strong and durable, glass bricks can be manufactured in all kinds of colours, thus giving a great variety of artistic effects.

In the future we may see factories, homes and skyscraper office buildings constructed of glass. Architects say that they will stand as long as, if not longer than, buildings of steel, concrete, and stone. They will, of course, be more beautiful to look at, and much more pleasant to work in, because of the greater amount of sunshine and daylight that will come through their walls.

And now we come to the

STAR ITEMS IN NEXT WEEK'S MAGNET!

The top-notch yarn of Harry Wharton & Co. is entitled:

"ORDERED TO QUIT!"
By Frank Richards,

and it's a mixture of fun, thrills, excitement and the thousand and one things which go to make a really good story. The extraordinary idea of having a professional gunman to keep watch and ward over a boy in his Form is far from pleasing to Mr. Quelch, who thinks it high time Poker Pike is given "marching orders." But Van Duck's bodyguard is not so easily got rid of, which, incidentally, is very fortunate for Mr. Quelch!

Following this star school story is a sparkling edition of the "Greyfriars Herald," and further thrill-packed chapters of our great new pirate yarn. Of course, we must not forget our clever Rhymester's verses—they're well up to standard.

A final word, order next Saturday's MAGNET in good time!

YOUR EDITOR.

ham and eggs. "I banged on the door and yelled through the keyhole, but nobody heard me till Mauleverer came in. And then he had to hunt for a key to let me out. Skinner took away my key."

Bunter gasped under the combined effects of wrath, indignation, ham, and eggs!

"But what did Skinner lock you in your study for?" asked Harry blankly.

"He did me out of a feed! You see, when Mauly got me out it was too late to start for Courtfield. That beast went instead!"

"He was going to Courtfield when we met him on the road over the common," said Harry. "But what feed are you talking about, and how could Skinner diddle you out of it?"

"Oh!" Bunter paused—not with the ham and eggs, but with his outburst of indignation. It occurred to his fat brain that as Van Duck was present, less said about that little scheme to annex his spread the better. "Oh, nothing! I—I mean——"

"Well, what do you mean?"

"Oh, nothing!" gasped Bunter. "I mean, I'll have some more ham."

"Is that all you mean?"

"No; I'll have some more of the eggs, too!"

Bunter had some more of the ham and eggs. There was consolation in ham and eggs! Bunter took a lot of consolation.

"I say, you fellows," he went on, "Mind you don't forget about batting Skinner! Not because he did me out of that feed at the Courtfield Hotel, you know, but because he's a rotten slacker!"

"A feed at the Courtfield Hotel!" ejaculated Wharton. "Who the dickens was standing a feed at the Courtfield Hotel?"

"Oh, nobody!" said Bunter hastily.

"Wha-a-t?"

"Nobody at all! Nothing of the sort, you know!"

"Is that fat gink loco?" asked Van Duck, in wonder.

"Oh, really, Van Duck——"

"He's telling lies, of course," said Bob. "That's nothing new. But why? What are you rolling them out for now, Bunter?"

"Oh, really, Cherry——" Bunter gobbled. "If you fellows were as truthful as I am—grooogh!—you'd do! Any more ham?"

"No, you cormorant!"

"I'll try that cake! It's nothing like the cake I should have had at Courtfield, if that tick Skinner hadn't diddled me——"

"So there was a cake?"

"Well, a rich American would be bound to stand a pretty decent spread, I suppose," said Bunter. "Skinner jolly well thought so, or he wouldn't have dished me, and gone instead. Treacherous beast, you know—listening to the whole thing, and then barging me into the study and locking the door——"

"A rich American!" repeated Wharton.

"Oh, no!" Bunter remembered caution again. "Not at all! I don't know anything about an American at Courtfield to-day—the fact is, I've never heard of Mr. Coot at all——"

"What?"

"Never heard the name!" said Bunter. "It's quite new to me."

The juniors stared at Bunter. Bunter blinked at them. He could see that they doubted his statement, though he did not know why!

"Well, that fat idiot takes the cake!" said Bob. "Isn't Coot the name of the American johnny your father knows in London, Van Duck?"

"Sure! I never heard that he was going to be in Courtfield to-day, though," answered Putnam. "Might have been in that letter that was lost yesterday — the one that fat gink chucked out of the window—I never found it."

"Looks as if Bunter did!" grunted Johnny Bull.

"I didn't!" roared Bunter.

"Then how do you know that Mr. Coot was to be in Courtfield to-day?"

"I didn't know!" explained Bunter. "I've never heard of Ezra Coot—I've told you so. I hope you can take a fellow's word!"

"Carry me home to die!" gasped Van Duck.

"I never saw that letter after it went out of the window!" said Bunter warmly. "And as if I'd read a fellow's letter, too! I hope I'm incapable of it—not like some fellows I could name! Taking a telephone call is quite another matter! Anybody might take a telephone call."

"You took a phone call from Coot?" demanded Van Duck.

"Oh, no! You see, I wasn't in Quelch's study——"

"Not when you were asleep in his armchair?" asked Bob.

"Oh!" gasped Bunter. "I—I mean—I mean I was fast asleep when I heard the telephone bell, and—and—and never heard it, you know. Besides, I had to take the call, or else some of the beaks would have come in—cackling like a lot of geese at Wiggins' door!"

Harry Wharton & Co. were concentrating their attention on the fat and fatuous Owl now. They could see that they were getting at something—though as yet they could hardly make out what.

"So Mr. Coot phoned," said Harry, "and you took the call?"

"Oh! No—nobody phoned!" said Bunter. "The bell never went at all, and I never thought the beaks might step in. I wasn't in the study. I hope you fellows don't think I'd even dream of bagging another fellow's spread! It was Skinner's idea, entirely."

"If that burbling bandersnatch means anything," said Bob thoughtfully, "he means that Mr. Coot telephoned from Courtfield, and Bunter took a call meant for Van Duck. If Coot's in Courtfield, he may have meant to ask Van Duck to tea! Is that the spread you're talking about, Bunter?"

"No! Coot never phoned!" explained Bunter. "The call I took was from—from the grocer's. They rang up Quelch's number by—by mistake! Not that I took a call, you know! I wasn't in the study, so how could I? Besides, the idea of going instead of Van Duck never occurred to me——"

"Going instead of Van Duck!" stuttered Wharton.

"Never even dreamed of such a thing!" said Bunter cheerfully. "How could I? You see, Coot never mentioned on the phone that he hadn't ever seen Van Duck, and wanted to make his acquaintance. So, of course, I never thought of anything of the kind."

"Great pip!"

"You locoed fat gink!" roared Van Duck, in great wrath. "You was going to string old Coot along, by making out that you was me—letting him figure that I was a pie-faced fat geck of your heft——"

"Well, I like that!" said Bunter warmly. "I should think you'd be glad to let Mr. Coot think you were a good-looking, athletic fellow—even if it was a mistake, and it wasn't you!"

"A—a—a—what——" gasped Van Duck—"a—a—a which?"

"Ha, ha, ha!"

"Blessed if I see anything to cackle at!" said Bunter. "If Coot had taken me for you, he would have gone away thinking you were a jolly decent-looking fellow—instead of what you are, you know!"

"Oh, search me!" gasped Van Duck, while the Famous Five yelled with laughter.

"In fact, that's really why I was going, so as not to disappoint Mr. Coot when he was expecting a fellow to tea," said Bunter. "As for the spread, I never gave it a thought! I'm always doing these kind, thoughtful things, and I never get any thanks. Is that all the cake, you fellows?"

"Mean to say that that gopher-faced geck Skinner has gone along to see old Coot, making out he was me, to snaffle that tea!" ejaculated Van Duck, as the truth dawned on him.

"Of course, that was his game," said Bunter. "That's why he locked me in the study. I hope old Coot spotted him and kicked him out! Getting it all out of me, you know, and then sticking me in a study, and going himself! Not that I personally thought of doing anything of the kind, you know. It was Skinner's idea from the very start—I dare say that was why he cut the paper-chase! I say, Wharton, mind you don't let him off that batting! It's up to you, as captain of the Remove, to see that a man's batted for slacking. I hope you're going to do your duty. A jolly good batting, see—a jolly good one!"

"Right-ho!" assented Harry Wharton.

He rose from the table and took the fives bat from the bookcase.

Bunter blinked at him.

"I say, you won't want that yet," he said. "Skinner's not here now——"

"You are!" pointed out the captain of the Remove.

"Oh," gasped Bunter, "I didn't mean——"

"I do!"

"Ha, ha, ha!"

Billy Bunter made a bound for the door. A grasp on his fat neck hooked him back. A swing of the arm landed him face down over the armchair.

"Yarooooh!" roared Bunter, in anticipation, "I say—— Whooop!"

Whack!

"I was thinking of letting you off," explained Wharton; "but, as you're so particular about my doing my duty——"

Whack!

"Ow!" roared Bunter. "I ain't! Not at all! Leggo!"

"Ha, ha, ha!"

Whack!

"Yaroooooooooop!"

Bunter's fat neck was released, and he squirmed away.

"Hold on!" said Harry. "I haven't given you a jolly good batting yet!"

"Yaroooh!"

"You said a jolly good one, didn't you?"

"Beast!"

Billy Bunter did not hold on. He flew. He seemed to have changed his mind about a jolly good batting being due to slackers. He fairly whizzed out of the doorway of Study No. 1, and vanished up the Remove passage, followed by a roar of laughter.

"By gum!" said Putnam van Duck. "I guess I'm wise to the how of it now! That guy Skinner was on his way to string old Coot along when we met up with him! I guess I'll hand him a few when he moseys in! I shall have to get old Coot on the long-distance and explain some. By the great horned toad, I'll sure make that pie-faced gink Skinner feel like he was an odd piece

Skinner rose from the bed as the gangsters entered. " I—I say——" he stammered. " You cheap skate ! " roared Chick Chew, turning on him savagely. " You two-cent remnant ! And me figuring that we'd cinched that gilt-edged young gink, Van Duck ! " Skinner fairly trembled as he faced the three disappointed gangsters.

that the cat brought in and left lying around!"

But that dire threat, as it turned out, could not be immediately fulfilled. For when the Greyfriars fellows assembled in Hall, for calling-over, one fellow in the Remove failed to answer to his name. That fellow was Harold Skinner.

Skinner was missing!

THE FIFTEENTH CHAPTER.

Not Gilt-Edged !

MR. CHEW smiled, with a gleam of teeth and gold stoppings.

"Did I mention it was pie?" he asked.

"Yep!" said Bud.

"Mebbe," said Chick complacently—"mebbe you'll get to remember, in the long run, Bud, that this baby never gets left! Mebbe you'll chew on that, Bud Parker, and quit grousing. I'm telling you!"

"We've sure got by!" said Bud.

"Sure!" said Tug. "I'll say it was easy!"

The gangsters were standing in the garage, where the Daimler now stood by the little black car. Chick was grinning with satisfaction—Bud was bright with newly revived confidence—Tug was beaming! It was as happy and satisfied a party of gangsters as could have been found anywhere in Chicago.

Tug took a key from his pocket and stepped towards the inner door. Chick and Bud followed him.

"I got him cinched safe!" said Tug. "And, you want to believe me, he allowed that he wasn't Putnam van Duck when I got him here! I'm telling you, he wanted to put that across! I sure been snickering a few over it!"

Chick and Bud chuckled.

Tug unlocked the door and threw it open.

A junior rose from the edge of the bed as the gangsters entered.

"I guess I'm glad to meet up with you, young Putnam!" said Chick blandly. "I'll tell a man—— Great Gophers! Great jumping snakes! What you got here, you Tug? Where's that Putnam van Duck?"

Chick stared at Skinner. Bud goggled at him through his horn-rimmed glasses. Tug stared at them.

"Say, what's biting you?" he demanded. "That's Putnam van Duck!"

"What?" yelled Chick.

"Hay?" roared Bud.

Tug looked bewildered.

"You ain't telling me that that young guy ain't Putnam van Duck!" he stuttered. "That's the guy what came along the road, and give me his name as Putnam van Duck, going to see old Coot! He sure is Putnam!"

"Putnam nothing!" yelled the enraged Chick. "You telling me you cinched that pie-faced, slab-sided cheap skate, figuring that he was Putnam van Duck?"

"He sure allowed he was that very identical guy when I met up with him," gasped Tug.

"Carry me home to die! Buy me a pine packet, and put flowers on it!" groaned Chick Chew. "You pesky, dog-goned bonehead——"

"I—I say——" stammered Skinner.

Chick turned on him savagely.

"You cheap skate!" he roared. "You two-cent remnant! Who're you? And what's this here game?"

"I—I told him I wasn't Van Duck!" groaned Skinner. "It was only a lark when I said I was. I told him afterwards——"

"A lark!" said Chick ferociously. "I guess if you was in Chicago, a feller about your size would be fished out of the lake to-morrow morning for that there lark! Sure! Tug, you bonehead——"

"How'd I know?" gasped Tug, with a glare at Skinner. "That pesky guy sure strung me along——"

"Aw, can it!" snorted the gangster. "Pack it up, you! Me figuring that you'd cinched that gilt-edged young gink—and you landing me like this with that cheap skate! Aw, you pesky bonehead!"

Skinner stood trembling.

The three disappointed gangsters withdrew into the garage, where they held a whispered consultation.

Skinner waited—shivering. His fate depended on the outcome of that consultation. He wondered dismally what it was going to be.

Finally, Tug came in to him.

He did not speak. He collared Skinner, hooked him into the garage, and bundled him head over heels into the little black car. Skinner squealed with apprehension as he was bound again—till his squeals were cut short by the gag. Then the rug was thrown over him.

He heard the engine start. He felt the car in motion—rapid motion. He was being taken away—somewhere! Where?

Centuries, once more, seemed to pass, as he lay suffocating under the rug. Of the direction the car took, he had not the remotest idea.

But it stopped at last.

The rug was taken off; he was released. This time Tug did not ask him to light down. He took Skinner by the neck and slung him bodily out.

Skinner sprawled and yelled.

He blinked round him. Grass and trees met his dazzled eyes in the bright May sunset. Where was he? It flashed into his mind that he was on Courtfield Common—hardly a couple of miles from Greyfriars! He realised that the gangsters did not want him, and had taken him back as the easiest method of getting rid of him. Chick wanted a millionaire's son—a cheap skate was no use to Chick!

Tug grasped him again, and set him on his feet.

(*Continued on page* 28.)

START READING THIS THRILLING STORY OF MODERN PIRACY TO-DAY !

CAPTAIN VENGEANCE!

By JOHN BREDON

A Short Life and a Merry One !

FOR a split second young Roderick Drake found himself looking Death in the face as Von Eimar, pirate and master-spy, glared ruthlessly down the sights of his automatic pistol.

In the cruiser Zermac, Roy Drake had voyaged to the famous penal island settlement of Nemesis Island, belonging to the Republic of Varland, there to interrogate Convict No. 333—otherwise Von Eimar—who had been sent there by the activities of his father, Morgan Drake, mystery man of the British Secret Service. Little had Roy supposed that Von Eimar, on that very day of the cruiser's arrival, had organised a mutiny among the convicts that had thrown the whole island settlement under his sway. Nevertheless, it was a fact, and now, having by a masterly bluff secured possession of the cruiser itself, Von Eimar had revenge in his reach.

Roderick Drake sat rigid. He had known nothing of the startling events that had taken place in the penal colony. But there, incredible as it seemed, was his father's old enemy, Von Eimar, scowling over the levelled automatic, and the arch-mutineer's finger on the trigger.

Then all at once a sinewy brown hand caught the convicts' leader by his broad, square wrist. Twisting his bull neck, Von Eimar scowled into the face of Ronald Westdale, his English lieutenant.

"Cut it out, Von Eimar !" said Westdale, smiling a little wearily. "That sort of thing won't do, you know. Cold-blooded murder, and all that. I'd pack it up !"

The piggy little eyes of Von Eimar narrowed to mere slits.

Roderick Drake, slowly realising the situation, glanced quickly from one to the other as he assessed his chances. For one moment it seemed as if all the pent-up storm of Von Eimar's rage was to be exploded upon the daring Englishman's head. Then the arch-mutineer eased the tension by uttering a short, guttural laugh, slipping the gun back into its holster.

"I thank you, Mr. Westdale !" He clicked his heels, Teutonic fashion, and bowed stiffly from the waist, thumbs to the seams of his white trousers. The ghost of a smile hovered around his thin lips. "You have done me a service, my friend. Ach ! A moment ago I might have done a most foolish and regrettable thing—shot one who should prove to be a useful hostage—and, more than a hostage, a decoy ! It is not often that my temper masters me. But"—and this time a steely hint of a threat sounded in Von Eimar's silky voice—"another time you will be pleased to remember that I am now your captain—Captain Vengeance, the pirate, Mr. Westdale. Although myself a mutineer, I do not tolerate mutinies against myself. Bear that in mind for the future, my impulsive and over-generous friend."

With that, the smile upon his hard, masterful features was more ominous than the blackest frown would have been.

"As you will, Von Eimar," answered the Englishman, with a shrug of his broad shoulders. "I'm not so sure that it matters so much, so far as I'm con-

Like wild beasts, the escaped convicts sprawled and lolled about the deck of the cruiser, laughing, drinking, and singing riotously !

cerned. A convict; then a pirate !" He spoke harshly and bitterly. "Life's not so sweet a thing for me these days, Captain Vengeance, that I'm likely to hug it too closely to heart; as you may guess from the circumstance of my being in your company."

Von Eimar made no answer to that. Instead, ignoring both Westdale and Roderick Drake, the arch-mutineer, or Captain Vengeance, as he now called himself, strolled from the chart-room out on to the bridge and gazed sardonically upon the mob of released convicts who were talking, laughing, and arguing in groups upon the steel-plated decks of the Varland cruiser.

Roy Drake heaved a sigh of relief. He had been within a hairsbreadth of death; that much he had seen in Von Eimar's glare when the Englishman, whose face seemed vaguely familiar, had jerked aside the pirate's pistol. Carelessly Ronald Westdale lounged aside, resting his elbows on the narrow wooden ledge beneath the chart-room windows. But before Roderick Drake could stammer out his thanks there came a sudden interruption to attract both of them.

It was the sharp, clear blast of Von Eimar's whistle, summoning the convicts in lounging knots and groups to the base of the forebridge.

Captain Vengeance surveyed them grimly through his monocle. The scum of the world was gathered there; brown, scarred, bitter faces in the soft yellow glow of the deck lights—thieves and murderers, traitors, spies, gun-runners, dockside rats, and "con" men from the big cities of Europe; in a word, hardly a man of them that was not a hardened criminal of some sort or the other.

Glancing through the dull glass of the chart-room windows, Roy Drake saw the faces of all types and nationalities, with their penal numbers and the crimson dagger of Varland branded on their naked, shaggy breasts. Every one was armed with bayonet, carbine, and revolver, loaded around their bare shoulders with belts of brass-clipped cartridges glowing in the light of the slush-lamps, broad knives glittering as they stood in massed ranks, evil faces uplifted to the stocky, hard-faced man on the bridge.

It would need a hand of iron and nerves of steel, Roy thought, to handle such a pack of reprobate and hardened villains. Well, Von Eimar was assuredly the man to supply such qualifications. Not for nothing had the erstwhile international spy set all the chancelleries of Europe by the ears in his time.

He spoke in English, that being the tongue understood by most of the polyglot gang, though the number that owned it as their native language was few.

It was a deep, attentive silence that settled upon those lawless ruffians as his sharp, trenchant voice cut the atmosphere of that warm tropical night.

Now it was that Von Eimar showed his powers of leadership and organisation, to say nothing of the almost uncanny, retentive memory that the master-spy possessed. For the past two years he had been in charge of all the records and card-indexes of Governor Zarda's prison office. By name and number he knew every man of the convict settlement, together with his criminal record and his nationality—and, what was now of the utmost importance, the trade or calling, apart from crime, which he normally followed.

In quiet, incisive tones he assigned to each man his particular duties. Killer Moran, the giant American racketeer who had once held a first mate's ticket on a rum-runner in the old days of Prohibition, was made Von Eimar's first lieutenant. Ronald Westdale became gunnery lieutenant; Mikhail Lebedoff, late Russian naval artificer, was appointed chief engineer, with a black squad of Chinese and negroes. The villainous Dr. Nieuwe, of course, retained the post of medical supervisor that he had held in the prison hospital.

As for the rest, quite a number had followed the sea at some time or other, many as smugglers or gun-runners, some even as slavers in the Red Sea. These were made inferior officers according to their qualifications. Not only that, but some even of the naval men of the Zarmac, dissatisfied with their conditions and pay, which last was several months in arrears, signified their willingness to join in with the mutinous convicts.

With these instructors Von Eimar had quite a respectable nucleus for his pirate crew.

The arch-pirate concluded with a short speech, leaning over the bridge-rail, with the glowing butt of a cigar in his plump fingers.

"Men, I'm not going to disguise from you the fact that this enterprise of ours is a desperate, life-or-death, sink-or-swim business.

"In my younger days—that is, when my criminal activities had gone no farther than what you English"—he glanced with a faint smile towards Westdale and Roderick Drake, both interested bystanders in the glow of the binnacle-lamp—"call, I believe, 'scrumping'—I was an inveterate devourer of all those books concerning the old-time gentleman of fortune who flew the skull and crossbones on the high seas.

"One of their sayings recurs to me—'A short life and a merry one, bullies!' It is a trite illustration of our position. This is the twentieth century, the age of wireless transmission, aeroplane bombers, and battle-cruisers that can do their forty knots to the hour. The times are past when our amiable predecessors could gut a ship, murder a crew, and sail away for some convenient port with nobody any the wiser for perhaps six months or more. A pursued vessel to-day has only to send out one S O S, and a dozen warships will be on the spot within twenty-four hours."

He flicked the ash out of his cigar and smiled grimly.

"I am not saying this to discourage you, but merely that you should understand the clear facts. One advantage, however, we have over our forbears. Every ship that crosses our bows, unless it chances to be a man-o'-war, is certain to be unarmed and helpless. And there are some rich prizes afloat in these seas, carrying millionaire passengers, and laden with bullion into the bargain!"

He paused, raising an impressive forefinger.

"With reasonable luck, we should make some rich hauls in the brief time that is open to us. Understand this! I am master here! If any man fails me in the discipline and efficiency I shall require—well, that man had better never to have been born! We shall make our fortunes in a month, my friends, or we shall make Davy Jones' locker!"

A Talk with a Traitor!

RODERICK DRAKE felt a hand upon his shoulder. Turning, he saw the handsome, yet lined and drawn features of the fellow-countryman who had not long since saved him from Von Eimar's passing fit of fury.

"You'd better come with me, youngster," said Ronald Westdale, with a faint smile, as Von Eimar, concluding his speech, strolled into the charthouse, without a glance at them. "It won't be safe above decks for you among all these two-legged sea-wolves! Scum of the earth!" He flung a withering glance over the bridge-rail at the ragged rascals who were dispersing from under the fore-bridge, animatedly discussing Von Eimar's words. "There's hardly one of the dogs that doesn't cheat the hangman with every breath that he draws!"

Nodding, Roy followed Westdale as the convict descended the bridge-ladder to the gun-deck.

The boy was puzzled. Somehow Westdale's clean-cut, good-looking features were vaguely familiar to him, yet he did not remember to have met him before. He could not place the man. Quite obviously, the tall, upstanding Englishman, with the clear grey eyes and pugnacious jaw, did not belong to this rogues' republic of unhung cutthroats.

The escaped convicts, three hundred ragged rogues in all, were enjoying themselves after the manner of their kind. Like wild beasts they sprawled and lolled upon the riveted deck-plates, about the cowled ventilators, the hatches, and the shielded four-inch guns on the well-deck battery.

All were talking, laughing, drinking, and singing in riotous orgy. They had looted the stores from the cruiser and from Governor Zarda's private quarters, and now these calloused scoundrels, straight from the hardships and privations of Nemesis Island, were smoking expensive Havanas, guzzling whisky, brandy, and claret neat from shivered bottle-necks.

After a preliminary examination of the cruiser's maps and charts, Von Eimar had retired to the captain's cabin of the Zermac, which he had now renamed the Vengeance.

Scowling, suspicious glances followed Ronald Westdale and Roderick Drake as the two descended the after companionway to the 'tween decks, dimly lighted by evil-smelling slush-lamps. Surlily the ruffians drew in their outflung naked feet as they passed, paused in their drinking and oiling of rifles, and fingered sharp knife-edges as they glanced from squinting eyes and muttered together in low tones.

But none ventured to interfere. Almost as much as Von Eimar and his ready automatic, they feared Ronald Westdale and his hard, quick-to-fly fists.

Through a narrow gallery lined with racks of rifles, Westdale led his charge into a small cabin that had once belonged to the first lieutenant of the Varland cruiser.

The English lad showed no signs of fear. Young as he was, in his fifteen years of life he had known many strange perils and adventures as the son and assistant of Morgan Drake, Britain's master-mind and secret agent, who had sent many a spy besides Von Eimar to justice.

Ronald Westdale unscrewed a brass-rimmed circular cabin-port, and, lighting a cigarette, seated himself upon a flapped table that he lowered from a bulkhead.

"So you're young Roderick Drake, Morgan Drake's son," said the Englishman, as a cooling breath of sea air pervaded through the open port. "I've heard of you, even here on Nemesis Island. And I dare say you will remember the name of Ronald Westdale."

There was a faint twitching of Westdale's lips as he spoke.

"I've heard it before," reflected Roy, searching his memory.

"Well, if I'm to sail under the Black Flag, I shan't sail under false colours, at all events," Shamefacedly Westdale avoided the boy's eyes, gazing steadily through the portlight. "In case you don't remember it all, I'll refresh your memory a little. I've good cause to remember every little incident, every single detail, only too well.

"A few years ago I was a naval lieutenant, with a promising career in front of me. But I was a fool—an utter, complete fool! I got into debt—what with cards, horse-racing, and the deuce in general. Then there was a girl. I thought the world of her. Of course, she was a spy for some foreign power. Before I realised what I was doing, she got some important dockyard secrets out of me. Then she bolted, and left me to stand the racket."

With a reckless laugh he swung away from the portlight, pitching the stub of his cigarette into the sea.

"That's how I came to find myself on Nemesis Island, chum," he finished bitterly. "The spy gang she was in with helped me to get away to Varland, up in the Baltic. There I was safe for a time, till your father induced the authorities there to pass their criminal refugees' law, and, like the rest, I was shipped off here. Now I'm branded as a spy and a traitor—a convict on Nemesis Island, and the next thing I'm likely to become is a pirate." He laughed in fierce derision and self-contempt. "Pretty good, isn't it?"

Roy Drake didn't answer. Now that Westdale had outlined the facts, he remembered the case fully. In a way he couldn't help feeling very sorry for Westdale, who, more fool than rogue, had paid such a terrible price for his crime.

Ronald Westdale scowled moodily at the strip of carpet on the cabin floor, burying clenched fists into the pockets of his white uniform jacket.

"But if I met that girl again, or, better, the blackhearted villain who was behind her," he muttered, between shut teeth, "I'd—well, I think there'd be murder done!"

A shadow fell athwart the threshold

of the cabin. Both looked up sharply. It was Luis Ramiro, the South American crook, padding softly on light, cat-like tread. He had changed his convict rags for the gaudiest clothing he could find aboard the cruiser, and, with a pair of gold ear-rings he had just stolen, and a vividly hued handkerchief swathing his black, greasy curls, the swarthy Latin looked the part of a pirate to the life.

"So! And what is this I see, companero mio?" he asked, purring in soft, sibilant English, with a flash of dark and smouldering eyes. "The little Ingles senor with the tall Ingles bravo, is it? Do we talk treachery, amigo? Do we seek to make terms for ourself with the son of the so cunning Morgan Drakue?"

His voice hissed like that of a mountain cat between his sharp, white filed teeth.

"I suppose you can't help being a sea-snake, Don Dago?" Westdale was openly contemptuous. "Treachery is in your blood, and you measure others by the same standard that you find good enough for yourself. But keep your suspicions to yourself, Ramiro, or there will be mourning in your ancient and illustrious Castilian family, which was founded by a South American peon and knifer way back in the Argentine!"

"Caramba!" The South-American's eyes blazed like lighted coals. "You insult my family! I am a hidalgo by birth! Ah!"

Like lightning his snaky, brown hand flew to the richly hilted knife that was thrust into the silken folds of his scarlet cummerbund.

But as his fingers closed upon the dagger-sheath, it was to discover it empty. Roy Drake had snatched it from under his very hand.

"Is this yours, senor?" asked the boy politely, holding the hilt towards the startled South American.

Westdale's gravity and angry contempt dissolved into an explosion of laughter.

With a throaty snarl Ramiro accepted the proffered dagger-hilt, and fell back a pace, not daring to make a movement with it under the cold grey eyes of Ronald Westdale. As suddenly as it had flared up, his rage oozed out in fierce, muttered curses in sibilant Spanish.

"Now, d'ye mind sayin' your book o' words out in the passage? I asks ye." It was Hilarity Hinton, or 'Ilarity 'Inton, as he called himself, the grinning little Cockney, who took the muttering Ramiro by the arm and piloted him gently into the passage-way. "An', if ye don't mind, my old canary, take that manicure-set with you."

With a snarl, Luis Ramiro thrust the dagger back into its elaborately worked sheath, and, darting a malignant glance over his shoulder, climbed a steel ladder to the gun deck above.

Hat on one side of his head, thumbs resting in his belt, Hilarity Hinton surveyed him whimsically as he went.

"Narsty-tempered cove, that dago, Mr. Westdale," he said, with a grin to the ex-naval lieutenant, as Ramiro heaved his lithe body through a scuttle. "Sort o' bloke as'd cut your throat behind your back, as the Irishman said, out o' sheer kindness of 'art. Rot me billy-kin if he wouldn't, the dirty furriner!"

Westdale laughed tersely.

"We'll be having trouble before long with Von Eimar's crew of cutthroats," he said grimly. And with that he closed the cabin door.

Von Eimar Shows the Iron Hand!

THE trouble came sooner than even Westdale anticipated—in fact, the very next morning.

The piercing notes of a bugle roused Roy Drake from his slumbers at the very first flush of daybreak. Climbing to the dewy-damp gun deck in the chill mists of morning, the lad found the convicts scowling and muttering as they mustered under the bridge, rubbing their tired eyes and yawning.

"What in blazes is t' matter wi' Von Eimar?" growled one close-cropped, evil-eyed rascal as he passed beside the English lad. "Fond o' discipline, h'ain't he? Thinks he's prison governor hisself, belike. P'r'aps 'e forgets 's 'ow theer's been a mutiny on this island once, an' mebbe will again."

Growled oaths from his companions sounded in agreement.

Unleashed now from galling prison discipline, the convicts were disposed to sink into idle lethargy, eating, drinking, and sleeping. But that was not Von Eimar's way, and it was significant that all the growls and grumbles subsided suddenly as the convicts caught sight of his stocky white figure stalking the upper bridge.

The shrill squeal of a pipe belonging to the one-eyed Finn sailor man, whom Von Eimar had promoted to be boatswain, stiffened them into something like orderliness. In a few curt words the pirate captain assigned the men to work-parties under officers. Some were set to polishing the brass fittings and the anchor cable, others to swabbing the decks, while parties were sent ashore to ransack the prison stores.

Others, under the eye of Ronald Westdale and a master gunner, who had been in the Varland Navy, were put to working the electric ammunition hoists, cleaning, oiling, loading and unloading the great eight-inch and six-inch guns, and receiving their first lessons in elementary gun-drill.

Murmurs there were in plenty, but it was hidden by shading hands. And sudden glances were flung from eye to eye, only when the broad back of the arch-mutineer was turned from them.

Roy Drake, finding himself alone and unheeded, paced forward to the iron fore deck, where unwilling convicts were scraping the rust off the hawsers, and busy with brushes and paint-pots under the eye of the Finn. Leaning on an iron rail stanchion, the boy gazed over the waters of the lagoon towards Nemesis Island.

Above the feathery crowns of coconut-palms loomed the cool, white prison buildings, and the tall observation tower, etched against the intense, dazzling blueness of the sky.

Warily the boy glanced around him. One dive into the jade-green, translucent waters of the bay, a short swim to the shore, and he would be hiding in the thick, green tangles of tropical jungle that clothed the island like a leafy net. Was it worth chancing it? Fever, hunger, thirst, the prospects of a bullet from the convict sentry patrolling the quarter-deck, months perhaps of being marooned on this island of evil fame until help arrived.

He decided that it was. Better, at least, than sailing as a prisoner and hostage under Von Eimar's pirate flag, with the probability of sinking with the pirate cruiser when at last it foundered under the gun-fire of avenging warships.

He took off his shoes. The convicts working within a yard of him knew nothing until a loud splash into the water announced the boy's escape. Yells resounded from the decks of the convicts' cruiser.

But luck was not with Roy Drake in his desperate attempt. Round from under the stern of the cruiser came scudding a motor-launch, with the outboard engine thundering at full revolutions as it propelled in his wake.

Two minutes later, dripping, kicked, and buffeted, Roy found himself dragged up the accommodation-ladder to the deck of the cruiser, where a mob of howling convicts surrounded him.

"This be he!" snarled the same evil-eyed ruffian whom Roy had heard muttering discontentedly a short half-hour before. "Morgan Drake's brat! Who's got a rope? We'll swing him up to the yard-arm—ay, an' Gov'nor Zarda an' t' admiral with him! An' Von Eimar, too, if he says a word——"

The words died on the man's lips, as he suddenly noticed Von Eimar standing within a yard of him.

"You were about to say———" inquired the arch-pirate, with suave and mocking politeness, as the man faltered. And the convicts holding Roy released the English lad.

Wildly the man glanced around him, nerving himself for the defiance. The smoothness of Von Eimar's voice deceived him. A mutter from behind heartened him to glare savagely into Von Eimar's calm, smiling face.

"Look ye here, Von Eimar, ye're carryin' things too far!" he said chokingly. "Ye're ridin' wi' too 'igh a 'and. So thinks I, an' so thinks the others!"

"Ay, ay!" rumbled three or four men behind him.

"So?" Von Eimar spoke with disarming blandness. "Is that the case? How many are with you? Let me see."

Shifting and shuffling, a small group lined up behind the sullen mutineer.

"You men are dissatisfied with my leadership?" Von Eimar's light blue eyes ran over them pleasantly.

"Ay, that's so! You've got too 'igh an' mighty a way with you, Von Eimar!" said one gruffly.

And the others nodded assent.

"Very well." Von Eimar nodded his square, shaven head. "I will constrain no one to follow my leadership."

There was a sigh of relief from the men. They had been dreading an explosion. But their relief was short-lived.

"Of course, you cannot sail with me on the cruiser," Von Eimar ran on quietly. "But there is an easy way out of the difficulty. You can remain here, on Nemesis Island."

The little group of malcontents gasped. Suddenly they realised the trap into which they had fallen.

"Remain—remain 'ere?" gulped the first spokesman, paling. "On Nemesis Island? Oh, no, cap'n—not that! We climbs down. You wins, Cap'n von Eimar. D-don't leave us on t' island, cap'n—oh, don't!"

Obdurately Von Eimar shook his head.

"You have made your choice, men. Get off the ship! You remain on Nemesis Island till the Varland Government sends a ship!"

Printed in Great Britain and published every Saturday by the Proprietors, The Amalgamated Press, Ltd., The Fleetway House, Farringdon Street, London, E.C.4. Advertisement offices: The Fleetway House, Farringdon Street, London, E.C.4. Registered for transmission by Canadian Magazine Post. Subscription rates: Inland and Abroad, 11s. per annum; 5s. 6d. for six months. Sole Agents for Australia and New Zealand: Messrs. Gordon & Gotch, Ltd., and for South Africa: Central News Agency, Ltd.—Saturday, May 16th, 1936.

In horror the men protested. Von Eimar was unbending. They fell on their knees, crawling to him on the deck-plates while their convict companions stood around, silenced and awed. No punishment that the arch-mutineer could invent would have been half so dreadful as leaving the wretched recalcitrants ashore on the penal settlement to await the vengeance of the Varland authorities.

Curtly Van Eimar ordered Ronald Westdale to see them into a boat, then turned abruptly on his heel and left them.

Roy Drake, stunned, stood watching the glumness and dismay among the convicts; and then Krunow, the Finn bos'un, approached him, jingling a pair of handcuffs.

"Dis way, boy," he said, in his difficult English, clipping the irons on the lad's wrists and urging him down the ladder to the ship's brig. "Der capt'n, him say 'Keep dat younker safe, or you be moroon', too!' So gum on!"

There was no help for it, and Roy Drake accompanied the Finn forward.

Seeing him safely locked in the steel-walled cell under the foredeck, Krunow grunted in his shaggy beard and returned to his duties.

At War with the World!

TWO days after Von Eimar's well-planned and highly successful coup, the Government supply ship arrived at Nemesis Island.

It had been Von Eimar's intention to escape in this ship, but the unexpected arrival of the Varland cruiser had not only caused him to alter his plans, but had given him a powerful man-o'-war into the bargain.

Never was there a more surprised man than the skipper of the Government steamer, as the long, grey, sinister warship which he recognised as the Zermac suddenly boomed out an eight-inch shell from one of her gun-turrets, and hundreds of ragged convicts and renegade naval men put out in boats to board his vessel as it steered into the bay.

The crew were too utterly bewildered to offer any resistance, and the newly fledged pirates swarmed all over the vessel, hauling down the Varland flag.

Fore and aft the supply ship was filled with giant iron cages. Trained upon these barred pens—which were crammed with hungry, half-naked convicts—were brass nozzles that, at a given signal, could spurt jets of blinding, scalding steam upon the helpless occupants. They had short methods with convict recalcitrants aboard that ship.

Fifty International criminals destined for Nemesis Island were huddled like wild beasts in these closely packed cages. They howled like madmen as their fellow convicts boarded the vessel, and wild babble, explanations, and yells of joy ensued as they were released.

Rescuers and rescued alike danced and embraced one another on the iron, rusty decks, and the horrified guards and crew, stripped to their skins, were hustled into the cages in their place.

Von Eimar stepped into the wheel-house, followed by Ronald Westdale and Killer Moran.

"This ship will supply us with all we require for months," he said to his two lieutenants. "Food, ammunition, clothing, coal for the cruiser's bunkers—everything. Fortunately, we surprised her before she was able to send off a wireless message. She is not expected back in port for three weeks, and so we have that much grace before the alarm is spread throughout the world. The question arises—what shall we do with the prisoners?"

"I guess thar's one short way, Cap," growled Killer Moran. "Lock the pesky galoots in the cages; gov'nor, admiral, an' all, and turn the steam jets on 'em an' open the sea-cocks so as she'll sink!"

Von Eimar rubbed a square, prominent chin.

"The plan has its advantages," he admitted. "'Dead men tell no tales'—that was the motto of our forerunners in the days of Morgan and Captain Kidd. And in this delectable game of piracy we are bound to swing in any case if we're caught. What is your opinion, Mr. Westdale?"

The face of the ex-naval lieutenant expressed his contempt and disgust.

"That's the advice of a Chicago gangster," he said shortly. "And it suits him. But it doesn't suit me, nor you, I hope, Von Eimar. We're none of us saints. But cold-blooded killing of hundreds of men, sailors, officers, warders—no, that's too thick by a long way!"

Killer Moran snarled in his thick throat. But he avoided the cold, fearless eyes of the Englishman.

"A little thick, as is your English saying—true!" agreed Von Eimar. "But what then? I don't like it, but we can't carry all those men as prisoners—we can't spare the provisions, for one thing; for another they outnumber us now by two to one, and it's too dangerous!"

"Then maroon them on the island," urged Westdale. "What can they do? If we wreck the wireless station and all their tools, they can neither send for help nor build a boat. They'll have to wait until a ship arrives to inquire after the missing cruiser."

Slowly Von Eimar nodded his shaven, straight-backed head.

"That will serve our purpose," he said in agreement. "Very well! I rejoice to find a way out of the difficulty. Have the prisoners set ashore, Westdale, and then we'll scuttle this hulk after gutting it of everything that we need."

A day of hard work then followed for Von Eimar's gang of pirates and released convicts.

Derricks were set to work, and the cargo of the supply vessel was transhipped from her hold to that of the pirate cruiser. While teams of the prisoners thus strained and sweated under the rifles of the late convicts; others of Von Eimar's men were busy at the prison quarters. The stores were rooted out, and everything required was carried aboard the cruiser. Dynamite was used to shatter the walls of the fort and prison; and such huts and storage sheds that remained were set on fire.

Every tool or instrument that might be used for the making of a boat was either destroyed or carried away. They were particularly careful about the wireless transmission set. Every delicate instrument and switchboard was smashed almost to powder by the time they had finished.

By sunset, the sailors of the cruiser and the supply ship, and the warders of the prison, were left stranded disconsolately on the beach. With them were the half-dozen hapless convicts who had dared defy Von Eimar. Supplies were left, sufficient to keep them on short rations until help should arrive.

As Westdale had said, there was no fear that the marooned men would be able to spread the alarm. Nemesis Island was far out of any of the recognised shipping routes. Even if they managed to construct a raft of sorts out of the island timber, the convicts had seen to it that they had neither compass nor chart to guide them over the trackless ocean, nor so much as a boat's barrico to hold the precious water.

For a month, at least, the castaways would be cut off from all communication with the outside world.

"What about Ol' Man Zarda an' t' Admiral, boss?" asked Killer Moran, as the newly appointed engineers, greasers, and stokehold hands were getting up steam under the watchful eyes of Mikhail Lebedoff.

"Send them down to the black squad," said Von Eimar with a grim smile.

And Governor Zarda and Admiral Mericski found themselves hustled down to the darksome, furnace-heated stokehold, there to endure the nightmare of slavery among the blacks and Chinese detailed for that duty.

The Zermac, or Vengeance as she was now called, was not exactly a modern cruiser, but she was sufficient for the pirates' needs. She carried four long eight-inch guns in her armour-plated turrets, two forward, and two on the after-deck; six six-inchers to starboard and port on her well-deck battery, besides searchlights, quick-firers, machine-guns, and two anti-aircraft guns. She was capable of thirty knots on her powerful turbines, the boilers being fired with coal instead of with oil as in the more modern fashion; but that, as it transpired later, was an advantage rather than otherwise.

Certainly it is safe to say that she was the most formidable man-o'-war that ever flew the black flag of piracy.

It was as sunset was melting into night that she steamed out into the Indian Ocean, deck-lights ablaze, her crew making merry. On the control-top Von Eimar watched contemptuously as her iron stem curled up the phosphorescent water under the light of the stars, the Southern Cross, bright in the heavens, trailing a stream of light behind her taffrail. Let the dogs drink and debauch to-night, he decided. To-morrow he would apply the curb tightly enough. They had had already a taste of his humour. Woe betide the man that withstood him a second time.

Leaning against a steam-winch on her after-deck was Roy Drake, released now that there was no chance of his escaping, keeping apart from the hilarious crew as he watched the receding, indigo shadow that was Nemesis Island. Probably he was the only person alive that ever regretted leaving the place. His thoughts were troubled. A prisoner, and an enemy, among these wild, savage, lawless cut-throats and pirates who held life cheaper than dirt. Nor had he forgotten Von Eimar's ominous hint of using him as a hostage and a decoy.

Silently the lad descended to Ronald Westdale's cabin as a black tarpaulin, crudely painted with a white death's head, was hoisted to the masthead in a riot of drunken cheers.

For the first time for over a hundred years a pirate man-o'-war was taking the seas to wage war against the world.

(Piracy in the twentieth century! Von Eimar has certainly taken on some job! But the arch-mutineer has already shown the iron hand! Look out for another feast of thrills in next week's chapters of this modern pirate story.)

THE GANGSTERS SWOOP!

(Continued from page 23.)

He wasted no words on Skinner. He let out his foot, delivering a kick that started Skinner well on his way home.

Skinner yelled, and ran.

He heard the car roar away as he went, but he did not look back. He ran and ran till he arrived at the school gates at last, and tugged frantically at the bell.

THE SIXTEENTH CHAPTER.

Better Late Than Never!

"SKINNER!"

Mr. Quelch, who was taking the roll in Hall, repeated the name.

But there was no answering "adsum."

The Remove master, frowning, marked Skinner as absent, and went on with the roll. After which the Greyfriars fellows streamed out of Hall.

The Famous Five could not help wondering what had become of Skinner. They knew from Bunter where he had gone, and why. But there seemed no reason why he should not have returned long ago.

There was another man missing from his usual place, as well as Skinner—and that was the Greyfriars gunman.

The pack had been relieved on Putnam's account when they arrived at the school, and found the hares waiting for them at the gates, but that relief had not been shared by Poker Pike.

Poker had not come back after them. With the belief fixed in his mind that Chick Chew had, somehow, "got away" with the millionaire's son, Poker was busy. As he had not come in, Harry Wharton & Co. guessed that he was hunting for the car that had carried off Chick and Bud; a task that was likely to keep him busy.

Putnam van Duck joined the Famous Five as they were going up to prep. His face was very grave.

"Say, old-timers," he remarked, "I guess there's some sort of a gum game been going on this afternoon. I been getting old Coot on the long-distance."

Putnam had asked leave to telephone to Mr. Ezra Coot in London. His talk on the telephone seemed to have disturbed him.

"I was sure going to explain to old Coot how he'd been spoofed, and that it wasn't this baby that tea'd with him at Courtfield!" went on Putnam. "And I'll mention that you could have knocked me down with a coke-hammer when he allowed that he hadn't been in Courtfield to-day."

"Hadn't!" ejaculated Bob Cherry.

"Nope! Nor he never wrote to me yesterday," said Putnam. "Nor he never phoned to-day. He don't know a thing about it."

The chums of the Remove stared at Putnam van Duck.

That communication rather took their breath away.

"But——" gasped Wharton.

"Somebody phoned, or Bunter couldn't have taken the call!" said Nugent.

Van Duck nodded.

"Sure! Some guy has been using old Coot's name! And I guess that guy's name is Chew!"

The juniors jumped.

"Chick Chew!" exclaimed Harry.

"What'd it look like?" demanded Van Duck. "A guy phones in old Coot's name to me here to get me along to Courtfield—there was a car with an Amurrican in charge waiting on the road—and Chick and Bud was found hanging about on the common! Add it up!"

Harry Wharton whistled.

"The whole thing was a trick of the kidnappers!" he said.

"That's the size of it! And me being away, Bunter wanted to walk into it instead—and Skinner dished him and walked right in!" said Putnam.

"Oh, my hat!" gasped Bob. "Then Skinner——"

"He's missing!" said Van Duck.

The chums of the Remove all looked very grave now. Now that they knew that the genuine Ezra Coot had not been concerned in the matter at all they could not help seeing what it looked like. Where was Skinner?

"That guy with the car wasn't wise to my frontispiece!" said Van Duck. "If he had been he wouldn't have let me pass as Smith, I guess. I'll say he met Skinner next and——"

"And took him for you!" gasped Bob.

"Sure thing."

"Then Skinner——"

"They got him! That's why he ain't blown in."

The juniors went up to the studies in a thoughtful and worried mood.

But prep had not been going on a quarter of an hour when the sound of a bell was heard. A few minutes later footsteps were heard in the Remove passage—and six juniors fairly jumped out of their studies to see whether it was Skinner.

It was!

Skinner was looking tired and pale and worn. It was easy to see that he had not enjoyed his afternoon out. Other fellows came out of their studies; all the Remove were curious to know what had happened to Skinner.

All but six were astounded when he told them. There was a buzz of amazement in the Remove passage.

"But how did they come to take you for Van Duck?" asked Bob Cherry, with a private wink at the Co.

Skinner shook his head. He had not explained that to Mr. Quelch—who had been very sympathetic—and he did not intend to explain it to the Remove.

"Can't make that out!" he answered. "But they did."

"He, he, he!" came from the doorway of Study No. 7.

Skinner gave the grinning Owl of the Remove a glare.

"He, he, he!" cackled Bunter, in great enjoyment. "He, he, he! I say, Skinner, was it worse than being locked in a study? He, he, he!"

Skinner made no reply to that question. He tramped on to his own study and slammed the door.

Putnam van Duck chuckled as he went back to Study No. 1 with Wharton and Nugent.

. . . .

"Search me!" gasped Poker Pike.

It was a sunny morning, and Harry Wharton & Co. were taking a trot round the quad after brekker, when a tired man came in at the gates.

They had forgotten Poker

Now they remembered him.

Poker's slits of eyes opened wide and his bowler hat almost fell off as he gazed at Putnam van Duck.

"Carry me home to die!" stuttered Poker.

Poker, it seemed, had made a night of it. He had been searching for Putnam van Duck! Naturally he had not found him, as Putnam had been asleep in the Remove dormitory all the time!

Putnam grinned at him cheerfully. The Famous Five chuckled Poker Pike rubbed his eyes and stared again.

"How'd you get away, you Putnam van Duck?" gasped Poker.

"From what?" asked Putnam.

"Them dog-goned kidnappers——"

"Who's been kidnapped?" asked Putnam.

"Ain't you?" howled Poker.

"Not a whole lot!"

"You ain't?" yelled Poker.

"Not so's you notice it!"

Poker gazed at him.

"I'll tell a man!" he said at last. "I'll tell all Chicago! I'll tell the whole United States!"

And the juniors, chuckling, resumed their trot, leaving the Greyfriars gunman still gazing after them, dumbfounded.

THE END.

*(The next yarn in this grand new series is more thrilling than ever. On no account miss reading: "ORDERED TO QUIT!" It's the finest yarn Frank Richards has yet written—and that's saying something.—*ED.)

HARRY WHARTON & CO. AT GRIPS WITH GANGSTERS!

(Thrilling School-Adventure Yarn Inside.)

No. 1,475. Vol. XLIX. EVERY SATURDAY. Week Ending May 23rd, 1936.

ORDERED to QUIT! By FRANK RICHARDS

Introducing HARRY WHARTON & CO., the Cheery Chums of GREYFRIARS.

THE FIRST CHAPTER.
Poker, Too!

"NONSENSE!" rapped Mr. Quelch.

The Remove master frowned.

The Remove, on the other hand, grinned.

They were amused, if their Form-master was not.

On that bright, sunny May afternoon the Remove had gathered in the quad, while less lucky fellows in other Forms sat in the Form-rooms at the usual grind.

It was a "walk."

Mr. Quelch, master of the Remove, was taking his Form for a Form walk—and every fellow in Mr. Quelch's Form was looking unusually spick-and-span, as befitted such an occasion. Even Billy Bunter was wearing a clean collar.

Nobody, of course, liked a Form walk in charge of a Form-master, but as an alternative to grinding Latin in the Form-room it had its attractions.

Bob Cherry remarked that it was, anyhow, out of doors, even if a fellow had to sport a topper—and anything out of doors appealed to Bob. Most of the Greyfriars Remove agreed. Putnam van Duck, the new junior from Chicago, guessed that it was the goods, especially as it gave him a chance of mosey-ing around without Poker Pike, his gunman guardian, treading on his tail for once.

But it soon transpired that that was a little error on the part of Putnam van Duck.

For as Mr. Quelch led his flock down to the gates a figure seated on the bench by Gosling's lodge rose, scanned the procession with a pair of very keen eyes that looked like slits in his hickory face under the brim of a clamped-down bowler hat, and stepped forward.

Mr. Quelch looked freezingly at Poker Pike.

Poker Pike gave him a genial nod.

"I guess I'm horning in," he remarked.

It was then that Quelch rapped out "Nonsense!" and frowned, and the Re-movites grinned.

"There is no occasion whatever," said Mr. Quelch, "for you to accompany my Form, Mr. Pike."

"Says you!" remarked Mr. Pike.

"I am aware," snapped Mr. Quelch, "that you are here to guard a boy in my Form against possible danger from kidnappers. But Van Duck is perfectly safe in charge of his Form-master."

"You packing a gun?" asked Poker Pike.

"Wha-a-at?" ejaculated the Remove master.

"Ha, ha, ha!" came from the Remove in a yell. They really could not help it. The bare idea of Henry Samuel Quelch, a sedate and middle-aged Form-master, packing a gun took them by storm. They roared.

Mr. Quelch's gimlet eyes turned from the gunman to his hilarious Form.

"Silence!" he hooted.

The juniors suppressed their merriment with difficulty. Mr. Quelch frowned still more portentously at Poker Pike.

"Certainly not!" he snapped.

"Then I guess I got to mosey along," said Poker. "Ain't you wise to it that Old Man Vanderdecken over in Chicago is paying me to keep tabs on that Putnam? Ain't the star kidnapper of the United States watching for a chance to cinch that infant? You figure that I'm letting Chick Chew get a holt on him? Forget it, big boy!"

Mr. Quelch breathed hard and deep.

"I repeat," he said, "that there is no occasion whatever for your presence, Mr. Pike! I repeat that Van Duck is not—and cannot be—in any danger under the charge of his Form-master. I am very far from approving of your presence in this school at all, and I certainly shall not allow you to intervene in matters affecting my Form. I trust I make myself clear?"

"You sure have spilled a hatful!" said Poker Pike. "I'll say you're the guy to chew the rag a few, and then some!"

"Kindly stand back!" rapped Mr. Quelch.

"Can it, Poker, you geek!" broke in Putnam van Duck. "What you got to do is a fade-out."

"I guess not!" said Poker Pike.

"Van Duck will be all right with a crowd like this, really, Mr. Pike," said Harry Wharton.

"Mebbe," said Mr. Pike, "and mebbe not."

"You need not speak, Wharton!" rapped Mr. Quelch. "Van Duck, be silent! Mr. Pike, stand out of the way at once! I will not allow you, sir, to join in this walk! Go away!"

Poker Pike stepped aside.

Mr. Quelch, with a sniff, marched past him. After Mr. Quelch marched the

Remove. The procession passed out of gates.

Then, after the procession, marched Poker Pike. The Greyfriars gunman brought up the rear.

"He, he, he!" gurgled Billy Bunter, as he blinked round through his big spectacles. "I say, you fellows, he's after us!"

"Shut up, ass!" murmured Bob Cherry.

There were suppressed chuckles and giggles in the procession. Mr. Quelch, tall and angular and stiff, walked ahead. Not having glanced round to the rear of the procession, he was unaware that Poker Pike had joined up at the tail thereof.

Evidently the Remove master was under the impression that his stern rebuke had had its effect, and that the gunman had remained behind, as bidden to do.

The juniors wondered what would happen when Quelch looked round and spotted him.

Mr. Quelch was not a man to have his authority disregarded. Poker Pike, on the other hand, was absolutely determined not to let the son of the Chicago millionaire get out of his sight. So it looked as if a tug-of-war was coming.

This Form walk was going to be more entertaining than most Form walks.

Quelch, stately and dignified, marched ahead. Poker Pike, his hard-boiled face serious under his bowler hat, lounged in the rear. Between them were about thirty smiling faces.

The procession processed down Friardale Lane. It was heading for the wood, where there was an old ruined priory. At that spot there was going to be a halt while Mr. Quelch discoursed to his Form on the historical associations of the place, giving them a spot of archæology.

If there was any fellow in the Greyfriars Remove who was keen on archæological information, he di dnot betray the fact by any expression of happy anticipation.

Still, it was, as Bob had declared, out of doors—and even archæology out of doors was better than Latin indoors on a fine May afternoon.

Much more interesting than archæology was the anticipation of what was going to happen when Mr. Quelch discovered that Poker Pike was in the offing.

Nobody was in a hurry to "put him wise." Indeed, the Removites began to wonder whether he would discover Poker's presence before they reached the priory. The longer he marched on unaware of Poker the funnier it seemed to his Form. But Billy Bunter had to spoil the joke.

"He, he, he!" came Bunter's chuckle.

"Shurrup, fathead!" hissed Johnny Bull.

"Oh, really, Bull——"

Mr. Quelch's head turned.

"Bunter!"

"Oh! Yes, sir?" gasped Bunter. It had not been his intention to draw his Form-master's attention specially to himself. That argument with Poker at the gates had not improved Quelch's temper, and nobody was keen to get his special attention—least of all the fat Owl of the Remove. But Bunter had done it.

The gimlet eyes glittered at Bunter.

"You were laughing, Bunter!"

"Oh, no, sir!" gasped Bunter. "I never made a sound, sir! I—I was coughing."

"At what, Bunter, were you laughing?"

"Oh lor'! I—I wasn't, sir!" groaned Bunter. "I—I—I was only sneezing, sir! I—I mean coughing! That is, I never made a sound, sir!"

"I shall——" Mr. Quelch broke off.

Having turned, he had the tail of the procession under his eyes, and he suddenly became aware of Poker Pike. Thunder gathered in his brow. He could guess now at what Bunter had been laughing. He strode back towards the gunman.

"What does this mean?" he rapped. "What are you doing here?"

"I'll say I'm keeping tabs on that Putnam van Duck," answered Poker.

Mr. Quelch's lips set in a tight line. He had a thick walking-stick under his arm, and for a breathless moment the juniors fancied that he was going to slip it down into his hand and give Poker the benefit of it.

The procession came to an irregular halt. Hilarity faded away from the faces of the Removites. Quelch, with his authority thus flouted under the eyes of all his Form, was bitterly, intensely angry.

Poker, quite a genial "guy" in his own way, was not angry at all—only quietly determined. He did not want to get this hombre's goat! But he was going to keep tabs on Putnam van Duck! Nothing was going to stop that.

The tug-o'-war was coming—and it looked as if it were going to be serious when it came! The Removites looked on breathlessly.

The idea of hiring a professional gunman as bodyguard to a boy in his Form, seems absurd to Mr. Quelch, master of the Greyfriars Remove, who considers it time that Poker Pike is given THE ORDER OF THE BOOT!

THE SECOND CHAPTER.

Hop It!

"GO!"

Mr. Quelch's voice was not loud, but deep.

He slipped the stick from under his arm, but it was not, as some of the juniors expected, or as some, perhaps, hoped, to land it with a whack on Mr. Pike's bowler hat! He lifted it to point back down the lane to the school.

Poker Pike, with his hands on his hips, regarded him thoughtfully.

"Meaning beat it?" he asked.

"I mean what I say—go!" breathed Mr. Quelch. "I will not allow your presence here, sir! I will not permit you to intervene in matters affecting my Form! I will not permit you to flout my authority! I order you to go, and at once!"

Mr. Quelch did not raise his voice, but it was sharp and intense with anger. He did not approve of Poker's presence at Greyfriars. He regarded it, in his own secret thoughts, as an act of weakness on the part of the Head to have acceded to Mr. van Duck's urgent request, and allowed a gunman to be posted at Greyfriars to keep guard over the millionaire's son.

That Putnam was in danger from kidnappers was certainly true; it had been proved, since he had been at the school, by the attempts of Chick Chew and his gang to get hold of him.

Mr. Quelch was aware of that. But the extraordinary idea of hiring a professional gunman to keep watch and ward over a Greyfriars boy did not please Mr. Quelch at all.

It was so very much out of the common. Mr. Quelch did not like things out of the common. He had reached a time of life when he preferred to stick to a groove. The whole thing was, in Quelch's opinion, absurd!

He could not tell the Head so! But he could, at least, exert his own authority in his own sphere. And he was going to!

Hardly doubting that even the obstinate gunman would obey a direct order, Mr. Quelch waited for him to go, his stick still at a level, pointing the way!

Poker did not go.

He stood like a rock!

"You understand me?" said Mr. Quelch, his voice trembling with anger.

"I sure get you!" assented Poker.

"Are you going?"

"Not so's you'd notice it, bo!"

They stood face to face—the Removites looking breathlessly on. One of them had to give way, that was clear. Neither of them intended to do so. It really looked like the case of the irresistible force brought to bear upon the immovable object!

Mr. Quelch's face reddened. He could not, if he would, surrender, under the staring eyes of all his Form. On the other hand, he could not descend to violence.

Even if he descended to it, in fact, it would not buy him anything, as Poker would have expressed it. For Quelch, though no weakling, would have crumpled up like tissue paper in the hefty grasp of the gunman.

It looked like a riddle without an answer—a problem minus a solution. It was then that the Bounder weighed in.

Herbert Vernon-Smith, the Bounder of Greyfriars, probably cared less for authority than any other fellow in the Remove. But he was keener on a row than any other fellow at Greyfriars. Smithy was prepared to vindicate his Form-master's authority, if the vindication of the same afforded a chance for a royal row!

"We weigh in here, you men!" he whispered. "Back me up, and we'll soon stop that blighter cheeking Quelch!"

"A lot you care for a blighter cheeking Quelch!" grinned Skinner. "Catch me tackling that hefty brute!"

"I guess he's got to can it!" said Putnam van Duck.

"He sure has!" grinned Bob Cherry.

"Quelch won't like us chipping in!" murmured Frank Nugent.

"We can't let our Form-master be cheeked like that!" argued the Bounder.

"You never cheek him?" asked Skinner.

"Oh, shut up, Skinner! I'm going to shift him, if he won't clear, and you fellows will have to back me up!" said Smithy.

"The shiftfulness is the proper caper," agreed Hurree Jamset Ram Singh, "and the back-upfulness will be terrific."

It was a long pause—while the juniors whispered and looked on. Mr. Quelch was waiting for the gunman to go. Poker, it seemed, was waiting for the walk to be resumed, fully intending to follow on. Slowly Mr. Quelch lowered the pointing stick. As Poker took no heed of it, that attitude began to be a little ridiculous. Redder and redder grew Mr. Quelch's speaking countenance. His anger grew more and more intense.

He was only too conscious of the keen, breathless interest of the whole Form in this scene. He could not back down. Yet what could he do?

"Will you go?" he demanded at last.

"Nope!"

"I order you to depart instantly."

"You got another guess coming, big boy!"

"I will not allow you," said Mr. Quelch, "to take another single step in this direction! I shall prevent you, by force, if need be."

"You phoned the ambulance afore you started?" asked Poker Pike.

"What—what?"

"I guess you'll need it."

"Upon my word!" Quelch's temper, hard-held, flamed out. He advanced on the gunman in majestic wrath. "Go! Go instantly!"

It was simply incredible to Mr. Quelch that this man would stand rock-like in his way, unmoving. But Poker Pike did! Quelch, advancing, met the gunman, unmoved, and bumped on him. Poker put out a hand and gave him a push.

It was only a push! But it seemed to take the Remove master by surprise. It could not be called a hard push! But it was sufficiently hard to cause Mr. Quelch to stumble, lose his footing, and sit down!

He sat down in Friardale Lane, the most astonished Form-master that ever was!

"Oh!" gasped Quelch.

"I guess," said Poker Pike gravely, "that I don't want no trouble with you, big boy! I guess I got to keep tabs on that Putnam van Duck! Surest thing you know! I'll say—— Yurrrrrroooop!"

The Bounder led the rush.

Smithy was keen, as usual, on a shindy. And surely no fellow ever had a better excuse for one! His Form-master had been pushed over—was sitting breathless in the dust! If that was not a jolly good excuse for a shindy, Smithy would have liked to know what was!

Smithy led—and the Famous Five followed. Putnam van Duck rushed with them. Putnam, though the object of Mr. Pike's watchful care, was as fed-up with Poker as anyone—more so, perhaps! Anyhow, he took a hand.

Up-ended by that sudden rush of the juniors, Poker Pike went over on his back, raising the dust of Friardale Lane in a cloud.

He smote the county of Kent with a hard and heavy smite.

"Say, you pesky piecans!" howled Poker, struggling wildly.

Twice before, since Poker Pike had been "keeping tabs" at Greyfriars, he had fallen foul of the Remove—once in the Form-room, where he had horned in during class; once when he had wanted to stop Putnam running as hare in a paper-chase. Now he fell foul of them a third time. Third time is said to be lucky; but it was not lucky for Poker Pike!

For, hefty as he was, he was pinned down by the Famous Five, the Bounder, and Putnam, with hearty assistance from Peter Todd, Squiff, Tom Brown, Lord Mauleverer, Russell, and Ogilvy, and, in fact, almost every fellow who could get a hand on him.

With about twenty hands holding him Mr. Pike wriggled wildly, but wriggled in vain. As he was held, the Bounder produced a whipcord from his pocket.

With that cord Smithy coolly tied Poker Pike's wrists together. Then, bending the gunman's hefty right leg at the knee, he tied the ankle to Poker's belt.

"Now let him get up!" chortled the Bounder.

"Yurrooop!" gasped Poker dizzily.

He was heaved to his feet. He stood on his only available leg, hopping to keep from falling, amid a roar of laughter.

Harry Wharton turned him round in the road.

"Travel!" he said.

"Urrgh! I guess—urggh!" spluttered Poker.

"Hop it!"

"Ha, ha, ha!"

Poker hopped. He had to hop, or go over! So he hopped! His hickory face was crimson with wrath under his bowler hat. He hopped and hopped.

Mr. Quelch had staggered to his feet. He leaned on a tree, gasping for breath. He hardly realised what was going on for some minutes. Certainly he was not the man to be a party to such a playful trick as tying up a fellow's leg and setting him hopping! But when the crowd of yelling juniors surrounding Poker Pike set him hopping back to the school, Mr. Quelch woke up, as it were, to what was going on.

"Boys!" he gasped. "Boys!"

"All right now, sir!" said the Bounder. "We're not letting that ruffian check our Form-master, sir!"

"No fear!" grinned Bob.

"What—what have you done?" Mr. Quelch fairly blinked at the enraged, hopping gunman in the middle of the lane. "What—what——"

"Hop it, you guy!" yelled Putnam van Duck.

"Hop home!" chuckled Johnny Bull.

"Ha, ha, ha!"

"Boys!" gasped Mr. Quelch. "Cease this—this absurdity at once! I—I am obliged to you, but—but cease this immediately! Release that man! Mr. Pike, will you return to the school at once?"

"No!" roared Poker. "Not by a jugful! I guess I'm keeping tabs on that Putnam van Duck feller!"

Mr. Quelch's eyes glinted.

"I will order the boys to release you, Mr. Pike, if you will immediately take your departure!" he snapped.

"Guess again!" roared Poker. "Pack it up, you pesky guy! I'll say that I'll beat them young piecans up a few."

"Then," said Mr. Quelch grimly, "you may release yourself at your leisure, Mr. Pike! I wash my hands of the matter. Boys, follow me!"

"Ha, ha, ha!"

"Silence, please!"

The procession formed up again. The Removites marched after their Form-master—leaving Poker Pike frantically hopping, to keep his balance. Still determined, Poker hopped after the procession. Looking back, the Removites shrieked at the sight of him.

"Ha, ha, ha!"

"He's hopping after us!"

"The hopfulness is terrific!"

"Ha, ha, ha!"

Mr. Quelch, flushed, angry, annoyed, yet scarcely able to find fault with his hilarious Form in the peculiar circumstances, marched on, with head erect, affecting to hear and see nothing.

Few of the juniors, however, looked where they were going. Everybody was staring back at the weird hopping figure in the rear—dropping behind, but keeping desperately on.

Hop, hop, hop, came the Greyfriars gunman; panting and perspiring, but desperately hopping on.

Mr. Quelch was glad—though the Remove did not share his gladness in the least—when they reached the stile and crossed it into Friardale Wood. The stile stopped Poker.

Even the determined Poker could not hop over a stile. He was brought to a halt there as the Remove walked up the footpath with their Form-master. His bull voice roared in the rear:

"Say, you ginks! You come and let a guy loose! You hear me toot? Say, you pesky young piecans, you let up on a galoot! I got to keep tabs on that Putnam van Duck!"

"Ha, ha, ha!"

Poker's voice died away behind. Mr. Quelch led his flock on to the old priory; and Poker was left to hop!

THE THIRD CHAPTER.
Not Pie!

HANNIBAL CHEW—known to his friends in Chicago as "Chick"—stared, and stared again. Then, with an agility and swiftness remarkable in so fat and bulky a gangster, he dodged out of sight behind a massy fragment of moss-grown wall in the old ruined priory in Friardale Wood.

Chick could hardly believe the little piggy eyes that gleamed from the rolls of fat on his podgy face.

Such luck as this was really too much of a good thing. Chick Chew was in the old priory, embosomed in the midst of the green woods that sunny May afternoon, not with any idea that his intended victim might fall into his podgy clutches that day. He was making himself better acquainted with the vicinity of Putnam's school.

It was Chick Chew's way to be thorough. This sort of a dog-goned old ruin, Chick reckoned, was just the sort of spot that a schoolboy might visit on a half-holiday—especially a schoolboy from the western continent. There was nothing of the kind in Putnam's own country.

Towering skyscrapers, Chick guessed, made a more pleasing view than mossy old ruins. But a young guy raised on skyscrapers would naturally want to give such queer things the once-over when he was in the pesky old island where such things were to be found.

That was why Chick was there—picking up local topography, with the idea of "laying" for the millionaire's son on another occasion. Certainly he had not the remotest idea of seeing anything of Putnam van Duck that afternoon.

And now he saw him!

It was not a half-holiday. Chick had picked up a lot of information about Putnam's school. He knew that Wednesdays and Saturdays were half-holidays; and that Tuesday wasn't. This was a Tuesday. So Chick guessed that Putnam, like the rest of the school, would be in his class-room, at lessons! He was quite surprised to see him.

However, one "squint" at the procession of schoolboys, winding down the green woodland path to the old priory, made it clear to Chick, as he noted the stiff, angular schoolmaster with them.

The master was taking his boys for a walk in the time usually devoted to classes. Chick jumped to that at once!

And the master was Putnam's master—the boys were Putnam's Form-fellows, and with them walked Putnam van Duck.

Walking fairly into the hands of the kidnapper!

Chick grinned as he disposed his bulky person in cover behind the mossy wall and watched through clambering ivy.

Chick's luck had not been good since he had transferred his activities to the old-fashioned, law-abiding side of the Atlantic. In fact, it had been bad. Now, it seemed, fortune was smiling again, suddenly and unexpectedly making up for past frowns.

"Search me!" breathed Chick, as he watched.

His hand slid to his hip, where he packed his automatic. He watched keenly as the Remove-master and the Remove marched in at the ancient gateway through the moss-grown fragments of the old stone arch that had long since fallen. He feared to see the hickory face and bowler hat of Poker Pike in company with the schoolboys.

Chick was not afraid of gun-play. He was prepared, if necessary, to pull on Poker Pike, and exchange whizzing lead with him. But he was not honing for it, as he would have expressed it. Poker was a handy guy with a gun—quite as handy as Chick! And Poker had the law on his side!

Law mattered little in Chick's native land; but in this pesky old island, he knew that it mattered a lot. In Chicago gun-play was his first resource—here, it was his last!

It was really hard to believe in his good and unexpected luck when he ascertained, beyond doubt, that the watchful gunman was not with the party.

The whole crowd of schoolboys came into the ruins, with Mr. Quelch, and nobody followed them in. For once, at least, Poker Pike was not keeping tabs on the millionaire's son.

If this wasn't pie, Chick would have liked to know what pie was!

A mile away he had a car waiting, with Bud Parker at the wheel. Here was the gilt-edged schoolboy in his grasp. He had only to cinch Putnam, walk him off through the wood, and park him in that car. In an hour's time, he would be safely landed at the hidden retreat long ago prepared for him. It was as easy as falling off a log.

"Pie!" murmured Chick. "Clam pie! I should smile!"

He drew out the automatic. There was no occasion to use it—the sight of it would be enough! Chick could picture the blanched terror in the faces of the schoolboys at the sight of the deadly weapon. He could see the bony knees of that stiff old gink of a schoolmaster knocking together! Chick could see all this with his mind's eye. He was not, in point of fact, destined to see it with any other eye! But he did' not know that yet.

An old gink of a schoolmaster, with a stick under his arm, a crowd of unarmed, frightened schoolboys! It was pie to the gangster who had, in his time, held up armed men at the point of a gun. All he had to do was to make them stick their hands up, and walk off with Putnam van Duck under their noses—leaving them with their hands stuck up. Fortune was making up, at last, for a lot of bad luck, at one fell swoop.

Chick Chew's expensive American teeth gleamed as he grinned with glee.

The unsuspecting schoolboys were wandering towards the mossy fragment that hid his bulk. They were due for a sudden surprise soon!

Mr. Quelch's voice reached his ears. The Remove master was pointing out objects of interest with his walking-stick—of interest, at least, to the Remove master. It appeared, from Mr. Quelch's discourse, that several styles of architecture were combined in that old priory. Early English, it seemed, had Norman superimposed on it.

In the broken wall behind which Chick crouched, was the remnant of an ancient window, clustered with ivy, through which Chick was peering.

Mr. Quelch's stick pointed to that very spot!

"Here," said Mr. Quelch, "is a very excellent example of Early English!"

He was quite unaware of the extremely modern American side by side with the Early English!

The juniors looked as interested as they could. Mark Linley, indeed, was actually interested—he had tastes that way. Harry Wharton & Co. could not help feeling that since classes were off, the time would have been better spent at cricket. Skinner and his friends would have preferred to spend it with cigarettes, in the study. Billy Bunter had not the slightest doubt that it could have been better spent in the tuckshop.

Still, it was better than Latin prose. All the Remove agreed on that. Sunshine and green foliage and mossy ruins beat Latin prose hollow—even with archæology added thereunto!

"Early English——" Mr. Quelch was going on, when he broke off in sudden surprise. Chick Chew weighed in just then, and Early English was completely discarded, as an object of attention, for modern American!

Chick stepped through the gap in the old wall, the sunlight gleaming on the levelled automatic in his fat hand.

"Stick 'em up!" he rapped.

Mr. Quelch gazed at him dumbfounded.

His stick, extended to point out that excellent relic of Early English architecture, remained extended, pointing at the sample of modern American gangsterism. He seemed petrified.

There was a howl from the juniors.

"Chew!" yelled Bob Cherry.

"Chick Chew!" gasped Harry Wharton.

"Gee!" ejaculated Putnam van Duck.

Up went Van Duck's hands over his head. Van Duck had been trained in a land where the command to "stick 'em up" was understood immediately, and

Chick Chew stepped through the gap in the old wall, a levelled automatic in his fat hand. "Stick 'em up!" he rapped. Mr. Quelch stared at the kidnapper, dumbfounded. His stick, extended to point out an excellent relic of Early English architecture, remained extended, pointing at a sample of modern American gangsterism instead!

obeyed with promptness. The black muzzle of the automatic was enough.

But Van Duck's hands were the only hands that went up. Greyfriars fellows were quite unaccustomed to hold-ups! They had not learned, as it were, how to play their part in the game.

They stared.

Billy Bunter, with a howl of terror, revolved on his axis and flew. Skinner and Snoop stood with knocking knees. Lord Mauleverer smiled—as if he found the startling scene amusing. The Bounder clenched his hands, his eyes gleaming. Most of the fellows stood stock still. It was a complete surprise—and all the fellows knew that a pressure of Chick's fat finger would spray death among them, if the gangster chose.

"What—what——" stuttered Mr. Quelch.

His eyes almost popped from his face at the gangster. Chick's gleamed over the levelled gun.

"I guess I said stick 'em up!" came his grating voice. "I'll mention that I ain't waiting."

"Who—who—who are you?" stuttered the Remove master. "What—what does this mean? How dare you produce a deadly weapon in the presence of schoolboys?"

"It's Chick Chew, sir!" gasped Putnam.

"The kidnapper, sir!" said Harry.

All the Famous Five knew the fat gangster by sight.

"You hear me toot, you schoolmaster guy?" hooted Chick. "Stick 'em up! You hear me say stick 'em up?"

"Certainly I hear you!" snapped Mr. Quelch. "But I do not follow your meaning. If you are threatening me with that weapon——"

"Hay?"

"If you have the audacity, the effrontery, to threaten me with that weapon, I will have you taken into custody——"

"Wha-a-t?" stuttered Chick. "Carry me home to die! Loco, I guess! I'm saying stick 'em up, you pie-faced old geck!"

"I hear you distinctly," answered Mr. Quelch coldly. "But, as I have said, I do not follow your meaning."

Chick gazed at him over the gun. This guy, a schoolmaster, who taught boys in school, did not know what was meant by "stick 'em up!" Such abysmal ignorance amazed Mr. Chew. But, really, it was quite natural. Mr. Quelch knew many languages. English was his mother-tongue; French was familiar, he was a whale at Latin and Greek. But he had never learned American. Actually, he did not know that "stick 'em up" meant that he was to put his hands up over his head!

Neither was he frightened. His bony knees were not knocking together. His grip closed hard on his stick. His gimlet-eyes glittered. Not frightened in the least, Mr. Quelch was very angry.

"Carry me home to die!" gasped Chick. "You pesky old piecan, I guess I mean grab atmosphere! Got that?"

Quelch only stared at him.

"Does anyone here know what this man means by such extraordinary expressions?" he inquired.

"He means put up your hands, sir!" gasped Bob Cherry.

"Sure!" snapped Chick. "Put 'em up! Stick 'em up! Grab atmosphere! Claw the air! Reach for the sky! Got it now?"

He stepped nearer to Mr. Quelch, the levelled gun looking the Remove master full in the face His piggy eyes glittered over it. Mr. Quelch's hands did not move.

"I understand now," he said coldly and contemptuously. "Certainly I shall obey no such order. You must be strangely ignorant of this country, my man, if you imagine, for one moment, that you can terrify an English schoolmaster, in charge of his boys. I conclude, if you are the man named Chew, that your object is to kidnap this American boy. I think you must be insane if you think you will be allowed to take a Greyfriars boy away from the protection of his Form-master."

"You sure have spilled a bibful," said Mr. Chew, "and I'll mention that I ain't here to chew the rag. Stick 'em up! I'd sure hate to spill your juice, but if you don't stick 'em up instanter I——"

Crash!

Quelch had not stirred till that moment. Now he stirred—suddenly. Before Chick Chew could begin to guess that the schoolmaster aimed at trouble Mr. Quelch's stick crashed on the automatic, knocking it out of his hand.

There was a gasp from the Remove.

It was done so swiftly, so suddenly, that even the wary gangster was taken by surprise. The automatic crashed down five or six yards away.

Even as it crashed Mr. Quelch leaped forward, stick upraised. It came down on Mr. Chew's soft, slouched hat, banging on the head within, and Mr. Chew, with a wild yell, staggered back. As he staggered Mr. Quelch followed him up, lashing again and again with the stick, crash on crash on the head of the howling gangster.

It was not, after all, pie for Chick! It felt like anything but pie!

THE FOURTH CHAPTER.

Putting Paid to Chick!

"WAKE snakes!" gasped Putnam van Duck.

"Oh crumbs!"

"Oh crikey!"

"Good old Quelch!"

"Oh, my hat!"

The Removites gazed and gasped. Quelch was no coward, they knew. And they knew that he had a tart temper. But they had never seen him coming out like this. Putnam van Duck was the most surprised. He had seen many things strange to him since he had been in the Old Country; but he had never dreamed of seeing a schoolmaster, armed only with a walking-stick, putting paid to an armed and desperate gangster—and that gangster Chick Chew, the star kidnapper of the United States.

But Quelch was putting paid to him. There was no doubt about that. Quelch had, as the grinning Bounder expressed it, his monkey up!

Indignant wrath glowed in his face.

In his own native city Chick might be a terrifying character; he might be, in his own language, a bully boy with a glass eye, and a tin terror on ten wheels! He might be a whole team and a cross dog under the wagon! But to the indignant Remove master he was an impudent ruffian, who had had the unparallelled audacity to think of kidnapping a boy while in his Form-master's charge! Such audacity called for chastisement. Mr. Quelch handed it out, with vigour.

Whack, whack, whack, rang his stick on the gangster.

Chick Chew jumped, and dodged, and bounded. Had his automatic been in his hand, the Remove master would have rolled over, riddled by lead. But his automatic lay far out of reach, and Bob Cherry had already planted a prompt foot on it. Physically, no doubt, the hefty gangster would have been more than a match for Quelch, if they had clinched. But Chick had no chance of clinching. The lashing stick knocked him right and left.

Neither would a clinch have helped him, for the whole Remove were there, ready and eager to lend helping hands.

"Come on!" shouted the Bounder.

"Stand back!" rapped Mr. Quelch over his shoulder. "Keep back, all of you! Leave this man to me!"

Unwillingly the juniors held back. But their aid was not needed. Chick was jumping back, jumping away, dodging, winding, twisting, to save his aching head from the crashing stick—without being able to save it.

Quelch followed him up, lashing and lashing.

Chick's frantic yells awoke the echoes of the ruined priory and the surrounding woods He staggered, he stumbled, he jumped and bounded. He roared and he howled.

He fairly turned tail at last, and ran!

Guys in Chicago joints could hardly have believed it, had they seen it—but there it was. Chick Chew, gangster and kidnapper, racketeer and bootlegger, Kidnapper No. 1 of the United States, was running as if for his life, panting, gasping, and howling—with an angry schoolmaster on his track, whacking him as he fled.

Lashes descended like rain on Chick's podgy back as he went. They rang like the crack of his own automatic.

Whack, whack, whack, whack!

It was fortunate for Chick that Mr. Quelch was past the sprinting age. He won the race!

Quelch's last lash missed him. The Remove master halted, panting for breath. Chick, yelling, disappeared into the wood. He did not even pick the direction of the car in which Bud Parker awaited him. He did not know what direction he took! He did not care! All he cared about was getting out of the reach of that surprising schoolmaster guy.

He got out of it at last. He vanished into the thick wood. Mr. Quelch, breathing hard after his exertions, tucked the stick under his arm, and walked back into the old priory, where the breathless Remove awaited him.

The Removites gazed at their Form-master as he came. Quelch had surprised them, as well as the gangster. They were rather proud of Quelch at that moment.

"Three cheers, you men!" gasped Harry Wharton.

"What-ho!"

"The cheerfulness is the proper caper!" said Hurree Jamset Ram Singh.

And the Remove gave them with a will.

"Hurrah! Hip, hip, hurrah!" The old priory and the woods rang with the roar.

Mr. Quelch frowned. He stared grimly at his cheering Form. Quelch's only feeling was annoyance at the whole occurrence.

"Boys!" he rapped.

"Hurrah!" roared the Remove.

"Silence!" snapped Mr. Quelch. "What do you mean? Why are you making that ridiculous noise?"

"Oh!" gasped Wharton. "Only cheering you, sir."

"Nonsense!"

"I guess you're the only guy that ever put it across Chick Chew, sir!" said Putnam van Duck.

"Do not be absurd, Van Duck! And I shall be glad if you can contrive, now that you are a Greyfriars boy, to speak English, or something like it!" snapped Mr. Quelch. "I find it difficult to follow your meaning."

"I—I—I guess——"

"Say no more! Be silent, all of you! Cherry, what are you doing with that dangerous weapon? Hand it to me at once!"

"Only shoving on the safety-catch, sir!"

"Give it to me immediately. It must be handed over to the police!"

Mr. Quelch took the automatic, and put it in his pocket. Then he glanced at his watch.

"Time has been wasted!" he snapped. "Are we all here? Where is Bunter? Where is Skinner? Where is Snoop? Where is Fish?" Quelch's gimlet eyes glittered round. Several of the Form were missing. "Is it possible that any boys have taken advantage of the late occurrence to disperse?"

"I guess they had the wind up, sir——" began Putnam.

"If you cannot speak to your Form-master in English, Van Duck, do not speak at all. I noticed, Van Duck, that you placed your hands above your head when that ruffian uttered the extraordinary words which I did not, at the time, comprehend. You should not have done so."

"I guess he had us covered with his hardware, sir——"

"I have told you to speak English, Van Duck, or to be silent. You should have done nothing of the kind. Such an absurd action could only encourage the man. Do not let it occur again!"

"Oh!" gasped Putnam.

"We will now," said Mr. Quelch, "resume." He pointed with his stick to the mossy wall, from behind which Chick Chew had so startlingly emerged. "Give me your attention, please, and cease staring about and whispering. We are not here to waste time in idle talk. Now, this is an excellent example of the Early English style——"

Putnam van Duck gazed at his Form-master. It was difficult for the boy from Chicago to believe that he was going to carry on as if nothing had happened. But Mr. Quelch certainly was. He would have disdained to allow any gangster to flatter himself that he would be allowed to interrupt an English schoolmaster, engaged in giving instruction to his boys.

Quelch—a little breathless, certainly—carried on. But his boys did not give him a lot of attention, and remained rather vague on the subject of the Early English style in architecture. They were feeling excited, if Mr. Quelch disdained to feel anything of the kind. Some of them were wondering, too, whether the gangster might not reappear.

But there was no danger of that. Chick Chew, in an exhausted state, was taking a rest in the deep wood, and when he got going again, it was to totter away, with his fat hands pressed to an aching, spinning head.

Mr. Quelch finished his lecture to the Remove, and they walked on their homeward way, without seeing anything more of the man from Chicago. It had been quite an entertaining and thrilling Form walk—and, for the first time in history, the Remove looked forward to the next time when their Form-master would take them for a walk.

THE FIFTH CHAPTER.

Revenge is Sweet!

"HE, he he!" chuckled Billy Bunter.

Poker Pike frowned.

It was the day after the Form walk, and all that day Poker Pike's hard-boiled countenance had worn a grim frown.

Many other faces at Greyfriars had worn smiles—fellows smiled whenever they sighted Mr. Pike about the quad, or sitting on his usual seat by Gosling's lodge.

Poker was a serious-minded guy, and he saw nothing of a comic nature in his experience as a hopper. Everybody else did.

Poker, really, had had an awful time. He had hopped and hopped for quite a long time, till a kindly disposed passer-by had at last released him. Not knowing where to look for the Remove, he had gone back to the school, deeply concerned for Putnam—though his concern was relieved, when, a little later, the Remove came marching home, Putnam safe and sound along with them.

All the school had heard the story by the following day, and all the school smiled over it. Wingate and the great men of the Sixth smiled—even the masters smiled; and the fags chuckled and chortled. Dozens of fellows asked Poker how he liked hopping as a pastime. Hobson of the Shell asked him whether his favourite game was hop-scotch. Poker was tired of the subject—more than tired, when Billy Bunter happened along, and cackled.

Serious guy as he was, Poker had a cheerful nature, and liked to see smiling faces round him. But that day he had had more than his fill of smiling faces. His hard-boiled face grew grimmer and grimmer—and now, as Bunter cackled, it was at its grimmest.

"He, he, he!" chuckled Bunter. "I say, how do you like hopping? He, he, he! I say, you looked an awful ass! He, he, he!"

Grunt from Poker.

He was walking by the elms, with his bowler hat screwed down on his head, over a knitted brow. The fat Owl of the Remove, had he been a little less shortsighted, and a little less obtuse, might have taken warning by his grim look. But Bunter rattled on cheerily:

"He, he, he! I say, if you knew what a silly idiot you looked—he, he, he! I saw—— Ow! Leggo!"

Poker reached out with a long arm, and caught the fat junior by the collar. Having had enough on the subject of hopping, he was going to give Bunter a strong hint to that effect.

"Ow! Beast! Leggo!" roared Bunter, wriggling in the mighty grasp. "I say, I'll kick your shins, you beast! Leggo my neck!"

"I guess," remarked Poker, "that you spill too much, big boy! I guess I'm going to shake you up a few, and then some."

Shake, shake, shake!

"Urrrgh!" gurgled Bunter, as he shook. "Gurrgh! Leggo! I say, if you make my specs fall off—gurrggh!—you beast!—and bust them—urrggh!—you'll have to pi-pip-pay for them—wurrrggh!"

Shake, shake, shake!

"Yaroooh! Help!" roared Bunter. "I say, you fellows—whoooop!"

Mr. Pike released Bunter suddenly, and he sat down with a bump that almost made the quadrangle shake.

"Wow!" gasped Bunter.

Mr. Pike resumed his walk under the elms. Bunter sat and gasped for breath, spluttering, and blinking at him through his big spectacles.

The Greyfriars gunman took no further heed of Bunter. He was done with him.

Bunter, on the other hand, was not done with the gunman. Bunter was breathless, shaken, wrathy.

He tottered to his feet at last.

"Beast!" he roared.

Mr. Pike, sedately pacing under the elms, passed him by, like the idle wind which he regarded not.

Bunter rolled away to the House. Poker, if he regarded him at all, regarded him as done with. But that was an error on Poker's part. Bunter was not done with.

Even the worm will turn! Even Bunter was not to be shaken by the neck without getting his own back, if he could.

He would have liked to punch Poker's nose. But that was too large an order for Bunter. Indeed, he could not have reached it without a ladder, or at least a pair of steps. But there were other ways.

In Study No. 7—Bunter's study in the Remove—there remained an egg uneaten. It was remarkable for anything of an edible nature to remain in Bunter's study uneaten. But that egg was no longer edible. It had been overlooked in the study cupboard for some weeks. When it turned up, Peter Todd declared that it was no longer fit for active service, so to speak. Even Bunter regretfully had had to agree. There was no need, however, to waste it. Toddy declared that it would come in useful next time Coker of the Fifth barged into the Remove passage looking for trouble.

So there it was! When Billy Bunter rolled out of the House again that egg was clutched in his fat hand, and there was a truculent gleam behind his big spectacles.

"Hallo, hallo, hallo! What have you got there?" inquired Bob Cherry, as the fat Owl rolled past him in the quad.

"Oh, nothing!" answered Bunter hastily. "Don't you barge in, Cherry! I haven't got an egg here——"

"What?"

"And I'm not going to chuck it at that beastly Yankee," added Bunter. "You mind your own business."

"Oh, my hat!" ejaculated Bob.

He stared after Bunter as the fat junior rolled hurriedly on.

"Bunter, you ass!" he roared. "Chuck it! I mean, don't chuck it! Do you hear, you blithering bandersnatch?"

Billy Bunter heard, but he did not heed. He blinked at Poker Pike, still sedately pacing, with one eye on the gateway. Poker seemed to fancy that Chick Chew might walk in at that gate, any day or any hour, with the intention of cinching the millionaire's son—an idea that made Greyfriars fellows smile.

Poker certainly was not regarding Bunter; but Bunter was regarding Poker with a deadly glare through his big spectacles.

Standing by one of the elms, he waited for Poker to pass. Bob Cherry, from a distance, stared at him.

Poker walked past the tree where Bunter stood. Up went the fat hand with the ancient egg in it.

Whiz!

Even Bunter could not miss at point-blank range.

The egg landed fairly on Poker Pike's nose. It burst there. The shell flew to fragments; the contents splashed and spurted over the hickory face.

"Yooo-yooop!" spluttered Poker, staggering. "Wake snakes and walk chalks! Gurrggh! What the great horned toad—— Yurrrggh!"

"He, he, he!" cackled Bunter breathlessly.

He stayed only for one cackle, then he flew. He headed for the safety of the House as fast as his fat little legs could move.

"Whoooough!" spluttered Poker, dabbing wildly at the streaming egg, and half-suffocated by the scent that arose therefrom. "Urrrggh!"

"Ha, ha, ha!" yelled Bob Cherry.

Poker spluttered and dabbed, and glared round for the hurler of the egg. With egg-streaming face he rushed in pursuit of Bunter.

Bunter flew. After him flew the Greyfriars gunman.

Bunter had a good start, but Poker Pike's wiry legs simply flashed. He gained on the fat Owl hand over fist.

Bunter, as he reached the House steps, cast a terrified blink over a fat shoulder. He saw an eggy and infuriated face only a yard from him. With a squeak of terror he bolted up the steps.

After him leaped Poker Pike.

"Ow! Help! Wow!" gasped Bunter, as he bolted into the House, like a fat rabbit into a burrow.

Coker, of the Fifth, who was just coming out, barely escaped a collision. He dodged just in time, and glared at Bunter.

"You young ass!" roared Coker. "You——"

Then Poker Pike flew in.

Coker had barely escaped a crash from Bunter. He did not escape a crash from the second comer. Poker hit him fair and square.

"Oh!" gasped Coker, as he rocked. "Ow! What——" He rocked and rolled, and over him stumbled Pike.

"Search me!" gasped Poker.

"Ow! Oh! Yow! What the—— Yooop!" spluttered Coker.

Poker was up quickly. Coker was still gurgling as the gunman leaped up, glaring round for Bunter.

But the delay, brief as it was, had given the fat Owl time. Bolting into the Rag, Bunter slammed the door and turned the key.

The next moment there was a bang at the door.

"Say, you young gink!" roared Poker Pike.

"Beast!" gasped Bunter.

"I'm sure going to lam you a few!" yelled Poker.

"Yah!"

Bang!

A dozen fellows in the Rag stared at Bunter. Bunter, safe behind a locked door, howled defiance at his enemy.

Bang! came at the door.

"Yah! Rotter! Beast!" howled Bunter, through the keyhole. "Go away, you cheeky rotter! Get out of it, you ruffian! Yah!"

"By the great horned toad, I'll sure——"

"What is this disturbance?" It was Mr. Quelch's voice. "Pike, what are you doing here? How dare you make such a disturbance! Leave the House!"

"I guess——"

"Leave this House, I say! Go at once! How dare you bang on that door in such a way! Leave the House immediately!" barked Mr. Quelch.

Bunter listened breathlessly. There was a sound of retreating footsteps. Poker Pike was gone.

"He, he, he!" chuckled Bunter. "I say, you fellows, I bunged an egg right on his boko—he, he, he!—a jolly whiffy egg—he, he, he! I say, he got it right on the boko—he, he, he!"

From the window of the Rag the fellows there had a view of Poker Pike, tramping away from the House, dabbing at his hickory face as he went. They chuckled as they watched. Poker headed for his quarters in Gosling's lodge—doubtless in search of a wash, which he certainly needed. Billy Bunter cackled loud and long.

The beast had had the cheek to shake him! Bunter had bunged an ancient egg at him in return and got away with it. But the happy Owl of the Remove would probably not have cackled so joyously had he known what was to follow.

THE SIXTH CHAPTER.

"Skip!"

"I SAY, you fellows, wait for me!"

"Gym, fathead!"

"I'm coming!"

"Oh roll on, then!"

The Famous Five could not help being surprised. Generally Billy Bunter avoided the gymnasium like a plague-spot. There were occasions when he was not allowed to avoid it, and then he went unwillingly, and with many discontented grunts. Physical jerks, really, were not in Bunter's line.

Now he seemed quite keen.

Surprised as they were, the chums of the Remove were quite ready to encourage Bunter in this new stunt. Bunter did not like exercise, but there was no doubt that he needed it. The more physical jerks he did, the less likely he was to burst his gym outfit.

The fat Owl blinked round through his big spectacles as they went down to the gym. It did not occur to the juniors for the moment that Bunter was in search, not of physical jerks, but of a bodyguard.

The fact was, that Bunter, having enjoyed his success in retaliating on Poker Pike, had discovered that there was a fly in the ointment, as it were. Mr. Quelch had ordered the gunman out of the House, and Poker, rather surprisingly, had gone. But Bunter was not intending to pass the rest of his natural life in the Rag, and he had a rather uneasy foreboding of what might happen next time he encountered Poker.

He had glimpsed the gunman in the Remove passage, and given that passage a wide berth, guessing that Poker was looking for him. Now he blinked round uneasily for the hickory face and the bowler hat. But Poker was not in the offing at the moment.

"I say, you fellows, if that beast turns up you'll barge him off, won't you?" said the fat Owl.

"Which beast?" asked Harry. "Loder of the Sixth after you?"

"That beast Pike!" said Bunter. "He cheeked me, you know, and I bunged an egg at his chivvy! I shouldn't wonder if he's shirty."

"He looked shirty when he got after you!" grinned Bob Cherry. "So that's why you've hooked on for gym, is it, you fat spoofer?"

"Oh, no! I'm fearfully keen on gym!" said Bunter hastily. "I don't need it so much as you fellows, of course, being so athletic. Still, I'm keen on it! I haven't come along with you fellows simply because I want you to keep that beast off. It's because I like your company, you know."

"Ha, ha, ha!"

"Blessed if I see anything to cackle at!" grunted Bunter. "If it comes to gym practice, I fancy I could leave you standing."

"Good!" said Bob. "We'll see what Bunter can do on the trapeze, you men."

"I'm not thinking of the trapeze exactly——"

"Well, the parallel bars!"

"I don't care for that specially——"

"A bit of vaulting!" suggested Bob.

"Well, no," said Bunter, "not to-day!"

As the automatic flew from Chick Chew's hand, Mr. Quelch leaped forward, stick upraised. It came down on the gangster's soft slouched hat, banging on the head within, and Mr. Chew, with a yell, staggered back. The Remove Form-master followed him up, lashing again and again with the stick. "Ooooh! Whooooop!" Chick's frantic yells awoke the echoes of the ruined priory.

"Then what the thump are you going to do in the gym?" asked Harry.

"Well, I'll put you fellows through your paces and give you some tips," said Bunter, as they entered the gym.

The Famous Five looked at Billy Bunter as if they could have eaten him. They were great men in the gymnastic line, and the idea of being put through their paces and given tips by Billy Bunter seemed to get their goat, as Putnam van Duck would have expressed it.

"You cheeky fat idiot!" growled Johnny Bull.

"Oh, really, Bull——"

"The cheekfulness of the esteemed fat Bunter is terrific!" remarked Hurree Jamset Ram Singh.

"Oh, really, Inky——"

"Right as rain!" said Bob Cherry cheerfully. "Bunty shall put us through our paces. We'll do everything Bunter does——"

"Eh! I didn't mean that!" said Bunter.

"I do!" said Bob.

"Oh, really, Cherry——"

"Ha, ha, ha!"

"Gather round, you men!" bawled Bob Cherry. "Bunter's going to put us through gym practice. Get going, Bunter!"

A dozen fellows gathered round, with grinning faces. Billy Bunter cast a blink at the doorway. A bird in hand is said to be worth two in the bush, but Bunter was beginning to think that the playful Bob in hand was worse than Poker Pike in the bush.

"I—I say, you fellows, I—I think——" began Bunter.

He broke off, as he glimpsed a bowler hat passing the open doorway.

"Oh lor'!" gasped Bunter.

Poker was in the offing!

"You can cut, you fat ass!" said Harry Wharton, laughing.

"Oh, no!" gasped Bunter. "I—I'm frightfully keen, you know." A moment before, Bunter had been thinking of cutting. But that glimpse of a bowler hat outside had decided him to remain.

"Well, get on with it," grinned Bob. "We know you can teach us a fearful lot, Bunter; but example is better than precept any day. What about skipping? I'll keep it up as long as you do."

"Kids' game!" said Bunter.

"Jolly good exercise—none better! Here's a rope!"

"I—I don't want it!"

"You do!" declared Bob. "And you can have it round you, like that——"

"Yarooh!"

"Or handle it in the usual way. Which do you prefer?"

"Beast!"

"Ha ha, ha!"

Billy Bunter took the skipping-rope. Skipping was, as Bob declared, a jolly good exercise. It was likely to do Bunter a lot of good. But, like many people, Bunter did not care much for the things that did him good.

Still, there was no doubt that he preferred the skipping-rope in his hands rather than laid round his fat legs. So he took it.

"Begin!" said Bob.

"I—I say——" gasped Bunter.

"Go it! I'll count up to a thousand!"

"You silly idiot!" gasped Bunter, almost overcome at the bare idea of skipping up to a thousand. "Look here——"

"Hallo, hallo, hallo, here's the gun merchant!"

"Oh lor'!"

Poker Pike lounged in at the doorway. The fellows in the gym stared at him. It was the first time that the Greyfriars gunman had honoured that building with a visit. Evidently he had spotted the fact that Bunter was there—and he was on the fat Owl's trail. The egg had been washed from Poker's hickory face, but the grim frown remained.

"I—I say, you fellows!" gasped Bunter. "I—I say——"

"Want anything, Pike?" asked Harry Wharton.

Poker nodded in his slow way.

"Yep!" he answered. "I guess I'm looking for that fat guy. Say, you going to skip, big boy?"

"Ow! Yes—no—gerrout!"

"Here, what are you up to?" yelled Bob, as the Greyfriars gunman slipped his hand to his hip and jerked out his celebrated six-gun.

"You guys stand clear!" said Poker. "I guess that fat piecan is my mutton."

"Yaroooh!"

"Vamoose this here ranch, you Bunter!" said the gunman. "I guess bullets would skip some on this floor when I fan you."

"Fuf-fuf-fan me!" gasped Bunter. "Why, you beast—I say, you fellows—oh crikey——"

"Step outside!" said Poker, flourishing the gun.

Bunter did not step out of the gym—he bounded! That flourish of the six-gun was enough for Bunter.

"Look here, you ass——" gasped Bob Cherry, as the crowd of juniors followed Poker Pike, after Bunter.

"Pack it up, you'uns!" said Poker stolidly. "I'm saying that that fat gink passed me an egg on my frontispiece, and I'm sure going to fan him a few! I guess you guys want to stand clear."

"I say, you fellows——" spluttered Bunter.

His little round eyes almost popped through his big, round spectacles. Bunter knew what "fanning" was like! Poker on one occasion had "fanned" Loder of the Sixth with his gun in the quad. Bunter had thought that funny. But he did not think this funny.

"Look here, Pike——" gasped Harry Wharton.

"Park it!" said Poker.

He waved the gun at Bunter.

"Skip!" he roared.

"I—I say——"

"Skip!" roared Poker Pike.

"I—I—I——" stuttered Bunter.

Bang!

There was a gasp from the crowd of Greyfriars fellows as the six-gun roared. The bullet crashed on the ground, hardly an inch from Bunter's foot. The fat Owl of the Remove let out a squeal of terror—and skipped!

THE SEVENTH CHAPTER.

Fanned a Few!

"SKIP!" roared Poker Pike.

"Ooooogh!" gasped Bunter. He skipped.

There was a surge back of the crowd of juniors as the gun began to roar. Nobody wanted to stop a chance bullet.

Guns were familiar to Poker Pike. He handled a gun just as he breathed. But they were not quite so familiar at Greyfriars School. Everybody preferred to be out of the line of fire.

Bunter, unfortunately, could not get out of it. He was right in it, and had to stay right in it.

He skipped. Some of the fellows were laughing—some were breathlessly excited. Poker Pike was quite serious. "Fanning a guy" was an old game with Poker, and he did not seem to realise that what might be quite the thing in a Chicago joint, or out in the wild and woolly West, was rather out of place in a school quadrangle. Dr. Locke had spoken to him with great severity on the occasion when he had "fanned" Loder of the Sixth. But perhaps Poker had forgotten that severe lecture. Anyhow, he was going to "fan" Billy Bunter, and that was that!

Crash!

Bunter tangled his clumsy fat legs in the rope, and came down suddenly and hard. There was a roar.

"Yarooop!"

"Ha, ha, ha!" came from the onlookers.

There was a snort from Poker Pike.

"Get going, you pesky young piecan! You hear me hoot?"

"I—I can't!" gasped Bunter. "I—I've broken my—my leg! And—and some ribs! And—and my neck——"

"Ha, ha, ha!"

Bang!

The six-gun roared again, and the bullet almost grazed a fat leg. Bunter bounded.

He was on his feet in a twinkling, with a swiftness and agility surprising in a fellow who had just broken his leg, his ribs, and his neck! Perhaps, however, there were not really so many breakages as that!

"Urrggh!" gasped Bunter. "I say—urrrggh!"

Poker flourished the smoking gun.

"You skipping?" he roared.

"Ow! No! Yes! Oh lor'!"

"Ha, ha, ha!"

"Go it, Bunter!" yelled Bob Cherry.

"Oh crikey!"

Bunter skipped again. This time he did not tumble. He dared not. With desperate energy, Bunter skipped, amid yells of laughter. The only serious face present—apart from Bunter's—was Poker Pike's. The Greyfriars gunman was quite serious.

"Oh lor'!" spluttered Bunter. "Oh crikey! I say, you fellows—grooogh! I say—oooch!"

With his eyes almost popping through his glasses, his fat face streaming with perspiration, Bunter skipped, and skipped, and skipped—but he gasped and spluttered for breath—but he skipped!

He slowed down at last—but only for a second!

Bang!

The six-gun roared: and it had an electrifying effect on Bunter! He skipped again with redoubled energy. A bullet crashing an inch from his feet was more than enough to spur the fat Owl on to exertion.

"Urrrrrrrgh!" he gurgled as he skipped.

"Ha, ha, ha!"

"Go it, Bunter!"

"Keep it up!"

"Blessed if I ever knew Bunter could keep it up like that!" gasped Bob Cherry. "Some skipper!"

"The skipfulness is terrific!"

"Ha, ha, ha!"

Skip skip, skip, went Bunter, frantically—skipping for his fat life! Grimly the gunman watched him, gun in hand.

Again Bunter slowed down. Exercise like this was more than flesh and blood could stand—Bunter's flesh and blood, at any rate. But he was quickly spurred on again!

Bang!

"Yarooooooh!"

"Skip!" roared Poker.

"Ow! Oh crikey! Ooooogh!"

Bunter skipped and skipped! More and more fellows gathered round—at a safe distance from the gun! They stared, and chuckled, and yelled. Everybody at Greyfriars—except Bunter—knew that the fat Owl was badly in need of exercise! He was getting it now!

The rope fairly whizzed! Up and down went Bunter, skipping, the hickory face under the bowler hat watching him grimly.

Far in the distance, the Head stood at his study window—staring. The reports of the six-gun rang all over Greyfriars, awakening every echo in the old school. At another window, stood Mr. Quelch, petrified. Wingate of the Sixth came rushing on the scene.

"What the thump——" yelled the Greyfriars captain.

"Keep clear, you!" rapped Poker Pike.

"But——" stuttered Wingate.

"I—I—I say——" gurgled Bunter. He slowed down again. "I say——"

Bang!

"Yarooooooooh!"

Bunter accelerated.

"Go it, Bunter!" roared Bob. "Skip, old fat bean, skip!"

"Ha, ha, ha!"

"You can't do this!" howled Wingate. "Stop it at once! Do you hear, you mad ass? I tell you, stop it!"

He grabbed at Poker's shoulder. Poker swept round his left arm, and the Greyfriars captain sat down suddenly.

"Man down!" chuckled the Bounder.

"Ha, ha, ha!"

"Urrrrggh!" gurgled Billy Bunter, skipping wildly. "I—I s-s-say, you f-f-fellows, I kik-kik-kik-can't kip-kip-keep it up! I—I—I—grooogh! Oh lor'! Oogh!"

"Skip!" roared Poker.

"I—I—I——"

Bang!

"Oh crikey! Stoppit, you beast, I'm skipping, ain't I?" shrieked Bunter. And he skipped with frantic energy.

Bump!

The fat Owl stumbled, caught his feet, and rolled over. Poker Pike regarded him thoughtfully.

"I guess that lets you out, big boy!" he remarked, and he packed his gun. "I'll say you done got some exercise you was wanting."

"Urrrrggh!"

"Ha, ha, ha!"

"Hallo, hallo, hallo! Here comes Quelch!" gasped Bob.

From the direction of the House, Mr. Quelch was striding on the scene, coming down like a thunderstorm. But the performance was over. Poker had packed his gun: and he walked away as the Remove master came. Mr. Quelch was left to gaze at Bunter—sitting and spluttering in a tangled skipping-rope, and a sea of perspiration, amid a yelling crowd.

THE EIGHTH CHAPTER.
Quit !

"IMPOSSIBLE!" said Mr. Quelch.

"I fear so!" agreed the Head.

"Such absolutely outrageous conduct——"

"I agree!"

"Such outrageous, unparalleled——"

"Quite so, Mr. Quelch!" said the Head, soothingly. "I perfectly understand your feelings in the matter. I share them. But——"

The Head paused—and Mr. Quelch's eyes glinted. He was in the headmaster's study—and the topic, of course, was Poker Pike, and the fanning of Billy Bunter. That was the one topic at Greyfriars at the moment. Even cricket—even First Eleven matches—paled into insignificance, as a topic. Not for the first time, the Greyfriars gunman had brought down the house. gunman had brought down the house. Mr. Quelch, his voice trembling with anger, "this—this—this person discharged firearms in the quadrangle, and he was plainly warned that if it occurred again, he would have to leave the school."

"True!" assented the Head.

"Now, sir, it has occurred again, more outrageously than before. On the former occasion, the victim was a Sixth Form prefect! On the present occasion, he is a junior boy in my Form! I have a right, sir——"

"Quite so, Mr. Quelch! I agree! Yet the matter presents difficulties," said the Head, slowly. "This man Pike is a—a—a somewhat unusual character, but I am sure that he means no harm. He has strange ways——"

"A ruffian, sir——"

"Hem! No actual harm has been done, and I am convinced that it was not his intention to do any, Mr. Quelch! Nevertheless——"

The Head paused again. Mr. Quelch compressed his lips bitterly. He was resolved that the weird proceedings of the Greyfriars gunman should come to an end! He was absolutely determined upon that! He was prepared to go to the length of handing in his own resignation, unless Poker Pike was ordered to go. He had never approved of the gunman's presence in the school. Now the gunman had transgressed all limits: passed unheeded the headmaster's solemn warning—and he had to go! Quelch was determined on that!

"It is a difficult matter, sir!" went on the Head, slowly. "Mr. Vanderdecken van Duck undoubtedly has reason to believe that his son is in danger from kidnappers! Several attempts have been made by the man—Bite— is his name—Bite——"

"Chew, sir!"

"Chew!" agreed the Head. "The man Chew! The boy Van Duck undoubtedly is in danger from this man Chew—what a very singular name! Indeed, your own experience only yesterday, sir——"

"My experience yesterday, sir, is a sufficient proof that no reckless and lawless ruffian from Chicago is required here, to protect a boy in my Form!" said the Remove master.

"But——"

"Against my wish, sir, against my order, the man Pike persisted in forcing his company upon my boys, in a Form walk! He was guilty of what amounted to violence towards me personally. But he was not required, sir! He was not on the scene when the man Chew appeared, in the old priory. I am quite capable, sir, of protecting a boy under my charge! I think, sir, that as much was clearly demonstrated on the very occasion to which you refer."

Dr. Locke nodded.

"That is certainly true, Mr. Quelch."

There was a pause.

"Personally," said the Head, at last, "I should be disposed to speak very seriously to the man, and give him another chance. But I acknowledge that you have the right to insist, my dear Quelch. If you insist, I shall tell Mr. Pike that he must leave the school immediately."

"The decision is entirely in your hands, sir," said Mr. Quelch. "But so far as I am concerned, I do insist, most emphatically, that this lawless man should leave Greyfriars without an hour's delay."

"Very well!" said Dr. Locke. "That decides the matter, and I will see Mr. Pike and request him to leave."

"Thank you, sir."

Mr. Quelch left the Head's study—satisfied. Poker Pike was to go! That was settled now.

Quelch was very far from being a vindictive man. But a gunman from Chicago was altogether too far outside his experience for Henry Samuel Quelch to make the necessary allowances for his wild and woolly ways.

Had Quelch been convinced that the safety of a boy in his Form depended upon Mr. Pike remaining in the school, no doubt he would have swallowed his wrath and indignation from a sense of duty. But he was not convinced of anything of the kind.

His firm belief was, that Putnam van Duck, within the walls of Greyfriars School, was perfectly safe from all the kidnappers in the United States. He was perfectly safe under the care of his Form-master—and no wild and woolly gunman was needed.

Really, Mr. Quelch had some grounds for thinking so. Had he not, with his own hand, beaten off, and, in fact, chased Kidnapper No. 1 of the United States, when that enterprising gangster attempted to rope in the millionaire's son?

He had! Poker Pete was superfluous! He was not needed—and if he was not needed, what was the use of keeping so extraordinary a character about the school?

The Head did not feel so sure. Still, after what had happened, he had to admit that Quelch had the argument on his side. Quelch had saved the American junior from kidnapping. Poker had kicked up a tremendous shindy. Talking to the gunman seemed of no use—the Head had already talked to him at very considerable length; he had, as Poker described it, spilled a hatful! And this was the result! Poker had to go!

Having reached that decision, it only remained for Dr. Locke to carry it into effect. He left his study, left the House, and walked down to Gosling's lodge.

Immediately he was outside the House there was a breathless squeak from Billy Bunter.

"I say, you fellows! The Beak's after him."

But Bunter's warning was not needed. Scores of eyes were upon the headmaster at once. The gravity in his majestic countenance, and the direction he was taking, left no doubt of his object! He was going to see Poker!

There was a buzz of excitement, and a rush from all sides. Ever since the "fanning" of Billy Bunter, an hour or more ago, there had been a buzzing crowd in the quad, breathlessly discussing what the Head was going to do. They had no doubt that he was going to do something drastic.

Loder of the Sixth told his friends, Carne and Walker, that the ruffian would have to go this time! He ought to have been kicked out for having fanned Loder a week or two ago; but he had been let off with a caution, as it were! Now he had broken out again! The Head could not possibly overlook it, Loder declared, with great satisfaction.

Other fellows, however, were not so pleased. Coker of the Fifth said that it was rather a shame. Coker had been down on that gunman, but he had come to change his opinion, and when Coker changed his opinion, of course he expected everybody else to follow suit. So Coker told Potter and Greene that it was a shame, and glared at them as if daring them to deny it.

Harry Wharton & Co. were quite sorry. They liked Poker Pike! He was rather a coughdrop, they admitted! He had manners and customs that were wildly out of place in a school. They had cheerfully lent a hand making him hop, when he cheeked their own special Beak. But they liked him all the same, and they realised, too, that he was far from conscious of having given serious offence.

"After all, what does Bunter matter?" argued Johnny Bull.

"Beast!" was Bunter's rejoinder to that.

"I dare say Pike thought a little exercise would do him good," argued Johnny. "And if he thought so, he was right."

"The rightfulness was terrific!" grinned the Nabob of Bhanipur. "The esteemed Bunter does not matter at all."

"Yah!" said Bunter. "I can tell you fellows he's jolly well going to be kicked out, and I'm jolly glad, so yah!"

Quite an army followed the headmaster, at a respectful distance, as he progressed majestically towards Gosling's lodge. Most of the fellows, it seemed, were sorry that it was the boot for Poker—if it was!

Loder of the Sixth was glad. Billy Bunter was glad. But really, they seemed to be the only fellows who were.

The Head seemed unconscious of the army behind him. He did not glance round. He arrived at Gosling's lodge, where he found Mr. Pike on his usual seat in his sunny corner, with an eye on the gates.

Poker rose to his feet as the headmaster arrived.

He did not remove his hat. Poker's hat was a fixture. It never seemed to occur to him to take it off, indoors or out. But he touched the brim with a finger. Hard-boiled hombre as he was, Poker Pike had a great respect for the silver-haired headmaster of Greyfriars. He had never seen such a guy before coming to Greyfriars, and at first he had almost doubted whether he was real! He was something utterly outside all Poker's previous experiences. But he had shown, on many occasions, a deep respect for the Head, and he showed it now. Which made the Head's task a little more difficult.

"Squat, sir!" said Poker hospitably, pointing to the bench from which he had risen.

"Eh!" ejaculated Dr. Locke.

"I guess you come to chew the rag a piece," said Poker amiably. "And I'll say, sir, that there ain't no guy around this here caboodle that I like better to hear spilling chinwag."

"Bless my soul!" said Dr. Locke.

"He, he, he!" came a fat chuckle.

Dr. Locke glanced around; apprised by that fat cackle from William George Bunter that he had an audience.

He frowned, and waved a hand.

The "army" retreated to a more respectful distance. They could not hear, but they could see! They watched with the deepest interest. Several fellows kicked Bunter, and he squeaked.

"I guess," said Putnam van Duck, "that it's pulling up stakes for Poker! I reckon I shan't be sorry not to have him treading on my tail. But I sure do hate to see him booted."

"Same here!" said Bob.

"The samefulness is terrific."

"I say, you fellows——"

"Shut up, Bunter!"

"Beast!"

And the Head's majestic back being turned again, the army encroached a little nearer, intensely anxious to hear as well as to witness the interview between the Head and the Greyfriars gunman.

THE NINTH CHAPTER.

To Go or Not to Go!

"QUIT?" said Poker Pike.

He stared at the Head. His slits of eyes opened wide. His gash of a mouth set like a closed trap. Standing with his hands on his hips, the gunman faced the Head.

"Quit?" he repeated.

"I am sorry!" said Dr. Locke gently. "But you will recall, Mr. Pike, that on the last occasion when you discharged firearms here——"

"When I—what?" interjected Poker. "Oh! I get you! You mean when I burned powder?"

"Hem! Precisely? You are aware that I warned you very seriously that if such a thing occurred again, I should be compelled to request you to take up your quarters elsewhere——"

Poker Pike rubbed his pimple of a nose thoughtfully. The old guy had him there. That was a cinch!

"You don't mean that you want me to beat it?" he asked.

"I regret very much——"

"Put your cards on the table, sir!" said Poker. "You aiming to say that you want me to vamoose the ranch?"

"To—to—to what?"

"Absquatulate!" said Poker.

"I—I hardly follow your meaning, Mr. Pike! What I desire to say is——"

"I got to git!"

"Git!" repeated the puzzled headmaster. "Oh! Get! No, Mr. Pike, I do not want you to get anything! I simply desire you to find other quarters as soon as possible. Say to-morrow——"

"Meaning that I got to git—to quit—to absquatulate—to vamoose the ranch—to hit the trail?" asked Poker. He wanted to get it clear.

"Oh!" gasped the Head. "Quite!"

"Waal," said Mr. Pike slowly, "there ain't no guy I'd sooner oblige than you, sir! I think a whole lot of you, sir, and then some. But I ain't quitting!"

"Eh?"

"I guess I got to keep tabs on that Putnam van Duck!" explained Poker. "How'd I keep tabs on him if I quit?"

"The boy is quite safe here, Mr. Pike——"

"Says you!" remarked Mr. Pike.

The Head coughed.

"Yes, certainly I say so, Mr. Pike! In any case, I can no longer permit your presence here. Deadly weapons are out of place in a school. The discharge of firearms in the quadrangle is excessively dangerous and alarming. If you care to take up your residence in the vicinity of the school, I have, of course, no objection to make. But you must leave Greyfriars."

Poker shook his head.

"I'll say I'm powerful sorry to disoblige a gent I respect as much as I respect you, sir!" he said. "But it don't cut no ice! I got to keep tabs on that Putnam van Duck."

"Really, Mr. Pike——"

"Nor I guess it don't hurt that fat young piecan Bunter to skip a few!" said Poker. "Forget it, bo! I ain't vamoosing this here ranch."

"Sir!" gasped the Head.

"Same to you!" said Poker.

"I am in authority here, Mr. Pike." Dr. Locke's manner was growing stiff and very firm. "I request you to leave."

"Request all you like, sir!" said Poker cheerfully. "I ain't got no kick coming, fur as that goes."

"You will leave to-morrow."

"Nunk!"

"You will not presume to remain here Mr. Pike, now that my permission is withdrawn?"

"Surest thing you know!" answered Poker.

There was a breathless gasp among the Greyfriars fellows—many of them within hearing of this remarkable conversation. The Head, with his back to them, did not see them. Poker, with his hickory face to them, saw them, but did not heed them.

All the fellows knew that Poker was a tough guy. But few had anticipated that he would venture to pass by the commands of the august headmaster, like the idle wind which he regarded not.

But he did! His manner was respectful, but determined—quite determined. He was there to keep tabs on Putnam van Duck! He respected the Head—but where Putnam was concerned, the Head did not come into the picture. He was sorry—powerful sorry, as he said—to displease this silver-haired old guy! But he wasn't quitting! Not by a jugful!

There was a long pause. The pink showed in Dr. Locke's cheeks.

"You must go, Mr. Pike!" he said at last. "I shall expect you to vacate your quarters here to-morrow."

"Forget it, sir!" said Poker.

Dr. Locke breathed hard.

"You cannot remain here, Mr. Pike," he said.

"Says you! You see," said Poker, as if he were patiently explaining matters to an obstinate child, "I got to keep tabs on that Putnam van Duck! I guess I got to hang up my hat where he hangs up his hat! That's a cinch! You get me?"

Dr. Locke breathed harder.

"I shall expect you to be gone to-morrow, Mr. Pike," he said.

"I should smile!" said Mr. Pike.

"I have no more to say!" said the headmaster of Greyfriars, with great dignity.

"You've sure spilled a bibful!" agreed Poker.

Breathing still harder, the Head turned, to pace majestically back to the House. He found himself face to face with more than half Greyfriars.

He stared at the army.

"Bless my soul!" he ejaculated. "What are all you boys doing here? What——" There was a general scamper, before he could complete the question.

With an unusually high colour, the headmaster walked back to the House. It was seldom that he was at a loss; but he was rather at a loss now. Poker Pike, ordered to quit, declined to quit. Exactly how that extraordinary man from Chicago was to be dealt with was rather a problem to the Head! Indeed, he was feeling a little annoyed with Mr. Quelch for having put such a problem up to him.

As soon as he was gone there was a rush back to the lodge. Poker Pike, seated on the bench, was surrounded by excited juniors.

"Poker, you pie-faced geck, you got to quit!" Putnam van Duck hooted at him. "You hear me, Poker? You got to beat it, you big stiff!"

"Forget it!" answered Poker.

"But you can't stay here against the Head's orders!" exclaimed Bob Cherry.

"You got another guess coming!" said Poker.

"You'll be shifted fast enough, if you don't go!" called out Loder of the Sixth.

Poker glanced at him.

"You honing to do the shifting?" he asked. "You asking me to fan you a few, like I did before, you piecan?"

Poker's hand went to his hip. Loder of the Sixth walked away rather fast. Apparently he did not want any more fanning.

"Then you're not going?" exclaimed Bob.

"Not so's you'd notice it."

"Oh, my hat!"

"I say, you fellows, we'll jolly well chuck him out!" squeaked Billy Bunter. "I say, we'll jolly well——"

"It's all Bunter's fault," said Bob Cherry. "Let's kick Bunter!"

"Oh, really, Cherry—— Yaroooh! Beast! Stoppit! Yoop!" Billy Bunter fled for his fat life.

In the studies at tea there was only one topic—Poker Pike, and his order to quit, which evidently he was going to disregard.

What would the Head do?

That was a question of intense and burning interest. Obviously the gunman, ordered to quit, had to quit! Equally obviously, he wasn't going to quit! No doubt he could be, as Loder remarked, shifted. But a guy like Poker would require some shifting! Excitement on the subject was intense—every fellow wondering what was going to happen on the morrow.

On the morrow, in the sunny May morning, Poker was seen taking his usual pasear, as he called it, in the quad. His hickory face showed no perturbation.

There was quite a buzz of excitement in the Form-rooms that morning. Never, or hardly ever, had the fellows been so keen to get out in break.

Was Poker still there? That was the question!

He was!

When the classes were dismissed and the fellows came out with a rush, the rush led almost everybody down to Gosling's lodge.

There sat Poker on his usual bench.

"Not gone yet?" gasped Peter Todd.

Poker glanced at Peter.

"Nope," he answered briefly.

"Not going?" yelled Bob.

"Nix!"

It looked as if Poker was right! The Greyfriars fellows went in for third school—and when they came out again Poker was still there. He was still there when the bell rang for dinner!

When the juniors came out after dinner there he still was—quiet, calm, unperturbed. Evidently Poker meant what he had said! He was not going! He had to go—but he wasn't going! And in breathless excitement the whole school wondered what was going to be the outcome!

As Poker Pike was about to pass the tree, Billy Bunter's fat hand went up, with the ancient egg in it. Whiz! The egg landed fairly on the gunman's nose and burst there. "Yooo-hooop!" spluttered Poker Pike, staggering. "Gurrgh! Yurrrggh!"

THE TENTH CHAPTER.

Corn in Egypt!

"I SAY, you fellows!"

"Just the man we want!" said Bob Cherry.

"Just!" said Frank Nugent heartily.

"The justfulness is terrific!"

Billy Bunter blinked at the Famous Five through his big spectacles, and backed away a pace. This cordial greeting did not seem to reassure him—it seemed to alarm him a little.

"I say, you fellows, no larks!" he exclaimed.

Bunter had been looking for the Famous Five. A postal order he had been expecting that morning had failed to arrive. Bunter was stony! And, as misfortunes never come singly, Bunter had not had enough dinner that day!

Shakespeare has remarked that when sorrows come they come not single spies, but in battalions! Thus it was with Bunter!

Broke to the wide, unable to raise even the price of a single, solitary jam-tart, Billy Bunter had been kept short of grub at dinner! He had only eaten enough for four or five fellows when Quelch stopped him.

Quelch fed with his Form! Often he had had a sharp eye on Bunter, and cut short the helpings when, in Quelch's opinion, they too far exceeded the limit. Bunter, left to his own devices, would have had helpings after helpings, till they ran almost into astronomical figures. Quelch had often barged in, in the most disagreeable way, before Bunter was able to bring about a famine in the land. To-day he had barged in earlier, and more sharply, than usual. He was shirty—and Bunter got the benefit of it.

In the Form-room that morning the Remove had found Mr. Quelch very tart. At dinner Bunter had found him tarter.

Bunter had rolled out dismally, with an aching void under his usually well-filled waistcoat. He had eaten hardly as much as the Famous Five together! It was all that beastly gunman's fault, for making old Quelch so shirty!

Bunter hated that gunman with a deadly hatred. Lynching, Bunter thought, was too good for him. Something lingering, with boiling oil in it, was more suitable for a man who was the cause of Bunter going short of foodstuffs!

That was why Bunter was looking for the Famous Five! He felt that if he did not get a snack before afternoon school, something serious might happen! In such an emergency he hoped that even those beasts would play up.

So when the chums of the Remove, instead of telling Bunter to buzz off, or roll away, as usual, greeted him smilingly, the fat Owl ought really to have been pleased!

Instead of which, he backed away in alarm! He suspected a rag!

"No larks!" he repeated, backing out of reach. "I say——"

"The larkfulness is not terrific, my esteemed fat Bunter!" Hurree Jamset Ram Singh assured him solemnly.

"Hungry, old man?" grinned Bob Cherry

"Hungry ain't the word!" said Bunter dismally. "Famished is more like! You fellows saw me at dinner! I ate nothing! Not that I ever do eat much, as you know——"

"Oh crikey!"

"I'm not greedy—like some chaps," said Bunter. "But a fellow wants enough to eat! You heard Quelch! He stopped me at the fifth helping——"

"Wasn't it the fifteenth, as usual?" asked Bob.

"No!" roared Bunter. "It wasn't! It's all that putrid gunman's fault! He's got Quelchy's rag out! I'm starved, in consequence! That's what they call justice here! I say, you fellows, I've been disappointed about a postal order——"

"Ha, ha, ha!"

"Blessed if I see anything to cackle at! I'm hard up at the present moment—actually stony! And hungry—hungry as a ——"

"As a Bunter?" asked Bob sympathetically.

"Beast! Hungry as a hunter! I feel quite faint!" said Bunter pathetically. "I say, you fellows, this isn't a time to be mean! You wouldn't like to see me collapse in the Form-room this afternoon from sheer weakness, brought about by want of food, would you?"

The Famous Five chuckled. Certainly they would not have liked to see such a harrowing catastrophe. But they did not really think that there was any danger of it.

"You can cackle!" said Bunter bitterly. "Cackle—while I've got a tummy-ache from sheer hunger! Talk about Pontius Pilate fiddling while Berlin was burning!"

"Ha, ha, ha!"

"Beasts!" roared Bunter. "If you can't do anything but cackle at a chap——"

"Come on, old fat bean!" said Bob Cherry. "Didn't I tell you you were just the man we want?"

"Where?" asked Bunter suspiciously.

"Tuckshop!"

"Oh!" gasped Bunter. "I—I say, you fellows standing a feed?"

"Exactly!"

"Oh!" repeated Bunter.

It was great news—welcome news; it

(*Continued on page* 16.)

FALSE FACES!

This week's Rib-Tickling Instalment of Young Dicky Nugent's Full-of-Fun Serial :

"THE SPARTANS OF ST. SAM'S!"

Sports Day dawned at last, and St. Sam's awoke to find that the weather was simply topping. The fags had an extra wash in honner of the grate occasion, and the playing-fields were bathed in sunshine. Everything seemed faverable to a day of good, clean sport.

Only one thing marred the complete happiness of the St. Sam's fellows—the fact that the Head, like the silly old fogey he was, had insisted on St. Sam's being represented by his so-called Spartans!

"If only we had Burleigh's team instead of those nocked-need wrecks!" sighed Loyle of the Fourth, as he gazed across to the playing-fields from the dormitory winders. "Then we'd be sure of the old skool beating all comers to-day!"

"Perhaps the Spartans will do well," remarked Trew, hoapfully. "Considering all the training the Head has given them, they shouldn't be so dusty."

"Nevertheless, old chap, I'm afraid they'll drag our name into the mud," said Loyle, with a rewful larf.

Similar sentiments to these were being eggspressed all over St. Sam's. But there was one who held quite the opposite opinion—namely, Doctor Birchemall. The Head's mood, as he scampered across to the Skool House, was one of soopreme optimism.

"Jevver see a better day, Lickham?" he chortled, as he found Mr. Lickham having brekker in his study. "This is just the weather we needed to ensure the triumf of our splendid Spartans!"

"Really, sir?" sniffed Mr. Lickham, who was one of the many who disapproved of the Head's tackticks. "I shouldn't have thought the weather made much difference to games of tiddley-winks or noughts-and-crosses!"

The Head stared.

"Tiddley-winks and noughts-and-crosses, Lickham? Whatever makes you think that tiddley-winks and noughts-and-crossesfigger in to-day's programme?"

"Meerly the fakt that you eggspect the Spartans to score a big triumf, sir!" grinned Mr. Lickham. "They're the only games in which I can imagine them scoring a triumf and —yarooooo! Leggo by dose!"

"Perhaps that will learn you not to make rash remarks about the team I trained myself!" said Doctor Birchemall sternly, as he gave the Fourth Form master's nose a final savvidge tweak. "Consider yourself lucky, Lickham, to get off so lightly as this. Only the fact that your remarks were not rasher has saved your bacon!"

He then left Mr. Lickham to finish his interrupted brekker and went upstairs to Burleigh's study in the Sixth Form passidge. There, he was serprized to find the kaptin of the Sixth wearing his outdoor clobber and packing a suitcase.

"Going out, Burleigh?" he asked.

"Oh, no, sir!" said Burleigh, with crushing sarkasm. "I'm just coming in!"

"Then why are you packing your suitcase?"

"To brane the next caller with!"

The Head frowned.

"I trust, Burleigh, that you are not trying to be dispertinent to your headmaster. My reason for calling on you was to find out what you and your colleagues in the old St. Sam's athlettick team are going to do to-day. I hoap that like trew sportsmen you will be present to cheer on the Spartans who have replaced you, to a grate and glorious viktory!"

"Well, I must say you've got a nerve to make such a rekwest!" remarked Burleigh. "But if it's any satisfaction to you to know it, sir, all the fellows conserned will be present—including myself!"

"Honest injun?" asked the Head.

"Really and trewly! We shan't be to the fourfront, of corse, sir; you can hardly eggspect that, under the circs. But you can depend on it, we shall all be there!"

"Burleigh," said Doctor Birchemall, with quite a catch in his voice, "I congratulate you on a wise and sportsmanlike decision—and also on escaping the flogging I should have given had you decided otherwise! See you later!"

And Doctor Birchemall farely danced out of Burleigh's study—as eggsited as a Second Form fag at the thought that Burleigh had come to heal at last!

If the Head had looked back again a few seconds later he mite have had his doubts about his supposed viktory, for he would have found Burleigh stretched out in his armchair, larfing fit to bust!

"Ha, ha, ha!" Burleigh was roaring. "He's as pleased as a dog with two tails becawse we're all going to the Sports! I wonder what he'd say if he knew we were going, not as specktators, but as rivals to his precious Spartans! Ho, ho, ho!"

After he had had his larf out, Burleigh finished his packing, then quitted the study, carrying his suitcase with him. Taking a little-used roote, he made his way stelthily out of the Skool House and proseeded across the quad to a side gate. There he found a crowd of St. Sam's fellows waiting for him, all carrying suitcases like himself.

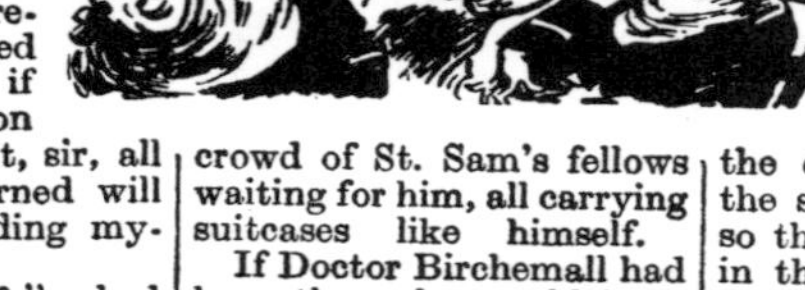

If Doctor Birchemall had been there, he would have been amazed to reckernise the very athletes he had banned when he had started the St. Sam's Spartans. Forchunitly, the Head was by this time bizzily engaged in feeding his face in the dining-hall—without a suspishon of the deep plot that was being hatched against him!

With Burleigh and Tallboy, his bosom pal, tramping ahead of them, the athletes marched across the fields to Muggleton. Strapper and Hardnut of the Sixth were amongst them, Fleetfoot of the Fifth and Jolly and Fearless of the Fourth, and many another stalwart of the turf and cinder-track. They all looked in the pink; the meer site of them would have made the Head's Spartans turn green with envy and the Head himself feel mitey blue!

"This way, you fellows!" cride Burleigh, as, arriving in Muggleton, he led the way into a shop which bore the intreeging sign "BEWTY PARLOUR" on its portals.

Why Burleigh and his merry men should be going into a bewty parlour would certainly have puzzled those who were not in the secret; but the athletes of St. Sam's showed no trace of serprize as they followed their leader into the shop. They knew what was coming. They knew that Burleigh had already arranged for the eggspert who owned the shop to disguise them so that they could compete in the Sports at St. Sam's without a sole suspecting their real eyedentity!

Everything was ready for them. Several bewty eggsperts, armed with huge tins of greasepaint and other aids to the art of altering faces, were
beside the empty
chairs; and very so
were bizzily at w
the first batch of cu

The way they
the appearance
St. Sam's fellows
fare nock-out! L
putty were de
wacked on to al
shape of their
false eyebrows
cunningly stuck o
glue; and wigs we
fully pinned on t
heads to cover u
real hair. And, as
put it, before the
where they were
hardly knew who
were!

The bewty eg
work was finished
and-one and all
agree that it was a
peace. Whatever
held in store for the
day, they felt jol
that nobody would
nise them as the St
fellows who had
with Burleigh that
ing!

It was a jolly
wheeze of Burleigh's
was no doubt abou
But Burleigh had son
else up his sleev
After he and his m
left the bewty
and arrived at the
where their sharrab
waiting, he drew ou
pocket a bill on whi
printed the words
ALF'S ATHLE
TEAM."

"My hat You
of everything, old c
remarked Tallboy
ingly, as Burleigh pr
to stick the bill
windscreen of the

"What a rude awa
for Birchy when h
covers he's been hoa

WOULD YOU BELIEVE IT?

Following a rumour that a dangerous criminal was loose near Greyfriars, Fisher T. Fish startled the Remove by coming into class with two six-shooters strapped to his waist! In response to Mr. Quelch's inquiry, Fishy said his "smoke poles" might be useful in the event of danger. Quelch was in danger of "catching fire" with vexation!

Before retiring, Bob Cherry takes a dozen deep breaths before the open dormitory window. He had only taken six the other night, when Temple & Co., of the Upper Fourth, burst in! Bob lent a hand in repulsing the raiders with heavy losses—and then returned to the window to complete his dozen breaths—rather "breathlessly"!

A difficult problem which baffled the Upper Fourth wa
to the Remove by Mr. Qu
Mark Linley was successfu
solving it. Remove are j
proud of their "star" class-
—and "Marky," by scorin
for Remove against the U
Fourth that afternoon, showe
can shine at sport, too.
"made a hit"!

'It's just a matter of ...nes!" said Burleigh, ...shing under his grease-...nt. "All aboard, every-...y, now—and don't for-... that you're supposed ... be from St. Alf's! ... you all remember the ...es we've agreed on?" Yes, rather!" Good! Let's get going ...n!"

...he disguised skoolboys ...bed up into the sharry, ... a few moments later ... were on their way ... to the skool.

... harty welcome ...ited them at St. Sam's. ...ering crowds swarmed ... from all directions as ... drove through the ... way, and Doctor ...hemall himself wel-...ed them from the steps ...he Skool House.

Ah! The boys from ...Alf's!" he cride, greet-...hem without a sign of ...ernition. "Welcome ...St. Sam's, my boys! ...se make yourselves at ...e! I want you to ... this place just as if ...ere your own skool!" Thanks awfully, sir!" Burleigh, in a disguised .... "That'll be easy, ...t it, you fellows?" What-ho!" grinned ...St. Alf's team.

...d they dessended from ... sharrabang and ...led with the crowds ... were now arriving ... St. Bill's and St. ...'s and treated the ... just as if it had been ... own. And nobody ...ned for a single moment ... it was that the boys ... St. Alf's felt so much ...me at St. Sam's!

(...on't miss the concluding ...ment of Dicky Nugent's ...ing serial in next ...s number!)

Why Not A Continental Tuckshop?

Asks FISHER T. FISH

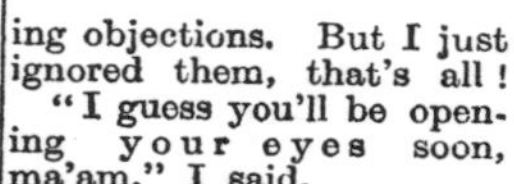

When Ma Mimble told me trade was a little quiet last week, she couldn't have hit on a better guy to put her wise on what was wrong—no, sir!

"Ma'am," I said. "What you need around this little joint is a guy who'll bring it bang up to date. You got a show here that ought to bring you in a roll as fat as that ham on your counter! I'll say it's a cinch. Gimme a leetle break. Lemme horn in just a few, and I guess I'll show you how."

The dumb dame looked at me like she didn't understand English, so I started to show her what was on my mind.

"I guess I'll increase your profits by fifty per cent," I explained, as I got busy. "It's a deal, huh? O.K.!"

Boy! What a money spinner I'd worked out. I figured that just what was wanted was al-fresco features—table and chairs outside the shop—the well-known Continental atmosphere! Get it?

I rolled up my sleeves and piled in. I lugged chairs and tables out of that shop like I meant it—yes, sir! For some reason, Ma Mimble wobbled about all over the joint, registering objections. But I just ignored them, that's all!

"I guess you'll be opening your eyes soon, ma'am," I said.

Was I on the mark? I'll tell the world! Why, I hadn't got the thing half-fixed before guys were sitting right down in them chairs and calling for a waiter! But something had to happen. It always does in this sleepy old shebang. Along comes the Big Shot, with his eyes jumping right out of their sockets.

"Fish!" yelps Doctor Locke. "How dare you?"

I guess I did my best to tell him. But what's the use in a one-horse burg like this? All I collected for my trouble was two hundred lines and strict orders not to do it again!

Anyway, there's the idea for the lucky guy who can use it when the Big Shots around here learn a little horse-sense! Why not a Continental Tuckshop? Hear me holler! WHY NOT?

GREYFRIARS FACTS WHILE YOU WAIT!

...g the descent of a cloud ...s in his native South ...iet Delarey said they con-...rything eatable. Smithy ...nter had the same ...istic when raiding a ...pboard. When Smithy ... to his study later, he ...bare—Bunter had acted ...ggestion! The Owl is ... under a "cloud"!

Cecil Reginald Temple, skipper of the Upper Fourth, is a born boaster. He tells the story of how he crossed the Channel last vac., in a gale, and the boat nearly stood on end. Dabney and Fry have already listened to this for hours "on end." They feel as "sick" of it as they secretly believe Temple was at the time!

When Hobson of the Shell told his musical study-mate, Hoskins, that he could get a foreign symphony orchestra on his new radio set, Hoskins looked pleased. The terrific groans and shrieks which Hobson got, however, drove Hoskins out. When Hobson at last got his station, Hoskins was "broadcasting" himself from the music-room!

BOB CHERRY Tells You

WHY BUNTER LOST HIS MEMORY

The first I heard about Bunter suffering from lapses of memory was when he failed to recognise me in the quad.

"What cheer, my old Prize Porker?" I called out, in a friendly kind of way; and all Bunter did was to give me a blank stare!

"I—I'm sorry, old chap," he said. "But I'm afraid you have the advantage of me."

"Wha-a-at?"

"The fact is, I don't recall your face!" explained Bunter. "Would you mind telling me your name?"

"You silly fat chump!" I gasped. "What's the game? You know me all right. I'm Cherry—Bob Cherry!"

Bunter passed his hand across his brow.

"Bob Cherry!" he said dreamily. "That seems to strike a chord of memory somewhere, too! Yes—it's coming back! Slowly and dimly, you know—ah, now I remember you again! Hallo, Bob, old chap!"

"Well, my hat!" I breathed. This was a new one on me and no mistake!

"Sorry I forgot who you were," said Bunter, with a kind of wan smile. "I seem to be suffering from loss of memory quite a lot lately, you know!"

And Bunter rolled on his way, leaving me holding on to the nearest tree-trunk for support!

After this little incident Bunter's lapses of memory became frequent and alarming. He failed to recognise nearly all his old acquaintances, forgot the name of his Form-master and the whereabouts of familiar places like the gym and the Rag. In fact, the only thing he seemed to be able to remember without difficulty was the whereabouts of the tuckshop.

Wharton summoned the fat idiot before a Form meeting in the end and told Bunter that something would have to be done about it. Bunter then revealed that he had already taken steps to put things right.

"I've written my pater," he said. "To tell you the truth, I've seen a memory course advertised in the papers that seems just the very thing I want. The cost of it is a mere trifle compared with the good it will do me—ten quid, to be exact!"

"Ten quid? Ye gods!" ejaculated Wharton. "Do you think your pater is going to cough up ten quid to provide you with a memory course, then?"

"Oh, really, old chap—I forget your name! Ten quid is jolly cheap for what they do. My pater ought to be jolly glad to be let off so lightly."

"Well, we'll wait and see what he says," said Wharton rather dubiously.

On the following day a bulky envelope arrived in the post for Bunter. The fat Removite grabbed it eagerly.

"I say, you fellows, it's from the pater! I knew he'd do the right thing!"

And Bunter slit open the envelope and examined the contents. But no ten quid came to light. All that the envelope contained was a bundle of printed papers and the following letter:

"Dear Billy,—I am sorry to hear your memory is so bad, but luckily there is no need to spend ten pounds on the course you mention. I happen to have that very course by me, you see. I am sending it herewith, and I am sure it will improve your memory wonderfully. Your affectionate FATHER."

The ten-quid memory course dropped from Bunter's nerveless hands. He uttered a strangled sort of groan. Black ingratitude was registered all over his countenance.

"Beast!" he roared. Then he bolted without even troubling to take a second look at the memory course!

Since that time the dear old Porpoise remembers as well as ever he did.

Having told you that, I don't think you'll need any further enlightenment on why Bunter lost his memory!

WHAT A "LARK"!

Hobson is in bad odour in the Shell for allowing his team to be licked by the Remove at cricket. One indignant Shellite says Hobson must be a complete *cuckoo* to allow a lot of *sparrows* like us to *crow* over him. So it really sounds as if Hobson has got the "bird," doesn't it?

(*Continued from page* 13.)

came like corn in Egypt in one of the lean years. But Bunter was still a little doubtful. It was such good news, that it seemed rather too good to be true! Fellows often saw Bunter scoff their tuck; but seldom or never did they show enthusiasm on the subject!

At the present moment the chums of the Remove looked as if they regarded Billy Bunter as a man they delighted to honour! That, of course, was just as it should have been! Still, it was unusual! Billy Bunter could not help thinking that there was a catch in it somewhere!

"Come on!" said Harry Wharton.

"I—I say, you fellows, no larks! If—if you mean it——"

"Honest Injun!" said Johnny Bull solemnly.

"Oh, all right!"

Bunter's fat face beamed. With a cheerful, grinning countenance, he rolled away with the Famous Five to the school shop.

Really, it was a very happy coincidence! On the very occasion when Bunter was most in need of something substantial in the way of refreshment, the Famous Five were actually looking for him, to feed him! No coincidence could have been happier!

They entered the tuckshop together—five fellows smiling, and one grinning from one fat ear to the other! This clearly was Billy Bunter's lucky day.

"Now, before you start——" said Harry Wharton.

"Eh?"

"There's something I want to say——"

"Leave it till afterwards, old chap!" said Bunter. "I say, what about beginning with a cake? Those plum-cakes——"

"Hold on a minute! You see——"

"I say, you fellows, I'm fearfully hungry," said Bunter, "and we haven't much time, either—it's not much more than an hour to class!"

"Oh crikey!" gasped the Five.

Bunter, it seemed, was prepared to go on demolishing foodstuffs for an hour or more!

"No sense in wasting time!" urged Bunter. "It would be rather rotten to hear that beastly bell for classes before we've finished the feed——"

"Oh crumbs!"

"I'll have that plum-cake—it's only a two-pound one—and while I'm scoffing it, you fellows can order the feed!" suggested Bunter.

"Oh scissors!"

"Look here, Bunter, I was going to say——" gasped Harry.

"Well, you look here, Wharton," said Bunter warmly, "if you've brought me here to jaw, I can say it's pretty rotten, after making out that it was going to be a feed. I jolly well think——"

"Stuff him with cake, and shut him up!" said Johnny Bull. "He won't leave off talking till his mouth's full."

"Oh, really, Bull——"

"One of those plum-cakes, please, Mrs. Mimble——" said Harry.

"Oh good!" Bunter started on the cake at once. "I say, you fellows, you order the feed—I shall be ready in a minute!"

A two-pound cake evidently did not constitute a "feed," in Billy Bunter's estimation. It simply occupied his attention while the feed was got ready! He gobbled, but, at the same time, blinked anxiously at the chums of the Remove through his big spectacles. Bunter liked plum-cake—and it was a nice plum-cake—but he was anxious about a feed.

"Well, get on with it, then," said Bunter. "I shall be ready in a minute."

"But you've got to play up on your side!" explained the captain of the Remove. "We want a quid pro quo from you—see?"

"I haven't a quid at the present moment——"

"Eh?"

"But I'll lend you a quid with pleasure, when my postal order comes," said Bunter. "Remind me!"

"Oh, my hat! I don't mean a quid!" gasped Wharton. "Quid pro quo—see? I mean, something in return! It's about Pike——"

"Pike!" repeated Bunter. "What about Pike? Blow him? Look here, you're not asking Pike to this feed! Besides, he wouldn't care for jam-tarts, doughnuts, and meringues! We're going to have jam-tarts, doughnuts, and meringues, ain't we?"

"If you like, but——"

"I'll have jam-tarts after this cake, then! A dozen to begin with," said Bunter. "I say, I'm nearly ready for that feed."

"About Pike!" said Harry Wharton firmly. "Look here, Bunter, we don't want the chap to be booted out of the school——"

"I do!" said Bunter.

"He's not a bad lad, really," said Bob.

"Awful rotter!" said Bunter, his voice a little muffled by cake. "Putrid Yankee! I hate him!"

"There'll be an awful row, if he won't go, when the Head's told him to go," said Nugent. "We don't want that."

"I don't mind," said Bunter.

"Now, look here," said Harry, "we all know jolly well that the Head would go easy with Pike, only Quelch is so ratty with the man. And Quelch is so jolly ratty, because of what Pike did to you yesterday——"

"Yes, the beast!"

"Well, we all think," said Harry, "that if you went to Quelch and begged him to overlook it just this once, it would be all right. You see, it's on your account that he's so awfully down on Pike! You, as the injured party, have a right to beg him off—see?"

"I'll watch it!" said Bunter.

"Ten to one, Quelch would go easy, and we know jolly well that the Head would, if Quelch did. Then the whole trouble would blow over, and the Head would withdraw his order, and Pike would stay on, and——"

"I don't want him here!"

"Never mind that——"

"I do mind it!" said Bunter firmly. "Don't talk rot, you chaps! I say, what about those jam-tarts next?"

"You'll go to Quelch——"

"No fear!"

The Famous Five looked at Bunter. He was finishing the cake, and was ready for the next item on the programme. But he was not ready to go to Mr. Quelch and beg off the gunman.

And as that was the single, sole, and solitary reason why the chums of the Remove were wasting foodstuffs on Bunter, there was a pause in the proceedings. Bunter wiped an ocean of crumbs from a fat face with his sleeve.

"I'm ready!" he said.

"To go to the esteemed Quelch?" grinned Hurree Jamset Ram Singh.

"No, you ass! For the feed!"

"Good-bye, Bunter!" said Harry. "Come on, you men! Nothing doing!"

The Famous Five walked to the door. Billy Bunter gazed after them, through his spectacles, in consternation, almost in horror. The feed was off! That gorgeous spread was gone from his gaze like a beautiful dream! It dawned on Bunter's fat brain that begging off Poker Pike, with Quelch, was a sine qua non—without that nothing!

It was not because he was such a nice chap that the chums of the Remove were feeding him. It was because they wanted him to beg off Poker Pike—and, as the fellow who had been the victim of Poker's gun-play, he was the only fellow who could do it!

"Oh!" gasped Bunter. "I say, you fellows! Don't go! I say, I'll go to Quelch this minute—I mean, as soon as I've fed! I say, come back, old chaps—I say, I'm hungry—I say, I like that beastly brute no end—I mean, that splendid chap Pike—I've always admired him! I—I quite enjoyed what he did yesterday—I—I'm going to ask him to do it again! Honest Injun! I say——"

The Famous Five, exchanging grinning glances, came back. And Billy Bunter, with a gasp of relief, started on jam-tarts!

THE ELEVENTH CHAPTER.

Not a Success!

BILLY BUNTER was looking sticky and shiny when he rolled out of the tuckshop with the chums of the Remove.

He was breathing with some little difficulty, but with great satisfaction. It had been a great spread—a gorgeous spread—a tip-top spread. For nearly half an hour Billy Bunter had parked foodstuffs—and even Billy Bunter had no room for more.

Harry Wharton & Co. had watched him, without joining in the spread. They were not keen on feeding so soon after dinner, for one thing; and funds would not run to it, for another. They were rather in funds, fortunately; but they had to pool resources, to see Bunter through.

Which was really very kind-hearted and disinterested of the Five. If this wheeze worked—and they did not see why it should not—it would save a lot of trouble all round. They liked Poker, and did not want to see him booted out. They liked Van Duck, and believed that he would be safer with Poker on the spot They had a very strong impression that the Head would be perfectly willing to allow Poker to carry on, if only the angry Remove master could be placated. And as Quelch was so deeply incensed, on account of what had happened to Bunter, surely he would take a milder view, if Bunter, the injured party, begged him to do so!

It looked hopeful, at least!

Such a happy ending to the trouble would be a general benefit. For if the Head remained determined that Poker should go, and Poker remained determined that he wouldn't quit, it was clear that serious trouble was ahead.

The Famous Five had the happy feeling of being public benefactors—if only this stunt worked successfully.

They walked Bunter off to the House—at a slow pace! Bunter had exerted himself in the tuckshop—but his exertions there had tired him. He crawled.

Moreover, Bunter was not in a hurry to arrive at Quelch's study. He had been quite enthusiastic about the feed—he was less enthusiastic about seeing Quelch. The "quid" appealed to Bunter less than the "quo."

"I say, you fellows," Bunter ventured, as they neared the House, "on second thoughts—you know second thoughts are best, old chaps—I—I think that brute Pike had better go. You see——"

"Stick to it, old man!" said Bob Cherry.

"You—you see, Quelch may be ratty——"

"Bit too late to think of that!" growled Johnny Bull. "If you don't go to Quelch, you'll have to hand back that spread."

"Eh? How can I hand it back, you silly ass!" ejaculated Bunter.

"We can up-end you, old fat man, and shake it out of you!" explained Johnny. "And we jolly well will, if you don't go to Quelch!"

"Oh, really, Bull——"

"A bargain's a bargain, Bunter," said Harry, "and if it comes off all right, there's tea in the study."

"Oh!" said Bunter.

Even Bunter was not hungry at the moment. But he knew that he would be hungry again by tea-time.

Wharton had touched the right chord!

"Of course, I'm a fellow of my word!" said Bunter, with dignity. "Having given you fellows my word, I'm not likely to break it, I hope."

"Hear, hear!" grinned Bob.

And the fat junior rolled into the House—and the Famous Five guided him, slowly but surely, to Masters' Studies. But at the end of Masters' Passage, Bunter paused again.

"I say, you fellows——"

"Come on!"

"Oh, yes! But, I say, if old Quelch is shirty——" Bunter seemed uneasy on that score. "You never know with a beak, you know! They—they're safer to keep away from, you know, like—like those Alsatians——"

The Famous Five chuckled. They wondered what Quelch would have thought of that comparison.

"You never know, with an Alsatian!" Bunter argued. "They might bite, and they might not! It's the same with beaks! I'll tell you what, you fellows, we'll talk it over again—later—over tea, f'rinstance."

"Quelch doesn't bite!" grinned Bob Cherry. "And, ten to one, he will think it jolly decent of you to speak up for the man who made you skip yesterday."

"It will look jolly generous and decent!" remarked Nugent.

"Noble!" said Bob.

"Oh!" said Bunter. He had no objection to looking generous and noble. "I—I say, if you fellows think so, all right! After all, it is rather noble, ain't it, to speak up for that beast that popped off his gun at me? Do you fellows think Quelch will think it noble?"

"Well, what else can he think?" said Nugent.

"That's so!" agreed Bunter. "After all I always was a noble chap——"

"Eh?"

"I dare say Quelch has noticed it, you know, and he won't be surprised to see me act in a noble manner! What?"

"Oh! Ah! Yes! Hem! Come on!"

Bunter came on, at last. He seemed to need an escort right up to Mr. Quelch's door. But the Famous Five were there to give him the necessary escort; and as he seemed a little slow to tap, Harry Wharton tapped for him.

"Come in!"

Mr. Quelch's voice answered from within the study. Certainly, it did not sound like the growl of a disturbed Alsatian. But it seemed to have a rather disconcerting effect on Bunter.

"I—I say, you fellows——" he stammered.

"Get in, you fat ass!" breathed Johnny Bull. "If you don't go in, Quelch will think it's somebody larking——"

"Oh lor'! But I—I say——"

Bob opened the door, stepping back quickly. Billy Bunter, in the open doorway, was revealed to the gaze of his Form-master.

"Bunter! What do you want?"

"Oh, nothing, sir!" gasped Bunter.

"What?"

"I—I mean—— Ow!" A surreptitious push started Bunter into the doorway. He rolled into the study.

Mr. Quelch stared at him not agreeably. It was only too clear that the Remove master was "shirty." As it happened, he had a view, from his study window, of Poker Pike in the distance—evidence that the Greyfriars gunman was not gone, and was not, apparently, thinking of going. Which, naturally, in the circumstances, roused Quelch's deepest ire.

"What is it, Bunter?" he asked curtly.

"I—I—I——" stammered the hapless Owl. "I—I—I've come here, sir——"

"What do you mean, Bunter? I can see that you have come here! Have you anything to say?" rapped Mr. Quelch.

"Oh! Yes! No! I—I mean, I—I was going to ask you, sir, about that beast——"

"What?"

"I—I mean Pike, sir—that man Pike——" stammered Bunter.

Mr. Quelch's brow registered thunder.

"Pike! Upon my word, has that man been guilty of some fresh outbreak of ruffianism?" he exclaimed. "This is too much! Speak! Tell me at once what has occurred, Bunter!"

Outside in the passage the Famous Five exchanged dubious glances. They had had great hopes of this wheeze! But they could not help feeling that this did not sound encouraging.

"Oh! Yes! No, sir!" gasped Bunter. "I mean——"

"What has he done now?" exclaimed Mr. Quelch.

"Oh! Nothing, sir!"

"Nothing! Then what have you to complain of?"

"Oh, dear! I didn't—I don't—I mean, I wasn't—that is, sir, I—I mean—I—I—I came here to say—— Oh lor'!"

A pair of gimlet-eyes almost bored into Billy Bunter. Mr. Quelch was very keen of hearing, and faint sounds from outside warned him that Bunter had not come alone to his study. He suspected a "rag." Already Quelch was far from being at his bonniest. And the mere suspicion of a rag brought a look to his face that terrified the fat Owl almost out of his podgy wits.

"If this is some absurd jest on your Form-master, Bunter——" began Mr. Quelch, in a voice like unto that of the Great Huge Bear.

"Oh, no, sir!" gasped Bunter. "I wanted to say—— Oh crikey! I—I mean, about that man Spike, sir—I mean Pike—I—I want to put in a word for him, sir! I—I thought you'd think it noble, sir!"

"Wha-a-t!"

"And—and generous, sir!" gasped Bunter. "Being a noble chap——"

"Bunter!"

"Yes, sir! The beast gave me an awful time yesterday, sir, and I'd be jolly glad to see him kicked out. I—I mean, if you'd be so kind as to give him another chance, sir! Speak to the Head——"

"Bunter!"

"Wharton thinks the Head would let him stay, sir, if you asked him. All the fellows think the Head's a bit soft, sir——"

Mr. Quelch, bereft of speech, gazed at his hopeful pupil. Outside, in the passage, five juniors brandished helpless fists, out of sight. Bunter was not a whale on tact, at the best of times; and now, reduced to a state of almost hopeless confusion by Mr. Quelch's thunderous glare, he hardly knew what he was saying at all.

"That—that's how it is, sir!" stammered the hapless Owl. "I—I—I've come here to beg him off, sir, if—if you don't mind! Not because they stood me a feed at the tuckshop, sir, or anything of that kind, but because I'm a noble chap, sir! I mean—I—I wish I hadn't come now!" groaned Bunter, as Mr. Quelch rose from his table with an expression on his face that might have made the fabled Gorgon green with envy.

Bunter had reason to wish he hadn't come!

Mr. Quelch found his voice.

"The boys outside will step into this study!" he said, very distinctly.

"Oh!" gasped the boys outside, taken by surprise. It was their first intimation that Quelch knew that they were there.

They stepped in! There was no help for it. Gimlet-eyes glittered at them as they entered. Nobody looked happy.

"Wharton! I gather, from the absurd and ridiculous remarks of this foolish boy, that you and your friends instigated him to this act of impertinence!" thundered Mr. Quelch.

"We—we——" stammered Wharton.

"I shall cane Bunter——"

"Oh lor'!"

"But I shall cane you with greater severity, as you are chiefly to blame," said Mr. Quelch.

"Oh!"

"Bunter, you will bend over that chair!" Mr. Quelch picked up his cane. "Bend over immediately!"

"I—I say, sir, it—it wasn't me!" gasped Bunter. "I wasn't—I mean, I didn't—I—I—I mean, I—I never——"

"Bend over!"

"Oh crikey!"

Billy Bunter bent dismally over the chair.

Swipe!

"Yarooooh!"

"You may go, Bunter!"

Bunter bolted.

"Now," said Mr. Quelch grimly, "you first, Wharton——"

It was quite a painful scene. How the wheeze might have worked if Billy Bunter had been blessed with as large an allowance of common sense as an ordinary bunny rabbit, remained unknown. Certainly it had not worked!

Quelch, so far from being placated, looked absolutely implacable. He had given Bunter one swipe! He gave the Famous Five three each! He put quite a lot of beef into them! The juniors could only wonder, dismally, where an elderly sportsman like Quelch packed all the muscle.

A little breathless after his exertions, Mr. Quelch pointed to the door with his cane. Five suffering juniors wriggled away.

They wriggled down the passage.

In the Remove Form Room that afternoon, half a dozen juniors sat very uncomfortably on the forms. In a wriggling, painful state, they were not thinking much of the valuable instruction Mr. Quelch was handing out. They were thinking still less of rescuing Poker Pike from the order of the boot! The career of the Famous Five as public benefactors had been cut short suddenly.

THE TWELFTH CHAPTER.

Cinched!

"YOU—are—not—gone!"

Mr. Quelch seemed to bite off the words, one by one, as he stopped to address the hickory-faced man sitting in the sunset by Gosling's lodge.

Mr. Quelch, in hat and coat, was going out. He had to pass Poker Pike as he went; and his natural impulse was to pass him with calm, unseeing disdain. But he paused to speak.

The state of affairs was extraordinary. It was intolerable. Ordered to quit, Pike had not quitted. That day he was to have gone—and he had not gone! True, the Head had not specified exactly at what time of day he was to go! But the day was drawing to its close, and he showed no sign whatever of vacating his quarters at Greyfriars School.

Excitement on the subject was growing keener. Dozens of fellows came along, from time to time, to give Poker the once-over. Generally, he was to be seen, either walking in the quad, or sitting on Gosling's bench. If he was out of sight for ten minutes, a wild rumour spread that he was gone. But he always turned up again.

His hard-boiled face was expressionless as he met Mr. Quelch's glittering glance. Every other guy at Greyfriars might be excited, but Poker was as calm as usual. It might almost have been supposed that he had forgotten that the Head had given him notice to quit.

He shook his head and his bowler hat in reply to Mr. Quelch's question. Really, it hardly needed an answer, as Pike was there, under Quelch's eyes. And the gunman was a man of few words.

"Are you going?" breathed Mr. Quelch.

Another shake of the bullet head and the bowler hat!

Quelch breathed hard and deep. He had a secret misgiving that the Head would have been willing to make wide, very wide allowances, for the gunman guard of the millionaire's son.

And he wondered, with bitter anger, whether the Head might possibly let the matter slide—might let this unspeakable, lawless person, remain. The mere thought was intensely irritating to Mr. Quelch. If the Head showed signs of any such weakness, Quelch was the man to keep him up to the mark!

"Will you answer me, sir?" rapped Mr. Quelch, not satisfied with head-shakes.

"Sure!" said Poker.

"Are you leaving?"

"Nope!"

"You have received instructions—orders——"

"I got to keep tabs on that Putnam van Duck!" said Poker simply. "I'm sure powerful sorry to get that old schoolmaster duck's goat! Surest thing you know. But I ain't vamoosing the ranch none."

"I am going now to Courtfield," said Mr. Quelch; "unless you are gone when I return, force will be used!"

"Forget it, big boy!" answered Poker. "I guess that don't cut no ice with this baby! Mebbe you'd like to put in a word with the schoolmaster guy."

"What?"

"I sure do hate to get his goat," explained Poker. "I respect that old guy a whole lot. Mebbe if you chewed the rag with him a piece, and put it to him square, he'd get another guess."

Mr. Quelch gazed at the gunman. Poker, in the cheerful simplicity of his heart, was suggesting to Mr. Quelch to make his peace with the Head!

The Remove master did not answer. Words could not have expressed his feelings. He turned away with compressed lips, and walked out of the gates.

Several Greyfriars fellows, who were out of gates after class, glanced at him in the road. It was not Mr. Quelch's custom to walk along a public road with Jove-like thunder on his brow. On the present occasion, he was doing so. He was so deeply incensed, that he quite forgot his usual careful regard for appearances.

"I'll say the guy's got his mad up!" whispered Putnam van Duck, who was there with the Famous Five.

Putnam certainly did not intend his remark to reach his Form-master's ears. The juniors were on the other side of the road, and the boy from Chicago only whispered, but Mr. Quelch seemed to be endowed with almost superhuman keenness of hearing that afternoon. He spun round towards the Removites.

"Van Duck," he rapped, "what did you say?"

Putnam jumped.

"Oh great snakes!" he ejaculated.

"What! You said nothing of the sort!" exclaimed Mr. Quelch, apparently taking that as an answer to his question. "You made a disrespectful remark, Van Duck."

"I—I—I guess——" stammered the American junior.

Mr. Quelch pointed to the gateway.

"Go in at once! Remain within gates! You other boys will also go in! You are gated!"

"But, sir——" exclaimed Harry Wharton. Putnam had—unintentionally—asked for it, but the other fellows had said nothing. Evidently Quelch was not in a mood of sweet reasonableness.

"Silence, Wharton!" he rapped.

"But, sir——" began Bob Cherry.

"Go in immediately, all of you!"

With deep feelings the six juniors went in at the gates. Mr. Quelch watched them grimly till they had gone in, then he walked away with his long strides by the road over the common.

Courtfield common looked very green and pleasant under the May sunset, but the beauties of Nature were entirely lost on Mr. Quelch in his present angry and bitter mood.

He did not notice the red-and-purple glow of the sunset, he did not notice the green of the grass, or the glimmer of the foliage in the trees, neither did he notice other pedestrians on the road; he was quite wrapped up in his own incensed reflections.

He remained, therefore, in complete ignorance of the fact that a clean-shaven man with very keen eyes, loafing among the furze by the wayside, stepped into the road and walked after him.

Even had Quelch looked round, he would not have taken any particular notice of that clean-shaven man. He had never seen Tug Keary before, but Tug had seen him. Tug had been keeping "tabs" on the school for some days, watching comings and goings. Now he was strolling behind Mr. Quelch on the road across the common, which grew rather lonely at a distance from Friardale and the school.

Unaware of the fact that he was shadowed, Mr. Quelch walked rapidly on. He was half-way to Courtfield when he heard a shrill, prolonged whistle behind him.

He gave it no heed.

But a man in horn-rimmed glasses who was smoking a cigarette in a clump of trees off the road heeded it. As soon as he heard that whistle Bud Parker sat up and took notice, as it were.

Mr. Quelch, walking on his way regardless, noticed a man in horn-rimmed glasses step into the road ahead of him, but as he had never seen the man before he gave him no special attention.

The horn-rimmed man, however, gave Mr. Quelch some. He stepped into the Form-master's way, and Mr. Quelch paused to avoid walking into him.

"Excuse me, sir," said the horn-rimmed man politely, "mebbe I'm speaking to Mr. Quelch?"

"That is my name," said the Remove master curtly.

"I reckoned so," agreed the horn-rimmed man. "I'll say you're young Putnam van Duck's schoolmaster at Greyfriars."

Mr. Quelch looked at him hard. He noticed that the man spoke with a nasal twang, and did not need telling that he was an American. He could hardly suppose that one of the kidnapping gang had the audacity to address him on a public highway in broad daylight: but he was a little startled, though not at all alarmed. Quelch was not a man easily alarmed.

"I fail to see how that can concern you, a stranger to me," he answered stiffly. "And I have no time to waste."

"But it's so, ain't it?" asked the horn-rimmed man.

"I decline to be questioned, sir," answered Mr. Quelch. "Kindly allow me to pass."

He was aware of a sound of running feet on the road behind him, but he did not connect that sound with himself or his interlocutor. Tug was coming on at a run.

Bud Parker did not allow Mr. Quelch to pass; as the Remove master moved to go round him Bud shifted to block his way again.

Mr. Quelch's eyes gleamed. He was growing very angry, and he realised by this time that the man was a suspicious character. He slipped his walking-stick down from under his arm and took a business-like grip on it.

"Will you allow me to pass?" he rapped.

"I guess I want to chew the rag with you a piece, sir, if you got a few minutes——"

"I have no time whatever to waste, and I decline to converse with a stranger!" snapped Mr. Quelch. "Stand aside, sir!"

"Guess again!" said Mr. Parker.

"What?"

"I'll say you got another guess coming!" said the horn-rimmed man.

Setting his lips, Mr. Quelch walked straight at the man; he gripped his stick, prepared to use it if necessary. His war-like look seemed to daunt Mr. Parker, who backed quickly away, though still keeping in front of the Remove master and barring his progress.

Quelch marched on—and Bud Parker retreated before him, backing. It was the expression on Bud's face that drew Mr. Quelch's attention to the pattering footsteps behind him, now close at hand. He turned his head quickly.

Tug was almost upon him; as Mr. Quelch turned Tug leaped.

He staggered the next moment, with a fearful yell, as Quelch with startling swiftness landed out with the walking-stick. It was a hefty swipe, and it damaged Tug. He yelled and stumbled.

But at the same moment Bud Parker weighed in. Mr. Quelch's back was to him for the moment, and Bud leaped at it. An arm was thrown round the Form-master's neck from behind and he was dragged over in the road.

"Pronto, Tug!" panted Bud Parker.

Tug grasped the Remove master the next moment. The stick was wrenched from his hand and flung away. In the grasp of the two gangsters Mr. Quelch crumpled on the dusty road.

"Rascals!" he panted. "Scoundrels! Help!"

"Pack it up, you old gink you!" growled Tug savagely.

"Quick, you geek!" hissed Bud Parker.

In the grasp of the two gangsters the struggling Form-master was dragged off the road. Headlong, hardly knowing whether he was on his head or his heels, he was dragged into the clump of trees from which Bud Parker had emerged at the signal whistle of his confederate.

In the midst of that clump the breathless, panting Form-master was pinned down under Tug's knee. Bud lingered behind, glancing swiftly up and down the road and across the common, fearful that the scene, brief as it had been, might have been witnessed. But there was no one at hand, and the horn-rimmed man followed his confederate into the thick clump of trees, where they were screened from passing eyes.

Mr. Quelch—breathless, amazed, indignant, stuttering with wrath—still struggled feebly. But his struggles ceased as a cord was knotted round wrists and ankles and a gag was thrust into his mouth. Like a man in the grip of a horrid nightmare, he lay dazed and dizzy—and the voice of the horn-rimmed man came to his dizzy ears.

"Beat it, Tug! Get Chick and put him wise that we've got the schoolmaster. Burn the wind, you!"

"You said it, Bud!"

Tug disappeared. Mr. Quelch, hardly believing that this amazing happening was real, lay in the grass, wriggling feebly, watched over by the man in the horn-rimmed glasses.

THE THIRTEENTH CHAPTER.

Losing Poker!

PUTNAM VAN DUCK glanced out of the school gates.

Greyfriars fellows were to be seen here and there, but the tall, angular figure of the Remove master had disappeared in the direction of distant Courtfield. The American junior turned back and rejoined the Famous Five.

He gave no heed to the gunman seated impassive on the bench by Gosling's lodge, but Poker Pike was watching him; his eyes had been on Putnam in the road before Mr. Quelch ordered the juniors to go in. So long as Putnam remained in sight Poker remained where he was, but if the millionaire's son started to walk away Poker was ready to get into action at once—treading on his tail, as Putnam called it, wherever he went.

"Coast's clear, you guys!" said Putnam. "I guess that pesky old piecan has beat it."

"We're gated," said Bob Cherry.

"I guess that cuts no ice. You guys coming?"

The Famous Five paused. They were not feeling pleased at being "gated" for nothing at all. Still, orders were orders, and authority was authority.

Harry Wharton shook his head.

"It's rather thick," he said, "but we'd better stick in. We can get some cricket, instead of going for a walk, old bean."

"Guess again," said Van Duck.

"My dear chap," said Johnny Bull, "Quelch is shirty, and it can't be helped! We can get a walk on Courtfield Common any day. Chuck it!"

"Any day won't do, I guess," answered Van Duck. "I'll say it's now or never." He lowered his voice, though Poker Pike was not within hearing of the group. "You guys heard what Quelchy said to Poker. He's got his mad up. Poker's got to go—and he won't go! I got a stunt."

"Oh!" said Harry.

The Famous Five eyed Van Duck rather dubiously. Their own "stunt" for solving that difficulty had turned out a ghastly frost. They were still feeling twinges from the result.

"Wash it out!" said Johnny Bull. "I'm fed-up!"

"The fedfulness is terrific!" remarked Hurree Jamset Ram Singh, with a shake of his dusky head.

"Aw, pack it up, and let a guy spill a syllable or two!" said Putnam. "I sure don't want a rookus here. Poker's

(*Continued on next page.*)

GREYFRIARS INTERVIEWS

Once more our long-haired poet breaks into verse. This week he brings before your notice

HAROLD SKINNER,

the cad of the Remove.

(1)

If you ever want to shine
In the rotten rascal line,
Or to try your hand at posing as a blade,
You will find that Harold Skinner
Has a method that's a winner,
It's a pastime he has very often played.
You must learn to smoke and bet,
For a furtive cigarette
Is a very special sign that you're a man!
You must wander out at night
Though your kneeses knock with fright,
It's essential to the "sporting fellow's" plan!

(2)

You may call a chap a funk,
But be sure to do a bunk
If he shows an inclination for a scrap!
You'll employ your leisure time
In the heights of bliss sublime—
In a corner of the box-room, playing nap!
Don't care twopence for the Head,
Though you tremble and go red
Every time you feel in danger from the cane,
If you drink and bet and smoke,
You'll be always stony-broke,
But at any rate you won't have lived in vain!

(3)

When a fellow stoops to folly
It is always melancholy,
As the poet says, and really it is sad
That such poor delights as these
Have continual power to please
Harold Skinner, for he's quite a clever lad.
At his work he can be smart,
He has quite a turn for art,
He can act, as even Wibley will agree,
He can write and versify,
Though not quite so good as I,
(Or should it be not quite so good as me?)

(4)

Well, I sought him everywhere
Till I tried the box-room—there
I discovered him at last with Snoop and Stott.
Skinner said: "Come in, old chap!
Come and take a hand at Nap!"
But I only stared and answered: "Well, great Scott!"
There was reason in my cry,
And I'm going to tell you why
I was puzzled and surprised at what I saw.
It was not the dingy three
Or their cards which staggered me,
It was not the smokes they feebly tried to draw.

(5)

Three large trunks were open wide
With the lids back, and inside
They were empty,—or I should say, they were not!
For I saw those shady funks
Calmly sitting in the trunks,
There was one trunk each for Skinner, Snoop and Stott!
And between them, in its place,
Was an empty packing-case
As a table for the cards to rest upon.
"What's the big idea?" I cried.
"Have a smoke!" the cad replied.
"Take one now; in half-a-minute they'll be gone!"

(6)

Then I coughed instead of spoke
(For the air was thick with smoke),
"It is easier sitting on the trunks than in.
Are you potty then, or what?"
At which Skinner winked at Stott,
And the "sports" surveyed my features with a grin.
Then I heard a step outside.
"That's the Quelchy-bird!" I cried.
And said Skinner: "Yes, it's just as I had feared!"
Then they each ducked out of sight,
Closed the lids upon them tight,
And in half-a-tick they'd all three disappeared!

(7)

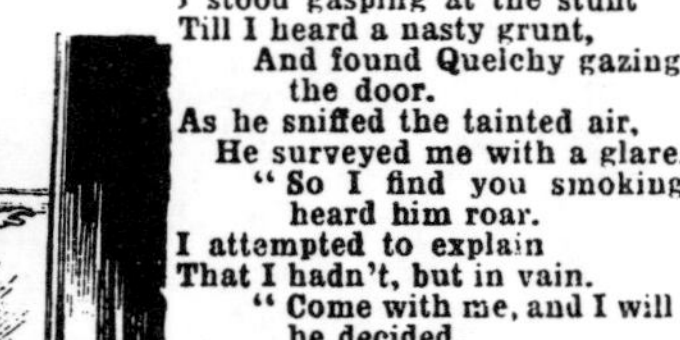

I stood gasping at the stunt
Till I heard a nasty grunt,
And found Quelchy gazing at me from the door.
As he sniffed the tainted air,
He surveyed me with a glare.
"So I find you smoking here!" I heard him roar.
I attempted to explain
That I hadn't, but in vain.
"Come with me, and I will cane you!" he decided.
But I locked each trunk before
I went with him, and what's more,
When I let them out they each got worse than I did!

an obstinate guy, and if he allows he won't beat it, he won't, and that's a cinch! If it came to gun-play——"

"Gun-play!" gasped Nugent.

"I guess Poker might forget that they don't handle guns in this country, if guys started in to boot him," said Putnam.

"Oh crikey!"

"Well, I got a stunt," said Putnam. "I guess it might be a winner. Poker won't absquatulate—you can bank on that! What's the big king-pin going to do, if he don't? Well, I reckon if we could take Poker out and lose him, that would make it O.K.—what?"

"He wouldn't be easy to lose," grinned Bob.

"S'pose I start on a leetle pasear with you guys—what's Poker going to do?" said Putnam. "Tread on my tail, as usual. Well, we lead him hoofing it a few miles, and then dodge him—drop him somewhere. I guess we can wangle it. What'll he do then? We get back without Poker being wise to it, I'll say he'll go on hunting for this baby."

"Surest thing you know," grinned Bob.

"And when he chucks it and hikes back, he finds the place all shut up, bolted and barred," said Putnam. "He won't be able to get in. It's outside for Poker, and without a row. How's that for high?"

"Not a bad wheeze," said Harry Wharton, laughing. "Goodness knows what's going to happen if he's still here when Quelch comes in! Quelch meant every word he said."

"So did Poker, I guess."

"We're gated!" said Harry. "But——" He glanced round at his chums. There was a general nod.

"Let's," said Nugent.

And the Famous Five and Putnam van Duck walked out of the gateway. Only Mr. Quelch knew that they were "gater," and Mr. Quelch was gone. They walked out, and took the road to Courtfield.

Looking back, a minute or two later, they beheld a hickory face under a bowler hat. Orders from the Head had no more effect on Poker Pike than water on a duck; but Putnam, starting for a walk, detached him promptly from his bench. The gunman swung along the road after the juniors.

They grinned as they walked on. Never once, since he had been at the school, had Putnam been able to get out of gates without the watchful Poker shadowing him, and only once had he been stopped—on the occasion of the Form walk, when he had been left behind, hopping. Gunman as he was, gangster as he had been, Poker was a faithful and dutiful guy.

Where the juniors were going, he had no idea; but he knew that wherever they went, he was going also, so long as Putnam was with them. A dozen yards behind the party he kept watch. Wary as he was, however, it was certain that Poker had no suspicion that the millionaire's son was taking him for a walk to "lose" him.

The juniors reached the corner of the common, and turned off into Oak Lane, which led past Popper Court to the river. They did not care to keep on across the common by the road, as that was the direction taken by Mr. Quelch. They did not want to risk meeting the view of the Form-master who had "gated" them, and supposed that they had remained obediently within gates.

They strolled cheerily along the shady lane till they were half a mile from the high road. At that distance the open spaces of the common were out of sight of anyone on the road. So at that point the Removites turned from the lane, and walked on to the green common.

After them walked Poker Pike.

It was quite a pleasant walk, and the juniors would have been glad to put in a good many miles, but for the fact that they had to get back to the school in time for calling-over. Once having "lost" Poker on the wide spaces of the common, however, a swift trot homeward by way of the towpath along the Sark, would land them at Greyfriars in time for roll.

"Here's the place," said Bob Cherry.

They reached the pond in the middle of Courtfield Common. Round it grew trees and bushes and bracken.

Grinning, the juniors disappeared into the thickets.

They heard a patter of feet behind them.

So long as they were in sight in the open, Poker Pike was content to keep his distance. But when they disappeared from view he put on speed at once. Poker would not have been surprised if the kidnappers had been lurking in those very thickets round the pond. Poker saw kidnappers everywhere.

Once out of the gunman's sight, however, the juniors acted swiftly. Instead of keeping on, they clambered into the branches of a beech.

They were deep in cover of the thick branches when Poker came trotting through the thickets below.

Through the foliage they had a glimpse of his bowler hat as he passed. He trotted on.

The juniors suppressed their chuckles.

Poker, quite unaware that their intention was to lose him, had not the slightest suspicion that they had taken to the branches. He figured that they had gone through the thickets, and continued on their way beyond.

Keeping silent, they listened. In a few minutes there was a sound of a calling voice.

"Say you Putnam van Duck!" shouted Poker. "Say, what's got you? You pesky young gink, you hear me toot? Say, what's come to you, you ornery young piecan?"

The juniors grinned in cheery silence.

Poker evidently was puzzled.

Beyond the thickets the common stretched before him, glowing in the May sunset. He saw nothing of the juniors there. But they might have dipped into any of a dozen hollows, or passed beyond any of the clumps of trees, or fringes of hawthorns. Puzzled and perplexed, the gunman strode on at last, searching for them.

"Gone!" murmured Bob Cherry, as he glimpsed a bowler hat from the beech beyond the edge of the thickets.

"The gonefulness is terrific!" grinned the Nabob of Bhanipur.

From the high tree the Removites watched for some time, while the bowler hat remained in sight. Poker Pike was trotting to and fro, quartering the ground like a hunting dog in search of the vanished schoolboys. He found no trace of them, and the black bowler disappeared at last across the common.

"I guess," remarked Putnam van Duck, "that we've sure lost that guy."

"Looks like it," said Harry Wharton, laughing.

It was clear that Poker had no idea of turning back. He was going on hunting for the juniors. No doubt it would dawn on him, sooner or later, that they had been deliberately pulling his leg; that they had dodged him somehow, and cut back to the school. Then, no doubt, Poker would hoof it back to Greyfriars—by that time, however, to find the school shut up for the night, and no admission for a gunman who had been ordered to quit.

The juniors slipped down from the beech, and cut off at a trot towards the river—the direction opposite from that taken by Poker Pike. They chuckled as they went. The wary gunman had fallen right into the trap, and the problem was solved. Whatever might have come of Poker's defiance of the Head's order to quit, it would not happen now.

Quickly the juniors trotted home, by way of the towpath. They reached the school in good time before Gosling came down to lock the gates. They strolled cheerily in to calling-over. Billy Bunter met them as they came in.

"I say, you fellows, heard?" asked Bunter.

"What and which?" asked Bob.

"He's gone."

"Who's gone?"

"That beastly gunman!" said Bunter, grinning. "I fancied it was all gas, you know. I jolly well knew he'd have to go! Well, he's gone!"

"Ha, ha, ha!"

"Blessed if I see anything to cackle at!" grunted the fat Owl. "I can tell you he's jolly well gone! You can believe me or not, but he's jolly well cleared. I knew he would, of course. You fellows didn't, but I did."

"What a lot Bunter knows," remarked Bob Cherry.

"The knowfulness is terrific!"

"Well, you'll find I'm right," declared Bunter.

And undoubtedly Bunter was right. Poker was gone. While Mr. Prout called the roll in Hall, and Harry Wharton & Co. answered to their names, Poker was still searching the wide expanses of Courtfield Common for them. And they wondered how long he would keep it up before he came back to Greyfriars, to find himself locked out of the school.

THE FOURTEENTH CHAPTER.

Third Degree?

MR. QUELCH blinked, in the midst of the tree-clump. The sunset was still red on the open common, but under the branches, in the clump of beeches and ashes, it was growing dim

The Remove master was still in a dazed and dizzy state of mind, hardly able to believe that he was not dreaming this awful occurrence

But it was no dream; it was only too terribly real! He lay in the grass under the shadowy trees, bound hand and foot, with a gag in his mouth. Near him was a horn-rimmed man, watching and listening

He was in the hands of the Chicago kidnappers—Mr. Quelch knew that; why, he could not begin to guess.

That the gang were watching the school for a chance to kidnap Putnam van Duck was pretty well known. But why they should have "cinched" Van Duck's Form-master was an insoluble mystery to Mr. Quelch.

Putnam, in the hands of the gangsters would have been worth half a million dollars to Chick Chew. Putnam's Form-master was worth nothing. But there he was—tied up like a turkey—waiting for the arrival of the leader of the kidnapping gang.

The sound of a car on the road came to Mr. Quelch's ears. He gave it no heed. A dozen times, at least, he had heard cars pass; the road was hardly more than twenty yards from the spot where he lay. But he was quite out of sight, and he could make no sound. There was no chance of help. He was in the hands of the gangsters till they chose to let him go.

This time, however, the buzz of the car stopped quite close at hand. Then came a brushing in the underwoods among the trees. Mr. Quelch realised that Chick had come.

It was Chick Chew! Leaving the car by the roadside, the fat gangster followed Tug into the clump of trees.

"You got him here?"

Mr. Quelch heard the voice. He had heard it only once before—in the old priory in Friardale Wood—but he knew the unmusical tones of Mr. Chew.

"Yep," answered Tug, "and Bud keeping tabs on him, Chick."

"O.K., Chick!" grinned the horn-rimmed man, as the fat gangster loomed up in the shadows.

"I should smile!" remarked Chick.

Mr. Quelch's eyes glittered up at him. If the Remove master was alarmed, his face did not betray it. All that was indicated in his face was a deep and intense anger.

"Stick him up!" said Mr. Chew.

Bud and Tug grasped the Remove master, lifted him from the grass, and backed him against a tree. At a sign from Chick, the gag was taken from his mouth.

"You don't want to yaup, feller!" remarked Chick. "I guess as soon's you yell, you get a tap on the cabeza that will keep you quiet!"

Mr. Quelch gasped for breath.

"Scoundrel!" he panted.

"I'll say you can cut that out!" said Mr. Chew. "I got you, bo, and I'm doing the talking! I'll tell a man, you're a mighty handy guy with a stick when you got your fins loose, and I'll mention that I got a lump on my cabeza as big as a turkey's egg, and then some! But you ain't cavorting around with a club jest now! Nope!"

"Rascal!"

"Don't spill any more! Leave it to me to chew the rag!"

"If this," gasped Mr. Quelch, "is an act of revenge, I warn you that there is a law in this country to deal with ruffianly rascals such as you!"

"Guess again!" said Chick. "You sure did land me a few sockdolagers with that stick of yourn, feller! But I ain't got no kick coming on that account. I sure wouldn't waste no time on you if that was the whole packet."

"Then what does this outrage mean?" exclaimed Mr. Quelch.

"You're going to be useful!" explained Mr. Chew. "That's where you come in, feller! I got to get a cinch on Putnam van Duck. You're his schoolmaster, and I guess that baby jumps to your orders, some!"

Mr. Quelch could only stare at him.

"You get me?" asked Chick. "I been after that bird, and I ain't got him. It sure ain't no easy proposition, him parked in a big school, and a gunman of Poker Pike's heft keeping tabs on him. Night I horned in, there was Poker loosing off lead, and I guess I had to beat it. I'd have had him sure, Toosday, but you put it across me with that stick of yourn. I ain't got him yet. But if you'd ever heard guys in Chicago talk about Kidnapper No. 1 of the United States, I guess you'd be wise to it that Chick Chew never gets left! You're going to help me cinch that young guy!"

"What?" gasped Mr. Quelch.

"That's why!" said Chick. "You seeing light, bo? I'll say we ain't cinched you because we like the colour of your hair! Nope! You being that young gink's schoolmaster, I guess he will hop when you say hop—what?"

"I fail to understand you! Certainly Van Duck will obey my orders, if that is what you mean."

"S'pose you write him a note, telling him you want him?" said Mr. Chew. "He sure will mosey where you tell him."

"I—I presume so. But——"

"That's the lay-out," explained Chick, with a nod. "That's why we got you, feller! You write a note to that young geck——"

"I shall do nothing of the kind!"

"You put it that you've seen the inspector of perlice at Courtfield, who wants to see him particular about this kidnapping business——"

"Nothing of the kind!"

"You're waiting at the police station for him," pursued Chick, utterly disregarding the Remove master's interruptions, "and you send that note by a taximan—him to come in the taxi."

"Never!"

(Continued on next page.)

"I guess he knows your fist all right, you being his schoolmaster——"

"Certainly! But I will never——"

"And a note from his schoolmaster, telling him to hump along to the police station, won't make nobody smell no mouse," said Chick. And Bud and Tug nodded and grinned. "Jest an ordinary taxi—all above-board!" Mr. Chew chuckled. "I'll say that young guy will start pronto for the police station, though I allow he won't get so fur."

Mr. Quelch gazed at the gangster in wrath and horror.

He understood now why he had been seized.

The scheme was one, indeed, that could not possibly fail if the Remove master did his part.

The local police had the kidnapping matter in hand. There would be nothing surprising in Inspector Grimes, at Courtfield, wanting to see the American junior on the subject. In any case, the boy had to obey instructions written by his Form-master, whom he would believe to be with the inspector, waiting for him to arrive at the police station.

That note was to be sent by a taximan from the rank at Courtfield. There would be nothing suspicious in the taxi or the driver—as likely as not, a man known by sight at the school.

The taxi-driver would know nothing, except that he was dispatched with a note to Greyfriars School

Putnam van Duck, it was absolutely certain, would step into that taxi, and would believe, as the taxi-driver would believe, that he was being driven to Courtfield Police Station

But on the lonely road across the common, lonelier than ever at the fall of dusk, three gangsters would be waiting for the taxi.

To hold up the taxi, knock the driver on the head if he offered resistance, and transfer the millionaire's son to a waiting car would be easy enough.

In horror and indignation, Mr. Quelch saw the whole scheme—saw that it could not fail, if that note was written and sent to Greyfriars. At the same time, he wondered that even a hardened and desperate crook could believe for one moment that a schoolmaster would, or could, lend assistance in kidnapping a boy under his charge.

He did not realise yet the methods Chick Chew was prepared to use to overcome the resistance he expected.

"You get me?" asked Chick, after giving the Greyfriars master a minute or two to get it down.

"I understand you," said Mr. Quelch, his voice trembling with anger, "but I fail to understand your folly, your crass stupidity, in fancying for one moment that I would lend myself to such a scheme!"

"Schoolmasters," said Chick, "ain't rich, as a rule. Any good offering you a pocketful of dollars?"

"Scoundrel!" gasped Mr Quelch.

"That don't cut no ice, Chick, with a guy of that heft!" said Bud Parker.

"You said it," agreed Chick "If that guy's asking for the third degree, I ain't the galoot to say nope! But I always was humane, and if that old piecan would click for a thousand dollars, I ain't mean."

"Rascal!" gasped Mr Quelch

Chick scanned his angry face A guy that could not be bought was, perhaps, something new in Mr Chew's experience. But he could see that this particular guy, at all events, was not to be bribed.

"I got a fountain-pen here, feller," he remarked. "We got it all cut and dried, ready for when we got a cinch on you. I better put you wise. You got to play up. You get third degree till you do! Get me?"

"Third degree!" stuttered Mr. Quelch.

"Jest that! If you'd ever been in the can at Chicago, with the cops trying to squeeze information out of you, you'd be wise to it! You're going to learn right now!"

Mr. Quelch gasped.

He had heard dimly of "third degree." He realised, though he could hardly believe, that he was to be put to the torture till he consented to play the gangster's game.

Chick Chew was a business man. He would not have taken the trouble to revenge that beating at the old priory. Revenge was not business, but in carrying out his plans he was absolutely ruthless.

Mr. Quelch understood now. The gangsters knew that neither threats nor bribery would be of the slightest use. They depended on third degree to gain their point. And it was evident that they depended on it with absolute confidence So far as Chick could see, it was simply a matter of time before the Remove master consented to do what was required of him. Probably, too, of a very short time.

"You getting down to brass tacks?" asked Chick.

"Villain!" gasped Mr. Quelch. "I am helpless in your lawless hands. Do your worst Not to save my life will I put pen to paper!"

"I'll say your life ain't in no danger, old-timer! But I guess you won't be able to use your arm ag'in for a month of Sundays if you keep us long at third degree," drawled Chick. "Stick that rag in his mouth, Tug. We sure don't want no publicity, and I'll say he'd yell a few if that trap of his wasn't corked."

The gag was packed into Mr. Quelch's mouth again.

Then, at a sign from Chick, Tug seized his left arm, and began, with perfect coolness, to twist it.

This was third degree!

The pain was excruciating. Slowly at first, then harder and harder the gangster twisted.

The perspiration started out on Mr. Quelch's forehead in great drops. He tried to cry out, but only a suffocated mumble came through the gag.

Chick and Bud watched him calmly. No doubt they had been through many such a scene before.

"Nod your cabeza when you're through!" said Chick. "Soon as you're ready to indite that leetle billy-do, jest give a nod. I'll sure wait."

Mr. Quelch made no sign.

He strove to struggle, but that was futile. His wrists were bound together. Tug's grip, like an iron vice, was on his elbow, twisting. It seemed to Mr. Quelch, as the pressure intensified, that the bone would crack. The pain was not merely terrible—it was intolerable, unendurable. It was more than human flesh and blood could stand.

Chick watched him coolly. He gave the hapless victim about a minute to surrender, but the Remove master made no sign.

Could he endure? He had to endure. He could not betray his trust. But as the torture intensified, Chick had no doubt that surrender was coming.

Was it coming? Mr. Quelch himself could hardly have told But with startling suddenness there came an interruption. There was a rustle in the trees, and as the gangsters spun round, the barrel of a six-gun glimmered in the dusk, and a sharp voice rapped:

"Stick 'em up, you'uns!"

THE FIFTEENTH CHAPTER.

"Hands Up!"

"STICK 'em up!" growled Poker Pike.

Poker's slits of eyes glittered over the levelled six-gun. His finger was on the trigger.

Bud Parker, his startled eyes almost bulging through his horn-rimmed glasses, shot up his hands above his head, almost before the words were out of Poker's mouth. Tug let go Mr. Quelch's elbow as suddenly as if Quelch's arm had become red-hot, and followed Bud's example with almost ludicrous swiftness

Chick Chew was the only man that hesitated His fat face purpled with rage. But his hesitation was brief, and it was well for the star kidnapper of the United States that it was brief. Up went the fat hands over the fat gangster's slouched hat.

The three gangsters stood, hands up. Poker was hardly six or seven feet from them, his gun swaying a little from side to side to cover all three. Chick rather prided himself on being "quick on the draw," but he had no chance to pull his automatic, and he knew it. Poker had what he would have called the "drop," and he would have loosed off lead without an instant's hesitation at a sign of gun-pulling. And only too well the Chicago gangsters were aware of it.

They obeyed like lambs!

"Keep 'em up!" drawled Poker.

Looking past the gangsters over the gun, he stared at Henry Samuel Quelch.

The Form-master, helpless in his bonds, leaned sagging against the tree. His face was white. His brain almost swam.

The sudden cessation of third degree made Mr. Quelch giddy with the relief. Poker Pike's voice was not musical, but the music of the spheres could not have sounded so melodious in the ears of the Remove master as Poker's metallic tones when he rapped out "Stick 'em up!" Poker was not handsome to look at, but never had so glad a sight dawned upon Mr. Quelch's vision as that of the hickory face under the bowler hat.

Poker's sudden appearance was a surprise to the gangsters, and certainly a surprise to Mr Quelch. And Quelch was a surprise to Poker!

Certainly he was not looking for Quelch, or thinking of him. He was looking for Putnam van Duck.

He had been looking for him ever since the playful Removites had "lost" the gunman on Courtfield Common. It was dawning on Poker's rather solid brain, by that time, that the juniors had pulled his leg, dodged him, and cut back to the school by unseen paths. But he was not sure, and he was going to keep on the search till dark. As like as not, Poker figured, young Putnam had fallen in with watchful kidnappers, and when from a distant knoll he spotted a fat figure getting out of a car on the road over the common, Poker had no doubt of it.

Poker had horned in, nothing doubting that the gangsters had Putnam van Duck in that clump of trees.

Now he saw that they hadn't. They had Putnam's schoolmaster, which was quite a surprise to Poker.

Surprise, however, did not make the Greyfriars gunman less wary. He looked at Mr Quelch, but he watched the gangsters like a cat at the same time. Any guy there who had reached for a gun would have "got his" sudden, as Poker would have put it.

They did not reach for guns. They stood with their hands up, gritting their teeth with rage.

"Villain!" gasped Mr. Quelch. "Not to save my life will I do what you require!" The perspiration started out on the Form-master's forehead, in great drops, as Tug twisted his arm. Suddenly there was a rustle in the trees; and as the gangsters spun round, the barrel of a six-gun glimmered in the dusk, and a sharp voice rapped: "Stick 'em up, you'uns!" Poker Pike had come to the Form-master's rescue!

Mr. Quelch gave Poker an eloquent look. He could not speak, but his look was eloquence itself.

"The schoolmaster guy!" said Poker. "By the great horned toad! Say, you, Chick, what's this game?"

Chick ground his teeth without replying.

"You got him dumb!" said Poker. "You, Tug, let him loose! See you don't play no monkey-tricks while you're doing it, or I'm mentioning you won't play no more on this side of Jordan! Surest thing you know!"

Tug silently stepped to Mr. Quelch. In a couple of minutes the Remove master was freed from the bonds and the gag.

He gasped for breath.

"Now, what's this here game?" asked Poker casually. "I guess I got to keep tabs on that Putnam van Duck, but I ain't the guy to horn into any other galoot's funeral. Nope!"

"These wretches," gasped Mr. Quelch, "these—these lawless dastards—seized me, to force me to help them in kidnapping the boy Van Duck!"

Poker Pike nodded.

"I reckon I was guessing that was it!" he remarked. "And if that's the game, I'll say they ain't getting by with it none. You been giving this ole piecan third degree, Chick?"

Snarl from Chick.

"I'll remark it's a low-down game, Chick!" said Poker. "That old guy ain't no friend of mine, but I'll say I'm seeing him through this entertainment. You'uns want to beat it, keeping your fins over your hats. I guess I'm seeing you go, and I'll mention that if you don't keep on reaching for the sky you get yours so sudden it will make your heads swim."

Chick Chew drew a deep, deep breath. His little piggy eyes sparkled with rage from layers of fat. He had been right on success—at least, he believed so. The intervention of the Greyfriars gunman had put paid to his best scheme. He was tempted to risk everything and pull a gun.

Poker read it in his fierce glare, and his hickory face set like iron. Bud Parker gave a gasp.

"Forget it, Chick! That guy has sure got us! Say, we don't want no gun-play."

"Surest thing you know!" said Poker grimly.

Chick controlled his rage.

He backed away, his associates backing on either side of him out of the trees to the open roadside.

Poker followed them with levelled gun.

Mr. Quelch, panting for breath, and rubbing an aching arm, followed after Poker with tottering footsteps.

Back and back went the gangsters, still "clawing the air," till they reached the car at the side of the road. All three were armed; all three watching for a chance to "pull" if Poker gave them a chance. But the Greyfriars gunman, watchful as a cat, gave them none.

"Keep going!" drawled Poker as Chick, having reached the roadside, made a movement towards the waiting car. "I'll mention that you're hoofing it, you'uns! You ain't travelling in no auto!"

"I guess——" hissed Chick.

"Can it!" said the gunman briefly. "You want to hit the horizon, and hit it quick. I ain't giving you long to get out of range of this here hardware."

But Parker was already running. After him ran Tug. And after them both, breathing hard with rage, ran Chick.

Poker's levelled six-gun saw them off.

"Say, you schoolmaster guy!" drawled Poker. "You pack into that auto, pronto! Mister Chew's sure lending us that auto."

"Bless my soul!" gasped Mr. Quelch. "Certainly, the car should be handed over to the authorities——"

"That don't cut no ice. Pack in! You figure them guys won't come gunning back, soon's they figure they got a chance! You want to stop a bullet?"

"Oh!" gasped Mr. Quelch.

He tottered into the car.

Three figures, black against the sunset, were running. They dared not halt or turn under the levelled six-gun. But once beyond effective range, Poker did not need telling what Chick would be doing.

Poker packed his gun, dropped into the driving-seat, and started the engine. Its roar caused three running gangsters to halt and whirl round. And in the May sunset they had the pleasure—or otherwise—of seeing the car vanish at fifty m.p.h. in the direction of Greyfriars School.

THE SIXTEENTH CHAPTER.

O.K.!

"I SAY, you fellows!" squeaked Billy Bunter.

"That's the bell!" said Bob Cherry.

"I say, think he's come back?" gasped Bunter.

"Quelch is still out," said Frank Nugent. "Perhaps it's Quelch!"

"Quelch would come in at masters' gate, with his key, after lock-up," said Harry Wharton.

"I guess it's Pike," grinned Putnam van Duck, "and maybe he'll get tired of ringing that bell."

(*Continued on page 28.*)

CAPTAIN VENGEANCE!

By JOHN BREDON.

"Surrender or Sink!"

A FLOATING leviathan, the giant Australian luxury liner, Sylvia Bay, steamed calmly and steadily through the long, glassy swell of the Indian Ocean, a plume of feathery smoke streaming from her squat yellow funnels, white enamel of her superstructure chequered against her black, glistening hull and rows of gleaming ports, a break of snowy foam piling away from the thrust of her lofty bows.

Captain Cooper, her master, immaculate in white drill and gold-peaked cap, smiled comfortably to himself as he paced the lofty bridge. He was a man with vast responsibilities, with £100,000 in bullion on board, destined for the Central India Bank at Bombay, to say nothing of the lives and comfort of a thousand passengers and crew to occupy his thoughts. Yet he could well afford to smile, for he had never known a more peaceful and uneventful voyage in all his forty years' experience of the sea.

On the promenade deck, undisturbed by the sonorous drone and throb of titanic engines, were gay and carefree passengers, sunning themselves, lounging in deck-chairs, laughing and chatting, playing at quoits. In the luxurious smoking-room Australian millionaires puffed at their cigars, lolled in padded leathern armchairs as they perused the latest news bulletin served up by the vessel's radio.

The Sylvia Bay was a floating luxury hotel, the pride of the Australian shipping line to which she belonged.

Captain Cooper turned on a heel, surveying the sunlit, shimmering violet-hued seas with his keen eyes.

All around, the vast, dark-blue bowl of the Indian Ocean was empty to the skyline, excepting a point on their port bow, where a long, grey warship was surging along on a course that would presently bring her athwart the luxury liner's bows.

The captain gazed at her long and steadily through the lenses of his powerful binoculars.

The man-o'-war was heading along at a fast rate, foam streaming from her sharp steel cutwater as she ploughed along at a full thirty knots. A few men in uniform could be seen about her decks and gun-turrets, and high up in her control top might be caught the glint of gold braid in the sun. But from neither her masthead nor at the ensign staff astern did she show any flag.

Exhilarated by the sight, and admiring her grim, yet stately lines, the liner's passengers crowded to the bulwark rails, laughing, commenting, taking snapshots—little dreaming, any of them, of the sinister doom that lurked in the steel belt of armour-plating that caught the sunny ripples of the waves as she rode along.

On the bridge, Captain Cooper pursed his lips.

"Strange thing, Brast," he said to his first officer, as he lowered his glasses. "What ship may that be, I wonder? She carries no flag, and I can see no name. I wonder what nationality she is?"

First Officer Brast gazed keenly at the oncoming cruiser.

Her stern lifted high in the air, smoke and steam pouring through her hatches, as the Sylvia Bay wallowed for her last depth-dive!

"I've seen that packet somewhere before, sir," he answered, his tones slightly puzzled. "Ah, I have it! It's the Zermac, of the republic of Varland, in the Baltic. Yes, I saw her once at Singapore, when she was coaling, on her way to Nemesis Island."

Nemesis Island! The captain and his first officer glanced at one another a little oddly, but without speaking. Almost it seemed as if a cold, dank shadow, in spite of the blazing heat, was cast over them at the very mention of the worst and most dreaded penal settlement in the world.

"The cruiser Zermac," muttered Captain Cooper, after a pause. "But that's peculiar, Mr. Brast. Why doesn't she show the flag of the Varland navy? And what is she doing in this part of the Indian Ocean, if her destination is Nemesis Island, three hundred miles to the south?"

The captain hesitated, half-turning on his heel.

"I'll send her a wireless message," he announced to Mr. Brast. "I don't know what she can want with us, anyway."

He beckoned to the quartermaster on the bridge.

But the order he was about to give never left his lips. Even as he opened his mouth there came from the distance a sudden, echoing crash, as of thunder.

Both ship's officers wheeled round, exclamations of wonder and incredulity breaking from their lips.

A white cloud of smoke had puffed out from one of the twin eight-inch guns, mounted in the cruiser's fore-turret, a jet of flame, and then a shell came screaming over the Sylvia Bay's bows, to plunge sullenly, in a spout of foam, to starboard.

Captain Cooper staggered, as though he had been struck. His eyes bulged unbelievingly. It was as though he had been strolling along the secure and orderly streets of Melbourne or Sydney and a policeman had suddenly hit him in the face.

Like an echo that rolled and grew in volume, his cry of astonishment swept the length of the crowded promenade deck. Passengers gaped and choked. Deck-hands ceased their polishing of brass and stared seawards, petrified.

A strange cruiser had fired upon the British flag!

"What—what on earth—— Is this captain mad?" Dazedly Captain Cooper asked that question of space. "She's fired on us—a British vessel! An act of war! Thunderation, what's the matter with that devil cruiser?"

"Look!" exclaimed Brast, pointing. "She's signalling to us. A message!"

The black-and-white semaphore on the

fore-bridge of the cruiser was twitching and jerking intermittently, snapping out a signal across the gentle sea-swells.

As in a trance Captain Cooper spelled out the signalled message.

"Heave to! The next shot will be in your hull, under the water-line. Surrender or sink!"

"By the Lord Harry, there's a crew of escaped lunatics on board! There must be!" Frenziedly Captain Cooper beat his temples with a tightened fist. "Anyway, it's no use, Brast. We've got to chuck up the sponge. If they're mad enough to fire on British colours they must be mad enough for anything. By heavens, though, I'll learn the rights of this, and if there's any power left in the British Empire, the Varland Republic will soon be needing a new naval captain."

It needed one already, though neither Captain Cooper nor the Varland Republic was aware of that circumstance. As yet the world was in ignorance of the fact that Von Eimar, the world's master-spy, had headed a mutiny among the convicts, and had now set out in a captured cruiser on his career as a pirate—in the twentieth century!

With a gesture of despair, Captain Cooper rang down the engine-room telegraph to "Stop!" A bell clanged below, and obediently the giant twin engines of the Sylvia Bay sank to a pulsating murmur as she glided slowly to a standstill.

"I've Come for your Gold, Captain!"

VALIANTLY Captain Cooper bridled his anger and indignation as a swift motor-pinnace came speeding alongside the tall black hull of the Sylvia Bay.

But, as his gaze rested upon the ragged and motley clad rascals, burned almost black by the sun, who nursed guns and knives across their knees as the craft slid alongside, his wrath gave place to wonderment, mingled with a strange, sinking dread.

Was it possible? But no! It was absurd! Piracy in the twentieth century—he was a fool even to entertain the idea! Resolutely he braced himself to meet the stocky, square-built man with the monocle in one eye, and wearing a white naval uniform, who came swinging up the accommodation-ladder with the agility of a captain.

Behind this newcomer swarmed the strangest pack of men Captain Cooper had ever seen, all half-naked, in dingy cotton slacks, some with broad straw hats, and others with rags of gaudy handkerchiefs twined round their greasy, unkempt heads. Every scowling, low-browed ruffian carried a carbine and ammunition belt, with a pair of revolvers, and a knife or cutlass; and there was not one but had a felon brand with a number burned upon his shaggy brown chest.

Captain Cooper caught his breath. His first fears revived as that burly, white-clad figure sprang up the bridge-ladder to salute him with podgy hand uplifted to gilt-peaked cap; and, with widening eyes he saw that the brass jacket-buttons were crested with the skull and crossbones, with a silver death's head in the stranger's hat-badge.

Pale blue eyes, twinkling in a broad Teutonic countenance, rested mockingly upon his tanned and startled face.

"Good-day, captain!" said the monocled intruder, speaking with only the faintest tinge of a guttural accent. "I must apologise for this somewhat startling and unexpected meeting. Pray allow me to introduce myself. For the moment I travel under the somewhat melodramatic nom-de-guerre of 'Captain Vengeance,' and this"—he indicated the grim, grey cruiser that lay-to with all her guns trained upon the ocean liner—"is my ship, the Vengeance——"

Captain Cooper exploded with wrath.

"What in the name of dickens does this mean?" he bellowed, reddening with anger. "D'ye know what it means to fire on the British flag?"

Captain Vengeance, as he called himself, lifted a plump hand with a deprecatory smile.

"I think that will render explanations unnecessary," he remarked, pointing over the bridge wing.

The captain's eyes almost started from his head as he saw a limp, black mass creeping to the masthead of the cruiser. A puff of wind blew out its sable folds, and there, brazenly in the bright light of the sun, flaunted the death's head, the grinning white skull with the crossed thigh bones—Jolly Roger, unseen on the seas for over a hundred years!

The tensed silence that had held spellbound every sailor and passenger aboard the Sylvia Bay, now broke out in a babble of excited exclamations.

"Great George!" ejaculated Captain Cooper, even now unable to credit the astounding truth. "D'ye mean to tell me——"

"Precisely!" said Captain Vengeance, with a smile. "You will pardon the vanity that is one of my besetting weaknesses. I am a pirate, so why should I not adopt the flag of my calling? You will understand that I am here to relieve you of the consignment of gold that you have on board. Movements of ships and their cargoes are reported at Nemesis Island——"

"Nemesis Island!" Light at last dawned upon Captain Cooper's mind. "You—come from——"

"The penal colony—yes!" Gold-filled teeth flashed in Von Eimar's smiling countenance. "We mutinied, and captured this cruiser. Is the situation clear? Then I need not remind you, captain, of the inevitable consequences should you refuse to comply. You know the sort of men who are sent to Nemesis Island——"

Choking, Captain Cooper turned to his first officer.

"Give him the keys, Mr. Brast," he said, forcing the reluctant words between his teeth. "We can do nothing. This confounded pirate has our hands tied. But, by Heaven, man," he growled, springing upon Von Eimar, "Captain Vengeance, or whatever you call yourself, you'll pay for this! I warn you!"

"That will do!" Von Eimar snapped out the words, and Captain Cooper penned his fury as best he could, as two villainous-looking convicts stood on either side of him with drawn automatics. "Luis Ramiro," the pirate leader added, to the gaudy, swarthy Latin beside him, "go to the liner's radio cabin, and see to it that she cannot send out an S O S after we leave. Make atoms of it! You others, follow the officer here, and have out those cases of specie. Look sharp about it!"

Captain Cooper smothered an oath as he watched the convicts hoisting out the heavily clamped boxes of bullion with the rope-handles slung over their broad, bare shoulders, under the round and wondering eyes of the passengers on the promenade deck.

Smiling, Von Eimar lighted a fat cigar, and strolled casually to and fro on the bridge, beaming upon the serene blue heavens.

The Sinking of the Sylvia Bay!

KILLER MORAN, American ex-gangster, and Von Eimar's pirate lieutenant, growled noisily in his thick throat as he hung over the bridge-rail of the Vengeance.

His ugly little eyes narrowed as he watched the bustle on the near-by liner.

"Say, she's coughin' up the boodle, bo," he said to Ronald Westdale, the English gun-lieutenant, who was standing on the foredeck beneath him. "I'll shore allow thet Von Eimar is the prize-packet, an' then some. Yep, sir! Thar comes the boss right now. I guess thar're heavin' the dust into the mo'-boat instanta."

Silently the one-time lieutenant of the British Navy nodded, watching the pirate-convicts as they lowered the heavy, rope-handled cases into the bobbing motor-pinnace. Beside him, sitting miserably on the flap of an ammunition-hoist, was Roderick Drake, son of Morgan Drake, of the British Secret Service, Von Eimar's prisoner and hostage.

As they watched, the launch cast off, driving towards the waiting pirate cruiser, with Von Eimar in the stern-sheets.

"Hey!" exclaimed the American suddenly. He was gazing at a short slip of paper that the wireless-room orderly had just placed in his hand. "Gosh, if they ain't sending out a S O S! Tha weasels! Let the galoots have the works. Say, you Britisher down there, send 'em a shot through thar hull-plates!"

Ronald Westdale glanced up suddenly, lifting his brows.

"What's that, Moran? S O S? What rot! The chief's sure to have seen to it that the radio's put out of action."

The Yankee, however, was yelling out orders to the pirate gunners, orders couched in the hottest gangster slang, which were incomprehensible to most of them. The men on the fore-deck looked to Westdale for instructions, but he waved them back.

In the well-deck, however, a late master-gunner of the Varland navy, who understood the American's import, if not his actual words, sprang to one of the big six-inch guns on the port battery. Already the murderous weapon was trained upon the defenceless passenger liner. Squinting along the gun-sights, the man pressed a thumb upon the firing-push. A stunning explosion followed, and as the smoke drifted away one of the squat yellow smokestacks of the Sylvia Bay crumpled up in a ruin of smoky vapours, rent fragments, and smouldering chips of steel.

Terror reigned upon the great liner. Captain Cooper, white-faced as he clung to the bridge-rail, supposed it to be an act of pirate treachery as he swiftly gave orders for the lowering away of the boats. But, as it transpired later, it was a thoughtless passenger, possessing a portable radio set of his own, who had locked himself in his cabin and sent out that fateful S O S, without the captain's consent or even knowledge.

Ronald Westdale sprang up the ladder to the fore-bridge of the pirate cruiser. Killer Moran was leaning over the bridge-rail, bawling vehemently through a speaking-trumpet. Stripped to the waist, the gunners were already slipping a copper-cased six-inch shell into the oiled breech of the gun.

Grasping Moran by the shoulder, Ronald Westdale twirled the giant American round, knocking his gun from his hand.

"You murderous thug!" His

narrowed, grey eyes glared into the rage-distorted face of the Chicago gangster. "Who are you to give orders to the gunners? I'm the gunnery-lieutenant!"

The Killer snarled between broken, tobacco-stained teeth. His left hand snaked quickly towards a second gun holstered to his hips. Before he could draw it, however, Westdale's fist crashed upon his heavy, bulldog jaw, and down he slumped, resting huddled against a stanchion.

"Donner! What is this?" Agilely Von Eimar bounded up the ladder, his pinnace having run alongside just before the six-incher was fired. He thrust his burly form between Westdale and Moran, light-blue eyes snapping viciously "Who gave orders for that gun to be fired? Ach! Answer me, one of you!"

Contemptuously Westdale pointed to the cowering American, who blanched at the look in Von Eimar's narrowed eyes. Slowly the Killer's fingers clutched at the crumpled slip of paper that lay beside him, passing it up to the frowning pirate chief.

"So!" Von Eimar grunted as he read the S O S. "I warned him. He has defied me, the fool!" Abruptly he swung to the bridge-end, grasping the megaphone Moran had dropped. "Ahoy, Sylvia Bay! Lower away your boats. I'll give you ten minutes. After that I'll send you a torpedo to answer your S O S!"

"Captain! Von Eimar!" gasped Westdale. "You can't do that! It's murder!"

Savagely Von Eimar slewed round upon him, showing the crumpled radio message in his opened palm.

"You see that, Mr. Westdale? He ignored my warning. Very well! I shall teach them that Captain Vengeance is not to be trifled with!" To his crew he lustily shouted: "Forrard torpedo-tube, stand by!"

Westdale fell back, biting his lip, fists clenched, face white and set. He could do nothing.

Already the Sylvia Bay was swinging out her boats. Captain Cooper knew that the threat was no idle one.

"Forrard torpedo-tube, make ready to fire!"

With gold watch ready in a podgy palm, Von Eimar stood waiting. Under the directions of a Varlander torpedo-layer, the convicts were sliding a long grey projectile into the sinister cylinder.

Roy Drake attempted to vault up to the bridge Westdale, at the ladder-head, threw out a restraining arm to check him.

"Steady, chum!" said the ex-naval officer quietly. "You can do nothing. You'll only make matters worse for yourself"

Roy struggled desperately, but Westdale's grip was of iron.

Von Eimar snapped his watch-case shut, and fobbed it.

"Forrard torpedo-tube, fire!" he ordered.

Like a silver fish the long steel harbinger of death flashed from the tube. It furrowed through the placid slides and ripples of water, heading for the tall black side of the doomed liner.

Crash!

A stricken leviathan, the Sylvia Bay staggered, then listed steeply to port. Cries of terror rose from her banking decks. Most of the boats had already been lowered, but some were still left. Smoke was pouring from her shattered funnels She was settling rapidly, her keel-plates breached in a tremendous gap, and exultantly the waters roared in through her shattered sides.

"That's settled her business!" growled Von Eimar, shutting his binoculars with a snap. One huge stride he took to the engine-room telegraph, and rang down "Full speed." "Let her rip, Lebedoff!" he snapped, unplugging the voice-pipe that communicated to the Russian engineer. "Get every ounce of steam out of her boilers that you can! That S O S has put a spoke in my plans. We've got to put a hundred miles between us and this spot before nightfall—before all the warships in these seas come hounding in our wake!"

Plugging the speaking-tube, he turned to fling a final glance at the sinking Sylvia Bay. Her stern was lifted high in the air, smoke and steam pouring through her hatches as she wallowed for her last depth-dive. Around, the sea was littered with lifeboats, fragments of wreckage, bobbing heads, and hastily improvised rafts, while seamen still leaped from her careened decks to flounder struggling in the warm seas. Most of the passengers and crew had got off in barely sufficient time, and the sea was smooth; but the death-roll must have been heavy, nevertheless.

From the scene of the tragedy Von Eimar focused his gaze upon the bridge-ladder, to see Roy Drake clinging to the steel rungs and struggling in the grasp of Ronald Westdale.

"You brute! You coward! You murderer!" Frantically the lad sobbed out his rage in Von Eimar's set, ruthless face. "You'll pay for this, you cutthroat pirate! You'll hang! Do you hear me—you'll hang!"

Emotion strangled his voice in a sea of sobs.

Von Eimar smiled sardonically, and turned on his heel.

Firmly Ronald Westdale dragged the boy away.

Realising the hopelessness of his position, Roderick Drake ceased his ravings, and relapsed quietly into a moody, abstracted apathy, eyes staring all unseeing before him. In silence he allowed Westdale to clamp a set of handcuffs on to his wrists, and then, stumbling through a blur of unbidden tears to the Englishman's cabin, he flung himself upon a bunk, with the door locked upon him, and turned his face to the wall.

His heart, after the terrible tragedy he had just witnessed, was too full for words.

Mysterious Strangers!

LET us leave Von Eimar and his crew of miscreants, racing through the Indian Ocean with all the speed of the Vengeance's pounding engines, and wing our way through space to the little seaside town of Chalmouth, on the Devon coast.

In a little by-street branching off the town square is a clean, pleasant little eating-house known as Old Joe's, and here, seated at one of its snowy-topped tables, are two men with whom we have business.

Ben Byrcraft, boatswain of Morgan Drake's private yacht, the Shadow, was a bluff, breezy, hearty old sea-dog who seemed to belong to old-time wind-jammer days, with his close-cropped, bullet head, mottled face, and grey flinty eyes that seemed to have borrowed the colour of Northern Seas, plying knife and fork in his horny brown fingers as he demolished a meal that might have sufficed for a crew of hungry castaways. Opposite him sat Ned Sparkes, who, in addition to the duties of quartermaster, was also master-gunner aboard the Shadow. Rather a superfluous post for a pleasure yacht, one might have imagined; but the Shadow, as will be seen, was no ordinary yacht.

"Tom's late, Ben," observed Ned, glancing at the clock on the mantelpiece as he stretched out a tattooed hand for a cruet.

He referred to Tom Silver, the young wireless operator of the Shadow, who was a great favourite with the two elder seamen—though a casual observer, noticing how they often wrangled and argued together, would hardly have supposed it.

The boatswain, a man of few words, nodded without speaking as he demolished the last egg and pushed back a greasy plate. A reply was not required, as it happened, for at that very moment Tom Silver burst upon them, and it was the manner of his entry that provided the two sailormen with the greatest perplexity

The wireless operator was young, fresh-looking, innocent and impudent looking at the same time, and as he approached the table, his air was more in the way of a member of a secret society than that of an ordinary, matter-of-fact ship's wireless officer.

Printed in Great Britain and published every Saturday by the Proprietors, The Amalgamated Press, Ltd. The Fleetway House, Farringdon Street, London, E.C.4. Advertisement offices: The Fleetway House, Farringdon Street, London, E.C.4. Registered for transmission by Canadian Magazine Post. Subscription rates: Inland and Abroad, 11s. per annum; 5s. 6d. for six months. Sole Agents for Australia and New Zealand: Messrs. Gordon & Gotch, Ltd., and for South Africa: Central News Agency, Ltd.—Saturday, May 23rd, 1936.

"'Ssh, you men!" he breathed, laying a finger to his lips with a dramatic gesture.

Ben Byrcraft and Ned Sparkes stared open-mouthed. There was no one in the room to overhear, even had Tom Silver spoken in his naturally pitched voice, except Old Joe, the proprietor, and he was busy at his till, besides being deaf as a post.

"Quiet, boys!" hissed Tom—each of the others was old enough to have been his father. "There's dirty work going on, or I'm a Dutchman!" He lowered his voice still further. "Spies!" he added, in a thrilling whisper, glancing around at the softly lighted room—as if in expectation of seeing a few dark, sinister-looking foreigners crouching about in dim corners and listening to his whispered warnings.

His companions did not seem impressed.

"I tell you it's serious!" Tom Silver was breathless with excitement. "They tackled me half an hour ago, asked me if I belonged to the Shadow, and said they wanted to see the Chief. Look for yourselves!"

Abruptly he crossed the strip of red faded carpet, and peeped through the flowered window curtains at two muffled figures who waited impatiently under the dim rays of a street lamp-post.

"There they are," he continued, as Sparkes and the boatswain joined him. "What d'ye make of them? If you want my opinion, they're a set of anarchists who want to bump off the Chief!"

The faces of his two friends changed. They became serious as they looked furtively through the cold, blurred glass.

"I wonder what they want, scuttle me!" growled Byrcraft. "Well look into this!"

The taller of the two strangers threw away his cigar-end impatiently as the suspicious three seamen approached.

"How much longer are we to be kept waiting?" he asked, with some asperity. "Our business is urgent! Are you Morgan Drake's men?"

His companion—a short, dapper individual, with long grey hair—whispered something into his ear.

"Fetch you along direct, sir!" said Byrcraft stolidly, as he touched his cap. "The yacht is in the 'arbour, off Holdthewind Head. This way, gentlemen!"

"And have the goodness to get us there as soon as possible, my good men," said the grey-haired one, as they followed a curving street to where the salty tang of the Channel was wafted to their nostrils. "Our business is of national importance."

"Ay, ay, sir!" rejoined Ben breezily. Sinking his voice, he added to his two companions in an undertone: "Watch 'em close, boys—that tall 'un, especially. If he draws a gun, 'it 'im 'ard in the elbows! I'll take charge of the old 'un. He's sure to be the artfullest."

Before long a swift motor-launch was foaming smartly alongside the accommodation-ladder of Morgan Drake's white, graceful yacht.

A millionaire's luxury toy, that was the Shadow, seen from a boat or from the shore. Nobody except her crew and a few—a very few—favoured individuals were ever allowed to set foot upon her snow-white decks. Newspaper reporters had long since discovered the futility of attempting to interview Morgan Drake, millionaire, adventurer, explorer, and mystery man, of whom much was rumoured, and yet nothing known for certain.

And for this there was a most excellent reason—for, unbeknown to the world, the Shadow was a pocket battle-cruiser. She carried six-inch guns fore and aft on disappearing platforms, with searchlights, machine-guns, quick-firers, and anti-aircraft guns. Her powerful twin engines could be worked up to a speed of forty knots, and her crew were all trained Navy men, silent, efficient.

Ben Byrcraft took a silver pipe and blew it smartly as they reached the clean, white deck. Shadowy, uniformed figures loomed up from the vagueness of deckhouses, ventilators, and boats neatly stowed on chocks. To a burly master-at-arms Byrcraft muttered something that caused that worthy to glance sharply at the two newcomers, and to flex mighty muscles under his blue sleeves as he set a heavy, bulldog jaw.

A door opened from the wireless cabin, and in a golden pool of light stood a tall, stalwart, aristocratic figure, cigar in mouth, hands in the pockets of his white yachting-suit.

"Ah!" cried the short grey man, advancing, with outstretched hand. "Morgan Drake!"

Morgan Drake stood for a split second, completely surprised. Then he, too, opened his hand, with a jovial, deep-chested laugh of welcome.

"Lord Carshire, of all people!" he exclaimed, taking the other's hand as he pitched the cigar over the ship's rail into the glimmering sea. "And Sir Basil Mitchell! What brings the Foreign Secretary and the First Lord of the Admiralty here at this hour of the night?"

In the shadows, three jaws dropped; three pairs of eyes started out of as many heads. Then with single accord three stunned and startled seamen melted away into the dusk.

"I thought somehow there was something distinguished about those two!" said Tom Silver musingly, as they made for their little cubby-hole between decks.

In his cabin, Morgan Drake poured out drinks for his distinguished guests. Through a haze of cigar-smoke the little grey Foreign Secretary gazed at the tanned, healthy, finely carved features before him, which showed nothing of the cares and responsibilities of the mastermind of Britain's Secret Service, except, perhaps, the nests of tiny crowsfeet that shadowed the kindly grey eyes and the silvery streaks about the temples.

"You have the news, Morgan Drake?" asked Lord Carshire.

Morgan Drake studied the slip of paper that the Foreign Secretary laid before him.

"SOS! SOS! SOS! Sylvia Bay stopped by pirate cruiser——" and there the radio message broke off with singular and ominous abruptness.

"Of course! The Shadow's wireless picked up the relayed message." Morgan Drake gazed pensively at the blue rings of tobacco-smoke that floated towards the cabin skylight. "But piracy—in the twentieth century! It seems fantastic!"

"Not so fantastic but that the Sylvia Bay has actually been sunk!" broke in the First Lord impulsively. "A British destroyer from the Andamans has picked up survivors. Incredible as it may seem, the Sylvia Bay was torpedoed by a strange cruiser, after having been robbed of her specie." Pausing portentously, after a moment he added: "Not only that, but the first officer, who was picked up, declares that he recognised the pirate for the Varland cruiser Zermac."

"Ah!" From a cabin locker Morgan Drake produced a chart of the Indian Ocean. Unrolling it, he described an arc on its surface with a pair of brass-mounted compasses. "The position of the Sylvia Bay when she was sunk was here," he said, indicating the latitude and longitude. Deftly he traced his finger to the south. "Nemesis Island is three hundred miles southward," he added significantly.

"Exactly!" Sir Basil thumped the table with his fist "We have got into touch with the Varland ambassador in London. For twenty-four hours his Government has tried to establish communication with both the Zermac and Nemesis Island—without result!"

COME INTO THE OFFICE, BOYS AND GIRLS!

Your Editor is always pleased to near from his readers. Write to him: Editor of the MAGNET, The Fleetway House, Farringdon Street, London, E.C.4. A stamped, addressed envelope will ensure a reply.

ALTHOUGH the space at my disposal this week is rather limited, I must reply to two important queries. A "Magnetite," from Richmond, Surrey, who has nothing but praise for the MAGNET, asks me if I can tell him anything about G. Manville Fenn, writer of so many stories for boys. My correspondent has just read "Devon Boys!" which he describes as the finest boys' yarn he has ever read. Is G. Manville Fenn still alive? Is he still writing? Are his books obtainable? If my Richmond chum will consult any bookseller's list, he will find mention of the works of this author. They are still read, and I often hear inquiries for them. Manville Fenn died in 1909. More than thirty years ago he wrote stories for certain papers of the Amalgamated Press. Like famous Frank Richards, he was a man of wide interests with experience gained in many walks of life.

In reply to a query from W. Woods, of Dublin, there is no such thing as "normal" height, weight, and measurements of a boy of twelve. It is, of course, possible to arrive at average figures. These, however, are not really of value, since it is quite normal for a boy to develop early owing to his environment—i.e., an athletic type develops younger than others. The only real guide is development of muscle and chest in relation to height, not age, though naturally a distinction must be made between juveniles and adults.

Now for

NEXT WEEK'S SPECIAL FEATURES!

The grand long story of Harry Wharton & Co., entitled, "BUNTER BEATS THE GANGSTERS!" is a real corker! Poker Pike, Putnam van Duck's gunman bodyguard, is a suspicious guy where his "charge" is concerned—prepared to suspect everyone from the Head of Greyfriars down to Gosling, the porter. And Pike has every reason to be suspicious, as you will learn when you read this exciting yarn. As usual, you can be sure of a whole heap of laughs in the "Greyfriars Herald," and a feast of thrills in our powerful modern pirate story. Our clever Greyfriars Rhymester winds up this bumper programme with an "Interview" in verse written around Sidney James Snoop. Don't get left through failing to order next Saturday's MAGNET in good time, chums.

YOUR EDITOR.

All three exchanged significant glances.

"Von Eimar!" they said, with a single breath.

Wearily Morgan Drake passed a hand over his damp brow. He seemed to have grown suddenly drawn and haggard.

"We know that your son Roy was aboard the Zermac——" the Foreign Secretary was beginning gently when there came a tap upon the cabin door.

"Excuse me, sir!" said the steward, as Morgan Drake bade him enter. "But Sparkes thinks this to be of importance to you, sir!"

Hastily Morgan Drake seized the slip of paper from the man's hand. His brow darkened as he passed it to his companions.

"S O S! Cruiser Zermac struck uncharted reef. Sinking rapidly. Von Eimar."

Then followed latitude and longitude.

Lord Carshire let out an exclamation.

"The pirate sunk!" Abruptly he checked the relief in his voice. "But, Morgan Drake, your son——"

Sir Basil boomed in, clumsily sympathetic.

"We'll send out a ship at once, Morgan Drake. He may have escaped."

Slowly Morgan Drake shook his head.

"You may send your ships, Sir Basil, but they will pick up no survivors. Wreckage, perhaps; a lifeboat with the Zermac's name upon it. Von Eimar is cunning enough to leave clues——"

"What do you mean?"

The statesman spoke in genuine bewilderment.

"I mean," said Morgan Drake, slowly and deliberately, "that the devil didn't rescue his servant Von Eimar from Nemesis Island just to pile him up on an uncharted reef! No! Such men as Von Eimar do not die in that way. That message was a fake, to throw off suspicion while Von Eimar makes for his burrow, wherever that may be. But I shall find him!"

A few hours later, with a purple plume of smoke trailing from her single white smoke-stack, the Shadow took the seas, out from Chalmouth Pool, bound on the track of Von Eimar and his crew of modern pirates!

(Be sure and join up in this exciting chase next Saturday, chums. It will be one long reel of thrills! By the way, are your chums reading this powerful modern pirate story? If not, why not?)

ORDERED TO QUIT!

(Continued from page 23.)

Harry Wharton & Co., in the big doorway, looked across the dusky quad, in the direction of the gates.

Clearly, through the still May evening, came the loud clang of the bell at the gates.

And the chums of the Remove grinned.

They had no doubt that Poker Pike had returned, now that darkness was falling—to find himself locked out of the school. Putnam's "stunt," it seemed, had worked like a charm!

"I sure hate it!" remarked Putnam. "Poker's a good little man, if only he'd keep his hardware packed. But he can't bulldoze the Head!"

"I guess he sure can't!" grinned Bob Cherry.

The bell ceased to ring. The juniors strained their eyes through the deep dusk in the quad. They did not suppose for a moment that Gosling would open the gates to the excluded gunman. Head's orders were Head's orders. Poker was out, and had to stay out!

"Hallo, hallo, hallo!" ejaculated Bob in astonishment. "W h a t—w h o—— Great Christopher Columbus!"

The lights of a car came gleaming up the drive.

At the wheel sat Poker Pike. Looking from the window was the face of Mr. Quelch.

"What the thump——" exclaimed Harry Wharton.

The stunt, after all, had not gone according to plan! Here was Poker Pike again, as large as life! But the amazing thing was that Quelch was with him! Evidently, they had returned to the school together.

The juniors could only stare.

"Oh crikey! Here comes the Head!" breathed Bob.

A crowd was gathering at the door. The news spread like wildfire that the gunman had come back. Perhaps the Head had spotted him from his study window. Anyhow, here he was, and the buzzing crowd of Greyfriars fellows made room for him to pass.

The car stopped. Poker Pike stepped down, and, to the general amazement, gave Mr. Quelch a hand from the car. The Remove master came up the steps, leaning heavily on the gunman's sinewy arm.

"Mr. Quelch!" gasped the Head.

He could scarcely believe the evidence of his majestic eyes.

"Sir!" gasped Mr. Quelch. "This man——"

"I see him!" said the Head. "Mr. Pike, I was under the impression that you had, according to instructions, taken your departure."

"Dr. Locke! Pray allow me to speak!" gasped Mr. Quelch. "This man has saved me from violence at the hands of those dastardly gangsters——"

"What?"

"I was seized, sir, by the ruffian called Chew Chick—I should say Chick Chew—who had the amazing effrontery, sir, to imagine that I could be forced into aiding his dastardly schemes——"

"Bless my soul!"

"I was subjected, sir, to what the wretch called 'third degree'—actual infliction of physical pain, sir, to compel me to accede to his demands——"

"Is it possible?"

"It is only too true, sir, and I hardly dare to think of what might have been my fate had not this—this excellent man——"

"This what?"

"This brave and dutiful man, sir, come to my rescue and driven off the ruffians——"

"Oh!"

"I owe my release to him, sir—to his courage, his devotion, to the generous aid he rendered to one who, I fear, has scarcely done him justice," said Mr. Quelch. "If, sir, you could possibly rescind your decision——"

"Eh?"

"And permit this excellent man to remain——"

"Oh!"

"I should take it, sir, as the greatest of favours," said Mr Quelch. "I should be very grateful, indeed, sir."

"Dear me!" stuttered the Head. "If the matter is as you state, Mr. Q u e l c h—hem!—Mr. Pike—hem!—at Mr. Quelch's request, I withdraw my —my instructions! Most certainly! You will remain."

Poker nodded.

"Surest thing you know!" he remarked.

And Putnam van Duck's bodyguard remained at Greyfriars.

THE END.

(Again and again has America's star kidnapper failed to capture his prize. But Chick Chew's a sticker! Look out for the next exciting yarn in this series, entitled: "BUNTER BEATS THE GANGSTERS!" You'll find it in next Saturday's bumper issue of the MAGNET, chums!)

BUNTER BEATS THE GANGSTERS!

No. 1,476. Vol. XLIX. EVERY SATURDAY. Week Ending May 30th, 1936.

THRILLING SITUATIONS AND LAUGHS GALORE IN THIS GRAND COMPLETE SCHOOL YARN OF GREYFRIARS !

BUNTER BEATS the GANGSTERS!

By FRANK RICHARDS

THE FIRST CHAPTER.

Important !

"VAN DUCK !" shouted Billy Bunter.

Putnam van Duck, the new junior in the Greyfriars Remove, did not heed. As he was standing at the wicket, with his bat in his hands, watching for the ball to come down from Hurree Jamset Ram Singh, he had no attention to waste on Billy Bunter.

Two or three other fellows, however, called out to the fat Owl of the Remove:

"Shut up, Bunter !"

"Buzz off !"

"Don't bother !"

Billy Bunter did not shut up. He did not buzz off. Neither did he cease to bother. Bunter had come down from the House at a run, and arrived breathless. Apparently it was an urgent matter that had brought him there. But to the Remove fellows, just then, the urgent matter was cricket.

It was only a practice at the nets. But Harry Wharton, the captain of the Remove, was watching Van Duck with a very keen eye. The American junior was taking to cricket like a duck to water. He wielded the willow like a fellow born to it. Now he was standing up to the bowling of Hurree Singh, the best junior bowler at Greyfriars.

Wharton was considering as he watched, whether Van Duck might not be a valuable recruit for the team going over to Rookwood the following week. Billy Bunter, always superfluous, was more superfluous than ever at the moment.

"I say, you fellows !" gasped Bunter.

"Get out !" hooted Harry Wharton.

"But I say——"

"Kick him, somebody !" snapped the captain of the Remove.

Billy Bunter jumped out of reach before anybody could oblige. His fat existence was forgotten at once. All eyes were on Putnam van Duck, as Hurree Singh sent the ball down.

It was a wily ball—one of the nabob's wiliest. But the junior from Chicago seemed equal to it. He patted it away, and grinned cheerfully.

"By gum, he can bat !" said Bob Cherry.

"By gum, he can !" agreed Harry Wharton. "I fancy we shall want him at Rookwood. We——"

"I say, you fellows——"

"Oh, my hat ! Is Bunter still there ? Blow away, Bunter !"

"But I say——" yelled Bunter.

"Kick him !"

"Van Duck's wanted !" howled Bunter.

"Rot !"

"Wanted at once—important !" spluttered Bunter. "Think I've come down here for nothing, you silly asses ? I tell you it's important !"

"Oh, blow !" growled Harry Wharton. "Here, Van Duck, this fat idiot says you're wanted !"

Van Duck came unwillingly away from the wicket. However, if his Form-master had sent for him, he had no choice in the matter. And he took it for granted that it was a summons from Mr. Quelch.

"Search me !" he grunted. "I guess Quelch might give a guy a rest on a half-holiday. What does the old gink want, Bunter ?"

"Eh ? 'Tisn't Quelch !"

"The Head ?" asked Van Duck.

"'Tisn't the Head !"

"Who the great horned toad is it, then ?" demanded Putnam. "If it's some pesky prefect sent for me, you can tell him to guess again ! I'll say I ain't chucking cricket to mosey around for any Sixth Form guy !"

"'Tisn't a prefect !"

"Then who——" roared Van Duck.

"It's a parcel !"

"A—a—a parcel !" stuttered the American junior.

"That's it !" gasped Bunter. "I came to tell you, at once, when I saw it taken to the House dame's room. You'll have to go to Mrs. Kebble for it, you know. It's tuck, of course."

"Tit-tut-tuck !" stuttered Van Duck, while the other Removites glared at William George Bunter as if they could have eaten him.

It was not a message from Quelch, or the Head, or even a prefect ! Billy Bunter had interrupted the cricket—to bring the news that a parcel of tuck had arrived for Putnam, and awaited him in the House dame's room. That was the important matter that had brought the fat Owl scudding breathlessly down to the nets !

From Billy Bunter's point of view, it was, of course, a matter of the very greatest importance and urgency. Cricket, in comparison, was a trifle light as air.

On that point Harry Wharton & Co. did not agree with Bunter.

"Tuck, of course," said Bunter, heedless of ferocious glares. "What else could it be ? 'Tisn't a hamper, though—too small for that ! Looks to me as if it might be a box of chocolates. Anyhow, it's jolly certain that it's tuck, old chap, and I came to tell you at once. Come on !"

"Come on ?" repeated Van Duck.

"Yes, come on, old fellow !" said Bunter.

"Carry me home to die !" ejaculated Putnam.

"You fat villain!" roared Bob Cherry.

"Oh, really, Cherry——"

"You pernicious porpoise!" yelled Johnny Bull.

"Oh, really, Bull——"

"Slaughter him!" said Harry Wharton.

"I say, you fellows, don't play the goat! Come on, Van Duck, old chap! I say, what are you waiting for? It's tuck!"

Evidently, Billy Bunter could not understand a fellow lingering, when he had news of the arrival of tuck! He blinked impatiently at Putnam through his big spectacles. Certainly, the Owl of the Remove was not wholly disinterested in the matter. He intended to be on hand when that parcel was opened—with an eye to the crumbs that fell from the rich man's table Bunter was in a hurry for that parcel to be opened.

"You—you pesky piecan!" gasped Van Duck. "You all-fired bonehead! You two-cent remnant! You—— Oh, sit down!"

"I say—— Yarooooooh!" roared Billy Bunter, as the exasperated American junior prodded him with his bat.

The prod took effect on the widest part of Billy Bunter's ample circumference. It tapped him on the equator, as it were. Billy Bunter sat down quite suddenly, with a heavy bump

"Urrrggh!" gasped Bunter.

"Now, you pack it up, you pie-faced piecan!" growled Van Duck, and he walked back to the wicket.

"Gurrrggh!" gurgled Bunter. "I—I say—— Oooooer!"

"Roll away, barrel!" grinned Bob Cherry.

"Urrgh! Beast! Wurrggh!"

"Gather round, my infants!" said Bob. "All of you kick him together—first kick to me! Keep still, Bunter! Hallo, hallo, hallo! Where are you going?"

Billy Bunter did not delay to reply; he went! Spluttering for breath, the fat junior burned the wind, as Putnam van Duck would have expressed it.

Harry Wharton & Co. turned their attention to cricket again. Inexplicable as it was to Billy Bunter, nobody cared two hoots, or one, whether there was a parcel of tuck unclaimed in the House dame's room, so long as cricket was the order of the day.

That parcel of tuck was immediately forgotten by everybody but Billy Bunter. But it was not the sort of thing that Billy Bunter could forget!

THE SECOND CHAPTER.

Luck—and Tuck!

"GO away, Master Bunter!"

"Oh, really, Mrs. Kebble, I——"

"Will you go away?" demanded Mrs. Kebble, with great asperity.

"Oh, certainly! But——"

"And shut the door, please!"

The House dame's room, surrounded by cupboards from floor to ceiling, was a nice cosy room. Mrs. Kebble, the House dame, was a nice, cosy old soul. But it was for neither reason that Billy Bunter had rolled in.

Half an hour had elapsed since Bunter's visit to the cricketers. During that half-hour he had paid no fewer than three visits to the House dame's room. Each time he had blinked at a parcel that lay on the House dame's table, with a longing blink through his big spectacles.

It was all very well for Putnam van Duck to pass a parcel of tuck by, like the idle wind which he regarded not. Van Duck was a millionaire's son, and no doubt had all the tuck he wanted.

It was quite different with Billy Bunter. Bunter never had all the tuck he wanted. Certainly, his wants in that line were rather extensive.

If Van Duck did not care about that parcel, Bunter did. He was, indeed, prepared to save Van Duck all the trouble of dealing with it.

On his first visit to the House dame's room, Bunter had stated that Van Duck wanted him to take that parcel up to his study. That statement had no effect whatever on Mrs. Kebble. Probably she knew her Bunter too well! She had simply asked Bunter to shut the door after him.

On his second visit, Bunter had asked for a clean handkerchief. That was rather more plausible, for there was no doubt that Bunter was in need of a clean handkerchief.

He was provided with one; but Mrs. Kebble, unfortunately, did not turn her back, so there was absolutely no chance of snaffling the parcel that lay on the table.

On his third visit Bunter asked for a clean collar. This, also, was plausible. Bunter needed a clean collar as much as he needed a clean handkerchief. Bunter's needs, in these lines, were perpetual.

In nine cases out of ten, William George Bunter, of the Greyfriars Remove, gets more kicks than ha'pence from his school-fellows. But, fat freak though he is, Bunter comes in useful sometimes, as is proved in this week's all-thrill school story of HARRY WHARTON & CO.

But Mrs. Kebble was getting rather impatient. Now, on Bunter's fourth visit, she bit, so to speak.

She was tired of Bunter as a visitor. New boys, lost and lonesome, often drifted to that cosy room, and were comforted, often with cake. But it was long since Bunter had been a new boy, though, certainly, he would have had no objection to being comforted with cake, like the newest of new kids.

"I say, Mrs. Kebble, I only came in for a clean handkerchief," said the fat Owl reproachfully.

"I gave you one not twenty minutes ago, Master Bunter!"

"I—I mean a clean collar——"

"I gave you one not ten minutes ago!"

"I—I mean——"

"Go away, Master Bunter!" said Mrs. Kebble severely. "I will report you to Mr. Quelch if you come here playing your little jokes!"

Mrs. Kebble did not seem to suspect that Bunter had designs on the parcel that lay on the table. She suspected a "rag."

"I—I say, what's that outside the window?" asked Bunter suddenly.

Mrs. Kebble turned her head to look at the window.

Billy Bunter made a swift movement towards the table.

But the House dame's head was turned back at once.

"There was nothing at the window!" she snapped. "And—and what are you doing, Master Bunter?"

"Oh!" gasped Bunter. "Nothing!"

"You must not touch Master van Duck's parcel! Go away at once! And if you come here again, I shall mention it to Mr. Quelch!" said the House dame, with intensified severity. "Shut the door after you, please!"

Billy Bunter suppressed his feelings, rolled out of the room, and shut the door after him with a bang. Which was very bad manners. But Bunter was feeling very angry and annoyed.

"Suspicious old cat!" murmured Bunter. "Looking at a chap as if she thought he was going to bag another fellow's parcel! Suspicious cat!"

As that had been precisely Billy Bunter's intention, the House dame's suspiciousness was really excusable.

But the fat Owl was annoyed.

Any minute now those beasts might come in from the cricket. They were going out of gates after cricket practice, Bunter knew, and they would come in and change. Then, no doubt, Putnam van Duck would consider it worth while to call for his parcel of tuck.

No doubt, if he was on the spot, he would be allowed a "whack." But with a lot of greedy fellows about, it would not be a large whack. Bunter liked the lion's share, when he could get it.

"Cat!" repeated Bunter, as he loafed morosely in the corridor, cudgelling his fat brains for another excuse to butt into the House dame's room.

"Bunter!"

"Oh!" gasped Bunter.

He spun round at the sound of his Form-master's voice. Mr. Quelch was coming up the passage, and he frowned at Bunter.

The fat Owl blinked at him. It really was annoying. Quelch had no business there, unless he was going to speak to the House dame. Of course, he had to butt in, just where he wasn't wanted—by Bunter! It was like a beak!

"Bunter, what are you doing here?" snapped Mr. Quelch.

Cheek, Bunter thought—as if a fellow couldn't do as he liked on a half-holiday. But he did not say that to Mr. Quelch.

"Oh! Nothing, sir!" he stammered.

"You should not be doing nothing, Bunter! I do not approve of boys loafing idly about the passages on a half-holiday!" said Mr. Quelch.

"I—I'm waiting for some chaps to come in from the nets, sir!"

"I do not see why you cannot join them at the nets, Bunter!"

"'Tain't a compulsory day, sir," said Bunter, as if that settled that.

"Nonsense!" said Mr. Quelch. "You are idle, Bunter! You would be much better occupied on the cricket field, or taking a healthy walk. At all events, do not loaf about the passages. I disapprove of it!"

"Oh! Yes, sir! I mean, no, sir!"

Mr. Quelch walked on to the House dame's door, and tapped. Billy Bunter blinked after him, with a vengeful blink through his big spectacles. He would have enjoyed telling the Remove master what he thought of him. It was not a flattering opinion. But that opinion Bunter had to keep locked up in his own fat breast.

"Er—Mrs. Kebble." Quelch did not enter the House dame's room; he spoke at the open door. "Mrs. Locke would be glad to see you in the Head's house, as soon as you are at leisure."

"Certainly, sir. I will go immediately!"

Billy Bunter heard both remarks. The wrath faded out of his fat face. He could have blessed Quelch. Quelch had come along just in time to solve his problem!

He rolled away, as Quelch came back down the corridor. But he rolled slowly, and the Remove master passed him and disappeared.

Once Quelch was out of sight, Billy Bunter stopped. He posted himself at a window in the corridor, and stood looking out. There was a view of the kitchen garden, and Mr. Mimble, the gardener, hoeing therein. Billy Bunter was, apparently, deeply interested in that view when, a few minutes later, Mrs. Kebble came rustling down the passage.

But when Mrs. Kebble had gone down the stairs, Bunter's interest in Mr. Mimble and his hoeing performance evaporated on the spot.

He gave one cautious blink round through his big spectacles, and rolled up the passage to the House dame's room.

Swiftness was not Billy Bunter's long suit! But on this occasion he was almost as swift as the swallow in its flight.

He whipped into the room, clutched the parcel from the table, and whipped out! He did the corridor almost at 50 m.p.h. On a half-holiday most of the fellows were out of the House, and no eye fell on Bunter as he bolted into the Remove passage with his prize. Breathlessly, he arrived in that passage.

Then, for a moment, Bunter paused, blinking at the parcel in his fat hand.

The label was addressed to Van Duck, in a "fist," that Bunter knew. It was the handwriting of Mr. Coot, an American gentleman in London, who sometimes wrote to the millionaire's son at Greyfriars. Bunter had seen that "fist" several times on letters put up in the rack. Van Duck had had a hamper from Mr. Coot on one occasion. This time it was a much smaller parcel—a box of chocolates, Bunter guessed.

Bunter was strongly tempted to roll on to Study No. 7, his own study, and devour his prey there. But he realised that it would not do. It always seemed to Billy Bunter that, if there was any tuck about, he had a sort of natural right to it. But he was aware that that view was not generally shared. It was, in fact, a rather serious matter to bag another fellow's parcel from the House dame's room.

Quelch had seen him in the passage, too! Mrs. Kebble would remember his many visits! He would be suspected!

Quelch, who did not approve of Bunter loafing about the corridor, would certainly have approved still less had he learned the object of Bunter's loafing.

On the other hand, though a fellow certainly couldn't snaffle another fellow's parcel, there was no reason why a fellow shouldn't take a fellow's parcel up to a fellow's study for him!

That was only good-natured.

There was no reason why he shouldn't open it all ready for him when he came in! That, too, was good-natured.

And, having good-naturedly done so much for a fellow, a chap might sample the contents of a parcel while he waited for a fellow to come in.

So Billy Bunter rolled into Study No. 1, the study that Van Duck shared with Wharton and Nugent. He shut the door, and in about a minute more, the packet was unwrapped on the study table.

It contained, as Bunter had already guessed, a box of chocolates—not a very large, but a very handsome box, and evidently expensive. The fat junior removed the lid. Within, beautifully packed in silver foil, lay the layers of lovely, luscious chocolate-creams! Not merely luscious, but scrumptious—the sort that melted in a fellow's mouth, and made him realise that life, with all its worries, was really worth while!

"Oh!" gasped Bunter. "Good!"

Bunter's capacious mouth watered. He grabbed a couple of the luscious chocs and crammed them into that capacious mouth.

Bunter gobbled.

It was his intention to sample a few of those chocs. The rest were to be left for the owner. But the sender of that box of chocs had concentrated rather on quality than on quantity. They were of the very best—which was good—but there were only about a dozen of them, which was not so good. Big and fat as they were, a dozen chocolate-creams did not go very far with Billy Bunter.

In five minutes Bunter was blinking through his big spectacles at an empty chocolate box. And as he blinked at it, there was a sound of tramping footsteps and cheery voices in the Remove passage.

"Oh lor'!" ejaculated Bunter.

Bunter had intended, really and truly, to leave the major part of that box of chocs for the owner. Somehow they had gone! It was clear that, with nothing but an empty box to show, it would not be useful to explain to Van Duck that he had brought that box up to the study and opened it for him out of sheer good nature!

Already it seemed to Bunter that he could feel a boot on his tight trousers. He blinked at the empty box—he blinked at the door, about to open—and in sheer desperation he grabbed the box and the unwrapped wrappings from the table, shoved them into the armchair, and sat on them. As the chocolate box crumpled under his weight, the door of Study No. 1 was thrown open, and Harry Wharton & Co. came in.

THE THIRD CHAPTER.

Ginger-Pop for Bunter!

"HALLO, hallo, hallo!"

"I—I say, you fellows——"

"How did Bunter know we were coming in for ginger-pop?" asked Frank Nugent.

"Ha, ha, ha!"

"Oh, really, Nugent——"

Billy Bunter did not rise from the armchair. It would have been polite, no doubt, to rise, when the owners of the study came in. But the fat Owl had his reasons for sitting tight!

"What's that fat bounder doing here?" asked Harry Wharton, with a suspicious glance at the fat Owl in the armchair. "If you've been scoffing the ginger-pop, you fat burglar——"

"Oh, really, Wharton! I never knew there was any ginger-pop in the cupboard. If you think I've touched your ginger-pop——"

Bunter, for once, was not guilty! Certainly, had he been aware that there was a supply of that refreshing beverage in the study cupboard, it would not have remained untouched. All was grist that came to the fat grub-hunter's mill. But he had been too busy in Study No. 1 to think about the possible contents of the cupboard.

"What are you doing here, then?" demanded the captain of the Remove.

"Oh! Just waiting for you chaps to come in!" said Bunter. "As you're going out after the cricket, I—I thought you might like me to come?"

"What the dickens put that idea into your head?" asked Johnny Bull.

"Oh, really, Bull——"

"My hat! It's still here!" exclaimed the captain of the Remove, as he opened the door of the study cupboard, and beheld the bottles of ginger-beer therein.

Considering that Billy Bunter had been found in the study, it was rather a surprising sight.

"Wonders will never cease!" said Nugent. "Like some ginger-pop, Bunter?"

"Yes, rather!" said Bunter promptly. A dozen large fat chocolate-creams had made Bunter thirsty.

"Go and scout for a glass, then," said Frank.

"Eh?"

"Get a glass from your study, fat-head! We haven't enough to go round."

"Oh!" gasped Bunter.

Bunter was lazy—the laziest man ever. But he was not too lazy to fetch a glass from a study a few yards up the passage, if the same was to be filled for him with fizzy ginger-pop on a warm afternoon.

But he did not move! He could not move from the armchair without revealing the ruins of Van Duck's box of chocolates.

Harry Wharton sorted out glasses. Study No. 1 was provided with six tumblers—quite an unusual supply for a junior study.

They were set out on the table, and the bottles lifted from the cupboard. After cricket practice in warm weather, ginger-pop was grateful and comforting; a pleasant refreshment before the juniors started to walk to Courtfield.

"I say, you fellows, you've got six glasses there," said Bunter. "No need to get any more."

"Van Duck's coming up, fathead—he's only cut off to the House dame's room to get his parcel."

"Oh crikey!"

"Is that what you're waiting here for?" grinned Bob Cherry.

"Oh! Yes! No! I—I say, you fellows, are you sure there was a parcel for Van Duck at all?" stammered Bunter.

The Famous Five stared at him.

"Why, you benighted ass, didn't you come down to the nets to tell Van Duck so?" exclaimed Bob. "Didn't you get prodded for it?"

"Beast! I—I mean, I—I might have been mistaken!" stammered Bunter. "I—I think, on—on second thoughts, you know—that—that perhaps there wasn't a parcel, after all. I don't suppose old Coot has sent Van Duck a box of chocolates."

"Old Coot!" repeated Harry.

"Yes, that old bean who writes to Van Duck, you know! It was his fist——"

"His fist—on the parcel that wasn't!"

"Ha, ha, ha!"

"I—I—I mean——"

"Well, what do you mean, you blithering owl?" asked Harry Wharton. "You can't have snaffled Van Duck's parcel under Mrs. Kebble's eyes, or, I should think——"

"I—I mean—that is—oh lor'!" Bunter broke off as Putnam van Duck came into the study. He came empty-handed, to the surprise of the Famous Five, though not to Billy Bunter's.

"Haven't you got it?" asked Bob.

"Nope! Kebble wasn't there, and I couldn't see anything of a parcel for me," answered the American junior. "I guess that fat gink was stringing me along."

"Oh! Yes! That's it!" gasped Bunter. "There—there wasn't a parcel, old chap. It was just—just my little joke!"

"You pie-faced bonehead——"

"Oh, really, Van Duck! If you're going to call a fellow names after he took the trouble to come and tell you about your parcel——"

"Ain't you just allowed there wasn't a parcel, you locoed geck?"

"Oh! Ah! Yes! I mean——"

"There jolly well was!" said Harry Wharton. "Bunter's seen Mr. Coot's fist on the label. He's let that out!"

"If Kebble isn't there, that accounts for the milk in the coconut!" chuckled Bob. "Bunter's snaffled the parcel."

"Oh, really, Cherry——"

"By the great horned toad——" began Van Duck, with a glare at the worried Owl in the armchair.

"I—I haven't!" howled Bunter, in alarm. "What I mean is, there was a

"If you can't take a fellow's word, you'd better let the matter drop," said Bunter, with dignity. "I say, you fellows might let me have some of that ginger-pop. Chocolates make a chap thirsty."

"Chocolates!"

"I—I mean, I haven't had any chocolates! I—I wonder what made me say—c-c-chocolates!" stammered Bunter. "I—I say, you might cut along to my study and get me a glass, Bob, old chap."

"You can't cut along and get one for yourself?" asked Bob.

"Nunno! I—I mean, I—I'm tired! I—I feel as if I couldn't get out of this armchair, old chap."

"That's all right! I'll help you out——"

"Keep off, you beast! I—I mean, I—I'm ill! I've got a pain!" gasped

"Only a dozen in it?" chuckled Bob.

"That's all," said Bunter. "Not that I know what was in it, you know. How should I know?"

"Ain't he a cough-drop?" said Bob. "I suppose he's sitting on it now, and that's why he can't get out of that chair!"

"Oh!" gasped Bunter. "Nothing of the sort! If you think I bunged it into this chair and sat on it when I heard you fellows coming——"

"Ha, ha, ha!"

Bob Cherry stepped behind the armchair, grasped the high back, and heaved. There was a roar from Billy Bunter as the chair tilted and he shot out on the carpet.

Bump!

After Bunter shot a crumpled chocolate-box and crumpled paper wrappings. But there was no sign of chocolates.

"Go away, Master Bunter!" said Mrs. Kebble, severely. "I will report you to Mr. Quelch!" But Bunter had designs on the parcel addressed to Putnam van Duck. "I—I say," he said suddenly, "what's that outside the window?" As the House dame turned her head, Bunter made a swift movement towards the parcel.

parcel, just as I told you, but I haven't been anywhere near the House dame's room. I wasn't within a hundred yards of the place when I saw it there——"

"Oh crumbs!"

"I—I say, you fellows, if the parcel's gone, I—I fancy it must have been the—the cat!" said Bunter. "You know that cat of Mrs. Kebble's—always sneaking about the House pinching something. I haven't been in Mrs. Kebble's room at all. You can ask her, if you like—she will remember giving me a clean kanky——"

"Oh crikey!"

"It's a bit thick, the way fellows always think of me if any tuck's missing," said Bunter warmly. "Unjust, I call it. It isn't as if I was a greedy fellow, like some fellows I could name. You, f'rinstance, Cherry——"

"Why, you fat slug——"

Bunter. "A—a touch of pneumonia in my right leg——"

"Ha, ha, ha!" yelled the juniors.

"Blessed if I see anything to cackle at! It's a fearful pain!" said Bunter. "My grandfather was lame with it——"

"Ha, ha, ha!"

"Oh, really, you fellows! Look here, I don't mind using the same glass as you, Wharton! I'll have it first—see?"

"Where's my parcel?" demanded Van Duck.

"How should I know?" retorted Bunter. "'Tain't my business to watch over your parcels, is it? I came and told you it was there, and a fat lot of thanks I got! If you'd come back to the House with me then, it would have been all right. I know absolutely nothing about it—no more than the man in the moon! Rotten fuss to make over a dozen chocolate creams——"

"Yow-ow-ow!" roared Bunter, as he rolled.

"Oh, my hat!" exclaimed Bob, as he picked up the crumpled box. "You needn't look farther for your parcel, Van Duck! Here's what's left of it!"

"I'll sure lambaste that fat piecan!" roared Van Duck.

"I—I say, you fellows!" gasped Bunter. He scrambled to his feet and backed hurriedly to the door. "I—I say, I—I brought that parcel up here to—to—to oblige you fellows! I mean, I don't know how it got in that armchair! It—it's quite surprising! I—I think I can hear Toddy calling me——"

"You're not going without your ginger-pop, I guess!" said Van Duck.

"Eh?"

Bunter was at the door, but he turned back at that. Van Duck picked up a foaming glass of ginger-pop from the table.

"Oh!" gasped Bunter. "I—I say, all right!"

Harry Wharton & Co. stared at Putnam van Duck. The American junior was a good-tempered and tolerant fellow, and, as he had heaps of money, no doubt the loss of a box of chocolates did not bother him very much. Still, it was rather surprising to see him take it like this. Few fellows, in the circumstances, would have offered Bunter ginger-pop in return for bagging a parcel of tuck, and that was what Putnam was doing.

Bunter was surprised. Still, he was going to get the ginger-pop, and that was the chief thing. He did not know yet how he was going to get it.

He halted in the doorway, and Van Duck stepped towards him, the glass of foaming fluid in his hand.

"I guess it's due to you, old-timer, after taking the trouble to bring that box of chocs up, and saving me all the trouble of eating them!" remarked Van Duck. "Here you are!"

He grasped Billy Bunter by the hair with his left hand and jerked his head forward. With his right hand he tilted the glass of ginger-beer down the back of the fat Owl's neck.

"Oooooooough!" spluttered Bunter. "Oooogh!"

"Ha, ha, ha!" yelled the Famous Five.

"Ow! I'm all wet! I'm all sticky!" yelled Bunter. "Ow! Ooogh! Why, you beast! Grooogh!"

"Hand me another glass!" said Van Duck. "Bunter's sure fond of ginger-pop, and I guess he can have all he wants!"

"Urrrrggh!"

Bunter did not stay for more ginger-pop. It was true that he was fond of that refreshing fluid, but he had had all he wanted—and more! A kangaroo had nothing on Bunter as he bounded out of Study No. 1.

THE FOURTH CHAPTER.

Amazing!

POKER PIKE, the Greyfriars gunman, rose from his bench by Gosling's lodge.

He gave his bowler hat a firmer clamp on his bullet head, and reached to his hip pocket to make sure that the six-gun was right and ready. Then he lounged down to the gates as six juniors arrived there in a cheery little crowd. After them rolled another—a very fat one!

Harry Wharton & Co. were starting on a ramble, which was to wind up in the bunshop at Courtfield. A walk up the towpath by the shining Sark, a short cut across Popper Court Woods, and tea at the bunshop seemed rather attractive on a sunny, fine half-holiday. To the fat junior who trailed after the party, the last-named item was the only attractive one—but that was very attractive indeed to William George Bunter.

Hurree Jamset Ram Singh, the happy possessor of a handsome remittance, was standing tea at the bunshop. Several Remove fellows, who were out and about in various directions, were to gather there at the prescribed time; it was going to be quite a party. From such a party, of course, Billy Bunter could not be left out—at least, from his own point of view.

Certainly, the dusky Nabob of Bhanipur had forgotten to include him in the list of guests. But that did not worry Bunter. That was a trifle light as air, or lighter.

Poker Pike, his hickory face serious as usual under his bowler hat, calmly joined the juniors as they went out of gates.

Harry Wharton & Co. smiled, though Putnam van Duck looked a little restive.

Putnam's popper, in far-off Chicago, had hired the gunman to keep watch and ward over his son at school, and Putnam admitted that he was needed there. The wiles of Chick Chew, Kidnapper No. 1 of the United States, were many and various. There was no doubt that the kidnappers would already have "cinched" the millionaire's son but for the watchful Poker.

Nevertheless, Poker Pike often seemed too much of a good thing to the gilt-edged American junior. He tired of having the gunman perpetually treading on his tail, as he called it. It was necessary, but not nice.

"You young guys hitting the horizon?" asked Poker.

"Some!" said Bob Cherry gravely, answering Poker in his own language. "Just a few, old-timer! Moseying around a piece."

"Me, too!" said Poker briefly.

"Aw, can it, Poker!" said Putnam restively. "I guess I'm safe enough with this crowd, and we're meeting more guys in Courtfield. You want to sit this one out, Poker."

"Forget it!" said Poker, with his usual brevity. Poker Pike was a man of few words, but unlimited determination.

"I say, you fellows!" Billy Bunter rolled out after the juniors. "I say, we don't want that dashed gunman! Look here, I don't want to show up at the best place in Courtfield with that blessed gunman, I can tell you!"

"You going to Courtfield, Bunter?" asked Bob.

"Oh, really, Cherry——"

"Going our way?" asked Harry Wharton.

"Oh, really, Wharton——"

"If the esteemed Bunter does not like the absurd company of the ridiculous gunman——" began Hurree Jamset Ram Singh.

"I jolly well don't!" grunted Bunter.

"Then the walkfulness in another direction is the proper caper!" suggested the Nabob of Bhanipur.

"Oh, really, Inky——"

Harry Wharton & Co. walked down to the river. Behind them walked Poker Pike, apparently deaf to the objections of Bunter—at least, completely regardless of them. The fat Owl rolled along with the juniors.

Bunter seemed to have forgotten the episode of the ginger-pop in Study No. 1, though it was only half an hour ago. Bunter was not the man to bear grudges or to remember offences when a spread was in the offing.

The fact that he was superfluous did not worry Bunter. If the good-natured nabob allowed him to hook on, that was good enough. And it was for Hurree Singh, as the founder of the feast, to decide. Bunter did not need a pressing invitation. Anything short of the boot was all right for Bunter.

Poker Pike lounged along the towpath behind the party, his slits of eyes very keen and watchful.

It was quite likely that the school was watched by some of the gang of kidnappers, and that hostile eyes were on Putnam van Duck as he walked out with his friends. Poker, at least, had no doubt of it.

He was not letting the gilt-edged youth out of his sight. He seldom, or never did.

"I say, you fellows, what's the good of walking?" asked Billy Bunter. "What about getting a car? I'll phone for one, if you like."

"Good!" said Johnny Bull. "You go back and phone for a car, while we keep on by the river."

"Jolly good idea!" said Bob Cherry heartily.

"I'll stand the car, if that's what you're worrying about," said Bunter. "Inky can lend me a pound——"

"The lendfulness will not be terrific," grinned the Nabob of Bhanipur.

"Well, if you're going to be mean, I——"

"The meanfulness is going to be preposterous!"

"Beast!"

"You silly ass!" said Frank Nugent. "We're taking Van Duck for a ramble through Popper Court Woods. He's never been there yet. If you're too jolly lazy to walk, sit down and shut up!"

"I could walk you off your legs, and chance it," retorted Bunter. "But the fact is, I'd like a car, and I'm willing to stand one."

"Inky's blowing his cash on the feed at the bunshop," said Bob. "He can't afford to stand cars, old fat man."

"Ha, ha, ha!"

Snort, from Bunter. He rolled on after the Famous Five and the American junior—slowly. The juniors started on a walk of two or three miles, which was nothing to the heroes of the Remove. But two or three yards, as a rule, sufficed for Billy Bunter. He was more heavily handicapped than the other fellows in the matter of weight.

He lagged and lagged. The juniors quite expected the fat Owl to lag, and probably to conk out in the first quarter of a mile.

"Come on, fatty!" called back Bob.

"Wait for me, you beasts!" squeaked Bunter.

The juniors waited for him to come up. Bunter rolled on slowly.

"If we're going at this rate, we'd better look for a night club instead of a bunshop," remarked Johnny Bull sarcastically. "We shan't be in Courtfield before midnight."

"I say, you fellows, there's no hurry," said Bunter. "The fact is I'm sleepy."

"Sleepy!" yelled the juniors.

"Yes." Bunter blinked at them through his big spectacles. "Blessed if I know what's come over me; but I feel fearfully sleepy!"

"Do you ever feel anything else?" asked Bob.

"Well, look here!" said Bunter. "We've lots of time on a half-holiday. What about resting for half an hour, while I have a nap? You fellows can sit in the shade, and brush the flies off me—see?"

"Ha, ha, ha!" yelled the juniors; and even Poker Pike's serious visage wrinkled in a grin.

The Removites could not quite see themselves giving up their ramble to sit round Bunter, and brush the flies off him while he snored.

"Blessed if I see anything to cackle at!" snapped Bunter. "I can tell you, I'm awfully sleepy. I can hardly keep my eyes open."

"You seem to be able to keep your mouth open."

"Beast!"

"Sit down and take a rest, old fat bean," said Bob.

"Will you fellows wait for me?"

"Oh, no!"

"Yah!"

Billy Bunter did not sit down and take a rest. Thick grass and shady trees looked very inviting. But Bunter did not want to arrive at the bunshop too late for the spread.

He rolled on. Behind the party walked the gunman, serious and sedate, and very watchful. But Bunter had forgotten the obnoxious gunman now. He was tired. That was nothing new, of course; but he was unusually tired, and he was sleepy, and growing sleepier.

Sleeping was Bunter's long suit. In the Remove dormitory his snore generally started as soon as his fat head was laid on the pillow, and continued, like a Wagnerian unending melody, till the rising-bell clanged out in the morning. And a nap after dinner was always welcome to Bunter. Still, it was very unusual for even Bunter to want to nod off while he was out for a walk in the afternoon.

But he did. He blinked, and blinked, and blinked, growing drowsier and drowsier. He came to a halt at last, and leaned on a tree as the juniors turned into the footpath through Popper Court Woods.

"I say, you fellows, hold on!" he squeaked. "I say, I'm really awfully, fearfully sleepy! I say, hold on!"

"What's the matter with the fat ass?" asked Bob Cherry. "He really looks sleepy." He stared at Bunter.

"Too much dinner," grunted Johnny Bull.

"I never had enough dinner," yapped Bunter. "Quelch stopped me at the fifth helping of steak-and-kidney pie, and he wouldn't let me have more than four helpings of pudding. I should be hungry now, if I hadn't had those chocs—I mean, I never had the chocs——"

"I guess we haven't moseyed out to listen to that fat guy chewing the rag," remarked Putnam van Duck.

"Come on!" said Harry.

"Beasts!" gasped Bunter.

With a tremendous effort he detached himself from the tree, and rolled after the juniors as they went down the shady path. He blinked, and blinked as he rolled. That strange, inexplicable drowsiness was growing on him. Sleepy-head as he was, this was quite a new experience for Bunter, and he did not know what to make of it. But he knew that he was fearfully sleepy, and that every time his fat eyelids closed, it was more difficult to get them open again.

The footpath, shaded by great branches, banked by nodding hawthorns, was very shady and pleasant after the sun glare on the riverside. Bunter was more and more tempted to take a rest. He began to feel that, feed or no feed, he would not be able to help it. He was almost falling asleep as he walked.

"Hallo, hallo, hallo!" ejaculated Bob suddenly, as he looked back at the fat Owl, who had fallen a good way behind. "What on earth's that game? Look!"

All the fellows looked. In fact, they stared blankly. Bunter was still coming on; but he was weaving his way blindly, like a fellow more than half-asleep. He lurched from side to side as he walked. He seemed hardly to know where he was going, and hardly able to keep his feet.

"What the dickens is the matter with him?" exclaimed Harry.

"Gammon!" grunted Johnny Bull. "Just gammon—to make us hang on for him."

Harry Wharton shook his head. They stood watching Bunter in amazement, and even Bull, after a few moments, doubted whether it was "gammon." But if it was not gammon—what was it? How could any fellow, even Bunter, be falling asleep as he walked in the middle of the day?

Poker Pike looked at him, and a strange expression came over the gunman's face. His look became very intent. But the amazed juniors did not notice the gunman. Their astonished eyes were fixed on Bunter.

"Hallo, hallo, hallo!" gasped Bob. "He's going over."

Billy Bunter gave another lurch, and went over in the grass. He was heard to grunt; then he lay still.

Harry Wharton ran back. He was rather alarmed, as well as astonished. He reached Bunter in a few moments. The fat Owl of the Remove lay still in the grass, fast asleep, and snoring.

THE FIFTH CHAPTER.
Who Doped Bunter?

SNORE!

That sound, familiar in the Remove dormitory at Greyfriars, now awoke the echoes of Popper Court Woods.

Harry Wharton & Co. stared down at the fat junior—in amazement, almost in stupefaction.

Poker Pike, standing with his hands on his hips, stared at him, his grim face setting grimmer and grimmer. His slits of eyes turned from Bunter to the amazed group of juniors, scanning face after face. Deep suspicion was written in Poker's look; and it would have made the chums of the Remove jump, had they guessed the thoughts that were passing in the Greyfriars gunman's mind. His glance lingered intently on the dusky face of Hurree Jamset Ram Singh.

"That's not gammon," said Bob. "He's really asleep."

"Kick him, and see," suggested Johnny Bull.

Had Bunter been spoofing, that suggestion would have been enough to wake him up. He would not have waited for the kick. But he gave no sign. He lay like a fat log in the grass, snoring.

Harry Wharton stooped, and shook him by a fat shoulder.

"Wake up, you ass!" he exclaimed.

Snore!

"Wake up, you blithering fathead!" roared Johnny Bull.

Snore!

Bunter did not wake. His little round eyes were tightly closed behind his big spectacles. He slept, and he snored. Bunter was never easy to wake—but now it seemed impossible.

"He can't be ill, I suppose?" said Nugent.

"He doesn't look ill," said Bob. "Besides, illness doesn't make a chap go to sleep—more likely to keep him awake, I should think."

"The absurd Bunter beats the celebrated Seven Sleepers at their own ridiculous game," remarked Hurree Jamset Ram Singh.

Bunter slept on regardless. Certainly there was no sign of illness about him. His fat face was as ruddy as ever. He had simply been overcome by that extraordinary drowsiness. He slept soundly, and he snored loudly.

"Well, we've got to get on!" said Harry at last. "But—what about that fat duffer?"

"Can't carry him!" remarked Bob Cherry.

The juniors chuckled. They were no weaklings, but certainly their combined strength would hardly have been equal to carrying Bunter's weight the length of that long, winding footpath.

"I guess we ain't standing around rubbering at that sleeping beauty," said Putnam van Duck. "If he wants to snooze, let him get on with it!"

"Can't do anything else, I suppose!" said the puzzled captain of the Remove. "Bunter beats Rip van Winkle, but I've never seen him like this before. Blessed if I can make him out. But he will be all right."

"The rightfulness will be terrific."

"We can make him comfortable in the shade," said Bob. "When he wakes up, he can trot home. Nothing else to be done."

"All hands on deck!" grinned Nugent.

All hands were needed! Six pairs grasped the sleeping Owl and lifted him out of the grass.

He stood on his feet—held! It was really amazing that it did not awaken him. But it did not. He sagged heavily in the grasp of the Removites, and would have pitched over had they let go. They gasped under the strain.

"Here, horn in, Poker, you gink!" snapped Putnam. "Can't you lend a hand, instead of standing there rubbering like you was a rural rube seeing Broadway for the first time!"

Poker Pike had his eyes glued to the nabob's dusky face, though quite unnoticed by Hurree Singh. But he started and nodded, and put a sinewy arm round Bunter's fat shoulders, taking the weight, which was a tremendous relief to the gasping juniors.

"This way!" said Harry.

The sleeping Owl could hardly be left in the footpath. The loss of his fascinating society on the walk did not, perhaps, worry the Removites very deeply, but they were willing to do everything they could to make him comfortable while he had his sleep out.

Bob pushed a way through the hawthorns that walled the footpath, and the others followed with Bunter.

They carried him round the massive trunk of an ancient beech that stood a few yards from the path

On the farther side of that beech the grass was high and thick, and made a comfortable couch.

Bunter was laid in it

The massive beech and the hawthorns hid him from the footpath, so he was not likely to be disturbed. In that quiet and shady spot he could sleep as long as he liked.

Bob Cherry, always good-natured, gathered a bunch of foliage to make him a pillow, and spread a handkerchief over the fat face to keep the gnats off.

Bunter, still fast asleep, settled down, snoring, his fat figure almost hidden from view by the high, thick grass. Poker Pike stared down at him, the grim, suspicious look more pronounced than ever on his hickory face. The Greyfriars fellows were surprised, but there was more than surprise in Poker's grim face.

Often enough, Bunter had been badly in need of a nap on a warm afternoon. This was a sounder nap than usual, but that, so far as the schoolboys could see, was all.

They walked on, and the rumble of Billy Bunter's snore died away behind them.

Poker Pike followed, his brow deeply knitted. He tapped Putnam van Duck on the arm, and the American junior oked round at him.

"Pull in a piece!" said Poker briefly. "I guess I want to chew the rag with you a few."

The schoolboys came to a halt.

"I'll say you guys can beat it!" added Poker.

Harry Wharton & Co. looked at him. Poker, it seemed, wanted to speak to Van Duck in private, unheard by other ears! They exchanged curious glances and walked on.

Putnam stopped unwillingly, with a frowning brow. But Poker Pike did not speak till the Famous Five were out of hearing.

"You pesky piecan!" exclaimed Putnam impatiently. "What's got you? Ain't you got no more manners than a grizzly bear, Poker?"

"I ain't worrying about manners none!" answered Poker. "I got to keep tabs on you, you Putnam van Duck, and I'll say that Chick Chew ain't cinching you by no shenannigan game. Nope! Ain't your popper, over in Chicawgo, paying me to keep you safe?"

"What the great horned toad——"

"You getting sleepy?" asked Poker.

Putnam jumped.

He did not look sleepy. He looked extremely wideawake as he stared at the gunman with wide-open eyes.

"Sleepy!" he ejaculated. "You gone loco, Poker? You figure I'm a guy to nod off to sleep a-walking, like that fat geck we've left in the wood?"

"You don't feel it coming on, like that fat gink?" asked Poker anxiously.

Putnam stared at him like a fellow in a dream.

"You gone loco?" he gasped.

"I guess you ain't got it!" said Poker, with a nod. "Mebbe they got that fat gink in mistake for you! The nigger, I reckon."

"You pesky piecan," said Van Duck savagely, "if you call Hurree Singh a nigger, I'll sure send the popper a cable to fire you!"

"Mebbe!" said Poker quietly. "But I ain't fired yet, and s'long's I ain't fired, I'm keeping tabs on you; and no darkey ain't going to play Chick Chew's game with me around. I ain't saying he's the nigger in the woodpile—I allow I don't know yet, but I sure don't like his colour a whole lot."

Poker Pike came from a country where the colour of a complexion was a matter of awful importance. He was aware, of course, that the Nabob of Bhanipur was an Indian, but in his own mind he classed him as "coloured."

So far, however, Poker had never allowed a hint of this absurd prejudice to escape him.

It astonished Van Duck. He could see that the gunman suspected Hurree Jamset Ram Singh of something, but he could not begin to guess what.

Poker made a gesture back along the footpath, in the direction where the sleeping Owl had been left.

"What you figure's got that fat gink?" he asked.

"He's gone to sleep——"

"Dope!" said Poker briefly.

"Great Jerusalem crickets!" gasped Van Duck. "You're sure loco! Who'd want to dope that geck?"

"Nobody, I reckon," answered Poker. "But he's sure doped! I guess they was arter you, and somehow that fat geck got it. I was feared that you'd got it along of him, but you look O.K. Anyhow, he's doped."

"Impossible!"

"He's doped!" said Poker calmly. "And I guess I'm wise to that brand of dope, too. I'll say I've knowed Chick Chew use it afore in his kidnapping stunts. Surest thing you know."

Van Duck gazed at him, dumbfounded.

"Nobody's watching out to kidnap that gink, I reckon," went on Poker. "He got it—but it was sure meant for you, Putnam van Duck. That's a cinch—how'd he get it? I'm telling you there's some guy in your school on Chick's pay-roll, playing Chick's game. One of that bunch, I reckon—and I guess most likely the coloured piecan! You get me?"

Van Duck could not speak; he could only stare.

Poker was a wary guy—and a suspicious guy. His training in the Chicago joints had not endowed him with faith in human nature.

He was prepared to suspect anybody and everybody where Putnam's safety was concerned.

Chick Chew, who stood to gain a ransom of half a million dollars for the kidnapped millionaire's son, was ready to spend money like water in bribes—and on his own happy side of the Atlantic that was extensively his method.

Certainly it seemed improbable, even to Poker, that schoolboys at Greyfriars could be bribed to help the gangster in his lawless game. But Poker was taking no chances.

Bunter had been drugged—doped, as Poker called it. The juniors never dreamed of suspecting it, but Mr. Pike was sure of it. Obviously, he had been doped in the school, before starting on that walk. By whom?

Poker did not know. He was trusting nobody till he knew. It was absurd to suppose that dope had been intended for Bunter. It had got to the wrong address. There was a scheme on foot to dope Van Duck and place him at the kidnapper's mercy. That was clear to Poker!

Who could have handled the dope except one of the fellows he associated with? And of those fellows, who was most likely? The coloured guy, of course! Poker figured that he had it pat!

"I guess," said Poker anxiously, "you want to forget this trip and walk back with this baby, you Putnam."

"You locoed geck!" said Putnam, finding his voice. "I'm going out to tea with Hurree Singh!"

"I'll say he's the very guy——"

"Can it, you bonehead!" snapped Van Duck. "I ain't believing any that Bunter's been doped. And if he was, my friends don't know a thing about it, as you'd understand, if you wasn't loco! Pack it up! I guess you'll be suspecting the Head next of being on Chick's pay-roll!"

"I wouldn't put it past him, if Chick aimed to buy him!" said Poker calmly. "But I sure got my eye on the coloured guy this time. That dope was aimed at you——"

"Aw, forget it! Pack it up and sit on the lid!" howled Van Duck. "Go and chop chips! Don't spill any more, or I will sure lam you a few!"

And, leaving the gunman, Putnam ran after his friends, and rejoined them, with a ruffled brow. Poker Pike, once his suspicions were aroused, was prepared to suspect everybody at Greyfriars, from the revered Head, Dr. Locke, down to Gosling, the porter. But his extraordinary suspicion made Putnam half angry, half inclined to laugh.

Poker stared after him, frowning, and then, with a grim face, followed on.

If there was a scheme on foot to dope

Van Duck stepped towards Bunter, the glass of foaming ginger-pop in his hand. Grasping the fat junior by the hair, he jerked his head forward. Then he tilted the glass of ginger-pop down Bunter's fat neck. "I guess you asked for it, old-timer!" he said. "Ooooooooogh!" spluttered the Owl of the Remove. "Beast—grooooogh!"

the millionaire's son that day, Poker was the guy to put paid to it! And he had no doubt whatever that there was!

THE SIXTH CHAPTER.

Not the Goods!

CHICK CHEW grinned—an expansive grin, that revealed his expensive American dentistry, gleaming in the shafts of sunlight that came through the foliage over the footpath in Popper Court Woods.

Chick Chew seemed in high feather.

His associate, or side-kicker, as Chick called him, walked by his side. The two gangsters were following the shady woodland path, the way the Greyfriars party had gone; but the latter were far ahead, out of sight. Had they seen Chick and Bud, however, they would hardly have recognised them. Chick and Bud were getting rather too well known in the vicinity of Greyfriars, and they had made some changes in their appearance. Except for Chick's extensive waist measurement, and Bud Parker's horn-rimmed glasses, they looked like their customary selves.

"I guess this journey is going to be the last trip, Bud!" remarked Mr. Chew, speaking in low, cautious tones.

"Sez you!" murmured Bud. Bud was pessimistic, as usual.

"I'll say you're some Dismal Jimmy, Bud!" grunted Chick. "Ain't that bird safe doped? I'm inquiring of you!"

"Mebbe!" said Bud.

"When a schoolboy gets hold of a box of expensive chocolates, what does he do with them?" demanded Chick.

"Parks 'em!" admitted Mr. Parker.

"Sure! That packet was addressed to the young gink, in a fist that old Coot, in London, would swear was his'n, if he piped it! He won't scent no mouse, that young gink won't! Soon's he parks them chocs, he's doped! There ain't no damage in that dope—but it's sure!" said Chick. "Didn't we use it on young Guggergummer, back in Noo Yark, and didn't he wake up where we wanted him?"

"You said it!" agreed Bud.

"It's holiday at that school," went on Chick, "and if young Putnam stayed in, he'd fall asleep there, faster'n Rip van Winkle, an hour after he parked that dope. Lying around to be picked up, Bud Parker."

"But——" murmured the more pessimistic Bud.

"But he started walking out afore the dope worked," went on Chick; "and I'll say nothing could have suited me finer. You want to know, Bud Parker, that I'd have picked him up, and walked his chalks, right in the middle of his school if it came to that! But I allow it comes easier with the young guy meandering around a mile out of the shebang."

"Poker's along of him!" muttered Bud uneasily.

"Aw pack that up!" growled Chick. "I allow I ain't honing for gun-play in this pesky country where a guy can't loose off an automatic without getting the whole pesky population rubbering around. But if Poker Pike stands between me and my bird he gets his sudden!"

Chick Chew slipped a fat hand into a pocket which sagged under the weight of his automatic.

"You keep your hardware ready, Bud! Mebbe it won't be wanted; but if it's wanted, it will be wanted bad! I'm telling you, that young guy Putnam is walking around doped, and we only got to foller on, to pick him up. Poker'll be keeping tabs on him, and we got to put paid to Poker!"

Bud Parker nodded, but rather dubiously. Putting paid to Poker did not seem to strike the horn-rimmed man as an attractive proposition.

But Chick was full of confidence.

He had no doubt that the doped chocolates had been consumed. He had still less doubt that the dope would work. It was, from his point of view, a stroke of luck that the doped schoolboy should have walked out of gates before the drug took effect; another stroke of luck that his walk should have led him to the lonely wood. When the drug overcame Putnam, the only difficulty in Chick's way was going to be the gunman guard.

That was, certainly, a considerable difficulty. But Chick was prepared to deal with it. If it came to gun-play, Chick was no slouch with a gun! The gangsters would be two to one, and the advantage of a surprise on their side.

"I'm telling you," said Chick. "It's pie this time! If we get Poker napping, he'll stick 'em up fast enough, with a gun lookin' him in the eye! Yep! And I guess he ain't wise to it that we're around."

"But——" murmured Bud.

"Lissen!" breathed Chick.

A rumbling sound from among the shady hawthorns reached the keen ears of the fat gangster.

It was a snore!

"You hear that?" breathed Chick.

"Sure!" whispered Bud.

"That's a guy asleep!"

"You said it!"

Chick's eyes gleamed; Bud's glistened

behind his horn-rimmed glasses. As they listened intently the sound of a snore from the shade came unmistakably. Evidently there was a sleeper there!

"By the great horned toad!" whispered Chick. "We got him! I guess that dope's got to work, Bud, and he's gone off—what?"

"Mebbe some hobo gone to sleep in the shade!" muttered Bud.

"Aw, can it!" growled Chick. He was not going to believe that that snore came from some tramp taking a rest. "Ain't we treading on the tail of them guys? Didn't they pass this way, jest ahead of us? Now we come on a guy gone to sleep! It's sure the guy that got the dope!"

Bud nodded. There could really be little doubt of it.

"I guess," went on Chick, "that the other infants would walk on, and leave him to it, if he wanted to doze! They sure wouldn't want to stand around all day watching him at it, Bud!"

"Poker wouldn't mosey on," said Bud.

"Nope! I guess Poker's squatting by him, O.K." admitted Chick. "We got to handle that hombre. But I guess we'll surprise him some, and get him covered afore he can pull his hardware."

"Looks good!" admitted Bud.

"You want to walk soft!" whispered Chick.

The fat gangster led the way, treading as lightly as a cat, in spite of his bulk. Still more lightly, the horn-rimmed man trod after him.

They wound silently through the hawthorn bushes, and reached the big beech that shadowed them.

From the other side of the massive trunk came the deep, continuous snore of a sound sleeper!

He was lying there, in the shade, as yet unseen! But he was there—the steady snore left no doubt on that point.

But no one was to be seen! Chick took it for granted that if Putnam van Duck wanted to go to sleep on that ramble, the other schoolboys would leave him to it. But Poker Pike, it was certain, would remain with Putnam. He might or might not suspect dope; but, in any case, he would remain on guard over the millionaire's son. But he was not to be seen.

Chick was puzzled.

Unless the gunman was standing on the other side of the beech, leaning against the trunk, he would have been visible. Chick concluded that that must be the case; though if Poker was there he was strangely silent, and obviously not on his guard as usual.

Snore!

So close to the spot Chick did not venture to speak, or even to whisper. He signed to his side-kicker what to do.

His automatic glimmered in his hand. Another glimmered in the hand of Bud Parker.

Poker, if he was there, was close up to the big trunk on the other side, standing by the sleeper. A sudden rush round the big beech, and Poker would be covered by two automatics before he had time to touch a weapon. Even the pessimistic Bud had to admit that this was "pie."

They rushed together—Chick on one side of the big beech, Bud on the other, automatics lifted.

"Stick 'em up!" rapped Chick Chew, as he came round the tree.

"Stick 'em up!" echoed Bud.

Two automatics were levelled at the hitherto unseen side of the big beech—and would have covered Poker had he been standing there!

But he was not there!

Chick stared—amazed! Bud's eyes almost popped through the horn rims of his glasses! Poker was not there! Nobody was there—except the sleeper in the grass, with the handkerchief over his face to keep off flies.

Chick's fat face crimsoned.

Never in all his career as a gangster and kidnapper, had Chick Chew felt such a bonehead as he felt now, with his deadly automatic levelled at the trunk of a tree!

That automatic disappeared quickly into Chick's pocket. Bud's followed it out of sight. Chick was red with annoyance. Bud grinned. Automatics, it was clear, were not needed.

"Beats me!" gasped Chick.

"To a frazzle!" agreed Bud.

"Poker ain't around——"

"He sure ain't!"

"I reckoned he was up agin that tree as we couldn't pipe him! But—but he ain't!"

"Not hide nor hair of him!" said Bud.

Chick stared round among the nodding hawthorns. There was no sound save the twittering birds and the buzz of the gnats. No one was at hand—except the sleeper, half hidden in the thick grass, with the handkerchief over his face. The sleeper's cap showed that he was a schoolboy and belonged to Greyfriars. Obviously it was the doped schoolboy. But there was no sign of Poker Pike!

"It's got me beat!" muttered the perplexed Chick. "Old man Vanderdecken, over in Chicawgo, is paying that gunslinger whole wads to keep tabs on his son here. Poker ain't the guy to throw him down while he's drawing his pay! But he ain't here! He's sure moseyed on and left him to snooze."

"I guess this sees us through," muttered Bud. "I'll say I ain't honing to throw lead with Poker! This here is clam pie!"

"That ain't no dream!" agreed Chick. "We got the goods!"

He grinned with satisfaction. Amazing and utterly unexpected as it was, for the watchful gunman to have left the doped schoolboy unguarded, it was "pie" to the kidnappers! They had only to pick him up and walk him off to the car that was waiting at a safe distance, with Tug at the wheel. Chick Chew grinned—and chuckled! He had "got the goods."

Then, as he bent over the sleeper, the grin faded from his face. The thick grass half hid the slumbering figure—the handkerchief wholly hid the face. But on a closer inspection Chick realised that the ample lines of that figure were not exactly those of Putnam van Duck.

With a sudden misgiving, he snatched the handkerchief away from the slumbering face.

He gave a yell of rage and disappointment.

The face that was revealed was that of a schoolboy, sleeping deep under the influence of "dope." But it was not the face of Putnam van Duck! It was a fat face adorned by a pair of big spectacles! It was the face of William George Bunter, the ornament of the Greyfriars Remove.

"Great snakes!" howled Chick.

He stared at Billy Bunter almost petrified. Bunter slumbered happily on. Chick stared at him with unbelieving eyes. He gritted his teeth, grasped the fat junior by the shoulder, and shook him savagely.

Bunter's snore was changed into an uneasy grunt. But he did not awaken. It was clear that he was doped.

Chick's face was a picture as he rose again, leaving the fat Owl snoring once more! Bud gazed at Bunter openmouthed.

"Carry me home to die!" murmured Chick almost faintly. "I'll say this is the elephant's side-whiskers, and then some! How come it that fat gink has got the dope instead of young Putnam? I'm asking you, Bud Parker! That's why Poker ain't around! I guess he ain't keeping no tabs on that slab-sided piecarr! But——"

"Search me!" said Bud.

"The dope's been took!" said Chick. "If it hadn't been took—— But it sure has! You can see that that lard-faced gink is doped! Doped to a frazzle! And—and young Putnam ain't! I'm asking you, Bud Parker, for the answer to that one."

"You can search me!" answered Bud.

Billy Bunter was at the mercy of the kidnappers—if they wanted him! But they didn't! They wanted the millionaire's son; but they would not have taken Billy Bunter at a gift!

With feelings too deep for words, Kidnapper No. 1 of the United States turned his back on the sleeping beauty. Bud Parker followed him. So did Billy Bunter's snore—for quite a distance. Unconscious of the gangsters, unconscious of a fly that had settled on his fat little nose, dreaming happily of a spread in a Greyfriars study, Billy Bunter slumbered on!

THE SEVENTH CHAPTER.

Poker Takes No Chances!

"ESTEEMED and ludicrous friends——"

"Hear, hear!"

"The delightful pleasure of beholding your ridiculous countenances round the festive board is absurd and terrific!"

"Ha, ha, ha!"

It was quite a large and happy gathering at the bunshop in Courtfield. Hurree Jamset Ram Singh had engaged his table by telephone earlier in the day, and a bowing waiter showed the Greyfriars party to it when they arrived. Other Remove fellows were already on the spot; Vernon-Smith and Redwing, Peter Todd and Tom Dutton, Tom Brown and Squiff and Hazeldene, and two or three more. It was a large table, but it was well packed.

On it were piled good things to eat—round it were packed the fellows to eat them. Hurree Jamset Ram Singh, at the head of the table, had Putnam van Duck on his right hand, Bob Cherry on his left. Two or three waiters gave the numerous party their attention; even the manager, a very portly and important person, hovered round.

It was rather a special occasion. The Nabob of Bhanipur, being in great funds, considered it a good idea to stand a handsome spread to his friends in the Remove—and all his friends in the Remove approved heartily.

It was really unfortunate that Billy Bunter could not be present. The mere sight of the eatables on the table would have delighted his eyes.

Hurree Jamset Ram Singh's graceful remarks were cheered. They also made the fellows smile.

In fact, all faces were smiling—except one! That was the hard-boiled, hickory face of Poker Pike.

Poker looked serious and grim. Politely the nabob had invited him to take a seat at the festive board. The juniors were prepared to make room for him. But the gunman curtly declined.

Probably Mr Pike did not care much, anyhow, for cakes and jam-tarts, cream puffs and eclairs and meringues. Probably he liked a stronger fluid than tea or coffee or lemonade or ginger-beer. In any case, Poker was there, not for pleasure, but for business. He was "keeping tabs"!

Never since he had been at Greyfriars had the gunman been so watchful and wary and suspicious. Bunter lay asleep in Popper Court Woods—doped! Whoever had doped him would be looking for another chance at the gilt-edged junior—and Poker was on the watch for it. His suspicions concentrated on the dusky nabob. It was one of the young piecans, Poker reckoned, and the coloured guy was the likeliest. And the dusky schoolboy was standing this feed —providing the food and drink that Putnam was to partake of! What did it look like? It looked, to Poker, as if there was dope about!

Like a lynx, the gunman watched the Nabob of Bhanipur. Hurree Jamset Ram Singh, after a time, had noticed that he seemed to have an unusual interest for Mr. Pike. But he never dreamed of suspecting the cause.

There were plenty of other customers in the bunshop. Many of them glanced towards the juniors' table. Many glanced at the stocky figure and hard-boiled face of the Chicago gunman.

Poker did not mind. He had no objection to publicity. Probably he did not observe that he was observed. His keen attention was fixed on Putnam and the suspected nabob.

Had Putnam been in the same state as Billy Bunter, miles from the school, he certainly would have been in danger from the kidnappers, even with his gunman guard to protect him. Poker did not intend to allow any risk of it.

"You won't want that here, old bean!" grinned Bob Cherry, as he noticed the gunman loosen the six-gun in his pocket, which looked as if Poker fancied that he might want it!

"Mebbe!" said Poker dryly. "And mebbe not!"

"Think Chick Chew is going to walk into a crowded bunshop and hook off Van Duck under our noses?" asked Vernon-Smith.

"I wouldn't put it past him!" answered Poker.

"Oh, my hat!" ejaculated the Bounder. "Look out for the gun-play, you men! Duck in time!"

"Ha, ha, ha!"

Poker grunted—and watched, posted near Van Duck's chair. Putnam gave him a fierce scowl, which left Poker quite unmoved.

"Can't you beat it, you pesky guy?" breathed Putnam. "You want the whole shebang rubbering at you?"

"I guess that cuts no ice," said Poker. "Let 'em rubber, if they want. I'll mention that you ain't going to be doped none."

"Pack it up, you bonehead!"

"What's that?" exclaimed Bob Cherry, staring round. "Who's going to dope whom, Van Duck?"

"That pesky guy figures that Bunter was doped," growled Van Duck. "He sure fancies some guy was after me and got Bunter. The pesky bonehead is sure haunted by Chick Chew, like he was a ghost."

"Oh, my hat!" said Bob. He stared at Poker. "What on earth's put that silly idea into your head, Pike?"

Poker shrugged his shoulders.

"I guess that fat gink was doped," he answered, "and I'll say I'm going to see that Putnam van Duck don't get the same, from the same galoot! Surest thing you know."

"Mad as a hatter!" said Bob.

"Madder!" growled Putnam. "You park it, Poker! Keep it parked!"

Poker stood silent—but very watchful. Some of the fellows who had caught what was said, grinned at one another. Poker Pike was taken rather as a joke at Greyfriars. But his extraordinary suspicion that the millionaire's son might be "doped" at a schoolboy tea-party in a bunshop seemed to the juniors a real shriek!

The spread proceeded merrily, fellows passing good things up and down the table. Putnam van Duck did as much justice to them as any other fellow—but Poker watched him so closely that he seemed to be counting the mouthfuls put away by the American junior.

So long as he received nothing from Hurree Jamset Ram Singh, the gunman appeared to be satisfied, though alert. Presently, however, the dusky nabob poured ginger-beer for the fellows who preferred that refreshing fluid to tea.

Foaming glasses were passed along, and Hurree Singh was handing one to Van Duck when suddenly he gave a jump as a grip of iron fastened on his dusky wrist.

"Forget it!" gritted Poker Pike.

The Nabob of Bhanipur stared at him in utter amazement. It seemed to him that the Greyfriars gunman had suddenly taken leave of his senses.

"My esteemed and absurd Poker——" he gasped.

"What the dickens——" exclaimed Harry Wharton.

"What the thump——" stuttered Bob.

Every face at the table was turned on Poker Pike. Every eye was fixed on him in amazement. He did not heed.

With a grip of iron on Hurree Singh's wrist he forced the tumbler down, and it was set on the table. Then, releasing the dusky wrist, Poker picked up the tumbler. Hurree Singh, lost in astonishment, fairly goggled at him.

Poker jammed the foaming tumbler to the nabob's mouth.

"Swaller!" he rapped.

"Wha-a-t——" stuttered Hurree Singh.

"Taste it, you!"

"Tit-tut-taste it!" stuttered the nabob.

"Yep! And pronto! I guess you ain't handing no dope to that Putnam van Duck while I'm around."

"Did-dud-dope!" gurgled Hurree Jamset Ram Singh. "My esteemed and idiotic gun-slinging fathead, the ginger-pop is harmless and necessary——"

"You tasting it?" demanded Poker, knitting his brows grimly. "I'm telling you to swaller half that packet, and swaller it pronto! Get me?"

"You pesky piecan!" shrieked Van Duck. "Will you let up?"

"Nope! Swaller!" rapped the gunman, while the tea-party stared at him, transfixed, almost petrified. "I ain't waiting! By the great horned toad, I guess I got you card-indexed, you doping guy! What's the harm in swallering, if there ain't no dope around? Swaller!"

"B-b-b-but——" gasped the astonished nabob.

"Swaller, or you get yours sudden!" snarled Poker.

With his free hand he jerked the six-gun from his hip.

There was a gasp from the tea-party as the gun glimmered in the gunman's hand. There was a stutter of astonishment from the waiters—a splutter of excitement from customers up and down and round about the bunshop. The portly manager almost fell down at the sight.

Heedless of all, Poker Pike jammed the six-gun almost in the dusky face of the Nabob of Bhanipur.

"Swaller!" he roared.

"Are you mad?" shouted Harry Wharton, jumping to his feet.

"Poker, you locoed gink——" gasped Van Duck.

"Swaller!" roared Poker. "By the great horned toad, you swaller instanter, or I'll sure spill your juice all over this here shebang! Surest thing you know."

He jammed the foaming glass at the nabob's mouth. A wave of ginger-beer went over the rim, and splashed into Hurree Singh's neck.

Utterly amazed and dumbfounded, Hurree Jamset Ram Singh gulped at the ginger-beer. With the glass tilted at his mouth, it was a hurried and liberal gulp, and it was not surprising that some of the ginger-beer went down the wrong way. Hurree Singh gurgled wildly.

Poker slammed down the tumbler, now half full. He watched the gurgling nabob grimly.

"Urrrggh!" came from Hurree Singh, as he choked. "Groogh! Woooooough!"

"I guess he's got it!" said Poker. "He's sure got his own dope! I'll say he's feeling it some! Surest thing you know."

"Grooogh! Hooooh! Oooch!"

Bob Cherry thumped the nabob on the back. He choked, and gasped, and gurgled, and recovered a little.

Poker Pike watched him. He seemed disappointed. His first impression was that Hurree Jamset Ram Singh had been immediately overcome by a liberal dose of "dope." Now he realised that it was simply a sudden gulping of ginger-beer that had made him choke. Whether dope was around or not, whether or not the dusky nabob was the doper, that ginger-beer, at all events, was quite innocuous.

"Gurrrggh!" gasped Hurree Jamset Ram Singh. "Wurrggh! You esteemed and ludicrous idiot, what is the meanfulness of these absurd proceedings? Oooogh!"

Putnam van Duck, his face crimson with wrath, picked up the tumbler half full of ginger-beer. Poker gave him a reassuring nod.

"I guess you can swaller that safe now, bud!" he remarked. "I guess——Ooooough! What—yoooooch!"

It was not Putnam's intention to drink the ginger-beer. He had another use for it! He glared at Poker, jerked his arm, and shot the ginger-beer fairly into the hickory face.

Splash!

"Gurrrrggh!" gasped Poker.

Taken by surprise, he staggered back. Bob Cherry kindly put out a foot, and the gunman stumbled backwards over it. Streaming with ginger-beer, Poker sat down suddenly and hard.

THE EIGHTH CHAPTER.
Painful for Bunter!

"HA, ha, ha!"

The tea-party roared.

Poker Pike sat blinking through ginger-beer. He was quite taken by surprise. Evidently he had not expected that from the gilt-edged youth he was protecting from the danger of "dope."

"Aw! Search me!" gasped Poker. "Grough! What the John James

Robinson—— Ooogh! You pesky young piecan—— Wooogh!"

"Ha, ha, ha!"

Van Duck was not finished yet. The other fellows were laughing, but the American junior had got his "mad" up! He grasped a bottle of ginger-beer and poured its contents over Poker as he sat. Foaming ginger-beer splashed all over the gunman, dripping from the rim of his bowler hat, drenching him from head to foot. Putnam followed up the ginger-beer with a jam-tart! There was a loud squashing sound as he plastered it on the hard-boiled face of his gunman guardian.

"Oh crikey!" gasped Bob Cherry. "Go easy, old bean!"

"You're wasting the tuck!" grinned Johnny Bull.

"I'll sure make that pesky guy skip!" howled Van Duck. "I'll give him dope! Take that, Poker, you locoed piecan!"

"That" was a large cream-tart! Poker, as he staggered blindly up, took it with his face.

He howled and gurgled.

The tea-party howled, too, with laughter. Poker's hickory countenance had disappeared, under jam and cream and pastry, mixed with streaming ginger-beer. His aspect was quite extraordinary.

"Urrgh! Say, what's the game?" gurgled Poker. "Let up, you young piecan! You want me to beat you up? Let up, I'm telling you!"

"Ha, ha, ha!"

"Gentlemen! Gentlemen!" The scandalised manager of the bunshop rolled up. "Gentlemen—I insist—this disturbance——"

"Kick that man out!" called out Temple of the Fourth, who was teaing with his friends, Dabney and Fry, at another table. "Kick 'em all out!"

"Rowdy lot, the Remove!" said Fry.

"Oh, rather!" said Dabney.

"Turn him out!" shouted Temple.

"This disturbance — really — I insist——" gasped the manager. It was a large and profitable tea-party, and Indian princes and American millionaires were more than welcome at the bunshop. But there was a limit.

"Now you beat it, Poker, you guy!" howled the exasperated Van Duck. "You hear me, you galoot? You beat it, and beat it pronto!"

Poker dabbed a sticky face, and spluttered.

"I guess not!" he gasped. "I sure ain't leaving you here to be doped by a coloured guy on Chick Chew's pay-roll."

"My only esteemed hat!" ejaculated the Nabob of Bhanipur. Hurree Jamset Ram Singh understood, at last, what was the matter with Poker Pike.

A flush came under the dusk of his cheeks, and his dark eyes flashed. He stepped towards the gunman.

"You ludicrous and preposterous fathead!" he exclaimed. "The absurd dopefulness exists only in your idiotic imagination——"

"Aw, can it?" said Poker, still dabbing. "I guess you ain't passing that Putnam van Duck nothing without tasting it first, and you can chew on that."

The gun was still in Poker's hand. But the Nabob of Bhanipur paid it no heed. Inky was the best-tempered fellow in the Remove—seldom or never was his Oriental calm ruffled. But it was ruffled now, with a vengeance. He clenched a dusky fist, and hit Poker Pike fairly on his pimple of a nose. It was a hefty knock, and that pimple of a nose felt as if it had been pushed through the bullet head.

Taken by surprise again, Poker Pike sat down, for a second time.

"Oh crumbs!" gasped Harry Wharton.

"Keep cool, Inky!" gasped Bob.

Poker sat and spluttered.

"I been knocked over!" he gasped. "Jumping toads! I sure been K.O.'d by a doggoned nigger! I guess I'll hand him a few!"

He scrambled up. With one accord the tea-party rushed on him. They piled on him right and left. Putnam van Duck swiftly annexed the six-gun. Other fellows flattened Poker Pike out. The portly manager of the bunshop almost danced round the scene. His expression indicated, quite plainly, that he was tired of that tea-party in his establishment.

"Go away!" he shrieked. "Get out! All of you! Stop this at once! I will send for the police! I will report you to your headmaster. Turn them out!"

Poker heaved and struggled furiously. Everybody in the bunshop was on his feet now, staring and buzzing. It was the wildest excitement that had ever been seen in that bunshop. Poker, not for the first time since he had been located at Greyfriars, had made a sensation.

"Fire him out!" roared Van Duck.

Heaving and struggling in the midst of the mob of schoolboys, Poker was heaved to the door. In a gasping heap he was hurled out on the pavement of Courtfield High Street.

Putnam brandished a fist at him from the door.

"Now beat it, you geck!" he roared. "Beat it, or you'll get run in! You want to be canned, you gink? Beat it!"

Poker staggered up.

"I guess I ain't beating it any, and leaving you here to be doped!" he gasped. "Not by a canful! I'm sure coming back!"

"Pack the goal!" grinned Bob Cherry.

The tea-party blocked the doorway, ready for Poker. Obviously, he was not going—he was coming back. Poker was a dutiful guy, and no odds could turn him from the path of duty. A crowd was gathering in the street—in the distance, loomed a policeman's helmet.

"Hold on!" gasped Van Duck. "I guess I'll beat it with the pesky guy—he sure won't let up without!"

Van Duck ran out and joined Poker. He grabbed him by the arm, and dragged him along the pavement.

"Step out, you gink!" he hissed. "There's a cop coming along——"

"I guess a cop don't worry me none!" answered Poker. "I'll say——"

"Come on, you pesky bonehead!" hissed Van Duck.

With Putnam along with him, Poker was quite ready to come on. Dabbing his sticky face, he accompanied the American schoolboy down the High Street.

"Well, my hat!" said Bob Cherry. "What an afternoon!"

"Nice man at a tea-party!" chuckled the Bounder.

"Ha, ha, ha!"

"My esteemed chums, now that that deplorable and disgusting gunman has departfully mizzled, let us resume the ludicrous spread," said the Nabob of Bhanipur.

The bunshop manager had to be placated, before the spread could be resumed. However, as Poker was gone, that was effected—especially as considerable items for damages were going to appear on the nabob's bill. The tea-party, rather breathless after their exertions, sat down round the table again—the cynosure of all eyes in the bunshop.

Meanwhile, Putnam van Duck hooked Poker Pike into a taxi, and eliminated him from the public gaze of Courtfield. Even Poker, indifferent as he was to publicity, was rather glad to get his sticky face out of the public view. All the way to Greyfriars Putnam filled in the time by telling Poker what he thought of him—Poker listening with an unmoved wooden face—the American junior's remarks having exactly as much effect on him as water on a duck.

THE NINTH CHAPTER.

Poor Old Bunter!

"BUNTER!"

Mr. Prout's rich and fruity voice boomed in Hall.

The Fifth Form master was taking roll.

But when Prout boomed "Bunter!" there came no answering "adsum." Remove fellows glanced round. Bunter was not present.

"Bunter!" came a deeper boom.

But it booted not. Billy Bunter was not there, and could not, therefore, answer to his name. Prout marked him absent.

Harry Wharton & Co., in the ranks of the Remove, exchanged rather startled looks. They had returned from the bunshop in ample time for calling-over, and had not seen Billy Bunter about when they came in. But, so far as they had remembered him at all, they had supposed that he was about somewhere.

They had taken it for granted that when he awoke from his nap in Popper Court Woods, he would roll homeward. He had not looked like awakening in time to arrive at the bunshop for the spread; but it had never occurred to them that he would not awaken in time to return to Greyfriars for calling-over. Yet he had not turned up.

Harry Wharton glanced at the big oak doors—closed while roll was taken. It was not infrequent for fellows to squeeze in at the last moment, and hurry into their places. But there was no sign of Bunter.

"My hat!" murmured Bob Cherry. "Bunter can't still be snoozing!"

"Not after hours of it, I should think," said Nugent.

"The snoozefulness would certainly be rather terrific!" remarked Hurree Jamset Ram Singh. "But the esteemed and idiotic Bunter is not here."

"Must be about somewhere," said Johnny Bull. "Perhaps he's found somebody's tuck in somebody's study, and it's kept him too busy to hear the bell."

Harry Wharton nodded. It was possible, and he could hardly believe that the Owl of the Remove was still out of gates, sleeping in the wood. If he was, it could hardly be a natural slumber. All the juniors had laughed at Poker's suspicion of "dope," but if Billy Bunter was still asleep out of gates, that put rather a different complexion on the matter.

The Famous Five were rather anxious now to ascertain whether Bunter had come in or not. As soon as the school was dismissed from Hall, they looked for the fat junior.

He was not to be seen.

"Seen Bunter?" they inquired up and down and round about the House, of every fellow they met.

"No!" was the general reply.

"Too often!" was Skinner's answer to the question; which was not a helpful variation.

Nobody had seen Bunter! Harry Wharton ran down to Gosling's lodge, to ask the porter whether he had seen Bunter come in. Gosling hadn't.

It was soon clear that Billy Bunter had not come back to the school. It was almost unimaginable that he was still

Hurree Jamset Ram Singh started the ball rolling, and the whole Form followed suit. Pudding after pudding, in sticky chunks, fairly rained on the Greyfriars gunman. He staggered and stumbled, blinded and choked by treacle-pudding. "Boys!" roared Mr. Quelch. "Cease this riot at once!"

asleep, under the shady beech where the juniors had left him. But if not, where was he?

"What the jolly old dickens——" said Bob Cherry. He gave his friends an uneasy look. "I say, there can't be anything in what that idiot Pike was jabbering——"

"How could there be?" said Harry. "How could Bunter be doped, as that fathead calls it? Who would play such a mad trick on him?"

Putnam van Duck whistled.

"I've sure called that guy Poker all the names I could remember," he remarked, "but I guess it looks as if he was on that mark. That gink Bunter is some sleeper, I allow, but if he's asleep now, he's sure been doped."

"But who — how——" exclaimed Nugent.

The chums of the Remove were uneasy and alarmed. "Dope," to their minds, was almost unthinkable. But where was Bunter?

Hurree Jamset Ram Singh's dusky face set a little, and he did not speak. The gunman's suspicion of the nabob, absurd as it was, was neither grateful nor comforting to him.

"We can't leave it at this!" said the captain of the Remove abruptly. "Bunter's got to be fetched in. It—it looks to me as if he's been drugged, somehow—goodness knows how. It looks as if Pike was right there——"

"But who—and how——"

"Goodness knows! But I'd better go to Quelch and let him know about Bunter."

That, it was clear, had to be done. Whatever was the truth of the matter, Billy Bunter could not be left out of gates, and the dusk was already falling. The Co. nodded assent, and the captain of the Remove went at once to his Form-master's study.

"Bunter hasn't come in yet, sir?" asked Harry, with a lingering hope that the fat Owl might have turned up.

"No, Wharton!" answered Mr. Quelch. Wharton noticed that a cane lay on the Remove master's table—evidently ready for Bunter when he did come in!

"I—I'm afraid there's something wrong with him, sir!" faltered Harry.

Mr. Quelch looked at him.

Hurriedly the captain of the Remove explained how Bunter had been left. Mr. Quelch's eyebrows rose, and rose more and more, as he listened in astonishment.

"But the boy cannot have remained asleep, out of doors, all this time!" exclaimed Mr. Quelch. "Absurd, Wharton!"

"I—I know, sir! But—that man Pike has an idea in his head that dope has been used——"

"Dope!" repeated Mr. Quelch blankly.

"I—I mean, a drug, sir! He thinks that it was meant for Van Duck, and Bunter got it somehow by mistake! The kidnappers——"

"Absurd!" said Mr. Quelch.

But he knitted his brows and looked very thoughtful.

"It is very singular that the boy has not come in," he said. "Very singular indeed! I think, Wharton, that I had better give you leave out of gates, to fetch him in, before it is quite dark."

"If he's unable to walk, sir——"

"I can scarcely think so. But"—Mr. Quelch paused—"I think you had better guide two Sixth Form prefects to the spot where he was left."

"Very well, sir!"

Five minutes later Harry Wharton left the school with Wingate and Gwynne of the Sixth. A crowd of fellows watched them go.

By that time everybody knew that Bunter was missing, and that he had been left asleep, hours ago, in Popper Court Woods.

Skinner declared that, once asleep, Bunter was not likely to wake till morning; but that was only Skinner's little joke. There could be no doubt that if the fat Owl was still asleep it was the result of drugging—quite an exciting idea to the juniors—especially to those who had been present at the party in the bunshop.

Poker Pike's amazing suspicion was not, after all, unfounded. Had Bunter, in some incredible way, fallen the victim to "dope" intended by the kidnappers for the American junior? It looked very much like it—and, in that case, it became a burning question whose hand had administered the dope? It seemed impossible that it could have been administered by anyone outside the school.

An eager crowd waited at the big doorway of the House for the return of Wharton and the prefects. If they had to carry Bunter home, they were not likely to return in a hurry. Skinner suggested that a breakdown gang would be required to go to their aid. But Skinner was frowned upon on all sides; it was no time for Skinner to be funny.

It was nearly time for prep, when, at

(*Continued on page* 16.)

VICTORS and VANQUISHED

Last Laughable Spasm of Dicky Nugent's Serial:

"THE SPARTANS OF ST. SAM'S!"

When Doctor Birchemall appeared on the St. Sam's Sports Ground, the eggsitement was at fever-pitch, though the cheers were not at all measley (joak!). Behind the Head came the rest of the judges; and behind them the athletes who were to compete in the day's events. Teams from St. Bill's and St. Pete's as well as St. Sam's marched side by side; and the misterious newcomers from St. Alf's—a skool nobody had ever heard of before—added just that spice of uncertainty to the results which was needed to complete the enthewsiasm of the specktators!

Deffening cheers rent the air as Doctor Birchemall led the procession down the track to the starting-post.

"Bash 'em, St. Bill's!"

"Smash 'em, St. Sam's!"

"Punish 'em, St. Pete's!"

The only skool that drew no cheers at all was St. Alf's; but the crowd were far too eggsited to notiss that pekuliar feetcher.

The Head, who was official starter as well as leading judge, soon got to bizziness.

"Ladies and jentlemen," he cride through a meggafone, "the first event on the programme is the Senior Hundred Yards race. Competitors will kindly line up immejately—or even sooner than that if they can!"

Four white-clad figgers detached themselves from the rest. The St. Sam's supporters groaned when they saw that Weekling, one of the puniest of the Head's so-called Spartans, was going to run for the home side. But Doctor Birchemall, who could see nothing wrong with the fellows he had trained himself, farely beamed as Weekling crawled up to the start.

"Bravvo, my brave Weekling!" he cride, clapping his bony hands enthewsiastically. "You look every inch a champion! Why, you ought to wack these mizzerable-looking spessimens hollow!"

Mr. Lickham, who was one of the Head's fellow-judges, coffed rather loudly and gave his chief a warning dig in the ribs.

"Not so loud, sir, or people won't like it!" he wispered. "The judges are supposed to be striktly impartial, sir!"

"Pooh! What does it matter on a day like this?" grinned the Head. "It's plain that none of the others stand a chance against the St. Sam's Spartans—as plain as your face, Lickham, if you don't mind my saying so!"

Mr. Lickham was not eggsactly an artist; nevertheless, Doctor Birchemall's remark made him culler furiously.

"Really, sir——" he began furiously.

But the Head had no intenshun of delaying the start for the plezzure of lissening to Mr. Lickham. Seeing that the runners were ready, he projoocedan old blunderbuss he had brought along from the skool armoury and fired.

Bang!

Like unleashed greyhounds, the runners leaped away from the start—or, at least, three of them did. The eggception was Weekling. Weeks of strenuous training under Doctor Birchemall had made poor old Weekling an even weaker weakling than he had been before the Head had enrolled him as a Spartan; and all he could do was to totter feebly along the track at the speed of a broken-down old cab-horse! The Head, who had only partly recovered from the shock of the blunderbuss going off, didn't notiss this at once and cheered wildly, under the impression that Weekling had won the race!

"Go it, Weekling! Attaboy! Look at his speed! Greased litening isn't in it with him! He's winning! He's winning! He wins! Hooray!"

The Head grabbed his nearest naybour, who happened to be Sir Gouty Greybeard, and started waltzing him roundandround out of sheer happiness!

It was Mr. Lickham who stepped in and eggsplained how matters really stood.

"Pull yourself together, sir!" he urged, pulling the Head back by the seat of his trowsis. "Weekling hasn't reached the half-way line yet. St. Sam's haven't won, sir; it's St. Alf's!"

Doctor Birchemall soon stopped his capers at this announcement. A garstly pallor spread itself over his cheeks.

"Impossibul!" he said, horsely.

"I'm afraid it's only too true, sir," sighed Mr. Lickham. "If you ask my opinion, this is only a fourtaste of what we may eggspect right through the programme. But, be that as it may, St. Alf's have won the first race!"

"Then I shall disqualify the winner!" declared Doctor Birchemall. "He won on a fowl! He deliberately ran ahead of Weekling! I'm not standing for tackticks like that on this track, Lickham! He's disqualified!"

"But even in that case, sir, St. Bill's or St. Pete's will take the honners!"

"That's all you know about it, Lickham! St. Bill's and St. Pete's will be disqualified for fowling in the same manner! Where's my meggafone?"

Doctor Birchema'l grabbed his meggafone, which was lying on the grass, and bellowed through it in a voice like that of the Bull of Bashem.

"Ladies and jentlemen!" he cride. "Here is the result of the Senior Hundred Yards race. St. Alf's:—disqualified for fowling. St. Bill's:—ditto. St. Pete's:—ditto. Winner:—Weekling of the St. Sam's Spartans!"

A mermer of indignation ran through the assembulled multitude.

"Shame!"

"Play the game, Birchemall!"

"Don't be a beastly rotter, sir!"

Then Sir Gouty Greybeard stepped in. Seezing the Head's meggafone, the vennerable old jentleman addressed the crowd himself.

"Ladies and jentlemen! Please—hah!—keep your seats!" he yelled, in his refined, aristocrattick voice. "As one of the—huh!—guvvernors of this—hah!—historical old skool, I take the responsibility of over-riding Doctor Birchemall's verdict! I award the race to St. Alf's, egad! Three harty cheers for the winner!"

Doctor Birchemall farely nashed his teeth with rage, as the crowd broke into frenzied cheering. But it was impossibul to do anything but bough to the will of an important jentleman like Sir Gouty Greybeard. His word was law, and the Head realised that if the Spartans were to win the day now, they would have to win on their merits. After a moment's reflecktion, he went off to the House. When he reappeared a little later, he was armed with two big birchrods! It was pretty obvious that for
the day the He
going to spare t
spoil his Sparta

From that m
wards Doctor
feetchered prom
every event.
Senior Quarter
the Junior 220
followed the Spa
dates half-way
course, flogging
the very dickens
their lagging
When the Junic
Yards came on
behind Littlegr
the Spartan run
pitchfork, and
violently into I
rear to make su
got away smartl
Tug-of-War, he
his plan a little
stuck pins into t
mies of the
opponents to pu
their stroke.

But all he did
avale. His vaw
tans simply coul
win, despite
efforts.

It was the mi
that carried c
honners—the
was supposed to
from St. Alf's.
went from trium
the crowd chee
and louder.
they cheered, th
wondered who t
men were, for
ever heard of
before.

At the end of
Alf's had won th
a huge margin
over all the c
bined. And i
they went up
their trofies of v
Sir Gouty Grey
the mistery of
dentity was at
up.

GREYFRIA

No. 190. EDITED BY

WOULD YOU BELIEVE IT?

Johnny Bull is justly proud of his physical development, which is remarkable in a junior. The other day he lifted a heavy weight which was too much for Bolsover major, Bulstrode, and other hefty fellows. Johnny says it's no good straining—he "lifts" with his shoulders.

A version of "The Three Musketeers," produced by William Wibley in the Rag "produced" some lively sword-play. When Bunter, getting excited, knocked "Wib's" wig off with the point of his sword, "Wib" looked "daggers"—but the audience roared. They saw the "point"!

Running the 440 yard
57 seconds, Peter Todd
defeated Wharton an
Singh. Toddy has the
and gawkiest—legs in th
but his spare frame c
reserve of power. B
Alonzo, though, coul
440 yards if he t

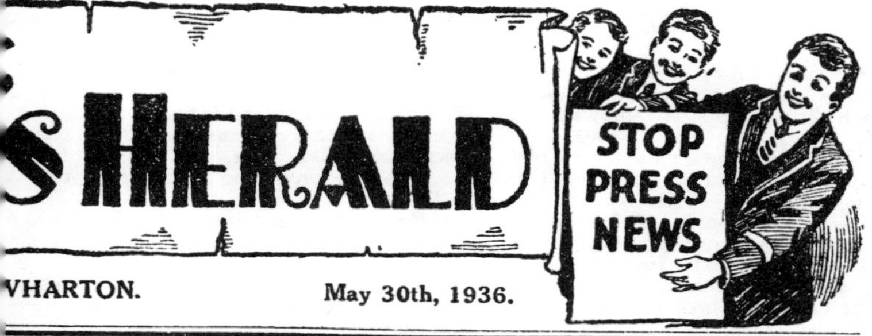

As they marched up to he platform, they started removing false wigs and eyebrows and rubbing off greasepaint ; and by the ime they were mounting he steps, they were reveeled for what they really vere. A yell of sheer amazement went up from he crowd as they reckernised their faces.

" Burleigh ! "

" Tallboy ! "

" Jolly and Fearless ! "

" It's the St. Sam's eam ! The team the Head struck out in faver of he Spartans ! "

" Ha, ha, ha ! "

The crowd shreeked.

At first, when he knew he truth, Doctor Birchemall looked awfully waxy.

But it wasn't long before e had recovered his usual song-froid.

" Ladies and jentlemen ! " e grinned, when the larfter ad at last died away. " I eggspect this is a grate serprize to most of you. But, of corse, so far as I am onserned, I must say I guessed it all the time ! "

" Wha-a-a-at ? "

" You did it very well, Burleigh—very well indeed ! " said the Head. ' But you have to get up early in the morning to hoodwink a wily old bird ike me ! I knew it all along ! But now that you ave come out in your true cullers, let me be the first to congratulate you ! You ave brought credit to St. Sam's to-day—and natcherally the credit is all nine ! "

For a moment the St. Sam's fellows could only gasp. Then there was a yell.

" Bump him ! "

Although it was not eggsactly the thing to bump

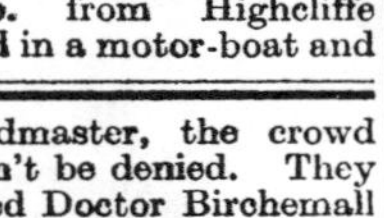

a headmaster, the crowd wouldn't be denied. They bumped Doctor Birchemall again and again.

Which made a very happy ending to the Sports at St. Sam's and also made it a pretty safe bet that Doctor Birchemall would be jolly wary of poking his nose into skool athletticks for a long, long time.

Mauly Lazy?—Never!

Says HARRY WHARTON

Anyone who tells me that Lord Mauleverer is lazy after what happened last Wednesday is in for a warm argument. Mauly is the very reverse of lazy when you get down to it ; and last Wednesday proved it up to the hilt !

Mind you, one might have been excused for thinking he was, in the first part of the afternoon. We had to drag him out of the House to get him to come down to the river with us ; and we had the dickens of a job to get him to do a little poling when we got into our punt. In fact, the idea that he's lazy was rather confirmed when he fell asleep over the job and landed himself in the water !

But after that—well, you should have been there to see him !

When we got to Popper's Island, Mauly changed into a bathing-costume Bob lent him and lit a fire to dry his clobber.

Later, when we left him to go exploring, Ponsonby & Co. from Highcliffe arrived in a motor-boat and

collared our tuck-hampers, and Mauly fought the whole crowd of 'em on his own !

Beaten by the overwhelming odds, he still mustered up sufficient energy to dive in after them and cling on to a rope that trailed from the stern of their boat. In this way he was drawn through the water with them till they landed at a spot farther up the river. Then he cheerfully climbed up on to terra firma again and waded into them once more !

What's more, he was able to draw them so far away from the bank as to give him a chance to race back ahead of them to the motor-boat, which he boarded and pushed off before they could catch up to him !

And so it was that Mauly returned to Popper's Island in triumph in Pon's motor-boat with our tuck-hamper intact ! And didn't we give him a welcome !

After all this, perhaps you can understand why I'm going to disagree with the next man who tells me Mauly is lazy.

Mauly lazy ? Never !

Or, at any rate, not always !

Look out for Laughs—

Says BOB CHERRY

IF QUELCH STARTS WRITING FICTION!

Rumour has it that the Quelch-bird is actually writing a detective thriller. It sounds almost too good to be true. But if it is true, I'm buying a copy the day the book comes out, I can tell you ! Quelchy describing gangsters ought to give the Rag the biggest laugh of the year ! Can't you imagine it, kids ?

" The great detective burst into the gangsters' den.

" ' Boys ! ' he thundered. ' Hold out your hands ! '

" At the sound of that dreaded voice, a cry of terror went round the room like wildfire.

" ' Cave ! '

" ' Gracious goodness ! It's the constable ! '

" Then the criminals recovered from their first shock of surprise and began to fight like cornered rats.

" ' Pray assist me to engage the constable in fisticuffs, dear friends ! ' cried out one murderous crook. But the great detective forestalled the move. With a cat-like spring, he flung himself at the rebel and gave him a good hard slap ; and the gangster, bursting into tears, desisted. Then another of the criminals struck a fighting attitude ; but our hero rapped him sharply on the knuckles with the handle of his umbrella, and the gangster slumped to the floor, weeping bitterly. The rest then gave in before further damage was done.

" ' Boys ! ' cried the detective, as his eyes swept triumphantly over his cringing captives. ' My task is done. Remorselessly, relentlessly, I have pursued you till at last I have you all in my grip. Now, wretched and depraved youths, you must pay the penalty !

" ' Take fifty lines ! ' "

Oh, yes, it ought to be great stuff, Quelchy's detective thriller ! I wouldn't miss it for worlds !

Fags' New Demands Are Too Modest!

Declares TOM BROWN

Listening-in to the open-air meeting of the newly formed Fags' Protection League under the elms the other afternoon, I couldn't help feeling that their demands are far too modest. Young Dicky Nugent, who was speaking, really surprised me by his moderation.

" Are we raising the banner of rebellion ? " his shrill treble asked. " The answer is NO ! All we want is justice ! "

Loud applause, varied by louder arguments between members of the audience, greeted this statement.

" We ask for an end to tyranny and bullying ! " said Dicky. " We ask for just a few modern comforts —a radio-gramophone in the Form-room, tickets for the pictures twice a week and a free tuckshop ! "

More loud applause, varied by one or two free fights.

" Just grant us these few simple wants and abolish prep and we shall be satisfied ! " declared Dicky. " Is there anything unreasonable about that ? "

No fear ! If you ask me, the fags are being a jolly sight too reasonable !

After all, the fags might well be asking for free motor rides and aeroplane trips and week-ends at the seaside and liveried footmen and no lessons at all !

They're too modest altogether—that's what's wrong with 'em. If the powers that be are wise, they'll agree to the requirements of the Fags' Protection League without a moment's delay !

What do you think ?

*(For the benefit of those who don't quite fathom the depths of Browny's sarcasm, we ought to say that he's really advocating that someone should go along to dust the fags' trousers with an ashplant ! This is just his funny way of saying it !—*Ed.*)*

GREYFRIARS FACTS WHILE YOU WAIT !

Cherry, the athletically nded, thinks " gym " classes the sands at the seaside a ndid idea—a stride forward, fact. Billy Bunter, who is fond of stride-jumping, is ly to take " strides " in the osite direction if he spots a holiday class !

Mrs. Mimble says Billy Bunter has put up a new record by calling in at the tuckshop seventeen times in one day to try to get some tarts " on tick." For the sake of peace, Mrs. Mimble let him have them. But she will have to " watch " Bunter—his idea of " tick " is limitless !

A game of handball on the sands at Pegg Bay settled a dispute between Remove and Upper Fourth. Harry Wharton & Co. showed themselves much " handier " with the ball than Temple & Co., however—with the result that the Upper Fourth " bit the sand " by 10 goals to nil.

(*Continued from page* 13.)

last, the tinkle of a bell was heard at the gate.

"They're coming!" said Bob Cherry.

Through the dusk of the quad, the returning party loomed up. Wingate and Gwynne were carrying a fat figure between them. Harry Wharton followed.

There was a buzz of excitement as they came up the steps. It was Bunter—and he had to be carried! The question of dope was settled now.

An eager swarm of excited fellows surrounded the prefects as they came in. Panting for breath, Wingate and Gwynne set Bunter down on his feet—still holding him, or he would have fallen.

Every eye was glued on the fat face. Billy Bunter's eyes were tightly closed behind his spectacles. He grunted and snored alternately. It was strange, startling, almost unnerving, to see the fat junior standing there fast asleep; but there was no doubt that he was deep in the deepest slumber.

"You found him there?" asked Bob, as Wharton followed in.

"Just where we left him," answered Harry. "Fast asleep under the beech. The handkerchief had slipped off his face, but that was all. He doesn't seem to have stirred."

"Poor old Bunter!"

"Is—is—is that Bunter?" Mr. Quelch rustled up with a startled face. "Bless my soul! He appears quite unconscious——"

"Quite, sir!" said Wingate.

"Please take him to his dormitory! I will telephone for the doctor immediately."

Plenty of willing hands helped to get Bunter to the Remove dormitory, where he was laid on his bed. A quarter of an hour later, Dr. Pillbury came buzzing from Friardale in his car.

Prep, that evening, claimed little attention. The fellows had to go to the studies—but the studies buzzed with excited conversation. Billy Bunter, in the Remove dormitory, lay unconscious—sleeping like Rip Van Winkle. The doctor's report was reassuring; he seemed to have suffered no harm, and could only be left till he came out of that strange slumber. He was still asleep when the Remove went to bed, and it was not till the rising-bell was ringing in the morning that Billy Bunter's eyes opened at last.

THE TENTH CHAPTER.

No Clue!

THAT day Billy Bunter had the spotlight.

The Owl of the Remove was the cynosure of all eyes.

His strange adventure had caused astonishment all round, but the most astonished fellow of all was Bunter himself!

He declined, at first, to believe that he had remained asleep in Popper Court Woods, and had been carried home by two Sixth Form prefects, unaware of what was going on.

But the fact that he awakened in bed in the Remove dormitory, and remembered nothing after falling asleep under the beech, convinced Bunter at last that it really had happened.

He had awakened feeling quite normal; the dope seemed to have left behind no effect whatever.

There was only one thing that mattered with Bunter. He was fearfully hungry, and more anxious for breakfast that morning than he had ever been before! And the breakfast he packed away was a record.

Mr. Quelch, who breakfasted with his Form, was very tolerant that morning with Bunter! Bunter was allowed a free run of the table.

As he had missed both tea and supper the previous day, he had a lot of leeway to make up. He did his best to make up for it.

At his tenth rasher and eleventh egg, however, Mr. Quelch called time, as it were. He was tolerant, kind, and sympathetic, but perhaps he was beginning to fear that Bunter might burst.

Bunter did not realise the danger! He blinked reproachfully at his Form-master through his big spectacles.

"I'm still hungry, sir!" he pointed out.

"You may have a little toast and marmalade," said Mr. Quelch, relenting.

Bunter did not have a little toast and marmalade—he had a lot! Again his Form-master called halt.

"I'm still hungry, sir!" ventured Bunter.

"Nonsense!" said Mr. Quelch.

And that was that!

But it was not quite "that," so to speak, for the fat junior annexed toast from Bob Cherry on one side of him, and a grape-fruit from Van Duck on the other. They grinned, and let him go ahead. But Skinner gave the fat Owl a warning whisper.

"Look out, Bunter!"

"Eh!" Bunter blinked round in alarm, fearful of Mr. Quelch's gimlet eye. But the Remove master had turned away at the moment to speak to Mr. Hacker.

"Better leave Van Duck's prog alone!" grinned Skinner. "That's how you got the dope, old fat man!"

"Oh!" gasped Bunter.

There was a chuckle up and down the Remove table.

Nobody doubted that the dope the day before had been intended for Van Duck. Somehow or other it had been introduced into something the American junior was expected to consume, and which Bunter must have consumed instead — not at all an uncommon happening!

Bunter blinked at the tempting grape-fruit uneasily. Then, slowly and reluctantly, he pushed it away from him. For the first time on record Billy Bunter refused foodstuffs!

"O.K., you fat gink!" said Van Duck. "Get on with it!"

"No fear!" said Bunter.

"You silly ass!" said Bob. "Do you think somebody's been doping the grub at the brekker-table?"

"Somebody doped something yesterday!" answered Bunter. "I don't know what it was, but I must have got it! No more for me, thanks!"

Van Duck, grinning, proceeded to deal with the grape-fruit himself. "Dope" had been about the previous day; but he was not feeling uneasy. Although far from being as keen on foodstuffs as William George Bunter, he was not likely to miss his meals for fear of dope!

But Billy Bunter had made up his fat mind to be very careful. For the present, at least, Van Duck's ample tuck was safe from the grub-raider of the Remove.

In Form that morning Billy Bunter began to feel rather glad that he had been through that strange adventure.

Quelch was very kind. Having done no prep the previous evening, Bunter could not be called on for his "con." Neither was he called on for anything else. Quelch gave him a very easy time in first and second lesson. Stiff and stern as Quelch looked, he could be very considerate when he saw just reason to be so.

Slacking in Form was sheer happiness to Billy Bunter. He could only hope that this would last.

He rolled out, in break, with a cheery grin on his fat visage.

And, in break, he realised what an important person he was. Fellows of all Forms came up to him in the quad to ask him about his weird experience. Fellows he hardly knew by sight were quite interested in him.

Even prefects of the Sixth, great men who lived in quite a different and superior world, gave Bunter a word. Even Coker of the Fifth, who regarded the Lower Fourth simply as troublesome microbes bestowed on Bunter some minutes of his valuable time.

Bunter found the spotlight rather agreeable.

He rolled back into the Remove-room for third school, feeling quite bucked. Quelch was still going easy.

He even affected not to notice that Bunter was sucking toffee—a gift in break from some sympathiser whose sympathy had taken a practical form.

Billy Bunter began to feel that he almost liked Quelch.

After morning school, he was called on to stay behind, when the Remove were dismissed. Such a summons would, at any other time, have filled Bunter with alarm. Now, however, he stopped quite cheerfully at his Form-master's desk. He wondered whether Quelch was going to give him an extra holiday or something of that sort!

Mr. Quelch stopped short of that. Bunter had been called up for questions to be asked.

The Remove master wanted to know about that dope! It was, of course, a matter that had to be investigated. The surreptitious hand had to be traced.

"Now, Bunter," said Mr. Quelch, "I wish you to answer me very carefully. There appears to be no doubt that some drug—fortunately, harmless—was introduced into something you ate or drank yesterday. No doubt you can remember what you may have eaten?"

"Oh, yes, sir! I don't eat much——"

"Eh?"

"I'm not always stuffing, like some fellows, sir," said Bunter. "I can remember everything I ate yesterday."

"It appears probable," said Mr. Quelch, "that the drug was intended for Van Duck—there appears to be no other way of accounting for it. Did you eat anything intended for Van Duck?"

"No, sir!" said Bunter promptly.

"You are sure, Bunter?"

"Oh, quite, sir! There are some fellows in the Remove who aren't a bit particular about snaffling another fellow's tuck, sir, but I've always been very careful about that sort of thing."

Mr. Quelch gazed at him. He was not so well acquainted with Billy

Bunter's manners and customs as the Removites were. But he had his doubts about the accuracy of that statement!

"This is a very urgent matter, Bunter," he said quietly. "Please try to remember carefully and answer truthfully."

"Oh, certainly, sir!"

"Van Duck's food or drink must, I think, have been tampered with yesterday, by some unknown means," said Mr Quelch. "If you took anything—ahem!—in a—a thoughtless moment, belonging to him——"

"Oh, no, sir!"

Bunter's answer was prompt—too prompt! He was beginning to feel alarmed.

"C-ca-can I go now, sir?" he asked.

Clearly it was not going to be an extra holiday. Bunter was anxious to get out of the Form-room.

His eye lingered on the cane on the desk. Certainly, Quelch had been very kind and considerate that morning; but Bunter doubted whether the kindness and consideration would last, if it came to light that he had snaffled a parcel from the House dame's room. Quelch was awfully strict about such things.

Fortunately—from Bunter's point of view—it was not likely to come out. Mrs. Kebble would naturally conclude that the American junior had taken the parcel addressed to him—unless she was informed otherwise.

Nobody was likely to inform her, of course. Van Duck had dealt with the grub-raider in his own way, and the matter was at an end.

Still, Bunter was not feeling easy in his fat mind. A whopping was due to him, and he did not want to be whopped.

"You are sure," said Mr. Quelch, "that you did not—h'm—consume anything that Van Duck might have been expected to take?"

"Absolutely certain, sir!"

"Did Van Duck, by any chance, give you anything that he might otherwise have taken himself?" asked Mr. Quelch. puzzled and perplexed.

"Only the ginger-beer, sir."

"Oh!" Mr. Quelch was alert at once. "Van Duck gave you some ginger-beer. Might he otherwise have drunk it himself?"

"I suppose so, sir, only——"

"A drug might very well be introduced into ginger-beer. This may be the clue of which we are in search!" exclaimed Mr. Quelch. "You drank the ginger-beer that Van Duck gave you, and——"

"Oh, no, sir!"

"You did not!" exclaimed Mr. Quelch.

"No, sir! You see——"

"I do not see!" snapped the Remove master. "If Van Duck gave you his glass of ginger-beer, why did you not drink it?"

"He—he put it down my back, sir——"

"What?"

"My b-b-b-back, sir!" stammered Bunter.

Mr. Quelch gave something like a snort. He had found a clue—to a schoolboy practical joke, apparently!

"Absurd!" he snapped.

"C-can I go now, sir?" gasped Bunter.

"If you can remember nothing else——"

"Oh, no, sir—nothing!"

"You may go!"

Bunter went—gladly! There was no danger now of the affair of the snaffled chocolates coming to light! And it did not occur to the fat Owl's podgy brain, for a moment, that it was the chocolates that had been doped! Mr. Quelch was left perplexed—without a clue to the mystery!

THE ELEVENTH CHAPTER.
Pudding for Poker!

"PIKE!"

"The absurd Pike!" exclaimed Hurree Jamset Ram Singh.

"Jolly old Pike!" grinned the Bounder.

Some of the fellows laughed. Some stared. Poker Pike, as he walked coolly into Hall at dinner-time, drew the general attention.

The gunman's hickory face was sedate as usual; almost expressionless. Poker was displaying his usual disregard for publicity!

He marched into Hall; glanced round him, and marched up to the Remove table, where that Form were already sitting down. Mr. Quelch, taking his seat at the head of the table, regarded him with surprised inquiry.

Fellows stared from the other tables. Even from the high table, where the great and glorious prefects of the Sixth sat in state, came curious stares and surprised murmurs.

The Removites grinned. Hurree Jamset Ram Singh frowned. Putnam van Duck looked at Poker as if he could have bitten him.

Heedless of all, the Greyfriars gunman stood there, giving the long table the "once-over."

"Do you—h'm—want anything, Mr. Pike?" asked the Remove master.

Mr. Quelch had never liked Poker's presence in the school; but of late he had been very civil indeed to Poker. That was since the gunman had got him away from Chick Chew, who had "roped-in" the Remove master, in one of his many schemes for getting hold of the gilt-edged American.

Even now, Quelch could not quite think that a Chicago gunman was in his proper place at a Public school; but after that eminent service from Mr. Pike, he could scarcely be anything but civil, and, indeed, grateful.

So now he addressed him with polite inquiry, instead of snapping at him as he would have done once upon a time.

"Sure!" said Poker, with a nod. "I guess I want to keep tabs on that Putnam van Duck!"

A ripple of merriment ran along the Remove table. It was checked by a gimlet-eyed glare from Mr. Quelch.

"But, really, Mr. Pike——" said the Remove master.

It was true that Poker saw kidnappers in every shadow, but he had not hitherto figured that it was necessary to watch the millionaire's son at meals.

"I reckon there's dope around, sir," explained Poker. "I got to see that that baby ain't doped none."

His slits of eyes rested for a searching moment on the dusky face of Hurree Jamset Ram Singh. The Nabob of Bhanipur was sitting only one or two places away from the American junior.

A flush came into Hurree Singh's dusky cheeks. That searching look, brief as it was, did not escape him.

"Dope!" repeated Mr. Quelch, with a start. He understood now why Poker considered it necessary to appear at meals. He coloured with vexation. "Really, it—there is not—cannot be—any danger!"

"Says you!"

"You can hardly suppose, Mr. Pike, that here, at the school dinner, anyone could possibly administer——"

"I guess I ain't taking no chances with that Putnam van Duck, sir!" said Poker stolidly. "His popper is sure paying me high to see him safe. I got to see that he ain't doped!"

"Ha, ha, ha!"

"Silence! Mr. Pike, if you desire to lunch at this table, I will direct a chair to be placed for you."

"I guess I ain't moseyed in for eats!" answered Poker. "I jest want to keep tabs! I'll say there's dope around in this here shebang, and I'll tell a man that it ain't going down young Putnam's neck!"

Mr. Quelch breathed hard and deep.

"You may stand there if you so desire!" he snapped.

"Surest thing you know!" said Poker.

Mr. Quelch desired to be considerate to the gunman. He could not forget the service Mr. Pike had rendered him, but undoubtedly he was very much perturbed and annoyed.

The bare idea of a suspicion that "dope" might be administered at the school dinner was really intolerable. Yet it could not be denied that dope had been handed out somehow the previous day. Bunter had got it instead of Van Duck, that was all.

How, when, and by whom was still an impenetrable mystery. But to suspect a Greyfriars servant or a Greyfriars boy of being a tool in the hands of the gangsters was absurd.

Absurd as it was, no other explanation was forthcoming. Mr. Quelch had to admit that. Poker's vigilance was justified, so far as that went.

Anyhow, he was going to keep "tabs."

The school dinner proceeded, with ripples of laughter. Poker stood like a statue, watching. He scanned everything that was passed to Van Duck. The American junior glared at him—without producing any effect. So long as Putnam was helped by a servant from the same supply that was handed out to the other fellows, Poker was satisfied. Wary and suspicious as he was, he did not figure that anybody was going to dope the whole Remove.

But when a dusky hand passed Van Duck the salt, Poker woke to sudden life. He reached over the table and knocked the salt-cellar out of Hurree Jamset Ram Singh's hand.

Crash!

"What——" gasped Mr. Quelch.

"You dog-goned geck!" roared Putnam van Duck.

"Silence! Mr. Pike, what——"

"O.K., sir!" said Poker calmly. "I guess I ain't taking no chances!"

"You silly ass!" exclaimed Bob Cherry indignantly.

"You howling fathead!" exclaimed Harry Wharton.

"Silence!" exclaimed Mr. Quelch. "Silence!"

Poker, once more immovable, watched. Many curious eyes turned on the dusky face of Hurree Jamset Ram Singh. The scene in the bunshop had not been forgotten, and Poker's action now was too pointed to be misunderstood. His suspicions centred on the dusky nabob.

"Mr. Pike," gasped the Remove master, "is it possible—is it imaginable—that you suspect a Remove boy?" Quelch choked with indignation.

"I ain't accusing no guy," said Poker calmly. "I'll say I don't know who handed out the dope. It was sure some guy that was around that Putnam van Duck, though the fat goob got it by mistake. Seeing that there ain't no pointer to no guy more'n any other guy, I guess it looks like it might be the darkie."

"How dare you suggest such a thing!" exclaimed Mr. Quelch, red with indignant wrath.

"I ain't taking no chances!" said Poker stolidly. "It was sure some guy in this bunch!"

"Nonsense!" hooted Mr. Quelch. "Absurd!"

Hurree Jamset Ram Singh rose to his feet.

Pudding was being served round the Remove table now—treacle pudding. Billy Bunter got busy on it at once. He was anxious to get through the first helping and bag a second, with an eye on a third. But no other fellow at the Remove table heeded the pudding. Most of the juniors were laughing, but the Co. were glaring at Mr. Pike in great wrath.

"My esteemed and idiotic Pike," said Hurree Jamset Ram Singh, his dark eyes gleaming, "the suspectfulness of any Remove man is absurd and ludicrous, and the suspectfulness of my humble self is terrifically offensive! The apologise is the proper caper!"

"Forget it!" said Poker.

"Please sit down, Hurree Singh!" gasped Mr. Quelch. "I recommend you to take no heed of this absurd, ridiculous, nonsensical——"

"With all respect to you, esteemed sahib, I am bound to take notice of the ridiculous and offensive insinuation!" said the nabob. "The absurd Pike has asked for it!"

Hurree Singh picked up his plate, on which lay a generous helping of treacle pudding.

Before even the wary gunman could guess his intention, the chunk of sticky pudding whizzed across the table and landed in the hickory face.

It was sticky, it was juicy, and it was hot! Poker Pike gave a roar as he received it on his wooden features.

"Good old Inky!" gasped Bob. "Go it, you men! Give him some more!"

Whiz! went Bob's pudding. It landed on Poker's right ear It was instantly followed by Wharton's, landing on his left.

"Boys!" shrieked Mr. Quelch.

But for once the Remove master was unheeded by his Form. Frank Nugent and Johnny Bull followed the lead of their comrades, and two generous helpings of treacle pudding squashed on Poker Pike.

"Go it, you men!" roared Bob.

"Hear, hear!"

"Ha, ha, ha!"

"Yurrrooough!" gurgled Poker, staggering, and clawing wildly at hot, sticky pudding. "I'll say—— Yrroogh!"

Squash! Squash! Squash! came chunk after chunk of pudding. The Bounder landed his on Poker's chin; Peter Todd's caught him in one eye, Squiff's in the other. Nearly all the Remove were on their feet now, hurling pudding.

Whiz, whiz! Squash, squash!

"Boys!" gasped Mr. Quelch. "Boys! I command you——"

There was a buzz from the other tables. Seniors and juniors were on their feet, staring. Even the prefects were standing up to look. Hall was filled by shouts of laughter.

Mr. Quelch waved his hands and hooted in vain. Every man in the Remove except Billy Bunter clutched up pudding to hurl. Poker's belief that the doper was "one of the bunch" might be ridiculous, but it was exasperating, too.

The Removites made it clear to Poker what they thought of him and his suspicions. Hurree Jamset Ram Singh had started the ball rolling, and the whole Form followed suit as one man. It was quite unusual for the Remove to disregard their Form-master, but they disregarded him now.

Pudding after pudding, in sticky chunks, fairly rained on the Greyfriars gunman. He staggered and stumbled, blinded and choked by treacle pudding. Pudding bunged up his eyes and nose and ears and mouth; it plastered his bowler hat, which Poker had not taken off in Hall; it ran down his neck; it stuck all over him from head to foot!

There was a howl of protest from Billy Bunter as Bob Cherry grabbed his plate away. Ammunition was running short, and Bunter was only half through his helping. It was needed for Poker Pike!

"I say, that's my pudding!" shrieked Bunter, in dismay. "I say—— Beast!"

Bunter's wild shriek was unheeded. His pudding squashed on Poker Pike. Then the Bounder grasped the pudding itself from the dish. About two-thirds of it had been served to the juniors. A third remained on the dish. Smithy seized it, and hurled it, amid yells of laughter.

"Gurrrrooogh!" gurgled Poker, as it spread all over his face, masking him with treacle.

"Ha, ha, ha!"

"Boys!" roared Mr. Quelch. "Cease this riot! Cease——"

"Pelt him!" yelled Bob Cherry.

"Give him the plate!" shouted the Bounder.

"Hurrah!"

"Go it!"

"Gurrrroooooogh!" gurgled the hapless gunman. "Urrrggh! I guess—wurrgh! Oooooooooch!"

"Ha, ha, ha!"

A plate cracked on his bowler hat. Poker dabbed and clawed treacle from his eyes, blinked round him wildly, and lurched for the doorway. He was in no state to keep tabs now! Even Poker realised it! He was a pillar of sticky treacle pudding from head to foot! Treacle was oozing down his neck. He lived, moved, and had his being in a world of treacle. Gasping and gurgling, spluttering and choking, Poker made for the door.

Howls of laughter followed him, and whizzing crockery. Poker tottered out of Hall, gurgling wildly.

"Ha, ha, ha!" roared the Remove.

"Ha, ha, ha!" echoed from one end of Hall to the other.

"Silence!" hooted Mr. Quelch. "Sit down! I order you to sit down at once! Resume your places! Silence!"

The Remove resumed their places. They had put paid to Poker, and they did not regret it; but now that the shindy was over, they rather expected a thunderstorm. After the feast came the reckoning; and they would not have been surprised at whoppings all round.

But Mr. Quelch surprised his Form. He astonished them. He opened his lips—and the Removites listened, waiting for the storm. But there was no storm. Mr. Quelch directed another pudding to be brought. Which was a great relief to his Form, especially Billy Bunter.

No doubt the Remove master shared his Form's indignation, and made allowances for it. Possibly he was even pleased to be relieved of the gunman's presence in Hall, even by such extraordinary measures.

Anyhow, he said nothing further on the subject, to the surprise and relief of the Remove.

When they came out after dinner they saw nothing of Poker Pike. He was not seen before they went in to afternoon school. Had Chick Chew "horned in" at Greyfriars just then, he would, for once, have found Poker off his guard. Poker Pike was very busy cleaning off treacle—and it kept him busy for a long, long time!

THE TWELFTH CHAPTER.

Bunter Tries It On!

"BEAST!" murmured Billy Bunter.

Shocking to relate, he was alluding to his Form-master. Needless to say, he did not let Mr. Quelch hear that remark.

It was the following day; and the Remove were in Form. It was a warm May afternoon, and Bunter was not the only Remove man who felt that there were nicer places than Form-rooms on a sunny day, and nicer things than Latin prose.

Bunter was peeved—very much peeved.

For a whole day, after his dope adventure, Quelch had been very considerate. He had slacked in Form as much as he liked.

It had seemed too good to last! And so it had proved! The next day Quelch was his old self again. Bunter was called on to construe in the morning, and handed out his "con"—for which he received a hundred lines. It was borne in on his fat mind that the happy period of slacking was over.

Which peeved Bunter very considerably. His fat brow wore a frown when he rolled in for afternoon school with the Remove. Latin prose had no attractions whatever for Bunter. Either in verse or prose, he loathed Latin. It seemed all the more putrid, after a happy day of slacking.

The day before Bunter had sucked toffee in class, unheeded. Now, when he ventured upon a single, solitary bullseye, Quelch was on him at once. He rapped fat knuckles with a pointer, and made Bunter throw a bag of bullseyes into the wastepaper-basket. No wonder the fat junior murmured "Beast!" It was quite a mild expression in the harrowing circumstances.

Now Bunter had a Latin paper before him—and never had a Latin paper seemed to him so weary, stale, flat, and unprofitable.

"Beast!" breathed Bunter.

A thoughtful wrinkle came into his fat brow. But he was not thinking of his Latin paper. Great thoughts were working in Bunter's podgy brain.

His eyes gleamed behind his spectacles.

If anything could set Billy Bunter's podgy intellect going at full pressure, it was the hope of dodging work. And Bunter had thought of a dodge.

A couple of days ago he had been doped. The doping was still a mystery. Poker Pike, at least, was expecting something of the kind to be tried again. So it might be! True, it was unlikely that another packet of dope, intended for Putnam van Duck, would get to Bunter's address. Still, it was possible! How was Quelch to know?

Quelch had been kind and sympathetic for a whole day, after Bunter's last doping. Now, if he was kind and sympathetic for a couple of hours, it would be all right.

And so the Remove, busy with Latin papers, were suddenly startled by a sound unaccustomed in the Form-room—a deep and resonant snore!

Every fellow jumped and looked round.

Mr. Quelch jumped, too!

Snore!

Quelch was quite unaware that his valuable instruction sometimes had a drowsy effect on his pupils. Certainly he never expected to see any fellow in his Form go to sleep at his desk!

"Oh crumbs!" breathed Bob Cherry. "That ass Bunter——"

There was a suppressed chuckle. The juniors supposed that Bunter, under the combined effects of Latin and warm weather, had nodded off to sleep. They had no doubt that Quelch would soon wake him up.

Bunter's fat head leaned on a fat arm on his desk. His little round eyes were glued shut behind his big round spectacles. And he snored.

Mr. Quelch gazed at him, transfixed, for a long moment. Then he hooted:

"Bunter!"

Snore!

"Bunter!"

Snore!

"Upon my word!" gasped Mr. Quelch. "Boys! Cease laughing at once! Do you imagine that this is a laughing matter?"

The grinning Removites looked as if they imagined that very thing. But Mr. Quelch saw no cause for merriment. He was deeply annoyed.

He strode over to Bunter's desk. Within a yard of the fat Owl he roared:

"Bunter!"

Snore!

Mr. Quelch had thoughtfully picked up his cane. Now he gave the fat junior a rap across his podgy shoulders.

"Oh!" spluttered Bunter.

"Bunter, how dare you go to sleep in class!" thundered Mr. Quelch.

Snore!

Mr. Quelch gazed at that hopeful pupil as if petrified. The Removites gazed at him, gasping.

If Bunter had been asleep, that whack with the cane certainly had awakened him, to judge by the howl he had uttered. But now he was going on snoring, as if still asleep. If Bunter hoped to get away with that, it showed that he had a very hopeful nature.

"Bunter!" gasped Mr. Quelch.

Snore!

"Bunter, you are not asleep!" stuttered Mr. Quelch. "What do you mean, Bunter, by this palpable pretence? Are you in your right senses?"

Snore!

"Upon my word, Bunter, if you do not sit up immediately, I shall cane you!" hooted Mr. Quelch. The cane swished in the air. "How dare you pretend to be asleep when I am speaking to you? I am perfectly aware that you are wide awake, Bunter!"

"Oh, no, sir!" gasped Bunter, alarmed by the swish of the cane in the air. "I—I—I'm fast asleep, sir!"

"Wha-a-a-t?"

"I—I can't open my eyes, sir!—I—I—I'm sound asleep!"

"Ha, ha, ha!" yelled the Remove.

"Silence! Bunter, how dare you!" roared Mr. Quelch. "How dare you make such a ridiculous statement!"

"'Tain't, sir!" gasped Bunter. "I—I'm asleep, sir. I—I can't wake up. I've been doped!"

"Doped!" shrieked Mr. Quelch.

"Yes, sir!" gasped Bunter. "Same as I was the other day, sir! I—I—I'm absolutely unconscious, sir."

The Removites fairly rocked. But Mr. Quelch did not share their mirth. For a moment or two he stared at Bunter; then the swishing cane came down, across the fat shoulders, with a mighty swipe.

Whack!

"Yaroooop!" roared Bunter.

He bounded.

If he had been asleep, he was awake now! He was wide awake! He bounded up from the form, roaring.

"Ha, ha, ha!"

"Ow! Wow! Yaroooh! Whooop!" roared Bunter.

"Bunter, you absurd, prevaricating boy——"

"Yooo-hooop!"

"Bend over that form, Bunter!"

"Oh crikey! I—I say, sir—— Wow!"

"Bend over!" thundered Mr. Quelch.

Whack, whack, whack!

"Yow-ow-ow! Whoooooop!"

"Now," said Mr. Quelch, "you may take your place, Bunter, and write your paper."

"Yow-ow-ow-ow!"

Bunter sat on the form again. He wriggled there painfully. And he did not go to sleep again! Brainy as that great idea was, evidently it failed to work with a downy bird like Quelch! For some reason—Bunter did not know why—Quelch hadn't believed that it was dope! That great idea was an absolute frost, and Bunter was sorry that he had tried it on! And dismal as Latin prose was, he did not think of trying it on again!

THE THIRTEENTH CHAPTER.

From Jest to Earnest!

"THE ludicrous ass!" growled Hurree Jamset Ram Singh.

And the Co. frowned.

They were walking in the quad after class, when Poker Pike appeared in the offing. The chums of the Remove were heading for the school shop, to refresh themselves with ginger-beer after Latin prose. Had the Famous Five been on their own, Poker would have taken no heed. But Putnam van Duck was with them, and Poker appeared suddenly from nowhere in particular and followed on.

Putnam breathed hard.

"I'll say I'm getting fed-up to the back teeth with that guy!" he said.

(*Continued on next page.*)

GREYFRIARS INTERVIEWS

Our long-haired poet is on the war-path again. This week his victim is

SIDNEY JAMES SNOOP,

one of the black sheep of the Remove.

(1)

To save myself trouble, I'll tell you at once
That Snoop is a toady, a weed and a dunce!
His will-power is weak and he's easily led
By any black sheep fairly strong in the head.
He hasn't the character, you will agree,
Of Smithy or any such fellow as he.
He follows their lead in their underhand stunts—
In fact, he's a toady, a weed and a dunce!

(2)

Once he decided to make a fresh start,
To turn a new leaf and be decent and smart.
That soon petered out, but we're glad to recall
That Snoop had the courage to try it at all.
Deep down in him somewhere he has a soft spot.
He's sometimes not happy with Skinner and Stott,
But not very often—the spot is too deep,
And usually Snoop is a thorough bad sheep.

(3)

In class-work he shines, but he shines the wrong way;
And Quelch says that Snoopey is turning him grey.
He's almost a genius at making mistakes
And, in his opinion, Canute burnt the cakes.
King Henry the Eighth told the waves to retreat,
And then walked barefooted to Cripplegate Street
Where Becket was waiting to kill the Black Prince,
Who died where he stood and has never smiled since.

(4)

With views such as these you'll discover, no doubt,
Why Snoop spends more time in detention than out.
And that's where he was when I sought him to-day—
In detention again in the usual way.
I stole in the class-room when Quelch had gone out,
For it's risky, of course, when a master's about.
Said Snoopey: "Trot in! You can give me a hand
With one or two things which I don't understand!"

(5)

I looked at the paper that Quelchy had set,
And some of his answers I'll never forget!
The first word was "ferret," which Snoopey had styled,
"A thing that eats rabbits!" No wonder I smiled.
Said I: "You will call it, if you've any sense,
A third person, singular verb, active tense,
The imperfect conjunctive of 'fero, I bear!'"
To which he replied with a gasp of despair.

(6)

I grinned and continued: "And 'possum' methinks
Is not a 'wild creecher resembling the linx!'
D'ye think it's a paper on nature, old man?
No, 'possum' is first person present, 'I can!'
And here again, 'ire' isn't 'anger,' you know!
But present imperative—'eo—I go!'"
And that word, at least, poor old Snoop understood,
For he brokenly murmured: "I wish that I could!"

(7)

I went on, with Snoop sitting silently glum,
"And 'venio' means——" And a voice said: "I come!"
'Twas Quelchy! He glared and said: "Thank you, my lad,
For construing Snoop's paper! Snoop ought to be glad!"
He tore up the paper (to Snoopey's content)
And, turning, said: "Snoop, you may go!"—and he went.
"And you," he remarked, with a frown on his face,
"Can write out irregular verbs in his place!"

(NOTE: The remainder of this poem, which consists of highly irregular adjectives about Quelch, is censored—Ed).

"He sure does get my goat. Here, you Poker, you beat it!"

The juniors came to a halt. Clearly the Greyfriars gunman was going to keep an eye on them in the tuckshop, wary of dope.

They liked Poker! With all his weird manners and customs they had taken a liking to him. But they were wrathy now. That the doping was a deep mystery, they admitted; but that Poker should suspect Greyfriars fellows of having a hand in it was the limit.

"Clear off, fathead!" said Harry Wharton.

"I guess not!" said Poker stolidly. "Nobody here ain't going to dope that Putnam van Duck with me around."

"You unspeakable idiot!" said Johnny Bull. "Do you think a Greyfriars man could be tipped by a kidnapper to dope anybody?"

"You said it!" agreed Poker calmly.

"You terrific fathead——" hooted the Nabob of Bhanipur.

"You can pack that up!" said Poker Pike. "I guess it was one of your bunch—I guess nobody else had no chance. And I'll mention I got suspicion that you was the guy. Mebbe you've got dope in your pocket this minute! You ain't passing it up on Putnam van Duck."

"Do you want some more treacle?" asked Bob Cherry.

"Aw, can it!" growled Poker. "I guess I'm a good-tempered guy, or I'd sure beat you up a few for treacling me that-a-way!"

"Fathead!"

"Ass!"

Heedless of those compliments, Poker Pike walked after the juniors as they walked on.

"Say," whispered Putnam, "you guys get on, and you come along with me, Inky. I guess I got a stunt for pulling that geek's leg a few."

The Co. went on to the tuckshop, and Hurree Singh changed his direction and walked down to the gates with the American junior.

After them walked Poker.

If Van Duck was going out of gates—especially in company with the dusky junior whom Poker distrusted—Poker was going to keep tabs on him, even more carefully than usual.

The two juniors walked out of gates and down the lane towards Friardale. The Greyfriars gunman hovered watchful in the rear.

"My esteemed Van Duck," murmured Hurree Jamset Ram Singh, "what is the wheezy idea?"

Putnam grinned.

"That pesky bonehead figures that you're in cahoots with the kidnappers," he answered. "I'll say he's sure suspicious that you're leading me now right where they're waiting to rope me in."

The nabob chuckled. He was exasperated, and at the same time amused, by Poker's suspicions.

"Waal, let him think so," said Van Duck. "We're going to lose this baby in the timber and give him a jolt. He sure will get mad with you when he comes on you alone and finds me missing—and it will surprise him some when I drop on his head from a branch. I'm telling you, that guy is going to have a lesson."

Hurree Singh grinned and nodded. They sauntered on down the lane, followed by the watchful Poker. They reached the stile that gave admittance into Friardale Wood. A man in a carter's smock, with a whip under his arm, was leaning on the stile.

He stepped aside for the juniors to pass, his eyes lingering on them as they went. They gave him no heed—men in carter's smocks were numerous enough about the village. And a shaggy beard and a quantity of grime quite hid the identity of Tug Keary!

They walked on by the footpath. The man in the carter's smock moved on towards the village as Poker came up, and his back was to the gunman. But he did not go far. He turned back again when the gunman had stepped over the stile.

Putnam and Hurree Singh walked some distance down the footpath, and then the American junior suddenly turned off into the wood.

Hurree Singh followed him, grinning.

They pushed a rapid way through hawthorns and bracken, and reached a big oak-tree a hundred yards or so from the path.

With a light bound Putnam caught a low branch and swung himself into the tree.

He was immediately out of sight in the foliage.

"Stick there, bo!" came his voice from above. "Wait till that pesky guy comes cavorting around! I sure am going to give Poker the surprise of his little life."

"The surprisefulness will be terrific!" chuckled Hurree Jamset Ram Singh.

He waited under the tree.

Poker was not long in coming. His suspicions, already aroused, were very keen now. The juniors had disappeared from his sight in the bracken—and Poker was in a hurry to spot them again.

A bowler hat appeared among the thickets, and Poker came panting up, his face alert with suspicion. He gave the dusky nabob a searching look, and stared round for the American junior. A glitter came into his slits of eyes as he failed to sight him.

"Say, where's that Putnam van Duck?" he barked.

Hurree Jamset Ram Singh leaned on the trunk of the oak, his hands in his pockets, and regarded the gunman with a cheery, dusky smile.

"The seefulness of the esteemed Van Duck is not great," he drawled. "He is not on this ridiculous spot."

"Where's that young guy?" barked Poker.

"The lookfulness is the proper caper," suggested the nabob, "and perhapsfully the findfulness will be the happy result."

Poker Pike's face set like iron. There was no sign of Van Duck—no sound to be heard from him. He had vanished. He had been out of the gunman's sight only two or three minutes—and in that short space of time he had disappeared.

"By the great horned toad!" breathed Poker. "I'll say I'm wise to your game, you doggoned darky! You got that young geek here for them kidnappers to cinch, and they got him! They sure got him!"

"The surefulness is not terrific, my esteemed and idiotic Poker."

"Park that!" snarled Poker. "Where's that young guy? You gotter lead me straight to him, or I guess I'll fill you so full of holes you'd do for a colander."

Poker Pike whipped out his six-gun.

"Now!" he snarled, gun in hand.

There was a rustle in the bracken behind the gunman, and he half turned. Before he could wholly turn there came a crashing blow.

With his attention fixed on the dusky schoolboy, the Greyfriars gunman was taken, for once, completely off his guard.

He had a glimpse of a man in a carter's smock, and at the same moment the butt of a revolver crashed on his head, and he spun over.

The six-gun went flying from his hand, dropping into the grass. Poker Pike went down with a crash, half stunned by that sudden, crashing blow which crushed in his bowler hat and banged like a hammer on the bullet head within.

It was such a blow as might have stunned any man. But Poker's head was hard—and he was not knocked out. He crashed over on the ground, his senses spinning, sprawling, but making an effort to rise.

But the man in the carter's smock leaped on him like a tiger.

Poker Pike was crushed down under a knee that was planted in his ribs, and the man in the smock threw up his right hand, with the revolver clubbed in it, for another smashing blow.

Had that terrible blow landed, it would have been the finish for Poker Pike for some hours to come; his dizzy senses would have been completely scattered.

But Hurree Jamset Ram Singh leaped forward.

It had all happened so suddenly that the dusky schoolboy, leaning on the oak, had been taken utterly by surprise. The assailant probably had not noticed him there; anyhow, his hands were full with Poker for the moment, and he had no time to attend to the schoolboy. A moment would have been enough for Tug; he needed no more to deal the blow that would have put Poker to sleep if it had not cracked his tough skull.

But in that moment the nabob leaped on him. Barely in time Hurree Singh grabbed the descending arm.

He was unable to stop the forcible descent of the blow, but he dragged the arm aside, and the heavy metal pistol butt crashed on the ground, inches from Poker Pike's head.

With a fierce snarl, Tug wrenched his arm loose and struck at the schoolboy. Hurree Jamset Ram Singh gave a panting cry as the pistol butt struck his dusky forehead, and he went over backwards, crashing.

Poker Pike heaved up, and Tug rocked. The gunman was hard hit, but he was still game. But the clubbed revolver was up again.

"I got you, Poker!" hissed Tug. "I got you, you big stiff! And I reckon I got that gilt-edged bird! You get yourn, Poker!"

There was a rustling and brushing in the branches of the oak above. A figure shot down, landing on the shoulders of the gangster, and Tug rolled off Poker Pike, grappling wildly with Putnam van Duck.

THE FOURTEENTH CHAPTER.

Poker Takes It Back!

HURREE JAMSET RAM SINGH strove to scramble up, but his senses were spinning. A big lump was forming on the nabob's dusky forehead. With a spinning brain, he sank back helplessly. Poker—less damaged, though he had had a harder knock—lurched to his feet.

The man in the carter's smock was rolling over in the grass, fiercely clutched by the American junior.

Tug had been taken quite by surprise by Putnam falling on him from the branches of the oak. That surprise had been intended for Poker Pike, but the game had changed suddenly from jest to earnest.

Putnam was strong and wiry, and he gave the gangster a tussle. Tug had dropped his revolver as he was hurled over, but his sinewy hands grasped at Putnam, and the struggle could not have lasted long. Putnam put every ounce into it, fighting like a wildcat, but the powerful gangster rapidly gained the upper hand.

There was no help from Hurree Singh; he was unable to get on his feet. Poker Pike heaved up and stood lurching, his head aching and spinning under the crunched bowler. But he pulled himself together with iron determination. He lurched towards the spot where his six-gun lay in the grass and stooped for it, almost pitching over as he stooped.

But he got hold of it and managed to straighten up. He lurched over to the gangster.

Crack! came the barrel of the six-gun on Tug's head.

The man in the carter's smock yelled and tore himself away from the breathless and almost exhausted American junior; he leaped clear, panting. The beard had been torn from his face in the struggle.

"Tug, you pesky scallawag!" panted Poker, and he fired as he spoke.

The report of the six-gun roared through Friardale Wood. But, for once, Poker's aim was not good; he was swaying as he pulled trigger. The bullet missed Tug by a yard.

Poker lurched towards him, pulling trigger again. The man in the carter's smock leaped away into the bracken. His own weapon lay in the grass, and Poker's dizzy eyes glared at him over the roaring six-gun. Tug sprang away just in time, missed by inches.

Poker Pike leaned one hand on the gnarled trunk of the oak to steady himself and pumped bullets after the gangster as he ran.

There was a wild crashing in the bracken as Tug fled for his life; bullets searched after him as he went, and some of them went close.

Bang, bang, bang! roared the six-gun. The hot lead tore screeching through bracken and bramble, speeding the gangster in his flight.

The rustle died away in the distance. Tug was gone. Poker loosed off his last shot and stood panting, leaning on the oak.

"Carry me home to die!" he gasped.

"Inky, old man!" Putnam scrambled over to the Nabob of Bhanipur and bent over him breathlessly with anxiety. "Inky, you're sure hurt!"

Hurree Jamset Ram Singh sat up dizzily, supported by the American junior's arm; his dusky hand went to his bruised forehead, and he grinned ruefully.

"You're hurt, old man!" panted Van Duck.

"The hurtfulness is not terrific," gasped Hurree Jamset Ram Singh. "Ow! There is an absurd bruise on my—ow!—idiotic napper, that is all."

Van Duck helped him to his feet. Hurree Singh leaned on the oak, tenderly rubbing his forehead. He was pulling himself together now, though he was still dizzy.

Poker Pike reloaded the six-gun; that was his first care. He packed it, and took off his crunched bowler and rubbed his aching head; then he punched out the bowler into a semblance of a hat again. When he replaced it he did not jam it down quite so tightly as usual.

Tug was gone; the sudden danger was over. Poker was more than alert now, ready for the whole gang of gangsters if they had turned up; but the wood was silent after the rustling of the fleeing Tug had died away.

There was a rather extraordinary expression on the hickory face of the Greyfriars gunman. He looked curiously and uncertainly at the Nabob of Bhanipur. Hurree Singh was in pain, but the look on the gunman's face made him smile.

"Putnam, you young guy, what was you doing in that tree?" growled Poker. It was dawning on him that the juniors had been "pulling his leg."

"You pesky piecan," retorted Putnam, "I was sure fooling you, like the ornery bonehead you are; and I'd sure have dropped on your cabeza if that guy hadn't horned in."

"You young gink!" grunted Poker. "You don't want to play no fool jokes on the guy what's keeping tabs on you. That galoot Tug was hanging around, watching for a chance—and I guess he came near getting by with it this time. He sure did surprise me some when he handed me that packet."

"Yep!" snapped Van Duck. "And who stopped him from plastering your fool brains all over this location?"

Poker Pike made no reply to that.

"Me, I got busy as fast as I could!" snapped Van Duck. "But it was this guy that horned in and stopped that galoot cracking your nut. Was it, or wasn't it, you pie-faced piecan?"

"Surest thing you know," admitted Poker.

"And you figuring that he was in cahoots with Chick Chew!" snorted Van Duck. "Say, you want to go round a corner and shake yourself."

Poker Pike nodded slowly.

He was slow to convince. But he had to be convinced. It was clear to even Poker's solid brain that it was Hurree Jamset Ram Singh who had defeated the gangster But for his prompt help, Poker would have lain in the grass like a log, stunned and senseless—leaving the gangster free to deal with the schoolboys. And, plucky as they were, they would have had no chance against an armed and desperate ruffian. Putnam van Duck would have been "cinched"—walked off by Tug—while Poker lay stunned, and probably the nabob stunned beside him. It was a surprise to Poker, but he had to chew on it and get it down.

"I guess," he said slowly, "that it wasn't that guy handled the dope. Nope! It sure was not that young guy. I'll tell that kid I take it back."

"And I'll tell you that you're the goob from Goobsville, and then some!" snapped Putnam. "Inky, old man, I guess we want to be hitting home—and hitting it quick. You want to doctor that prize-packet you got on your cabeza."

Poker Pike followed the two juniors back to the footpath and then to Friardale Lane. His hickory face was very thoughtful as he went. He did not speak a word till they reached the school gates.

Then, as they went in, he tapped the Nabob of Bhanipur on the elbow. Hurree Jamset Ram Singh glanced at him, with a faint grin on his dusky face.

"I'll say I'm sorry, big boy," mumbled Poker. "You sure did horn in like a little man, and you got a packet to show for it. And me figuring that you was in cahoots with them kidnapping hombres! I'm telling you I'm feeling jest now like a two-cent remnant."

"It is all right, my esteemed and idiotic Poker" grinned the nabob.

"I'll say I do feel like a piece that the cat brought in and left around," mumbled Poker, "and then some. I allow that you wasn't the doping guy—nor yet any of your bunch, I reckon. It's got me beat—but I guess I got to look farther for that doping guy."

"Mebbe you'll suspicion the Head next," suggested Van Duck sarcastically.

"Mebbe," said Poker.

"Oh, my esteemed hat!" ejaculated Hurree Jamset Ram Singh.

"Me suspicioning you, and you getting that packet on my account, it sure does make me feel a cheap skate," said Poker, who was evidently remorseful for his distrust of the nabob, now that the dusky schoolboy's good faith had been so indubitably proved. "I'm asking you to forget it, bud."

"The forgetfulness will be immediate and terrific," the nabob assured him. "The frown of absurd hostility and preposterous indignation will be replaced by the smile and friendship and kind regards."

"Search me!" gasped Poker. "You sure do spill a bibful when you start the machine."

And Poker went into Gosling's lodge, and the two juniors hurried to the House, where Mrs. Kebble's skilled services were called upon to deal with the nabob's bruise. But with all the House dame's skill and care that bruise was big and black and prominent, and it was likely to be a long time before Hurree Jamset Ram Singh got rid of the "packet" that Tug had handed him.

THE FIFTEENTH CHAPTER.

Light at Last.

"LOOK out, Bunter!" grinned Bob Cherry.

Billy Bunter blinked round through his big spectacles.

"That's Grimey," said Harry Wharton, with a glance at the stocky official figure that was crossing from the gates to the House.

A good many glances turned on Inspector Grimes, of Courtfield. Most of the fellows concluded that he had visited Greyfriars in connection with the activities of the kidnappers. But the spirit moved Bob Cherry to pull Billy Bunter's fat leg.

"Wonder who Grimey's after?" remarked Bob, with a wink to his friends, unseen by the fat Owl. "Looks bad for Bunter."

"Oh, really, Cherry——"

"The badfulness is terrific," agreed Hurree Jamset Ram Singh. "If esteemed Quelch has sent for honourable inspector to investigate mystery of missing grub——"

"Oh, really, Inky——"

"It was bound to come," said Johnny Bull gravely. "Tuck missing up and down the Remove passage——"

"I hear that Coker of the Fifth has missed a pie, too," remarked Frank Nugent, entering solemnly into the game.

"Well, if Quelch has called in Inspector Grimes, it's a pretty serious outlook for Bunter," said Harry Wharton. "As a first offender, they might let him off with a caution."

"Beast!" howled Bunter. "You jolly well know that old Grimey ain't come here for me! I never touched Coker's pie—measly thing, too, with hardly any gravy in it!"

"Ha, ha, ha!"

"I guess you had my packet from old Coot," grinned Putnam van Duck. "And if Quelch has got wise to it——"

"I didn't!" roared Bunter. "I never knew you had a parcel, and I never touched it. And that was two or three days ago, anyhow. They can't be raking that up now."

"Three months' hard for poor old Bunter," sighed Bob Cherry. "But I believe it's jolly good exercise on the treadmill. It will bring down his fat. He may come out only weighing a ton."

"Yah!" snorted Bunter.

Billy Bunter had many sins on his fat conscience—more sins than conscience, really. But he did not quite believe that a police inspector had been called in to handle the mystery of missing tuck in Remove studies. Still, he blinked rather uneasily after Mr. Grimes, as that portly official gentleman went into the House.

A few minutes later Trotter, the page, appeared, looking round. He came over to the group of Removites.

"Are they sending for Bunter?" murmured Bob.

"Oh crikey!" gasped Bunter.

The fat Owl eyed Trotter with great apprehension as he came up.

"Mr. Quelch wants——" began Trotter.

"Oh crikey! Is old Grimey with him?" exclaimed Bunter.

"Yes, sir. He wants——"

"I'm not going!" gasped Bunter. "I—I say, Trotter, you tell Quelch that I'm out of gates—see? I'll tip you half-a-crown when—when my postal order comes."

Trotter stared at him.

"Mr. Quelch wants——" he repeated.

"I—I won't go——"

"Master Van Duck——"

"Oh!" gasped Bunter.

"And Master Bunter——"

"Oh lor'!"

Trotter grinned, and went back to the House. Billy Bunter blinked at the juniors in great dismay.

"I—I say, you—you go, Van Duck," he stuttered. "Tell Quelch I've gone out. Tell him I've been run over. Say to him—— Ow! Leggo my arm, you beast! Stop dragging me along, you rotter! I won't go! I mean, I'm coming, ain't I?" howled Bunter.

"Ha, ha, ha!"

Billy Bunter went reluctantly. Evidently he had to go. He arrived at Mr. Quelch's study with Van Duck in a very uneasy frame of mind.

Inspector Grimes was in the study with the Remove master. Bunter gave him a dismal blink through his big spectacles.

"I say, it—it wasn't me——" began Bunter.

"What do you mean, you foolish boy?" snapped Mr. Quelch. "Be silent! Van Duck, as no discovery has been made with regard to the—the drug that was used last Wednesday, I have asked Inspector Grimes to make an inquiry into the matter. He has kindly consented to do so."

"Oh!" gasped Bunter, in great relief.

He realised that it was only the mystery of the dope that had brought the Courtfield inspector to the school. He was not on the track of missing tuck.

"Bunter is sent for, as he chanced to be the victim of the drug," said Mr. Quelch. "Both of you will answer Mr. Grimes' questions."

"Sure, sir!" said Putnam.

"Now, Master Van Duck," said Inspector Grimes, "your Form-master thinks, and I agree, that the drug must have been for you, and that this boy, Bunter, became its victim by some mischance."

"I guess so, sir."

"Master Bunter must, therefore, have eaten or drunk something intended for you," said Mr. Grimes. "This article, whatever it was, must have been drugged. It is scarcely possible that any person can have penetrated into the school, and tampered with the food. I think we may dismiss that, Mr. Quelch."

Mr. Quelch raised his eyebrows.

"Surely, sir, you do not suspect, like that ridiculous gunman, that any Greyfriars boy could possibly have——" he began.

"No, sir!" said Mr. Grimes, with a faint smile. "That would be the last idea to enter my mind."

"I am glad of that, sir! Yet, if you exclude the possibility that some extraneous person—— However, proceed, sir."

Inspector Grimes proceeded.

"Now, answer me carefully, Master van Duck! I understand that boys at school sometimes receive—hem—tuck, I think it is called—tuck by the medium of the post. Such as a hamper, or a cake! Hem! Have you received anything of the kind by post this week?"

Mr. Quelch started a little. He saw at once the drift of the Courtfield inspector's thoughts.

"There was a parcel on Wednesday, sir," said Van Duck.

"On Wednesday!" The inspector's eyes gleamed. "That was the day the drug was used. What was in the parcel?"

"A box of chocolates, sir, from Mr. Coot."

"Who is Mr. Coot?"

"An old friend of my popper, sir, who lives in London. He sends me things sometimes."

"You are sure that this parcel came from Mr. Coot?"

"It was his fist on the label, sir."

"Handwriting may be imitated," said Mr. Grimes. "Did you eat the chocolates?"

"N-n-nope!" stammered Putnam.

"Who did?"

"I didn't!" gasped Bunter, as Van Duck's eyes turned on him. "I never knew that Van Duck had a parcel on Wednesday. I never went down to the nets to tell him. You can ask Wharton, sir—he was there."

"Wha-a-at!" ejaculated Inspector Grimes.

"Bunter!" came Mr. Quelch's deep voice.

"Oh, yes, sir! I'm absolutely innocent, sir!" gasped Bunter. "You couldn't possibly suppose that I would snaffle a fellow's parcel, sir! You—you know me too well!"

"Bunter, I warn you to answer Mr. Grimes truthfully. Otherwise——"

"Oh, of—of course, sir!" groaned Bunter. "I hope I'm not a fellow to tell fibs. I haven't tasted chocolates this week, sir! I—I've almost forgotten what they taste like, it's—it's so long since I had any."

"I think, sir, that we are getting near the facts," said Inspector Grimes, with a faint grin on his official visage. "If Master Bunter consumed the chocolates sent by post to Master van Duck——"

"Oh, no!" gasped Bunter.

"Bunter, speak the truth at once!" exclaimed Mr. Quelch.

"I got you, Poker!" hissed Tug, raising his clubbed revolver. "I got you, and I reckon I got that gilt-edged bird, too!" There was a rustling and brushing in the branches of the old oak above as Putnam van Duck shot down!

"Yes, sir. I—I always do, sir. I—I've often got into trouble for being so truthful!" groaned Bunter. "I never went anywhere near the House dame's room on Wednesday afternoon, sir! Mrs. Kebble will tell you so, if you ask her—she's sure to remember giving me a clean handkerchief——"

"Bunter!" gasped Mr. Quelch. "You went to the House dame's room and——"

"Oh, no, sir! I went nowhere near the place," moaned Bunter. "I wasn't in the passage when you passed me, sir—you remember——"

"Upon my word!" exclaimed Mr. Quelch. "I remember now that I saw you in that passage, near the House dame's room on Wednesday afternoon, Bunter, and spoke to you. I remember clearly. And you were there for the purpose of——"

"Oh lor'! No, sir!" gasped Bunter. "Nothing of the kind! I never knew there was a parcel on Mrs. Kebble's table. Besides, I only took it up to the study to oblige Van Duck. You see, sir, he was at the cricket, and—and hadn't time to fetch the parcel himself, and being a good-natured chap——"

"Then you did take the parcel?"

"Oh, no, sir! I never touched it," stuttered Bunter. "I—I wouldn't! Some fellows in the Remove would, sir—but not me."

"Bless my soul!" gurgled Mr. Quelch. "This boy's stupidity and prevarication——"

"Oh, really, sir! I—I assure you I never touched the parcel! And it was all through my being good-natured, and wanting to oblige a chap! I knew Van Duck wouldn't mind me taking one or two, sir—and I was going to leave the rest for him, but—but somehow they all went! I—I was quite surprised, sir, when I saw the box empty. Not that I had them!" added Bunter cautiously. "I told Van Duck I never had them, and instead of taking a fellow's word, he shoved the ginger-beer down my back and——"

Inspector Grimes coughed. He was trying not to laugh. Mr. Grimes had questioned all sorts of offenders in his time; but the fat and fatuous Owl of the Remove was a new one on him!

"It appears, Van Duck," gasped Mr. Quelch, "that this box of chocolates, intended for you, was wholly consumed by this greedy and untruthful boy."

"He's told you so, sir!" said Putnam.

"I haven't!" yelled Bunter in alarm. "I've told Mr. Quelch I didn't, you beast! Don't you get making out that I had your chocs! As if I'd touch a fellow's tuck! I don't know how the box got in the study at all! I sat on it entirely by accident! I——"

"Be silent, Bunter!" roared Mr. Quelch.

"Oh, yes, sir! But I never——"

"Silence!"

"It seems fortunate, sir, that this—this extraordinary boy acted as he did," said Mr. Grimes, willing to put in a word for the hapless Owl. "Had Van Duck eaten the chocolates, as no doubt he would have done entirely without suspicion, he might have fallen helplessly into the hands of the kidnappers."

"That is quite true!" said Mr. Quelch. "You are then, assured that the chocolates——"

"Doped chocolates by post, sir, is an old trick, though doubtless new in the experience of a schoolmaster," said the inspector. "But a telephone call to this Mr. Coot will establish the fact beyond doubt."

"Quite!" said Mr. Quelch. "Bunter, I will deal with you later. You may both go for the present."

"I—I say, sir, I—I never——"

"Go!" thundered Mr. Quelch.

And Bunter jumped, and went.

The Owl of the Remove had one satisfaction, however—he had succeeded in beating the gangsters!

The mystery was elucidated at last; in fact, what had been a very deep mystery to Greyfriars School was rather a simple proposition to a police-inspector.

A telephone call to Mr. Coot, in London, drew from that gentleman a total denial of any knowledge of any box of chocolates sent to Putnam at Greyfriars.

Evidently that box of chocolates had not come from Mr. Coot; so there was no doubt that Mr. Coot's "fist" had been imitated by some person unknown—and there could be no doubt that that person was Chick Chew, star kidnapper of the United States! It was one more of the gangster's many wiles, and it had failed—through Billy Bunter!

For which Billy Bunter claimed the credit, as soon as he understood how the matter lay. According to Bunter, he had suspected those chocolates, and had snaffled them out of pure friendship for Putnam—really an act of devotion! Sad to relate, nobody believed Bunter.

THE END.

(The next yarn in this grand series is entitled: "THE VENGEANCE OF BUNTER THE VENTRILOQUIST!" Be sure to purchase your copy of the MAGNET *next Friday!)*

CAPTAIN VENGEANCE!

By
JOHN BREDON

"Your Fate is Sealed!"

WEARILY, and with his hands fettered, Roderick Drake lay in his narrow bunk in Ronald Westdale's cabin, listening to the throb and whir of gigantic engines as they lashed into fullest pressure, driving the pirate cruiser through placid seas.

Night shrouded the Indian Ocean. For twelve hours—twelve ages of mental agony, as it seemed—from the sinking of the Sylvia Bay, Roy Drake had been a prisoner in the gunnery lieutenant's cabin. In his mind's eye, he could still see the foundering of the giant Australian luxury liner, the passengers, lately so light-hearted and carefree, crowded into the lifeboats or struggling in the shark-swarming sea; on the bridge of the Vengeance, implacable as Fate, he saw Von Eimar, coolly surveying the scene of horror through his powerful binoculars.

Mentally the boy reviewed the sensational events that had taken place with such breathless rapidity since Von Eimar had organised the mutiny of convicts on Nemesis Island. and by stratagem captured the Varland cruiser which he had turned into a pirate warship. Already Captain Vengeance, as the world's master-spy now called himself, had shown himself to be capable of the tigerish ruthlessness so necessary to his desperate new trade.

One crumb of comfort alone remained to Roderick Drake. The Sylvia Bay had managed to flash out an SOS before the torpedo had shattered a breach in her keel-plates. By now the world would be aware that, for the first time for a hundred years, a pirate man-o'-war was out on the seas. Nor would it be long before Roy's father, Morgan Drake, the brain of Britain's Secret Service, would be engaged on the task of rescuing—or avenging—his kidnapped son.

A door clicked open in the tiny cabin, and the electric bulb blazed into life. Twisting in his berth, Roy saw Hilarity Hinton, the little Cockney ex-burglar who was Ronald Westdale's general factotum. In one hand he balanced a tray with a plate of sandwiches and a mug of steaming coffee.

"'Ow do?" asked the Cockney. Observing the boy's white, strained countenance, he grinned sympathetically. Laying the tray on a hinged table, he drew a tiny key from the pocket of his dingy white, reefer jacket. "It's hun-accommodatin' to wear the rings, chum," he added, fitting the key into the lock of the handcuffs. "I knows that from hexperience. 'Ere y'are, my bucko!" The steel bands clicked open, and thankfully Roy crept out from the bunk, rubbing his chafed wrists and stretching and flexing his cramped muscles.

"No, I wouldn't, if I were you, son," warned Hilarity, slipping a gun from his pocket, as instinctively Roy measured the Cockney's diminutive stature against his own well-developed limbs, for Roy was only a lad of fifteen. "I'm a nervous chap myself," Hilarity ran on, "an' if anything 'appened to you because of me I'd never recover from the shock. Park it, cocky! What's the good, anyway? You've a three-'undred-mile swim between you and the nearest land!"

Trrr-rrr-rrrh! Flame spurted from the depressed muzzles as the airman pressed his trigger, threshing the decks of the pirate cruiser with red-hot streams of lead. Screeches of sheer panic volleyed from the demoralised convicts!

Roy smiled a little as he sat down to his first meal since noon the previous day. As Hilarity had said, it was worse than useless to think of escape from this cruiser, with its crew of wolfish convicts. Later on, perhaps, when they made land—if ever they did—he would watch his chance.

Hungrily Roy devoured the supper before him—or breakfast it should be called, for it was within an hour to dawn. As he demolished the last crumb, and swallowed the final mouthful of coffee, Hilarity unlocked the cabin door and motioned him to follow.

"Now for a nice, quiet little constitootional in the moonlight," grinned the Cockney, following Roy up a vertical iron ladder to the gun-deck. "You takes your hexercise by moonlight, like the howls. The Big Bug, Von Eimar, wants a pleasant little chat with you in his cabin. Feels sociable, he does. Only mind how you speaks, cocky; he's got a narsty temper, he has!"

With this friendly warning, Hilarity Hinton led the way across the shadowed gun-deck.

Stars flashed bright in the dusky, purple vault. Through the placid swells where phosphorescent blue fires danced and flickered like will-o'-the-wisps, the Vengeance lunged her iron stem, sparklit smoke pouring from her squat, red-hot funnels.

Down in the blistering Gehenna of her stokehold, black and yellow firemen were toiling, naked, perspiring, staggering from one gaping, white-hot furnace maw to the other, clanging fire shovels, furnace rakes, and clinker bars to keep up the pressure of steam. Only men seasoned to the sun-heat of Africa and South China could have stood the strain.

In the engine-room, Mikhail Lebedoff, Russian renegade engineer, stolidly chewed a rank cigar as he swabbed his matted brow with a piece of oily waste and kept a bloodshot eye upon his dials and indicators.

"Full speed ahead" Von Eimar had ordered, and pistons pounded, valves and steampipes hissed, boilers strained and jumped on their bed-plates, while gasping, half-dead greasers squirmed in and out of the mazes of machinery as they oiled couplings and bearings.

Roy Drake, pacing behind Hilarity Hinton in the clean, fresh tang of the sea air, understood fully the reason for Von Eimar's haste. Like invisible waves, the S O S sent out by his victim was spreading across the world. For hundreds of miles every ship and wireless station would be flashing out the sensational, almost incredible news. Warships in Singapore, Colombo, and in the Dutch East Indies would be getting up steam. In a few hours retribution would be loosed in the wake of the daring modern pirate who had defied every sea law and tradition of the past hundred years.

Not a light was to be seen on the Vengeance from stem to stern. The bright starlight, glimmering ghostly upon her metal deck-plates and superstructure, provided the sole illumination; nor was there any of the song-roaring and drunkenness that had prevailed among the convicts during the first hours of the voyage. Von Eimar kept his crew of rascals and ruffians under an iron hand.

As they passed the inky blotch of shadow cast by the gun-shield of a big six-incher, Roy made out the close-cropped, bullet head of Killer Moran, and the gold ear-rings of Luis Ramiro as they squatted under the massive gun-breech.

They had been talking rapidly and in muttered tones, but at the approach of the two newcomers they became suddenly mum.

Roy wondered. Neither the American gangster nor the Argentine half-breed would he have trusted an inch. To see those two in secret conclave was a sinister sign. It boded mischief for someone!

Removing his peaked cap, Hilarity rapped his knuckles upon a steel-sheeted door, and as it was opened in response to a deep, strong, familiar voice, Roderick Drake found himself once more in the presence of the master-spy and master-pirate, Von Eimar.

With the inevitable cigar jutting from one corner of his tight-lipped mouth, Von Eimar sat at his ease in a swivel-chair, before a handsome oak desk in the cabin that had once belonged to Admiral Mericski, of the Varland navy. The admiral did not require it now, having changed his quarters to the stokehold, in company with Governor Zarda of Nemesis Island.

With the new captain sat the notorious Dr. Nieuwe, distinguished Brussels surgeon—and poisoner!

Roy Drake set his lips in a firm line as he met the suave and mocking glance of his father's sworn enemy.

"Be pleased to take a seat, Master Drake!" Von Eimar smiled blandly as he nodded towards a padded armchair, removing the black, strong cigar from his lips. "A drink? No? Well, there are some chocolates on the table. Help yourself. Hinton, you may wait within call."

Sedulously Von Eimar polished his monocle with a handkerchief, while Roy sat defiantly in the armchair.

"'Murderer and pirate,' I think you called me some hours ago," began Von Eimar, screwing his monocle once more into a pale blue eye. "A pithy exposition of my character, Master Drake, though you make no allowance for my other and better qualities. Almost I am inclined to like you. You are possessed of a truthful and refreshing candour, and you do not lack for spirit—two qualities which I have always admired. If you were not the son of Morgan Drake, I could wish that you were my own." Significantly he paused, to add: "It is a pleasing stroke of irony that has thrown into my hands the son of the man who sent me to Nemesis Island!"

"And so you intend to work your revenge upon me?" smiled Roy bitterly, as, squarely and directly, he looked Von Eimar in the face. "Well, get on with it! I shan't give you the satisfaction of seeing me snivel."

"You are mistaken, my dear boy." Dryly Von Eimar took a biscuit from the tray and snapped it between his white, gold-filled teeth. "With you, personally, I have no quarrel. It is your father who is my enemy, not you. You are merely the instrument of my vengeance. It is Morgan Drake, not his son, whom I wish to see squirming and snivelling."

"You mean to strike at my father through me?" asked Roy contemptuously. "To break my father by murdering me—is that it? Well, snivelling and squirming doesn't run in our family——"

Von Eimar raised a ringed, podgy hand.

"Who said you were to be killed, my impulsive young friend?" Smiling, he shook his square, shaven, straight-backed head. "I do not take so crude and clumsy a revenge. My methods are more subtle."

The smile upon his broad Teutonic features became coldly sinister, infinitely devilish in its mockery.

"I wonder what my old friend Morgan Drake will feel when he learns that his own son has joined my pirate crew?" he continued pleasantly. And with that he leaned back in his swing-chair, drawing at his cigar with intense satisfaction.

Roy felt puzzled. From Von Eimar he glanced to the Belgian doctor, who had taken no part in the discussion, and whose black, beady eyes glittered maliciously behind his pince-nez.

"I am a prisoner; not a member of your pirate crew!" Roy pointed out contemptuously and not a little surprised.

"So you say, my boy. And it is true. But truth does not always prevail in this sinful world."

Blandly suave, Von Eimar drew a handsomely bound book from a drawer in his desk, and rustled the leaves.

"Here are the laws and articles of my pirate crew, drawn up by myself and signed by every man under my orders. Your name occupies a prominent position on the list. You are surprised? But we have several most consummate forgers among us, and in your baggage we found several letters and documents with your signature to serve for a model. See for yourself!"

With amazed eyes Roy saw his own name, so skilfully imitated that he himself could not tell the difference, among those of the pirate leaders.

"If we should ever come to trial," Von Eimar purred softly, "that signature ought to be good hangman's evidence!"

Coolly he checked the hot words with which Roderick Drake would have interposed.

"I have no intention of allowing myself or any of my confederates coming to trial, if I can help it," he added. "But at times we shall take prisoners. I intend that they shall see this book. Perhaps I shall contrive it that one shall escape with this incriminating evidence. At all events, they shall see you, apparently holding an important post aboard this ship—with a gunman to watch you so that you have to play the part! Should you escape from us, your denials might be accepted; but I doubt it—emphatically I doubt it! If we should be captured, make no doubt but that every man of this crew will swear that you were one of us—out of spite, if for no other reason. Your fate is sealed. Better accept your destiny, and enlist with Von Eimar, the pirate."

Roderick Drake felt cold inwardly, and sick. In spite of the warm colour that burned in his cheeks, fear gripped at his heart-strings with icy fingers. This was a revenge fitting to the cold, calculating nature of Von Eimar. He knew the master-spy's devilish cunning, and how he could make it appear that Roy had actually and voluntarily joined the pirate crew.

As for Von Eimar's infamous proposal, he disdained to answer. Rather would he have followed the hapless wretches of the Sylvia Bay than joined that crew of outlaws, pirates, and murderers.

"How long do you think you will be able to play out this game?" he asked, in a burst of impulsive bitterness. "That S O S from the liner has done for you! There's not a port in the world where you can take this cruiser, and her coal and supplies won't last for ever. There will be warships on your track this very hour. All the navies in the world will be after you. You'll be sunk or forced to surrender within a week!"

Von Eimar shook his head.

"My dear lad, you really do not suppose that I embarked upon this desperate venture without calculating the immediate consequences? I am not so rash as all that. No! That S O S from the Sylvia Bay, I own, was an item outside my calculations; or, rather, a risk I had considered to be negligible. I did not suppose that Captain Cooper wished to commit suicide.

"But, all the same, if you were to look into our radio cabin at the present moment, you would see our operator giving out the message that the Vengeance has struck a sunken reef, and is foundering rapidly. That message may be believed or not at present. Probably not. The navies of the world, as you so aptly remark, will doubtless continue the hunt. But when they fail to find us, they will be forced to the conclusion that it is correct, and the search will be abandoned."

"But they are bound to find you!" Roy pointed out. "They'll rake every square mile of the seas, every island you can reach, every creek and lagoon!"

Again Von Eimar shook his head.

"I have provided for that contingency, my dear Roy Drake," he said. "I am not so poor a sea-fox that I have not my secret burrow. Where is it? Your curiosity will be satisfied within a few hours, my boy. The only thing I fear is that I may be intercepted before I reach it. It's a race against time!"

As he was speaking, Roy noticed a flush of rosy light upon the thick, glazed "bullseye" of the cabin porthole, which betokened coming day. It was as he noticed this circumstance when there came a sudden, startled shout from the Vengeance's control-top, the loud, insistent clangor of a ship's bell, and then the brazen peal of a bugle.

The door was slung violently open till it clashed on its hinges, and into the cabin plunged Hilarity Hinton.

"I say, capting," cried the Cockney frenziedly, as Von Eimar glared, "it's all up with us! Haireyplanes! Four of 'em. They're coming up to meet us, an' hevery one's a whopper!"

Forced to Surrender!

WITH a face like that of a balked devil, Von Eimar swung up the iron ladder to the cruiser's forebridge. Beneath him, under the forward gun-turret, the hastily aroused pirates swarmed in dismayed groups, all staring eastwards where the flaming half-disc of sun hove slowly over the gilded sea rim.

Ronald Westdale handed his chief a pair of binoculars, and with a grunt in his square, thick throat, Von Eimar leaned upon the bridge rail, focusing the lenses into the dazzling glare.

Out of the ruddily lit clouds swung four black specks, droning sonorously towards the solitary cruiser.

"Ach!" Von Eimar muttered an angry exclamation. "This is what I feared, Mr. Westdale. Bombers! Dutch, I make them out to be! Fokker fighting planes from Batavia, probably. This is bad!"

He swung round as a wireless-room orderly touched him on his sleeve.

"Well?" he grunted shortly.

The man handed him a slip of paper. Von Eimar glanced at it, uttered a short laugh, and crumpled it in a podgy fist, tossing it over the lee bridge-wing into the wind.

"From the Dutchmen!" he said to Westdale. "They want to know who we are. They'll find out soon enough." Briskly Von Eimar upcapped the engine-room speaking-tube. "I want every atom of speed you can give me, Mikhail Lebedoff! What's that?" he added, as a murmur floated up the pipe. "The boilers will blow up if you put on another ounce of steam? Let them! It's the nearest you'll ever get to heaven, Lebedoff, if they do. We'll have one or two messages of brotherly love dropping on to us from the sky before long."

He swung round on his heel to give sharp, guttural orders to the quartermaster at the wheel, a short, stocky German with a crooked scar on his cheekbone. Westdale had already descended to the deck where the Varland master-gunner and one or two of his mates were unrigging the weatherproof covers from the twin anti-aircraft guns. In a few brusque words the ex-lieutenant of the British Navy gave his orders.

Unnoticed and forgotten in the general bustle, Roy Drake stood apart, watching the swift approach of the four Dutch battleplanes. To and fro in the wildest confusion ran the convicts of Nemesis Island, arming themselves with rifles from the racks, falling up and down upright ladders, and impeding those few of the pirate crew, chiefly Varland navy deserters, who knew what to do.

Von Eimar, from the bridge, rapped out a few orders in stinging, caustic tones, and the convicts rallied a little, fumbling, however, as they rammed clips of cartridges into the magazines of rifles, with hands that shook with alarm and terror.

By now, with a thunder of powerful triple motors, the four Dutch Fokkers were almost upon them. The silence of the cruiser to their inquiries, and the bustled preparations on the gun-deck, no doubt convinced them that here was the modern pirate cruiser whose exploit of yesterday was already ringing round the world.

Larger they loomed, like giant bees hovering round a dog that had disturbed their hive—but with this difference, that their sting was far more powerful and deadly.

Through his lenses, Von Eimar could see the goggled and helmeted heads of pilots and gunners, the machine-guns swivelled above the cockpits, and the bomb-racks slung below. They were seaplanes, and, powerfully armed as she was, the Vengeance was especially vulnerable from the air.

Coolly and methodically, stripped to his shirtsleeves with the cuffs rolled up, displaying his muscular forearms, Ronald Westdale superintended the gunners as they slid a copper-cased shell into the oiled breech-chamber. Then, as the breech-block clamped shut, he took over the gun, tilting the long, lean barrel at a trajectory angle, till he focused the first-coming war-plane in his sights.

In silent rage he gritted his teeth, blinking his eyes as the fierce, blazing sunrays flooded the sights and blinded his vision. The Dutchmen knew their business. Not only did they come swooping out of the sun's eye, as it were, but they dipped, rolled, and soared as they zoomed along, sunlight flashing on their wings, offering the most difficult of targets.

Trrr-rrr-rrrh!

The foremost plane suddenly let out a rattle of machine-gun fire. It was only a preliminary warming-up, as the gunner gave warning of his hostile intentions, but it started another panic among the unsteady convicts. Down swooped the avenging angels from the sky.

Oblivious of the terrified howls, screeches, and yells of the pirates who were screaming at him to fire, Ronald Westdale waited, coolly, then calmly pressed the firing-push.

Crash!

A flower of smoke, petalled with flame, blossomed into view and obscured the enemy squadron.

Westdale suppressed an exclamation. The sun had baffled him. His aim had been all right, but he had misjudged the range by fifty yards. Except for one flying ribbon of canvas that flapped from a wing, the four Fokkers were undamaged.

The frightened convicts howled curses at him; but Von Eimar, up on the bridge, said not a word, knowing full well the difficulty that his English gun-lieutenant had to face.

Shrugging his massive shoulders, the captain rapped out an order to that stocky German helmsman, who had served aboard a raider in these seas during the Great War.

Over swung the cruiser to port, just as the leading Dutchman flattened out, zooming low over their smoking funnels and tripod masts.

Trrr-rrr-rrrh!

Flame spurted from the depressed muzzles as the gunner pressed his trigger, threshing the decks with red-hot streams of lead. Screeches of sheer panic volleyed from the demoralised convicts.

A few fired a ragged, futile fusillade; most threw themselves flat on the deck-plates.

Later on, Roy Drake smiled to think of the terror of these half-hearted sea-scum. At the moment he had other things to think about.

Pi-i-iing!

A bullet struck a ventilator cowling just beside him, glancing aside, and then flattened itself against the armour-plating. A smouldering flake from the ventilator spun upon the boy's jacket, burning a hole in his sleeve. With a musical twang a wire backstay swung to the deck, severed by a remarkable shot.

"'Oly 'orrors!" gasped Hilarity Hinton, ducking instinctively beside him. "F'ree shies a penny! It's like 'Appy 'Ampstead, only we're the cokernuts!"

One after the other, the Fokker war-planes thundered over the helpless cruiser, raking her decks with a zone of fire. A gunner beside Westdale slumped to the base of the gun-pivot, groaning as he nursed a broken shoulder. The steel deck-plates were splashed and dinted in rows with stars of lead.

The convicts scampered in a mad rush for the hatches. A few flesh-wounds were the sole result of that continuous machine-gun fire, but one man was stunned and another broke a leg as they jumped for the 'tween decks.

"Stand to quarters, you scum!" thundered Von Eimar through a speaking-trumpet, to the few who remained. "We're not beat yet! Mein blut! You fools, are you afraid of their bombs? They won't drop them if they can help it!"

His vigorous contempt infused some life into them as the Dutchmen ceased fire and wheeled. Grunting in his bull throat, he switched the glare of his light blue eyes on to Killer Moran, who stood on the bridge beside him, gnawing his trembling lips with fear.

"Have up our colours, Moran!" snapped Von Eimar curtly. "If we go under this time it will be with Jolly Roger flying to show our contempt for the world!"

Gulping something down that threatened to choke him, for he was a coward at heart, like all his murderous kind, the American plug-ugly did as he was ordered. As though to show the supremest contempt for the Dutchmen's fire, the sable flag with the death's head flapped to the morning breeze.

Standing exposed as he was on the pirate warship's deck, Roderick Drake experienced a curious sense of detachment. That he himself stood the chance of being killed by the fire of those who were really his friends, or of being drowned if the Vengeance was bombed and sunk, hardly occurred to him. It was as if he had been sitting in a comfortable seat, watching an exciting episode on the films.

Again the anti-aircraft gun exploded in smoke and flame. Tensed, and with grey eyes narrowed, a smear of cordite smudging his keen, clear-cut features, Ronald Westdale had aligned his sights upon the bombers as they circled overhead.

Von Eimar clapped a fist upon his open palm.

"Good shooting, Westdale!" he grunted, in guttural approval.

One of the Fokker planes suddenly lurched in her gliding flight, hovered, then swung completely over as one of her wings crumpled like paper. A flying piece of shrapnel had caught it as the Dutchman banked. Down she fluttered like a great wounded bird, rested upon the smooth sea-surface a minute, then slowly filled and sank.

"First blood!" croaked Westdale, his throat hoarse with sulphur and saltpetre, as he wiped the sweat and smoke from his face. "But it was more luck than anything else. Here come the mynheers again."

From three different directions at once the Hollanders converged upon the pirate cruiser, intent to avenge their fallen comrade. First to starboard, then to port, the Vengeance zig-zagged, a corkscrew of silver surf marking her erratic course.

Again and again Westdale pumped shells into the gold-and-blue of the tropic

Printed in Great Britain and published every Saturday by the Proprietors, The Amalgamated Press, Ltd., The Fleetway House, Farringdon Street, London, E.C.4. Advertisement offices: The Fleetway House, Farringdon Street, London, E.C.4. Registered for transmission by Canadian Magazine Post. Subscription rates: Inland and Abroad, 11s. per annum; 5s. 6d. for six months. Sole Agents for Australia and New Zealand: Messrs. Gordon & Gotch, Ltd., and for South Africa: Central News Agency, Ltd.—Saturday, May 30th, 1936.

sky. It was like trying to hit mosquitoes with tennis-balls, with one's eyes dazzled with the sun's radiance. Still the Dutchmen wheeled and hovered in the blazing zone of the sun, every now and then breaking away to swoop over the decks of the cruiser with a murderous storm of machine-gun fire.

As yet they had dropped none of the high explosive bombs slung to their carriages. Von Eimar surmised correctly that the Dutchmen would reserve those terrible projectiles for a last resort. For one thing, they wanted to recover the bullion stolen from the Sylvia Bay, and to bring the pirates to trial, if possible. For another, they did not wish for complications with the Varland republic, to whom the cruiser belonged.

But at last their impatience mastered them. Roy saw a plane thundering out of the golden dazzle, and then like flashing meteors, two bright objects came hurtling and whistling down.

Boom! Boo-oo-ooom!

Like a toy steamer the cruiser rocked, as with muffled thunder, pillars of spouting water hurled fountains of spray to lash upon the decks.

Disregarding the terror and dismay of his crew, Von Eimar drove the long grey cruiser about its winding course.

Deliberately the Dutchmen had refrained from dropping the bombs directly on to the cruiser. It was a threat and a warning; nothing more. Shouts of surrender came from the few convicts still remaining on deck, but Von Eimar stood like a statue, inexorable on the upper bridge.

Next time it was a grimmer warning they got. In vain, Westdale fired, the shell exploding over the tail of the plane as it volplaned down upon them from the sky. The glare foiled his aim again.

A steel bolt came hurtling from the overhead plane on to the cruiser's foredeck.

Losing his balance, Roy Drake was flung violently on to the metal deckplates as the Vengeance groaned and shivered in every rivet and girder. His ears were stunned by the reverberating crash of high explosive. Flame, smoke, and showers of bent, twisted, smouldering iron volcanoed from the bows.

When at last he scrambled to his feet, ears numbed and singing, so that for the moment he thought himself deaf for life, it was to see with misted, water-filled eyes the smoke drifting away and the forecastle revealed as a tangle of wreckage, with a blackened and perforated crater in her forward deck.

An engine-room bell clanged, and Von Eimar threw over the telegraph to "Stop!"

(Continued on next page.)

COME INTO THE OFFICE, BOYS AND GIRLS!

Your Editor is always pleased to hear from his readers. Write to him: Editor of the MAGNET, The Fleetway House, Farringdon Street, London, E.C.4. A stamped, addressed envelope will ensure a reply.

BEFORE getting down to real business this week, I must thank hundreds of you fellows for your letters expressing your genuine delight at being able to read the stories dealing with the early adventures of Harry Wharton & Co., at Greyfriars—now appearing in our great companion paper, the "Gem," published every Wednesday. These yarns, written in the early days of Frank Richards, are real gems. Are you reading them? If not, you're missing the finest treat ever!

From one of my Welwyn readers comes a query regarding

THE SALT OF THE EARTH.

He wants to know how long it is possible for anyone to live without salt. Not very long, I can assure my chum of that. The exact time is not known, because, as far as is known, no one has deliberately killed themselves by abstaining from salt. A little while ago some students decided to find out if it was possible to exist without salt. They lived entirely on food from which all salt had been excluded. Even their vegetables were boiled three times to extract every particle of natural salt from them. The results were amazing. They soon found that all food became absolutely tasteless. Then they began to suffer violently from cramp. After that they became so tired that it was too much of an effort for them to shave. Without doubt they would soon have died if they had not abandoned the experiment and built up their strength again on food which had extra large supplies of salt to counteract the lack of it in their bodies.

Salt is one of the most valuable things in the world. There are still many places in the world

WHERE SALT IS MONEY.

Blocks of salt are used as money in the Sahara desert, and also in certain parts of Abyssinia. Every year large caravans set out across the mighty desert, making for the salt pans. Here salt water, obtained from ponds in the desert, is placed in shallow pans. The water is evaporated by the sun, and the salt remains. It is then made into blocks of a certain size. There is a definite currency value for these blocks of salt, and when anything is purchased which is only worth a half or a quarter block of salt, the blocks are split up accordingly. By the time the year is out all the salt currency is used up—so off go the caravans again on their long march over the desert to renew the supply of currency for the Bedouin dwellers in the desert.

A LITTLE while ago I mentioned, in my chat, the smallest book in the world. A Manchester reader has now sent me particulars of

THE SMALLEST WRITING IN THE WORLD

—so small, in fact, that it seems hardly believable. It is just another case of the invaluable work that can be done by microscopy. Would you believe that the entire contents of the Bible could be so reduced that the whole lot could be reproduced fifty-nine times in the space of a square inch? A microscopical writing machine, invented by the late William Webb, a Fellow of the Royal Microscopical Society, could condense matter even to these infinitesimal proportions. Needless to say, a very high-powered microscope was necessary to read the writing. Webb destroyed his machine some time before he died, but many of the slides, containing the writing, still exist.

Although this apparatus has not been taken up by our own museum authorities, it is interesting to note that Russian scientists are now experimenting on the same lines. They can already reduce a whole page of an ordinary newspaper on to a microscopic slide, where it will only take up a square third of an inch. When anyone wishes to consult this, the slide is magnified and thrown on to a large screen, where it can be read with ease!

From one of my Manchester readers, who signs himself "Film-fan," comes a query concerning cinemas. He wants to know

HOW MANY CINEMAS ARE THERE

in the whole of the world? The United States Government have recently compiled a report on cinemas, and they estimate that there are no less than 87,299 cinemas in the world. These cater for a total population of 1,808,705,017. I don't know how they work out the presumed population of the world, but, anyway, those are their figures. This means that there is one cinema for every 20,718 people.

In Europe we have 60,150 cinemas for 557,608,191 inhabitants. The United States possesses 15,378 cinemas for a population of 127 million people. The country with the smallest number of cinemas in proportion to its population is China. There are only three hundred cinemas in China, and it is estimated that this means only one cinema per 1,582,624 persons!

Here are a few

RAPID-FIRE REPLIES

to various readers' queries:

What was the First English Newspaper? A journal called "Nathaniel Butter's Weekley Newes." The first issue was published on August 2nd, 1622.

What is the Greatest Depth that Men have Descended into the Sea? Three thousand and twenty-eight feet. Dr. William Beebe and Mr. Otis Barton reached this depth in a bathysphere in August, 1934. They remained at that depth for five minutes.

Is it True that there is a Country with only one Millionaire? Yes. There is only one man in Austria whose income is above a million Austrian schillings, about £40,000 in English money.

Can One Hire Umbrellas at Railway Stations? There is one railway station which hires out umbrellas on rainy days for the use of passengers. This is Streatham Station. A season ticket holder pays 2d. per day for the use of an umbrella. Ordinary passengers must leave a deposit of 2s. 6d.

What is "Sheet Lightning"? The same as "forked lightning," but seen at a distance or obscured by a cloud. Thus we only see the glare of the reflection, and not the actual striking of the lightning flash such as we see in "forked lightning."

I think you will be extra pleased with next week's issue of the MAGNET, chums. Frank Richards has written some rattling good yarns in the past, but I think that next week's yarn,

"THE VENGEANCE OF BUNTER THE VENTRILOQUIST!"

is easily the best he has ever written. Most of you fellows know about Bunter's gift of imitating fellows' voices and to what purposes he has put it to in the past. Well, the fat ventriloquist has not forgotten how Poker Pike "fanned" him and made him skip, and the idea of pulling Pike's leg by way of revenge is something not to be missed. Thrills and laughs simply tumble over each other in this ripping yarn, and if you don't vote it great you're real hard to please.

Next we come to Captain Vengeance and his convict crew who meet with more thrilling adventures aboard the pirate cruiser, Vengeance.

Of course, you can rely on the usual big bag of laughs in the "Greyfriars Herald" and plenty of pep in the Greyfriars Rhymester's verses written around William Stott.

YOUR EDITOR.

In a sea of white, scared faces the convict pirates massed under the bridge. Knives and rifles were brandished. Firemen and greasers came scrambling out of the engine-room hatch.

"Surrender! Haul down the flag! Surrender before they blow us out of the water, captain!"

Killer Moran, flourishing a long-barrelled Colt, led the panic-stricken rush, standing on the bridge-ladder, baying like a frightened dog, but still cowed by the fierce, white glare of Von Eimar.

"Dutchy's got us beat, cap'n! We've gotta throw in!"

Sweat beaded the American's brow. Clearly he was torn between two fears, but the backing of the crew helped him to face the ruthless arch-pirates.

"We've got no kick comin', Von Eimar," he insisted frantically. "Better to go back to Nemesis Island than be blown up like this!"

Roy Drake stood aside, looking on contemptuously. Westdale, lighting a cigarette with smoke-stained fingers, leaned against the breech of his gun. Wildly clamoured the mob. Plainly if Von Eimar did not surrender they would tear him to pieces.

Stolidly Von Eimar drew a whistle from his pocket. The hubbub died to a mutter as he blew a piercing blast.

"Strike the black flag, Moran," said the chief pirate, quietly and distinctly. "The Dutchmen have us by the throat. We surrender!"

Von Eimar Turns the Tables!

SHUTTING off her engines as she glided down, a big Dutch seaplane skimmed gracefully along the smooth sea-surface until she rested within a few yards from the surrendered pirate cruiser. Out of her cockpit leaned an officer with a megaphone.

"Send us a boat!" he roared across the short stretch of water. "I want to come aboard!"

Silently Roy Drake watched as Krunow, the Finn bo'sun, piped hands to man and lower one of the warship's boats.

The pirates, now that their first shock and terror was over, hung about moodily and in groups, scowling and muttering as they watched Von Eimar on the bridge. Evidently they wanted a scapegoat upon whom to wreak their rage and disappointment, though no one had the hardihood to speak a word to that grim, implacable figure who stood with one podgy hand resting on his sheathed revolver, monocle glinting in the sun.

"This is a rummy go," muttered Hilarity Hinton to Roy and Westdale. "We've fell out o' the fryin' pan into the fire! What'll they do to us when they get us nice an' safe back on Nemmy-sis Island, I wonder?"

Neither of them answered. Watching Von Eimar as he stood lighting a cigar, Roy wondered what was passing in the pirate captain's mind. Knowing how utterly such tame surrender was at variance with Von Eimar's crafty, tigerish nature, the boy wondered vaguely whether some dark scheme was hatching in the master pirate's mind.

The Dutch flying officer, a big, middle-aged man with a thick moustache, elbowed his way through the throng of pirates at the gangway and clambered briskly to the bridge. From his manner it was plain that he intended to stand no nonsense.

"You are the leader of this gang of—of pirates, I presume?" he said, addressing Von Eimar, and hesitating a little at the word that, in the twentieth century, verged upon the grotesque.

Von Eimar saluted, with the faintest flicker of irony.

"I call myself Captain Vengeance," he replied, as Killer Moran and Ronald Westdale joined him on the bridge.

"Well, whatever your name may be, you are captain no longer." The Dutchman spoke loudly and clearly for all to hear. "You and all the men in this ship are prisoners. From now on you will steer a course for Batavia. A Dutch cruiser is coming to meet us. And—be sure of this—at the first sign of treachery we'll blow you out of the sea!"

Whatever may have been Von Eimar's thoughts, his hard features remained inscrutable. He even smiled.

"I am at your orders," he answered, shrugging his shoulders. "But will you not come into the charthouse to advise me? I fear I am but a faulty navigator, and I am not altogether sure of the right course."

For a moment the Dutchman hesitated. Then, reflecting that even these desperate fellows, now driven to complete and ignominious surrender, would hardly dare to injure him, he nodded and followed Von Eimar into the chart-room.

A minute or two later a muffled and goggled figure descended the accommodation ladder and was rowed back to the waiting plane.

A thunder of triple engines, the suction of powerful air-screws drawing the giant seaplane through the water, and presently she soared aloft to rejoin her consorts circling above.

Westdale gave orders to the crew. It happened that the bomb had not done any irreparable damage to the Vengeance's forecastle. The bows were badly crumpled, but her underwater plates were still sound. Smoke volleyed through the twin funnels, the screws churned, and the surrendered cruiser commenced to surge forward on her altered course.

Westdale's gaze followed the big seaplane as it swung aloft and took up station at the rear of the other two Dutch aircraft, all three whirring along in V formation, circling round the cruiser.

"What is it, Ron?" asked Roy, struck by the Englishman's look.

"You'll see presently," countered Westdale, and strained interest, not unmixed with anxiety, was in his eyes as he watched.

Roy, glancing up to the bridge, was surprised not to see the stocky figure of Von Eimar. Was he hiding his chagrin and mortification in the charthouse, he wondered.

The next moment he nearly jumped out of his skin.

Scarcely able to credit his ears, he heard the sudden, continuous rattle of machine-gun fire. Then, with amazed eyes, he saw one of the foremost Dutch bombers suddenly crumple, burst into flame, and fall, spinning, in a swift death-dive to the sea.

Startled exclamations broke from the watching convicts.

"Wha-what—what——" stuttered Roy Drake dazedly.

Westdale caught him by the shoulder.

"It's Von Eimar!" he cried excitedly. "That Dutchman who boarded us. Von Eimar stuck him up with a gun, bound, and gagged him, and then took his place, disguised in his uniform and goggles!"

"But—but the Dutch pilot?" asked Roy, catching his breath.

Westdale shrugged his shoulders and bit his underlip.

"Can't you guess? Von Eimar couldn't take chances. The plane's fitted with dual controls, of course. Look!"

Fascinated, Roy Drake watched the duel between Von Eimar and the last remaining Fokker. It was short and sharp. Staggered by that sudden and unlooked-for development, the Dutch pilot and gunner were taken completely at a disadvantage. Von Eimar was upon their tail, shooting wings, fuselage, and propellers to pieces.

Before the gaze of the babbling convicts and Roderick Drake's horrified eyes she plunged to destruction in the wake of her consorts.

In a few minutes Von Eimar had returned to the bridge of the cruiser.

"Full speed!" he called down the engine-room tube, ignoring the delighted vociferations of his crew, who a short while before had been ready to rend him limb from limb. "Let her rip, Mikhail Lebedoff! We've got to find secret anchorage within twenty-four hours!"

(Von Eimar got out of that difficulty very well! What will be his next move? You'll be surprised when you read next week's exciting chapters of this stirring adventure yarn, chums!)

HOLIDAY FUN WITH BUNTER THE VENTRILOQUIST !

No. 1,477. Vol. XLIX EVERY SATURDAY Week Ending June 6th. 1936.

AMUSING AND AMAZING SITUATIONS IN THIS BRILLIANT SCHOOL YARN——

The Vengeance of Bunter the Ventriloquist!

By FRANK RICHARDS

——Featuring the World-Popular Favourites . . HARRY WHARTON & CO.

THE FIRST CHAPTER.

Billy Bunter Makes History!

"BUNTER!"

"Oh!" gasped Billy Bunter. And he bolted!

It was surprising.

It was, in fact, amazing.

Harry Wharton & Co. of the Greyfriars Remove stared blankly after the fat junior as he scudded across the quad.

"Bunter!" roared Bob Cherry.

Bunter did not heed. He hurtled on. It was not only surprising and amazing, it was astounding. For it was tea-time; and at tea-time Billy Bunter was always more anxious to be found than to be lost.

There was a cake in Study No. 1. Bunter knew that there was a cake—he had seen Harry Wharton take it in from the school shop.

So the Famous Five naturally expected to find Bunter haunting the vicinity of Study No. 1 at tea-time. Not finding him there, however, they came down to the quad to look for him. And immediately they sighted him, he fled as if for his fat life! Apparently, Billy Bunter, for the first time in history, did not want to be asked to tea!

"What's the matter with the fat ass?" asked Harry Wharton, in wonder. "Bunter!" he roared. "Bunter! You're wanted!"

"Cake!" shouted Johnny Bull; and the juniors chuckled.

It was a magic word—to Bunter! That ought to have stopped him, if anything could. But the magic seemed to have lost its power! Johnny's shout, instead of stopping Bunter, seemed to spur him on. He flew.

"After him!" said Harry.

And the juniors cut in pursuit.

Billy Bunter was wanted—for once! It was seldom that Bunter was wanted—especially at tea-time. Still more seldom was he missing at such a time, whether he was wanted or not. Now, as it happened, he was wanted; and, instead of rejoicing thereat, he flew!

"Stop, you fat duffer!" shouted Bob Cherry.

"Bunter, you fathead——"

Bunter tore on.

He was heading for the gates that stood wide open. He seemed to be bent on hitting the open spaces—to get away from the fellows who were going to ask him to tea, although he knew that there was a cake! It was really inexplicable.

"Stop him, Van Duck!" shouted Harry Wharton.

Putnam van Duck, the American junior in the Remove, was coming up from the direction of the gates. He had been there, chewing the rag, as he called it, with his gunman guardian, Poker Pike, who was sitting on his usual seat—the bench outside Gosling's lodge.

Van Duck was frowning—not, apparently, having derived much satisfaction from chewing the rag with Poker.

He glanced round as the captain of the Remove called to him, and stepped into Billy Bunter's way.

The next moment he wished he hadn't.

Bunter did not stop! He came on full-tilt, and crashed into the youth from Chicago like a fat cannon-ball.

"Aw, wake snakes!" gasped Van Duck, as he spun over backwards.

"Urrrrgh!" gasped Bunter, as he stumbled over Putnam.

He landed hard and heavy on the sprawling American junior. There was a horrible gurgle from Putnam, as every ounce of wind was driven out of him.

"Oh crikey!" spluttered the fat Owl.

He bounced up like an india-rubber ball and tore on, leaving Putnam van Duck on his back, gasping.

Billy Bunter was gasping, too. But he bolted on, reaching the gates well ahead of his pursuers.

"Stop him, Pike!" yelled Bob.

Billy Bunter was putting on unusual—indeed, amazing—speed. It *really* looked as if it was going to be a stern chase if Bunter got out of gates, and the chums of the Remove were not looking for a cross-country run! So they shouted to Mr. Pike to stop him.

Poker Pike rose from the bench and stepped into Bunter's way, as Putnam had done!

There was another crash! Bunter did not stop—he cannoned!! But this time he cannoned on an immovable object. The gunman stood like a rock, and did not even stir as he received Bunter's charge. Bunter cannoned on him like a billiards ball on a cushion. He flew off the rock-like Mr. Pike, and rolled over.

"Ooooooogh!" spluttered Bunter as he rolled.

"Got him!" gasped Bob.

The Famous Five came up with a rush and surrounded the sprawling, fat Owl. Poker Pike strolled back to his bench. Billy Bunter sat up, gurgling, and blinked at the Removites over the spectacles that had slid down his fat, little nose.

"I—I say, you fellows," he gasped, "I never had it! I——"

"You howling ass!" roared Bob. "What are you playing the goat for? Don't you want to come in to tea?"

"Tut-tut-tea!" stuttered Bunter.

"Tea in our study, you blithering bandersnatch!" said Frank Nugent. "We've got a cake——"

"Kik-kik-cake!"

"What did you rush off for, you howling ass?" demanded Johnny Bull.

"I—I didn't!" gasped Bunter.

"What?"

"I—I mean, I—I—— Urrrgh! I mean——" Billy Bunter staggered to his feet. "I say, you fellows, I—I don't want to come to tea!"

"You don't want to come to tea!" gasped Bob.

"No! I—I'm going out! Like that beast's cheek to stop me!" gasped Bunter. "I've a jolly good mind to punch his head! I don't think the Head ought to let that ruffian stay in the school at all! I've said so before! I jolly well think——"

"Never mind what you think—if you think at all!" said Harry Wharton. "Come on, you fat duffer!"

"I'm not coming! Look here, you gerrout of the way!" gasped Bunter. "I'm not a fellow for stuffing—like some chaps I could name! Lemme pass!"

The Famous Five did not let Bunter pass. They stood round him in an amazed circle. When Billy Bunter did not want to come to tea, although there was a cake, it was time for the skies to fall!

"But we've got a big cake——" said Harry Wharton.

"I—I don't want any of it."

"And a bag of jam tarts, too!" said Nugent.

"Blow your jam tarts!"

"And ginger-pop!" said Bob.

"I don't want any!"

They could only gaze at him. If Billy Bunter did not want cake, and jam tarts, and ginger-pop, it was clear that the age of miracles was not past.

"Is he off his rocker?" asked Bob, in wonder.

"Is he ever on it?" asked Johnny Bull.

"Must have gone potty!" said Nugent.

"Terrifically potty!" declared Hurree Jamset Ram Singh.

"Look here, Bunter——"

"Well, you look here," said Bunter. "You leave a fellow alone—see? I don't want to come to your study! Keep your measly cake! I'm going out for—for a walk! I never knew you were going to ask me to tea, of course, or I shouldn't have——"

"What?"

"Oh! Nothing! Look here, you clear off, and lemme get out!"

"I suppose this is some sort of a joke," said Harry Wharton, staring at the fat Owl of the Remove. "Blessed if I see it, if it is! Look here, Bunter, you're asked to tea—cake, and jam tarts, and ginger-pop! No larks! Honest Injun! Now come up to the study."

"Shan't!"

"We want you—we've got something to say——"

"Well, I don't want to hear it! Go and say it to somebody else," said Bunter. "I'm going out."

"Nobody else will do, as it happens," said Harry. "Come on!"

"Shan't!" roared Bunter.

"Take his other ear, Bob!"

"'Ear, 'ear!" said Bob, as he took it.

"Ow! Leggo! Beast! Leggo!" roared Bunter.

But the juniors did not let go. Any fellow, of course, was free to decline an invitation to tea, if he liked. But this change in Billy Bunter's manners and customs was altogether too sudden and surprising. The difficulty, generally, was to keep him away from a study at tea-time. It was quite a new experience to find difficulty in getting Bunter in to tea!

However, that difficulty was solved by taking hold of Bunter's ears. They were large, and gave a good hold.

"Will you leggo!" howled Bunter, as he was led by his fat ears back to the House. "Ow! Don't pull my ears off, you beasts! I won't come! See? I jolly well won't come! Beasts! Yaroooh! Ow! Wow! I'm coming, ain't I, you beasts?"

And Bunter, reluctantly, came.

THE SECOND CHAPTER.

Ventriloquist Wanted!

"LOCO, I guess!" said Putnam van Duck.

The American junior followed the Famous Five and Billy Bunter into Study No. 1 in the Remove.

Bunter entered that study unwillingly. He blinked longingly at the door through his big spectacles. But Bob Cherry spun the fat Owl to the arm-chair, into which he plumped.

Billy Bunter is chiefly famous for eating, drinking and sleeping. But there's no getting away from the fact that the fat and fatuous Owl of the Greyfriars Remove is a skilled ventriloquist!

"Ow!" gasped Bunter. "Beast!"

Bunter's reluctance to join up at that study spread was as pronounced as ever—indeed, more so. He had been reluctant to enter the study—and now he was evidently only anxious to escape from it. It was absolutely inexplicable—unless Bunter was bent on making history! Unless he was "loco," as Van Duck called it, or off his rocker, as Bob put it, it was an unfathomable mystery.

"Now, you fat ass——" began Harry Wharton.

"Beast!" hooted Bunter. "Lemme out of this study!"

"Let him see the cake!" suggested Frank Nugent. "Perhaps the blithering idiot doesn't believe there's a cake."

"He saw me bringing it in," said Harry Wharton. "I thought he'd be after it as usual——"

"Oh, really, Wharton——"

"Well, I'll get it out," said Nugent. "We can talk to him while he scoffs cake."

"I say, never mind about the cake!" exclaimed Bunter hurriedly. "If—if you fellows want to talk to me, you can go ahead—but don't get out that cake! I don't want any."

Nugent, who was stepping towards the study cupboard, stopped in sheer amazement.

"The—the fact is," gasped Bunter, "I'd rather not eat while we talk. I—I never was a chap for guzzling, as you know."

"Ye gods!" gasped Nugent.

"If you've got anything to say, say it, and let a chap clear!" said Bunter. "You can have your tea afterwards. Get it over, see! I—I've got to go and see old Quelch."

"You were going out of gates to see Quelch!" yelled Bob. "You jolly well know Quelch is in his study."

"I—I—I mean——" gasped Bunter. "I—I—I——"

"Well, what do you mean?"

"Oh! Nothing! Look here, you fellows, if you want to jaw, jaw, and get done with it. You can't expect me to sit here and watch you guzzling!"

"Don't you want any cake?" shrieked Bob.

"No, I don't—and I don't want to sit here while you guzzle cake, either! I've got no time to waste, with the Head expecting me——"

"The Head?"

"I mean Quelch—that is, I mean, I—I've got to go out! Look here, get it over before you start tea. What's it all about, anyhow?"

"Well, wonders will never cease!" said Bob. "No need to feed the fat ass if he doesn't want to be fed. But——"

"Some fellows are always guzzling," said Bunter. "I'm not that sort, I hope. Look here, what do you want? I've got to see Wingate of the Sixth, and you know prefects don't like to be kept waiting——"

"Right-ho," said Harry Wharton. "Now, look here, Bunter——"

"Cut it short!" said Bunter, with a longing eye on the door.

"Shut up and listen! We're taking the team over to Rookwood to-morrow, as I dare say you know, to play Jimmy Silver's lot——"

"Oh!" said Bunter. "Well, if you want me to play for the Remove, you needn't have dragged me up here to say so. It's all right—I'll play! If that's all, I'll be going."

"You howling ass!" roared Wharton. "We're going to play Rookwood at cricket, not at marbles, so you won't be wanted."

"You cheeky ass——"

"Van Duck's in the team for Rookwood," went on Harry.

"What rot!" said Bunter. "You'd better play me! Yankees don't know anything about cricket!"

"You pie-faced gink——" began Putnam van Duck.

"Yah!"

"Never mind that," said the captain of the Remove. "You're not wanted to help in selecting the team, Bunter. Van Duck's coming! Now, you know that Poker Pike is here to keep watch over him, because of the gangsters getting after him to kidnap him. Chick Chew——"

"I know all about Chick Chew! For goodness' sake get through, and let a fellow go!" snapped Bunter. "I can't keep Loder of the Sixth waiting long. You know what a beastly bully he is——"

"You can keep Loder waiting, along with Wingate, and Quelch, and the Head, as well as that walk out of gates!" said Bob Cherry.

"Ha, ha, ha!"

"I—I mean——"

"Never mind what you mean," said the captain of the Remove. "Shut up and listen! We don't want Pike over at Rookwood. Van Duck will be quite safe from Chick Chew and the kidnappers, along with a mob of Greyfriars fellows, and we don't want to spring that gunman on the Rookwood crowd. See?"

"He, he, he!" chuckled Bunter. "I wonder what the Rookwood chaps would think of him, with his gun and all. He, he, he!"

"Well, we want to leave him behind

to-morrow," said Harry, "and we think you can help us."

"I'll say he won't be left," grunted Putnam van Duck. "I've just been chewing the rag with him about that very thing; and I guess Poker will be along!"

"We've been jawing it over, old bean," said Harry, "and we think Bunter can help to keep him here."

"You can jolly well leave me out!" said Bunter positively. "If you think I'm going to handle that hefty brute, you're——"

"Ha, ha, ha!" yelled the juniors. The idea of Billy Bunter handling Poker Pike made them howl. Poker was quite able to handle two of the biggest Sixth Formers at Greyfriars School, one with each hand. Billy Bunter would have had about as much effect on him as a fat fly on an elephant.

"Blessed if I see anything to cackle at!" grunted Bunter. "I dare say I could handle him all right—an athletic chap like me! But I'm jolly well not going to do it!"

"Ha, ha, ha!"

"Look here, if you've got nothing to do but cackle at a chap, I may as well go!" hooted Bunter. "I've got to see Walker of the Sixth—I mean Loder—that is, Wingate——"

"They can all wait a bit," said Harry. "Now, this is the idea—Poker's got to have his leg pulled, and you're the only fellow that can do it. We've simply got to get off somehow and leave him behind—goodness only knows what might happen if he got an idea into his head that kidnappers were about, and started popping off his gun at Rookwood——"

"He, he, he!" chortled Bunter.

"He won't stay behind if he knows that Van Duck is gone. But if he fancies that Van Duck is still here, he will stay. See? Now, Van Duck's going to slip over the Cloister wall, and pick up the charabanc in the road, when we go to the station. So Poker won't see him start. Poker's got to believe that he's still in the school, and that's where you come in."

Billy Bunter shook his head.

"You can wash that out," he said firmly. "I'm not telling him any lies! I'm surprised at you, Wharton! I've never told a lie in my life!"

"What!" yelled Wharton.

"Never," said Bunter; "and I'm not going to begin now. I'm surprised at you! I know you ain't so particular about such things as I am——"

"You fat villain!"

"You can call a fellow names!" said Bunter scornfully. "But I've always been truthful, and I'm keeping it up. Like that chap Abraham Lincoln, who couldn't tell a lie——"

"George Washington, you fat gink!" said Putnam.

"Was it?" said Bunter. "Well, I knew it was some beastly Yankee. He couldn't tell a lie, anyhow; and it's the same with me. I just couldn't! Ask Smithy! He wouldn't mind. Now I'd better go—I promised Coker of the Fifth to see him in his study—I mean Loder's waiting for me—that is, Quelch——"

"Shut up, you fat frog! I tell you, Poker Pike's got to have his leg pulled," hissed Wharton. "Your rotten ventriloquism——"

"My what?"

"Your putrid ventriloquism," said the captain of the Remove. "Poker's never heard of it, of course, so you can pull his leg with it."

"If you mean my wonderful ventriloquism——"

"Any old thing!" said Harry. "You've been kicked up and down the Remove passage for imitating fellow's voices, and playing rotten tricks with your putrid—I mean, your wonderful—ventriloquism. Now, you've often imitated Quelch's voice, and the Head's, and a lot of fellows—and you can pick up Van Duck's, see? You can lock yourself in a study or somewhere, and talk to Poker through the door. He won't see you, but will hear——"

"Oh!" said Bunter.

The fat junior sat up and took notice. He understood now why he was wanted in Study No. 1.

Bunter's ventriloquism, whether is was putrid or wonderful, was rather at a discount in the Remove. It had earned him more kicks than ha'pence.

But there was no doubt that the fat junior, who could do nothing else, could do that and do it in a very remarkable way.

Most of the Greyfriars fellows knew about Bunter's weird gift. In the Remove they were fed-up on it, and discouraged Bunter promptly when he got going. A mysterious voice from behind a door, or the growl of an unexpected dog under a table, neither alarmed nor amused, but generally led to a boot being planted on Billy Bunter's tight trousers.

Poker Pike, as a stranger in the land, knew nothing of his ventriloquial trickery. It was certain that if Poker heard Van Duck's voice from a study, he would be assured that Van Duck was in that study. He would "keep tabs" on that study while Putnam got off to Rookwood with the Remove cricketers. And to the fat Greyfriars ventriloquist, such a jape was as easy as falling off a form.

And Bunter rather liked the idea of pulling Poker's leg. He had not forgotten how Poker had "fanned" him with bullets and made him skip.

It was like Bunter, however, to assume egregious importance as soon as he found that he was wanted. He was quite keen to pull Poker's leg and show off his wonderful powers. But he was not going to admit it. Not Bunter!

"Well, it's not a bad idea," he remarked. "I might do it, to oblige you fellows. I'll think about it, anyhow. Now I'll go——"

"If you think you can imitate Van Duck's voice——" said Harry.

"Oh, don't be an ass!" said Bunter.

"What?"

"I can imitate any voice I've heard, especially if it's got anything queer about it——"

"Eh?" ejaculated Van Duck.

"Like yours, you know," said Bunter, blinking at him. "I suppose you call it a voice? Sort of yowl through the nose is what I call it."

Van Duck gave the fat Owl a very expressive look. Possibly he was aware that he had a nasal drawl, like many Americans. But he had never regarded his voice as a yowl through the nose!

"You slab-sided, two-cent remnant of——" he began.

"Oh, chuck it!" said Bunter. "If you fellows want me to oblige you with my clever ventriloquism, you'd better be civil about it. I'm not at all sure I can find time to-morrow. I'm generally rather busy on a half-holiday. A lot of fellows will be wanting me——"

"I guess this is N.G.," said Van Duck. "Mean to say that that fat gink can do anything except guzzle foodstuffs and snore half his time and tell fibs? I guess I want to know!"

"It's a fact," said Harry. "Of course, it isn't easy to believe that that fat idiot can do anything——"

"Oh, really, Wharton——"

"But he can ventriloquise," said Harry. "Blessed if I know how he does it—it can't need brains, or, of course, he couldn't——"

"You cheeky beast!" hooted Bunter.

"I guess I'll believe it when I see it!" said Putnam sceptically. "I guess that——"

He broke off suddenly as a voice barked at the door.

The door had been left ajar, and no one had noticed a footstep in the passage. But from the Remove passage came a sudden barking voice—the well-known metallic tones of Poker Pike, the Greyfriars gunman!

"Search me! You figure you can string me along that-a-way, you young guys? I'll say you better forget it! Surest thing you know."

"Oh, my hat!" gasped Bob Cherry, in dismay.

The whole Co. spun round, staring at the door. If Poker Pike had overheard the plot to pull his leg on the morrow, it was clear that the game was up before it started! In utter dismay the chums of the Remove stared at the door, while from Billy Bunter came a fat cackle.

"He, he, he!"

THE THIRD CHAPTER.

Light on the Mystery!

"HE, he, he!" chortled Bunter.

The dismay of the Removites seemed to entertain the fat Owl. He sat in the armchair and chortled.

"He, he, he! I say, you fellows—he, he, he! There's nobody there!" chuckled Bunter. "I say, he, he, he! I——"

"You fat ass, it's Pike——"

"He, he, he!"

"I guess he's wise to the game now, if there was anything in it," said Van Duck, grinning. "Not that there was!"

"He, he, he!"

"I guess that gink couldn't work the riffle——"

"He, he, he!" cackled Bunter.

"Aw, can it, you fat piecan!" snapped Putnam. "Here, you Pike! Mosey in, you gold-darned geek! What are you sticking outside the door for, you big stiff?"

There was no reply from the passage. The door did not open. Billy Bunter's fat chortle sounded more explosively. And the Famous Five, looking at the chortling Owl, guessed! It was not Poker at the door at all! Nobody was there! It was a sample of Bunter's ventriloquism!

But Putnam van Duck did not think so for a moment. Bunter's voice-slinging stunt was a new one on him. He did not believe that Bunter could do it. Which was really rather natural, for the fat and fatuous Owl certainly did not give the impression of being able to do things that other fellows couldn't do. In every other respect, Bunter was a fathead, and the American junior was slow to believe that he was not a fathead in all respects.

"You hear me, Poker, you pesky piecan?" hooted Van Duck. "What you mean by crawling along without a guy hearing you, and horning in that-a-way? I guess you want beating up a few, you scallawag."

"He, he, he!"

Van Duck, angry and impatient, strode to the door and dragged it wide open. For he gazed out of an empty doorway into an empty passage.

The Famous Five grinned. They had already guessed how the matter stood—though so exactly had Bunter picked up the nasal bark of the gunman, that they had been quite deceived at first. But Putnam van Duck stared into the empty passage, his eyes popping with astonishment.

"Say, where's that guy Poker got to?" he exclaimed.

"He, he, he!" gurgled Bunter.

Van Duck put his head out at the door. On the landing at the end of the passage he could see Vernon-Smith and Tom Redwing of the Remove. He called to them.

"Say, you! You see that gink Poker around?"

The two juniors glanced along the passage.

"Poker?" said Redwing. "No, he's not about, that I know of."

"He was here a minute ago, yauping in at this door."

"He jolly well wasn't!" said Smithy, with a stare. "We've been standing here five minutes, and we should have seen him."

Van Duck, puzzled and mystified, looked in the other direction up the passage. Peter Todd was in the doorway of his study, No. 7, talking to Squiff and Tom Brown, who stood in the passage.

"You guys seen Poker go up the passage?" called out Van Duck.

"No; he hasn't passed us," called back Squiff.

"Carry me home to die!" ejaculated Van Duck, and he turned back into Study No. 1, to stare at five smiling faces, and one grinning from ear to ear.

"It's all right, old bean," said Harry Wharton, laughing. "That was only a sample of Bunter's ventriloquism."

"Can it!" said Putnam derisively. "You want me to swallow that that fat gink could get Poker's bark to the life, like that, and make me believe it was Poker yapping at the door? Forget it!"

"You silly ass!" hooted Bunter. "It was my wonderful ventriloquism——"

"Aw, pack it up! I can't make out where Poker is, but——"

"I guess I'm here, buddy!" came the nasal bark of the Chicago gunman, and Van Duck stared blankly as the voice came from under the study table.

"How'd he get in here without me seeing him?" howled Van Duck.

"Aw, I guess you don't see a thing, you young bonehead," came the voice from under the table. "I'll tell a man, you're the world's prize boob from Boobsville."

Van Duck made a jump at the table, grabbed it, and dragged it to one side. He almost fell down in astonishment as he stared at the blank space where the table had stood. No one was there.

"Search me!" stuttered Van Duck.

"He, he, he!"

Putnam turned to stare at the fat junior in the armchair. Belief was forced upon his doubting mind.

"Mean to say you did it?" he demanded.

"Yes, you ass!" grinned Bunter. "I'm a wonderful ventriloquist—really marvellous and wonderful, and——"

"I guess you know how to crack up your goods, at any rate!" grunted Van Duck. "But I'll say it's some stunt! I'd have told all Chicago that that was Poker's bark. Mean to say you could imitate my toot like that?"

"Bunter could do it on his head," said Bob Cherry. "The fat villain imitated Quelch's voice once, and gave me lines."

"I guess I don't believe that!"

Bob Cherry reddened.

"What the thump do you mean, Van Duck!" he exclaimed hotly. "I don't know the manners of Chicago, but I can jolly well tell you that at Greyfriars we don't call fellows liars——"

He broke off, staring at Van Duck's bewildered face.

"Great jumping frogs! Who was it spoke?" yelled Putnam.

"You did——"

"I did not!"

"You silly, cheeky ass——"

"He, he, he!"—from Bunter.

Johnny Bull gave a roar.

"Hold on, you men! It was Bunter! It was some more of his putrid ventriloquism. Bump him out of that chair!"

"I say, you fellows, you keep off!" yelled Bunter, in alarm. "Van Duck said I couldn't imitate his voice, didn't he? I was only showing you——"

"Oh!" gasped Bob Cherry. His red face grew redder. "Sorry, Van Duck, I- I thought it was you speaking! I'll kick that fat rotter for playing such a rotten trick——"

"Beast! You keep off! I——"

"Waal, search me!" gasped Van Duck. "If that was Bunter, the stunt's the best I've heard in a month of Sundays! Poker will sure figure that it's me talking to him, if that fat gink can throw it like that."

"I could ventriloquise your head off!" said Bunter complacently.

"I'll take an ear!" said Harry Wharton. "You take the other one, Bob!" "'Ear, 'ear!" said Bob Cherry, as he took it. "Will you leggo?" howled Bunter, as he was led back to the House. "I jolly well won't come! Beasts! Yarooooh! Ow! I'm coming, ain't I, you beasts?"

"'Tain't easy to imitate a common-place voice—like Nugent's, f'rinstance—but anything odd or weird, like your yowl through the nose, or Bull's grunt that he calls a voice, or Wharton's high-faluting way of speaking——"

"You silly ass!"

"You cheeky gink!"

"Bunter wants kicking!" said Johnny Bull. "He always wants kicking, and more than ever when he gets a chance of showing off! Let's kick him!"

"The kickfulness is the proper caper!" agreed Hurree Jamset Ram Singh.

"Oh, chuck it!" said Bunter. "If you want me to do this for you—the only fellow at Greyfriars who's got the brains to do it—you'd better be civil, I can tell you! I don't mind obliging you—I think a clever chap ought to be willing to help silly asses when they can't help themselves—but——"

"Oh, ring off, you fat frump!" growled Bob Cherry. "I've a jolly good mind to kick you along the passage! Anyhow, you can see now that the fat bounder can do the trick, Van Duck?"

"Sure!" agreed Putnam. "I'll say it's the elephant's side-whiskers!"

"That's settled, then!" said Harry Wharton. "Bunter will play up to-morrow. Now we'll feed him. He deserves a feed for what he's going to do. Let's have tea!"

The fat grin faded from Billy Bunter face, as if the mention of tea had alarmed him. He jumped hurriedly out of the armchair.

"I say, you fellows, I don't want any tea! I haven't come here to guzzle! If you're going to have tea, I'll clear!"

He rolled to the door.

"You howling ass!" exclaimed Wharton impatiently. "What are you playing that silly game for? You're always rooting after a feed. And you never do anything for nothing, either. Stay and feed, you fat ass!"

"Shan't! The—the fact is, I've had my tea——"

"You can always do with a second one, and generally a third!" snapped the captain of the Remove. "But if you mean it, get out, and be blowed!"

"Yah!"

Billy Bunter rolled out of the study and slammed the door after him. His footsteps died away—hurriedly.

Harry Wharton & Co. gazed at one another. They utterly failed to understand the fat Owl. He seemed quite a new Bunter.

"Blessed if I make the fat idiot out!" said Frank Nugent. "Anyhow, if Bunter doesn't want any tea, we do, so let's get going!"

He stepped to the study cupboard and opened the door. He looked into the cupboard. Then he stood staring into it with a fixed stare.

"The fat villain!" he gasped.

"Hand out the stuff, old chap!" said Harry.

It was rather late for tea, and all the juniors were ready.

"It's not here!" yelled Nugent.

"Wha-a-t?"

"That fat scoundrel! That's why he didn't want to come up to tea!" yelled Nugent. "He's snaffled it already!"

There was a rush to the cupboard. Six juniors stared into it.

Blank space met their view.

There was no cake! There were no jam tarts! There were ginger-beer bottles, but they lay uncorked and empty. The cupboard was in the same state as Mother Hubbard's. Only a litter of crumbs remained to show that somebody had stood at the cupboard feeding!

"The fat burglar!" roared Bob Cherry.

"So that was why——" gasped Wharton.

"The whyfulness was terrific!"

The mystery was explained now! Bunter had not wanted to come up for those good things, because they were already parked in his capacious interior. He had dreaded that the discovery would be made while he was on the spot!

That was why, for the first time in history, he had refused an invitation to tea—and fled from hospitality!

"The—the—the fat burglar!" gasped Wharton. "I—I—I'll burst him all over the passage! Get after him!"

There was a rush from the study. Up and down the passage half a dozen exasperated juniors sought the Owl of the Remove. But they found him not. Billy Bunter had had a good start, and he had vanished. And the cake, the jam tarts and the ginger-beer had vanished with Bunter—safely packed inside!

THE FOURTH CHAPTER.

A Case of Conscience!

"SAY, big boy!"

Harry Wharton & Co. smiled at Poker Pike.

It was the following morning—a bright and balmy summer's morning, giving promise of a scrumptious day for cricket.

When the Famous Five came out into the quad after breakfast, they were thinking chiefly of the journey to Rookwood School, and of the game there with Jimmy Silver & Co.

Members of the eleven had leave from second and third school. There was only one lesson that morning, for the fellows who were going over to Rookwood. All the arrangements were made, though the carrying-out of the same, so far as Putnam van Duck was concerned, depended largely on Billy Bunter.

Poker Pike, with his hickory face very wary and watchful, under his clamped-down bowler hat, came up to the juniors in the quad.

The Greyfriars gunman was well aware that Putnam did not want to arrive at Rookwood with his gunman guard. But that cut no ice with Poker.

Mr. Vanderdecken van Duck was paying him an enormous salary to guard his son from kidnappers; and Poker was going to earn that salary.

He had no doubt that Chick Chew, star kidnapper of the United States, would be on the watch, and would snap up the millionaire's son, if he went unguarded.

On that point the Remove fellows did not agree with Poker. They had no doubt whatever that Putnam would be quite safe, travelling with so numerous a party.

And they were quite fixed in their determination that Poker wasn't going to "horn in" at Rookwood. They liked Poker, and they respected his unbending sense of duty. But a Chicago gunman was quite out of place at a cricket match at another school.

Poker had caused a good deal of a sensation at Greyfriars. That could not be helped, so long as he was required to "keep tabs" on a junior menaced by kidnappers. But they did not want the sensation repeated at Rookwood. It was altogether too much of a good thing.

Poker was going to be left behind —and it was clear that he was suspicious. Van Duck had argued with him on the subject the previous day, producing no effect, except to make Poker extra watchful.

"Hallo, hallo, hallo!" said Bob Cherry cheerfully. "Nice morning, Mr. Pike."

"You said it!" agreed Mr. Pike. "Say, what time you hitting the railroad?"

"Ten o'clock at Courtfield!" said Harry. "We go to the station in a charabanc. Roll along and see us off!"

"I guess you'll make room for a guy in that hearse!" said Poker stolidly. "I'll mention that I'm travelling with that Putnam van Duck!"

"You fancy that Chick Chew will be waiting for us at Rookwood?" asked Frank Nugent, with a grin.

"I wouldn't put it past him!" said Poker.

"Come in the charabanc, if you like," said the captain of the Remove. "Your company's always a pleasure, Mr. Pike."

"The pleasurefulness is terrific!" declared Hurree Jamset Ram Singh solemnly.

Poker Pike looked at them. He was quite aware that the Greyfriars cricketers considered him superfluous at Rookwood. He had a strong suspicion that Putnam would dodge him if he could. So he was a little puzzled by this bland permission to accompany the party to the station.

"I guess I'll be around," he said. "And if you young guys figure that you can string me along, you got another guess coming!"

And the gunman walked back to the bench by Gosling's lodge, to wait and watch there till the charabanc started for Courtfield.

Harry Wharton & Co. exchanged cheery smiles.

Poker was wary and suspicious, but it was certain that he had not the faintest suspicion of the deep-laid plot for pulling his leg that morning.

"I guess he'll be on hand," remarked Putnam van Duck, when the gunman was out of hearing. "But he won't see this baby in the charabanc. I guess I——"

"I say, you fellows——"

Billy Bunter rolled out of the House, blinked round him through his big spectacles, and came up to the group of juniors.

"I'm rather sorry——" he began.

"Sorry you snaffled our tuck yesterday?" asked Harry. "It's all right, you fat spoofer. You're let off for that, as you're going to make yourself useful."

"Oh, really, Wharton, I never had the tuck! If you think I waited till you were gone down to the nets, and then went to your study, it only shows you've got a jolly suspicious mind! I never knew you had a cake——"

"You saw me take it in, you fat villain!"

"Well, I never knew you had any jam tarts," said Bunter. "I never knew anything about them till I saw them in the study cupboard. Not that I went to the study, you know. I wasn't in the Remove passage at all at the time. But, I say, you fellows, never mind that. I'm rather sorry that I shan't be able to oblige you, after all, to-day."

And Bunter shook his head.

Six separate and distinct glares were fixed on the Owl of the Remove.

This was Bunter all over. To the Remove cricketers, Billy Bunter was merely a pawn in the game. But that did not suit Bunter. It was seldom—very seldom—that Bunter was of any importance. When he was, he was the fellow to make the most of it.

"You fat ass——" began Johnny Bull, in a deep growl like that of the Great Huge Bear.

"You'd better not call a fellow names when you're asking favours of him!" said Bunter loftily. "I want to do the best I can for you fellows, of course. I always was kind and obliging; it's my chief fault. It's often taken advantage of. I never get any gratitude——"

"Is he wound up?" asked Bob.

"Beast! The fact is," said Bunter, "if I stick in your study, Wharton, I shall be late for second school. I can't very well do it."

"That's all right," said Harry. "Second lesson is French with Mossoo, and Monsieur Charpentier never rags a fellow for coming in late. You've come in late often enough to know that."

"That's all very well," said Bunter. "But what about my conscience?"

"Your whatter?" yelled Bob.

Nobody in the Greyfriars Remove had ever supposed that Billy Bunter had a conscience. But it was like Bunter to develop one at an awkward moment.

"You fellows ain't very particular, I know," said Bunter. "But if you think you're going to bring me down to your level, you're jolly well mistaken. A fellow ought to be punctual for classes. Quelch keeps on telling us so. Well, he's right. I'm afraid I can't be late for French with Mossoo. I don't think I ought, you know."

"You podgy spoofer——"

"If you're simply going to call a fellow names, that ends it!" said Bunter disdainfully. "I'm going to do what I think's right!"

"When did you start that?" asked Nugent.

"Beast!"

"I'm going to leave a tin of toffees in the study!" remarked Wharton.

"Oh!" Bunter's little round eyes gleamed behind his big round spectacles. "Of course, if you're going to do the decent thing, I shall do my very best for you. Anything beside the toffees?"

"No, you fat cormorant!"

"If you think you can bribe me with a tin of toffees, Wharton, I'm afraid you're rather unscrupulous!" said Bunter, shaking his head. "Wash it out! It's a fellow's duty to turn up on time for class unless he's unavoidably prevented, and you know I'm a whale on duty——"

"Kick him!" said Johnny Bull.

"You jolly well kick me, and I can jolly well tell you that you won't get any ventriloquism out of me!" said Bunter. "I might stretch a point, if you were really pally——"

"And a bag of doughnuts!" said Wharton.

"How many?" asked Bunter, very cautiously.

"Six!"

"If you're too jolly mean to stand a fellow a dozen doughnuts, you can't expect——"

"Well, a dozen!"

"Any jam tarts?"

Harry Wharton made a motion with his foot, and Bunter backed away promptly. But the captain of the Remove restrained his wrath. Billy Bunter for once was indispensable, and not to be kicked as he deserved.

"And a dozen jam tarts!" he said.

"Oh, all right!" Bunter became quite affable. "My dear chap, rely on me! After all, we've always been pals, haven't we? And I'm the chap to stand by a pal, as you know. You remember how I stood by you when you first came to Greyfriars. You weren't here then, Van Duck. Wharton's rather changed since then; he was worse then than he is now! You remember scrapping with him in the train, Franky, the day he came—— Yaroooh!"

Bunter broke off with a roar as Frank Nugent's foot landed.

His cheery reminiscences of Wharton's early days at Greyfriars did not seem grateful or comforting to Harry Wharton's special chum.

"Ow! Wow! Look here, you beast——" roared Bunter.

"Have another?" asked Nugent, drawing back his foot.

"Beast!"

Bunter did not stop for another.

He rolled away in haste, wrathful and indignant, and very much inclined to refuse to oblige those ungrateful fellows, after all.

But toffee and doughnuts and jam tarts had an irresistible appeal. Bunter's final decision was that he would oblige the fellows, ungrateful as they were. As for his conscience, which had awakened so suddenly that morning, the prospect of a feed in the study seemed to have satisfied it. Billy Bunter's conscience, fortunately, was a very accommodating one!

THE FIFTH CHAPTER.

Off to Rookwood!

MR. QUELCH had some rather inattentive pupils in first school that morning.

The Remove Eleven and a couple of lucky fellows who had leave to go over to Rookwood with the team were thinking very little of the poetical works of that great poet, P. Vergilius Maro, to which that lesson was devoted. Even Mark Linley handed out a very poor "con," and Bob Cherry's was as bad as Bunter's.

But Henry Samuel Quelch had been a boy himself in his time, though one would hardly have guessed it by appearances. He could make allowances for eager youth. To Mr. Quelch, cricket was very small beer compared with classical learning. But he could remember a time when he would have given all the works of all the classical poets to hit a sixer!

So he was patient with those eager youths who were thinking of cricket, and passed over mistakes that at other times would have brought down the vials of wrath on unthinking heads.

The Remove were dismissed after that lesson to go to Class-room No. 10, where Monsieur Charpentier was going to take them in French for second school.

They had five minutes for the changeover, and on such occasions they never hurried. Mossoo was known to be a "good little ass," never calling a delinquent to account unless absolutely driven to do so. Any fellow who had business on hand could be late for Mossoo's French sets. It was a sheer stroke of luck for the Remove plotters that second school that day was with the French master. Bunter had to be late, and it was a risky business being late with Quelch. With Mossoo, it was safe as houses.

The Remove streamed cheerily out. The fellows booked for Rookwood rushed off to get ready for the trip. The charabanc was already at the gate to take them to the station.

Cricket bags were pitched in, and fellows took their seats, under the watchful eyes of Poker Pike. Never had the Greyfriars gunman been more keenly on the alert.

He knew that Van Duck was down to play in the Rookwood match. He expected to see him start for the station with the rest of the cricketers. But he was quite prepared to discover that Putnam was dodging off by himself—in which case, Poker was going to be very quickly on his trail.

"Hallo, hallo, hallo!" roared Bob Cherry, as he arrived at the gates. "Van Duck here?"

That question was asked purely for the benefit of the watchful gunman. Bob was well aware that Putnam was elsewhere.

"He hasn't come along yet!" grinned Herbert Vernon-Smith. The Bounder, like all the party, was in the little secret.

"Seen Van Duck, Poker?" called out Bob blandly.

"Nope!" answered Poker. "I guess I'm waiting to see him."

Frank Nugent came up, with Johnny Bull and Hurree Jamset Ram Singh.

"Where's Van Duck, Franky?" called out Bob.

"He went up to his study for something. Where's Wharton?"

"Not here yet."

"Well, lots of time for the train," said Johnny Bull. "Here, make room for a chap! Hang one of your feet outside, Bob!"

"Fathead!"

"You coming, Mr. Pike?" called out Peter Todd.

"Surest thing you know," answered Poker.

"Well, hop in!"

Poker shook his bullet head and bowler hat.

"I guess I'm waiting till I see Putnam!" he answered.

And Poker waited and watched, while the cricketers packed in. Harry Wharton and Putnam van Duck had not yet appeared.

They were, as a matter of fact, in Study No. 1, in the Remove, at that moment. So was Billy Bunter.

While the cricketers were preparing for the journey to Rookwood, and less lucky fellows for French with Mossoo, Billy Bunter had rolled into that study, intent on things far more important than either cricket or French—to wit, toffee, and doughnuts, and jam tarts!

The fat Owl grinned with satisfaction at the sight of a heap of good things on the study table.

There was a tin of toffees, a bag of doughnuts, and another bag of tarts. Bunter beamed at them! It was worth while being late for French, to dispose of a snack like this!

"Lock the door, fatty," said the captain of the Remove, "and mind you put on Van Duck's voice when Poker comes up."

"Leave it to me!" said Bunter. He grabbed a doughnut, and started. "Easy as falling off a form! You couldn't do it, of course!"

"That's all right, so long as you can, old fat man!" said Harry. "Come on, Van Duck, all right now!"

"I say, you fellows—hold on!" exclaimed Bunter. "There's one thing I forgot——"

"Pronto!" rapped Van Duck.

Wharton gave the fat Owl rather a grim look. If Bunter was going to start more difficulties, at the last moment, he was in serious danger of getting the kicking of his life.

"Buck up!" said Harry curtly. "We've got to get off!"

"I was going to say—groooogh! Oooooch!" Bunter had packed in rather too much doughnut for easy speech. "I mean—urrrggh! I was going to say—wooooooch!"

"Is that all?"

"Grooogh! I mean—gurrggh!"

"Buck up, you fat ass, time's going!"

"Urrgh!" Bunter grunted his fat neck clear and resumed. "I believe I mentioned that I was expecting a postal order——"

"You howling ass!" roared the captain of the Remove.

He had no time to waste hearing anything more about Bunter's celebrated postal order.

"Oh, really, Wharton——"

"Beat it!" said Van Duck. "I guess we got to burn the wind."

"I say, you fellows!" gasped Bunter. "What I mean is, the postal order hasn't come. I suppose you could lend me five bob——"

There was a pattering of feet in the passage. Wharton and Van Duck were heading for the stairs, at a run.

"I say, you fellows!" Bunter put his head out of the study and yelled after them. "I say, about that postal order——"

They vanished down the stairs.

"Beasts!" roared Bunter.

They were gone!

The Owl of the Remove blinked after them wrathfully.

Toffee, and doughnuts, and tarts were all very well, but Billy Bunter did not see why his celebrated postal order should not be cashed, in addition. He was strongly tempted to follow them and explain that if they were too jolly mean to cash a postal order for a pal they could jolly well get somebody else to do their ventriloquism for them.

But it was already time for Mossoo's French class to be in Study No. 10, and the fat Owl could not risk being spotted out of class. That would have parted him from the toffee, the doughnuts, and the tarts!

So he expressed his feelings with an indignant snort, rolled back into Study No 1, and shut and locked the door. A moment more, and he was travelling through the doughnuts at express speed.

Meanwhile, Wharton and Van Duck cut out of the House. They parted, Van Duck cutting off towards the Cloisters, where he was to drop over the wall, into the little side-lane, and join the charabanc on the road.

Harry Wharton walked down to the gates.

He grinned at the sight of the watchful Poker.

"Hallo, hallo, hallo! Where's Van Duck?" bawled Bob Cherry.

"Van Duck!" repeated the captain of the Remove. "He knows the time we've got to start; he can't be sticking in the study all this time."

He turned to the gunman.

"Seen Van Duck?" he asked.

"Nope!" answered Poker Pike. "But I guess I'm going to."

Wharton got into the charabanc. Everybody was present now, excepting Van Duck. The driver was ready to start. All the fellows looked back towards the House, as if in expectation of another arrival.

"Somebody had better go and call him!" said the Bounder. "We can't wait here for ever."

Poker Pike's hickory face was growing more and more grim and suspicious. There were a dozen ways by which a fellow might have got out of the school unseen by the watchful eyes at the gate. Poker was by no means blind to the possibility of the charabanc picking up Putnam on the road, after he had dodged out unseen at some secluded corner.

"Say, you guys, what's this game?" he demanded gruffly. "I guess I want to know where that Putnam van Duck is."

"Cut up to his study, then, and call him!" suggested Wharton.

Poker grunted.

"And that young guy getting in while my back's turned!" he growled. "Not by a jugful!"

Evidently Poker was very suspicious.

Poker was in a difficulty. If he turned his back Putnam might clear off in the charabanc. On the other hand, he might already have got out, and started walking to the station. Poker was getting anxious. He wanted to spot the millionaire's son—and he wanted to spot him quick.

"Say, you pesky young scallawags," he grunted, "if that young guy ain't in the shebang, I guess I'll be arter you pronto."

And with that Poker walked off.

The cricketers grinned as they watched him go. There was plenty of time for Poker to ring up a taxi and follow the charabanc, if he failed to find Putnam in the House. That was the gunman's intention. But if the little scheme worked successfully Poker was going to be satisfied that Putnam was safe in Study No. 1.

"Time we got off!" remarked Bob Cherry, as the bowler hat disappeared into the House.

And the charabanc started. It rolled out of gates and along the road, to stop at the corner of the side-lane by the Cloisters, to pick up Putnam van Duck. And the plotters hoped that Poker was being kept busy by the Greyfriars ventriloquist.

THE SIXTH CHAPTER.

The Two Voices!

"URRRRGGH!" gurgled Billy Bunter.

He jumped, and some jammy tart went down the wrong way.

The door-handle of Study No. 1 was grabbed from outside, and turned. As the door did not open, there came a heavy bang on it from a hickory fist.

Billy Bunter had been two busy to remember Poker Pike, or anybody or anything else. But he was reminded of him now.

Bang, bang! came at the door.

"Say, you there, you Putnam van Duck!" came Poker's angry bark. "Say, you let a guy in! What you got this door locked for, you gink?"

"Urrrggh!" gurgled Bunter, struggling with jam tart. "Grooogh!"

Bunter's cue was to answer in Van Duck's voice—an easy task to the Greyfriar's ventriloquist. But the greatest master of the ventriloquial art could scarcely have got a good effect with his neck full of jam tart going the wrong way.

Instead, therefore, of imitating the voice of Van Duck, Bunter gave a very good imitation of a suffocating frog!

"Urrrggh! Oooogh! Grooogh!"

"Say, that ain't Putnam!" barked the gunman. "I reckoned them young scallaways was stringing me along." He banged angrily on the door. "Say, is that young guy there?"

"Grooogh!" gasped Bunter. "Beast!"

"You pesky, young lard-faced geek!" roared Poker. Evidently he was wise to it that Bunter was there. "Is Van Duck there? Spill it, you fat gink!"

Billy Bunter coughed his fat neck clear.

"Oh, go away!" he snapped. "Don't

bother! Don't open that door, Van Duck!"

The fat Owl had given away his own presence in the study. But that made no difference, so long as the gunman believed that Putnam was there as well. So Bunter addressed an imaginary Van Duck, for Poker to overhear.

Having spoken to an imaginary Van Duck in his own voice, the fat ventriloquist answered in Van Duck's voice.

"I guess not, Bunter, old-timer."

It was Van Duck's voice to the last tone. Poker Pike, as he heard it out in the passage, could have no doubt that the gilt-edged junior was there.

He thumped on the door again.

"Say, you, Putnam van Duck!"

"Tell that fathead to go away, Van Duck!" said Bunter to space.

natural voice. "I can tell you; they're good!"

"O.K.!" answered Van Duck's voice.

Poker Pike, outside the study door, was puzzled and irritated. He had no doubt that Putnam van Duck was in the study. He could hear him in conversation with Billy Bunter there.

But he was quite perplexed by the American junior's unexpected proceedings. With the cricketers waiting to start, it was extraordinary for Van Duck to lock himself in a study and devote himself to tuck.

Poker banged on the door again.

"Aw! Will you beat it, you big stiff?" came a voice from the study, which the gunman had not the slightest doubt was Van Duck's.

"I don't get you!" snapped the glimpse of the charabanc rolling away, obviously without Van Duck in it. "You pesky young geck, I want to know what this here game is. They're starting. You hear me toot! Them young gecks are going without you."

"I say, Van Duck! Are you really going to cut the cricket?" asked Billy Bunter, addressing empty space.

"Sure!" went on the fat ventriloquist. "I guess I ain't showing up at Rookwood with a gunman treading on my tail. If I can't go without Poker, I guess I ain't going none."

"Waal, I'll mention that you ain't going without this baby!" growled Poker through the door. "Not so's you'd notice it, you young gink. With Chick Chew, mebbe, hanging around and watching for you."

From the Remove passage came the well-known metallic tones of Poker Pike, the Greyfriars gunman. "Search me! You figure that you can string me along that-a-way, you young guys. I'll say you better forget it!" Angry and impatient, Van Duck strode to the door and looked out into the passage. But Poker Pike was not to be seen. "He, he, he!" cackled Bunter, the ventriloquist.

"Say, you, Poker, you beat it!" he followed up with the American junior's voice.

"I guess I ain't beating it," growled Poker. "I got to keep tabs on you, you pesky young gink!"

"Aw! Go and chop chips!"

"You big stiff!" barked Poker. "Them young guys are waiting to start, and I guess they got a train to catch at the depot. Ain't you going?"

"Beat it! And tell them I'm coming!"

"I guess not," growled Poker. "Now I got you cinched, I guess I ain't losing you again. Unlock this here door!"

"Aw! Go round a corner and shake yourself, Poker!"

"I say! Have some of these tarts, Van Duck!" said Billy Bunter, in his puzzled Poker. "Ain't you going with them young guys to play cricket?"

"Nope!" answered the voice. "I guess not! You beat it, and tell them I've changed my mind!"

"I ain't beating it any!" snapped Poker. "I guess you got some shennanigan game on, you young geck, though I don't get it. I ain't quitting this here door s'long's you're in that there room. Surest thing you know."

Billy Bunter chuckled.

"I say, Van Duck, tell that silly ass not to kick up such a row," he said. "We shall have a beak after us, at this rate."

"Say, you park it, Poker!" came the nasal tones from the study. "Pack up your chin-wag a piece."

"Search me!" muttered Poker. From the landing window he had a

"Have another tart, Van Duck?" grinned Bunter.

"Yep!"

Billy Bunter sometimes gave a ventriloquial dialogue, for the entertainment of the Remove—as often, in fact, as he could get an audience. Now he gave a dialogue for the entertainment of Poker Pike. It was quite easy to the Greyfriars ventriloquist. He made his remarks in the intervals of gobbling tarts and doughnuts.

Poker Pike rapped on the door again.

"Say, you, Putnam!" he barked.

"Aw, can it!"

"If you ain't beating it with them guys to play cricket, I guess you got to get into your class," said Poker. "Ain't that so?"

"Sure! But I ain't honing for class," came the voice from the study. "I guess I'm sitting it out, Poker."

"I'll say you're a doggoned young scallawag!" exclaimed Poker warmly. "You get leave from school to play cricket, and you park yourself here and chew eats. That's a low-down game, young Putnam!"

"You pesky bonehead, will you pack it up before you bring some beak rubbering around?" snapped the voice from the study. "I guess my popper didn't hire you to be my schoolmaster."

Snort, from Poker. Certainly, if Van Duck had changed his mind about going with the cricketers, his Form-master would have expected him to turn up for the French set with the rest of the Form. Poker was not surprised that Putnam did not want to go over to Rookwood, with a gunman "treading on his tail." But he was rather surprised at Putnam cutting class, when he was no longer entitled to do so. Not for a moment did it occur to him that the American junior was not in Study No. 1 at all. His voice, at least, was there.

"Waal," he grunted, "I guess I ain't losing you till you're safe in your class, you Putnam van Duck. You ain't getting no chance of beating it after them guys, and leaving me fooled. Surest thing you know. I'll say I'm keeping tabs on your door till you come out."

And Poker walked along to the landing, and sat down in the window-seat. From that seat he could keep his eyes on the door of Study No. 1. And he was not going to take his eyes off that door till Putnam van Duck emerged. Which looked as if Poker was booked for a very long watch as the gilt-edged junior was not in the study at all.

THE SEVENTH CHAPTER.

A Surprise for Chick!

CHICK CHEW, Kidnapper No. 1 of the United States, had met with many surprises and shocks of one kind and another in the course of his career as kidnapper, boot-legger, gangster, and racketeer. But it was the biggest surprise of a hectic life that happened to him that morning.

Poker Pike, always wary, figured that it was very likely that Chick was around, watching for a chance to carry out his scheme of kidnapping the Chicago millionaire's son.

And Poker was right; Chick was around.

While the cricketers were packing in the charabanc, and Billy Bunter was scoffing tuck in Study No. 1, Chick was quite near at hand.

He was, in point of fact, leaning on the old Cloister wall in the little shady side lane that ran along by the Cloisters.

Even Poker Pike, probably, would not have recognised Chick, had he seen him. The fat gangster was an adept in disguises.

In his proper person he was well-known by this time to a good many people at Greyfriars School. But skill in disguises was a part of Chick's peculiar profession.

Now he was dressed in plus fours, with a wide-brimmed, shady hat, and sported an eyeglass and a moustache, and a complexion quite unlike his own.

He looked, at a glance, like a rather well-dressed tourist, and certainly nothing at all like a gangster.

Such a tourist could stroll about the lanes, and give his attention to old Cloisters and such things, and pause to admire the beauties of Nature without exciting anybody's suspicions.

That was Chick's occupation now.

Chick was a patient man. And he could afford to give plenty of time to a stunt which was to bring in half a million dollars in the way of ransom, if successful. Failure after failure had not daunted Chick, nor lessened his determination. As soon as one scheme failed, Chick started another.

His explorations that morning had shown him that there was quite an easy way into Greyfriars School by clambering over the old Cloister wall. An easy way in, and an easy way out. Half a dozen times he had peered over that wall, and seen nobody—it was a secluded spot. Now he was leaning on the wall, his hands in his pockets, a thoughtful shade on his fat face.

Chick was a man for bold ventures.

By entering at that unexpected spot he would escape the lynx eyes of the Greyfriars gunman.

Lurking among the old stone pillars, watching for Van Duck, spotting him, grabbing him suddenly and whisking him off before the alarm could spread—that was the idea that was working in the gangster's mind.

The very suddenness and unexpectedness of such a venture might spell success! Unless Poker Pike chanced to be on the spot!

Leaning on the old stone wall, half hidden by the clustering ivy, Chick turned it over in his mind.

There was plenty of time to think it over, for he knew the time of morning break, when Van Duck would be out of the House with the other schoolboys. That was more than an hour ahead.

It was a dubious matter, and Chick Chew realised that he had to think it over very carefully, in all its aspects, before he acted.

He had not made up his mind, when his cogitations were suddenly interrupted.

Chick hoped that Putnam van Duck might fall into his hands that morning. But he neither hoped nor dreamed that Putnam van Duck would fall on his head!

But that was precisely what Putnam van Duck did!

That a fat man was leaning on the outside of the old Cloister wall, at the spot where it was easiest to climb, naturally never occurred to Putnam. All he was thinking of was to get out of the school unseen by Poker, and pick up the charabanc on the road, at the end of the little lane.

After Harry Wharton had left him, the American junior lingered in the Cloisters, and from the cover of one of the old stone pillars, had the satisfaction of seeing Poker Pike hurry off to the House.

As soon as the gunman disappeared, Putnam got going.

With a cheery grin on his face, he went along to that particular spot of the Cloister wall, grabbed the thick tendrils of old ivy, and swung himself up and over.

Chick, below, heard the rustle of the ivy, and stirred. Even as he moved, the active junior swung over and down.

Putnam expected to land on the earth. Chick Chew being in the way, he landed on Chick Chew!

The gangster hardly knew what was happening for a moment. A boot crashed on his ear, another clumped in the back of his neck. Then he rolled over under Putnam van Duck.

Putnam sprawled, with a startled howl.

"What the great horned toad——"

"Aw! Search me!" spluttered Chick. "Carry me home to die!"

Putnam was on his feet with a bound. He knew that rasping voice.

"Chick!" he stuttered.

He did not stay for even a glance at the gangster. He ran up the lane towards the road like a deer.

Chick staggered up.

The sudden and unexpected shock had startled him, and rather winded him. He stared after Van Duck with starting eyes.

"Jumping toads!" he gasped.

It was amazing to Chick! But he was quick on the uptake. It was Putnam van Duck—almost in his grasp!

He leaped in swift pursuit.

He had been considering a desperate venture into the school, to grab that very junior; and here was Van Duck coming out alone, dropping over the wall at the very spot where he stood!

It was such luck as Chick had never dared to dream of! It seemed too good to be true!

He tore after the American junior, gaining on him at every stride.

It was amazing to see the boy there, for he knew it was lesson-time! But Chick was not the man to lose such a chance!

He fairly bounded.

Van Duck ran his hardest. Once he reached the corner, where the little lane joined the high-road, he would be all right. The charabanc would be in sight.

Knowing nothing of the charabanc, or of the cricketers' arrangements that morning, Chick flew after him, gloating.

So far as he could see, the gilt-edged junior had fairly walked into his hands, by breaking school bounds in class-time!

At the corner he was only a yard behind Van Duck!

Panting, the American junior burst out of the shady little lane into the road. After him bounded the gangster.

At the same moment a charabanc, rolling along from the school gates, slowed down at the end of the lane.

A dozen pairs of startled eyes fixed on Putnam van Duck and the fat man charging after him.

"Hallo, hallo, hallo!" roared Bob Cherry.

"Van Duck!" yelled Harry Wharton.

"Look out!"

"What the thump——"

An outstretched hand was touching Van Duck as he leaped for the charabanc. Three or four of the Removites jumped down.

They did not recognise Chick. But his actions spoke for themselves. They rushed at him.

Chick had figured that it was too good to be true! And so it was! Only a swift, backward jump saved him from clutching hands.

Van Duck clambered breathlessly on the charabanc.

Chick Chew turned and crashed through a hedge. Kidnapping Putnam van Duck was a vain dream now. Chick was in danger of being "cinched" himself! He flew across the field faster than he had flown on the track of the American junior.

"Wake snakes!" gasped Van Duck, panting for breath in the charabanc. "I guess that was a close call! I'm telling you, I dropped on his cabeza——"

"But who——" gasped Bob.

"Chick!" grinned Van Duck. "I guess he's changed himself some, but I knew his toot! I'll say it's Chick Chew!"

"Oh, my hat!"

The startled juniors stared across the field. Chick had already vanished beyond hedges.

"Well, my hat!" gasped Harry Wharton. "Who'd have thought—— All safe now, anyhow, and we've got the train to catch! Get on, driver!"

The charabanc rolled on to Courtfield. Nothing was seen of Chick Chew or of Poker Pike when the cricketers packed into the train; and they rolled away for Rookwood, forgetful of both gangsters and gunmen, and thinking only of the game with Jimmy Silver & Co.

THE EIGHTH CHAPTER.

Poker Keeps Tabs!

BILLY BUNTER finished the tarts and the doughnuts He chewed toffee thoughtfully. Already a quarter of an hour late for class in Class-room No. 10, the fat Owl of the Remove realised that it was time to get a move on. The charabanc was long gone, Putnam van Duck was long gone. The scheme had worked like a charm, so far as the cricketers were concerned. But Billy Bunter, as usual, was thinking chiefly about his fat and important self.

He had heard Poker Pike tramp along to the landing and sit down there. He knew that the gunman was watching the study—keeping "tabs" on the door till Putnam should emerge. Putnam, already on the way to Rookwood with the Remove cricketers, was certainly not likely to emerge from that study! But Billy Bunter had to emerge, unless he was to cut the French set entirely—which he could hardly venture to do.

So far, Poker had no suspicion of the trick that had been played. But if he discovered it, Bunter could not help thinking that the results for him personally might be quite painful.

He had to get out of the study without Poker discovering that Van Duck was not there. It was quite amusing to think of the wary gunman going on watching an empty study. But it was necessary to be very cautious.

Billy Bunter chewed toffee, parked the remainder of the tin's contents in his pockets, to be devoured later at his leisure, and approached the study door on tiptoe.

Noiselessly he turned back the key.

Opening the door about a foot, he put out a fat head, like a tortoise from a shell, and blinked along towards the landing at the end of the passage.

There, in the window-seat, a dozen yards from him, sat Poker Pike, in his bowler hat, which was a fixture on Poker, indoors as well as out.

The gunman's eyes were on his fat face at once.

As the door opened inwards, the lock on it was out of Poker's sight, as he looked along the passage.

It was easy for Bunter to transfer the key to the outside of the lock, unseen by Poker, especially as the gunman, of course, had not the faintest idea that he had any motive for doing so.

Poker remained where he was. He was ready to get busy the moment he saw Van Duck; but Billy Bunter had no interest for him.

Bunter stepped into the passage.

"You coming, Van Duck?" he called into the empty study.

"I guess I ain't coming down to class!" came the answer from the fat ventriloquist, loud enough for Poker to hear where he sat.

"Well, I'm going!" said Bunter, in his natural voice. "Mossoo will report us to Quelch if we don't turn up."

"Aw, I guess that cuts no ice! I ain't going!" came the life-like imitation of Putnam's voice.

"Please yourself!" said Bunter.

And he jerked the door shut.

Poker Pike heard that brief dialogue without the remotest idea that only one person was speaking. He was keen and wary, but Bunter's ventriloquism was a new one on him.

Standing carefully to screen what he was doing from the gunman, Billy Bunter turned the key in the outside of the lock, drew it out, and slipped it into his pocket.

The door was locked now on an empty room; but Poker, assuredly, had not the faintest idea that the room was empty. So far as he knew, Putman van Duck was still there.

Billy Bunter rolled down the passage.

His fat heart felt a qualm as he passed the gunman on the landing. If Poker suspected that he was being tricked, a sinewy hand was certain to grab the fat junior as he passed.

But Poker had no suspicion.

Bunter rolled past him in safety, and breathed more freely as he went down the Remove staircase.

(*Continued on next page.*)

Poker watched him pass without interest. His keen eyes fastened again on the door of Study No. 1.

Billy Bunter grinned as he rolled cheerfully away to Class-room No. 10. He kept a wary eye open for Mr. Quelch, but the Remove master was occupied in his study during his rest from his Form. The fat Owl reached the French master's class-room unobserved.

Monsieur Charpentier gave him a severe glance as he rolled in. Mossoo was very patient with fellows who came in late, but Bunter was more than twenty minutes late, and nearly half the lesson had elapsed.

"Buntair!" rapped the French master. "Pourquoi—vy for you come so late? Vingt minutes——"

"So sorry, sir!" said the fat Owl. "I've been looking for my French book, sir."

"Mais—but it needs to have ze book ready for ze class, Buntair!" said Monsieur Charpentier.

"Yes, sir, but I think a fellow must have hidden it, for a joke on me, sir," said Bunter. "I've been hunting everywhere."

Monsieur Charpentier gave him a very suspicious look.

"I zink, Buntair, zat I must give you fifty lines from ze Henriade!" he said.

"Oh, sir!" Billy Bunter assumed his most injured expression. "I've been hunting and hunting for my book, sir, all over the place——"

"I zink zat you have also been eating ze toffee, Buntair."

There was a chuckle from the French class! When Billy Bunter had been eating toffee, the skill of Sherlock Holmes was not required to trace the same. There was plenty of sticky evidence on Bunter's fat face.

"Oh, no, sir!" said Bunter. "I haven't tasted toffee this week at all, sir. I hardly ever touch it. I—I don't like toffee, sir."

"Zere is stickiness on your face, Buntair."

"Oh!" Bunter passed a sticky hand over a sticky mouth. "Is—is—is there, sir? Oh lor'!"

"You vill take vun hundred lines from ze Henriade, Buntair!" said Monsieur Charpentier severely.

"Oh, really, sir!" exclaimed Bunter indignantly. "Mr. Quelch always takes a fellow's word, sir! I haven't been in Wharton's study, sir, and there wasn't any toffee there——"

"Vat?"

"You can ask Wharton when he comes back from Rookwood, sir! He knows, as he left the toffee there specially. I hope you don't doubt my word, sir," said Bunter warmly.

"Ha, ha, ha!" came from the class.

"Mon Dieu!" exclaimed Monsieur Charpentier. "Buntair, you vill take two hundred lines from ze Henriade. Now go to your place."

"Oh, really, sir——"

"Taisez-vous!" snapped Monsieur Charpentier. "Be silent viz yourself, you bad garcon! Zat you sit down!"

Billy Bunter snorted and rolled to his place. He had not expected lines from Mossoo, who was generally very easy-going. However, there was comfort in the toffees he had parked in his pockets—to which Bunter gave more attention, during the next half-hour, than to French verbs.

Meanwhile, Poker Pike continued to "keep tabs" on the door of Study No. 1 in the Remove. He was a patient guy, and he sat unmoved till a bell rang, and the Greyfriars fellows came out in break.

Then Poker at last rose from the window-seat and walked along to the study. He rapped at the door.

"Say, you Putnam van Duck!" he called out.

No answer.

Poker turned the door handle. As the door did not open, he supposed that Putnam had locked it on the inside after Bunter had left. Really, he could hardly suppose anything else.

"You pesky young gink!" exclaimed Poker. "I want to know what's this here game? What you sticking in there for, Putnam van Duck? I'm telling you the young gecks have come out of class. Say, what's the big idea in sticking in that there room?"

Still no reply.

"You hear me toot?" exclaimed Poker.

If he was heard, he was not heeded. He banged at the door.

"You got a tongue in your bully beef trap, Putnam van Duck?" he roared. "Say, you sing out!"

Silence.

"Search me!" muttered the puzzled Poker.

Van Duck was surely still in the study! He could not have got out unseen by Poker. Yet, listening, the gunman could not hear the faintest sound within. But he was there—he had to be there!

"You pesky young gink!" snorted Poker, at last, and he went back to his seat on the landing.

If Van Duck had cut a class, he would surely emerge when the fellows were all out in break! But he did not! Break was over, and the Greyfriars fellows went in to third school.

All through third school Poker sat and "kept tabs" on that study. He was growing more and more puzzled by Van Duck's extraordinary behaviour; but he still did not doubt—he could not doubt—that the American junior was locked in that study.

The clang of a bell announced, at last, the end of morning school. A buzzing swarm of boys streamed out into the quad. Poker Pike had no doubt that Van Duck would come out now.

But he did not!

When the dinner-bell rang, Poker rose from his seat. The junior in the study had to come out for dinner. Poker was prepared to see him safe to Hall.

But, to his utter amazement, the door of Study No. 1 did not open.

He tramped along to the door and banged.

"You pesky young geck!" he roared. "You coming out!"

No reply.

"Carry me home to die!" gasped Poker, the most astonished gunman in the wide world. "What's got the young gink?"

Poker had his own dinner to think of. But he was not thinking of that. He was puzzled, mystified, and a little alarmed. Unless his ears had deceived him, Putnam van Duck was in that study. If he was there, he must have heard the dinner-bell. Why did he not emerge—or, at least, speak? It beat Poker Pike to a frazzle. A sorely puzzled man, Poker Pike went down the stairs at last, and headed for the Hall.

THE NINTH CHAPTER.

Drawn Blank!

MR. QUELCH, at the head of the Remove table, raised his eyebrows as Poker Pike tramped into Hall.

Every eye in Hall turned on the bowler-hatted gunman as he came in. Billy Bunter grinned, and fixed his eyes, and his spectacles, on his plate. Mr. Quelch frowned as the gunman marched up to the Remove table. More than once Poker had "horned" into Hall to "keep tabs" on Putnam van Duck, regardless of frowns. But Van Duck was not there now, and the Remove master failed to see any reason whatever for this visit.

"Do you want anything here, Mr. Pike?" he asked, in his iciest tone.

"You said it!" agreed Poker. "I guess I'm worried a few about that Putnam van Duck."

Mr. Quelch's eyebrows, already raised, were elevated still more.

"Van Duck!" he repeated. "I do not quite follow you, Mr. Pike! It can hardly be necessary for you to keep watch over the boy while he is with so large a number of his Form-fellows; but if you desire to do so, there is nothing, so far as I am aware, to prevent you from going to Rookwood."

"Rookwood nothing!" grunted Poker. "Putnam ain't vamoosed out of this here shebang."

"You are mistaken, Mr. Pike," said the Remove master coldly. "Van Duck is a member of the junior cricket team, and he had leave to go to Rookwood with the others to-day."

"Sure, but he never beat it!" said Poker.

"I am assured that he did go with the others," snapped Mr. Quelch. "If any change in the arrangements had been made, and Van Duck had stayed behind, he would have been present in class. I have not seen him."

"You sure ain't!" said Poker. "I guess you wouldn't see him a lot, and him locked in a study."

"Locked in a study!" repeated Mr. Quelch.

"Surest thing you know."

Mr. Quelch's eyebrows really looked as if they would go over the top of his head at that startling statement.

"Impossible!" he exclaimed.

"I'm telling you!" said Poker.

Mr. Quelch glanced at the staring juniors at the table.

"Does anybody here know whether Van Duck failed to accompany the cricket eleven to Rookwood?" he asked.

The Removites could only shake their heads.

"Has anyone here seen him since the cricketers left?"

Nobody had.

"I'm sure he went, sir!" said Kipps. "He was in the team, and his name's still up in the list in the Rag."

"Must have gone, sir!" said Wibley.

"You hear, Mr. Pike?" said the Remove master.

"Sure!" said Poker. "But that Putnam van Duck never beat it, big boy. He sure was locked in his study, and I been talking to him at the door. He's sure parked himself in that room all the morning."

"But why——"

"It's got me beat," said Poker. "I reckon he didn't want this baby keeping tabs on him at another pesky school, and that's why he never went. But why he's parked in that study beats me to a frazzle. He won't answer a guy at the door! Mebbe he's throwed a fit or something."

"Nonsense!" said Mr. Quelch.

The Removites at the table were grinning. Putnam van Duck was as healthy as any fellow in the Remove, and certainly not likely to "throw a fit." But to Poker's puzzled mind that was the only possible explanation of the American junior's amazing self-imprisonment and silence in Study No. 1.

"I got away from Poker Pike by making Van Duck's voice come out of the woodshed—the silly ass thought Van Duck was there, you know, when I imitated his voice. That gunman is a silly fool——" "Sez you!" Bunter spun round in alarm to find a hickory face under a bowler hat looking at him. "Oh lor'!" gasped the fat junior.

"I'll say he's there!" grunted Poker. "You being his schoolmaster, mebbe he'll answer you, and if he don't, mebbe you've got a key that'll work the riffle! I reckoned I'd put it up to you afore I cracked the door open."

"Oh!" gasped Mr. Quelch. "Kindly do not think of doing anything of the sort. I will go with you to the study and ascertain whether Van Duck is there. I am perfectly certain that he is not. I have not the slightest doubt that he is at Rookwood playing cricket."

"Sez you!" grunted Poker.

Mr. Quelch rose from the table, his lunch unfinished, and followed the gunman from Hall. The Remove table was left in a buzz of surprise, and fellows at all the other tables stared.

Except for the cricketers, only Billy Bunter knew of that remarkable scheme for keeping Poker Pike away from Rookwood. Everybody else supposed that Poker was making some extraordinary mistake. The idea of a fellow locking himself in a study, instead of going to a cricket match was altogether too surprising.

Poker Pike tramped up the stairs again, followed by the frowning Remove master. They arrived in the Remove passage, and Mr. Quelch tapped at the door of Study No. 1, and turned the handle.

"Dear me!" he said. "The door is locked!" He rapped again, sharply. "If anyone is in this study, open this door at once!"

He did not expect an answer, for he had no doubt whatever that Van Duck was at Rookwood School—as, indeed, he was! But Poker Pike expected an answer. Unless Van Duck was in some strange sort of a fit, he was bound to answer his master's voice. But no answer came.

"Van Duck!" called out Mr. Quelch. "Are you there?"

Silence.

Mr. Quelch turned from the door with a sound suspiciously like a snort.

"You can see for yourself, Mr. Pike, that no one is there," he snapped.

"I guess not!" answered Poker. "What's the door locked for?"

"It is certainly very odd that the juniors should have locked the study door," said Mr. Quelch. "It is not usual. Nevertheless——"

"I'm telling you that young guy is locked in that there room."

"Nonsense!"

Poker Pike's slits of eyes gleamed.

"You getting that door open?" he asked. "I guess I'm giving the inside of that room the once-over. Putnam van Duck is sure there, and I guess I want to know why he won't toot none."

Mr. Quelch breathed hard.

"Van Duck assuredly is not there," he answered. "The very idea is absurd. You see that there is no key in the lock inside. The door must have been locked on the outside, and the key taken. Even if a boy locked himself in a study, which is absurd, he could have no reason for removing the key from the lock."

"He is sure there!" said Poker stolidly.

"I will obtain the key and open the door, and you may satisfy yourself!" snapped Mr. Quelch.

"That goes!" agreed Poker.

He leaned on the study door, and waited while Mr. Quelch went down the stairs, in far from a good temper. It was only the absolute certainty that Poker would force the door, if it were not opened, that caused the Remove master to trouble further with the matter at all.

It was several minutes before he returned, with the key in his hand. Poker Pike detached himself from the door and watched the key placed in the lock. Mr. Quelch turned it back and threw the study door wide open.

"Now, sir!" he snapped.

Poker Pike tramped into the study.

"You pesky young gink——" he began.

He broke off.

His slits of eyes opened wide as he stared round Study No. 1. The room was empty.

Poker stared blankly. He looked under the table, behind the screen in the corner—even into the study cupboard. He crossed to the window and examined it. It was twenty or thirty feet from the ground—but whether it was possible for Van Duck to have climbed down or not, he certainly had not done so, for the window was closed and fastened on the inside! Utterly bewildered, Poker Pike stood in the study, gazing round him blankly.

"Well, sir, do you find anyone in that study?" inquired Mr. Quelch's sarcastic voice from the doorway.

"Nope!" gasped Poker.

The Remove master walked away to finish his interrupted lunch, leaving Poker Pike to stare.

He stood and stared! Putnam van Duck had been in the study—had he not heard his voice there in talk with the fat gink, Bunter? He could not have

(Continued on page 16.)

DOCTOR BIRCHEMALL'S BANK HOLLERDAY!

By DICKY NUGENT

"Hurry up, you fellows!" cride Jack Jolly, as he burst into the Fourth Form dormitory at St. Sam's on Bank Hollerday morning. "The sharrabang waits without!"

"Hooray!" cheered the Fourth, as they started tumbling out of bed. Jack Jolly looked rather alarmed.

"Quiet, you asses!" he hist. "Remember that we want to get away without Doctor Birchemall knowing! If he guesses we're going out for the day in a sharrabang, it's ten to one in doenutts, he'll want to come with us. Hurry up!"

The Fourth needed no further bidding. They started washing and dressing at litening speed, grinning all over their dials at the meer thought of getting away for a day without arousing the Head's suspishons.

Little did they dreem that the man they wanted to dodge was lissening to every word they said! Nevertheless, it was so. Doctor Birchemall had seen Jolly going down to the gates that morning, and wondering what was in the wind, had hurriedly dressed and followed him up the stairs on his return.

A grim, sardonnick smile appeared on the Head's face, as he heard what was said in the dormitory.

"Aha! So the dispertinent yung raskals want to dodge me, do they?" he muttered. "It's like their cheek, I must say! Bank Hollerday or no Bank Hollerday, I'm going with 'em!"

Where Doctor Birchemall sneaked off to after that was a mistery not to be solved till a little later in the day.

There was no sign of him five minnits afterwards, when the Fourth Formers crept stelthily down the stairs, and the juniors were in grate glee when they mannidged to reach the gates without running into him.

"There's the sharrabang!" cride Jack Jolly, pointing to a wacking grate motor-coach that was drawn up at the side of the road. "All aboard!"

The Fourth swarmed into the sharrabang in a cupple of jiffies, and Jack gave the order to the driver to start; and soon they were tearing through the country-side at a spanking speed!

The yung hollerday-makers' spirits rose high, as the sharrabang took them further and further away from St. Sam's, and ti wasn't long before their voices were ringing out in many a lusty corus. Jack Jolly, who was famus as an organiser, had brought mouth-organs for himself and his pals, and these added grately to the mewsical efforts of the Fourth. Everything seemed set for a really ripping Bank Hollerday!

In their eggsitement, the fellows took little notiss of the driver. Had they done so, they mite have observed one or two pekuliar feetchers about him. To begin with, he was wearing goggles, although the windscreen made them souperfluous; then again, he had his coat-collar turned up, although it was a hot day; and as if these were not enuff, he kept on larfing to himself as though he was enjoying a secret joak of his own!

But it was not till afterwards that the fellows remembered all this about the driver. Consekwently, a long interval went by without anyone suspeckting a thing; and it was only when the sharrabang arrived at a big town and came to a stop outside a museum, that they got the first inkling that something was wrong.

"Look where we've stopped!" ejackulated Frank Fearless.

"Oh, crums! It's a museum!"

Everybody stared at the driver, who was just turning down his coat-collar and removing his goggles. Imagine their disgust when they reckernised the sellybrated beard and familiar feetchers of Doctor Alfred Birchemall himself!

"It's the Head!" gasped Jack Jolly.

"Little me!" nodded Doctor Birchemall, with a leer. "I thought I'd give you a plezzant little serprize, boys; so I sent the sharrabang driver to the skool kitchen to have breakfast, and took his place myself. I hoap you're all pleased to see me! We will combine bizziness with plezzure by spending the day visiting various museums and studying fossils!"

"Wha-at?"

"I know some topping museums where they keep awfully interesting fossils," rattled on Doctor Birchemall. "This is the first. Tumble out, boys, and we will go inside and see them."

"Oh, grate pip!"

The fellows tottered after the Head, with feelings that were too deep for words.

When they arrived inside the museum, their very worst fears were realised. Usually, when Doctor Birchemall gave a lecture, he could be relied on to entertain his lisseners with frekwent joaks and witty sallies; but this time he was fearfully boring and long-winded!

It wasn't long before the fellows were feeling in the mood for any move, however mad, that would get them out of the klutches of the Head.

"We've had enuff of fossils," Jack Jolly growled to Frank Fearless, sotto vocey. "Something will have to be done about it."

"Hear, hear!" muttered Fearless. "The question is: what?"

"Desprit diseases require desprit remedies," whispered Jolly. "My idea is that we ought to make a getaway in the sharrabang and leave the Head here on his own. Then he can study fossils by himself for the rest of the day, if he likes!"

Frank Fearless chuckled softly.

"It's a wheeze after my own heart, old chap! Let's pass the word round. I can drive the sharrabang all right!"

Jack Jolly nodded; and in the next few minnits the word was passed round for everybody to be ready to take to their heels on a given signal from the Fourth Form kaptin.

The hollerday makers' chance came swiftly. All of a sudden, Doctor Birchemall broke off to bend down to tie up his shoelace. While he was engaged in this task, Jolly gave the signal.

In a cupple of jiffies, the fellows were out of the room, farely racing for the street. They heard a yell from behind them: "Hi! Stop, you yung raskals!" But, heedless of the Head's order, they pored through the eggsit and swarmed back into the sharrabang.

Frank Fearless, in the driver's seat, pressed the self-starter; and before you could say "Nife!" they were off!

"So much for the Head!" larfed Jack Jolly, as the fellows settled back in their seats with sighs of releef. "We shan't see him again till we get back to St. Sam's!"

But the kaptin of the Fourth was mistaken, for, in actual fakt, the Head had rushed out as they were moving off, and just

mannidged to hang
spare wheel tied
back of the sharra
Not till they rea
seaside resort of W
did Jack Jolly & C
that. But they soo
it out, then, for
person in the town
them was Doctor
mall! He looked n
a nigger minstrel
headmaster. But
still very much a
kicking, and the ha
St. Sam's hollerda
sank right into the
when they saw him
"Boys!" cride t
"Oh, crums!"
"Please, si
thought——"
"You thought y
me behind in that n
eh?" thundered
Birchemall. "W
jolly well didn't, s
Now hear your sen
The dismayed
Formers waited in
trembling. Was th
going to order the
birched and egg
Or was he perchan
to make it even wo
that—something
with boiling oil in
instance?
But nothing like
fourthcoming. The
pekuliar glimmer in
Birchemall's ey
strangely yewman a
ly gleem that be
stern axxents! W
spoke again, the
found out the reaso
"I sentence yo
said the Head, in s
sollem tones, "TO E
TAIN ME FOR
REST OF THE
ENTIRELY AT
OWN EGGSPENS
A REALLY RI
BANK HOLLER

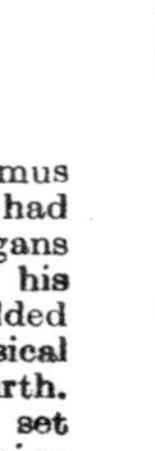

GREYFRIA
No. 191.
EDITED BY

WOULD YOU BELIEVE IT?

In a swimming gala held at Cliff House School, the winners were "Babs" Redfern for speed, Marjorie Hazeldene for style, and Phyllis Howell for endurance. Clara Trevlyn, the tomboy of Cliff House, unexpectedly won a prize for life-saving. Harry Wharton & Co. joined the girls at tea, and everything went "swimmingly"!

S. Q. I. Field, the Removite from New South Wales, has shown tremendous form this season at cricket. No matter how hot the sun, "Squiff's" fielding never loses its "edge." Against the Shell, he brought off a phenomenal catch which dismissed their best bat, Hobson. Hobson gasped and said "Squiff" was really the outside "edge"!

Horace Coker performed wh
in reality a difficult trick w
put his motor-bike into a "
side" in the Courtfield
Street, and escaped wit
person intact! The bike
a complete "wreck," and
Coker had listened to a "
jaw" from the Head, he
he had "recked" the
beforehand!

ARTON. June 6th, 1936.

'OP HAT CRICKET THRILLED CROWD

Declares LARRY LASCELLES

When I set out to convert fellow-masters to the of an Old-fashioned ket Match between ters and Boys in aid of the Courtfield Cottage Hospital, I had no idea I was organising a game destined to give the crowd the biggest thrill of the Summer Term. My first object was to provide laughs—not thrills. Unintentionally, I provided both!

Certainly nobody could complain of any lack of fun. The mere appearance of the Masters' Team, of which, by the way, I had the honour to be captain, drew roars of laughter from the crowd. And no wonder! For we all wore top-hats and frock-coats—and to complete the picture, most of us wore flowing whiskers as well!

As for the boys, they were, as I heard Cherry of the Remove put it, a sight for sore eyes! Some wore top-hats and tails, and others military and naval uniforms of a century ago. Loder, incidentally, with a humour which we masters didn't altogether relish, strolled out smoking a long church-warden pipe!

The game was hilariously funny at the beginning. There were only two stumps to a wicket, and the space between them was sufficiently wide to allow the ball through without shifting the single bail between the two; and Wingate, with the first ball of the game, was thus able to "clean bowl" Mr. Twigg without getting him out! The crowd became almost hysterical over that, and the laughter was continuous right through that over. Wingate and Mr. Twigg played to the gallery in fine fashion, Wingate bowling underarm and Mr. Twigg making very funny use of his bat. Others who followed them kept it up splendidly.

The game proceeded on these lines for most of the afternoon, and it was not until late in the day when the crowd had laughed till they were almost tired of laughing that the players sobered down to anything like serious work. What caused the change was Wingate's sudden waking up to the fact that his team were in danger of losing. It had been taken for granted that the boys, most of whom were regular First Eleven men, would beat the Masters without any difficulty. But we old stagers had taken advantage of the way the game was "guyed" to pile up the respectable total of 180 runs; and some determined bowling on the part of myself and Mr. Twigg had got the Boys out for a bare 115, and enabled us to put our opponents in again. When they scored only 130, leaving us but 66 to win the game, they began to treat it with a little more respect!

And so it came about, that as we drew near the finish, this comic cricket match developed—most unexpectedly—into a really thrilling struggle for victory. The crowd that had come to laugh stayed on to cheer; and Masters and Boys, infected alike by the new spirit of the game, both gave of their best.

The most exciting moment came when our score stood at 64, leaving us to get one run for a tie and two for a win—with myself facing the bowler! I can assure you I meant to get those two runs if it lay in my power.

Alas! North, the bowler, sent down a fast leg-break that left me standing, and shattered my wicket; and so the game ended in the narrowest of all possible victories for the Boys!

Well, we've no complaints to make on that score; and as everybody enjoyed it and the hospital will benefit considerably, I think we can justifiably regard the first Old-fashioned Cricket Match at Greyfriars as a great success.

Eh ?"

And if you don't give a really tip-top time, 'e's going to be trubble you when we get back St. Sam's!" added tor Birchemall. "Let eggsplain, boys! When ecided to join you to-, I had two ideas. The was to give you a e by making you think were in for a toor of eums. The other was ave a jolly good Bank lerday when the joak over. Twiggy-voo ?"

Oh, grate pip!" gasped Fourth.

Now get bizzy, boys!" ned Doctor Bichemall.

took the Fourth fully innit to realise that the d was in Ernest. But they did realise it, were all out to give Head a real good time! the rest of that day it one long round of iment—and, strange as emed, the revered and stick headmaster of Sam's threw himself the fun and frollick feasting with all the of a Second Form fag enjoyed himself as n as anybody!

they drove back to am's that nite, every-agreed—and Doctor emall was the loudest ing so—that the best orightest day out in all ry had been Doctor emall's Bank Holler-

GREYFRIARS FACTS WHILE YOU WAIT!

own is very fond of prac- the quad with the lariat ght from his native New . The authorities usually n plenty of "rope." But e inadvertently "roped r. Prout, Browney's head "spun" with horror! sing profusely, Browney ky to escape the "rope's end"!

Mr. "Larry" Lascelles, the maths. master, is a popular umpire in both senior and junior matches. "Larry" is never too busy—or too proud—to officiate on Little Side if he is needed. A "fin" damaged in the Great War prevents "Larry" from knocking up sixes as he used to do—but any Removite would give him a "glad hand"!

A quarrel between Skinner of the Remove and Angel of the Upper Fourth developed into a catch-as-catch-can fight. At one stage Skinner had his heel on Angel's neck. They were both scrambling on the ground when Mr. Capper arrived and severely caned them both. Harry Wharton & Co. were nearly "all in," too—with laughter!

TOM BROWN Calls for—

THREE CHEERS FOR COKER!

No, I'm not joking, chaps. I really mean it. I believe in giving credit where credit is due; and if three cheers aren't due to Coker for what he did when those sneak-thieves got away with our clobber at the swimming pool last Wednesday, I'll eat my Sunday best topper!

Let's set out the facts in their stark simplicity, without any trimmings whatever. There was a whole crowd of us in the water. Coker, fresh from the changing-hut in a bright, new swimming costume, was standing on the bank yelling out advice to all and sundry on the art of swimming.

Suddenly the noise of a motor engine made Coker look round. He was just in time to see a stranger, wearing a hat pulled well down over his eyes, slinging a load of clobber into a car that was standing by a changing-hut.

Coker yelled: "Hi! What are you doing?" and the man in the hat promptly jumped into the car, which then moved off down the cart-track towards the road.

Coker dashed to the hut and saw that every stitch of clothing we had left there had been taken. Without waiting even to sling a towel round his shoulders, he jumped on to his motor-bike and roared away down the cart-track after the clobber bandits!

Driving with his usual cheery recklessness, he caught up with the crooks on the road just before they reached Friardale. He then performed the acrobatic feat of jumping from his bike on to the running-board, gave the driver a sock on the chin that knocked him right out and brought the car to a stop. After that, he set about the man in the hat.

P.-c. Tozer, who rolled up just as Coker administered his second k.o., asked what was up, and was told. Five minutes later the crooks were driving back to the pool, with Tozer in the back and Coker bringing up triumphantly as the rear-guard on his still serviceable motor-bike. Not long after, we were all in possession of our stolen duds again, and the bandit pair were on their way to Courtfield police station!

Such are the bald facts about Coker's little adventure last Wednesday. Anyone who can read them and say it wasn't a brilliant achievement on Coker's part is jolly well prejudiced. The rest of you will doubtless be happy to join me in giving the old sport three rousing cheers!

THIS TALE RINGS TRUE!

On being told that Mr. Quelch had many "sterling" qualities, Skinner ruefully retorted: "Well, he's certainly a good 'tanner,' anyway!"

LOST!

Pump, Hoselines and Escape Ladder belonging to Remove Fire Brigade. Unless returned quickly in good order, we shall be "put out"—but the next fire won't.—Apply, H. WHARTON, Hon. Sec.

(*Continued from page* 13.)

left it unseen! Yet he was not there! It was a complete puzzle to Poker Pike—and it had got him guessing!

THE TENTH CHAPTER.
The Mysterious Voice!

"PUZZLE—find the Yankee!" grinned Skinner.

"Ha, ha, ha!"

Many eyes were on Poker Pike in the sunny quad.

It was a half-holiday that afternoon. Harry Wharton & Co. were away, busily occupied with cricket at Rookwood. But the Remove fellows at home were provided with an unexpected entertainment.

It was the sight of Poker Pike searching for Putnam van Duck!

That Van Duck had gone over to Rookwood with the cricketers all the fellows knew. Poker was absolutely certain that he hadn't.

He had heard Van Duck's voice in the study after the cricketers had gone. He had kept tabs on Study No. 1 ever since, till dinner-time. Yet when the door was opened Van Duck was not there. Poker could come to only one conclusion—the American junior had slipped quietly out of the study, locking the door after him, while he had gone down to call Mr. Quelch.

He had been gone little more than five minutes. Still, that was ample time, if the junior had been in the study waiting for an opportunity to dodge out unseen. That seemed the only possible explanation to Poker. Evidently—to Poker—Van Duck was "stringing him along"—playing jokes at the expense of his watchful gunman guardian. He had been in the study—he had dodged out quietly when Poker went down to Hall—and now he was deliberately keeping out of sight to puzzle and worry the over-dutiful and faithful Poker!

With a grim brow, Poker hunted for him up and down and round about the school — without finding him. He dreaded that Putnam might have gone out of gates—in which case Poker had no doubt that Chick Chew and his myrmidons were on the watch, looking for a chance to grab him. Certainly he did not succeed in finding him within the walls of Greyfriars.

A good many fellows had gathered on the cricket ground, and Poker, after a vain search in the House, proceeded thither—interested juniors following him with grinning faces. But a search of the cricket ground failed to reveal Van Duck—or anybody who had seen him.

Poker came back to the quad grimmer than ever. He looked in the school shop. A dozen fellows were there, but Van Duck was not among them. Billy Bunter was blinking in at the window through his big spectacles. Bunter's postal order was still in an unarrived state; and Bunter was in his accustomed hard-up state. Like a fat Peri at the gate of Paradise, he was looking at the good things he was unable to share, when Poker Pike came along.

The fat Owl gave a fat chuckle. Knowing what he did, Bunter was even more entertained than the other fellows by Poker's persistent search up and down the school for a fellow who was playing cricket at another school in another county.

Poker came out of the tuckshop again, puzzled and wrathy. A dozen grinning faces watched him. Poker frowned at them.

"You young guys ain't seen that Putnam van Duck?" he asked.

"Oh, yes, I've seen him!" answered Skinner.

"Where?" rapped Poker.

"In the Remove dormitory," answered Skinner airily.

Poker stared.

"I guess he ain't turned in to snooze—in the afternoon?" he ejaculated.

"Well, I saw him there," said Skinner.

Puzzled, Poker started off towards the House.

"What the dickens do you mean, Skinner?" asked Bolsover major. "Van Duck's over at Rookwood. You never saw him in the dorm."

"I jolly well did!" answered Skinner. "I forgot to mention to Pike that it was last night I saw him there, though."

"Ha, ha, ha!" roared the juniors.

Poker went into the House. He reappeared in about five minutes, looking grimmer than ever. He glanced round for Skinner, but that humorous youth had judiciously disappeared.

Billy Bunter was still regarding the good things in Mrs. Mimble's little window with a longing eye, when he felt a sudden grip of iron on his fat shoulder. He spun round with a startled squeak, and blinked at Poker Pike.

"Ow! Leggo!" he gasped. "Wharrer you want, you beast? Leggo!"

"I guess," said Poker grimly, "that I want to know! You was in that study with Putnam this morning, you fat gink——"

"I—I wasn't!" gasped Bunter. "I—I mean——"

"Aw, can it!" growled Poker. "I guess you're in this here game, you pesky piecan! Where's that Putnam van Duck? I reckon you know!"

"Ow! He's gone to Rookwood!" gasped Bunter, wriggling in the vice-like grip on his shoulder.

"Guess again!" growled Poker, compressing his grip, till the fat Owl of the Remove squeaked.

"Ow! Wow! I say, he's really gone to Rookwood!" spluttered Bunter. "Any of the fellows can tell you! Ask them, and they'll say—— Wow! Ow! Leggo!"

"I guess I'll sure beat you up a few if you don't spill it!"

Bunter blinked at him in dismay.

Poker, certainly, was not wise to the trick that had been played—he did not begin to guess what had really happened; but he had a strong suspicion that Bunter knew something of the matter.

It was not often that Bunter told the truth—it was generally his last resource. This time he did—and it was no use Poker was not going to believe that Van Duck had gone with the cricketers.

"I—I say, really!" gasped Bunter. "Really and truly—— Wow! I say—— Yow! He wasn't in the study when you heard him there!"

"What?" howled Poker.

"I—I mean, I don't know where he is—— Ow! Wow! Leggo! I mean, I know where he is!" gasped Bunter. "I—I'll take you to him, if you like, if—if you'll leggo!"

"I guess I'll keep a cinch on you till I see him!" grunted Poker. "I reckon that pesky young guy is keeping doggo, just to string me along! Ain't that the how of it?"

"No—— Ow! I mean, yes!" gasped Bunter.

"And you're wise to it?" hooted Poker.

"No—yes—— Ow! He—he—he's hiding in Gosling's woodshed!" gasped Bunter. "You—you go and look for him there, and—and——"

"I guess you're going to take a leetle pasear with me, to that there woodshed!" said Poker.

"Oh lor'!" gasped Bunter.

There was no help for it. Billy Bunter walked away to Gosling's woodshed with the gunman. But his fat wits were working as he went. Arrived at the woodshed, that building was found closed and locked.

Poker, holding Bunter's fat shoulder with one hand, tried the door of the shed with the other.

"You pesky young piecan——" he began.

"I—I say, he's really there!" gasped Bunter. "You—you call out to him, and you—you'll see."

Poker glared at him suspiciously. But he rapped on the woodshed door and shouted:

"Say, you there, you Putnam van Duck?"

He did not believe Bunter's statement that the American junior was there. But his doubts were dispelled the next moment, as a voice that Van Duck might have fancied was his own, answered, apparently from within:

"You said it, old-timer!"

Poker jumped.

"Aw, what's this game, you young piecan?" he roared. "What you hiding in that pesky shebang for, I want to know?"

"I guess I'm fed-up with you, Poker—go and chop chips!"

"Open this door here, you young geek!"

"Guess again!"

"Say, I guess you're going loco, young Putnam, playing this here fool game!" exclaimed Poker.

"Aw, can it, you big stiff! You sure make me tired!"

Poker Pike released Bunter's fat shoulder. He had found Van Duck now—at least, he was assured that he had! Amazed as he was by Putnam's extraordinary proceedings, in locking himself in one place after another, Poker had no doubt that he had cornered him.

"Beat it, you!" he grunted to Bunter; and the fat ventriloquist "beat it" promptly. He grinned as he went, leaving Poker Pike leaning on the locked door of the woodshed.

It was half an hour later that Gosling came along for something from his woodshed. He stared at Poker Pike.

"O.K., old-timer!" said Poker. "That young guy Van Duck is in this here shebang of yourn, and I guess I'm keeping tabs on him."

"He ain't!" said Gosling, staring. "How'd he be in there, and the shed locked, and the key on my bunch?"

"He sure is!" said Poker.

Gosling grunted, and unlocked the

shed. Poker Pike followed him in—and almost fell down as he discovered that the woodshed was unoccupied. He stared round the shed as he had stared round Study No. 1, but in still more hopeless bewilderment. This time he had not ceased to "keep tabs" for a moment; yet in some mysterious way, the junior whose voice he had heard was gone!

"Carry me home to die!" gasped Poker.

He almost tottered from the woodshed. It really began to look as if Putnam van Duck had vanished from Greyfriars, leaving only his voice behind him! His voice, certainly, had been there—Poker had heard it! But Van Duck wasn't! The mystified gunman began to wonder whether he was seeing things!

But he had no chance of getting further information from Billy Bunter. That fat youth had gone out of gates, sagely determined to give the Greyfriars gunman a wide berth for the rest of the day. And that afternoon, Poker Pike was a sorely puzzled and mystified gunman!

THE ELEVENTH CHAPTER.
A Puzzle for Poker!

"NONSENSE!" said Mr. Quelch.

"Sez you!" grunted Poker.

Quelch was annoyed.

After tea, he had retired to his study for a quiet hour with his favourite author, Sophocles. At ease in his armchair, his feet on a hassock, a ponderous volume open before him, Henry Samuel Quelch was back in ancient Greece, and had quite forgotten the modern world and all its many worries. He was reminded of them by the arrival of Poker Pike, who walked into the study without knocking, and with his hat on. Poker was a good man in his own way, but he had not learned polished manners in the Chicago joints.

Poker had never heard of Sophocles, and would not have given ten cents for all his classical works, anyhow. He was deeply worried about Putnam van Duck. Quelch was fed-up on that subject.

"Nonsense!" he repeated. "The boy is at Rookwood I have already told you so. He will be returning here shortly. You will see him——"

"Forget it!" said Poker. "I'll say that young guy is hereabouts, and he's sure been playing hide-and-seek to string me along. Now I can't spot him anywheres. I'm telling you, I want to know! I'll mention that I ain't sitting it out quiet while Chick Chew clinches that young geck! I'm shouting out to you that he's got to be found!"

Mr. Quelch lay Sophocles on the study table.

"If nothing else will convince you, Mr. Pike, I will ring up Rookwood School on the telephone!" he said tartly. "Kindly be seated."

Poker Pike remained standing. But he stood silent, while Mr. Quelch rang up and asked for a trunk call.

Quelch's face wore a deep frown. Really, it was hard lines that a hard-worked Form-master could not be allowed a quiet hour, undisturbed, with so entrancing an author as Sophocles. When the answer came through, he almost yapped into the transmitter.

"Is that Rookwood School? Mr. Quelch speaking from Greyfriars. Will you ask Wharton—Harry Wharton—to come to the telephone, if he is not at the moment on the cricket field?"

"Certainly, sir."

Mr. Quelch glanced round at Poker.

"No doubt you will be willing to believe my head boy's assurance that Van Duck is with the cricket team!" he snapped.

"Sure!" said Poker. "But I guess he ain't."

Grunt—from Quelch. He turned to the mouthpiece again, as a voice came through.

"Wharton! Is that you, Wharton?"

"Yes, sir," came the voice of the captain of the Remove. "Is that Mr. Quelch speaking? I was told——"

"Yes, yes I understand that Van Duck is with you, Wharton. Is not that the case?"

"Oh, certainly, sir!"

"Mr. Pike, for some reason I cannot fathom, doubts it!" snapped Mr. Quelch. "Kindly hold on and speak to him."

"Oh, my hat!"

"What—what did you say, Wharton?"

"I—I mean all right, sir."

"Mr. Pike, if you will kindly take this receiver——"

Poker kindly took the receiver. His hickory face was sorely puzzled. He barked into the telephone.

"Say, you young guy! You there? You allow that that Putnam van Duck is along of you, playing cricket?"

"Yes, rather!"

"Search me!" gasped Poker. "Say, if that young guy's there, when did he hit the spot?"

He was surprised to hear a chuckle over the wires; then the answer came:

"Van Duck travelled with the rest of the team this morning, Mr. Pike. We got here early. We took the first knock——"

"Eh?"

"Van Duck put up 30 runs in his first innings——"

"I guess I don't want to know——"

"We were 15 ahead on the first innings," went on Harry Wharton's cheery voice. "Jimmy Silver's lot knocked up 95 to our 110."

"Look hyer——"

"In our second innings——"

Poker Pike snorted. This schoolboy, apparently, at least, fancied that he was keen to hear the details of the cricket match—in which Poker really was not interested at all, knowing as much about the great game of cricket as he knew about that great author Sophocles.

"I want to know——" he barked.

"Yes, I understand," said Wharton, at the other end. "You're keen to know how Van Duck turned out at cricket——"

"Nope! I guess——"

"He turned out first-rate! I was jolly glad to have him in the team. He's taken to cricket like a duck to water——"

"I'm telling you——"

"He bagged 40 in our second innings, and——"

"Doggone your innings! I——"

"I can tell you the Rookwood men had to pull up their socks, but they never really had a chance after we put up 150 in the second knock."

"I guess——" howled Poker.

"I bet you don't guess how many we beat them by. They were 120 at last man in."

"You pesky young piecan, I tell you——"

"Jimmy Silver and Lovell were at the wickets," went on Harry Wharton, "and they may have fancied they were going to pull the game out of the fire. But Van Duck——"

"You allow that that young geck has been——"

"Van Duck brought off a catch——"

"Goldarn your ketches! I want to know——"

"He caught Jimmy Silver out——"

"You young piecan, I want to know——"

"We beat them by 45 runs," Wharton rattled on cheerily. "The game's been over only a quarter of an hour. You've rung up just right to get the news."

"I guess I don't want to hear nothing about your pesky cricket!" yelled Poker. "I'll say I want to hear about that Putnam van Duck."

"Oh, yes, I quite understand!" came the answer, with another chuckle. "You want to know how Van Duck did in the match."

"Nope!" shrieked Poker. "I guess I want to know——"

"He did fine—ripping—better than I expected! You'd have liked to see his game. Why didn't you trot over?"

Poker snorted.

"I guess I'd have come if I'd knowed he was there! You allow that that Putnam van Duck has been with you all day?"

"He couldn't have played cricket here otherwise, could he? We wanted him chiefly for batting, and it was a bit of a surprise when he brought off that catch and pushed Jimmy Silver out. It was in the slips——"

"Doggone the slips! I tell you I want to know!" raved Poker. "I don't get this! I heered that young geck talking here, behind a locked door, arter you was gone——"

"Ha, ha, ha!"

"Pack up the snicker, doggone you! If he's been with you all day, I don't get it! It's got me beat! You ain't stringing me along?"

"Not at all! He played a ripping game——"

"Look hyer——"

"Thirty in the first innings, 40 in the second—and a catch at the finish that knocked Rookwood right out——"

"Park it!" howled Poker. "I'll say I'm tired of hearing about your pesky cricket! Is that young guy Van Duck along with you now?"

"Oh, yes!"

"What's he doin'?"

"Mopping up ginger-beer."

"And he's been along all day?"

"Certainly! He was third on the list, after Smithy and Bob Cherry, and——"

"I guess I'm coming along to see him safe home."

"Better come by plane, then," suggested Wharton. "We're going for our train in a quarter of an hour."

"Say, you young geck, you keep where you are till I arrive; you keep that Putnam van Duck there till I hit the spot and——"

"Good-bye!"

"I'm telling you——" roared Poker.

"See you later, old bean! Can't miss our train!"

"I'm telling you——"

"Ta-ta!"

Harry Wharton, at the Rookwood end, rang off. Poker Pike stood staring at the telephone.

"Carry me home to die!" he ejaculated at last.

"Are you satisfied now, Mr. Pike?" asked the Remove master tartly.

Poker blinked at him.

"I don't get it!" he said. "It's got me beat! But I guess it's the straight goods! I'm telling you, big boy, I don't get it! This sure is the rhinoceros' side-whiskers!"

Mr. Quelch sniffed and sat down with Sophocles again. Poker Pike, in a state of dizzy astonishment, tramped out of the study and left him to it. Unless his ears had deceived him, Putnam van Duck had stayed behind at Greyfriars that day. Yet it was clear that he had been all day at Rookwood, playing cricket with the Remove team. It was a puzzle that even the hard-headed Poker could not possibly puzzle out.

All he could do was to tramp down to Courtfield and wait for the train to come in with the returning cricketers—which he did. And if a lingering doubt remained in his mind, it had to be dispelled when at last he saw Putnam van Duck step from the train with the Remove crowd. Evidently, obviously, and indubitably, the American junior had been at Rookwood with the cricketers—and how he had contrived to leave his voice behind at Greyfriars remained a mystery that the puzzled Poker could not possibly fathom.

THE TWELFTH CHAPTER.

Billy Bunter Talks Too Much !

"I SAY, you fellows——"

"Roll out, Bunter !"

"If that's what you call gratitude——" said Billy Bunter loftily and scornfully, his very spectacles gleaming with scorn.

"Oh, roll in !" said Harry Wharton.

There was a study supper in Study No. 1 that evening.

The Remove cricketers had returned from Rookwood in great spirits. They had had a good game and a big victory. Putnam van Duck had more than justified his selection as a member of the eleven. Everybody was pleased and satisfied, and the study supper was a celebration, and Study No. 1 was crowded, not to say overcrowded, with cricketers playing the game over again as they disposed of good things. Billy Bunter, as usual, was superfluous; but, also as usual, his superfluity did not worry Bunter. He was not going to miss that spread.

There was not much room for Billy Bunter to roll in. But he wedged in at the doorway. All available seats were taken up, some of the chairs having two fellows seated on them. The fat Owl of the Remove blinked round in vain for a seat.

"I say, you fellows——"

"Shut up, Bunter !"

"Beast ! I say, what am I going to sit on ?" squeaked Bunter.

"There's a rather nice oak floor——"

"Oh, really, Wharton ! I say, Toddy, you might let me have that chair."

"I might," assented Peter Todd; "but then again, I mightn't ! The betting is on the mightn't !"

"Inky, old chap, you might let me have that box——"

"The mightfulness is terrific !" grinned Hurree Jamset Ram Singh.

"If you fellows think I'm going to stand——" hooted Bunter. "Do you think I'm going to stand, Wharton ?"

"Eh ? I wasn't thinking about you at all, old fat man !" answered the captain of the Remove. "Dry up, there's a good porpoise."

"Well," said Bunter, in disgust, "I like that—after all I've done for you !"

"If you like it, what are you grousing about ?" asked Bob Cherry.

"Yah !" snorted Bunter. "Pass me over the cake, anyhow !"

"Couldn't possibly !" answered Bob, shaking his head. "I'm not a steam derrick, old podgy porpoise."

"You silly ass, you can pass me over the cake, can't you ?"

"Of course I can't ! It would take three or four fellows, and jolly hefty chaps, to pass you over the cake, or anything else."

"Ha, ha, ha !"

"You blithering idiot !" howled Bunter. "I mean, pass the cake over, you fathead—not me over the cake, you howling chump !"

"Oh, all right !" said Bob, who had evidently been joking—though it was no time for jokes, when Bunter was waiting for cake. "Here you are !"

Cake was passed over. Bunter leaned on the door, which was set wide open, and guzzled. Putnam van Duck, who was in the window-seat, glanced across the study to the door.

"Say, you cut off and cinch a chair, Bunter," he said. "You're nearest the door."

"Oh, I'll stand !" grunted Bunter, through a large mouthful of cake. "You needn't worry about that !"

"I guess I ain't !" grinned Van Duck. "I want a chair for Poker. We've asked him to come up to this supper."

"Rot !" said Bunter. "You don't want that rotten gunman here. I'm not going to fetch him a chair, anyhow."

"I'll get one from my study," said Tom Redwing, who was near the door.

"Get one for me," said Bunter. "That ruffian can stand, if he comes. I don't see what you want him for, Van Duck."

"There's a whole lot of things you don't see, even with your specs, old fat piecan !" answered Putnam.

"Yah !"

Redwing fetched a chair, which was planted just inside the doorway, ready for Poker when he came. Billy Bunter promptly sat in it.

Whether Mr. Pike was keen on a schoolboys' study supper was perhaps doubtful. But after what happened that day, Putnam and his friends wanted to be nice to Poker.

Putnam had got back from Rookwood safe and sound with the cricketers. Poker and his six-gun had not been needed to guard him. And all the fellows certainly were glad that the Greyfriars gunman and his gun had not shown up at Rookwood to cause a sensation there. Still, they realised that Poker was a dutiful guy, and he had had rather a worrying day; so they wanted to be as nice as possible. Poker was going to be an honoured guest at the study supper, if he cared to horn in.

He did not seem in a hurry to do so. At all events, he had not yet arrived. Meanwhile, Bunter deposited his fat person in the chair specially fetched for the honoured guest.

"I say, you fellows——"

"It was a ripping catch," said Frank Nugent. "Blessed if I thought Van Duck would bring it off !"

"Oh, do stop jawing cricket !" said Bunter peevishly. "I was speaking, Nugent."

"You generally are !" remarked Johnny Bull.

"Beast ! I think you might let a fellow have a chance at the cream puffs, after all he's done for you. I can tell you, that gunman would have come after you to Rookwood, if I hadn't stopped him. I say, you fellows, he was rooting all over the school after Van Duck."

"Ha, ha, ha !"

"Hunting everywhere !" grinned Bunter. "I say, I made him believe Van Duck was in the woodshed, with my wonderful ventriloquism, you know. I say, I'm waiting for those cream puffs."

Cream puffs were passed over to Bunter. For several minutes he was too creamy and sticky to talk, and cricket "jaw" was resumed. Three or four fellows talked at once, and there was plenty of noise in the study, and no one noticed footsteps coming along the passage from the stairs.

"I say," Bunter recommenced, "I say, if you won't let a fellow get near the table, you might pass him things. Are you going to scoff all the jam tarts, Squiff ?"

"Oh dear ! Pass him all the tarts, and perhaps he'll shut up for a minute or two !" said Bob Cherry.

"Oh, really, Cherry ! I can jolly well tell you, you'd have had that gunman after you at Rookwood if I hadn't pulled his leg !" snorted Bunter. "Fat lot of thanks I get for giving up my half-holiday to help you fellows. I say the beast suspected that I knew something about it, and he grabbed me—and I got away by making Van Duck's voice come out of the woodshed. The silly ass thought Van Duck was there, you know, when I imitated his voice. That gunman is a silly fool——"

"Sez you !" said a quiet voice over Billy Bunter's fat shoulder.

"Oh lor' !" gasped Bunter.

He spun round on his chair in the doorway, forgetful even of jam tarts. A hickory face under a bowler hat was looking into the study.

"Oh, my hat !" exclaimed Bob Cherry. "H'm ! Trot in, Mr. Pike !"

"Trickle in, old bean !" said Harry Wharton.

Poker did not trot or trickle in. His hickory face was grim.

It was clear that he had heard what Billy Bunter had said, and had jumped, at last, to the solution of the mystery that had baffled him all that day.

No doubt it had already dawned on Poker's rather solid brain that, as Van Duck certainly had been absent, the voice he had heard must have been a trick of some sort. Now he knew the trick that had been played.

"So that was the leetle game, was it ?" said Poker grimly. "You fat gink, I knowed you was wise to it ! So it was you putting up an imitation of that young geck's toot, to string me along."

"Oh ! No !" gasped Bunter, in alarm. "Nothing of the kind ! I'm not a ventriloquist at all, and as for imitating any chap's voice, I simply couldn't do it. You can ask any of these fellows—they've heard me lots of times."

"Ha, ha, ha !"

"Aw, don't you get your mad up, Poker !" grinned Van Duck. "I guess your gun wasn't wanted at Rookwood, and we jest had to pull your leg. Mosey in and sit down to supper, and smile a few."

"I guess," said Poker, "that I ain't stopping for eats ! I guess I'm going to lam that fat guy a few for stringing me."

"I say, you fellows !" yelled Bunter.

Billy Bunter wished that he hadn't rolled into that study supper, or, alternately, that he hadn't talked so much ! But it was too late for either wish. A sinewy hand grasped him, and hooked him off the chair. A swing of a sinewy arm whirled him over, face down across the chair. Then the gunman's other hand rose, and descended like a flail, on the tightest trousers at Greyfriars.

Smack !

"Yaroooh !"

Smack !

"Whoop !" yelled Billy Bunter. "Help ! I say, you fellows, help !"

"Hold on !" gasped Harry Wharton.

Smack !

"Stop !" yelled Van Duck. "Pack it up, you galoot !"

Smack !

"Yarooh ! Rescue !" shrieked Bunter.

Smack !

"Pile in!" shouted Bob Cherry, and he led the rush.

Billy Bunter sprawled roaring on the floor, as the rush of the Removites hurled Poker through the doorway into the Remove passage.

"Ow! Wow! You!" roared Bunter.

"Aw! You pesky young piecans!" gasped Poker, as he whirled in the passage. "I guess—— Aw, great jumping toads! I guess—yorrrroooop!"

Poker Pike had come as an honoured guest. But he looked like anything but an honoured guest as he departed—rolling down the Remove staircase. He came to a stop on the next landing—and his bowler hat, for once detached from his head, went rolling down the lower stairs.

"Aw! Carry me home to die!" spluttered Poker; and he followed his hat, gasping as he went. And the study supper finished without the Greyfriars gunman.

THE THIRTEENTH CHAPTER.

Bunter Knows How!

"JOLLY well rag him!" said Billy Bunter.

"Jolly well rats!" said Bob Cherry.

"I've been smacked!" roared Bunter.

"That's all right!"

"Is it?" howled Bunter.

"Right as rain!" said Bob cheerfully.

That was the sort of sympathy Billy Bunter received.

If ever a fellow had reason to feel wrathy and indignant, William George Bunter had.

It was the day after the Rookwood match. The sun had gone down and risen again, and Billy Bunter had let the sun rise on his wrath.

Bunter had often realised that it was an ungrateful world. Now this fact was borne in more than ever on his fat mind.

He had been smacked—hard! This was his reward for having helped the Remove fellows out of a difficulty with his wonderful ventriloquism. His view was that there should have been general indignation on the subject—and there wasn't!

Nobody seemed to think that it mattered very much whether Bunter was smacked or not. But to Bunter it mattered quite a lot.

His fat brow was morose in Form that morning.

When the Remove came out in break Billy Bunter's indignation intensified at the sight of the Famous Five and their proceedings. Poker Pike was taking a walk in the quad, and the chums of the Remove joined him, with smiling faces—just as if Poker mattered, and Bunter didn't!

Poker regarded the cheery juniors rather grimly.

"Sorry we had to roll you out of the study, old bean!" said Harry Wharton amicably. "But, you see——"

"Huh!" grunted Poker.

"You see, we couldn't let you smack Bunter. We put him up to pulling your leg yesterday," explained Wharton, "so we really couldn't let you go ahead. Sorry, all the same!"

"The sorrowfulness is terrific, my worthy and ludicrous Poker!" assured Hurree Jamset Ram Singh solemnly.

"Huh!"

"So don't be shirty, old man!" said Bob Cherry.

"Huh!"

"Let not the frown of infuriated wrath replace the smile of idiotic friendship!" urged Hurree Jamset Ram Singh.

Poker grinned.

"O.K.!" he said. "I guess I ain't got no grouch. You sure won't be able to string me again that-a-way, now I'm wise to it. Forget it!"

So peace was established—which was satisfactory to the chums of the Remove, who liked Poker, and not at all satisfactory to Billy Bunter, who didn't!

"I say, you fellows," began the fat Owl, when the juniors left Poker—"I say, if you think I'm going to stand a——"

"Bow-wow!" said Bob.

"If you think I'm going to stand——" roared Bunter.

"Ring off, old fat man!"

"I'm not going to stand——" yelled Bunter.

"Right-ho! Sit down!" said Bob. And Bunter sat down suddenly in the quad, with a little assistance from the exuberant Bob. "That all right?"

"Ha, ha, ha!"

"Ow! Beast!" roared Bunter.

Apparently, it was not all right!

"Well, if you're not going to stand, and you don't want to sit down, what do you want?" demanded Bob. "Some fellows are never satisfied!"

"Beast! I mean, I'm not going to stand——"

"You're repeating yourself, old fat

(*Continued on next page.*)

GREYFRIARS INTERVIEWS

Skinner and Snoop have already come under the eagle eye and pen of our long-haired poet. Now comes the turn of the third member of this "select" trio . . .

WILLIAM STOTT,

another Black Sheep of the Remove.

(1)

The last two poems from my pen
Have dealt with Skinner and Snoop,
And now I've got to write of Stott,
And thus complete the group;
So let's get on with it, and then
We'll finish with their troupe.

(2)

The three Black Sheep of the Remove,
Are always more or less
Together, and I understand,
It's through that letter S.
The same initial well may prove
The same attractions—yes?

(3)

Not that it works with Hurree Singh
(Though he's a "Black Sheep," too),
But Smith (if he is S. not V.)
Is counted with the crew,
And you may see this kind of thing
In other forms on view.

(4)

There's Hobson-Hoskins in the Shell,
There's Blundell thick with Bland;
But this is by the way, for I
Must keep my work in hand,
And William Stott's the subject—well,
Now ain't life really grand?

(5)

I've no desire to write of Stott,
There's nothing to attract
The poet's muse, and I refuse
To do it, if I'm sacked!
No, sir, I tell you I will not!
I mean it, that's a fact!

(6)

The Editor has told me I
Must interview this pest,
I'll say I won't, but if I don't,
He'll soon lose interest.
On second thoughts I think I'll try,
And second thoughts are best!

(7)

There's nothing much to say of him,
He's just a weedy tick,
Who often smokes until he chokes,
And finds he's feeling sick,
Then takes, in Quelchy's study grim,
His medicine—the stick!

(8)

'Twas in the woodshed I espied,
Him smoking all his might!
I clapped a hand upon him, and
His smoke dropped out of sight!
That cigarette had dropped inside
His collar—still alight!

(9)

Then Stott began to dance and shout,
I watched him, with a grin,
He spun around with frantic bound,
Just like a Harlequin!
That cigarette had not gone out,
It rested on his skin!

(10)

To me the words he used were fresh,
They showed me that he felt
A sense of pain! He made that plain!
And as he danced I smelt
A smell resembling burning flesh,
And Stott began to melt!

(11)

"Yarooh! I'm burning! Help!"
he screamed,
His voice like pistol shots!
He jumped and howled, he shrieked
and scowled,
He tied himself in knots.
I grew quite dizzy, for it seemed,
I saw a dozen Stotts.

(12)

I had to do my best, of course,
To save the wretched chap,
And so I rose, took Gosling's hose,
And screwed it to the tap!
The water, bursting out with force,
Wiped Stott clean off the map.

(13)

He rolled and grovelled in the pool,
That gathered on the spot,
I'd put him out without a doubt,
But grateful? He was not!
He trailed back dismally to school,
A drenched, but wiser Stott.

bean! Hallo, hallo, hallo! There's the bell!"

And the juniors scampered away.

"Beasts!"

Billy Bunter's fat brow was wrathy as he followed the Remove into the Form-room for third school. Third lesson was Latin prose papers under the eye of Mr. Quelch. But, to the relief of the Remove, the Form-master, having set them going, glanced at the clock, and called to Wharton, his head boy.

"Wharton, I shall leave you in charge for a quarter of an hour," he said. "I have to see the headmaster."

Mr. Quelch left the Form-room.

There was a general relaxation at once. The papers had to be written, but the Remove did not exert themselves unduly in Mr. Quelch's absence. In such matters the master's eye was essential.

Bob Cherry and Smithy and several other fellows began to discuss the previous day's game at Rookwood—a more interesting subject to them than Latin prose. Lord Mauleverer closed his eyes for a gentle doze. Skinner manufactured an ink-ball to project at Mark Linley, the only fellow in the Remove who was still concentrated on Latin. Ogilvy handed round a packet of toffee.

Billy Bunter—wonderful to relate—did not heed the toffee. He rose to his feet and made for the door.

"Hold on, fathead!" called out Harry Wharton. "You can't go out of the Form-room!"

"I've forgotten my Latin grammar, and——"

"There it is—on your desk."

"Oh! I—I mean, I—I've left the tap running in the passage——"

"Not much difference!" said the head boy of the Remove sarcastically. "Well, whatever you've done, sit down and shut up!"

"Shan't!" retorted Bunter.

And he opened the Form-room door and rolled out.

"You fat ass!" roared Wharton. "Come back!"

"Yah!"

Bunter disappeared.

"Anybody left any tuck in his study?" grinned the Bounder. "If he has, he won't see it again!"

And there was a chuckle. But, as it happened, Billy Bunter was not thinking of raiding tuck in the studies.

The fat Owl blinked round him cautiously through his big spectacles as he rolled down the passage. Cautiously he made his way to Mr. Quelch's study. Quelch was with the Head, the other masters were with their Forms, and the coast was clear.

No eye fell on Billy Bunter as he rolled into his Form-master's study and shut the door.

He rolled across to the telephone.

Poker Pike had declared that, now he was "wise" to the trick, it would not be possible to "string him along" again by such a stunt as imitating a voice. But the Greyfriars ventriloquist had his own ideas about that.

He rang up Gosling's lodge.

The ancient porter of Greyfriars answered.

"Mr. Quelch speaking!" Bunter barked into the telephone, in so exact an imitation of Henry Samuel Quelch's curt tones that Henry Samuel, had he been present, might have supposed that it was himself speaking.

"Yessir!" grunted Gosling.

"Tell Mr. Pike I desire to speak to him at once!"

"Yessir!"

Poker, who had his quarters in Gosling's lodge, generally sat on the bench outside that lodge while Putnam van Duck was in class. In less than a minute his voice came through.

"Yep!"

"Mr. Pike, I am called away from my class for some time this morning," barked the Greyfriars ventriloquist. "I should be much obliged if you would come to the Remove room and take charge of the Form during my absence."

"Sure!" said Poker.

"If you will kindly come at once——"

"Surest thing you know!"

"Thank you, Mr. Pike!"

"O.K.!"

Billy Bunter rang off and rolled, grinning, out of Mr. Quelch's study. His fat face was wreathed in grins as he rolled into the Remove Form Room.

"What have you been up to, you fat villain?" asked Harry Wharton.

"Oh, nothing!" answered Bunter. "I say, you fellows—he, he, he!—I say, you remember how wild old Quelch was the time that beast Pike barged into our Form-room? He, he, he! He was as mad as a hatter! He, he, he! I say, you fellows, what do you think Quelch will say if he finds that gunman here when he comes back?"

"Pike won't come here again, you fat duffer!" said Harry, staring at him. "There was too much of a row about it last time."

"He, he, he!" chuckled Bunter.

"Say, that pesky guy ain't horning in again, is he?" exclaimed Van Duck.

"He, he, he!"

"Have you seen him coming?" exclaimed Skinner. "My hat! There will be a row if Quelch finds him here again!"

"He, he, he!"

There was a heavy tread in the corridor.

The Form-room door opened, and a bowler hat and a hickory face dawned on the staring Removites. Lord Mauleverer opened his eyes; the cricketers forgot cricket; Mark Linley forgot Latin prose; all the Remove stared at Poker Pike. The Greyfriars gunman walked cheerfully in.

"What the thump——" exclaimed Harry Wharton.

"Poker you bonehead, you beat it!" yelled Putnam. "You honing for another rookus with our Form-master, you pesky piecan?"

"Aw, forget it," said Poker. "I guess I'm here to take charge of you young ginks!"

"For goodness' sake, clear off!" exclaimed Harry anxiously. "Look here, you don't want another row with Quelch——"

"O.K.!" said Poker. "I guess that guy asked me to come here and take charge while he was out."

"Quelch asked you?" gasped Wharton.

"Surest thing you know."

"Oh crumbs!"

"He, he, he!"

"But—but—but Quelch can't have asked you!" stuttered the head boy of the Remove.

"He sure did! Pack it up, you!" said Poker. "Go and sit down! I guess I'm put in charge of this bunch—and I don't want no back chat!"

"But——" gasped Wharton.

"I'll mention that I said pack it up, bo!"

And Wharton, in great astonishment, "packed it up," and went to his place. And the Greyfriars gunman, with his usual sedate seriousness, took charge of the amazed, staring Remove.

THE FOURTEENTH CHAPTER.

Poker Pike—Form-master!

"QUIT chewing the rag!" barked Poker.

There was a buzz in the Remove. Mr. Quelch would have called out "Silence!" but Poker had brought his own variety of the English language to Greyfriars with him

A ripple of merriment ran through the Form. Certainly, the Remove had no objection to being "up" to Mr. Pike instead of "up" to Quelch, for a lesson. It was likely to be much more entertaining.

Poker, as usual, was in deadly earnest. He saw no occasion for merriment. The juniors could not help thinking that some mistake had been made—some extraordinary misunderstanding—for it was scarcely possible that Quelch really had requested the gunman to take his class in his absence.

But Poker, it was clear, was acting in good faith. He believed, at least, that that was what Mr. Quelch wanted. And it was not so surprising to him as to the Removites. In book-learning, certainly, Poker was no great shakes. But he had great stores of what he regarded as much more useful knowledge.

The blackboard stood on its easel before the class. Quelch had intended to chalk Latin verbs there. Mr. Pike knew nothing of Latin verbs—if, indeed, he had ever heard of the Latin language at all. When he picked up the chalk the juniors wondered what was coming.

"What you young guys been doing?" asked Poker, staring at the Latin papers on the desks.

"Latin prose!" grinned the Bounder. "Are you going to take us in Latin, Mr. Pike?"

"Ha, ha, ha!"

"Can it!" snapped Poker. "I guess I've got no use for snickering! Say, you fat guy, you want to pack it up, pronto!"

"He, he, he!"

Smack!

"Yarooooh!" roared Bunter, his fat chuckle changing into a terrific bellow as a hefty hand smacked. "Ow! Wow! Beast! Yarooooh!"

"I guess I'm keeping order while I'm riding herd on this bunch," said Poker. "Chew on that, you young ginks!"

"Ow! Wow! Ow!" gurgled Bunter.

Billy Bunter had expected things to happen when he played that trick on the unsuspicious gunman. But he had not expected the smacking of his own fat head to be an item in the programme. He rubbed his head and glared at Poker through his big spectacles.

The Remove suppressed their merriment. Poker's methods with a class were rather heavy-handed, and nobody else wanted a swipe from that hefty hand.

"I guess you can forget that guff," said Poker. "I guess it wouldn't help you none if you was crowded into a rookus."

If Mr. Quelch had asked Poker to take his class, certainly he would hardly have expected him to dismiss Latin prose as "guff." But the Remove fellows were quite prepared to dismiss Latin prose.

They watched Poker with great interest as he chalked on the blackboard.

Having, somewhat slowly and laboriously, chalked up a gem of useful knowledge, Poker stepped aside, to reveal it to the rapt gaze of the Lower Fourth.

The juniors fairly gasped as they read:

"ALWAYS
BE QUICK
ON THE DRAW!"

"Oh crikey!" stuttered Bob Cherry. "Oh, my only hat! I wonder what Quelch would think of that?"

"Ha, ha, ha!"

"Pack it up, you 'uns!" roared Poker. "I guess you ain't got no call to snicker when you're l'arning in school! Ain't your schoolmaster guy put me in charge of this bunch, and ain't I teaching you?"

"Go it!" chortled the Bounder. "This is better than Latin!"

"The betterfulness is terrific!"

"Hear, hear!"

"I'll allow I ain't wise to Latin, whatever that might be," said Poker Pike. "But I guess a guy wants to learn to be quick on the draw. Now you lissen! S'pose you was in a rookus in some joint, and maybe two or three hoodlums crowding you, like I've been a whole heap of times."

"Oh dear!" gasped Harry Wharton.

Poker was handing out instruction with great seriousness. But it was difficult for the Removites to take it seriously. They really could not quite imagine themselves in a "rookus" in a "joint," with "hoodlums" crowding them. Instruction on such subjects had been absolutely left out of the curriculum at Greyfriars School.

"Figure that you're fixed up that-a-way!" went on the learned lecturer. "I guess book-learning wouldn't help you none! Surest thing you know! A guy may not want his gat for weeks at a time—but when he wants his gat he wants it bad."

"Please, what's a gat?" inquired Smithy demurely.

"Hay? You been to school, and don't know what a gat is?" demanded Poker. "Carry me home to die! It's sure a gun. Now, you want to pack a gun handy in a pocket you can reach mighty sudden——"

"But a gun's too big to go in a pocket!" said Smithy.

"Search me!" gasped Poker. "What do you learn in this here school if you don't know that a gun's a revolver?"

"Only want to get it clear," said the Bounder, while the Remove chuckled. "A gat is a gun, and a gun is a pistol. What's a pistol?"

"Ha, ha, ha!"

Smack!

"Yoop!" yelled Smithy.

"I guess I mentioned that I don't want no back chat!" said Poker. "We ain't here for funning. I'll say I'm teaching this bunch. Now you watch me and get it card-indexed."

The Remove watched as Poker slid his hand to his hip, and, in the twinkling of an eye, whipped out his six-gun. There was no doubt that Poker was quick on the draw!

There was a general jump as he levelled the revolver at the class, his finger on the trigger.

"Now——" he went on.

"Yarooh!" roared Billy Bunter. "Turn that beastly thing another way, you silly idiot! It might go off!"

"I guess you'll be cinching another sockdolager if you don't quit chewing the rag, you pesky gink. Now, s'pose you was a gang of hoodlums, crowding me in a dive in Chicago, I got you covered!" said Poker. "You lissen! This here is a lesson for you young guys to chew on! Keep your gun handy, and always be quick on the draw——"

"Ha, ha, ha!"

"Never be in a hurry to start anything," went on Poker, "but if the other guy aims to start anything, get in first. Always aim low, and if you don't get him in the midriff you'll get him in the cabeza!"

"Oh crikey!"

"Now you read over what I've wrote, and chew on it!" said Poker; and, using his six-gun instead of a pointer, he pointed to the valuable instruction chalked on the blackboard.

The Form-room door opened.

Mr. Quelch stepped in.

Poker's back was to the door, and he did not see the Remove master enter. Mr. Quelch stared blankly at the extraordinary scene that met his gaze.

"Chew on it!" went on Poker. "Always be quick on the draw——"

Mr. Quelch came round the blackboard. The Removites gazed at him, breathless. They wondered what the Remove master would think of the extraordinary instruction his Form was receiving. It seemed to take Henry Samuel Quelch's breath away.

"Wha-a-a-a-t——" stuttered Mr. Quelch.

Poker glanced at him, and gave him a cheery nod.

"Say, I guess we're getting on fine, big boy!" he remarked genially. "You don't want to worry about this here bunch while I'm riding herd. I'll say these young geeks are learning a whole lot."

"What—what—what does this mean?" gasped Mr. Quelch. "How dare you enter this Form-room? I repeat—how dare you? Go away at once! Upon my word, this is too much! How dare you?"

Billy Bunter was still rubbing his head; but he grinned as he rubbed it. The thunderstorm was coming now.

THE FIFTEENTH CHAPTER.

High Words!

POKER PIKE stared at the Remove master. Perhaps he had expected Mr. Quelch to thank him for having taken charge so efficiently during the Form-master's absence. Anyhow, he had not expected this. The genial expression faded from his hickory face.

"Say, what's biting you?" he demanded gruffly. "Ain't you satisfied with what I'm teaching them young geeks?"

"Satisfied!" gasped Mr. Quelch. "Are you insane? Are you mad? I will tolerate no more of this! I shall insist that you leave the school. On the last occasion when you had the audacity to enter this Form-room——"

"Aw, can it!" snapped Poker. "What you getting at? I guess I ain't horned in without being asked."

"What! Van Duck did you venture—did you dare to ask this—this person to enter the Form-room——"

"Nope!" gasped Putnam.

"Wharton, you——"

"Oh, no, sir!" stuttered the captain of the Remove.

"I left you in charge of this Form, Wharton. You should have informed me immediately when this—this man came here. You should have——"

"But—but he said, sir——"

"It matters nothing what he may have said, Wharton!" thundered Mr. Quelch. "You are my head boy, and you are perfectly aware that I should allow nothing of the kind. I shall cane you——"

"Aw, pack it up!" hooted Poker. "That young gink knowed that you asked me to ride herd here."

"What!" stuttered Mr. Quelch. "I—I asked you to—to—to—— How dare you make such a statement? Wharton, did this—this man tell you that I had asked him to come here?"

"Yes, sir!" gasped Wharton.

"Upon my word! You actually made such a statement to my Form that——"

"Say, didn't you ask me, you pesky old geek?" roared Poker.

"Certainly not! Nothing of the kind! How dare you make such a statement?" shrieked Mr. Quelch.

"You allow you never asked me to horn in here, and ride herd while you was out?" roared Poker indignantly.

"Nothing of the kind! The statement is utterly false!"

"You calling me a liar!" howled Poker. "By the great horned toad, I guess if you don't take that back, I'll sure beat you up a few! You doggoned old geck, you sure did ask me——"

"I did not!" shrieked Mr. Quelch. "Nothing could have been further from my thoughts. I did not!"

"You sure did!" roared Poker.

"I repeat that I did not! How dare you pretend that I ever made such a request?" Mr. Quelch almost raved with wrath.

"Beat it, Poker, you gink!" shouted Putnam.

"Aw, can it!" snarled Poker. "You figure that I'm going to be called a liar by a doggoned guy of a schoolmaster? I'll say I've shot up guys for less'n that! Here, you! Stick 'em up!"

Mr. Quelch jumped almost clear of the Form-room floor as the angry and indignant gunman thrust the six-gun almost in his majestic face.

"For a Continental red cent!" said Poker savagely. "I'd sure fill you so full of holes that you'd do for a colander! Yep! You ask a guy to come here and ride herd over your bunch——"

"I did not! I——"

"You sure did. And me being an obliging guy I horned in, like you asked me!" roared Poker. "And I guess I been teaching these young gecks more useful stuff than they ever got before, too. I guess their Latin and such wouldn't help them a lot if they was crowded in a rookus. Surest thing you know."

"Go!" gasped Mr. Quelch. "Go! I shall place this matter before the headmaster. I—I shall——"

"Can it!" yapped Poker. "You can't call this baby a liar and get by with it. You're taking it back—get me?"

"Poker!" yelled Van Duck.

"Park it, you! I'm sure talking to this doggoned old piecan! You taking it back—you, Quelch—or you wanting me to beat you up till your Uncle George wouldn't know you from a carpet?" roared Poker.

"Bless my soul!" gasped Mr. Quelch.

The Greyfriars gunman glared at him over the levelled six-gun. Poker's hickory face was crimson with wrath and indignation. There was a step in the doorway, and a gasp from the juniors.

"The Head!" breathed Bob Cherry.

Dr. Locke rustled in. Poker's angry roar had reached his august ears. Seldom did the headmaster of Greyfriars lose his calm, lofty composure. But his eyes almost bulged from his countenance at the scene in the Remove Form Room.

"What is this?" gasped the Head. "What—what—what——"

Poker Pike looked round.

At sight of the headmaster his lifted arm was lowered, and the six-gun disappeared as if by magic into his hip-pocket. Poker was as quick on packing a gun as pulling one. Poker was a tough guy, but he had a deep respect for the silver-haired headmaster of Greyfriars. The six-gun vanished, and the gunman looked a good deal like a schoolboy caught in a prank.

"Aw!" he gasped. "I'll say you don't want to horn into this here rookus, sir. Not by a jugful. I guess I wasn't going to shoot up that old guy none. I was jest handling my hardware promiscus——"

"Mr. Quelch, what——"

"That—that person," stuttered Mr. Quelch "that—that—that man declares that I requested him to take charge of my Form, and——"

"You sure did!!" howled Poker.

"Such a statement is, on the face of it, ridiculous!" exclaimed the Head. "You have made some extraordinary mistake, Mr. Pike."

"Don't I know his toot?" roared Poker. "Ain't it jest like the filing of a saw? That old geck sure asked me——"

"Impossible!"

"I cannot account for the man's delusion, sir," stuttered Mr. Quelch. "But, in any case, this ruffianly outbreak in my Form-room——"

"It is quite intolerable!" said the Head. "Mr. Pike, leave this Form-room at once! Immediately, sir!"

Poker Pike eyed the Head a good deal like a savage bulldog. It was clear that he was very keen on "beating up" the Remove master, unless he "took it back," as Poker expressed it. But there was a calm authority in the majestic headmaster of Greyfriars that was not to be denied. Slowly Poker turned to the door.

In the doorway he paused.

"I'm telling you——" he began.

"Please go at once!"

"That old guy spoke to me over the phone to the lodge, and he asked me to horn in and ride herd——"

"Please go!"

"I ain't starting no rookus with you, sir," said Poker. "I respect you a whole lot, and then some. But when you ain't around, I sure am going to beat up that guy a few for calling me a liar! I'll say that's a cinch!"

"Bless my soul!" murmured Mr. Quelch.

And the Remove gasped.

"Kindly go!" rapped the Head. "Mr. Quelch, you may rely upon it that no such scene will be repeated here. I shall dispatch a cable to Mr. Vanderdecken van Duck, in Chicago, requesting him to recall Mr. Pike immediately."

"Very good, sir!" gasped Mr. Quelch.

Dr. Locke followed the gunman from the Form-room. He closed the door after him.

Mr. Quelch wiped a spot of perspiration from his scholastic brow. There was a buzz in the Remove. Harry Wharton & Co. glared at the grinning fat Owl.

They had been quite puzzled by Poker's extraordinary misapprehension. But as soon as he mentioned that Mr. Quelch's request had been made over the phone to Gosling's lodge, they understood at once that the Greyfriars ventriloquist had been at his tricks again. They did not need telling now why Bunter had left the Form-room.

"You fat villain!" breathed Bob Cherry. "You've been pulling Poker's leg over the phone."

"He, he, he!" gurgled Bunter.

"Silence!" exclaimed Mr. Quelch. "Cherry! You are talking! Take fifty lines! Bunter! How dare you laugh? Take a hundred lines!"

"Oh lor'!"

Mr. Quelch was very much disturbed. But he was not too disturbed to carry on with Latin prose. And during the remainder of that lesson his temper was tart—very tart indeed! Seldom had the Remove been so glad to be dismissed.

THE SIXTEENTH CHAPTER.
After the Feast the Reckoning!

"BUNTER!"

"He, he, he!"

"You fat scoundrel!"

"He, he, he!"

"You burbling, blinking bandersnatch!"

"He, he, he!"

Bunter was amused. But the fellows who surrounded him in the quad, after the Remove came out, did not look amused. They looked wrathy.

The previous day Billy Bunter's ventriloquism had come in useful. On the present occasion it was too much of a good thing—altogether too much! A jape was a jape; but the consequences were altogether too serious.

The view of the Famous Five was that Billy Bunter ought to own up. But no such view presented itself to William George Bunter.

"You can't let this go on," said Harry Wharton. "Last time Poker rowed with Quelch, he was ordered to go, and Quelch let him off. This time he won't!"

"No fear!" grinned Bunter.

"If the Head sends that cable to my popper, in Chicago, it's U P with poor old Poker!" said Putnam van Duck.

"Jolly good thing, too!" said Bunter, grinning. "Who wants him here? I don't!"

"Waal, I guess I do!" said Putnam. "I'm sure tired of the gink treading on my tail, but I ain't got no hunch to be cinched by Chick Chew and his bunch! Poker's got to stick!"

"He, he, he!"

"Stop cackling, you fat frog!" growled Johnny Bull. "You've got to go to the Head before he sends that cable——"

"I'll watch it!" chuckled Bunter.

"And own up!" said Frank Nugent.

"He, he, he!"

"Quelch has gone to the Head now," said Harry Wharton. "Bet you they're concocting that blessed cable together. It's too rotten! You can see that you've got to own up, Bunter!"

"Shan't!"

"Or we'll jolly well rag you baldheaded!" roared Bob Cherry.

"I say, you fellows, no larks!" exclaimed Bunter, in alarm. "The fact is, I—I had nothing to do with it. If I had, of course, I—I'd go and own up like a shot! But I never went to Quelch's study this morning, and I never called up Gosling's lodge on his phone!"

"You did!" howled Bob.

"I didn't!" hooted Bunter. "You can ask Gosling, if you like! He knows, as he answered the phone."

"Oh scissors!"

"The fact is, I know no more about it than the man in the moon. I can't go to the Head and say I did it, when—when I didn't! It wouldn't be truthful! I'm a bit more particular about that than you fellows."

"Oh, scrag him!" said Bob.

"You're not getting by with a rotten trick like this, you fat frump!" exclaimed the captain of the Remove. "Quelch is as mad as a hatter now, and the Head's in a bate, but they'll be all right as soon as they know that it was a trick on Poker. You've got to own up and set it right."

"Well, look here," said Bunter. "If you want somebody to own up, you can go and own up yourself—see? Go to the Head and own up that you did it."

"But I didn't!" howled Wharton.

"Well, I didn't, either!" said Bunter. "I never even thought of getting that beast into a row with Quelch, to pay him out for smacking me yesterday. I wasn't in Quelch's study at all when I did it—I mean, when I didn't do it! If you fellows can't take my word, I prefer to let the matter drop."

"Collar him!" said Bob.

"Yaroob!"

The matter did not drop. It was Billy

Bunter that dropped. He sat down on the quadrangle with a heavy bump.

"Ow! Beasts! Wow!" roared Bunter.

"Are you going to own up?" demanded Bob.

"Beast!"

"Oh, kick him!"

"Yaroooop!"

Billy Bunter scrambled up and fled for his fat life.

Harry Wharton & Co. were left in a worried group. They knew what had happened, but the headmaster and Form-master had no suspicion of it. Giving Bunter away to the beaks was not to be thought of—it was against all laws, written and unwritten. And it was clear that Bunter wasn't going to own up. A flogging was due to a fellow who played such a trick as impersonating his Form-master on the telephone and causing a shindy in the Form-room.

"Can it!" yapped Poker Pike. "You can't call this baby a liar and get by with it. You're taking it back! Get me!" The Greyfriars gunman was glaring at Mr. Quelch over his levelled gun when Dr. Locke rustled into the Form-room. "What is this?" gasped the startled Head. "Mr. Quelch—Mr. Pike—what is this?"

Bunter did not want to be flogged! He had the strongest possible objections to anything of the kind.

"Hallo, hallo, hallo, here comes jolly old Poker!" murmured Bob.

The Greyfriars gunman was walking in the quad, with a frown of deep thought on his hickory face, under the bowler hat. Some of the fellows who saw him wondered whether he was waiting for Quelch to come out, to carry out his dire threat of "beating him up."

Harry Wharton & Co. were silent as the gunman came up to them. Poker Pike eyed them thoughtfully.

"Say, you young guys," said Poker, "I guess I been chewing it over a few! That schoolmaster guy of yourn ain't the galoot to tell lies, I reckon."

"Hardly!" said Harry Wharton.

"He allowed he never asked me to ride herd over his bunch," said Poker. "And he sure did, over the phone!"

The juniors did not answer. They could not give the fat and fatuous ventriloquist away.

"I sure knowed his toot!" said Poker. "And I guess I was glad to oblige. I'll tell you, I was surprised some when he went back on it! I sure was going to beat him up a few——"

"You locoed geck!" growled Putnam van Duck.

"But I guess I been chewing it over," went on Poker calmly, "and I kinder reckerlect that while that young gink Van Duck was away yesterday, his voice was left lying around. Mebbe I mentioned to you young guys that a galoot couldn't string me along twice in the same way."

Poker nodded his bowler hat slowly.

"I'll tell a man, I'm sure wise to it, now I been chewing it over," he said. "Mebbe I'm a bonehead, and can be strung along like a rube from Rubesville, and mebbe I ain't! That fat gink Bunter is sure spry at putting over another geck's toot. Mebbe if he could play young Putnam ahind a locked door, he could play the schoolmaster on the phone."

The chums of the Remove exchanged glances. Evidently Poker Pike had "chewed it over" with results.

"I reckon I got on to it," said Poker, with another nod of the bowler hat. "Surest thing you know! I guess that fat guy is going to cough it up!"

Poker walked away, looking for Billy Bunter.

A few minutes later a terrific howl awoke the echoes of the Greyfriars quadrangle.

It proceeded from Billy Bunter.

"Yarooh! ! Leggo!" yelled Bunter. "I say, you fellows! Help! Whooop!"

"Oh, my hat!" gasped Bob Cherry. "Poker's got him!"

"He sure has cinched that fat guy!" grinned Putnam.

"Yoo-hooop!"

Billy Bunter, with a grip of iron on the back of his fat neck, was being propelled towards the House. He wriggled wildly as he went; but he had to go; the sinewy arm of the Greyfriars gunman was not to be denied. Dozens of fellows rushed up, to stare at the scene.

"I say, you fellows, rescue!" shrieked Bunter. "I say, I ain't going to the Head! I never did it! Besides, the beast smacked me! I say—— Yarooh!"

Still roaring, Bunter was propelled into the House!

"That's that!" remarked Bob Cherry. And that, undoubtedly, was that!

THE SEVENTEENTH CHAPTER.

O.K.

"WHAT!" ejaculated the Head.

"W-what!" stuttered Mr. Quelch.

They were in the Head's study, and the cable intended for Mr. Vanderdecken van Duck, in Chicago, lay on the table. The study door was pitched open all of a sudden, and the two masters stared round blankly as a fat, wriggling junior was projected into the room.

(*Continued on page* 28.)

CAPTAIN VENGEANCE!

By JOHN BREDON

Armed with a lash, Killer Moran stood over the convict pirates while they got busy replenishing the coal bunkers of the cruiser Vengeance!

A Secret of the Great War!

IN the chart-room of the pirate cruiser Vengeance, Von Eimar, arch-pirate and world's master-spy, bent over the chart table with a thoughtful frown, compasses and dividers in his plump hands.

The pirate cruiser ploughed through the calm sapphire of the sea, as her giant engines rolled and thundered at fullest pressure. Down in the engine-room, dials and gauges indicated that every ounce of steam was being harnessed in that fierce, intense race against time. In the chart-room with Von Eimar was Ronald Westdale, his English gunnery lieutenant, Killer Moran, an American, Dr. Nieuwe, and Luis Ramiro; and in the doorway, cap in hand, stood the stockily built German quartermaster, Dietz by name.

"This is the secret refuge for which we are heading," grunted Von Eimar at last, his monocle glinting as he glanced up and tapped the chart with podgy forefinger. "Inaccessible Island it is called. Dietz," he nodded his square, smooth-shaven head towards the quartermaster, "is the only man in the ship who has ever been there, and it is he who will guide us into its secret harbour."

Ronald Westdale, his brow corrugated by a puzzled frown, glanced interestedly at the dot marked by Von Eimar's compasses.

"Inaccessible Island!" he repeated thoughtfully. "But if this island is marked on all Admiralty charts, as it must be, how can we be safe there? All the warships in these seas are searching for us. They'll comb every island and lagoon before they give up the search."

Von Eimar grinned with the smile of superior knowledge.

Thick and fast had events crowded upon one another since that memorable night when Von Eimar had planned and led the uprising of convicts on Nemesis Island, the notorious penal settlement, and seized the Government cruiser which he had turned into a pirate man-o'-war. Already he had opened his piratical career by the sinking of the Australian luxury liner, Sylvia Bay, after taking the hundred thousand pounds' worth of bullion that she had on board. But on one event he had miscalculated. Just before she was torpedoed, the Sylvia Bay had managed to send out an S O S, and now cruisers and destroyers of half a dozen nations had joined in remorseless pursuit of the modern pirate.

Two hours before, with his usual masterly combination of bravery and cold-blooded, calculated cunning, Von Eimar had destroyed four Dutch seaplanes that had attempted to intercept his flight. But now, as every man aboard the cruiser knew, the pirates were nearing the end of their tether. At any moment a trail of smoke upon the skyline might herald the advent of pursuing warships. Gangs of convicts, slaving in relays, had piled up the fires in the furnaces, driving the cruiser at her utmost speed; but the coal in her bunkers was becoming ominously low, and, so far as the others in the chart-room knew, they had no means of replenishing their depleted supplies.

Von Eimar smiled as he polished his monocle, noting the anxiety that his lieutenants did not attempt to hide.

"My dear friends," he murmured in his low-pitched, guttural English, jamming the glass once more into his light blue eye, "I had really thought that you rated my intelligence at a higher scale. You may be sure that I did not organise our little insurrection at Nemesis Island without foreseeing the obvious; also, you may be assured that I did not leave so important a matter as an ultimate refuge to chance. As you say, my dear Westdale, Inaccessible Island is marked down on every Admiralty chart. What you may not know, however, is that no warship will trouble to search round it, for the simple reason that it will be deemed impossible for us to be in hiding there."

Delicately he dusted his nostrils with a scented handkerchief, enjoying to the full the fretting impatience of his subordinates.

"Inaccessible Island," he ran on, "has been known to geographers since the eighteenth century. From its first discovery it has always been described as a small island, five miles by four, bounded on all sides by high, inaccessible cliffs—hence its name—and that, what with strong and treacherous currents and cross-currents, and innumerable coral-reefs, it is impossible for a ship to get within two miles of it. Only a small boat can approach the cliffs, and then only with the greatest danger. Consequently, all books of reference on the subject will tell you that Inaccessible Island has never been explored, and that no human foot has ever been set upon its shores."

Von Eimar smiled blandly and lit a cigar. The faces of his companions lengthened.

"Dios mio!" blazed Luis Ramiro excitedly. "You will lead us into the trap, Von Eimar? A barren island, inaccessible, without harbour? Is this the joke, senor capitan?"

The pale blue eyes of Von Eimar glinted like polished steel. The South American's torrential eloquence died away promptly and abruptly like the jamming of a machine-gun.

"If you do not mind, Luis Ramiro—I have not finished yet!" Von Eimar spoke with all that icy, gentle suavity that his hearers knew to be a danger signal; and Luis Ramiro wilted.

"That is Inaccessible Island, my friends, as it is known to the world," resumed Von Eimar. "But it happens that the world does not know everything. Some years ago—four years before the Great War, to be precise—a German vessel happened to be surveying these waters. The professor and hydrographer in charge paid particular attention to Inaccessible Island. That attention amply repaid him.

"In brief, he discovered that Inaccessible Island, so long considered to be uninhabitable, had, in fact a most secure and natural harbour hidden from view by a projecting headland, and connected with the open sea by a narrow and intricate channel through the shoals and coral reefs. He found that, with care, a large vessel could be navigated into this unknown and unsuspected harbour, and that once inside it could remain absolutely lost to the outside world."

The others hung intently on his words.

"At this time I may say that this government vessel was surveying the seas in preparation for the Great War, which everyone then knew to be imminent. The German Admiralty at once decided to utilise Inaccessible Island as a secret naval base, and to that end large quantities of imperishable war materials, coal, oil, ammunition, and other stores, including, I believe, a seaplane in parts ready for assembling, were sent out and housed in one of the innumerable caves that honeycombed the island shores.

"As it happened, however, the need for this secret island base never materialised. Your British Navy," Von Eimar bowed stiffly towards Ronald Westdale, "remained unchallenged in the Southern Ocean. But the secret was still kept, and while I was engaged in Secret Service work during the War, I had full access to all charts, maps, and records of the island—the subject interested me. By a curiously lucky chance when on Nemesis Island, I found that Dietz, who is now our quartermaster, was one of the crew who surveyed and mapped that island in 1910."

With that he paused and looked grimly from one to the other, then let his clenched fist fall with a crash to the table.

"The secret harbour still exists upon Inaccessible Island. The stores are still there—the coal, for instance, which we so greatly need. Inaccessible Island shall be our secure bolt-hole until the naval hunt for us has died down."

There was a pause for one minute, and then came a loud hail from the look-out in the top:

"Land ahead!"

The Hidden Harbour !

It was about four in the afternoon when the Vengeance, her engines now slowed down to five knots, steamed in under the lee of Inaccessible Island.

Ronald Westdale, coming forward on to the iron foredeck, which still bore the bomb-hole made by the Dutch warplanes, found young Roderick Drake, the son of Morgan Drake, Britain's master-agent, whom Von Eimar was holding as a hostage and prisoner, gazing intently upon the high, serrated peaks of the island etched against the blue skies.

"So this is Inaccessible Island, chum," observed the English ex-naval lieutenant, resting his hand on Roy's shoulder as he followed the direction of his gaze. "A barren, lonely spot, it looks, doesn't it? Even now I can hardly believe in this secret harbour of which Von Eimar speaks."

"You're right, Ron." Roy Drake nodded.

With the exception of Hilarity Hinton, the cheery little Cockney ex-burglar, Ronald Westdale was the only one among that lawless, murderous crew for whom Roy Drake could have the slightest sympathy or regard.

Forward, crowding in a mass, with staring eyes, the convict pirates gazed upon the rugged, purple contours of the island before them.

Soaring high above the silver masses of foam that lashed its rocky base, Inaccessible Island towered upwards in sheer, perpendicular heights into the windy blue, four or five hundred feet at the lowest. Inexpressibly silent and lonely it looked amid the vastness of watery wastes. Here and there were clefts and narrow breaks in the precipitous bluffs and cliffs, but there was not an inch of beach; and sharp, jagged fangs of rock guarded its foot, like the teeth of sea dragons half submerged, bathed in thunderous waves and eternal spray. Little wonder that for two centuries it had been Inaccessible Island, in fact as well as by name.

With Von Eimar on the fore-bridge, in close consultation with Dietz at the wheel, and the little petrol launch leading the way with a man heaving the lead, slowly the Vengeance nosed its threading way between the mazes of sea shoals and treacherous undertow and sword-sharp reefs of coral. The slightest deviation from the proper course would have spelt disaster for the Vengeance and all her crew.

Fifteen fathoms, ten fathoms, five fathoms. Listening to the shouted calls of the leadsman in the motor-boat, Roy Drake felt the hair on his scalp stiffen. In and out of the underwater labyrinth with its treacherous tidal races Von Eimar guided his pirate cruiser.

"Look!" exclaimed Westdale, catching Roy by the arm. "The harbour mouth. Would you believe it? It's like magic!"

Giant cliffs boomed with the echoes of the Vengeance's steam siren as the craggy portals of the harbour unfolded before them. A great, rocky promontory, curving seawards like a mountainous sickle, effectively hid the entrance from the most powerful binoculars of any ship that might be riding off-shore. As they glided in, it was just as if the peaked summits and precipices were swinging round upon a hidden pivot.

A deep, narrow, winding gorge, like a miniature Norwegian fiord, let the slowly steaming pirate cruiser into the inner mysteries of Inaccessible Island.

Utter astonishment found voice in the babbled cries of the convict pirates as they found themselves gliding into a calm, still, beautiful lagoon of sapphire blue shored in by steep cliffs and sandy coves, a shell of exquisite grandeur.

From the sea Inaccessible Island was grim, bare, sterile, a stony outcrop of rock breaking from the waters. Within, by a most amazing contrast, it was an island fairyland. Green, feathery cocoa-nut-palms clothed the slopes of the ringed hills in a garment of luxuriant verdure. Silver-white sands of dazzling brightness ran down to the breathless pool of sapphire waters that mirrored the grey, grim lines of the pirate warship as she glided to a full stop.

Yells rent the clear, warm, invigorating air. Even those hardened and calloused scoundrels from Nemesis Island could not fail to appreciate the beauties of the island forests and ravines as they dropped anchor with a reverberating boom that shook echoes from every rocky cliff and precipice, causing scores of brilliant tropical birds to rise, screaming, like handfuls of jewels tossed up into the bright glare of the sun.

"What a refuge!" cried Ronald Westdale. "All the navies in the world could be hanging about outside and never dream that a ship could be hidden here. The only possibility of discovery is that of an aeroplane flying directly overhead; and that's one chance in a million!"

The Burying of the Bullion !

Great fires roared and crackled, red and smoky against the stars. Around, the serried rows of hills forming the outer ring of Inaccessible Island looked on in hushed majesty, as the moon silvered their peaks.

"We're pirates now, and who cares how?
Yo ho for a bottle, and let's have our fling.
We've got all the gold, secure in the hold,
So, ho for the bottle! And let it go with a swing!"

Leaping, flame-lit rays and inky shadows played upon the tanned, unshaven, villainous faces of the convicts and pirates as they lolled upon the crisp, warm sands, and sang their pirate song.

A little apart, resting his back upon the stem of a coconut palm, Roderick Drake sat aside and watched. The strains of a piano-accordion tinkled faintly through the riotous clamour. Near to him stretched Mikhail Lebedoff, sleeping heavily in spite of the uproar. For the past forty-eight hours the Russian ex-naval officer had superintended his pounding, flogging engines, dozing only in fitful snatches, during that nerve-straining flight after the sinking of the Sylvia Bay, and now he slumbered as only a man could who was utterly worn out by fatigue and tension.

A few yards away, too, squatted Governor Zarda, once prison-governor of Nemesis Island; and with him Admiral Merieski, former commander of the Vengeance, when she had been the cruiser Zermac, of the Varland republic. Both men were shackled by iron rings clamped round their legs, and stapled by a chain to a palm-tree.

Few who had known these two in their glory would have recognised them now, ragged, coaly black, and broken with the hellish toil and heat of the stokehold.

Roderick Drake, watching through the ruddy fire-flickers, beheld a stack of heavy, oaken, rope-handled cases piled on the fringe of the camp. These, he knew, contained the bullion taken from the ill-fated Sylvia Bay. Atop of them sat Killer Moran, speaking rapidly and in low, animated tones to Luis Ramiro and a group of others.

Just then the flap of a tent under the palms stirred, and Von Eimar, immaculate in white ducks, strolled towards the group.

Killer Moran did not notice the pirate captain until he was close upon the group, within a few feet of Roderick Drake, who sat on the sands.

When he did, he stopped speaking as though paralysed.

"Pray go on, Moran," said Von Eimar easily, waving a plump hand. "Don't mind me. I like men who speak their minds. A little meeting, I perceive. Well, well! I am glad that some of you, at least, take an interest in the enterprise, instead of swilling and wallowing like those pig-dogs yonder," and he jerked a fat thumb contemptuously towards the rowdy revellers in the firelight.

Ronald Westdale, Dr. Nieuwe, Hilarity Hinton, and several more, attracted by the scene, strolled up at this juncture, and Roy's view was blocked by the gathering figures. Quite a crowd was ringed round in a few seconds.

Noisily Moran cleared his throat. His close-set little eyes were like those of a cat about to spring.

"It's about the durocks, boss," he said thickly and defiantly.

"I beg your pardon, Moran?" Von Eimar smiled indulgently. "You will have to speak in the English language. I fear I am not conversant with the American language."

"About the bullion, chief." Killer scowled at the subtle mockery and implied contempt in Von Eimar's steel-smooth tones, but he dared show no open resentment. He continued, expressing himself in English as best he could, banging thick, horny fingers upon one of the cases to emphasise his words. "This hyar bullion, boss. We wants you to put us wise. It's not what you'd call anyhow safe as the Bank of England on these hyar sands. How long will we be coolin' our toes on this pesky island, cap?"

Von Eimar reflected, pulling at his underlip with a fat finger and thumb.

"For a month at least, men. First"—he ticked off the items on his fingers, speaking loudly and clearly for all to hear—"the seas hereabouts will be thick with warships for weeks to come, until they come to believe our fake wireless message that we had struck a reef and were foundering. Secondly, until the alarm has been lulled, no other ships will we find to capture—at least, none with bullion and such-like aboard, which is what we want. Third, the damage caused by the Dutchmen's bombs must be repaired. Last of all, not one in ten of you is a trained seaman. Westdale and I must knock some idea of handling the guns into you, in case we meet with a warship in one of our future raids."

Killer Moran glared furtively out of one half-closed eye at Von Eimar.

"Thet bein' so, cap, I'd like to pass a suggestion. This hyar bullion! Let's park it—cache it somewhar in some likely hide-out. If the cruiser were sunk, an' we made a getaway in the boats—fur instance—it would be o' no manner o' use to us at the sea bottom. So I says, put it away somewhar, in secret. I'm sayin' nuthin' of any man in pertickler, but thar's men hyar I'd trust about as far as I could throw a ton o' coals with my li'l finger. You parks it, cap, an' twelve selected men o' the crew is witnesses. Is thet fair?" And he glanced over the massed faces of the pirate crew, most of whom were by now drawn to the scene.

A shout of approval greeted his inquiry.

Slowly Von Eimar nodded his straight-backed head.

"Excellent, Moran. As it happens, I was about to make some such suggestion myself. You have merely forestalled me. Let us choose the twelve witnesses, and we will set about locating a secret cache immediately."

Ronald Westdale, Killer Moran, Ramiro, Dr. Nieuwe, and Hilarity Hinton, the Cockney, were all among the twelve chosen by the crew. The cases of bullion were at once transhipped into the petrol-launch, and, with a hurricane lamp hoisted to the masthead, Von Eimar himself steered them under the shadowy arch of a cavern that burrowed far under the mountainous cliffs.

"The island is honeycombed with these sea caves," the leader said, as the lantern rays quivered over inky swirls and eddies as the motor-boat chugged forward, diving into a maze of rocky arches and caves. "In one of them is hidden the secret supplies of coal and other stores which the German Government so thoughtfully provided many years ago. Choose one of these clefts in the cave walls, my friends, and we will duly bury the bullion and draw up the necessary map."

A spot was chosen, and deep in the sable shadows of the sea-cave they laboured, with clink of spade and pick, dragging the heavy bullion-cases over the rough rock in the lantern-light, and burying them deep in a dark fissure under piles of stones and boulders. The location of the hiding-place was carefully noted, and drawn up on a map by Von Eimar, eager, sweat-streaked faces peering over his broad shoulders as he scrawled in his note-book.

Like men with some guilty secret on their conscience, they sat silently as the boat throbbed and foamed once more on the inky, lapping waters to the outlet of the caves.

With his close-set, shifty eyes peering slyly upon Von Eimar as he sat at the tiller, Killer Moran lowered his bullet head and whispered something into the ear of Luis Ramiro, which might have interested the chief pirate had he overheard it. Significant, too, were the glances the pair exchanged as they fondled the holstered guns in their belts.

The motor-launch shot out from under the beetling cliff, and her bow-ripples flashed milky white under the radiant moon.

"I wonder if my friends entertain the same charming thoughts for me as I do of them?" Von Eimar soliloquised grimly, as, after the launch had been tied up by the beach, he stalked back to his tent under the twinkling stars. "Twelve men on this island, besides myself, know the secret of this treasure cache—that is, twelve men on this island know too much!"

The Monster of the Deep!

"HEAVE-HO, there! Heave! Steady! Careful with those sacks, now!"

Weird echoes rumbled and reverberated hollowly throughout the natural, rugged vaults and arches of the sea-cavern. Flaring torches illuminated the caves with flickering patterns of red and black, hovering and quivering over the pitchy, still water.

Tons of coal, intended for that German war raider that never came, were piled into the shadowy recesses of the caves of Inaccessible Island. Under the supervision of Killer Moran and Luis Ramiro, the convict pirates were shovelling out the black lumps and blocks, filling sacks to replenish the coal bunkers of the Vengeance, nearly emptied in that wild rush to the secret island harbour. Files of black, dusty, half-naked men ran to and fro, stooping as they balanced the hundredweight bags on their backs; and, one after another, they dumped them into the waiting boats that ferried them under the cave-arches to the cruiser in the lagoon.

It was heart-breaking work. The Killer, with a black cigar jutting out from his mouth, stood upon a jut of rock overlooking the cave passage, with a lash coiled in his big fist, and any convict that skulked or faltered felt its stinging knots cracking round his legs.

Luis Ramiro, his black eyes glittering, stalked to and fro like a cat, playing with his long, slender stiletto.

Outside, in the blazing sunshine, Von Eimar was drilling some of the best fighting-men of the convicts; on the cruiser's gun-deck, Westdale was giving instruction in the loading and sighting of the long six-inch and eight-inch guns in the turrets. On a high, naked spire of rock that dominated the island a watchman was posted, ensconced in a hidden cleft, and sweeping the ocean rim with his glasses.

Roderick Drake rubbed his sore and blistered palms as he unshipped the oars and allowed the dinghy to float gently against the flat rock ledge in the cave that served as a landing-stage. At Von Eimar's orders he had been spared the task of handling the coal-sacks, though the rowing of the heavily laden boat was hard work enough.

"Whe-e-ew!" Hilarity Hinton, the Cockney, gasped stertorously, as he swung a hundredweight sack over his head and shoulders into the boat.

He paused a moment, rubbing his perspiring brow with a blackened hand, stretching his muscles and sinews as he gazed across the inky cave waters. Then his eyes rounded, and he let out a whistling gasp of surprise and confusion.

"Lor', lumme! W-what — is — it? Blow me, I've got the 'orrors! I'm seeing things! D—do you see wha-what I see?"

Surprised, Roy Drake slewed round on the thwart amidships, following the direction of the Cockney's pointed, shaking finger.

Then he, too, uttered a gasp of amazement and horror. His eyes started in his head. His hair stiffened, and his tongue clove to the roof of his mouth.

Coal-sacks crashed and clashed to the rocky, fissured floor; men yelled, staring and pointing into the shadowy depths of the water cavern. Killer Moran let the cigar fall from his dropped jaws, his fingers trembling as they fumbled for the guns holstered in his belt.

A strange, nightmare horror was uncoiling from the surface of the cave pool.

Peering through the half-light, Roy Drake saw, first, what appeared at one glance to be a huge, writhing sea-snake, but which afterwards resolved itself into a long, flexible, pendulous tentacle waving in the air; secondly, a metallic, globular head, topped with a horny protuberance between the round and glowing eyes. Before their startled and terrified gaze, this monstrous object floated on the inky swirls and eddies, and then the first tentacle was joined by others, five or six wriggling upwards, and jointed with curved spikes like claws.

The panic was indescribable. Hardened convicts threw themselves flat upon the rocks, cowering and babbling in their terror. Slowly the Thing swam towards the rocky platform, glassy eyes fixed upon the paralysed humans, barring the outlet to the lagoon. The claws wrenched a jut of rock from a ragged column, and, brandishing this boulder above its head, the Thing floated so close that the water ripples lapped against the rock of the landing-stage.

One man let out a screech that was hardly human, magnified a thousand-fold by the echoes of the dim cavern vaults.

That released the tension. In mad, unreasoning panic the pirates ran for the higher and dry caves, jamming

Printed in Great Britain and published every Saturday by the Proprietors, The Amalgamated Press, Ltd., The Fleetway House, Farringdon Street, London, E.C.4. Advertisement offices: The Fleetway House, Farringdon Street, London, E.C.4. Registered for transmission by Canadian Magazine Post. Subscription rates: Inland and Abroad, 11s. per annum; 5s. 6d. for six months. Sole Agents for Australia and New Zealand: Messrs. Gordon & Gotch, Ltd., and for South Africa: Central News Agency, Ltd.—Saturday, June 6th, 1936.

together in a hopeless confused mass at the narrow passage-ways. Men fell gasping, and were trampled underfoot.

With the snapping of that tautened stillness, Roy Drake acted. Instinctively as the boat rocked with the wash of the slowly gliding monster, he tore a carbine from the nerveless hands of one of the guards, who was cowering like a jelly in the bows.

Crack! Cra-a-ck! Crack, crack!

Thunderous echoing reports revolved around the caves as he pressed trigger. Flames spurted from the muzzle as he aimed for the monster's goggling eyes.

Pi-i-ing!

Either his startled nerves had caused his hands to shake, or the rocking of the boat on its keel spoiled his aim.

The bullets glanced off that smooth, round, metallic head as if it had been made of reinforced steel. None of the staring eyes were touched. Above him flourished one of those hovering tentacles, and, losing his footing, he pitched head-first into the water as the gunwale was crunched like paper.

Rising in a mist of dripping water he paddled for the rock ledge, gripping its rough, uneven surface with his fingers. A loud scream rang on his ears.

Glancing around as he hauled himself flat upon the rock, Roy was appalled to see a limp human form wriggling and dangling in the monster's grip. It was the convict from whom he had snatched the carbine. The man hung poised in midair, screaming in peals of terror as the clawing talons gripped him round the waist, arms and legs beating wildly and hopelessly.

Another tentacle shot out, swooping towards Roy. He ducked, darting into the inkiest shadows, scrambling over boulders and coal-sacks towards the cave openings high above the pool.

He reached it just in time. Over a barrier of rocks and stones he plunged, to stumble upon Killer Moran and Hilarity Hinton as they crouched in the narrow archway.

Killer Moran, who was a coward at heart, like most gunmen, simply groaned and grovelled in terror.

Coolly Roderick Drake picked up a magazine rifle that had been dropped in the panic flight of the convicts, and squirmed into a firing position between two boulders.

When he looked down into the cavern pool, it was to see that the monster had sunk under the surface, though the tentacles and the spiked protuberance between the eyes was still visible. The convict in its grip had ceased to scream and struggle. Either he had fainted, or he had died of fright.

Rapidly, and yet carefully, Roy Drake fired, emptying the magazine, with every buttress and dome of the great cavern ringing with the echoes.

Lowering the smoking rifle he gazed down into the disturbed pool, flashing an electric torch that he borrowed from Killer Moran.

The monster of the pool had disappeared. One solitary tentacle alone remained in sight, carrying the limp form of its victim aloft. That, too, began to descend. Slowly it sank from sight. In a revolving suction of waters it followed that hideous head, drawing the insensible figure of its victim to the depths, till at last only a few swirls and eddies remained to show that it was not some nightmare dream.

Roy shuddered, and felt sick, the rifle sagging in his loosened grip. Though the convict he had just seen dragged to his death-dive had been guilty of a dozen crimes, culminating in treason and murder, he could not but feel for the wretch in his dreadful fate.

After a while, and very reluctantly, dismayed groups of convicts climbed down the rugged and natural steps from the coal-storage caves. Among them, at least, no word of pity or sympathy was heard for their lost comrade. All they were concerned for was the safety of their own valuable skins.

Killer Moran sprang from the rock platform into the petrol launch, which was tethered to a boulder.

"Cool on it, yuh bo's!" he snarled, his wicked eyes glinting, drawing and cocking his long-barrelled Colts as the rest of the convicts made a rush. "I'll say yuh don't swamp this boat! I'm gonna fetch the boss. He's got all the grey matter in thet bonehead of his, so he kin deal with this—whatever it is. Start up thet engine, young Britisher."

Obediently Roy threw open the throttle, and, leaving the rest of the convict pirates in a halting mass on the rocky ledge, the motor-launch foamed through the shadowy sea caves out to the vivid sunlight of the lagoon, where Von Eimar was drilling his men on the sandy beach.

Von Eimar rubbed his nose, and

(*Continued on next page.*)

COME INTO THE OFFICE, BOYS AND GIRLS!

Your Editor is always pleased to hear from his readers. Write to him: Editor of the MAGNET, The Fleetway House, Farringdon Street, London, E.C.4. A stamped, addressed envelope will ensure a reply.

WELL, chums, I've just spent a pleasant hour going through my post-bag. Among the many letters is one from John Jefferies, of Horsham, who writes to ask if I can supply him with issues of the MAGNET dealing with the early adventures of Harry Wharton at Greyfriars. He says that he is willing to pay half-a-crown apiece for such copies. Evidently my chum is unaware of the fact that these stories are being republished in our companion paper, the "Gem." Save your money, John, by purchasing a copy of the "Gem" each week! I strongly urge all you fellows who have recently swelled the ranks of the happy band of "Magnetites" to take advantage of the opportunity of reading the splendid yarn dealing with:

"THE MAKING OF HARRY WHARTON!"

now running in our champion school-story companion paper—the "Gem." You'll say thanks for the tip, believe me!

A query regarding an old superstition comes from "Magnetite," of Newark. He wants to know

ARE PEACOCK FEATHERS UNLUCKY?

Not any more than anything else. The superstition of peacock feathers being unlucky comes from the days when people believed in the "evil eye." Even now, in certain parts of the world, people believe that if the "evil eye" is cast upon them they will suffer a variety of ills. The opened tail of a peacock is dotted with many marks which have the appearance of eyes. Superstitious people believed that these were reflections of the "evil eye," and thus the peacock's feathers gained the reputation of being unlucky!

Here is an interesting item of news which I came across the other day.

DO YOU WANT TO BUY AN ISLAND?

If you do, now is your opportunity! And it will be a British island, too! There are three of them for sale—Mingalay, Pabbay, and Berneray, and they are situated in the Outer Hebrides, sixty miles from the mainland. These three islands are owned by an Englishman, who is getting tired of the loneliness. And I don't blame him, for on Mingalay, where he lives, there is only a four-roomed cottage, a disused chapel-house, and one landing ground. A boat calls once a week in the summer, and once a fortnight in the winter. Occasionally, a shepherd lives on the island, and there are men tending the lighthouse on Barra Head. If any of you are feeling like living a Robinson Crusoe existence, you can do so—and have three islands to yourself instead of one! But it will cost you about £3,000, the sum the owner is asking for the islands!

Of course, you've heard the old saying:

"EVERY DOG HAS HIS DAY!"

Well, the dogs of a town in Hungary have certainly had their day! The local councillors decided to increase the tax on dogs. But dog-owners—and their dogs—weren't going to take that lying down. The owners held an indignation meeting. The next time the local council met, along went the dog-owners and their dogs. The dogs were let loose in the council chamber. Then the fun started!

The dogs chased the councillors round and round the room. One big Alsatian picked on the burgomaster, and finally chased him into a cupboard, where he was forced to lock himself in. The rest of the councillors took to their heels and were chased by the indignant dogs.

And the dogs won the day! In consequence of this, the council held another hasty meeting and altered the bye-law which they had made. So the dog tax remains the same as it was before the uproar! Three cheers for the dogs!

And now we come to next week's bumper bill-o'-fare. Although

"THE BOGUS BEAK!"

By Frank Richards,

is the last story in our present series featuring Putnam van Duck and his ever-watchful gunman guardian, Poker Pike, I feel fully justified in saying it is unquestionably the best. So far, Poker Pike has put "paid" to all Chick Chew's enterprises. But Kidnapper No. 1 of the United States is a sticker with a professional pride to study. His final scheme to bring about success is a real corker!

Our supporting features, too, are as good as ever; further exciting chapters of our modern pirate story, a topical issue of the "Greyfriars Herald," an effusion from our Greyfriars Rhymester, and lastly, another chat with

YOUR EDITOR.

turned to Westdale. Around them crowded the excited, uneasy convicts. In the light of electric flashlamps the cavern pool looked as calm and innocent as a mill-pond.

"What do you make of it, Westdale?" he asked.

Ronald Westdale shrugged his broad shoulders.

"It's hardly believable," the English ex-naval lieutenant said. "But obviously some queer creature has its existence at the bottom of this pool. There are strange things in the sea. Some underwater monster, perhaps, unknown to science, that normally lives at the bottom of the ocean."

Von Eimar thrust out his broad underlip, and nodded.

"That is the likeliest explanation, Westdale," he agreed. "Donner! There is no safety for us on this island while this creature remains alive. We'll see what a depth-charge can do towards shaking it up."

"Hey!" Killer Moran let out a fervent protest. "Thet won't do, cap! Yuh're likely to bring the roof of this hyar cave down onta us."

Von Eimar turned on him with an ugly scowl.

"I want none of your timid suggestions, Moran!" he rasped harshly. "I have no use for cowards, either. Get ready with that depth-charge, Westdale."

The whole subterranean world seemed to rock as that depth-charge exploded at the bottom of the pool. The echoes stunned them. They watched intently. When at last the whispered echoings died away, and the agitated surface of the underground lake became still once more, there was not a sign of the monster or its victim.

Ronald Westdale drew in a deep breath.

"We called this island a paradise when we landed yesterday," he said aside to Roderick Drake. "But it seems as though the devil's got it with a complimentary ticket."

(Has the depth-charge destroyed the hideous, unknown sea-monster, or is it lurking under the surface waiting to strike again? Boys, you're booked for a real feast of thrills in next week's chapters of this powerful modern pirate yarn!)

THE VENGEANCE OF BUNTER THE VENTRILOQUIST!

(Continued from page 23.)

"Ooooogh!" gurgled Bunter. as he came.

Mr. Quelch jumped to his feet. The Head, more slowly, rose in majestic wrath. Poker Pike, still gripping the back of Bunter's fat neck, followed the Owl of the Remove in.

"What——" thundered the Head.

"Ow! Leggo! I didn't—I wasn't!" spluttered Bunter. "I—ow—leggo!"

"I guess I've brung this here guy to put you wise, sir!" said Poker calmly "Mebbe you'll listen a piece!"

"This outrage——" gasped Mr. Quelch.

"Aw, pack it up!" barked Poker. "This here gink has got a stunt of imitating other guys' toots, and he sure did string me yesterday about that Putnam van Duck. I guess it was this here fat gink what phoned me, making me believe it was Quelch——"

"Impossible!" exclaimed the Head.

"Sez you!" grunted Poker.

"I cannot believe——"

"One moment, sir!" exclaimed Mr. Quelch, his eyes gleaming with a gleam that made Billy Bunter wish, from the bottom of his fat heart, that he was not so wonderfully clever a ventriloquist. "It is certainly possible that a trick has been played. This boy Bunter has an absurd trick of imitating voices—he has been punished for playing such tricks."

"Oh lor'!" gasped Bunter.

"Bunter, did you leave the Form-room during my absence this morning?"

"Oh, no, sir!" gasped Bunter. "Not for a moment, sir! And—and I couldn't have got on your phone, sir, in your study, without getting out of the Form-room, sir, could I? I never left the Form-room, sir, for a second! You—you can ask Wharton. He—he called me back."

"Bless my soul!" said the Head.

"Then you left the Form-room?" exclaimed Mr. Quelch.

"Oh, no, sir! I—I've just told you I didn't!" wailed Bunter. "Besides, the beast smacked me yesterday, sir——"

"What?"

"He smacked me on my bags, sir," gasped Bunter, "just because I imitated Van Duck's voice for—for a joke, sir! But I never thought of paying him out! The idea never came into my head, sir! I didn't think you'd be frightfully wild if you found him in the Form-room again, after the row last time, and I never phoned to Gosling's lodge, sir."

"You may leave Bunter to me, Mr. Pike," said the Head, in a deep voice. "Mr. Quelch, as it is clear that a trick was played, and Mr. Pike was deceived into supposing that you had requested him——"

"Oh, certainly. sir!" said Mr. Quelch. "I am, indeed, very sorry that Mr. Pike has been the victim of an absurd, practical joke, played by a boy in my Form. So far as I am concerned, the matter is at an end. Mr. Pike, I express my regret——"

"O.K.!" said Poker, and, with a duck of the bowler hat, he walked out of the study.

The Head slid the cable into the wastepaper-basket.

"C-c-c-can I go now, sir?" stuttered Bunter.

"You may go with your Form-master, Bunter!" said the Head grimly. "Mr. Quelch, I think I can rely upon you to administer adequate punishment——"

"You can, sir!" said Mr. Quelch, with equal grimness. "Come with me, Bunter."

"Oh lor'!" gasped Bunter.

The Head's reliance on Mr. Quelch proved to be well-founded. From the terrific howls that proceeded from Quelch's study, a few minutes later, it was clear—painfully clear—that adequate punishment was being administered. To Billy Bunter it seemed more than adequate!

THE END.

(So much, then, for Billy Bunter and Poker Pike. But what's Chick Chew lying doggo for? You'll be surprised when you read: "THE BOGUS BEAK!" the final yarn in this exciting series. Be sure to order next week's MAGNET *early, chums!)*

Billy Bunter and Harry Wharton & Co. in Another Sensational School Adventure. **"THE BOGUS BEAK!"**

No. 1,478. Vol. XLIX. EVERY SATURDAY Week Ending June 13th, 1936.

The BOGUS BEAK!

By FRANK RICHARDS

—Featuring HARRY WHARTON & CO., the Cheery Chums of GREYFRIARS.

THE FIRST CHAPTER.

Caught Bending !

"SEARCH me!" murmured Putnam van Duck.

The American junior stared into his study—Study No. 1 in the Remove.

It was after prep, and the Remove studies were deserted. Most of the Removites were gathered in the Rag, downstairs

Putnam had come up to the study for a "Holiday Annual." But he forgot that entrancing volume now.

As his study-mates, Wharton and Nugent, were in the Rag, he naturally expected to find the study dark and vacant. Instead of which, the light was on, and someone was in the study.

That someone was in the study cupboard. He was, in fact, half in it, reaching to the shelf at the back.

Putnam had a view chiefly of an extensive pair of trousers.

He stared at those trousers.

There were plenty of fellows who could not be recognised merely by a back view! But in this case, there was no doubt on the question of identity. Those extensive trousers could only have enclosed the ample proportions of Billy Bunter.

Putnam van Duck stepped into the study.

"Urrrggh!" came a grunt from the fat junior reaching deep into the cupboard.

Putnam grinned.

Billy Bunter was a tall fellow sideways. But he was not long in the reach. He seemed to have difficulty in getting at that back shelf. His feet were off the floor as he reached deeper in and reached for the pot of jam on that shelf.

"Urrgh! Beasts!" grunted Bunter. "Packing things out of a fellow's reach—just as if they fancied that a fellow might be after them! Suspicious beasts!"

Billy Bunter was busy—too busy to blink round through his big spectacles. He had not heard the American junior arrive. And Putnam made no sound.

While Bunter, grunting stertorously, reached for the jam, Putnam reached for a cricket stump.

Stump in hand, he stepped towards the fat junior, still making no sound. Up went his right hand, with the stump in it.

It came down suddenly, and it came down hard, landing with a terrific whop on the tightest trousers at Greyfriars School, just as Bunter captured the jam.

Whack!

"Yooo-hoooooop!" came a startled roar from Billy Bunter. "Ow! Who—what—yarooooop!"

The fat little legs kicked frantically in the air.

Whack!

"Yow-wooop!" yelled Bunter as the stump landed a second time. "Ow! Beast! Stoppit! I ain't after your jam! Yow-ow-ow!"

The fat Owl of the Remove rolled out of the cupboard, roaring. He sat down on the carpet with a bump that almost shook Study No. 1. After him rolled the jam-jar, cracking as it landed on the floor.

Putnam van Duck grinned down at him.

"Get up and have another, you pesky piecan!" he said.

"Ow!" roared Bunter. "Beast! Ow!"

"I guess you was after that jam, and I'll say you sure can have it now, Fat Jack!" remarked Putnam.

He picked up the cracked jar. Jam was streaming from it. Billy Bunter squirmed hurriedly away.

"Keep off, you beast!" he roared. "I don't want the jam! I wasn't after the jam! Don't you mop that jam over me, you beast! Oh crikey! Ooooogh!"

Jam from the broken jar streamed over a fat face, as Billy Bunter squirmed. Some of it went into his mouth, where Billy Bunter intended all of it to go. But some went into his nose, and his ears, and his hair, and plastered on his spectacles. That was not what Bunter had intended at all! Taken like that, even strawberry jam, of the best quality, was not nice.

"Oh crikey! Ow! Beast! Stoppit! I'm all sticky!" yelled Bunter. "I'll jolly well punch your nose! Ooooogh! Grroooogh!"

The fat junior scrambled wildly to his feet and bounded for the door. Jam dripped from him as he bounded.

"Hold on!" called out Putnam. "There's some marmalade in the cupboard. You can have that, too, you fat piecan!"

"Urrrggh!"

Billy Bunter did not stop for the marmalade! The jam was enough for him. He bounded out of Study No. 1 into the Remove passage and tore along to the stairs. He dabbed and clawed frantically at the jam as he went.

Putnam, grinning, threw the jam-jar into the waste-paper basket, picked up the "Holiday Annual," and followed him from the study.

Billy Bunter, on the Remove landing, blinked round at him, with a jammy blink. Bunter's vision was limited, especially with jam on his spectacles.

"Keep off, you beast!" he roared. "Keep that marmalade away from me, you beast!"

"Ha, ha, ha!" yelled Putnam. It was a "Holiday Annual" in his hand, but to the Owl of the Remove it was a jar of marmalade, to be added to the jam!

Bunter was feeling sticky enough already! As Putnam arrived on the landing, Bunter bolted down the stairs.

If Bunter had stopped to think, he would have realised that he was in too jammy a state to show up in public. But Bunter did not stop to think. He flew!

Putnam, chuckling, followed. He was done with the grub-raider of the Remove, but he had to go back to the Rag with the book he had come to fetch.

Billy Bunter blinked back from the middle of the landing.

"Beast!" he gasped.

And he flew down the lower stairs.

In the lighted hall below, a dozen pairs of eyes, at least, turned on Billy Bunter's jammy face. Among them was a pair of very keen eyes, often likened by the Removites to gimlets—those of Mr. Quelch, the master of the Remove.

Quelch was talking to Prout, the master of the Fifth. Both of them stared at the jammy Owl.

Prout gave a sniff, which implied that this sort of thing was to be expected in Quelch's Form. Quelch, with a brow of thunder, strode towards the jammy, fat junior.

"Bunter!" he thundered.

"Oh lor'!" gasped Bunter.

"You—you—you disgusting boy!" exclaimed Mr. Quelch, in withering accents. "I have spoken to you many times, Bunter, on the subject of your gluttony, and your slovenliness——"

"I—I—I never——" stuttered Bunter.

"Now, you dare to let me see you in this—this revolting state!" hooted Mr. Quelch. "You have been eating jam—I should say devouring it—in enormous quantities. Your face is smothered with it——"

"I—I haven't——"

"You are reeking with jam!" exclaimed Mr. Quelch. "You are positively smothered with jam! You are in a disgusting and revolting state, Bunter!"

"I—I—I——"

"Go to your dormitory at once, and wash yourself clean! Go immediately! I will not allow you to appear in public in that revolting state! You are a disgrace to your Form, Bunter! Go and wash yourself!"

"I—I—I——" gurgled Bunter.

"Go!" thundered Mr. Quelch.

"Oh crikey!"

Bunter went!

He passed Putnam van Duck on the stairs, and gave him a jammy, sticky, and infuriated blink.

"Beast!" he hissed.

Putnam chortled, and Billy Bunter trailed away to the Remove dormitory to wash off the jam.

THE SECOND CHAPTER.

Loder is Late!

"WHAT'S the time?"

"Twenty-past nine, fathead!"

"Sure that clock's right?" demanded Billy Bunter.

"Ass!"

That was not a polite answer, to a fellow who wanted to know the time. But as it happened, Billy Bunter had asked the time three or four times over, in the last ten minutes. For some mysterious reason the fat Owl of the Remove was very anxious about the time.

Most of the Remove fellows were in the Rag. Harry Wharton & Co. were gathered in a cheery group round Van Duck's "Holiday Annual," which was open on the table. The Famous Five were reading a story therein, together, and incessant interruptions from Billy Bunter were not required.

Billy Bunter was taking his ease in an armchair. His fat face had a newly washed appearance—unusually clean at so late an hour. Generally Bunter grew grubbier and grubbier towards bed-time.

But washing off the jam had given the fat Owl a newly swept and garnished aspect. He was still sticky about the hair and the ears, but most of the jam was gone.

Sitting in the armchair, Bunter blinked continually at the clock. But he was too far from it to see the time with his limited range of vision. There was no reason why Bunter should not get up and step towards the clock, and blink at it at close range—except that he was lazy! But that was a very strong reason. It was easier to ask other fellows the time.

"I say, you fellows," Bunter began

So far, Poker Pike has put "paid" to all Chick Chew's stunts to capture Putnam van Duck, son of a Chicago millionaire. But Kidnapper No. 1 of the United States is a sticker with a professional pride to study. It's success or the "stone jug" with him, and he decides to make a supreme effort!

---

again, after two or three minutes, "I say, that ass Loder's late!"

It was up to Loder of the Sixth, that evening, to see lights-out for the Remove in their dormitory. Loder was not a very dutiful prefect, and was often unpunctual. But as bed-time for the Lower Fourth was nine-thirty, Loder of the Sixth was not due yet.

A dozen fellows glanced round at Bunter. Juniors were not, as a rule, keen on dorm. Hardly a fellow would have objected to staying up a little later than usual. Even Bunter was not usually keen on going to bed, though, once there, he was never willing to get out again.

"Loder's not late!" said Bob Cherry. "It's more than five minutes yet. What's the hurry, fatty?"

"Oh, nothing!" said Bunter. "I say, my watch says half-past."

"Your watch is like its owner—it can't keep to the truth!" remarked Frank Nugent.

"Yah!"

"Shut up, Bunter!" said Johnny Bull. "We're reading—or trying to read!"

Bunter was silent for about a minute.

"I believe that clock's slow!" he said, after that brief pause. "I say, Mauly, what's the right time?"

"Goodness knows!" answered Lord Mauleverer.

"Haven't you got your watch?"

"Yaas."

"Isn't it right?"

"Yaas."

"Then why can't you tell the right time by it, you fathead?" demanded Bunter.

"Because I'm not lookin' at it, old fat bean," yawned his lazy lordship, who was seated in an armchair, with his noble head resting on his hands clasped behind the noble head. When it came to laziness, Mauly was quite a good second to Bunter.

"Well, look at it, ass!" yapped Bunter.

"You look at it!" suggested Mauleverer.

"Yah!"

If Mauly was too lazy to stir, so was Bunter.

"I say, you fellows——"

"Cheese it!"

"What's the time, Smithy?"

"Time for you to shut up!" answered the Bounder.

"That slacking ass, Loder, is late!" said Bunter peevishly. "Prefects oughtn't to be late! Somebody ought to go and call him!"

"If you're sleepy, you fat ass, go to sleep in that chair, and dry up!" suggested Peter Todd.

"Oh, I'm not sleepy!"

"Then what do you want to get to dorm for, ass?"

"Eh! Oh, nothing!"

"What's biting the fat guy?" asked Putnam van Duck, staring at the fat Owl of the Remove. "Have you parked a packet of tuck in the dorm, Bunter?"

"Beast!"

Billy Bunter gave the American junior a withering glare through his big spectacles. It was more than half an hour since the cricket stump had smitten his tight trousers, at the cupboard in Study No. 1. But Bunter was still feeling painful twinges.

The Famous Five finished the "Holiday Annual," and Bob Cherry closed that volume with a bang. They strolled across to the window, which stood open, to let in the balmy summer air.

"Hallo, hallo, hallo, there's jolly old Poker!" grinned Bob.

In the dusky quadrangle, a figure in a bowler hat loomed up. It was Poker Pike, the gunman from Chicago. His hickory face and bowler hat glimmered at the open window, and his keen slits of eyes searched the room within.

"Say, you O.K., you Putnam van Duck?" he called out.

"O.K., you bonehead!" answered the American junior. "Walk your chalks, you gink! You figure that Chick Chew has come down a chimney after me?"

"I wouldn't put it past him!" answered Poker stolidly.

And the juniors chuckled. Since Putnam van Duck had been at Greyfriars, several attempts had been made by Chick Chew, star kidnapper of the United States, to "cinch" him. But only the watchful gunman fancied that even the enterprising Chick would dream of venturing into the school after the millionaire's son.

"We haven't seen him about, Mr. Pike!" said Harry Wharton, laughing.

"Mebbe you've seen him, without being wise to it!" retorted Poker Pike. "I'll say that guy Chick can make himself up like a pesky actor, and I sure wouldn't be s'prised if he horned in as a gasman or an insurance collector."

Bob Cherry chortled.

"There was a man came to mend a window in our dorm yesterday," he said. "Think that was Chick Chew?"

"Ha, ha, ha!"

"Mebbe, and mebbe not!" grunted Poker.

And the bowler-hatted gunman disappeared into the shadows of the quad, leaving the juniors laughing.

"I say, you fellows——"

"Shut up, Bunter!"

"But I say, what's the time?"

"Blow the time!"

"Well, look here, we oughtn't to be late for bed!" said Bunter. "Early to bed, early to rise, you know! Loder ought to be called! Lazy rotter, you know, slack as they make 'em; he's never on time!"

"What is that fat ass blithering about?" asked Bob Cherry. "If you've got tuck in the dorm, Bunter——"

"Oh, no! I haven't been up to the dorm!" said Bunter. "Quelch didn't tell me to go there and wash off the jam that beast Van Duck plastered over me, and I never went. Besides, I only went there to wash. If you think I've done anything to pay that beast out, you're jolly well mistaken!"

"Ha, ha, ha!"

"Blessed if I see anything to cackle at! I say, you fellows, one of you cut off to the Sixth, and tell Loder he's late."

"What has that fat duffer been up to in the dorm?" asked Vernon-Smith.

"Eh! Nothing!" said Bunter. "I haven't been to the dorm—we're not allowed to, as you know. And I never did anything while I was there. So far as I know. Van Duck's bed hasn't been ragged."

"Ha, ha, ha!" yelled the Removites.

They understood now why the fat Owl was so anxious to get to the dormitory. Evidently he had planned a deadly vengeance for the jam.

"You pesky piecan!" exclaimed Van Duck. "If you've been japing with my bed——"

"Nothing of the kind! How could I, when I haven't been to the dorm?" demanded Bunter. "If there's any soot in your bed, I know nothing about it. I never went to the dorm, and I only washed while I was there——"

"Ha, ha, ha!"

"Oh, shut up cackling!" exclaimed Bunter. "Look here, that slacking ass, Loder, is late——"

"Quiet!" hissed Bob, as Loder of the Sixth appeared in the doorway of the Rag. "Shut up!"

But Billy Bunter did not see Loder, and he did not shut up.

"I think it's jolly disgraceful for a prefect to slack like this!" he said warmly. "Loder always was a rotten slacker! I wonder the Head keeps him on as a prefect! He jolly well wouldn't if he knew what he was like. I dare say he's smoking in his study this blessed minute, with Carne and Walker. That's the sort of rank outsider Loder is——"

Billy Bunter stopped. He did not see Loder at the door, but the horrified silence of the Remove warned him something was amiss.

The juniors gazed at Gerald Loder. The expression on Loder's face was really extraordinary as he listened to Bunter's opinion of him.

Seldom did a Sixth Form prefect get such an unsolicited testimonial.

Loder strode in.

"I say, you fellows, what's the matter?" asked Bunter.

"Bunter!" roared Loder.

Then Billy Bunter knew what was the matter!

"Oh lor'!" he gasped.

Bunter had been too lazy to get out of the armchair to look at the clock. But he forgot that he was lazy now. He fairly bounded out of it.

"I—I say, Loder, I—I wasn't saying anything," he said. "I never knew you were listening at the door——"

If Billy Bunter hoped that that would improve matters, he was disappointed. Loder of the Sixth had his ashplant under his arm. He slipped it down into his hand and flourished it.

"Bend over that chair, Bunter!" he roared.

"Oh crikey! I—I say, Loder, I—I wouldn't have called you a rank outsider if I'd known you were listening!"

"Bend over!" bawled Loder.

"Oh jiminy!"

Whack, whack, whack, whack!

"Yow-ow-ow-ow!"

"Now get off to your dormitory, you young sweeps!" growled Loder, tucking his ashplant under his arm.

And the Remove marched off to their dormitory, Billy Bunter bringing up the rear, and looking as if he was trying to shut himself up like a pocket-knife as he went.

THE THIRD CHAPTER.

Soot for Somebody!

HARRY WHARTON & CO. were grinning when they arrived in the Remove dormitory.

Billy Bunter, who had his own weird and wonderful ways of keeping a secret, did not seem to be aware that he had given away his deep and deadly scheme of vengeance on Van Duck. But all the juniors looked at Putnam's bed as they came in.

At first glance, there was nothing amiss with it. At the second, traces of sprinkled soot could be seen. It was easy to guess that more was hidden inside.

Putnam turned back the bedclothes and looked. Then there was a ripple of laughter.

A large shovelful of soot had been deposited in the middle of the bed. The sheets were black with it.

"Great jumping toads!" ejaculated Van Duck.

"Ha, ha, ha!"

"I guess I can't turn into that bed!" said the American junior. "That pesky, pie-faced piecan——"

"Bunter, you howling ass!" exclaimed Harry Wharton.

"I say, I don't know anything about it!" exclaimed Bunter, in a hurry, as the American junior turned a grim look on him. "I haven't the faintest idea how that soot got there! I certainly never got it from the box-room. So far as I know, there isn't any soot in the old box-room chimney."

"There's less than there was, anyhow!" chuckled Bob.

"You pesky gink!" hooted Van Duck.

"Oh, really, Van Duck——"

"Think I'm going to turn into that bed after you've banked it up with soot, you fat piecan?"

"I didn't!" howled Bunter. "I told you in the Rag that if there was any soot in your bed, I knew nothing about it. All the fellows heard me."

"Ha, ha, ha!"

Loder of the Sixth looked in at the door. He was chatting in the passage with Walker, but the merriment in the dormitory drew his attention.

"Now, then, stop that row!" called out the bully of the Sixth. "Turn in! Do you hear? I'm not waiting long!"

From the doorway Loder, fortunately, could not see the sooty bed. No one wanted to draw the prefect's attention to it.

"I say, you fellows, don't you make out I did that!" gasped Bunter, as Loder turned away again. "There'll be a row about it, you know!"

"The rowfulness will probably be terrific!" chuckled Hurree Jamset Ram Singh.

"You blithering ass!" said Frank Nugent. "Mrs. Kebble will want to know who made those bedclothes sooty to-morrow!"

"Well, I know nothing about it!" said Bunter. "I wasn't in the dormitory at all when I came up here to wash——"

"Oh crikey!"

"And if that beast pitches into a fellow with a cricket stump, he can jolly well take what's coming to him!" said Bunter. "Not that I know anything about it, of course."

Grinning, the fat Owl of the Remove prepared to turn in.

Some of the fellows expected Van Duck to show signs of wrath. It was certain that whoever slept in that bed was going to have a rather sooty and uncomfortable time. But the American junior did not seem to be unduly worried or wrathy.

He was taking that fatheaded jape with unexpected indifference. His indifference, however, was explained when he was ready for bed.

He did not approach his own bed. He went to Bunter's.

Billy Bunter's eyes almost bulged through his spectacles as he saw the American junior turn into that bed.

"I—I say, you fathead, that's my bed!" he squeaked.

"Mine for to-night, I guess!" drawled Van Duck.

"Ha, ha, ha!" shrieked the Removites.

It was really a very simple way out of the difficulty for Van Duck. But it had evidently never entered the fat Owl's fat and fatuous head that this would be the outcome of his activity with the soot.

The expression on Billy Bunter's fat face was worth more than a guinea a box as he glared at Van Duck.

"Why, you—you cheeky beast!" he gasped. "Think you're going to have my bed?"

"I guess you can have mine!"

"It's all sooty!" howled Bunter.

"Waal, if you don't like soot, what did you bank it in the bed for? You figure that I like it?"

"Ha, ha, ha!"

"You—you beast! You gerrout of my bed!" gasped Bunter. "I say, you fellows, you turn that cheeky beast out of my bed!"

"Turn the soot out of Van Duck's first!" chuckled Harry Wharton.

"How can I, you silly ass? Look here, you Yankee beast, if you don't get out of my bed, I'll jolly well pull you out!"

"Get on with the pulling!" grinned Van Duck. "I guess you'll have to pull a whole lot, and then some, and a few over!"

"Loder'll make you get out, you beast! He knows that ain't your bed!"

"O.K.! If you want to tell Loder that you've banked soot in a bed, go ahead! I ain't stopping you!"

"Oh, you beast!" gasped Bunter.

Four from Loder's ashplant in the Rag were enough for Bunter. He did not want to draw Loder's attention to himself any more.

The Remove turned in, chuckling, leaving Billy Bunter blinking in dismay at the sooty bed. Pulling Van Duck out was rather too large an order for the fat Owl. But getting into a bed smothered with soot was horribly unpleasant. Billy Bunter was not fearfully particular on the subject of cleanliness, but even Bunter jibbed at a sooty bed.

"I say, you fellows——" he squeaked, in dismay.

"Jolly old Shakespeare says, 'tis

sport to see the engineer hoist by his own petard !" remarked Peter Todd.

"Blow Shakespeare! I say, I shall get all sooty if I get into that bed!" wailed Bunter.

"You'll have to wash in the morning, that's a cert!" said Bob Cherry. "Awful hard lines, old bean! You've had your wash for the term, haven't you?"

"Ha, ha, ha!"

Loder put in his head again, and reached the switch by the doorway to turn off the light.

"I—I say, Loder, I—I'm not in bed yet!" stuttered Bunter.

"Get in in the dark, then!" snapped Loder.

A more dutiful prefect might have

A pale glimmer from the high windows of the dormitory faintly revealed the fat figure in striped pyjamas.

"Oh lor'!" said Bunter.

There was a chuckle from the rows of beds. Billy Bunter's predicament, of his own making, seemed to entertain the Remove.

"I say, Wharton, you're head boy—you make that beast Van Duck get out of my bed!" howled Bunter. "You know jolly well Quelch wouldn't let a fellow bag another fellow's bed!"

"Think Quelch would let a fellow put soot in another fellow's bed?" inquired the head boy of the Remove.

"Beast! Look here, you Yankee rotter, I'll jolly well have you out of

He sat on the edge of the empty bed, rubbed his nose, and grunted.

"I say, you fellows——"

"Shut up!" said Bolsover major. "We want to go to sleep, if you don't!"

"But I do!" wailed Bunter. "But I can't go to bed in a heap of soot."

"Ha, ha, ha!"

"If you beasts are only going to cackle——"

"Ha, ha, ha!"

"Oh lor'!"

There was no help for it! Bunter had to go to bed in that sooty bed, or else sit up all night! Grunting with wrath, the fat junior groped at the bed, rolling up the heap of soot in the sheets, taking them off and depositing them under the bed. A great deal of the soot was

Up went Putnam van Duck's right hand with the cricket stump in it. It came down suddenly, and it came down hard, landing with a terrific whop on the tightest trousers at Greyfriars. Whack! "Yow-wooop!" yelled Bunter. "I ain't after your jam! Yow-ow-ow!"

noticed that one of the juniors was in the wrong bed. At the foot of each bed in the Remove dormitory was a box with the owner's name plainly inscribed thereon. So the name of W. G. Bunter was on the box at the foot of the bed now occupied by Putnam van Duck, and the name of P. van Duck was on the box at the foot of the empty bed at which Billy Bunter was blinking in dismal dismay.

But Loder, who was anxious to get back to his study to resume an important discussion on the subject of "gee-gees" with Walker and Carne and Price of the Fifth, noticed nothing, and would not have cared, anyhow. He had given the Lower Fourth time to turn in, and now he was going.

He switched off the light.

The dormitory door closed, and Loder walked away with Walker. Bunter was left standing in the dark

that bed if you don't gerrout!" hooted Bunter.

"Wade in!" chuckled Van Duck.

Billy Bunter rolled to the annexed bed. He was getting desperate. He groped for Van Duck to pull him out.

A finger and thumb fastened on a fat little nose.

There was a sound of squeaking and squealing in the Remove dormitory. Then Bunter's voice was heard in muffled tones:

"Wurrgh! Led do by dose, you beast!"

"Ha, ha, ha!"

"Pull away!" said Van Duck. "I guess I can pull a few, too."

"Ooooooooooogh!"

"Ha, ha, ha!"

Billy Bunter got his nose away. He immediately departed with it to a safe distance. He had had enough of pulling Van Duck out of his bed.

spilled over the blankets, but that could not be helped.

Bunter slid his fat figure into sooty blankets and laid his fat head on a sprinkled pillow. He grunted and snorted in an atmosphere of soot. For once Bunter's hefty snore did not awaken the echoes of the Remove dormitory a minute after his head touched the pillow. Almost for the first time in history Billy Bunter was the last man in the Remove to go to sleep.

THE FOURTH CHAPTER.

Easy Work for Chick!

"DARK!" murmured Chick Chew.

"You said it!" agreed Bud Parker in a cautious whisper. "Suits us fine!"

"I guess I'd like to see whether that

guy Poker is around!" muttered Bud, staring round him uneasily through his horn-rimmed glasses.

"I'll say that the less we see of that galoot the more I like it!" said Chick. "He sure won't see us to-night, unless he's a doggoned cat."

It was a fine summer night—but very dark. The two gangsters could hardly see one another in the shadowed quadrangle of Greyfriars.

At midnight the school was deep in silence and slumber. The last light had long been extinguished. The only sound that broke the stillness was the faint murmur of the wind from the sea in the branches of the old Greyfriars elms.

Standing by a little window—that of the lobby at the end of the Sixth Form passage—Chick Chew and Bud Parker watched and listened. They had entered the precincts of the school easily enough, by way of the old Cloisters. The deep darkness favoured them if watchful eyes were abroad. They stood silent in black shadow.

But for the presence of Poker Pike at Greyfriars the kidnapping of the Chicago millionaire's son would have been simply "pie" to an experienced kidnapper like Chick. But the gunman guardian had, so far, put "paid" to all Chick Chew's enterprises in that direction.

Mr. Vanderdecken van Duck, in far-off Chicago, had known what he was about when he hired a gunman to keep watch over his son at school in the old country.

But Chick was a determined guy. He admitted that that astute move on the part of the millionaire made his task more difficult. But he was not going to be left. Half a million dollars was the figure fixed for Putnam's ransom if the gangsters succeeded in "cinching" him. But that was not all. It was a matter of professional pride, too. Kidnapper No. 1 of the United States was not going to register his first defeat!

"O.K.!" murmured Chick. "I guess that guy Poker is fast asleep in his leetle bunk, and snoring."

"Sez you!" murmured Bud.

The horn-rimmed man was doubtful and uneasy. He had been pessimistic ever since the activities of the kidnappers had been transferred to the old-fashioned side of the Atlantic. Bud Parker would willingly have thrown down the enterprise and beaten it for Chicago, where a gangster had little to fear from "cops," and could buy his way out of the "can" if he found himself in that abode.

"Aw, park it!" growled Chick. "You figure that that guy Poker sits up all night with his optics propped open? Can it! I guess we got an easy run! That guy is located at the porter's lodge, and I'll say that suits me fine. He ain't nowhere around this shebang!"

Bud stared uneasily into the shadows.

Chick got busy with the lobby window.

That window was secured inside. But no window fastenings offered much difficulty to Chick. Chick had dabbled in all sorts of things before he found his true vocation as star kidnapper of the United States. Cracking cribs was an old game to Chick. No doubt the schoolmaster guys fancied that the House was safely secured from midnight intruders. Such an idea made Chick smile. The lobby window was open in a few minutes.

Chick was fat and bulky, but he was extremely active. He was through the window almost in a twinkling. He leaned out to whisper to Bud.

"You stick around and wait, Bud! I guess I'll be through in two shakes of a cat's tail.

Bud refrained from replying "Sez you!" But it was clear that he had his doubts and was in incessant dread of seeing a hickory face and a bowler hat loom up in the shadows.

"Ain't we got it all cut and dried?" whispered Chick. "Ain't I given the shebang the once-over and located that young gink in his dormitory? Did I heave a rock at a winder of that room three days ago and crack out a pane, or did I not?"

"You said it!" agreed Bud.

"Did I fix it with the builder's man to hand me his job of mending that winder, or did I not?" further inquired Chick.

"I'll say you did!" admitted Bud.

"Did I horn in here as a winder-mender, and nobody the wiser, or did I not?" pursued Chick. "Did I spot young Putnam's bed in his dormitory, or did I not? Was his name wrote fair and plain on the box along of his bed, or was it not? Do I know where to lay my finger on that gilt-edged young geck, or do I not, Bud Parker? I'm asking you."

"Yep!" admitted Bud.

There had been rather a "row" a few days ago over the cracking of a window in the Remove dormitory by a stone hurled by an unknown hand.

But nobody, certainly, guessed for a moment that the hand had been the fat hand of Chick Chew.

Neither, certainly, had anyone the remotest suspicion that the man who had come—or had been supposed to come—from the builder's at Courtfield was the star kidnapper of the United States in one of his many disguises.

By that astute device Chick had learned what he wanted to know—the exact location of Putnam van Duck's bed in the House.

With that knowledge clear in his astute mind, the rest was pie to Chick, if only the watchful gunman could be eluded.

"Waal, then," grunted Chick, "you want to believe that we're getting by with it this time, you Dismal Jimmy! You stick around till I hand you that young guy from this here winder."

"You got the chloroform pad?" whispered Bud.

Chick grinned, with a gleam of expensive American dentistry in the gloom.

"You figure I've left it at home on the grand pianner?" he retorted. "You stick around and don't ask fool questions."

Chick disappeared in the darkness within, leaving his horn-rimmed side-kicker to "stick around."

With a stealthy lightness amazing in so bulky a gangster, Chick threaded his way silently through a sleeping House.

His peculiar profession had given Chick an almost cat-like faculty of getting about in the dark without a sound and without a false step. Only once had he been able to give the interior of the House the "once-over"—when he had come there as a glazier to mend the dormitory window! But once was enough for Chick; all that he needed to know was clearly mapped in his keen and retentive mind.

The door of the Remove dormitory opened silently under Chick's stealthy hand.

All was densely dark within.

Only the palest of glimmers came from the high windows. The beds were merely darker shadows in darkness.

But Chick knew his way.

Noiselessly he stepped towards Putnam van Duck's bed.

In a dormitory occupied by about thirty boys it was likely enough that one might wake at any moment, if only to turn his head on the pillow. Chick could not venture to turn on the faintest glimmer of light, even for a moment. One startled voice would have given the alarm and knocked all his plans into a cocked hat.

Chick had a length of lead-piping at hand in the gangster style. He would have had no hesitation in using it. But in the present circumstances it was useless.

On the occasion when he had "cinched" Putnam at Wharton Lodge the American boy had had a room to himself. Then it had been easy.

In a school dormitory the matter was quite different. Chick was an active man in handling a length of lead-piping, but thirty heads were rather too many for the most active gangster to tap.

One shout would alarm the House—and once the alarm was given, Poker Pike would be very rapidly on the scene with his six-gun. All depended on carrying the enterprise through without an alarm.

Silently Chick stopped at the foot of Putnam's bed.

If any eye had opened, it would not have spotted him in the deep darkness. And he made no sound.

He knew which was Putnam's bed. There was no doubt on that point. He had made a special note of that.

But careful caution was second nature to Chick. He stooped over the box at the foot of the bed. He dared not show the faintest glimmer from a flash-lamp, lest an eye should open at an unfortunate moment. But he strove to read the name on the box.

Knowing what to expect to see there, he was able to make out enough to satisfy him that there was no mistake.

It was undoubtedly Putnam van Duck's box. It was, therefore, undoubtedly Putnam van Duck's bed.

Equally undoubtedly, the occupant of that bed was fast asleep—for a deep snore was proceeding from him.

Chick stepped soundlessly along the bed. He could not see the sleeper's face, except the palest glimmer. But the snore was an easy guide.

There was a faint, sickly smell as the chloroform pad approached the sleeping face. And Billy Bunter glided from deep into deeper sleep—from which he was not likely to waken for many hours!

THE FIFTH CHAPTER.

The Wrong Pig by the Ear!

"YOU got him?" breathed Bud Parker.

He stared in at the lobby window through his horn-rimmed glasses. Within, a shadow loomed up from the dark.

It was Chick Chew.

The fat gangster was breathing hard. Carried like a sack across his shoulder was a still figure wrapped in blankets.

"I should smile!" answered Chick.

"Wake snakes!" breathed the horn-rimmed man. "You got away with the goods this trip!"

"Sure thing!"

Chick rested his burden in the window. The chloroformed junior was rolled in the blankets from his bed. From one end of the roll of blankets the crown of his head showed; from the other end protruded his feet and a glimpse of striped pyjamas.

The fat gangster panted.

"I'll say they've fed him a few since he's been located in this here shebang!" he gasped. "I'll tell a man, I'd never have figured that he weighed half as much! Nor a quarter! They sure have fed him up like he was a prize turkey, judging by his doggoned weight."

"Say, you got the right guy?" Bud was uneasy and anxious. Failure after failure had damped his enthusiasm and his confidence in his leader.

Chick gave an angry grunt.

"You pesky bonehead, you figure that I moseyed around picking up a guy promiscus?" he demanded. "I got this baby out of Putnam van Duck's bed. You want to know whether some other guy was snoozing in his bed, and him out of it? Don't you waste your breath on fool talk, Bud Parker!"

"O.K.," murmured Bud. "If you got him dead to rights, the sooner we hit space the better for our health. I sure don't feel any too easy in my mind about that guy Poker."

"Poker nothing!" grunted Chick. "Take a holt on this guy, and get him off'n my hands."

Bud Parker took the bundle in the blankets, and fairly staggered under the weight as he received it.

Bud was not nearly so hefty as the fat gangster. And the weight of his prize had astonished Chick and made him pant for breath. Bud staggered under it, and almost collapsed.

He swayed, and lowered the blanketed bundle to the ground. It bumped there rather suddenly.

"Search me!" gasped Bud. "They sure have fed him up to the back of his neck, and then some! I'll tell a man, he's some weight!"

Chick clambered out of the window.

He wiped a spot of perspiration from his fat brow. Bud Parker panted for breath. Still and silent at their feet lay the figure rolled in blankets.

Bud, as he panted, listened anxiously. There was no sound of alarm. If Poker Pike was on the alert, he was nowhere near at hand.

Only too well the gangsters knew that Poker "moseyed" around at all hours of the night, on the watch for possible intruders. But if the gunman was on watch that night, the thick cloak of darkness favoured the kidnappers. Wherever Poker Pike was, he had not spotted them.

"Get to it!" muttered Chick.

He stooped, and took one end of the blanketed bundle. Bud Parker lifted the other.

Carrying the unconscious junior between them, they trod softly away.

Chick's eyes gleamed with satisfaction. At last, at long last, he had got away with the goods! Bud shared his satisfaction—but he also shared the weight of the kidnapped junior, and he found, like Cain of old, his burden almost more than he could bear!

"I'll say he weighs some!" he breathed stertorously. "I guess it's got me beat, Chick, that young guy putting on all this weight."

"He's sure fattened a lot!" said Chick. "I guess they feed 'em well at this here school, and a few over."

Bud opened his lips—and closed them again. It did not seem possible that Chick had made a mistake. Who but Putnam van Duck could have been sleeping in Putnam van Duck's bed?

What Van Duck weighed Bud did not know, but on his looks he would have expected the American junior to weigh less than half of this terrific weight. He could not help feeling a lingering doubt.

Chick Chew took the weight without undue exertion, but the weedy Bud almost crumpled under it.

"I guess I'll be mighty glad when we get him to the car!" he breathed. "I'll tell a man, this is making me tired."

"Aw, can it, and get on!" grunted Chick.

Bud canned it, and they got on. They passed silently into the black shadow of the old Cloisters.

There Bud lowered his end of the fat prize. Chick, not unwilling to take a brief rest, hefty as he was, followed his example.

"Say," murmured Bud, "it's sure safe here to turn on a glim——"

"What'll you want with turning on a glim?" grunted Chick.

"I guess it won't cost us anything to give him the once-over——"

"Aw, park it!"

"I'm telling you, Chick Chew, I don't get on to that guy Van Duck being so doggoned heavy!" panted Bud. "Looking at the young guy, who'd figure he weighed like he was a prize ox? Mebbe——"

Chick glared at him.

"Mebbe I'm a bonehead, and got the wrong pig by the ear!" he snarled. "And mebbe you know more about the kidnapping game than I do, Bud Parker! And mebbe you figure that some other guy was snoozing in Van Duck's bed! Say, you park your chin-wag, and don't talk foolish!"

"I guess I'd like to give that young guy the once-over!" urged Bud. "It sure has got me guessing, him being so goldarned heavy. He never looked it when I seen him."

Snort, from Chick.

"I guess a glim wouldn't be seen here," he growled. "Give him the once-over, doggone you, and then quit chewing the rag!"

Bud gave a cautious stare round through his horn-rimmed glasses. The old cloisters were dark and silent. The blanketed figure had been laid down behind one of the old stone pillars. It was safe to turn on a brief light.

The man in the horn-rimmed glasses bent over the sleeper and pulled the rolled blanket down to reveal the face. Then he jerked a flash-lamp from his pocket and turned the beam on the sleeper's face.

"Satisfied now?" grunted Chick.

"Search me!" gasped Bud, staring at the fat face revealed by the flash-lamp. "That ain't Van Duck!"

"Pack it up, you pesky stiff!" snapped Chick. "I guess——" But the next moment he broke off, his fat jaw agape, as he stared at the face of the sleeper in the gleam of the flash-lamp.

He stared at it in stupefaction.

It was not the face of Putnam van Duck! It was a face the gangsters had seen before—the face of William George Bunter! The prize had been hooked out of Putnam van Duck's bed in the Remove dormitory! But, only too clearly, it was not Putnam van Duck!

For a long moment Chick stood stupefied. That startling discovery bereft him of speech.

"You hit the wrong bed!" hissed Bud.

"I did not!" gasped Chick. "I'm telling you, Bud Parker, I hit the right bed! I'm shouting out to you, Bud Parker, that I hit Putnam van Duck's bed and got that guy out of it. They must have changed beds, and it ain't no use asking me why. It's got me beat!"

But Parker snarled.

"You got the wrong guy, you Chick! And if I hadn't made you stop and give him the once-over here, you'd have got him to the car. That fat gink, that's no use to nobody! I'll tell a man! You doped him once in mistake for Van Duck—now you've done hooked him out of bed in mistake for that young guy! You sure do seem to have a hunch for cinching that fat geck, Chick Chew!"

"How'd I know they changed beds?"

"How'd you know anything?" hissed Bud. "I guess the sooner you throw down kidnapping, and buy a candy store, the better! Mebbe you could sell candy without mistaking it for chewing-gum!"

Chick glared at his follower, and clenched a fat fist.

"If you're honing to have them arc-lights of yourn pushed back through your cabesa——" he snarled.

"Aw, can it!" sneered Bud. "What we going to do with this lard-faced boob? What's the use of him?"

"He ain't no more use than you are, Bud Parker! I guess I'm going back for the guy I want!" hissed Chick. "Turn that doggoned light off, you bonehead! You figure that we want publicity, and you playing at being an illuminated advertisement on Broadway?"

Bud, in his anger and dismay at finding Billy Bunter in the place of the millionaire's son, had forgotten the flashlamp in his hand.

He shut off the light.

"Now leave that fat gink there, and come back!" snarled Chick. "I guess——"

"Lissen!" breathed Bud.

"Aw, can it, you scared rabbit! I'm telling you——"

"Lissen!" hissed Bud.

There was a sound in the silence—a stealthy footfall. Bud's uneasy ears had caught it first—but Chick heard it now. Suddenly, from the darkness, came the blaze of a light—bright as a searchlight, backed by impenetrable darkness.

But the gangsters did not need telling who was behind that sudden glare of light. And they did not need telling that there was a gun in his other hand!

Chick forgot his idea of returning to make another attempt. He bolted along the shadowy Cloisters. After him scampered Bud.

"Stick 'em up, you 'uns!" came the deep roar of Poker Pike.

They ran hard.

Bang!

The six-gun roared, the bullet whistling among the stone pillars. The glare of light followed the gangsters, picking them up as they ran.

Poker, it was clear, was up and on the watch that night! Had the prisoner been Van Duck, no doubt the gangsters would have got him away before Poker established contact.

But that error in the dark dormitory had spoiled everything, from the kidnappers' point of view. In that startling and dismaying discovery, that they had the wrong pig by the ear, they had forgotten caution for a few moments.

Perhaps Poker had had a glimpse of Bud's flashlamp—perhaps he had caught a sound of angry voices. Anyhow, there he was!

There he was—picking up the gangsters as they fled, with the powerful light of the electric torch, following fast on their fleeing footsteps, and loosing off his six-gun as he followed!

Bang, bang, bang!

Chick Chew swung himself over the wall, and dropped, a breathless heap, into the lane outside the Cloisters. As he dropped, he heard a frantic yell and a fall on the inner side of the wall.

"I got it!" came Bud's howling voice. "I sure got it in the laig!" And another wild yell followed.

Chick bounded up.

He was on the safe side of the wall. Bud was on the unsafe side, with a bullet in his leg. Bud was a gone coon—but Chick was not the man to throw away his more valuable self on account of a lame duck who had been so injudicious as to stop a bullet! Chick Chew bounded away in the darkness, and did not stop running till he reached the car where Tug waited at the wheel. But Parker was in no state for running.

"I guess," remarked Poker Pike, as he stared down at the horn-rimmed man, in the glare of the electric torch. "I guess I got you, Bud Parker! Surest thing you know! I guess you want to be glad that we ain't in Chicago now, Bud, or you'd sure have cinched that pill in a place where you live. But they're powerful pertickler in this hyer country about shooting up a guy and making it last sickness for him! You want to be pleased that I let you have it in the laig, Bud!"

Bud groaned. No doubt he had reason to be pleased. But he did not look pleased, and he did not feel pleased. His wound was nothing to make a song or a dance about—only sufficient to stop his flight and hand him over to the grip of the Greyfriars gunman. But Bud's game was up—Chick Chew was hitting the open spaces, no doubt to try again; but Bud Parker was through with kidnapping for some years to come!

From the day they had transferred their activities to the old-fashioned side of the Atlantic Bud had been pessimistic. He had felt that England was no country for a gangster. And he had been right! Chick had overruled his objections—but he had been right! A country in which a guy could not buy his way out of the "can," was no country for gangstering!

And the hapless Bud, in the lowest of spirits, realised that he was booked now for a "can" from which there was no exit to be bought—he had to come before a judge who could not be bribed and a jury who were not for sale—and the dismal prospect made Bud feel like a two-cent remnant!

THE SIXTH CHAPTER.

An Alarm in the Night!

"THAT geck Poker!" exclaimed Putnam van Duck.

Every fellow in the school was awake.

The roar of Poker Pike's six-gun rang and echoed far and wide. It was followed by the flashing of lights and the banging of doors.

The Remove fellows sat up in bed and listened.

The echo of the firing in the quad died away; but there were many sounds from downstairs, hurrying feet and a buzz of voices.

"The jolly old kidnappers!" remarked Bob Cherry. "Poker wouldn't be blazing away for fun at this time of night!"

There was a patter of rapid feet in the dormitory passage.

The door was flung open, and the light flashed on. Mr. Quelch, in dressing-gown and slippers, hurried in.

He made straight for Van Duck's bed.

"Good heavens!" he ejaculated, as he saw that the bed was empty. "Then it is not a false alarm—the boy is gone!"

"Great pip!" gasped Bob, as he stared at the empty bed.

"Bunter's gone!" gasped Wharton.

Until the light was switched on, the juniors had had no idea that anyone was missing from the dormitory. Now all eyes turned on the empty bed.

"Wharton!" rapped out Mr. Quelch. "Van Duck appears to be missing. Have you any knowledge——"

"He's here, sir."

"What?"

"O.K., sir!" said Van Duck.

The Remove master spun round towards him, his eyes bulging in astonishment at the sight of the American junior sitting up in Bunter's bed.

"Oh!" he gasped. "I feared—I am glad to see that you are safe, Van Duck. But what does this mean? Why are you not in your own bed?"

"I guess I changed beds with Bunter, sir."

"What? You should have done nothing of the kind!" exclaimed Mr. Quelch. "You are very well aware that no such change is permitted! Why——"

"Some guy had been spilling soot in my bed, sir, and—and——"

"This is extraordinary!" exclaimed Mr. Quelch, with a glance at the empty bed. "Certainly, it appears to be sooty! Some foolish boy—— But never mind that now You caused me a moment of very painful alarm, Van Duck—seeing your bed empty, I feared that you had fallen into the hands of a kidnapper!"

"Sorry, sir——"

"But where is Bunter?" asked Mr. Quelch. "If you have changed beds, why is not Bunter in your bed, as you are in his? Bunter!"

Mr. Quelch stared round the dormitory. But there was no sign of the fat Owl of the Remove.

"Where is Bunter?" he rapped.

"I—I—I'm afraid that—that——" stammered Wharton. "Bunter was in Van Duck's bed, sir, when we went to sleep, and—and if the kidnapper has been here——"

"Oh!" gasped Mr. Quelch.

Bunter evidently was not in the dormitory. It was not difficult to guess that, occupying Van Duck's bed, he had been taken for Van Duck in the dark. That was, indeed, the only way of accounting for his absence.

Mr. Quelch hurried from the dormitory.

There was a buzz of voices from the excited juniors. Most of them turned out of bed, and gathered in a crowd at the doorway.

"I guess they got him!" muttered Van Duck. "I guess they been here, and they got that fat gink in the dark——"

"He was in your bed," said Nugent. "But how the thump would they know which was your bed, Van Duck? If they turned on a light, they would see that it wasn't you in the bed."

"Waal, they didn't see that it wasn't me, so I reckon they knew which was my bed," said Putnam. "I'll say Chick Chew has been around taking notes, some time or other. He knew which bed to hit. But I reckon that even Chick never guessed that a guy had changed beds."

The man in the horn-rimmed glasses jerked a flash-lamp from his pocket, and turned the beam on the sleeper's face. "Satisfied now?" grunted Chick. "Search me!" gasped Bud, staring at the fat face revealed. "That ain't Van Duck! You got the wrong guy, you Chick!"

"Hardly," said Harry Wharton. "If you'd been in your own bed——"

"I guess it would have been a cinch."

"But Bunter——" said Bob.

"They got no use for Bunter," said Van Duck. "As soon as they find they ain't got the right packet, I guess they'll drop it."

The juniors waited anxiously. Billy Bunter's fatuous jape on the American junior's bed had had an utterly unexpected result. It looked as if it had saved Van Duck from the clutches of the kidnappers, and caused the fat Owl to fall into those clutches.

Meanwhile, Mr. Quelch had hurried down the stairs. The great door of the House stood wide open, and light streamed out into the dark quadrangle.

Masters and prefects were up, half-dressed, staring out into the quad. The voice of Mr. Prout, the master of the Fifth, was booming.

"Absurd! An absurd alarm! I have been awakened by a sound of firing! Absurd, ridiculous!"

"A boy from the Remove dormitory is missing, Mr. Prout," said the Remove master. "Something has happened——"

"That gunman," said Mr. Wiggins. "Such a disturbance is really—really—really——"

"Here he comes, sir!" said Wingate of the Sixth.

A bowler-hatted figure loomed up in the light from the doorway. Every eye was fixed on it.

Poker Pike came up the steps, carrying what looked like a roll of blankets on his hefty shoulder.

He walked in and deposited the bundle on the floor, at the feet of the Remove master.

"Yourn, I reckon," he remarked.

"Bunter!" exclaimed Mr. Quelch.

He stared at the fat, unconscious face that looked from the roll of blankets.

"Chloroform, I reckon," said Poker tersely. "I guess it's got me beat how Chick picked up that fat gink, instead of the guy he was after; but I reckon he did. Say, where's that Putnam van Duck?"

"He is safe in his dormitory!" gasped Mr. Quelch. "I have just seen him and spoken to him."

"O.K.!" said Poker.

He lounged out of the House again into the dark quadrangle.

Billy Bunter was picked up by some of the masters, and carried up the stairs to his dormitory. There was a buzz among the Removites as Quelch, Prout, and Capper were seen coming up the corridor, breathing hard under the weight of the unconscious Owl.

"Hallo, hallo, hallo! Here's Bunter!"

"Thank goodness he's safe!"

The crowd of excited juniors surged back from the doorway as Bunter was carried in. The fat junior was placed in his own bed. It was clear that he was under the influence of chloroform; its faint, sickly odour was still clinging about him. It was likely to be some time before he returned to consciousness.

"You boys will return to bed," said Mr. Quelch severely.

The juniors went back to bed—though not to sleep. Mr. Quelch went down to his study to ring up the school doctor at Friardale.

He had finished his call, and was putting up the receiver, when there was a trampling of feet, and a buzz of voices in the passage. A bowler-hatted head looked into the study.

"Mebbe you'll ring up the cops?" suggested Poker Pike.

"The—the what?" ejaculated Mr. Quelch.

"The bulls," explained Mr. Pike.

"I—I fail to understand. I am about to ring up the police station."

"You got it," assented Mr. Pike. "You put them wise that I got a bird for them."

"A—a—a bird?"

"Surest thing you know."

Poker Pike turned back from the doorway, leaving Mr. Quelch staring. Then he reappeared, helping in a man in horn-rimmed glasses, who limped on one leg. Mr. Quelch stared blankly at Bud Parker.

"Who—who—who is this?" he stuttered.

"Chick's side-kicker," explained Poker briefly. "I guess I got him in the laig when he was hitting the horizon."

"Doggone you!" groaned Bud.

"Pack it up!" said Poker. "I guess you come out at the little end of the horn this trip, Bud. But you ain't got no kick coming."

"Is—is—is that one of the—the kidnappers?" stuttered Mr. Quelch.

"You said it."

"Bless my soul! And—and——"

"I guess I handed him a pill," said Poker. "But he ain't damaged a whole lot. Jest spilled some juice. Mebbe you'll let him stick here till the cops come along to tote him to the 'can.'"

He deposited the groaning Bud in Mr. Quelch's armchair.

"Bless my soul!" repeated the Remove master dazedly.

He rang up the police station at Courtfield. Half an hour later, Inspector Grimes arrived in a car. And in another half-hour Bud's dismal forebodings were realised, and he was safe in a "can," from which there was no escape.

THE SEVENTH CHAPTER.

Ginger-beer for Poker!

"HE, he, he!"

"Shut up, you fat ass!"

"Looks like an owl, doesn't he, in those barnacles?" grinned Billy Bunter.

Whereat the other fellows grinned.

The white-haired old gentleman who was pottering about in the quadrangle certainly had rather an owlish look, with a large pair of glasses perched on his nose. But that remark from the Owl of the Remove made the juniors smile.

It was several days since the excitement of the gangsters' visit to the school.

Bud Parker, safe in what he called the "can," was awaiting trial. Chick Chew, in parts unknown, was doubtless laying plans for another attempt on the Chicago millionaire's son at Greyfriars.

Dr. Locke hoped that his failure, and the capture of his associate, would discourage Chick, and cause him to give up his enterprise, and retire to the safety of his own country. Mr. Quelch shared that hope, and considered it probable.

Nothing, at all events, had been seen or heard of the gangsters since that eventful night.

But Poker Pike, keeping "tabs" on the heir to the Van Duck-millions, was as watchful and wary as ever. And Putnam did not believe for a moment that he was "through" with Kidnapper No. 1 of the United States.

Coming out of class in the summer afternoon, a good many fellows glanced at the old gentleman, whose white hair showed under his shining silk hat. He was peering through his glasses at an ancient date cut on the granite basin of the fountain. Some of the fellows smiled as he took out a magnifying-glass to give it a closer scrutiny. He was a stout, pink-complexioned old gentleman.

It was not uncommon for some old gentleman of archæological tendencies to visit the school, and potter about its antiquities. Greyfriars fellows regarded such old sportsmen with toleration.

"I say, you fellows, that gunman's got an eye on him!" remarked Billy Bunter, with another chuckle.

Poker Pike strolled over from the porter's lodge. His keen slits of eyes searched the harmless-looking old gentleman as he passed him.

Harry Wharton & Co. could not help grinning as the Greyfriars gunman came up to them. Poker was a wary guy, and they could see that he wanted to know about that stout, venerable-looking archæologist.

"That silly ass thinks everybody who comes to the school is after Van Duck," grinned Billy Bunter. "I've seen him squinting into the grocer's cart at the tradesmen's gate."

And the juniors chuckled.

"Say, who's that old guy?" asked Poker, jerking his thumb towards the old gentleman at the fountain.

"Some giddy archæologist!" replied Harry Wharton. "He blew in this afternoon."

"You wise to him?"

"Eh! I've never seen him before, if that's what you mean."

"You figure that he's one of Chick's side-kickers, you bonehead?" grunted Putnam van Duck.

"I guess Chick uses all sorts to play his game," answered Poker. "Mebbe that old guy's on the level, and mebbe he ain't. I'll say I'm keeping tabs on you, Putnam van Duck, while he's around."

"Aw, can it!" said Putnam. "You sure make me tired, Poker!"

"I say, you fellows, I know who he is," said Billy Bunter. "I heard him speaking to the Head in his study."

"Of course Bunter knows," grunted Johnny Bull. "He always will, so long as they make keyholes in the doors."

"Beast! I happened to be under the Head's study window, and it was open," said Bunter. "So I couldn't help hearing what they said. You see, the window was wide open, and I had stopped to tie my shoe-lace——"

"Lucky for you the Head didn't spot you listening under his window!" grunted Johnny Bull.

"I wasn't listening!" hooted Bunter. "I hope I'm not the fellow to listen. I couldn't help hearing what they said when I had stopped just under the window to pick up my handkerchief."

"As well as to tie your shoe-lace?" asked Bob.

"I mean, to tie my shoe-lace! Well, while I was picking up my shoe-lace—I mean, tying my handkerchief—that is, while I was tying my shoe-lace, I heard them jaw. He's Professor Belknap, and belongs to the Archæological Association, and he said that being in the neighbourhood, he took the liberty of calling——"

"I suppose the Head knows him!" said Harry.

"He jolly well doesn't," said Bunter, "because he said that he was pleased to make his acquaintance, and had heard of him."

"You heard a jolly lot, while you were tying that shoe-lace!" said Johnny Bull sarcastically.

"Beast! And the Head said——"

"Kick him!"

"Beast!"

Billy Bunter rolled away, just in time. Poker Pike lounged away, but he did not go very far. Evidently he was going to keep a special eye on Putnam, while the stranger was within the gates. Even a white-haired member of the Archæological Association was not above suspicion, in the wary eyes of the Greyfriars gunman.

Mr. Prout came out of the House and glanced round him. He stopped to speak as he passed the group of Removites.

"Wharton!"

"Yes, sir!" answered Harry.

"I understand that Professor Belknap, of the Archæological Association, is here," said the Fifth Form master. "Have you seen him? Can you tell me where he is?"

"Over there by the fountain, sir."

"Thank you, Wharton."

And the portly Prout rolled away to the fountain in the quad, no doubt to place his stores of knowledge at the disposal of the learned professor.

"That old bean will be sorry he called when Prout starts wagging his chin," remarked Bob Cherry. "What about ginger-pop?"

"Good egg!"

The chums of the Remove walked across to the school shop. After them walked Poker Pike.

Putnam van Duck gave a snort.

Putnam acknowledged freely that the Greyfriars gunman was necessary to his safety. More than once already, the watchful Poker had saved him from the wiles of Chick Chew. But he could not help feeling that Poker overdid the watchfulness, and "treading on his tail" within the school walls was rather too much of a good thing.

"Beat it, you bonehead!" he snapped, turning at the door of the tuckshop. "You big stiff, you figure that that old white-whiskered guy is going to snap me up and tote me off in his silk topper?"

"Ha, ha, ha!"

"Mebbe, and mebbe not!" answered Poker stolidly. "I guess I ain't losing sight of you, you Putnam van Duck."

"Vamoose, I'm telling you!"

"Forget it!" said Poker.

And the gunman followed the juniors into the school shop. A good many fellows were there, and there was a general grin at the sight of the gunman.

"Here comes the kid and his nurse!" said Skinner.

"Shut up, Skinner!" said Bob Cherry, as the American junior reddened.

Poker did not mind. He was quite indifferent to Skinner's little jokes, and the grinning faces of the other fellows. He was there to keep tabs on Putnam, and nothing else mattered to the dutiful Poker. But it was not surprising that Putnam was fed-up occasionally, with tabs being kept on him to such an extent.

The gunman stood like a graven image, while the juniors ordered ginger-pop.

Putnam, as he took a bottle of that refreshing liquid, gave him a glare.

"Say, you guy, you want to take a walk!" he snapped.

"Forget it!" answered Poker.

"You beating it?" demanded Van Duck.

"Not so's you'd notice it."

Putnam's eyes gleamed over the ginger-beer bottle. The cork was removed suddenly.

Fizzzzzzz!

Squish!

Splash!

"Yurrrooooop!" roared Poker, as the sudden stream caught him in his hickory face. "Say, what the thunder—gurrrrggh!"

"Ha, ha, ha!"

"Gurrrrggh! I guess—oooch!" spluttered Poker. "You pesky young piecan—urrrrggggh!"

"Ha, ha, ha!" yelled the juniors.

Poker staggered back, dabbing wildly at streaming ginger-beer. There was a howl of laughter in the tuckshop.

"Urrgh! You young gink, I guess I'll beat you up a few!" spluttered Poker. "I'll sure lam you, you Putnam van Duck! I guess——"

Poker was interrupted. There was a sudden roar of voices from the quad—

excited voices shouting from a dozen directions.

"Hallo, hallo, hallo! What's up?" exclaimed Bob Cherry. He rushed to the door, and the other fellows rushed after him. Putnam van Duck rushed with the rest, and Poker, dabbing streaming ginger-beer from his hickory features, for once failed to "keep tabs."

THE EIGHTH CHAPTER.

Some Surprise!

"LIKE this!" said Coker.

"For goodness' sake," said Potter of the Fifth, "mind what you're doing with that cricket ball."

"For the love of Mike——" urged Greene.

"If you fellows will shut up!" said Horace Coker, "I'll show you the trick of it! I'm not going to bowl, you silly asses! Think I'm ass enough to chuck cricket balls about in the middle of the quad?"

Potter and Greene dodged away from Coker.

Their opinion, it appeared, was that Coker of the Fifth was ass enough for that, or for anything else!

Certainly, they seemed very anxious not to stand in front of the great Horace while he was brandishing that cricket ball.

"What are you jumping about like kangaroos for?" demanded Coker angrily. "I'm simply going to show you the trick of it. I shan't let the ball leave my hand! Think I want to break windows, or knock that old sportsman's hat off, or bung Prout in the eye?"

"Well, mind you don't!" said Potter.

Potter and Greene were uneasy. They had cause to be uneasy. Even in the cricket field, nobody liked to be near Horace Coker when he had the ball in his hand. Unexpected things happened when Coker of the Fifth handled a cricket ball—unexpected, at least, by Coker. In such circumstances, only the wicket was safe.

Handling it in the quad was still more dangerous. Fellows were not allowed to buzz cricket balls about in the quad.

True, Coker was not going to carry his demonstration to the actual length of bowling! But his friends, knowing their Coker, were uneasy, and were likely to remain uneasy so long as Coker handled what—in his hands—was not merely a cricket ball, but a deadly weapon.

There were a lot of people about in the summer sunshine, after class. Dozens of fellows of all Forms were in the quad. A crowd of Remove juniors had just gone into the tuckshop, but the quad was well populated.

Quelch and Capper were walking by Masters' windows. By the fountain in the middle of the quad, Mr. Prout stood in conversation with the white-haired old gentleman, who, according to Bunter, had introduced himself to the Head as Professor Belknap, of the Archæological Association. Wingate and some of the Sixth were grouped in one spot—other fellows spotted about. If that ball left Coker's hand, with Coker's beef behind it, it was fairly clear that somebody was going to get damaged.

Any fellow, of course, could have demonstrated a bowling trick without letting the ball go. But with Coker, you never could tell. Potter and Greene, at all events, preferred to act on the maxim of safety first!

They hopped away from Coker, giving him plenty of sea-room. That action caused Horace to snort with annoyance.

"Watch me!" he snapped.

"We're watching!" called back Potter. They preferred safe-distance watching—still, they watched. It was only prudent to watch Coker when he was brandishing a deadly projectile.

"You get it like this," said Coker. "Your finger on the seam—see?"

"Oh! Yes!" said Greene. "I say, be careful."

"Don't be an ass, Greene!"

"Well, look here——" said Potter.

"Don't jaw, Potter!" said Coker. "Just watch! Like this!"

Coker's powerful arm swept.

As a bowler Coker of the Fifth might with luck have hit the side of a house, provided that it was quite a large house and Coker not very far off from it. But Coker's own idea was that he could bowl. A large-hearted fellow like Coker, in possession of valuable knowledge, naturally desired to impart some of the same to his less-gifted friends. Lack of enthusiasm on their part did not discourage Coker.

"Like this," repeated Coker.

Perhaps that tricky way of getting his finger on the seam prevented Coker from getting a very secure grip on the ball; or perhaps Coker was, as usual, simply a clumsy ass.

Anyhow, the ball flew. Coker did not intend it to leave his hand; but a cricket ball never heeded Coker's intentions—in Coker's grip it seemed to have a will of its own.

Whiz! went the ball.

"Oh!" gasped Coker.

He seemed surprised.

Potter and Greene were not surprised, they were only alarmed; they had quite expected something of the sort. They could only hope that if Coker hurled that deadly missile across a crowded quadrangle it would fail to find a billet—as a bullet is said always to do.

But there was no such good fortune; there were too many billets about for that whizzing ball to fail to find one.

Crash!

Yell!

"Oh crumbs!" gasped Coker.

"You've done it now!" stuttered Potter.

Coker had!

He had done it brown!

For a split second after that ball so unexpectedly left Coker's hand it was a painful problem who would stop it; then it was stopped as it crashed on the side of a venerable-looking head.

It missed Prout by a foot and banged on the head of the archæological gentleman with whom he stood in conversation at the fountain.

The crash and the frantic yell were followed by a heavy fall. Coker of the Fifth, if he lacked other qualities, had plenty of beef. There was lots and lots of beef behind that cricket ball. It banged on the white-haired head like a blacksmith's hammer.

The shining silk hat flew off and floated in the fountain; its wearer rolled at Prout's feet.

Prout gazed at him transfixed.

There was a roar all over the quad. Fellows rushed up on all sides; they shouted and stared.

Coker stood rooted, overwhelmed. He had not intended to do this, but he had done it—only too evidently he had done it.

"G-g-g-goodness gracious!" gasped Prout.

The Fifth Form master jumped to the fallen man; he dropped on his knees by his side; he raised a dizzy head in his hands.

Then he gave what could only be described as a squeal of amazement; for as he raised the half-stunned head of the archæological gentleman the venerable mop of white hair came off in his hands.

It revealed a close-cropped dark head.

Prout, on one knee with a white wig in his hand, remained a fixed figure of astonishment.

"What—what—what——" stuttered Prout.

"Oooooh!" gasped the sprawling man. "Oh! Great snakes! Ow!"

"What the thump——" gasped Wingate of the Sixth.

"I say, you fellows, it's a wig!" yelled Billy Bunter.

"Who——"

"What——"

Professor Belknap—if that was his name, which was very doubtful—raised himself dizzily on an elbow and blinked round him; his glasses had fallen off, but he did not seem to need them.

"Oh!" he gasped. "Oh! Oooogh!"

"What——" gurgled Prout.

"Seize him!" Mr. Quelch came hurrying up.

Prout was not quick on the uptake, but the Remove master was. A man in the school in disguise was enough to tell Quelch how the matter stood.

"An impostor! Detain him!"

The loss of his venerable white hair had strangely changed the visitor's looks. The close-cropped dark head was that of a man at least twenty years younger than he had appeared to be. An old gentleman with a bald head might have worn a wig for very good reasons, but a younger man with a good crop of natural hair could only have one reason for doing so. It was clear to Quelch and to others that the man was not Professor Belknap, of the Archæological Association, at all, but one of the kidnapping gang.

That he was a much younger man than he looked was proved when Mr. Quelch reached him and grasped at him.

Dizzy as he was from the crash of the cricket ball on his head, he dealt promptly and effectively with the Remove master.

A fist that seemed to Mr. Quelch like a lump of iron lashed out, and Henry Samuel Quelch went over backwards, almost heels over head.

He crashed on his back and lay gasping.

The disguised man scrambled up.

He was a stout man, but evidently extremely active. There was a lump on his head where the cricket ball had smitten, and his brain must have been spinning from the shock, but he leaped away with the activity of a kangaroo.

"Collar him!"

"Kidnapper!"

"He's downed Quelch!"

"Bag him!"

It was a roar of voices all over the quad. It brought Harry Wharton & Co. helter-skelter from the tuckshop.

Putnam van Duck gave a yell as he saw the stout figure, hatless, streaking for the gates.

"Chick!"

"What?" gasped Harry Wharton. "That old bean——"

"Chick Chew!" shrieked Putnam.

"After him!" roared Bob Cherry.

Five or six fellows, nearer to the spot, sprang at Chick as he ran. His powerful arm swept round; Wingate of the Sixth reeled in one direction, Gwynne in another. Blundell of the Fifth jumped in his way, and spun over like a ninepin. With a yelling mob at his heels, the disguised gangster ran like a deer for the gateway.

"Secure him!" Prout was booming.

"Secure the scoundrel! In disguise—a palpable disguise! An impostor! Secure him!"

But it was not so easy to secure Chick. Gosling appeared in the gateway—and jumped promptly aside as the desperate man came speeding at him. Chick flew out into the road.

"Poker!" yelled Putnam.

But Poker Pike was mopping streaming ginger-beer from his hickory face.

Running like a deer, the gangster disappeared out of the gateway. A shouting mob poured out after him—and crowded back as a car driven at a reckless speed roared down the road. The hatless man leaped on the running board as it reached him, and the car vanished in the distance in a cloud of dust. Chick Chew was gone!

THE NINTH CHAPTER.

Hard Lines on Quelch!

"POOR old Quelch!"

"Quelch is hurt!"

"I say, you fellows, old Quelch is knocked out!"

A crowd gathered round the Remove master.

Mr. Wiggins and Mr. Capper raised him from the ground. Dr. Locke was seen hurrying down from the House. Greyfriars buzzed and rang with excitement from end to end. Prout stood with the white wig still in his hand. Potter of the Fifth captured the silk hat that floated in the granite basin of the fountain.

Chick Chew was already far away, and he had left those relics behind him. Poker Pike, still dabbing ginger-beer, looked at them grimly. Coker of the Fifth blinked at them. Coker had little dreamed what was going to be the result of his demonstration of that trick of bowling to Potter and Greene.

"What—what has happened?" The Head came up. "Mr. Quelch—— Bless my soul! He appears to be unconscious!"

"Poor old Quelch!" breathed Bob Cherry.

Chick had hit the Remove master only once—but Chick was a hard hitter. Quelch hardly knew what had happened to him. It might have been the kick of a mule. He was half-stunned; and he sagged, a helpless weight, in the supporting arms of Wiggins and Capper.

"Who threw that ball?" Prout was booming as the Head came up. "It was most fortunate—most fortunate! I was completely deceived by that wretched impostor! But who——"

"I did, sir," stammered Coker. "I—I—I——"

"What—what——" exclaimed the Head. "Who—who——"

"An impostor, sir!" boomed Prout. "A rascal, sir, in disguise! Evidently, sir, one of the kidnapping gang, and certainly not Professor Belknap at all!"

"Bless my soul!"

"I'll say it was Chick!" grunted Poker Pike. "It was sure Chick! I guess he was here after that Putnam van Duck."

"But—but——" gasped the Head. He had not had the remotest doubt of Professor Belknap's bonafides, when that archæological gentleman had introduced himself.

"Surest thing you know!" grunted Poker. "And I'll mention that if I'd been around he wouldn't have vamoosed the ranch so easy! You pesky young piecan, you Putnam van Duck——"

"A boy of my Form, sir, exposed him!" boomed Prout. "This boy, sir—Coker of my Form, sir—knocked him over, sir, with a cricket ball. How Coker discovered that he was an impostor, sir, I do not yet know; but undoubtedly, sir, Coker acted with great presence of mind—a boy of my Form, sir."

"Oh crikey!" gasped Coker.

Horace Coker realised that this matter was not going to turn out so badly, after all!

Had the archæological gentleman been genuine, certainly Horace would have been booked for very serious trouble, for nearly braining him with a cricket-ball. It was rather fortunate for Coker, if not for Quelch, that that archæological gentleman had proved to be Chick Chew in one of his many disguises.

"Bless my soul!" said the Head.

"A boy of my Form, sir!" boomed Prout, evidently greatly pleased by the fact that it was a Fifth Form man who had revealed the trickery of the impostor, by displaying such presence of mind. "This boy, sir, Coker—— But for this boy Coker, sir, the cheat would not have been discovered—the wretch would have been here carrying out his dastardly plans——"

"Please bring Mr. Quelch into the House!" said the Head. "My dear Quelch——"

"I—I can walk, sir!" panted the Remove master. Quelch hated fuss, and had no desire whatever to figure as a lame duck.

"My dear Quelch——" said Wiggins.

"My dear fellow——" said Capper.

They assisted Quelch to the House. In point of fact, Quelch found that he needed assistance. A sympathetic crowd followed—Prout still booming.

"A boy of my Form—remarkable presence of mind—very remarkable indeed—a boy of my Form!"

"Good old Coker!" said Bob Cherry. "But how the thump did Coker know that he was a jolly old gangster? He didn't look it."

"The howfulness is terrific."

"How did you know, Coker?" a dozen fellows demanded, as Mr. Quelch was taken into the House.

Coker gasped.

"I—I didn't!"

"You didn't!" howled Bob.

"Nunno! It was an accident!"

"Oh crikey!"

"Ha, ha, ha!"

"Better not tell Prout that!" chuckled Nugent.

"Ha, ha, ha!"

"Wonderful presence of mind to weigh in with an accident!" chortled the Bounder. "Were you chucking that cricket ball at Prout, Coker?"

"No, you young ass! I was showing Potter and Greene a bowling trick, and it slipped from my hand somehow——"

"Ha, ha, ha!"

Everybody was concerned about Mr. Quelch; but Coker's explanation furnished a little comic relief!

When the juniors went in to tea, it was rumoured that Quelch had been taken into "sanny" and the school doctor telephoned for. Billy Bunter rolled into Study No. 1 with news, while the Famous Five were at tea there with Putnam van Duck.

"I say, you fellows, Quelch has got the K.O.," announced Bunter. "This may mean a day off to-morrow. I say, I'll have some of that cake! I say, I wonder if we shall get a holiday. Just like the Head to fix us up with extra French if Quelch can't take us! You know these schoolmasters! Still, I'd rather have Mossoo than Quelch, so that's all right, really."

"You fat villain!" said Bob.

"Oh, really, Cherry! I say, I hear that old Prout has let Coker off some lines! He, he, he! First time he's ever been pleased with Coker. Bet you Coker won't tell him it was an accident and Prout might have got it himself! He, he, he!"

"Poor old Quelch!" said Harry Wharton.

"Oh, yes, sorry for old Quelch!" assented Bunter. "But if we get off Latin to-morrow, it won't be so bad! There's a silver lining to every cloud, you know. I say, I'll have some of those doughnuts. Quelch is going to have a pair of black eyes! I saw him going into sanny. Fancy Quelch with black eyes! He, he he! I say, Van Duck, Quelch will be fed up with having you here. I say, you fellows, do you think Quelch will turn up in the Form-room with his eyes blacked? Bit undignified, what? We may get out of Latin for a week or more!"

"Kick him!" said Johnny Bull.

"Beast!"

Billy Bunter rolled out of Study No. 1, to carry further the glorious news of the possibility of getting out of Latin for a week or more!

"Poor old Quelch!" said Putnam van Duck. "I'll say it's fierce for him! I reckon I wish Poker had been on the spot with his gun, when that bonehead Coker knocked Chick over. If he'd got Chick, I guess the kidnapping game would be up and I'd have a chance of seeing Chicago again."

"Tired of Greyfriars?" asked Bob, with a grin.

"Nope! But I guess popper wants me home," said Van Duck. "But the United States ain't no place for me so long as Chick's on the warpath! He ain't got me here, but he'd sure cinch me fast enough on the other side of the pond. It wouldn't be any use if the cops got him—Chick is rich enough to buy himself out of the 'can.'"

"Nobody in England is rich enough to do that!" chuckled Bob.

"You said it!" agreed Van Duck. "I guess Pop is wise to that! If they get Chick on this side of the pond Chick will be parked safe, and the popper can have me home. I'm telling you, the popper knew what he was about, when he sent me here. But they ain't got Chick yet—though I reckon that Poker would have got him, if I hadn't been fooling around with that pesky ginger-beer."

After tea, the juniors went down to get news of Quelch. They learned that he was in "sanny," and that the school doctor had attended him. It was rumoured that he was booked for the school hospital for some time. No doubt Mr. Quelch was suffering from severe shock; and still more probably, he was unwilling to show up in public with blackened eyes. Anyhow, the Remove had lost their Form-master for the present.

And that they had lost him for some time to come was clear, when it was learned that the Head had telephoned to Leggett & Teggers for a temporary master to take his place.

Which Billy Bunter declared was just like a schoolmaster! Bunter declared that if they were going to have a new beak in the place of the old beak, Quelch might just as well not be ill at all! But as the Head omitted to ask Billy Bunter's advice in the matter, a temporary master for the Remove was due to arrive at an early date.

Poker Pike drew back a few paces, and launched himself at the door. A hefty shoulder, with all the gunman's beef behind it, drove on the oak, with a terrific crash. "Oh crikey!" gasped Bob Cherry, as the door flew open. Saloman, in a dressing-gown, was standing in the middle of the room, his eyes blinking behind his glasses.

THE TENTH CHAPTER.

Missing Mr. Saloman!

"SALOMAN!"

"That's the name!"

"I say, you fellows, is he a Jew?" asked Billy Bunter.

"Shut up, fathead!" growled Bob Cherry.

It was a couple of days later; and the news had spread that the temporary master of the Remove was arriving that afternoon. The firm of Leggett & Teggers supplied temporary masters, or any sort of masters, at short notice; and Mr. Saloman—whoever Mr. Saloman might be—had been duly supplied by that well-known scholastic agency. Some of the Removites were discussing the matter, and wondering what the temporary "beak" would be like. As Monty Newland of the Remove was in the group, and Monty was of the ancient race of Israel, Billy Bunter's question was not in the best of manners.

"Oh, really, Cherry! It sounds rather like a Jew!" said Bunter. "If he is, I dare say Newland will get on with him, what? He, he, he! I don't think much——"

"Why say much?" asked Newland. "You mean you don't think at all."

"The muchfulness is not terrific!" grinned Hurree Jamset Ram Singh.

"I was going to say I don't think much——"

"First time I've ever heard Bunter tell the truth!" remarked Frank Nugent.

"I was going to say I don't think much——"

"Tell us something we don't know!" suggested Johnny Bull.

"Will you let a fellow speak?" howled Bunter. "I don't think much of Jews! Look at Newland, f'rinstance! Stingy! Only yesterday, I asked him to cash a postal order for me, and he said he would cash it as soon as he saw it——"

"Ha, ha, ha!"

"Blessed if I see anything to cackle at! Speaking of postal orders," went on Bunter, "I told you fellows I was expecting one, I think. If you'd like to let me have the five bob, Van Duck——"

"Guess again!"

"I suppose Americans are as stingy as Jews," said Bunter. "You'll let me have that five bob, won't you, Wharton?"

"No!"

"If you're going to be as stingy as Van Duck and Newland——"

"Just!" agreed Wharton.

"I say, Bob, old chap——"

"No good old-chapping me!" said Bob Cherry sadly. "I haven't got five bob."

"Ha, ha, ha!"

"Nugent, old fellow——"

"No good old-fellowing me!" grinned Nugent. "I haven't, either."

"I say, Johnny——"

"Go and eat coke!" grunted Johnny Bull.

"I say, Monty, old bean——"

"If you call me Monty, I'll kick you, Bunter!" said Newland.

"Beast!"

Evidently Billy Bunter's celebrated postal order was not going to be cashed till it arrived. And that distant date was no use to Bunter.

"What about walking down to the station?" asked Harry Wharton. "I hear that Saloman is coming by the four-thirty."

"Catch me walking miles to meet a Jew!" grunted Billy Bunter.

"Nobody asked you, sir, she said!" sang Bob Cherry. "Let's! It will show the Saloman-bird what nice chaps we are, and how we love our kind teachers, which always does a beak good."

"Rot!" said Bunter.

But it did not seem rot to the Famous Five. A walk across the green common in the June sunshine was pleasant enough; and they were rather interested to see the new beak, who was to take Mr. Quelch's place in the Remove Form-room for a week or more.

As they were going to have at least a week of him, such a polite attention on his arrival might make a good impression, which might prove useful when they came to deal with him in the Form-room. And as they had nothing special to do till tea-time, the chums of the Remove decided on the walk.

As the Famous Five and Van Duck went down to the gates, a bowler-hatted figure rose from the bench by Gosling's lodge.

"Moseying out?" asked Poker Pike.

"Yep!" answered Bob Cherry gravely. "Surest thing you know, old-timer."

And the juniors grinned as they walked out—the Greyfriars gunman walking after them.

Van Duck made a grimace. Mr. Saloman might be pleased at being met at the station by members of the Form he was to take at Greyfriars. But he was likely to be more surprised than pleased

(Continued on page 16.)

DOCTOR BIRCHEMALL AND THE GIPSIES!

A Side-Splitting Story of St. Sam's

By DICKY NUGENT

"The Head's a beest!"

"Hear, hear!"

Doctor Alfred Birchemall frowned. It was a hot summer's day, and the revered and majestick headmaster of St. Sam's was taking his ease amongst the branches of a tree in Muggleton Woods. He had a bag of toffy in his lap into which he was dipping with grate relish.

In his enjoyment the Head had almost forgotten where he was. But the voices beneeth him woke him up with a vengenz.

Peering down cautiously through the leaves, he saw that several juniors belonging to St. Sam's were sawntering through the woods towards the skool.

"Sawcy yung raskals!" said the Head to himself. "How dare they refer to me as a beest! I wonder what I've done to call fourth such disrespective langwidge?"

As if in answer to that question, Bill Bright's voice came floating up to him.

"It's just like Doctor Birchemall to go and detain Fearless on the very day were were relying on him to play kricket!" said Bright. "Why couldn't the old fogey detain Tubby Barrell or someone else who didn't matter?"

"'Old fogey'!" choked the Head. "And me only ninety-nine next birthday! Why, I'll slawter 'em! I'll——"

"The old buffer couldn't have chosen a worse time for detaining Fearless," he heard Merry saying from far beneeth him. "They say the St. Pete's team are as hot as mustard this year, and we can't possibly lick them without Fearless. Is it any good appealing to the Head, I wonder?"

"Some hoaps!" said Stedfast, with a merthless larf. "You'd stand as much chance as if you appealed to Nero!"

From his seclooded nook high up in the branches of the tree, Doctor Birchemall cullered with vexation. Before he had time to yell down an indignant protest, however, Jack Jolly was speaking—and Jolly's words made Doctor Birchemall decide to keep quiet a little longer.

"Got it!" was Jolly's eggsclamation. "I've got a brane-wave, you fellows—a brane-wave for diddling the Head and setting Fearless free for the afternoon!"

"The dickens you have!"

"Coff it up, old chap, then, for goodness' sake!"

"Seeing those gipsies near the skool this morning gave me the idea," grinned the kaptin of the Fourth. "Breefly, the wheeze is this: we'll disguise ourselves as gipsies——"

"Wha-a-at?"

"Then wait for the Head when he comes back from his walk to Muggleton and kidnap him!" went on Jack Jolly, eggsitedly. "We can easily lock him up somewhere for the afternoon, and once he's out of the way, Fearless can play kricket for us without the slitest risk of anyone interfering. Afterwards, of corse, we can pretend to find the Head by axxident. He'll never suspect that we were the real kidnappers all the time!"

"My hat! What a spiffing wheeze!"

"It's a corker, old chap, and no mistake!"

"Glad you like it!" chuckled Jack Jolly. "If you're all in faver, then, we'd better get bizzy at once. Forchunitly, we've some gipsy costumes among the drammattick society's props. Let's hop back and fetch them. Then we can change in the woods and lie in wait for the Head!"

"Right-ho, old fellow!"

The juniors tramped off; and as their voices died away, Doctor Birchemall gave vent to his feelings in a long, gloating larf.

"Ho, ho, ho! So, my bewties, you plan to lay hands on the sacred person of your headmaster, do you?" he muttered, leering, as he helped himself to another toffy. "What a shock you'll get when you find that my eagle eyes have pennytrated your disguises! Ho, ho, ho!"

Doctor Birchemall remained up the tree for nearly half an hour to give Jack Jolly & Co. time to change into their costumes and prepare their ambush. Then he lowered himself down to the ground and strolled at a lezzurely pace along the footpath leading to St. Sam's.

When he saw a number of pictcheresque figgers taking cover behind some bushes and trees ahead of him, he nearly busted himself larfing. But, with a grate effort, he mannidged to put an innersent eggspression into his face, as he walked into the ambush.

"Grab heem, brothers!"

It was a horse shout from the bushes. Doctor Birchemall stopped and glanced towards them like a startled fawn. A moment later half-a-duzzen darkskinned gipsies sprang into view and made a rush at him.

The Head of St. Sam's pretended to be scared out of his life, though inwardly he was larfing fit to bust.

"Spare me!" he cride. "Have mersy, kind friends!"

"Seeze the dog, brothers!" wrapped out the leader of the gipsies. "Take heem to our camp an' there we weel hold heem to ransom!"

"Lumme! These lads can certainly act!" thought Doctor Birchemall to himself, as the gipsies seezed him. "As for their disguises, it is impossibul to see through them. But that duzzent matter much. They'll be all the more serprized when I call out their names and order them to let me go! Ha, ha, ha!"

And the Head marched along in the midst of his swarthy captors, pretending to weep, whereas he was in reality shaking with larfter!

After marching for about five minnits, Doctor Birchemall decided that the joak had gone far enuff. He came to a sudden stop and glared at the gipsy band.

"Boys!" he roared. "How dare you"

"What you say, dog?"

"How dare you attack your own headmaster like this!" stormed the Head. "You thought you'd hoodwink me, disguising yourselves! But your disguises are useless when you're dealing with a lynx-eyed person like me! Jolly! Merry! Bright! Stedfast! I reckernise all of you!"

"Maledictos! The dog, he ees mad!"

"So will you be, my pippin, when you feel my birch-rod dusting your trowsis!" grinned the Head. "Ha, ha, ha! Gipsies, indeed! Why, you're no more like real gipsies than I am myself! Fall in, you young welps!"

Then Doctor Birchemall receeved a seveer shock. For, instead of falling in, the gipsies seezed him more tightly than ever, and, to add to the Head's serprize, whipped out daggers and nives, which they started flurrishing in a most alarming fashun!

"To the camp with heem!" cride the gipsy leader.

Doctor Birchemall gave a yell.

"Yarooooo! I'll birch you black and blue! Wait
till I get you bac
skool, you yung
and I'll——"

Then the truth
dawned on the H
his few remaini
stood up on end
horror.

"I—I say, you
he stuttered. "A
Jack Jolly and his
then?"

"Jack Jolly?
know thees Jack
snarled one of the

"M-m-my hat
you're real gipsies

"What you th
were, dog?"

The Head's nee
wobbled. He le
frenzied howl.

"Help! Murde
lice! Reskew, St.

And then to th
releef there was a
ing shout from th

"This way, you
Coming, sir!"

A few seconds la
a-duzzen juniors,
Jack Jolly, came
into view and, wit
slitest hezzitatio
themselves at
Birchemall's would
nappers.

Plonk!

Jack Jolly's fis
with terribul force
leader's jaw, and t
dropped to the gr
a log.

Bang! Crash!

Merry and Bri
Stedfast felled thr
with blows that w
felled an ox. The
and Trew nocked
maining two uncor

"So much for
remarked Jack Jo
temptibly. "Shal
the perlice, sir, a
over the scound
justiss?"

WOULD YOU BELIEVE IT?

Tom Dutton made his study-mates grin when he said he never believes a word he hears from Bunter. Dutton is rather hard of hearing, and rarely catches Bunter's mumble, whether it is the truth or not! But, in spite of his disability, Dutton's judgment is shrewd. He had "heard" aright about Bunter!

Scoring a brilliant century against St. Jim's, George Wingate enabled the Greyfriars First XI. to win by three wickets. Kildare, of St. Jim's, hit up 65—but as Removites watching loyally said, there was no batsman to compare with Wingate. Getting his 114 not out, he looked set for "centuries"!

**Billy Bunter was sayin
summer holidays ought
greatly extended, when Mr.
overheard him. Quelch re
Bunter that as he cannot
as much as the other fello
term of the present leng
would be almost a complet
if it were any shorter!
looked—and felt—"idioti**

ARTON. June 13th, 1936.

'Nunno, Jolly, don't
bble; perhaps they've
rned their lesson from
s!" gasped the Head.
.et's return to St. Sam's,
vs, and thanks awfully
what you've done!"
'Don't mensh, sir!"
ned Jack Jolly. "It's
lezzure!"
Doctor Birchemall's
newhat greenish eyes
on a portmantoe the
iors were carrying, bear-
the label "Fourth Form
matick Society," and
coffed.
'Ahem! I feel all the
e that I should like to
something to commem-
te this suspishus oc-
on," he said. "Per-
s the best way of doing
will be to cancel Fear-
' detention this after-
n. You may tell Fear-
, my boys, that he is
to play kricket this
rnoon if he wishes!"
Honest injun, sir?"
Honner bright!"
ned the Head.
Hip, hip, hooray!"
nd Jack Jolly & Co.
rned to St. Sam's,
ring. Frank Fearless
turned out against St.
's that afternoon and
ed the home team to
a grate viktory against
visitors. And nobody
had the slitest idea
Doctor Birchemall
v all about Jack Jolly's
e wheeze for kidnap-
the Head.
hich only went to
that even an old
t like Doctor Birch-
ll had his good points!

ook out next week for irst instalment of Dicky ent's rib-tickling new l, "DOCTOR BIRCH-ALL'S DUBBLE!")

ALONZO TODD says—

BUNTER SHOCKS—NAY, DISGUSTS ME!

It has always been my earnest endeavour to help fellow creatures in distress. But I must confess that the juvenile known as Billy Bunter causes me at times to entertain serious doubts as to the wisdom of that aim!

The incident which occurred yesterday, is alas, typical! Whilst directing my pedal extremities towards Greyfriars, I caught up with Bunter and found him wheeling along the mangled remains of an article of vehicular locomotion, to wit, a bicycle. He appeared to be in a mood of despondency; but he brightened up at my approach.

"I say, 'Lonzy, would you mind wheeling this jigger back to the bike-shed for me?" he asked. "I've had an accident with it."

"So I observe, my dear Bunter," I remarked. "I trust that you suffered no personal injury?"

Bunter's response was to supply me with a list of supposed injuries of such imposing dimensions as to give me the melancholy impression that he could

not be adhering to the strict truth. Nevertheless, I agreed to assist him, and accordingly wheeled the damaged vehicle to the bike-shed.

Alas! I had scarcely taken a dozen steps before that impetuous juvenile, Vernon-Smith, assaulted me with very great severity and deprived me of the custody of the bike.

Now mark the sequel! When I informed Bunter about this extraordinary episode, he was affected not by sympathy but by risibility—in fact, he laughed quite immoderately. On inquiring the cause, I elicited from him the distressing facts that the damaged bicycle belonged to Vernon-Smith and that he had borrowed it without that juvenile's permission and handed it to me so that Vernon-Smith should assume that I was the person responsible!

Truly, such behaviour can be described as nothing less than reprehensible. I must say that Bunter shocks—nay, disgusts me!

FOR SALE!

Asbestos Suit, guaranteed fire and heat-proof. Just the thing for your fag to wear when he's making your morning toast.—Write or call, OLIVER KIPPS, Study No. 5, Remove.

TOM BROWN explains—

WHAT WINGATE MEANT BY ENTOMOLOGY!

Remove cricketers were sadly disappointed the other "halfer" when Wingate came down to Little Side to say he couldn't keep his promise to spend the afternoon coaching them.

"What's the matter, old bean?" asked Bob Cherry, seeing that Wingate was dressed for going out. "Taking up hiking?"

"No. I'm taking up entomology as a matter of fact!" was Wingate's reply, and the crowd stared.

"Entomology?" said Wharton. "That's the study of insects, isn't it?"

"Just that! But don't get alarmed, kid," added Wingate, noting the look of dismay in Wharton's face. "I'm only doing it for this particular afternoon—in fact, if I catch the specimens I'm after I may get back in time to give you an hour. Let's hope for the best!"

And Wingate, with a nod, marched off.

Frankly, the fellows were staggered. Hobbies like insect-collecting had always in the past been associated with guys like Alonzo Todd. Certainly nobody had ever imagined a chap like Wingate going in for entomology. But there it was, anyway; Wingate himself had said it, so presumably it was true. The chaps could only hope it was a passing fad and that Wingate would soon get it over.

They needn't have worried! Wingate came back within a couple of hours with the specimens he had set out to capture and, after handing over the said specimens to the tender mercies of Mr. Quelch, he duly trotted down to Little Side and coached the Remove for the rest of the afternoon. Wingate's spasm for entomology, it seemed, was completely at an end.

Incidentally, I ought to explain that by entomology Wingate didn't mean collecting insects of the usual kind. Oh dear, no!

What had actually taken him out was a rumour that certain Remove chaps had planned a card party in the woods. And the "specimens" of "insects" he had brought back were Skinner and Snoop and Stott.

That's what Wingate meant by entomology!

RIVER MEN—BE REFINED!

Pleads LORD MAULEVERER

River manners are deplorable. I mean it, dear men! When I went punting with Wharton and some other sportsmen the other day, it stood out a mile!

The shouting and singing and larking about that goes on is enough to give pain to any sportsman of the old school, so to speak. And the raucous arguments that ensue when boats bash into each other! And the way chappies sling tomatoes and whatnot at chappies across the water! Really, it's enough to bring the bright blush of shame to the cheeks of a man who believes in good manners on the cheery old river.

What I saw convinced me that it's time we had a code of the river as well as a code of the road. Here are one or two rules I'm going to suggest if such a code is started:

Don't have comb-and-paper bands on your boat. Mouth-organs are much more aristocratic.

Don't squirt ink at each other. Water is so much more pure and plentiful.

Don't whistle across to other boats; be gentlemanly and yell "Hi!" instead.

Don't shout "You clumsy idiots!" when a collision occurs. Just be dignified and yell: "Why don't you look where you're going, blow you!"

In brief, river men, be refined!

(We have a suspicion that Mauly is pulling our legs, but it's so rare for the dear old languid lord to summon up sufficient energy to write anything for us that we simply can't leave it out!—ED.)

GREYFRIARS FACTS WHILE YOU WAIT!

nuel Vernon-Smith, the ire, anchored in Pegg his new steam yacht and ed his son Herbert—y"—and the Famous er the week-end. The es had special per- and enjoyed themselves ull, swimming and sun- ing. "Yacht"-ho!

Peter Todd's long legs served him in good stead when batting for the Remove against Rookwood. A terrific spurt and a dive at full length just got him to his crease to save him being run out—after which "Toddy" settled down and knocked up 40 before being caught. Toddy fields—rightly—at "long leg"!

Mark Linley, the lad from Lancashire, says the North offers everything to holidaymakers, from Blackpool sands to the tors and caverns of North Derbyshire. Linley spent much of his last vac exploring the latter—and though he tackled some tough climbs, "Marky" was not the chap to "cave" in!

(*Continued from page* 13.)

at the sight of a Chicago gunman in attendance.

Still, Chick Chew's latest stunt, in entering the school in disguise, made it clearer than ever that Poker's watchful care was a stern necessity; and nobody raised objections. Not that objections would have had any effect on the stolid Poker.

It was quite a pleasant walk across Courtfield Common, and the party of juniors arrived at the station in good time for the train.

Taking platform tickets, they went on the platform to wait for the train to come in from Lantham Junction. Poker Pike followed them on the platform. Perhaps he figured that Chick Chew might be hanging about the station, ready to whisk the millionaire's son off in an express train! Poker wouldn't have put it past him!

"Hallo, hallo, hallo! Here she comes!" said Bob Cherry, as the express from Lantham came steaming down the line.

The train stopped in the station; doors flew open, and passengers alighted. The juniors watched them as they got out, trying to pick out Mr. Saloman.

It was known that he was to arrive by that train, so there could be no doubt that he was among the passengers. But, if so, it was not easy to pick him out.

There were only eight passengers alighting from the train. Three of them were of the gentle sex. Of the other five, one was Mr. Pilkins, the estate agent; another was Dick Trumper, of Courtfield School; one was a stout farmer, one was a commercial traveller, and one was a florid gentleman who looked like an auctioneer.

"Is that the merchant?" asked Bob doubtfully.

"Doesn't look the part!" remarked Harry Wharton.

"Well, these temporary masters are all sorts of odds and ends," said Bob. "It can't be one of the others; we'd better ask him."

And Bob stepped towards the man who looked like an auctioneer, raised his hat very politely, and asked:

"Mr. Saloman, sir?"

"Eh? No! Get out!" said the florid gentleman, And he walked on.

"Floored!" said Bob. "He hasn't come!"

Harry Wharton laughed.

"Missed the connection at Lantham, I suppose," he said. "He will come along in the next train—that's an hour."

"Blow the next train!" grunted Bob. "We've had our walk for nothing."

"And we shan't be able to show him what nice fellows we are, and how we love our kind teachers!" grinned Nugent.

"What about tea at the bunshop, and coming round for the next train?" asked Harry. "That will fit in all right."

"I guess that's O.K.," said Van Duck. And the party having agreed that it was O.K., there was an adjournment to the bunshop in the High Street for tea—shadowed by the watchful Poker.

Tea filled in the interval nicely till the next train from Lanthom was due. Then, still under Poker's watchful eye, the juniors returned to the station to see the five-thirty from Lantham come in.

This time they had no doubt of spotting their man. But again there was a surprise and a disappointment. Only three passengers alighted at Courtfield—and not one of them could possibly be imagined to be a schoolmaster. The chums of the Remove watched them pass down the platform—a young lady typist from Chunkley's, a horsy-looking man chewing a straw, and Sir Hilton Popper, of Popper's Court! Certainly Mr. Saloman was not one of the three!

"Well, my only hat!" said Bob, in disgust. "Has the foozling ass missed another train or what?"

"Must be a chump!" remarked Johnny Bull.

"There's another train in another hour!" said Nugent, with a grin.

"Oh, rats!"

Nobody was disposed to wait for the six-thirty. The Greyfriars fellows left the station, and walked back to the school. Either the temporary master was a man with a genius for losing trains, or else something had happened to delay his arrival.

Billy Bunter met the juniors as they came into the House. His fat face was wreathed with grins.

"I say, you fellows, did you go to the station?" he inquired.

"Yes, ass!"

"How did you miss him, then?"

"He never came."

"He, he, he!"

"Anything to cackle at in that?" grunted Johnny Bull.

"Well, you must be silly asses!" grinned Bunter. "He must have walked out under your noses! He, he, he!"

"You giggling gorgon, he never came!"

"He jolly well did!" chuckled Bunter. "He's with the Head now!"

"He's here?" exclaimed Harry Wharton, in astonishment.

"He, he, he! Yes, rather! I've seen him—he's a Jew all right!" said Bunter. "Too jolly stingy for a taxi-fare! He, he, he! He walked from the station."

"You blithering ass!" hooted Bob. "He never came!"

"Well, he's with the Head now, whether he did or not!" chortled Bunter. "I heard him say to Prout, after he came in, that being such a fine day, he had walked from the station. You fellows must have been as blind as owls."

The juniors stared at Bunter. They were utterly astonished to hear that the new master had arrived during their absence. They were absolutely certain that he had not arrived at Courtfield by the four-thirty, at all events.

"Is that fat ass gammoning?" asked Johnny Bull.

"Here, Smithy!" called out Bob Cherry. "Has the new beak blown in?"

"Yes, an hour ago," answered the Bounder. "I believe he's with the Head."

"What's he like?"

"Fat old codger, with a boko!" grinned Smithy. "Looks a good-tempered old bean—we shall have an easier time with him than with Quelch, I fancy."

"Well, my hat!"

It was quite a puzzle to the chums of the Remove. A "fat old codger with a boko" could hardly have passed unnoticed under six pairs of eyes. Yet he must have done so, if he had walked from Courtfield to the school. Still, they knew that he hadn't, and couldn't have. So it really was a puzzle.

THE ELEVENTH CHAPTER.

A Little Mysterious!

MR. SALOMAN was seen at calling over.

He was in Hall, with the other masters, when the school gathered for call-over; and most of the Remove eyed him with interest—especially the Famous Five and Putnam van Duck.

He looked, as the Bounder had said, a good-tempered old bean. He was a stout gentleman of uncertain age, with a dark, and rather shiny complexion, and—undoubtedly—a "boko." Judging by his features, at all events, Mr. Saloman had a strong dash of the Oriental in him. He wore glasses, and a beard; and his nose, was, to say the least, prominent.

Certainly he was not a man to have passed unnoticed when six fellows were waiting and watching for him.

"So that's the sportsman!" murmured Bob Cherry.

"That chap never came by train to Courtfield!" said Johnny Bull. "We couldn't possibly have missed him."

"Bunter says he walked from the station——"

"Bunter's an ass!"

"Oh, really, Bull! I heard him say to Prout——"

"Rats!"

"Old Prout barged in to jaw—he always does, you know. He said that Saloman had been expected earlier, and the old bean said he had walked from the station because it was such a fine day——"

"Rot!"

"Blessed if I make it out!" said Harry Wharton.

After calling-over the Removites, in the Rag, discussed their new "beak." There was general agreement that, on his looks, they were likely to have an easier time with him than with Quelch. Which was quite a consolation for the temporary loss of their Form-master.

Harry Wharton, as head boy of the Remove, rather expected to be sent for by the new master. As the summons did not come, he decided to call on Mr. Saloman, when time for prep drew near. He was in point of fact rather interested to learn how the new beak had blown in, without being seen by six fellows who had waited for him at the station.

He tapped at the door of Mr. Quelch's study, now occupied by the temporary beak.

"Come in!" came a rather high-pitched and wheezy voice.

The head boy of the Remove entered.

Mr. Saloman was seated in Mr. Quelch's armchair, by the window. He was looking out into the quad, red in the sunset.

At a distance a bowler-hatted figure was lounging by the elms, and Mr. Saloman seemed interested in that figure.

His profile was to the junior, as he entered, and Wharton could not help being struck by the ample curve of his nose. There was no doubt that Mr. Saloman was blessed with a good allowance of "boko."

He glanced round at the captain of the Remove. His eyes were very keen, behind the large glasses he wore, and it seemed to Wharton, for a moment, that there was a glint of recognition in them.

But that could scarcely be possible, as the temporary master from Leggett & Teggers was a stranger at Greyfriars, and Wharton, assuredly, had never met anyone named Saloman before.

"What is it?" asked the new master. There was quite an agreeable smile on his fat, shiny face.

"I thought you might wish to see me, sir, as head boy of your Form," answered Harry.

"Oh, quite!" said Mr. Saloman. "Your name is Wharton, then? Your headmaster referred to you. I am glad to make your acquaintance, Wharton."

He rose from the armchair, and shook hands with his head boy, with a large, fat hand.

"I hope you had a pleasant journey down, sir!" said Harry, chiefly by way of politeness.

"Oh, quite, quite!" said Mr. Saloman. "We are getting beautiful weather."

"We expected you rather earlier, sir."

"Indeed!" said Mr. Saloman. "Yes, no doubt. But the fine weather tempted me to walk from the station, so I fear that I arrived a little late."

"You did not walk from Lantham, sir?" exclaimed Wharton, in surprise.

"Oh, no!" Mr. Saloman smiled, with a gleam of gold-stopped teeth. "I am quite a good walker, but such a distance would be too much for me. I walked from Courtfield."

Wharton stood dumb.

Why this man, a new master, employed for a week or two to take Quelch's place, supplied by the agency that always supplied Greyfriars on such occasions, should tell lies, was an utter mystery to him.

But he knew that the man was not speaking the truth. That was impossible. He stated that he had walked from Courtfield, and he could not have done so, as he had not arrived there.

Wharton was quite taken aback.

The new master, of course, knew nothing of the fact that a party of his Form had gone to the station to meet him. But for that circumstance, his statement would have passed muster without question. But as the matter stood, Wharton knew that it was not true.

The keen eyes behind the spectacles narrowed almost to pin-points, as the new master scanned Wharton. He could see that the junior was surprised, and it seemed to make him strangely alert.

"A very pleasant walk," said Mr. Saloman. "The scenery about here is very fine. I quite enjoyed my walk across the common."

"But—but you did not come by the four-thirty, after all, did you, sir?" stammered the captain of the Remove, quite bewildered.

"Certainly; that was my train!" answered Mr. Saloman, raising his eyebrows, which were very thick and bushy. "Why do you ask?"

"Oh! I—I thought——" stammered Harry.

He hardly knew what to say. The man was lying—why, he could not begin to guess.

He had not come by train to Courtfield, and had not walked across the common; yet he stated that he had. He must have come by some other route, and why he should make a secret of it, at the expense of telling lies, was a mystery. But the head boy of the Remove could not, at all events, tell his new beak that he knew that he was not speaking the truth.

"I—I thought——" He floundered. "I—I thought you might like to discuss Form matters, sir, with your head boy, as you will be taking the Remove in the morning."

"Quite so!" said Mr. Saloman. "But I am a little fatigued from my journey, Wharton, and I think I will defer that till to-morrow."

"Very well, sir!"

Wharton left the study, still bewildered. Mr. Saloman watched the door close on him, and then his gaze returned to the bowler-hatted figure by the elms across the quad.

So long as the Greyfriars gunman remained in sight, Mr. Saloman sat there watching him—and he allowed his glasses to slip down his ample nose, and watched the gunman without their aid. The new master of the Remove seemed to be keenly interested in the Greyfriars gunman, and did not seem to need the assistance of the big glasses he wore to scrutinise Poker Pike.

THE TWELFTH CHAPTER.

Bunter the Bold!

"THIS is the dormitory, sir!" said Loder of the Sixth.

"Very good!" said Mr. Saloman.

The Remove were in their dorm, and had expected Loder to see lights out for them that night. The fat figure, large glasses, and beaky nose of the new master loomed in the doorway, however. The new master of the Remove had come up to see his Form go to "roost."

Loder was by no means displeased. As a prefect, he had duties to perform; but he was never keen on them.

"If you would care to see lights out for your Form, sir——" he suggested.

"Quite so!" said Mr. Saloman. "Please leave it to me."

"Certainly, sir."

And Loder willingly departed, leaving it to Mr. Saloman.

The stout gentleman blinked benevolently at the juniors, through his big glasses. Harry Wharton avoided meeting his glance.

Wharton hardly knew what to make of the new man. But he could not help having his own opinion of a man who told untruths, whatever might be his motive, or lack of motive, for doing so.

The man seemed good-tempered enough, and quite agreeable in his manners; but a man who told untruths was untruthful, and the captain of the Remove did not like that kind of man. He hoped that he would have very little to do with the temporary beak who had taken Quelch's place.

When the new master was about to switch off the light, there came a squeak from Billy Bunter.

"I say, sir! The door has to be locked."

"What is that?" exclaimed Mr. Saloman.

"The door's locked every night now, sir!" squeaked Bunter. "Ever since that kidnapper came in after Van Duck, sir."

"Dear me!" said Mr. Saloman. "The headmaster mentioned to me that there was a boy in my Form who had been threatened by kidnappers. Which boy is it?"

"Little me, sir!" answered Van Duck.

The new master blinked at him.

"Are you Van Duck?" he asked. "I think that was the name Dr. Locke mentioned."

"Sure!"

"The kidnapper got in here one night, sir!" said Bob Cherry. "Ever since then the door has been kept locked at night."

"A very prudent precaution," said Mr. Saloman. "I shall certainly lock the door, and take away the key. Good-night, my boys!"

"Good-night, sir!"

The stout gentleman trod heavily out of the dormitory, shut the door, and locked it on the outside. The juniors heard the key withdrawn, and the heavy tread die away down the passage.

Then there was a creaking and rumpling, as a fat junior turned out of bed. Billy Bunter turned on a flash-lamp, and by its illumination, carried a couple of chairs to the door.

He piled one on top of the other, just inside the door.

The door could not now be opened without knocking over the upper chair—with a crash that certainly would have awakened every fellow in the dormitory—except perhaps Bunter himself.

Billy Bunter did not like turning out of bed, and did not like exerting himself. But he had done both, regularly, every night since Chick Chew had dabbed the chloroform pad over his sleeping face. The Owl of the Remove was taking no more risks, if he could help it.

"At it again, you fat ass?" yawned the Bounder, from his bed.

"I'm not jolly well going to be snaffled by that kidnapping beast again!" grunted Bunter. "I say, you fellows, you turn out, if you hear him."

"He won't snaffle you any more, you fat duffer!" said Peter Todd. "He was after Van Duck, and only got you because you were in his bed. He made a mistake in the dark."

"He jolly well isn't going to make another, if I can stop him!" said Bunter. "We ought to have bolts on the door, really. I thought of asking Quelch! I think I'll ask that man Saloman to-morrow—he's a Jew, but he looks good-tempered—much better-tempered than old Quelch."

Billy Bunter rolled back to bed.

"Fathead!" said Bob Cherry. "It's all right with the door locked—even if the blighter comes again, which isn't likely."

"He got in by the fastened window that night!" retorted Bunter. "A locked door wouldn't stop him."

"Well, that's so!" admitted Bob.

"Safety first, you know!" said Bunter. "It wouldn't matter if he got one of you fellows; but he might get me again, and —I mean, of course, I'm only taking all this trouble for you fellows' safety. I'm not afraid, so far as that goes."

"Ha, ha, ha!"

"Oh, cackle!" snorted Bunter. "I fancy you'd cackle on the other side of your mouths, though, if you heard that chair crash over in the middle of the night, and knew that he was coming. You'd call me fast enough, to protect you!"

"Oh, my hat!" gasped Bob. "I can see you doing it, if we did!"

"You'll see it all right, if he comes!" said Bunter. "Last time he caught me napping! If I'd been awake I'd have handled him all right! Well, I shall be awake next time, and you'll see."

"We shall see you dive under the bed-clothes, you mean!"

"No, you won't!" roared Bunter. "You'll see me jump and tackle the brute, while you're all sticking in bed shivering with funk!"

Bob Cherry, grinning in the dark, sat up in bed.

"Hark!" he exclaimed dramatically. "Did you hear a footprint—I mean, a footstep?"

"Ow!" gasped Bunter. "I—I—I say, you fellows, pip-pip-pip-perhaps it's only Saloman coming back. Or Loder! I—I say—I—I can't hear anybody!"

"That's easily explained," said Bob cheerfully. "You see, there isn't anybody. At least, I can't hear anybody!"

"Ha, ha, ha!"

"Beast! Trying to pull a fellow's leg!" snorted Bunter. "I jolly well knew you were fooling. You can't frighten me!"

"Bunter the Bold!" chuckled Bob. "Can you fellows see him plunging into the fray—or can you see him popping under his bed?"

"The popfulness would be terrific!"

"Ha, ha, ha!"

"Yah!" retorted Bunter. "Wait and see! I fancy I'm the only chap here who would have the pluck to tackle him, and chance it!"

"What a fertile fancy!"

"Ha, ha, ha!"

"Well, you'll see, if he comes here again!" sneered Bunter. "You can cackle now, but you'll howl to me for help if he comes, so yah!"

Bob Cherry stepped quietly out of bed.

In the darkness he tiptoed towards the door. Half a dozen fellows glimpsed him, in the gloom; but not the Owl of the Remove. Billy Bunter had no idea that anyone was out of bed.

Suddenly, in the silence of the dormitory, came a crash.

It came from the door. It was caused, obviously, by the upper chair tumbling off the one it was piled on. There were startled exclamations from many beds, and a howl of terror from Billy Bunter.

"I say, you fellows, he's come!" howled Bunter. "I say, call Quelch—I mean, the Head—the prefects—the police! Yaroooh!"

"Play up, Bunter!" yelled Bob. "Tackle him!"

"Protect us, Bunter!" gasped Frank Nugent.

"Collar him, Bunter!"

"Bag him, Bunter!"

"Quick, Bunter—oh, quick!"

"Oh crikey!" gasped Bunter.

The Owl of the Remove did not leap from his bed to tackle the intruder. He plunged wildly under the bedclothes, dragging sheets and blankets over his terrified head. From under the pile came a series of terrified squeaks.

"Ha, ha, ha!"

"It's all right, you fat ass!" roared Bob. "Nobody's here——"

"Yarooh! Help! Fire! Murder! Help!" came in muffled squeaks from under Bunter's bedclothes.

"You silly ass, shut up!"

"Help!"

"There's nobody!" shrieked Bob.

"Fire! Kidnappers! Murder! Help!"

"Ha, ha, ha!"

"You blithering idiot, I knocked the chair over!" howled Bob. "Do you want to bring the whole House here?"

"Yarooh! Help! Yoop!"

Bob Cherry grabbed at the protecting bedclothes, and dragged them off the Owl of the Remove. Two fat little legs in striped pyjamas kicked up, in frantic terror.

"Yarooh! Keep off! It ain't me—I mean, I ain't Van Duck! He's in the bed next to Wharton! Help!"

"Ha, ha, ha!" yelled the whole dormitory.

"You frabjous frump!" gasped Bob. "Will you shut up? You'll have the prefects up here if you kick up that row. Don't I keep on telling you that I knocked the chair over, to pull your silly leg?"

"Oh! Beast!" gasped Bunter.

"Ha, ha, ha!"

"I—I—I jolly well knew you did! That—that's why I didn't turn out!" gasped the fat Owl.

"Ha, ha, ha!"

"If you fellows think I was frightened——"

"The thinkfulness is terrific, my esteemed, funky Bunter!"

"Ha, ha, ha!"

Bob Cherry, chuckling, went back to bed. Bunter sat up.

"I say, you beast, if you knocked that chair over, go and stick it up again!" he yapped.

"Rats!"

"Beast!"

Bunter rolled out of bed once more, and piled up the chair at the door. Then he scrambled into bed, and gathered up bedclothes. And in a few minutes more his deep snore was rumbling through the dormitory. After which a practical joke would have been a sheer waste of energy, for a dozen falling chairs would hardly have awakened Billy Bunter, when he was once safe in the embrace of Morpheus.

THE THIRTEENTH CHAPTER.
In the Dead of Night!

CRASH!

Harry Wharton started suddenly out of slumber.

So did a dozen other fellows in the Remove dormitory.

It was past midnight. Every fellow at Greyfriars was fast asleep. There was no sound in the Remove dormitory, save the regular breathing of many sleepers, and the steady snore of Billy Bunter—till the crash came! It came suddenly and loudly in the silence.

Wharton sprang up in bed.

In the dim glimmer from the high windows he could see little or nothing. But he knew that the door—left locked by Mr. Saloman—had opened from outside, and that the chair so cautiously piled up by Billy Bunter had crashed over.

It was not a practical joke this time—no fellow was out of bed playing pranks after midnight. Wharton, with a thrill at his heart, knew what it was—what it could only be! It was the kidnapper!

Billy Bunter's snore continued uninterrupted. But every other fellow in the dormitory started out of slumber. The crash of the chair on the old oak planks was more than enough to awaken the Remove.

"Search me!" came a gasp from Van Duck's bed.

"It's him!" panted Bob Cherry, breathlessly and ungrammatically.

"Turn out!" yelled the Bounder.

"Back up, you fellows!" shouted the captain of the Remove. He leaped from his bed, grasping a pillow for a weapon.

A dozen fellows were jumping out. Nothing could be seen, but they knew that the door was open. A sound came to their ears—the sound of swiftly retreating feet in the passage.

Whoever had come to the door had been even more startled than the juniors by the crashing chair. And he had realised at once that, with a crowd of schoolboys awakened, his game was up before it started. Prompt retreat was the kidnapper's cue, and he was retreating promptly.

Harry Wharton dashed across to the door and switched on the light. The dormitory was instantly flooded with illumination.

He ran into the passage.

The fleeting footsteps were dying away down the long corridor, in the direction of the landing at the end.

Wharton flashed on the passage light.

Then, staring down the corridor, he had a glimpse of a vanishing figure—a bulky man, dressed in black. The fugitive turned his head to glance back as he ran out of the passage on the landing, and the captain of the Remove saw, for a flashing instant, the face of Chick Chew.

"Follow on!" shouted Harry.

He raced down the passage in pursuit.

After him came the Co., helter-skelter, with Smithy and Redwing, Peter Todd and Squiff, Lord Mauleverer and Tom Brown, and a dozen more of the Remove at their heels.

They did the passage as if it was the cinder-path.

Wharton groped for the switch, and turned on the landing light.

"There he is!" roared Bob Cherry.

The bulky figure was vanishing across the landing, into the corridor that led to Masters' quarters.

"After him!" panted Harry. "We've got him now!"

He led the rush across the landing.

So swift had been the pursuit that the bulky man had not had time to escape unseen. But for that glimpse of him the juniors would have taken it for granted that he had fled downstairs to escape from the House.

They were utterly surprised to see him dodge into the passage that led only to Masters' bed-rooms. In that direction there was no escape, except by clambering out of a high window. It looked as if Chick Chew, in his haste and hurry, had made an error of judgment.

All was dark in the passage when the juniors ran into it, but a light was swiftly switched on, illuminating it from end to end.

Even as the light came, a door was heard to close. Frank Nugent gave a startled gasp.

"He's dodged into Quelch's room."

"We've got him!"

"Keep your eyes peeled," panted Van Duck. "If Chick's cornered, you want to watch out for his gun."

"Bother his gun!" said Bob. "Come on! He may damage old Saloman—that old bean couldn't tackle him! He's got Quelch's room now."

The juniors tore down the passage, to the door of Mr. Quelch's bed-room, now the quarters of the temporary master. Wharton turned the door-handle, but the door was locked on the inside.

He knocked hastily.

"Mr. Saloman! Mr. Saloman! Wake up, sir!"

There was no answer from within. But other doors along the passage were opening, and startled voices were heard. Mr. Prout, in flowing dressing-gown, came out of his room, his eyes almost bulging from his plump face at the sight of the excited mob of Removites.

"What—what does this mean?" thundered Prout, purple with wrath. "This—this riot, in the middle of the night—this—this——"

"The kidnapper, sir!" gasped Harry Wharton.

"What? What? Nonsense!"

"Chick Chew, sir—I saw him!" panted the captain of the Remove. "He's dodged into Mr. Quelch's room—I mean Mr. Saloman's—and locked the door after him! He's there now."

"G-g-goodness gracious!" gasped Prout. "Wait—wait till I get a weapon of some sort! I have a golf club in my room! Wait!"

The Fifth Form master rushed back to his room. A loud bump, and a louder exclamation, floated back. Prout's feet, apparently, had become entangled in his flowing dressing-gown.

Mr. Capper, Mr. Wiggins, and Mr. Hacker were out of their rooms now. Prout came charging back, with a hefty-looking driver in his grasp.

"Now, stand back!" boomed Prout.

As the Fifth Form master was flourishing the golf-club in warlike way, everybody stood back. Nobody wanted to be brained by the warlike Prout. Mr. Prout was given plenty of room as he barged along to the locked door. He banged on it with the club.

"Mr. Saloman!" he boomed. "Are you awake?"

This time there was a reply.

"Dear me!" came the wheezy voice of Mr. Saloman. "What ever is the matter? Is the house on fire?"

"No! No! A miscreant—a kidnapping miscreant—has taken refuge in your room! Pray open the door at once!"

"Goodness gracious!"

"Please open the door!" boomed Prout.

"Certainly! At once—at once! I do not think that there is anyone in my room, however——"

"We saw him dodge in, sir!" called out Harry Wharton.

"Goodness gracious! Are you sure?"

"Quite sure, sir. Is the window open?"

"The window! Yes, the window certainly appears to be open! That is very singular, as I left it shut——"

"He's getting away!" roared Bob Cherry. "Climbing down the ivy! For goodness' sake, open this door, sir!"

A gleam under the door showed that Mr. Saloman had turned on the light. He could be heard moving in the room. But the door did not open. Prout pounded again with the golf club.

"Mr. Saloman—kindly make haste!" he boomed.

"Certainly—certainly! But I cannot find the key. The key appears to be gone from the door—and the door is locked! I will endeavour to find the key——"

"Fat lot of use, when he's bolted by the window!" grunted Vernon-Smith. "Let's get down, and call that jolly old gunman! We may get him in the quad."

"No one is in the room," came Mr. Saloman's wheezy voice. "I have looked in every corner, but the window certainly is open——"

"Come on, you men!"

"Boys!" boomed Mr. Prout.

But nobody heeded Prout. There was a scampering rush down the stairs, of a mob of fellows in pyjamas. After them lumbered Prout, golf-club in hand; and after Prout followed Wiggins, Capper, and Hacker—and in the rear came Monsieur Charpentier, uttering a series of startled squeaks. Downstairs, Sixth Form men were turning out, at the alarm, and a crowd of the Fifth and Fourth had turned out of their dormitories, shouting to know what was on. The great door of the House was flung wide open, and an excited crowd of fellows rushed into the quad under the summer stars.

THE FOURTEENTH CHAPTER.

The Vanishing Trick!

"SEARCH me!" ejaculated Poker Pike.

He stood staring up at the ivy-clad old stone wall, his slits of eyes very keen, under the rim of his bowler hat. His gun was in his hand, ready for use, if he had spotted the escaping man. But there was no sign of a clambering figure on the thick old ivy—no sign of any stranger within the gates.

Round the gunman clustered a crowd of fellows, half-dressed, wildly excited. A dozen hands pointed to the ivy-clad wall under the window of the room occupied by Mr. Saloman.

Poker Pike, quick to take the alarm, had turned up at once when the crowd came rushing out of the House. Very quickly he learned of what had happened within. But not quickly enough, it seemed, to intercept the escape of the kidnapper, for nothing was to be seen of Chick Chew.

That the man was Chick, Harry Wharton was positive, and Poker had no doubt of it. But what had become of him?

Poker wrinkled his brows grimly under his bowler hat as he stared up the wall, thick with ancient ivy. That thick old ivy offered good handhold to a daring climber—and Chick had plenty of nerve. None of the juniors doubted that he had passed through Mr. Saloman's room, locking the door after him, and escaping by the window. But the swiftness with which he had done it was amazing. They had fully expected, when they reached the quad, to find him still clambering down. Minutes had been wasted at Mr Saloman's door; but surely it was more than a matter of minutes for a bulky man like Chick to clamber down sixty feet of ivy—feeling his way, groping for tendrils strong enough to sustain his heavy weight!

Yet he was gone.

Fellows were scattering over the quad, looking for him. But there could be little doubt that, if he had climbed clear, he had escaped from the school.

"Beats me!" muttered Poker. "I

(*Continued on next page.*)

GREYFRIARS INTERVIEWS

"It's not always the clothes that make the man . . . it's what is under his hat!" says our long-haired poet. And I think you will agree with him when you read the following clever verses written around

CECIL REGINALD TEMPLE,

the Aristocratic Captain of the Upper Fourth.

(1)

Attend, all ye who list to hear!
Your humble now presents
To loyal readers, far and near,
The best of ornaments,
Bow down with reverence!
And tremble, grovel, shake with fear
In case he takes offence!

(2)

To east and west and south and north
His name be blazoned far!
Yea, Temple of the Upper Fourth!
Hail, Temple, Cecil R.!
He shineth like a star!
A thousand voices volley forth
His praises! Har, har, har!

(3)

Oh, glossy, glossy are the hats
That sit upon his head!
Of virgin whiteness are the spats
That dignify his tread.
His garments are well bred!
His voice is silent, too; but that's
When he's asleep in bed.

(4)

One sound is certain to rejoice
Our Temple all day long,
And that's the sound of Temple's voice,
Which charms him, going strong,
Just like a siren's song.
In Temple's view, his tones are choice;
That view, of course, is wrong.

(5)

His study-mates are now resigned
To hear his jawbone wag,
Although at times they feel inclined
To fit him with a gag.
Perhaps it's too much fag,
Or possibly they do not find
It pays to start a rag.

(6)

For Temple's uncle's very rich,
And that's the reason why,
Though Fry's and Dabney's fingers itch
To dot their leader's eye,
They're careful not to try!
He often gets a tenner, which
Appeals to Dab and Fry!

(7)

I sought this youthful autocrat
And soon encountered him
Out in the open, where he sat
Upon the fountain's rim,
So elegant and slim.
As I approached, he murmured: "Scat!"
His tones were bored, but grim.

(8)

"Removite fags I bar!" he drawled.
"Oh, rather!" Dabney cried.
"What kind of object are you called
At Whipsnade?" I replied.
That wounded Temple's pride.
"Oh, kick him, somebody!" he bawled.
Upon the fountain's side.

(9)

I jumped and started to retreat,
But Fry, and Dab as well,
Lunged out with hard and heavy feet.
They hurt me, I can tell!
I reeled, and as I fell
I knocked old Temple from his seat!
He vanished with a yell.

(10)

When I sat up again, I found
We four were now we three!
We all were lying on the ground,
But Temple, where was he?
Ask of the waves that rolled around
The marble statuary!

(11)

A drenched and dripping object rose,
A wet and woeful mess!
With water pouring from its nose,
It cried in dire distress.
It scared me, I confess.
What was the object? Goodness knows!
Perhaps you'd like to guess!

guess it beats me to a frazzle! Chick is spry—I'll say he's sure spry! But I reckon he never vamoosed by that winder! Nope!"

"He sure did, Poker!" exclaimed Putnam van Duck. "I'm telling you, we was on his heels to Saloman's room, and we saw him dodge in."

"Mebbe!" said Poker. "If you did, he's sure still there! I'm telling you, he never hit that ivy."

The gunman turned on a powerful torch and scanned the ivy on the wall with a keen and scrutinising eye.

"He must have, Poker!" said Harry Wharton.

"I'll mention that Chick ain't no feather-weight!" grunted Poker. "Mebbe that ivy would hold him, but I guess it would show signs. There ain't a ornery piece pulled out of place."

"Might have dropped the last bit!" said Bob.

"Mebbe," grunted Poker—"and mebbe not!"

Every eye was fixed on the ivied wall, and Poker played the light over it. So far as the glare of the torch extended, no sign of disturbance in the ivy could be noted. Which was very singular if it had supported the weight of a bulky man like Chick Chew in a desperately hurried clamber.

"Might have got away over the roofs!" suggested Johnny Bull.

"Mebbe!" said Poker briefly.

"Anyhow, he certainly was in Saloman's room!" said Frank Nugent. "And he locked the door after him. He never got out by the door."

"I guess I'm going to give that room the once-over," said Poker grimly. "Some of you guys watch that winder and let out a howl if he makes a break."

Evidently the Greyfriars gunman did not believe that Chick had escaped by that window. It seemed absurd to the juniors, for obviously Mr. Saloman, now that he had turned his light on, must know whether anyone was in the room with him. But Poker was an obstinate guy. He tramped away—with the intention of giving the new master's room the once-over.

"Boys," came Prout's boom, "go back at once! Go into the House immediately! Al! but the Sixth Form prefects—at once!"

The juniors, in the excitement of the moment, might have passed Prout's boom unheeded; but they were keen to follow Poker Pike, and they trooped after him into the House. That he would discover the gangster within the House they did not believe, but it was clear that Poker believed that Chick was still within.

Poker Pike tramped up the stairs, followed by a buzzing crowd. He tramped along the upper passage that led to Mr. Quelch's old room. The door was still locked; it did not open when he jerked at the handle. He banged on the panels with the butt of his six-gun.

"Say, you open up!" he hooted.

"Goodness gracious!" came Mr. Saloman's wheezy voice. "Who is that?"

"It's Poker Pike, Mr. Saloman," called back Harry Wharton. "He wants to search the room."

"Dear me! I cannot find the key—I fear that the miscreant must have taken it with him—I cannot unlock the door."

"Ten to one he's taken it after locking the door!" remarked Nugent. "Of course, he must have got away by the window."

"Sez you!" grunted Poker.

"Think he went up the chimney?" grinned the Bounder.

Poker Pike made no reply to that. He gave another bang on the door with the butt of his revolver.

"You opening up?" he roared.

"Impossible! I am sorry—I cannot unlock the door!"

"I guess I'm getting through, bo!"

Poker drew back a few paces, and launched himself at the door. A hefty shoulder, with all Poker's beef behind it, drove on the oak with a terrific crash. It was quite a strong door, but it was not built to withstand the crash of a human battering-ram.

"Oh crikey!" gasped Bob, as the door flew open.

Poker Pike, gun in hand, stepped in. Mr. Saloman, in a dressing-gown, was standing in the middle of the room, his eyes blinking behind his glasses. Poker gave a keen, searching look at the shiny face, the big, aquiline nose, the beard, the spectacles, taking in all details of Mr. Saloman at that single searching glance.

Then he proceeded to search the room.

The Remove fellows, clustered at the door, watched him. Mr. Saloman watched him also, blinking owlishly through his spectacles.

Nobody expected Poker to discover a gangster hidden in the room. And he did not make any discovery.

Having given the room the once-over, he gave Mr. Saloman another keen, searching stare.

"You never saw that guy?" he asked.

"No! No!" gasped the new master of the Remove. "I was quite surprised—astonished—alarmed—when I was told——"

"I guess you would be!" agreed Poker, and he turned and tramped out of the room. "Here, you Putnam van Duck, you beat it back to bed. I guess I'm sittin' on the foot of that bed till sun-up."

"You figure that Chick's still around?" grinned Putnam.

"I guess he ain't as fur off as Chicago!" answered Poker Pike. "And I'll mention that I'm keeping tabs on you till morning, young Putnam! Surest thing you know."

And Poker did! When the excited Greyfriars fellows were got back to the dormitories at last Poker Pike installed himself in the Remove dormitory, and sat there on the foot of Putnam's bed, with his gun in his hand on his knee. He was still sitting there, like a graven image, when the last of the Removites dropped off to sleep.

THE FIFTEENTH CHAPTER.
Walking Into the Trap!

"UP early after a wild night!" remarked Bob Cherry, with a grin.

Mr. Saloman was walking in the quad when the Remove fellows came out in the morning. The plump figure in cap and gown caught their eyes at once.

Putnam van Duck chuckled.

"I guess the old bird was surprised some last night," he remarked. "I'll say he never expected such a spot of excitement his first night here."

"Hardly!" said Harry Wharton. "Must have spoiled his beauty sleep."

"Just a few!" grinned Putnam.

Harry Wharton & Co. were the first down of the Remove, and there were few fellows to be seen out of the House. A gentleman of Mr. Saloman's ripe years might have been expected to put in a little extra sleep in the morning after the disturbance of the night. But it seemed that he was an early riser.

He came towards the juniors, and they capped him respectfully.

"A very extraordinary occurrence, my boys," said Mr. Saloman in his wheezy, high-pitched voice. "I was very, very much disturbed. A most extraordinary experience."

"Sorry we disturbed you, sir," said Harry, "but——"

"Oh, quite, quite! It was quite unavoidable, in the very peculiar circumstances," said Mr. Saloman. "But it was a very strange and startling experience for a man of my age. It is very singular that a boy here should be exposed to such perils—very singular indeed. Are you not very nervous, Van Duck?"

"Not a whole lot, sir!" answered Putnam.

"You Americans are very cool-headed, very self-possessed," said Mr.

Saloman. "It is very fortunate, in the strange circumstances. While I am here, Van Duck, I shall make it a point to be very careful of you and to keep you under my own observation—though I understand that you are already watched over by that very, very peculiar man who forced a way into my room last night. A very singular person indeed."

The juniors smiled. They could understand that a temporary master, coming to a school to take up a temporary job, had been considerably surprised and disturbed by Poker Pike and his strenuous manners and customs.

"Poker wants getting used to, sir!" said Putnam. "But he's a dutiful guy, and he sure has kept me safe from Chick Chew."

"Oh, no doubt, no doubt! I did not, of course, expect anything of the kind here when I accepted the temporary post offered me by Leggett & Teggers," said Mr. Saloman. "It is very unusual—very unusual! Very surprising indeed! I should be glad to know more of this very peculiar matter, Van Duck, as you will be under my charge for some little time. Please walk with me for a few minutes, and tell me all the circumstances of your danger from this man Chook——"

"Chick, sir!" said Putnam.

"Yes, yes, quite so, quite so!"

Putnam made rather a grimace at the Famous Five. He did not want to be walked off for a "jaw" by the new Form-master.

But it was scarcely possible to hint as much to a Form-master, and the American junior walked away with the stout gentleman, and the Famous Five scampered off for a trot round the quad before brekker.

Walking in the quadrangle, Mr. Saloman, in his high-pitched voice, put a good many questions to the millionaire's son. Keeping the American junior in talk, he walked down the path that led to Masters' gate.

Putnam walked with him, answering his questions.

They arrived at the little gate to which only masters had keys. Rather to Putnam's surprise, Mr. Saloman produced a key and unlocked the gate.

"What a very beautiful morning!" he remarked. "I have not yet seen the river. I think we might walk as far as the river, Van Duck."

"Yes, sir, if you like," answered Putnam.

He followed the stout gentleman out of the gate, which Mr. Saloman closed after him.

He was a little surprised that the new master chose to take a walk abroad in cap and gown, but that was no business of his.

Mr. Saloman talked incessantly as they walked down to the bank of the Sark, keeping the American junior busy answering his questions.

"That's the bell for prayers, sir," said Putnam, as a distant clang came from the direction of the school.

"Dear me!" said Mr. Saloman. "Yes, yes! I am not yet fully acquainted with the routine here. Perhaps we had better turn back."

"Sure!"

"No, no!" added the new master. He smiled. "As your Form-master, Van Duck, I can excuse you. I am extremely interested in what you have been telling me, and it is necessary for me to know the circumstances. Let us walk on for a few minutes."

"Yes, sir!"

Putnam walked on along the river-bank with Mr. Saloman. He could not help being surprised. If the new master was beginning at Greyfriars by a disregard of the rules of the school, he was not likely to give much satisfaction to Dr. Locke.

But it was not for a junior to argue the point with his Form-master. And Putnam had no objection to a walk by the river in the dewy freshness of the June morning. He walked on cheerfully.

A few minutes later Mr. Saloman looked at his watch.

"Perhaps we had better get back, Van Duck," he said. "I think this is a short cut back to the school."

He turned into a footpath under thick, leafy trees.

"Oh, no, sir!" said Putnam. "I know that path, sir. It doesn't lead towards Greyfriars; it leads through the woods towards Friardale, sir."

"I think you must be mistaken," said Mr. Saloman. "I am sure that it will lead us directly to the school. We shall sight the buildings in a few minutes."

Putnam grinned.

"The only building on that path, sir, is an old cottage, which is let to holiday folk in the summer. I've passed it more than once."

"I feel sure that you are mistaken, my boy. I have a very good sense of direction," said Mr. Saloman. "Let us ascertain, at all events."

"O.K.!" said Putnam.

He did not mind extending the walk, so far as that went. But he wondered what Poker Pike would have thought had the Greyfriars gunman been aware that he was walking out without Poker "keeping tabs" as usual.

So far as he knew, Poker had not seen him with Mr. Saloman that morning. Certainly, a fellow might have been supposed safe in the company of his Form-master. But Poker was not the man to take that view. Poker never regarded Putnam as safe unless his own eye was on him.

They walked by the deep, shady path through the wood. Mr. Saloman quickened his pace, as if in haste now to get back to the school.

But as the path led away from Greyfriars, every step took them farther and farther away from the school—deeper and deeper into the solitary wood.

"Goodness gracious!" exclaimed Mr. Saloman at last. "I think you must have been right, my boy. We have missed the way."

"You said it, sir!" grinned Putnam.

Mr. Saloman stopped at a spot where a little gate stood in the hedge by the footpath. Beyond it was a long garden and a small cottage—the one to which Putnam had referred.

"Does anyone live here, my boy?" asked Mr. Saloman, blinking at the little building through his big glasses.

"I don't think so, sir," answered Van Duck. "I've heard it's let to somebody for week-ends, but I don't know."

"We may find someone of whom to ask our way, at all events," said Mr. Saloman, opening the little gate.

"I guess I know the way, sir," said Putnam. "We're more than a mile from Greyfriars now, but I guess I know every foot of it."

"Possibly, possibly," assented Mr. Saloman. "But I think it would be more prudent to inquire our way, as I am a complete stranger in this locality. Come with me, my boy."

Putnam followed him up the garden path, into the trellised porch at the cottage door. The new master of the Remove tapped at the door.

"Nobody there, sir," said Putnam.

"It appears not," said Mr. Saloman.

He turned the door-handle, and the door opened to his touch. It opened into the living-room of the cottage.

Putnam van Duck glanced in carelessly.

He saw a small, plainly furnished room, with a table, a few chairs, and a looking-glass on the wall. The room, and evidently the cottage, was unoccupied.

"Nobody at home, sir," said Putnam.

"Nope!" said Mr. Saloman, with so startling a change of voice and manner that Putnam van Duck jumped clear of the ground in his amazement. "Nope! But I reckon somebody's going to be at home mighty soon, and I'll say that you're the identical guy!"

And as Putnam fairly tottered in his amazement at hearing the voice of Chick Chew proceed from the bearded lips of Mr. Saloman, the new master of the Remove, he received a violent shove. It sent him spinning into the room, and Mr. Saloman, alias Chick Chew, followed him in and slammed the door.

THE SIXTEENTH CHAPTER.

Foiled at the Finish!

PUTNAM VAN DUCK stumbled across the room, and fell with a bump. Amazed and bewildered, he scrambled up, to feel a grip of iron on his shoulder.

"Don't you bank on starting anything, bo!" came the rasping voice of the gangster. "I guess you get yours mighty quick if you do!"

"Carry me home to die!" gasped Putnam.

He struggled, but only for a moment. That powerful grip on his shoulder held him like a vice. And Chick Chew's left hand jerked from his pocket, under the gown, a short length of lead piping—the gangster's favourite weapon.

"You win, Chick!" said Putnam coolly.

The gangster grinned.

"You said it!" he agreed.

Putnam stared at him. Even now he knew that the man was Chick Chew, Kidnapper No. 1 of the United States, he could scarcely believe it. Not the remotest resemblance to Chick could be traced in Mr. Saloman—except in his stout build, which even the cunning gangster could not disguise.

The Semitic-looking face, with its beard and spectacles, was evidently a masterpiece of the art of make-up.

"You sitting this one out, Putnam?" asked Chick, with a flourish of the lead pipe.

"I should smile!" said Putnam.

"I'll say that's hoss-sense!" agreed Chick. "I ain't wanting to crack your cabeza, and you worth half a million dollars to me, if you sit it out quiet, big boy!"

"Quieter'n a lamb, s'long's you've got that lead pipe handy!" answered Van Duck.

The gangster grinned, and slipped his weapon back into his pocket. He led the kidnapped junior to the wall, where a coat hung. Throwing the coat aside, he revealed an iron staple in the wall, from which hung a length of rope.

Coolly, quickly, and methodically, he bound the junior's arms behind him with the rope.

Putnam, standing with his back to the wall, was secured to the staple, a helpless prisoner.

"I'll say that's a cinch!" remarked Chick complacently.

"You're shouting!" agreed Putnam, cool as an iceberg. "I'll tell a man, that ain't no dream, Chick."

The gangster, grinning, sat on a bench facing the kidnapped schoolboy. Evidently Chick was full of satisfaction at his success, after so long a list of failures.

"If it wasn't for your toot, Chick, I guess I wouldn't believe it was you now," drawled Van Duck. "I reckon you figured on playing a game of this sort when you moseyed in as an archæological professor. You had this shebang fixed up all ready if you got me going on a walk."

"You said it!" grinned Chick.

"But I'll say this has got me beat!" said Putnam. "Poker's a smart guy, but I guess he'd never jump to it that a master in the school was Chick Chew with a new set of features. The guys have been joking about that nose of yours, Chick. Where did you buy it?"

Chick chuckled.

"You got me guessing," went on Putnam. "How'd you work that riffle, Chick? How'd you fix up as a master to come to the school? What you done with the guy you've borrowed a name from?"

"I guess he's O.K.," said Chick Chew, "and I'll own up I figure that this was some stunt, and a few over! Your schoolmaster horned in that day I was calling as Professor Belknap, and I sure handed him a sockdolager that I reckoned would last him some time!"

"You sure did!" agreed Putnam. "He's laid up in sanny now."

"That was what I figured! And I sure figured, too, that, with a schoolmaster on the sick list, mebbe the king-pin of the outfit would want a guy in his place."

"I get you!" assented Putnam. "But how'd you know——"

"I guess there ain't much about your school, young Putnam van Duck, that I don't know!" grinned Chick Chew. "I sure did learn my lesson like I was a boy at school, and I'll mention that I got wise to the whole caboodle. Being wise to it that that school got masters, when wanted, from Leggett & Teggers, and figuring that mebbe the king-pin would want a noo man in place of the one I put to sleep, I sure concentrated on Leggett & Teggers. It was jest pie to my jackals to pick up the noos that a guy named Saloman was going to the school in a temporary post."

"I guess so," agreed Putnam, with a nod.

"That guy," went on Chick, "was watched for at Lantham Junction, and picked up there, with a tale that his headmaster had sent a car for him."

"Pie!" assented Putnam.

"Clam-pie!" grinned Chick. "He never smelled no mouse till he had a gat at his head in a nice lonely spot; and then he was in quite a hurry to agree to any remarks I made. I borrowed his outfit, and hit for Greyfriars. I was fixed up ready for the circus. I guess I don't look a lot like the real Saloman guy, but as nobody knew him at the school, that cut no ice. I guess I was satisfied s'long as I didn't look like Hannibal Chew."

"And you sure do not!" said Putnam.

"Not a lot, I allow! This here nose is more'n twice as big as my own, and I'll say it's dandy!" said Chick. "I guess I done with it now. But it sure has been useful, if it ain't pretty to look at!"

"So that's how Mr. Saloman came to miss the train for Courtfield!" said Putnam grimly. "I guess I was surprised some when I heard from Wharton that our noo beak had told a heap of lies about that train!"

Chick gave another chuckle.

"I guess I had to lose Saloman's train, handling Saloman and seeing him safe," he answered. "I hit for the school in a car, got out a mile from the shebang, and walked the rest. I allowed that I'd walked from Courtfield, and I guessed nobody was the wiser."

"There was a bunch of us that was the wiser!" retorted Putnam van Duck. "But I allow we never guessed why Mr. Saloman was telling lies about it. I sure never did dream of seeing you horn in as a schoolmaster, Chick."

"Nor yet that smart guy Poker!" grinned Chick. "Though I'll mention that I had my hand mighty near a gun when he horned into my room last night."

Putnam whistled.

It was clear to him now, of course, how the midnight intruder in the dormitory had escaped.

No wonder Chick had fled into Mr. Saloman's room—as he was, in point of fact, Mr. Saloman!

He had discarded his schoolmaster disguise, when he made his attempt on the Remove dormitory—baffled so unexpectedly by Billy Bunter's astute precautions!

But having escaped into his own room, the locked door had given him ample time to replace the disguise, long before Poker's hefty shoulder drove the door in.

"I'll say Poker's smart," went on Chick complacently. "But there's a smarter guy in the United States, and I'll mention that his name's Hannibal Chew. I'll say I got Poker guessing!"

Putnam made no reply to that. He was wondering.

Poker Pike had asserted that Chick had not escaped by way of Mr. Saloman's window. He had searched the room. And then he had seemed content to drop the matter, and to remain for the rest of the night watching over Van Duck in the Remove dormitory. And Putnam wondered whether, after all, the keen, wary gunman had some lurking suspicion of Mr. Saloman. It rather looked to Putnam as if Poker had.

Chick, evidently, did not suppose so for a moment. Chick's belief was that he had all Greyfriars fooled, including the Greyfriars gunman, and that he had won his game at last.

He looked at his watch and rose from the bench.

"I guess I'll leave you parked safe here, Putnam," he remarked. "They'll sure be hunting for you soon; but I reckon they won't be looking into this shebang. I got to get word to Tug that I got you, and get the auto around.

"You won't be here more'n an hour or two. Then I guess I got a safe place, fur enough away, to park you, till you can be packed safe on a gentleman's private yacht and put on the home-trail. Your popper will sure sit up a few when he gets a letter from you with a United States postmark, mentioning that I'm waiting for half a million dollars!"

"You ain't got by with it yet!" said Putnam.

"I'm banking on it!" drawled Chick. "If that guy Poker can horn in on my game again, I'll sure allow he's the best man! But I'm telling you that I've left Poker guessing."

Chick Chew turned to the looking-glass and began to remove his disguise.

Putnam watched his reflection in the glass as he removed the false nose, the beard, the eyebrows, the spectacles. Slowly the genuine appearance of Chick Chew came to light.

Neither of them heard the door softly open.

But suddenly Chick gave a wild and violent start, and Putnam a gasp. In the looking-glass, beside the reflection of the gangster, appeared the mirrored, hickory face of a man in a bowler hat—with a levelled gun!

As if paralysed by that sudden and unexpected vision in the mirror, Chick stared at it, dumbfounded, the disguise he had just removed frozen in his fat hands.

"Stick 'em up!" came a quiet, metallic voice behind the gangster.

Putnam gave a breathless yell:

"Poker!"

Chick spun round.

Instinctively he reached for a gun.

But the levelled revolver looked him in the face with Poker Pike's icy eyes glittering over it, under the bowler hat.

"Stick 'em up, Chick!" said Poker evenly. "You get yours sudden, if you don't!"

And Chick realised it only too clearly! Slowly his hands went up over his head.

Red with rage, he stared at the Greyfriars gunman.

"Poker, old-timer!" panted Putnam. "You sure was keeping tabs!"

Poker nodded.

"Surest thing you know, big boy! I guess I suspicioned that guy a whole lot last night—and if a guy couldn't be sure enough to cinch him then, a guy could watch him like a guy was a cat looking arter a mouse!

"Yep. I'll say I was not fast asleep when you started on a pasear with that hombre, and I sure did tread on your tail all the way—and, mebbe, it'll interest you, Chick, that I did not feel sure it was you till I heard your toot—and I been listening to you, outside that here door, while you been chewing the rag with young Putnam—and I ain't no objection to saying that you are an entertaining guy when you're chewing the rag! And if you got more to spill, I ain't objecting to wait while you cough it up!"

But Chick had no more to spill.

In silence, in utter rage and dismay, he glared at the Greyfriars gunman and his levelled gun—his hands above his head! It was borne in upon the mind of Hannibal Chew that his career as the star kidnapper of the United States had reached its end—for some years to come, at least! Kidnapper No. 1 was booked for the "can" from which there was no exit!

THE SEVENTEENTH CHAPTER.

Chick in the "Can"!

"WHERE'S Van Duck?"

"Goodness knows!"

"The wherefulness is terrific!"

A place at breakfast was vacant at the Remove table. Putnam van Duck did not turn up.

Neither was Mr. Saloman seen.

Only one sharp pair of eyes had observed them leave by Masters' gate—Poker's. Nobody else knew that they had left the school. Harry Wharton & Co. were puzzled; but they could only conclude that Van Duck was showing the new master about the school. That he could be in any danger, in company with the new master of the Remove, crossed nobody's mind.

But when the fellows came out after

His hands tied behind his back, the muzzle of a six-gun prodding him in the rear, the prisoner was led through the school gateway. Up to the neck he was a master; above the neck he was quite a different person. Breathless with amazement, the chums of the Remove stared. "Chick Chew, the kidnapper!" gasped Harry Wharton.

breakfast, and Van Duck was looked for, and not found, the alarm began. Harry Wharton hurried to his Form-master's study, to see whether Mr. Saloman was there; but he found the study vacant. Neither the new master, nor the American junior, was to be seen anywhere.

"They can't have gone out!" said Harry, as he rejoined his friends in the quad. "Why should they? But where are they?"

"Echo answers where!" said Bob Cherry. "What the dickens is that man Saloman up to? He will be due in the Form-room soon."

"We left Van Duck with him!" said the captain of the Remove. "Blessed if I can make it out! Poker may know where Van Duck is—he generally does! Let's go and ask Poker."

The Famous Five went down to Gosling's lodge. But they learned from Gosling that Poker Pike was not there. Gosling had not seen him since that morning at all.

"Better go to the Head!" said Bob. "Something's happened to Van Duck, that's pretty clear. Can't tell Saloman, as he's not there! You'd better cut off to the Head, old bean."

"If Van Duck doesn't turn up for class——"

"Hallo, hallo, hallo!" roared Bob suddenly, his eyes fixed, with a startled stare, on three figures that arrived at the gateway

One of them was Putnam van Duck. Another was Poker Pike. But the third was an amazing figure.

Up to the neck he was. Mr. Saloman; the stout figure in a master's gown. Above the neck he was quite a different person.

Beaky nose and beard and spectacles were gone. Only the shiny complexion remained of his disguise, and that did not prevent the Famous Five from recognising Chick Chew.

His hands were tied together behind him. Poker Pike, walking with him, prodded him with a muzzle of a six-gun when he lagged. Putnam van Duck was grinning. But Poker's hickory face was as serious as usual, and the gangster's was convulsed with fury.

Breathless with amazement, the chums of the Remove stared.

Fellows came scampering up on all sides. There was a roar of amazed voices as Poker Pike marched his prisoner in.

"Chick Chew!" gasped Harry.

"The esteemed and ridiculous Chick, and——"

"Saloman——"

"It's the new beak——"

"It's Chick Chew——"

"I say, you fellows——"

"Great pip!"

"Chick's latest, you guys!" grinned Van Duck, as Poker Pike marched his prisoner on towards the House, through a staring, buzzing crowd. "Say, did any guy here tumble to it that Saloman was Chick in a noo outfit?"

"No fear!" gasped Bob.

"He took me for a walk," grinned Putnam. "And I'll say it would have been a long trip if Poker hadn't horned in. I'm telling you, it's Chick for the 'can' this time."

"Oh, my hat!"

A buzzing swarm of fellows followed the captured gangster to the House. Dr. Locke met the gunman and his prisoner as they entered, his eyes almost bulging from his majestic face.

"What—what—what——" stuttered the Head.

"Chick, sir," said Poker.

"Bless my soul! The—the—the kidnapper!"

"You said it, bo. I guess he horned in here calling himself Saloman. And I'll say he's got the real goods parked somewhere, and mebbe he'll mention where when he's packed in the 'can.'"

"Mr. Saloman!" The Head almost fell down. "Bless my soul! I—I fail to understand. I—I——"

"Mebbe you're s'prised a few," admitted Poker. "But it's sure Chick, and I got him safe and sound. I guess I'll borrow a room to lock him in, while I get on the phone, big boy. The cops will sure be pleased to intervoo Chick."

"Bless my soul!" said the Head feebly.

In the quad an excited swarm of fellows surrounded Putnam van Duck, eager to hear every detail of what had happened. Never had the bell for classes been so unwelcome at Greyfriars.

Chick Chew was gone when the fellows came out in break—safe in the official hands of Inspector Grimes at Courtfield. Chick was never likely to be seen at Greyfriars again, nor, indeed, to meet the public view at all, for a good many years to come. Too late Chick realised that he would have done well to heed the forebodings of his side-kicker, Bud Parker, and to

(*Continued on page* 28.)

ROUSING RED-HOT ADVENTURES WITH CONVICT PIRATES and—

CAPTAIN VENGEANCE!

By John Bredon.

"Well," snapped the man in the horn-rimmed spectacles, stepping from the doorway of the strange under-water craft and looking Roy Drake up and down, "who are you, boy, and what do you want? How did you get here?"

The Second Victim!

RONALD WESTDALE, gunnery lieutenant of the pirate cruiser Vengeance, pushed the glazed peak of his cap back over his damp, curly brow, and lighted a cigarette.

"No signs of the Monster, as yet," he said, with a short, forced laugh, as he watched the cold white beam of the searchlight playing over the inky ripples and rugged, rocky arches of the subterranean lake on Inaccessible Island. "If it wasn't for the fact that French Louis is missing from the muster-roll, I should be inclined to put it all down to a bad dream."

"It's here, right enough." Roderick Drake, the pirates' prisoner, lay flat upon a jutting ledge of rock, shading his eyes from the bright, white glare. "Lurking in one of these unexplored sea caves, down under the surface. Unless it's got some secret outlet to the sea bed, and only comes to the island occasionally. That depth charge must have given it a jolt. But it's neither dead nor badly injured, or we should have seen some sign in the water."

Two days had elapsed since Von Eimar and the convict pirates from Nemesis Island had taken up their refuge in the secret harbour of Inaccessible Island, in their captured cruiser. They had not been twenty-four hours on the island before they learned that it contained some mysterious inhabitant besides themselves; a hideous, unknown sea monster that dwelt in the labyrinthine caves of the underground lake that branched off from the lagoon. Already one of the convicts had fallen a victim to its frightful tentacles, and been dragged to the coal-black depths, never to be seen again.

The pirates, under the direction of Von Eimar, had set up a small generating station in one of the dry caves to provide power for the searchlight that ever since had incessantly swept the cavern pool. A six-pounder quick-firing gun, too, had been mounted upon the rocky landing-stage by the channel that wound under serrated arches to the island lagoon, where the cruiser lay anchored.

Keen eyes constantly scanned the lake as heavily laden boats and rafts ferried to and fro, loaded with coal-sacks, drums of oil, and other stores that had been secreted in the caves by German agents in the days before the Great War.

"You should have seen it, Ron," continued Roy, examining the breech and sights of the quick-firer as he spoke. "I never saw anything like it in all my life. Half a dozen tentacles like steel hawsers, goggling eyes that gave you the creeps, all glowing like lamps. Believe me or not, I fired my rifle point-blank, and the bullet glanced off the monster's head like a pebble off a rock. Just as if it had been made of triple armour plating."

"You're right in that, sir—right as rain!" agreed Hilarity Hinton, the Cockney, as he glanced uneasily over the hovering cave shadows. "I saw'd it, I did! 'Orrible, it was! Fair frightened me!"

Westdale laughed, slapping the gun-breech with a brown hand.

"Well, whatever it is, chum, Barking Bully will soon put paid to its antics if it shows up again. If its head can stand up to one of these six-pounder shells, I give it best! Why—what—what's that?"

Westdale's sharp eyes had caught a ripple of disturbed water at the distant end of the cavern pool.

With a bound, Roy Drake leaped to his feet, and pivoted the searchlight full upon the low cave arch whence the swirling eddies came.

"That's it! The Monster!" cried the boy excitedly, as a short, cylindrical object, surrounded by waving and flexible tentacles, floated into the full white blaze of the searchlight. "Ahoy, there!" he shouted to the crew of a raft, who were rowing slowly towards the outlet that led to the lagoon. "Get ashore at once! Quickly! It's the Monster!"

The irregular, domed roof of the giant cavern reiterated his shouts in thunderous, booming echoes. They were redoubled by alarmed warnings from the armed guards stationed at various points on the rocks.

Ronald Westdale, eye upon the gun-sights of the quick-firer, thumb resting upon the firing-push, muttered under his breath with vexation. The raft, with its human occupants, was directly in the line of fire, between him and the Monster.

One by one the four men of its crew jumped from the lashed logs into the water, struggling and splashing towards the rocky shore.

Still Westdale hesitated. The resultant explosion once his shell struck the sea beast spelt almost certain death for the swimming men.

Crack! Brrrang! Cra-a-ack! Crack! Crack!

The cavern echoes rolled and crashed as the sentries, kneeling on the rocky landing-stage, or higher up in the clefts and cavities, fired their rifles again and again. The shadows of the caves were lit by pulsating flashes like lightning. Bullets droned. Water sprayed and spurted all over the underground lake.

But Roy Drake, watching beside Westdale, as the latter fumed and growled, knew perfectly well that they were only wasting their ammunition. For one thing, the men were firing too wildly and hurriedly to take effective aim; and the only mark was those coiling, undulating tentacles, and the short, round object, like a bottle floating upright in the water, which he recognised for the spiky crest or protuberance between the round, glowing eyes, which were invisible under the water.

Only a direct hit from one of the six-pounder shells could destroy the under-sea monster, with its hide like armoured steel.

Westdale still muttered and cursed impatiently. He could not fire a shot while those four men, convicts and criminals though they were, lay between him and his objective. One of the men, a strong swimmer, breasting the tide as it swirled towards the lagoon, had already reached the base of the rocks, and was hauling himself up. Two more were swimming steadily as the raft drifted away on the suction of the powerful current.

A loud, frenzied squeal came from the fourth and last, who splashed and kicked wildly as he clung to one of the wooden paddles.

Hilarity Hinton leaped to his feet, with horror delineated upon his usual cheerful countenance.

"By gum, it's old Lakowski! The Poleski! 'E can't swim—not a stroke! The Monster'll get him!"

"Can't swim!" gasped Roy Drake, staring across the troubled water.

The man, clinging to his paddle, was being rapidly drawn into the race of the tide as it swept through the cave portals. Behind him the Monster floated leisurely, closing in upon the man relentlessly.

"My hat! The poor devil! He hasn't a chance!"

Roy braced himself on his toes by the brink of the rock ledge, arms stretched, fingers meeting, as he poised for a dive.

"What are you doing, Roy, you fool?" roared Westdale, jumping up to check his impulse. "Stop, you young ass! You can't do anything! The Monster will get you as well!"

His warning fell upon deaf ears. Even as he spoke, Roy Drake projected lightly from the rocky edge, curving cleanly as he dived. With a splash he struck the surface of the pool, the waters muffling Westdale's cry of dismay and warning in his ears, as he swooped into the black depths.

Rising to the top, he swept aside the curtain of water that ran from his hair over his eyes, gazing around him eagerly. A few yards away floated Lakowski, the Polish convict, a little, wizened old man, with a bald head and cropped ears, his face distorted with terror.

"Steady!" cried Roy.

With a few rapid strokes, he diminished the distance between himself and the frightened man, who screamed and clutched frantically.

The boy glided away, avoiding the desperate, grabbing hands that would have drawn them both to the black depths. Then, watching his opportunity, he swam in and caught the man by the shoulders. Turning him over on his back, he seized him under the armpits and struck out with his legs for the shore.

Terror seemed at last to have numbed the Pole's faculties; he lay quiescent in Roy's arms.

They neared the low cliff, Roy dreading every moment to feel that crushing, appalling grip of the tentacles upon him.

"Quick, lad!"

Westdale and Hilarity Hinton lay flat upon the ledge, stretching out their hands to grasp the Pole's sagging, insensible form. Westdale was staring fixedly over Roy's head, and, though he said not a word, the boy knew that he was watching the Monster as it glided slowly and inexorably in their wake.

The dazed and drooping Pole was hauled like a sack of firewood out of the water, over the rugged brink to the ledge. Roy's fingers gripped at the glistening, corrugated sides of the rock.

Even as he did so he felt that cold, frightful, paralysing clutch upon his ankle.

His friends cried out with alarm and dismay.

With the sweat bursting out on his forehead, Roy Drake clawed desperately at the ineffectual handhold of the rock-side.

Westdale, his face transformed in a paroxysm of rage, blazed rapidly with his automatic at the coiling tentacles and at the huge, globular head, just visible under the surface. He might as well have fired at the bare rocks.

The Cockney, with that sublime self-sacrifice that comes to men at such moments, leaned precariously over the edge, holding out his hand, knowing full well that it only meant his own death if the boy grasped it.

The steel-like, inexorable grip on Roy's ankle dragged him down as in a vice. Scraped and bleeding, his fingers slipped, and slid from their hold upon the rough surface of the rock. His last cry of horror was strangled in his throat as his head vanished from sight, and slowly, remorselessly, he was drawn down into the black oblivion of the cavern lake, leaving his companions to stare and stare at the black ripples and eddies where he had disappeared, like men bereft of their senses.

The Mystery Unfolded!

DIMLY conscious though he was that he was only prolonging his agony, Roy Drake fought hard to preserve that vital spark which we call life as he was drawn down rapidly through the black ocean depths.

His ears buzzed. An intolerable weight seemed to be pressing against his close-shut mouth, his closed eyes, and nostrils. His lungs swelled to the point of bursting. Then at last, after minutes which seemed measured out in hours, the grasp on his ankle suddenly released.

Upwards he shot to the surface. For a while he paddled about in a darkness, gratefully inhaling deep gulps of fresh, sweet air.

At once he knew that he must be in one of the innumerable sea-caverns that branched off from the lagoon of Inaccessible Island—the Monster's lair, no doubt. He had been drawn through an under-sea tunnel like a cork down a drain-pipe.

But where was the Monster? And why, if this was a cave connected by a submarine channel with the main cavern, was the air so fresh and sweet instead of being thick and foul, as it should have been in such a case?

By air-shafts piercing the cave roof, he answered his last question. And then, as he swam in circles, a bright, white, dazzling light suddenly blazed from above.

For one minute Roy was almost blinded; then, his eyes becoming at last accustomed to this unaccountable glare, he espied slabs and ledges of lava rock rising up from the inky water, surmounted by the mouths of caves and crevices in the rugged wall. Quite evidently, Inaccessible Island was riddled by these caves and underground lakes—a not surprising phenomenon, remembering that the island was the result of some bygone volcanic upheaval.

Swimming towards a flattish pile of rocks, Roy Drake hauled himself to the top, and, wringing out his saturated clothing, stared around for the Monster.

There it was, climbing the rocks a short way distant.

Roy cried out hoarsely in his surprise.

Seen now by the penetrating light that illuminated the cavern, the Monster, with its spidery tentacles and huge, globular head, resembled a gigantic diving-suit.

Yes; diving-suit it was, though such a one as the boy had never seen before.

Twelve feet in height, bolted together with plates of polished steel, the tentacles were its arms, no doubt manipulated by mechanical devices from within. Its motive power was a tripod of hinged pillars that acted as legs. And what Roy had first taken to be a horned protuberance between the thick glass port-holes was, in reality, a periscope like that of a submarine.

At the same time, Roy realised that the bright electric light came from powerful arc-lamps fitted to the cave roof.

So paralysed was the lad by his unexpected discovery that he remained squatting on the slab of lava as sliding-doors glided open in the steel trunk to reveal its crew.

The occupants, two in number as they stepped from the doorway, looked as strange as their under-water craft. One was a burly, dwarfish Chinaman, slant-eyed, clad in overalls of blue canvas. The other was a lean, lanky man, with a straggly beard, blinking, watery eyes behind huge, horn-rimmed spectacles, and with a domed bald head that was fringed by long, grey locks falling to his narrow shoulders.

With a spring, Roy rose to his feet, looking to right and left for a chunk of rock that might serve him for a weapon, since these strangers would hardly be friendly. But he found nothing.

"Stop!" It was the man in horn-rimmed spectacles who barked out the word.

Seeing that escape was hopeless, Roy stood his ground and waited while the strangers approached.

Slowly the tall white man looked Roy up and down.

"Well," he snapped, speaking English with a strong foreign accent, "who are you, boy? What do you want? And how did you get here?"

Professor Oskar Vorst.

SILENTLY the Chinaman glided behind Roy, tensed and poised, hovering ready to spring.

"My name's Roderick Drake—called Roy for short—if you want to know," answered the boy brusquely. "As to how I got here, you should know better than I do. And if you want to know what I want, I'd ask nothing better than to dot you one on the nose for your dashed cheek. After that I'd like a bite to eat. I'm hungry."

"Ah, bah!" The man in the horn-rimmed spectacles clicked his teeth. "You are English, of course. That explains it. All the English are mad." Swinging round to the Chinese, he added: "Show him the way, Li."

With that he climbed a series of rude, natural steps up to one of the caves that overlooked the lake.

Watching Roy like a bulldog on the heels of an intruder, Li motioned the boy to follow.

Ducking his head under a rocky arch, Roy found himself in a roomy, irregular chamber hollowed out from the rock, lighted by an electric bulb from the ceiling, and barely furnished with a plain, deal table, stools, chairs, chests, and trunks, and benches that were littered with phials, test tubes, and various scientific instruments, mostly unknown to him. Another rugged archway showed further caves beyond. Inaccessible Island was like a gigantic sponge.

"Ach! Feed him, Li!" grunted the white man, standing in the middle of the cave with arms folded on his pigeon breast. "The animal must be fed, I suppose, before it will bark. Eat, boy, eat; but do not take all day about it! Tell me the truth! Tell me how that warship came to this island to disturb my privacy, and my work!"

Roy sat on a stool as Li, the Chinaman, sorted out a change of clothing from a box. Then he tackled some bully beef and bread, while from a battered coffee-pot Li poured out some steaming brown liquid into a mug.

Between mouthfuls Roy told the strange, white man all that he knew—how Von Eimar had led the revolt of the convicts on Nemesis Island; seized the Varland cruiser, Zermac, and renamed her the Vengeance, and started out upon the amazing career of a modern pirate. Briefly Roy sketched out the story of the sinking of the Sylvia Bay, the battle with the Dutch aircraft, and the hiding of the Australian liner's bullion in the caves of Inaccessible Island. He was careful to add that he was only a prisoner aboard the pirate cruiser, though, for obvious reasons, he omitted to state that this was because his father was Morgan Drake, the hand and brain of the British Secret Service.

When he had finished, his bearded, spectacled captor let out a snort like that of an angry horse.

"A strange tale," he grunted—"very strange! As strange a one as ever I have heard in sixty years. Von Eimar—Nemesis Island—a pirate cruiser. Um! Von Eimar! Ha!" Excitedly he stalked about the little cave swinging his long, lean arms, and muttering excitedly to himself in German. "Von Eimar! I know that name! Years ago I met him in Berlin. What is he like—a squat, strongly built man; like a Prussian officer, with pale blue eyes? He smiles—ah, yes, a smile that you never forget—an ugly smile as though he plays with you. Is that your Von Eimar?"

"Von Eimar to a hair," said Roy Drake. "Do you know him, then?"

"I know him—yes. He was in the Secret Service, many years ago. He it was who questioned me when I discovered the secrets of Inaccessible Island."

Roy Drake pricked up his ears.

"You discovered the secrets of Inaccessible Island?" he echoed.

His interrogator lifted up his small, bald head, blinking through the thick lenses of his glasses.

"Ach, yes! I did. I am Professor Oskar Vorst, the cartographer. It was I who explored this island, years before the Great War. Von Eimar—that explains it. I had supposed that none besides myself knew of this hidden harbour on Inaccessible Island. But, if Von Eimar is the man who incited the convicts to rise and run away with this cruiser, as you say, then naturally he would make for this island as a refuge. Von Eimar is a man who forgets nothing."

Once more Professor Oskar Vorst, as he named himself, resumed his nervous, uneasy pacing about the cave, his chin sunk on his breast as his lips worked convulsively.

"This is bad," he muttered to himself, over and over again—"very bad. All my plans it spoils—yes."

"But, I say, professor!" exclaimed Roy, after a few minutes, the professor still rambling about restlessly.

"Well?" Professor Oskar Vorst wheeled around and glanced at him irritably. "What is it? You are interrupting my thoughts, boy. What do you want? Don't sit there gaping!"

"It's just this," began Roy. "You say that the presence of the pirate cruiser spoils all your plans. Well, there is a way in which you can rid yourself of Von Eimar and all his pirates and convicts. Haven't you any communication with the outside world?"

"Well?" rapped the professor again. "Don't speak to me in riddles, boy. Well, what of it?"

Apparently the professor didn't see the obvious inference.

Roy explained further.

"I've told you that warships are out hunting for Von Eimar and his pirate cruiser. The search will be kept up for weeks. They won't trouble about Inaccessible Island, because everyone supposes that it is a barren rock, where nobody can approach—what with the currents and the sunken coral reefs. But you've a wireless installation, I suppose? Send out a radio message, and Von Eimar will find himself bottled up like a rat in a trap."

It cost Roy a pang as he said this. Even as he spoke, he realised that destruction for Von Eimar and his pirates must also mean destruction for Ronald Westdale and Hilarity Hinton, the Cockney. In the few, but exciting days that had elapsed since the mutiny on Nemesis Island, there had sprung up a warm attachment between the lad and these two. They were the only two friends that he had among the cutthroat, lawless crew of the Vengeance, and he owed them both a deep debt of gratitude.

All the same, Roy's duty was clear and unmistakable. At all costs, he must send out the message that would encompass the destruction of Von Eimar and his pirate crew before this enemy of all mankind could wreak such another atrocity as the sinking of the Sylvia Bay.

Ron Westdale and Hilarity Hinton must take their chance—he realised that. Such men as Von Eimar, Killer Moran, Dr. Nieuwe and Luis Ramiro, with their hang-dog followers, must be wiped ruthlessly out of existence.

But Roy was to discover that their downfall was not to be accomplished so easily as all that.

Slowly and deliberately the professor fixed him with a suspicious glare, and above the horn rims of his spectacles his shaggy brows contracted into a knitted scowl.

"What is this that you suggest, boy?" he grated angrily. "What treachery is behind this move of yours? You want me to help in the destruction of your pirate comrades?"

"Treachery? My—my pirate comrades?" Roy was frankly puzzled. "I've told you already—they are no friends or comrades of mine. I'm a prisoner on the pirate cruiser—a hostage! Von Eimar is my enemy!"

"Ah, bah!" Contemptuously Oskar Vorst snapped his fingers. "Do you think that you can hoodwink me with so thin a tale? Do you take me for a fool—an idiot? A prisoner—a hostage!" he scoffed mockingly. "Of course, when Von Eimar and his pirates, are captured and brought to justice, they will all swear that they are prisoners and hostages, from the captain downwards. But do you think their judges will believe them? Of course not. As little as I believe you now, boy."

Indignantly Roy began to protest, but the professor silenced him with an impatient wave of his hand.

"And, moreover, even supposing that your absurd statement could be believed," Oskar Vorst went on, "and assuredly I do not credit it for one moment—what then? Do you suppose that I want battleships and aeroplanes battering this island to pieces with bombs and shells and high explosives, ruining all my carefully prepared plans and achievements? Do you imagine that I want all sorts of fools and scoundrels prowling round Inaccessible Island, to nose and pry into my secrets?"

Roy was puzzled.

"I'm sure I don't know," he said, after a pause. "What are you doing here? Have you found a gold-mine on Inaccessible Island? Or pearls—at the bottom of the lagoon," he added, in a flash of inspiration.

Fanatical rage blazed for a moment in the watery eyes behind those huge, thickly lensed spectacles. Then the professor jarred the silence with a jeering, contemptuous laugh, mimicking the boy's words.

"Pearls? Gold?" he echoed, sneering "Of course! That is just the idea that would emanate from the speck that you call a brain! No appreciation, in this barbarous world, for the higher mysteries of science—nothing but a lust for gold, for pearls, for money, and yet more money! But why should I blame you? I see that you are a clod among clods. Come, I have wasted enough time as it is. Li!"

At the word, the Chinese servant pounced upon Roy with all the lithe, supple strength of a panther. The boy struggled furiously, the stool crashing over in the scuffle. But those yellow, muscular arms coiled round him and locked his limbs in a powerful, immovable wrestler's grip.

With Li's heavy knee pinned between his shoulder-blades, Roy felt a strap wound about his elbows, drawn close, and buckled tightly and firmly. Ropes were deftly looped around him, fastening wrists, knees, ankles, till he looked as if he were enmeshed in a hempen net.

Turning him upon his back, Li forced his jaws apart, and then jammed a piece of wood into his mouth, and lashed it so tightly that it seemed to Roy that his skin was being drawn from his skull.

"Take him away!" grunted the professor.

The Chinaman swung Roy on to his broad shoulder, and then stepped lightly from the living-cave into a rough-hewn passage that gaped between buttresses of lava.

Hanging head downwards, Roy found himself carried into a further cavity, a mere fissure or hollow in the passageway.

With a grunt the Chinese dropped him unceremoniously on to the cracked and

Printed in Great Britain and published every Saturday by the Proprietors, The Amalgamated Press, Ltd., The Fleetway House, Farringdon Street, London, E.C.4. Advertisement offices: The Fleetway House, Farringdon Street, London, E.C.4. Registered for transmission by Canadian Magazine Post. Subscription rates: Inland and Abroad, 11s. per annum; 5s. 6d. for six months. Sole Agents for Australia and New Zealand: Messrs. Gordon & Gotch, Ltd., and for South Africa: Central News Agency, Ltd.—Saturday, June 13th, 1936.

uneven floor, leaving him alone with a dim and flickering hurricane-lamp for company, and his thoughts that were as dismal and foreboding as the shadows that hovered around.

At last, feeling almost crushed in those galling bonds that cut like knives into his skin, Roy gazed around in the shadow-filled cave.

Squirming, wriggling, he tried to saw through the stout-fibred ropes with a loose piece of sharp lava that he found pricking into his back. But the only result was to scar once more his already bruised and bleeding flesh, and at last he desisted in despair.

As he did so, a thought struck him. The lump of rock, slipping from his numbed fingers, tinkled faintly on to the floor. Slight as the sound was, it sent a series of echoes through the mazes underground.

What if this system of caves was a gigantic whispering-gallery, connecting to the main cavern where Von Eimar and his pirates were encamped?

It was a chance!

Taking the piece of lava once more in his stiffened fingers, Roy Drake clinked it against a jutting knob of the wall, tapping out a message in Morse to those who, though he could hardly call them friends, were at least preferable as gaolers to the fanatical and merciless German scientist.

Trapped!

AN answer came swifter than Roy expected.

But it was not of the kind which he had hoped for and half expected.

In his excitement the boy had forgotten that Oskar Vorst and the Chinaman were nearer, and therefore more likely to pick up his surreptitious message than Von Eimar and his pirates. Abruptly Roy ceased his tap-tapping as he heard the soft pad of Li's feet along the rocky lava, striving unsuccessfully to conceal his "transmitter" beneath his body.

The Chinaman's yellow, calloused foot spurned him to one side, and then, with one of his expressive grunts, he jerked the tool away.

"So you try to communicate with your fellow-rascals, do you?" Oskar Vorst glared down upon him, with his pale, watery eyes blinking rapidly and angrily beneath his shaggy brows. "And you would have deceived me into

(*Continued on next page.*)

COME INTO the OFFICE, BOYS—AND GIRLS!

Your Editor is always pleased to hear from his readers. Write to him: Editor of the "Magnet," The Amalgamated Press, Ltd., Fleetway House, Farringdon Street, London, E.C.4. A stamped, addressed envelope will ensure a reply.

FROM north, south, east and west, letters come pouring in from readers praising the good old MAGNET and Frank Richards' yarns of the chums of Greyfriars in particular. "If only the MAGNET could be published twice a week!" writes a Tottenham reader. I wonder if this particular chum is reading the rousing yarns dealing with the early adventures of Harry Wharton, now running in the GEM? If not, he's missing the treat of a lifetime!

"THE MAKING OF HARRY WHARTON!"
By Frank Richards,

is one of the star features in our grand school-story companion paper, and "Magnetites," one and all, are strongly advised to read it.

In last week's chat I mentioned that there were three islands for sale. Now John Adams writes to ask if it is true that there is

A VOLCANO FOR SALE?

Yes, John is quite right. The volcano of Mount Popocatepetl, in Mexico, has been up for sale for thirty-six years. It is the fifth highest mountain in North America, having a height of 17,540 feet. If any of my readers feel like buying it, they can have it for ten million dollars of Mexican money. That works out at somewhere near a million pounds in English money.

I don't think I'd like to pay a million pounds to live on top of a volcano, would you?

What was

THE BIGGEST CIGAR IN THE WORLD?

That's the question that comes from "Constant Reader," of Manchester. Ever seen a cigar that was eight and a half feet in length? I haven't—but one was made some time ago by a firm in Cuba. It would have cost you £500 to purchase it! There was enough tobacco in that particular cigar to have provided an ordinary cigar smoker with three cigars a day for no less than ten years!

Do you know which is

THE MOST VALUABLE STAMP IN THE WORLD?

Arthur Higgs, of Leicester, asks me to tell him. This is considered by philatelists to be the one cent magenta-coloured stamp issued in British Guiana in 1856. So far as is known, there is only one stamp of that issue now existing, and it has a rather interesting history. It was first bought for £140 by an Italian, who willed it to a Berlin museum. The Great War was in progress when the Italian collector died, and the stamp was in France with the rest of his collection. The French Government seized it as enemy property, and sold it by auction. It was bought by an American for £7,150. The purchaser is now dead, but his widow, who owns the stamp, recently refused an offer of £7,500 for it. The stamp is now insured for £9,600, and no offer less than £10,000 will be considered. "Some!" price to pay for a stamp which was once sold for a halfpenny, what?

Many of my readers are interested in philately, so here are a few

SHORTS ABOUT STAMPS

which I have collected for their benefit:

Three of the Most Famous Stamp Collectors in the World were the late King George V, the former King Alfonso of Spain, and the present President Roosevelt of America. Roosevelt's collection is valued at £5,000.

A Large House in Exchange for a Postage Stamp was recently offered by a London collector—but the stamp had to be worth the value of the house!

A Complete Collection of the World's Stamp Issues would cost something like £600,000 to buy—assuming that other collectors were willing to sell their rarest specimens.

A Country which Existed on the Sale of Stamps to Collectors was the Government of Fiume, which had practically no other revenue except what it made from the sale of stamps.

The World's First Postage Stamp was the British "Penny Black," issued on May 6th, 1840. It is not so rare, however, as many other issues brought out some time later.

Here is an idea for those of my readers who get sudden "brain-waves." I have just been informed that a certain railway company has already paid out

£800 FOR IDEAS!

Just of late railway companies in this country have been trying out all sorts of new suggestions—and most of them have proved most beneficial both to the companies and their passengers. At first the railway companies offered prizes of from one to ten guineas for ideas that would lead to better railway services. So many valuable ideas were sent in that the maximum award has now been raised to thirty guineas. Most of the awards, of course, go to railway servants who get a "brain-wave" while they are at work, and suggest means whereby the company can improve its service, and, at the same time, make money. In fact, the railway company in question admits that the amount of money saved by the adoption of these ideas is many times more than the amount of the awards they have paid out.

When the ideas are considered by the Suggestions Committee, the names of the senders are not disclosed. So it frequently happens that a porter puts up a much more useful idea than even the district manager!

And now for next week's all-star programme. The piece-de-resistance is

"BILLY BUNTER'S BURGLAR!"
By Frank Richards.

This is truly a great yarn right from the word "go." Billy Bunter's career as a grub-hunter has often landed him in trouble. But never has our tame porpoise been in such a predicament as he finds himself next week—stranded on an island with a burglar! What actually happens I'm not attempting to explain here. Frank Richards can do that much better next Saturday. It's a corking yarn, though, and that's enough to go on at present.

The only fault you'll find with our big thriller "Captain Vengeance!" is that there are not enough chapters. But I must leave space for the "Greyfriars Herald" supplement, another "Interview" by the Greyfriars Rhymester and my usual weekly chat.

YOUR EDITOR.

supposing that you were a prisoner among them—eh? Ach! I am no fool, I, Oskar Vorst!" Deliberately he struck the boy across the face with his bony knuckles. "You want to join your friends, is that it, boy? Very well, you shall! Von Eimar and his crew of pirates shall see what is in store for them. Bring him along, Li!"

Ruthlessly, the Chinaman dragged Roy along at the heels of the lanky, stringy professor, hauling him along by his feet, with his back scraping and bumping over the rough, sharp lava, his tied hands unable to protect himself. The lad's shirt was in ribbons, and his back cruelly bruised and gashed by the time they reached the shores of the cavern-pool.

Professor Oskar Vorst stood by the sliding doors of his gigantic mechanical diving-suit, his eyes blazing with a wild light.

Looking at him now, as he stood in the full glare of the electric roof-lamps, Roy realised that—as he already had begun to suspect—the professor was well over the wrong side of the borderline that separates mere eccentricity from real insanity.

"Bring him inside," barked Oskar Vorst.

The Chinaman, slashing with a big knife the ropes that bound Roy's legs, hustled the boy into the narrow, cylindrical trunk that formed the body of the diving-suit.

It was like the conning-tower of a submarine, only on smaller dimensions, with a periscope-mirror attached to the projecting pipe that the pirates had mistaken for the "monster's" crest, and with all its geared controls and appliances for manipulating the cunningly contrived "tentacles" as well as the motive power, there was just room for three, and no more. They were able to breathe by means of a suction-pipe connected to a tube of compressed air affixed to the back.

Roy was thrust up against the steel wall, his wrists still bound, and the professor glared at him with maniacal triumph as Li, seated on a kind of saddle, manipulated with his feet the treadles that operated the "legs," what time the contrivance waded through the black, lapping waters, and, submerging, trod the undersea passage that connected the professor's refuge with the subterranean lake.

"You shall see something very interesting soon, I promise you!" Oskar Vorst cried exultingly, as the electric bulb overhead glared full upon the polished glass of the periscope mirror. "In a few seconds we will have passed through this underwater tunnel into the cavern where your villainous companions are. Only the tip of our periscope will show above water when we reach it.

"Let them use their searchlight and their poor little rifles and machine-guns! These plates are bullet-proof. Soon will you see more of your friends and fellow-pirates struggling in the grasp of our tentacles—and this I promise you, I shall take no more prisoners to betray me!"

Stolidly, Li, the Chinaman, sat with his hands at the controls, as the professor, with a contemptuous crack of his finger-joints under Roy's nose, turned to rivet his gaze upon the periscope-mirror as they emerged from the under-sea passage.

Furiously the boy chewed upon the immovable gag that bridled his mouth. But he could not warn the half-mad professor of the knowledge that was seething and burning in his brain—of the quick-firing gun that Ronald Westdale and his gunners had mounted upon the landing-stage rocks, with its deadly muzzle trained upon the spot where the "monster" had last emerged.

The domed steel turret that was the head of Oskar Vorst's diving-machine might well be impervious to steel-cased bullets, as the professor had gloatingly boasted, but a quick-firer was a very different matter. One well-planted six-pounder shell, and in one second they and the machine would be blasted into eternity.

Roy bit into the gag and chewed upon the hard wood, but it was useless, and he had to ease his aching jaws.

With bulging, staring eyes, he fixed his gaze upon the periscope-mirror, watching the black, wavery line as the periscope thrust above water, the bright blaze of the ever-hovering searchlight; and then the machine jolted unexpectedly, hurling them sideways in a floundering heap, and the pitchy water outside the thick glass windows churned furiously as the tentacles struggled and grappled above water.

"Mein Gott, we are trapped!" Recovering himself, Oskar Vorst stumbled towards the mirror, steadied it, and glared into its glossy surface with eyes of baffled hate. "Von Eimar—that cunning devil! I should have thought of this. They have fixed up a net, and we are caught—caught like rats in a trap!"

He ground his teeth in impotent fury, and clawed at his straggly beard till the blood ran, while Roy Drake, bound, gagged, and helpless, braced himself up against the round steel wall and waited, with starting eyes and tensed nerves, for the crashing explosion that would be the last thing he would know in this world!

(Von Eimar has had things all his own way so far. But what chance has he got against Oskar Vorst and his strange underwater machine? Don't miss a line of this all-thrilling story, chums!)

THE BOGUS BEAK!

(Continued from page 23.)

beat it for the safe side of the Atlantic while the going was good.

* * * *

"Glad and sorry," said Harry Wharton in Study No. 1 a week or two later.

"Jest how I feel," agreed Putnam van Duck. "I sure do like this school a whole lot, and I'll say that I never struck a bunch I liked better than I like you guys. But the popper wants me home, now that Chick's in the 'can,' and it's safe for me in Chicago. And I guess I got to hit the steamer."

"Glad you're safe from the jolly old kidnappers, and sorry to lose you," said Bob.

"Mebbe you'll hit Chicago some day, and I sure will enjoy showing you round the little old town," said Van Duck. "I guess I shan't forget this school, and you guys. And I'll say I think a whole lot of this little island where they keep a kidnapper safe in the 'can,' once they get a cinch on him."

The capture of Chick Chew was the end of the kidnapping enterprise. The other members of the gang, deprived of their great leader, were only too glad to "beat it," while the going was good—as Chick, too late, fervently wished that he himself had done. Mr. Saloman, the genuine gentleman of that name, was released from the quiet and secluded residence where he had been "parked," while the enterprising Chick was using his name and identity, with such disastrous results to Chick. But the temporary master of the Remove was gone, and Mr. Quelch back in his old place when the day came for Van Duck to depart.

Harry Wharton & Co., and plenty of other fellows, were sorry to lose their American chum—sorry, too, to see the last of Poker. But Putnam was booked for home, and with him went Poker Pike.

"We shall miss Van Duck," remarked Harry Wharton.

"Yes, rather!" said Nugent.

"The ratherfulness is terrific!"

"What rot!" said Bunter. "You've still got me;" he added reproachfully.

"Ha, ha, ha!" yelled the Famous Five.

The fact that they had still got Bunter did not seem to afford them any enormous amount of consolation. But the fat Owl had, at least supplied a little comic relief.

THE END.

(Now look out for "BILLY BUNTER'S BURGLAR!" another topping Greyfriars yarn by Frank Richards in next week's MAGNET. *You'll vote it grand! Be sure to order your copy early!)*